THE MINORITY OF HENRY III

THE MINORITY OF

HENRY III

D. A. Carpenter

Lecturer in History, King's College, London

University of California Press
Berkeley and Los Angeles

22446773

To Jane and Kate

First U.S. edition published 1990 by
University of California Press
Berkeley and Los Angeles

Library of Congress Catalog Number 90-50247
ISBN 0-520-07239-1

Typeset in 11/13pt Baskerville
by Hewer Text Composition Services, Edinburgh
Printed in Great Britain by
St Edmundsbury Press Ltd, Bury St Edmunds, Suffolk

CONTENTS

LIST OF ILLUSTRATIONS   *page*   ix
PREFACE   xi
PRINCIPAL DATES   xiii
PRINCIPAL CHARACTERS   xvi
GENERAL MAPS   xix
NOTE ON REFERENCES   xxiv

1. **Introduction**   1
   King John, Magna Carta and the civil war   5

2. **Winning the War, 1216–17**   13
   i.   The new government   13
   ii. The military situation   19
   iii. Magna Carta, 1216   21
   iv. The period of stalemate, November 1216–February 1217   24
   v.   Louis in France, 27 February–23 April 1217: the
          movement to the young king   27
   vi. The nature of the civil war   31
   vii. Decision by battle: Lincoln and Sandwich   35
   viii. The peace of Kingston/Lambeth, 12/20 September 1217   44

3. **The Government of the Regent, 1217–19**   50
   i.   Government problems and structure after the war   50
   ii. Settlement, October–November 1217: individuals   56
   iii. Magna Carta and the Charter of the Forest, November
          1217   60
   iv. The restoration of government, October–November 1217   64
   v.   The settlement with the king of Scotland, December 1217 69
   vi. Disputes over the sheriffdoms; the proclamation of
          Magna Carta; January–February 1218   70
   vii. The treaty of Worcester, March 1218   74
   viii. The failure to control wardships and sheriffdoms,
          March–May 1218   78
   ix. The great council of May 1218   81
   x.   The siege of Newark, July 1218   84
   xi. The problem of the forest, July 1218   89

xi. The count of Aumale and the siege of Bytham, December
1220–January 1221   227

xii. The achievement of the triumvirate, May 1220–
January 1221   234

6. **The Triumvirate: Dissolution**   239
i. The tensions within the triumvirate   239
ii. The alliance with the earl of Pembroke, May 1221   243
iii. The fall of Peter de Maulay, June 1221   249
iv. Retreat and advance, summer 1221   252
v. Pandulf's resignation and achievement   254
vi. The end of the king's pupillage and the watershed in
English politics   256

7. **The Government of the Justiciar, 1221–23**   263
i. Archbishop Langton and Hubert's government   263
ii. The conflict in Poitou   266
iii. The resumption of the demesne, October 1221: failure   268
iv. Crisis, December 1221–January 1222   270
v. The recovery of the county farms, November 1221–
February 1222   274
vi. The Yorkshire protest over the forest eyre, May–
June 1222   276
vii. The resumption of the demesne, June 1222: success   279
viii. The emergence of the king and the London riots, July
1222   289
ix. The Michaelmas exchequer of 1222; Wales; Poitou   292
x. The confirmation of Magna Carta, January 1223   295

8. **The King and His Castles, 1223**   301
i. The papal letters of April 1223   301
ii. The earl of Pembroke's conquest of south Wales   306
iii. The death of King Philip, July 1223   309
iv. Montgomery castle and the end of the Welsh war,
September–October 1223   311
v. Hubert's opportunity, October–November 1223   314
vi. The collapse of Hubert's initiative, November 1223   316
vii. Archbishop Langton's intervention, December 1223   319
viii. The king receives control of his seal, 10 December
1223   321
ix. The king resumes his castles and sheriffdoms, 30
December 1223   325
x. The resumption of the castles and sheriffdoms:
perspectives and conclusions   329

xii. The inauguration of the king's seal and the revival of
the general eyre, November 1218   93

xiii. The end of the regent's government, December 1218–
April 1219   103

xiv. The crisis facing English kingship   108

4. The Triumvirate, 1219–20: The Verge of Anarchy   128

i. The establishment of the triumvirate, April–June 1219   128

ii. The triumvirate: attitudes and ambitions   134

iii. Abortive initiatives, June–July 1219   146

iv. Pandulf and Scotland, July–August 1219   151

v. Poitou, July 1219   153

vi. Alarms and excursions: Staines, Northampton, Lincoln
and Tickhill, July–August 1219   157

vii. The Michaelmas term of 1219: exchequer and bench   161

viii. Poitou; the forest; November–December 1219   167

ix. The triumvirate apart, December 1219–January 1220   169

x. The triumvirate in London; Philip of Oldcoates;
February 1220   174

xi. The renewal of the truce with the king of France,
March 1220   176

xii. The process of conciliation, April 1220   179

xiii. The justiciar and the council, October 1219–May 1220   182

xiv. The frustration of the triumvirate, April 1219–April
1220   184

5. The Triumvirate 1220–21: Success   187

i. The king's second coronation, May 1220   187

ii. Wales and Poitou, May 1220   191

iii. The settlement with the king of Scotland; the surrender
of Mitford; June 1220   194

iv. The siege of Rockingham, June 1220   198

v. Philip of Oldcoates and Poitou, July 1220   200

vi. The great council of August 1220   203

vii. The north of England: counsel, consent and dissent,
August–September 1220   207

viii. The king's recovery of Cornwall; the despatch of Philip
of Oldcoates to Poitou; August–September 1220   211

ix. Llywelyn's campaign in south Wales; the earl of
Pembroke's surrender of Fotheringhay; Hugh de
Lusignan's delivery of the king's sister; August–
November 1220   217

x. The Michaelmas exchequer of 1220 and the
proceeds of the carucage   222

9. **Bedford and Poitou, 1224**   343
  i. Confrontation or conciliation? The situation of the new
    government   343
  ii. Confrontation, February–March 1224   344
  iii. The settlement of April 1224   348
  iv. The attack on Falkes, April 1224   351
  v. The defection of Hugh de Lusignan, May–June 1224   355
  vi. The siege of Bedford, 20 June–15 August 1224   360
  vii. The loss of Poitou   370

10. **Gascony, Taxation and Magna Carta, 1225**   376
  i. Gascony, 1225   376
  ii. The fifteenth on movables and the recovery of
    government   379
  iii. Magna Carta and the Charter of the Forest, 1225   382

11. **The End of the Minority**   389

12. **The Minority and its Aftermath**   396

  APPENDIX: Financial Tables   413
  GENEALOGICAL TABLES   419
  BIBLIOGRAPHY   425
  INDEX   441

ILLUSTRATIONS

PLATES

1. Matthew Paris's drawing of the battle of Lincoln. (*The Master and Fellows of Corpus Christi College, Cambridge*)
2. The eastern gateway of Lincoln castle. (*John Bethell*)
3. Matthew Paris's drawing of the sea battle off Sandwich. (*The Master and Fellows of Corpus Christi College, Cambridge*)
4. Pandulf's letter of 11 June 1219 to Ralph de Neville. (*Public Record Office, London*)
5. Effigy (c.1230s) probably representing the regent, William Marshal, earl of Pembroke, in the Temple Church, London. (*Courtesy of the Board of Trustees of the V&A*)
6. Dover castle from the north-west. (*A.F. Kersting*)
7. Newark castle from across the Trent. (*A.F. Kersting*)
8. The only surviving example of Magna Carta 1217. (*The Bodleian Library, Oxford*)
9. Montgomery castle. (*Janet and Colin Bord*)
10. Skenfrith castle, the keep. (*Janet and Colin Bord*)
11. Matthew Paris's drawing of the hanging of the garrison of Bedford castle in 1224. (*The Master and Fellows of Corpus Christi College, Cambridge*)
12. The Close Roll for December 1223 at the point where the king took over the attestation of royal letters. (*Public Record Office, London*)
13. Effigy (c.1230s) in Salisbury cathedral of William Longespee, earl of Salisbury (d.1226). (*The Dean and Chapter of Salisbury Cathedral*)
14. Matthew Paris's drawing of Falkes de Bréauté's death in 1226. (*The Master and Fellows of Corpus Christi College, Cambridge*)
15. Magna Carta 1225. (*British Library*)

MAPS

1. Counties, sheriffs and castles of England, 1218   xx
2. The royal forests in the mid-thirteenth century   xxii
3. Poitou and Gascony in the minority   xxiii

4. The battle of Lincoln, 20 May 1217   38
5. Southern Wales, 1218–23   75
6. Montgomery and central Wales in the Minority   312
7. Northern royal forests in the minority   391

GENEALOGICAL TABLES

1. The Angevin royal house   420
2. The Marshal family   421
3. The Braose family   422
4. Llewelyn, prince of North Wales and his children   423
5. Sons and grandsons of Lord Rhys of Deheubarth   423

PREFACE

In the spring of 1986, having completed the research, I began to write a biography of King Henry III. By the end of the summer it was clear that I was in fact writing a history of Henry III's minority. Rather than begin all over again, I decided that the importance of the period, and the richness of its source material, fully merited a separate work: the more especially since the only other book on the subject had been published before the First World War. Although I am now writing a biography of Henry, I do not see the present book as in any way a 'Henry III part I'. Rather it is a self-contained work on a vital period of English history, a period with its own themes and setting.

In writing this book I have incurred many debts. My first is to J. O. Prestwich, who supervised my thesis on the sheriffs of Oxfordshire and who has been a valued friend, supporter and critic ever since. My second debt is to Barbara Harvey, who read a very early draft of the book and combined constructive criticism with timely encouragement; without that encouragement I am not sure that the work would have been completed. Subsequent drafts were read by David Crook, J. C. Holt, J. R. Maddicott and Nicholas Vincent, and the book has profited considerably from their suggestions. I was particularly lucky that Nicholas Vincent was working on his thesis on Peter des Roches at the time I was writing. He generously allowed me to read drafts of his chapters and I owe much to his discoveries. Like many other historians, I have been greatly helped by David Crouch, who, apart from reading Chapters 2 and 3, has always been ready to share his knowledge and provide access to the vast amount of material that he has assembled in the course of his Leverhulme project on the English aristocracy. To Robert Stacey I am grateful for comments on Chapter 3, xiv. I have also learnt much from his recent book on politics, policy and finance under Henry III, where, indeed, the method of adding up the revenue in pipe rolls was so superior to my own that I began my sums all over again. Others who have kindly helped me in letters or discussion include Mary Cheney, Stephen Church, Michael Clanchy, Anne and Charles Duggan, Richard Eales, Robin Frame, Judith Green, Andrew Hershey, Simon Lloyd, Michael Prestwich and Robin Storey, while W. H. Liddell was so good as to lend me his thesis on royal forests north of the

Trent. I have received constant help from the staff of the Institute of Historical Research: my financial calculations were aided both by the loan of the Institute's pounds, shillings and pence calculator and by the patient instruction in how to use it. The staff of the Public Record Office have been similarly helpful, not least in allowing me to work on large numbers of rolls simultaneously. Finally, on the academic side, I owe an especial debt to Paul Brand and David Crook, who, over many years, have fielded my telephone calls, at all hours of the day and night, asking for help on difficult points. They have rarely failed to come up with answers.

At Methuen itself I was grateful for the constructive calm with which Ann Mansbridge reacted when a book very different from the one which she had commissioned arrived on her desk. Ann Wilson, in editing the book, has saved me from numerous errors, made many useful suggestions, and in general smoothed the path towards publication. Sarah Hannigan has worked indefatigably on the illustrations and taken many other pains. It is a pleasure to acknowledge a most generous grant towards the costs of publication from the Isobel Thornley fund of London University. A grant from the Leverhulme trust facilitated a year's leave in 1987–88 during which a very rough draft of the book was put into presentable form. Lastly, I would like to thank all those to whom I have taught medieval history over the years at Christ Church, Oxford, St Hilda's College, Oxford, the University of Aberdeen, Queen Mary College, London and now at King's College, London. Likewise I am grateful to the members of my special subject class on the reign of Henry III drawn from the several colleges of London University. If, as I hope, my research and writing have made me a better teacher, the ideas and enthusiasm of those I have taught have constantly encouraged and improved my writings and research.

David Carpenter, King's College, London   December 1989

PRINCIPAL DATES

1207	October 1	Birth of Henry III
1215	June	King John concedes Magna Carta
1216	May	Prince Louis lands in England
1216	October	Death of King John
		Henry III's coronation at Gloucester
		William Marshal becomes governor of the king and kingdom
	November	Henry III concedes a version of Magna Carta
1217	May	Battle of Lincoln
	August	Sea battle off Sandwich
	September	Peace of Kingston/Lambeth
	November	Henry III concedes the Charter of the Forest and a version of Magna Carta
1218	March	Treaty of Worcester
	July	Siege of Newark
	November	Inauguration of the king's seal; launching of a general eyre
1219	April	First papal letters urging act of resumption; William Marshal's resignation as regent
	April–June	Hubert de Burgh begins to attest royal letters; formation of the triumvirate
	November	Geoffrey de Neville's resignation as seneschal of Poitou
	December	Commissions appointed to determine bounds of forest
1220	March	Renewal of truce with King Philip Augustus of France
	May	Hugh de Lusignan's marriage with Queen Isabella
		Henry III's second coronation
	June	Settlement with King Alexander II of Scotland; Philip of Oldcoates surrenders Mitford; siege of Rockingham

	August	Concession of carucage by a great council
	September	Expulsion of Henry fitz Count from Cornwall; Llywelyn's invasion of Pembroke
1221	January	Hugh de Vivonne appointed seneschal of Poitou; rebellion of count of Aumale; siege of Bytham
	May	Proposed marriage between earl of Pembroke and king's sister
	June	Peter de Maulay's expulsion from Corfe
	July	Pandulf's resignation
	October	Henry III's fourteenth birthday
		Bishop of Winchester ceases to be king's tutor; Savari de Mauléon appointed seneschal of Poitou
1222	January	Archbishop Langton restores peace after crisis
	March	Pandulf arranges a truce with Hugh de Lusignan
	June	Yorkshire protest over forest eyre; resumption of royal demesne
	August	Riots in London
1223	January	Henry III verbally confirms the Charters
	April	Papal letters giving the king control of his seal and commanding the resumption of his castles; earl of Pembroke begins conquest of south Wales
	July	Death of King Philip Augustus
	October	Building of new castle at Montgomery; submission of Llywelyn
	November	Hubert de Burgh's attempt to resume the king's castles
	December	King Henry begins to attest royal letters; resumption of the king's castles and sheriffdoms
1224	April	Attempted political settlement
	May	Earl of Pembroke becomes justiciar of Ireland to put down revolt of Hugh de Lacy; King Louis VIII refuses to renew truce; defection of Hugh de Lusignan
	June–August	Revolt of Falkes de Bréauté; siege of Bedford; King Louis VIII conquers Poitou

1225   February   Henry III confirms Magna Carta and
                        Charter of the Forest; concession of a
                        fifteenth on movables
1227   January   Henry III proclaims that henceforth he
                        will issue charters
1228   October 1   Henry III's twenty-first birthday

PRINCIPAL CHARACTERS

Kings
John, king of England, lord of Ireland, duke of Normandy and
 Aquitaine, and count of Anjou 1199–1216
Henry III, son of King John, king 1216–72
Philip Augustus, king of France 1180–1223
Louis VIII, son of King Philip Augustus, king of France 1223–26
Alexander II, king of Scotland 1214–49

Popes
Innocent III, 1198–1216
Honorius III, 1216–27

Legates in England
Guala Bicchieri, 1216–18
Pandulf, 1218–21

Bishops
Stephen Langton, archbishop of Canterbury 1207–28
Walter de Grey, archbishop of York 1215–55
Jocelin of Wells, bishop of Wells 1206–42
Richard de Marsh, bishop of Durham 1217–26
Richard le Poure, bishop of Salisbury 1217–28; of Durham 1228–37

Supporters of King John and his son during the war
i. Great barons:
William Marshal, earl of Pembroke 1199–1219, regent 1216–19
Ranulf, earl of Chester 1187–1232
William de Ferrers, earl of Derby 1190–1247
Robert de Vieuxpont, lord of Westmorland (d.1228)
Walter de Lacy of Ewias Lacy and Meath (d.1241)
John of Monmouth (d.1248)
Hugh de Mortimer of Wigmore (d.1227)
Henry fitz Count, illegitimate son of Reginald earl of Cornwall (d.1222)
ii. Foreigners:
Peter des Roches, bishop of Winchester 1204–38
Peter de Maulay (d.1241)
Engelard de Cigogné (d.1244)

Philip Mark (d.1234)
Falkes de Bréauté (d.1226)
William de Cantilupe (d.1239)
Robert de Gaugi (d.1218)
Hugh de Vivonne (d.1249)
iii. English *curiales*, sheriffs and castellans:
Hubert de Burgh, justiciar 1215–32 (d.1243)
William Brewer (d.1226)
Philip de Albini (d.1236)
Brian de Lisle (d.1234)
Ralph Musard (d.1230)
Geoffrey de Neville (d.1225)
Philip of Oldcoates (d.1220)

Rebels
Robert fitz Walter (d.1235)
Saer de Quincy, earl of Winchester 1207–19
Roger Bigod, earl of Norfolk 1189–1221
Hugh Bigod, son of Roger, earl of Norfolk 1221–25
Gilbert de Clare, earl of Hertford and Gloucester 1217–30
Henry de Bohun, earl of Hereford 1200–20
Humphrey de Bohun, son of Henry, earl of Hereford 1220–75
Geoffrey de Mandeville, earl of Essex and Gloucester 1213/14–16
William de Mandeville, brother of Geoffrey, earl of Essex 1216–27
Robert de Vere, earl of Oxford 1214–21
Reginald de Braose (d.1228)
John de Braose, nephew of Reginald, prisoner during war (d.1232)
William de Beauchamp of Bedford (d.1260)
Henry de Coleville of Bytham

Northern rebels ('The Northerners')
Roger Bertram of Mitford (d.1242)
Gilbert fitz Reinfrey (d.1220)
William of Lancaster, son of Gilbert fitz Reinfrey (d.1246)
Gilbert de Gant (d.1242)
Maurice de Gant (d.1230)
John de Lacy, constable of Chester, earl of Lincoln 1232–40
Roger de Montbegon (d.1226)
Thomas of Moulton (d.1240)
William de Mowbray (d.1224)
Robert de Percy
Robert de Ros of Helmsley (d.1226)
Nicholas de Stuteville I (d.1217)
Nicholas de Stuteville II (d.1233)
Richard de Umfraville of Prudhoe (d.1226)

Conspicuous trimmers in the war
William Longespee, earl of Salisbury 1196–1226
William Marshal junior, earl of Pembroke 1219–31
William de Albini, earl of Arundel 1193–1221
William de Fors, count of Aumale 1214–41
William de Warenne, earl of Surrey 1202–40
Hugh de Neville (d.1234)

Officials of the chancery, exchequer and bench
Ralph de Neville, keeper of the seal 1218–38; chancellor 1226–44; bishop of Chichester 1224–44
Eustace de Faukenburg, treasurer of the exchequer 1217–28; bishop of London 1221–28
Martin of Pattishall, senior professional justice at the bench 1218–29

The Welshmen
Llywelyn, prince of North Wales (d.1240)
Rhys Gryg, son of Lord Rhys of Deheubarth (d.1233)
Maelgwn ap Rhys, son of Lord Rhys of Deheubarth (d.1231)
Rhys Ieuanc, grandson of Lord Rhys of Deheubarth (d.1222)
Morgan of Caerleon (d.1248)

Irish rebels 1223–24
Hugh de Lacy, earl of Ulster 1205–44
William de Lacy, half-brother of Hugh (d.1233)

Justiciars of Ireland
Geoffrey de Marsh 1215–21
Henry of London, archbishop of Dublin 1221–24
William Marshal, earl of Pembroke 1224–26

The Poitevins
Hugh de Lusignan, lord of Lusignan, count of La Marche 1219–48
Savari de Mauléon, seneschal of Poitou 1221–24 (d.1233)
Aimeri VII, vicomte of Thouars (d.1226)
William l'Archevêque, lord of Parthenay
Guy de La Possonière

GENERAL MAPS

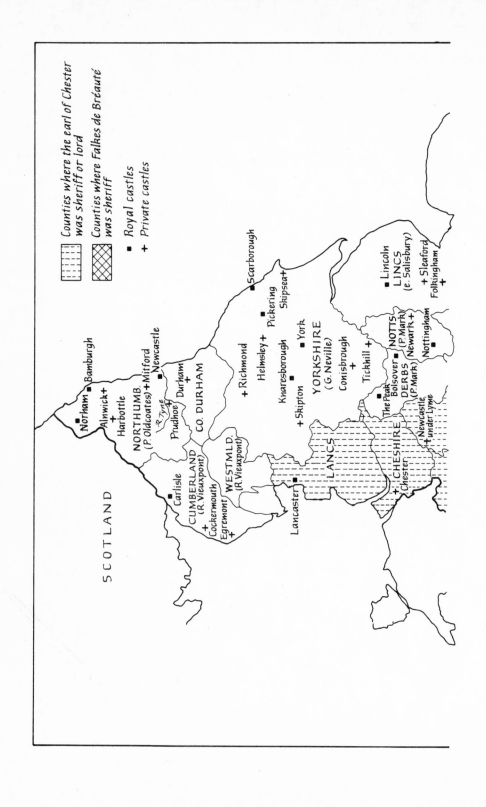

SCOTLAND

Counties where the earl of Chester was sheriff or lord

Counties where Falkes de Bréauté was sheriff

■ *Royal castles*
+ *Private castles*

NORTHUMB.
(P. Oldcoates)

■ Bamburgh
■ Norham
Alnwick +
+
Harbottle

Mitford
+ ■ Newcastle
R. Tyne
Prudhoe + ■ Durham

CO. DURHAM

Carlisle ■

CUMBERLAND
(R. Vieuxpont)
Cockermouth
+
Egremont +

WESTMLD.
(R. Vieuxpont)

+ Richmond

Scarborough ■

Helmsley + ■ Pickering
Skipsea +

Knaresborough
+ + York
+ Skipton

YORKSHIRE
(G. Neville)

Conisbrough
+
Tickhill +

Lancaster ■

LANCS

The Peak ■
Bolsover ■
DERBS
(P. Mark)

Newcastle
+ under Lyme

CHESHIRE
+ Chester

Newark +
(P. Mark)

■ Nottingham
NOTTS
(P. Mark)

■ Lincoln
LINCS
(e. Salisbury)

+ Sleaford
Folkingham
+

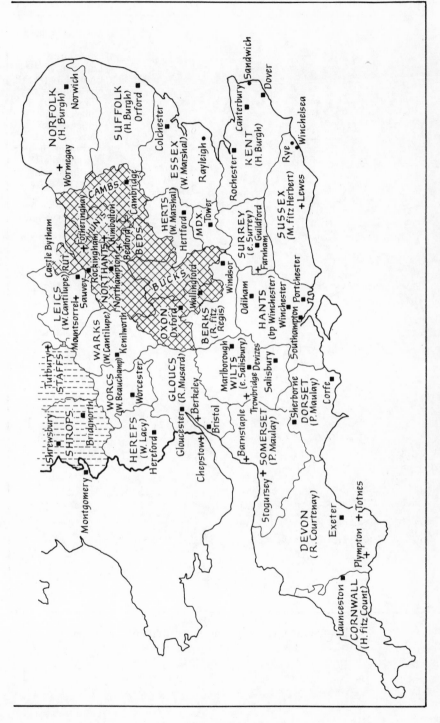

1. Counties, sheriffs and castles of England, 1218

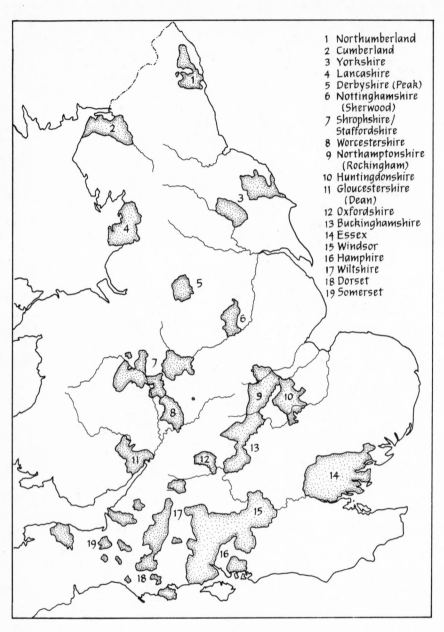

1 Northumberland
2 Cumberland
3 Yorkshire
4 Lancashire
5 Derbyshire (Peak)
6 Nottinghamshire
  (Sherwood)
7 Shrophshire/
  Staffordshire
8 Worcestershire
9 Northamptonshire
  (Rockingham)
10 Huntingdonshire
11 Gloucestershire
   (Dean)
12 Oxfordshire
13 Buckinghamshire
14 Essex
15 Windsor
16 Hamphire
17 Wiltshire
18 Dorset
19 Somerset

2. The royal forests in the mid-thirteenth century

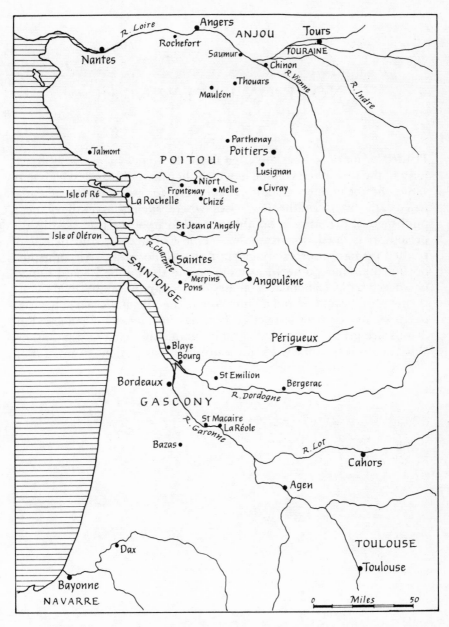

3. Poitou and Gascony in the minority

NOTE ON REFERENCES

Printed primary sources are cited in the footnotes by an abbreviated form of the title of the volume in which they are published, which may sometimes be no more than the first letters (for example, *PR* for *Patent Rolls 1216–1225*). In the few cases where such sources have been published in periodicals, an abbreviated form of the title used in the periodical is cited (for example, 'Cerne Cartulary'). Full details of printed primary sources are given in the Bibliography. All unprinted documents, unless otherwise stated, are in the Public Record Office, Chancery Lane, London. Secondary sources are normally cited by the surname of the author and a short form of the title: italicized in the case of books, placed within inverted commas in the case of articles. Full details are given in the Bibliography under the name of the author. Where a multi-volume work has continuous pagination or numeration the volume number is not cited.

Chapter 1

INTRODUCTION

The minority of King Henry III was a pivotal period in English history. It determined that England would be ruled by the Plantagenets, rather than by the Capetian kings of France. It rescued England from anarchy and saved royal power from almost total collapse. Yet it also saw both the establishment of Magna Carta and the genesis of more radical schemes of political reform, schemes which were still at the forefront of politics in the seventeenth century.

King Henry III, the son of King John, came to the throne in October 1216. He was only nine years of age and more than half the country was controlled by Louis, the eldest son of King Philip of France, to whom the rebellious barons had offered the crown. It seemed more than likely that Henry would be swept away and England and France be ruled by the Capetian dynasty. Yet, within a year, Louis had been decisively defeated and Henry was universally accepted as king.

Once the war was won, the issue became the future power and structure of English kingship. During the war that structure had disintegrated. The king was left penniless, a fact which had serious implications for his position in Wales, Ireland and further afield in Poitou and Gascony. Within England, the king's personal authority was in abeyance. Henry himself, in 1219, was 'called, by way of derision, not a king but a boy'.[1] Many castellans and sheriffs believed that they could not be dismissed until he came of age. There was also a view that the only legitimate decisions were those taken by great councils and that only 'reasonable' orders of the king should be obeyed. Those controlling central government for the young king thus faced appalling difficulties in impressing their will on the localities. In areas where the rebels had been strong, the king's local agents were frequently impotent. Elsewhere, paradoxically, they were sometimes over-mighty. The great men who had carried the young king's cause through to victory remained in control of his castles, sheriffdoms and manors, and drew off their revenues for themselves. They proved almost impossible for the centre to either remove or control. In these circumstances, it was more than likely that the country would remain divided between semi-independent principalities under great sheriffs and castellans, on the one hand, and areas where the authority of the

[1] SC 1/1, no. 39.

king's agents was negligible on the other. Even more pressing was the danger that England would simply disintegrate into anarchy, an anarchy composed of recalcitrant sheriffs and castellans, private wars, unlicensed tournaments, and barons and knights encroaching on the rights of the king. The parallels between this period and 'the anarchy' of Stephen's reign are numerous.

Before the minority was over, however, this collapse of central authority had been arrested and reversed. The structure of royal government had been repaired and its resources reassembled. As a consequence, having lost Poitou, the king was able to mobilize the funds to retain Gascony, which thereafter remained in English hands another 225 years.

If, however, royal government recovered strength, its authority was qualified in a new and fundamental way. Magna Carta 'took root during the minority of Henry III'.[2] King John had conceded the Great Charter in 1215 and had almost immediately persuaded the pope to quash it. This was a major cause of the civil war and, in order to win the war and secure the peace, the minority government changed tack completely. It issued a version of the Charter soon after the young king's accession and another version at the end of the war, this time linked with an entirely new Charter regulating the extent and administration of the king's forest. Thus the name Magna Carta first appears in the minority in order to distinguish it from the smaller Charter of the Forest.[3] In 1225 the two Charters of 1217 were issued once again in what became their definitive form. It is clauses of the 1225 Charter, in Edward I's confirmation of 1297, which are still on the Statute Book today, the most significant being that which forbids the denial, delay and sale of justice and the outlawry, exile, imprisonment and disseisin of a free man save 'by lawful judgement of his peers or by the law of the land'.[4]

In promulgating these new Charters the government was far from casting bread from the stern of the ship and hoping that sea-gulls would appear, for the gulls were already following the ship, screaming for food. A key feature of the minority is the determination displayed by magnates and gentry to safeguard and exploit the provisions in the Charters. By the end of the period, treasured by the king's subjects and conceded on several occasions by the king, they had indeed taken root.

When Henry III, therefore, assumed full regal power in January

[2]   Holt, *Northerners*, 3.

[3]   *RLC*, 377–377b.

[4]   *Halsbury's Statutes*, 14–17 (clause 29 of the 1225 Charter, having been 40 and 39 in that of 1215). The other clauses still on the Statute Book are numbers 1 on the liberties of the church, 9 on those of London and part of 37, which forms the conclusion. For the relevance of clause 29 today, see Lord Hailsham's article 'How the security services are bound by the rule of law', in *The Independent*, 3 February 1988.

1227, the authority of kingship had been restored and the Charters were in place. The two processes were intimately connected. Fundamentally, men accepted the recovery of royal power, indeed supported central government in turning the tables on the great local governors, because they believed that they were getting a moderate form of kingship which they could limit and control. Given that fact, they were able to appreciate its benefits. They realized that unless the rights and revenues of the king were secure he could not guarantee and safeguard their own rights. Equally, he would lack the power and authority to maintain peace and dispense justice. This compromise was implicit in Magna Carta itself. It sought to limit rather than destroy the king's sources of revenue and expand rather than contract the king's role as the dispenser of justice.

After the minority of Henry III the Charters were an inescapable fact of English political life. Already in 1225 Henry was sensibly working within them and turning them to his advantage. In that sense the minority fashioned a new *modus vivendi* between the king and his subjects. There was, however, nothing permanent about the arrangement and its terms, in the minority itself, had changed under conflicting political pressures. It was already clear that the ambiguity of the Charters on some important issues and their silence on others meant that they provided no comprehensive solution to contemporary grievances. There was constant conflict, for example, between the king's government and the counties over just how much deforestation the Forest Charter sanctioned. Such conflicts, moreover, highlighted another problem. If there were disagreements over what the Charters meant, if, indeed, the king plainly transgressed them, there was no constitutional remedy. This was because the new Charters of Henry III omitted the 'security' clause of 1215: the clause under which twenty-five barons, chosen by their fellows, were empowered to force the king to emend breaches of Magna Carta. After 1227 other defects of the Charters became apparent. They had virtually nothing to say about how the king should appoint ministers, dispense patronage and decide policy. This, indeed, was to be the main area of conflict between Henry and his opponents in the period down to the revolution of 1258.

The minority, therefore, for all the implantation of the Charters, failed to place relations between the king and his subjects on any permanently satisfactory footing. By 1244 far more radical schemes of political reform were being propounded. It was, however, precisely the governmental structure of the minority from which these schemes derived. The most novel and important feature of that structure was the role played both by great ministers and the great councils to which they were, in effect, accountable. It is clear that in the minority great councils, that is, assemblies of the lay and ecclesiastical magnates of the kingdom, both appointed the king's chief ministers and sanctioned a wide range of other decision. Indeed, according to one view, without such sanction, decisions had no validity. Thus in 1220 Robert de Vieuxpont complained that an order had been issued 'without the common counsel and assent of the magnates of England who are held to be and are of the chief council of the king', while the earl of Salisbury added that, without his own counsel and assent as part of the chief council, 'such an order is not held to be done rightfully'.[5] In essence, programmes of constitutional reform, in and after 1244, envisaged a return to the minority system, requiring the direct, or indirect, appointment of the king's ministers by great councils or parliaments. Indeed, this remained a central demand of the king's opponents into early modern times. In that sense the minority of Henry III both secured the formal acceptance of Magna Carta and created the political programme which would follow it.

The minority influenced the future in other ways. In the short term it created factional struggles which determined the course of politics down to 1234. It also did much to encourage English national feeling, fomenting resentment against foreigners and stimulating the belief that England was for the English, sentiments which formed the background to many of King Henry's later difficulties. The role played by papal legates in helping to win the war and rebuild royal power afterwards gave Henry the exaggerated respect for the papacy for which he was later famous. The retention of Gascony laid the foundations for the Hundred Years War.

'History is a story with a beginning and an end.' Although this book has many analytical sections, its core lies in a detailed narrative account of the minority, written from the viewpoint of central government. For the fact is that the minority has a very pronounced story: on the one hand, the struggle of those ruling in the king's name to win the war, maintain the peace and rebuild the structure of royal government; on the other, the process whereby Magna Carta and the Charter of the Forest became integrated into English political life. The complexity and drama of these events can only be grasped when they are told in a detailed narrative. Only then can one appreciate the range and scale of the difficulties faced by the government in the years after the war and how nearly the country dissolved into anarchy; only then can one see how the problems of Wales, Ireland and Poitou interacted with domestic politics and how the ultimate objectives of the government interlocked with questions of finance, justice, appointments, patronage and political alliances. A more analytical approach to the period would bring familiarity with individual bricks but give little idea of their place in the construction of the building.

In tracing and understanding the course of events, the vast range of primary sources are utilized here for the first time. The main work on

[5] SC 1/2, nos 10, 17. See below p. 209.

the period, Kate Norgate's *The Minority of Henry The Third* (1912), and the briefer accounts by Sir Maurice Powicke (1948 and 1953), although impressive in their different ways, were based almost exclusively on printed materials.[6] This meant that neither historian made use of the huge amount of financial evidence contained in the pipe, memoranda and receipt rolls of the exchequer. They were unaware of the cripplingly small size of the king's revenue after the war and the consequent scale of the collapse of royal power. Equally, Norgate and Powicke had limited recourse to legal records and thus failed to appreciate that the course of national politics was frequently influenced by private quarrels. They also made no use of perambulations of the royal forest and consequently could not demonstrate the central role played by the forest in the politics of the period. Finally, neither author looked at the considerable number of unprinted private letters to and between those in control of central government.[7] The interest of this private correspondence is worth stressing, for it has few parallels in the thirteenth century, being partly produced by the unique circumstances of the minority when ministers, separated geographically, had to exchange their views and co-ordinate their activities by letter. In the medieval period historians have often to accept that the pressures and discussions behind decisions are closed to them; they can merely see the results in the king's letters and charters. In the minority, by contrast, it is possible to hear the debates and see something of the inner workings behind events. Out of those events the important results of the period – the winning of the war; the recovery of government; the taking root of the Charters; the ideas about great councils – emerged. It is the sequence of those events which this books sets out to examine.

King John, Magna Carta and the civil war

'In this year [1215] a great discord arose between the king of England and the barons . . . for in the time of his father and more especially in his own time [the free customs and liberties conceded by previous kings] had been corrupted and diminished. For some [barons King John] had disinherited without judgement of their peers; some he had condemned to a cruel death; of others he had violated their wives and daughters; and so instead of law there was tyrannical will.'

---

[6] Powicke, *King Henry III*, chs I, II, and *The Thirteenth Century*, ch. 1. For earlier pioneering studies, see the two articles by G. J. Turner, 'The minority of Henry III (part I)', 245–95, and 'The minority of Henry III (part II)', 205–62. For more recent work, see particularly Holt, *Magna Carta*, 269–82; Stacey, *Politics*, ch. 1; Eales, 'Castles and politics', 23–43.

[7] This private correspondence is contained within the Public Record Office's class of Ancient Correspondence: SC 1. Only the selection printed in *RL* was employed by Norgate and Powicke.

Thus the Waverley abbey annalist, looking back from the early minority of Henry III, explained the beginning of the war between John and the barons.[1] The annalist was right to believe that John's predecessors and, in particular, his father bore some responsibility for the grievances which exploded in 1215.[2] He was equally right to realize that many of the barons had highly personal grievances against John himself. John was licentious, cruel, impious, suspicious, cunning and graceless. It is impossible to cast aside the belief that his seduction, or attempted seduction, of the wives, sisters and daughters of his barons had political repercussions. The rebellions of Robert fitz Walter, Eustace de Vesci, Hugh de Neville and the earls of Salisbury and Surrey may have had greater or lesser tinges of this kind.[3] But more important were harder, material grievances. A long list of barons – Nicholas de Stuteville, the earls of Hereford, Hertford, Essex, Winchester and Huntingdon, the count of Aumale, Robert fitz Walter, William de Mowbray, Richard de Muntfichet, William de Lanvallei and William Mauduit, for example, believed, with greater or lesser justification, that they had been unjustly deprived by John or his predecessors of castles, lands, rights and liberties.[4] They had been disinherited, as the Waverley annalist put it, without judgement of their peers by the king's tyrannical will.

An equally long list of barons – Gilbert de Gant, William de Mowbray, Peter de Brus, John de Lacy, Robert de Vaux, Giles de Braose, bishop of Hereford, and the earls of Essex and Norfolk, to make but a start – had grievances against the king of a financial kind. They either had been finally forced to pay their old debts to the crown or had been saddled with huge new burdens by way of reliefs or proffers for favours.[5] The manner in which indebtedness to the crown could be used to break even the mightiest baron had been dramatically demonstrated in the case of William de Braose. Even in John's own account of the affair, which made out that he had acted perfectly lawfully, there was something chilling in the revelation that William's wife, Matilda, had been made to offer 50,000 marks for the king's grace when her total resources amounted to 24 marks and a few pieces of gold. Matilda's misfortunes had begun when she refused to hand over

---

[1] *Ann. Mon.*, ii, 282.

[2] For John's reign and Magna Carta, see Holt's *Northerners, Magna Carta* and his collected articles in *Magna Carta and Medieval Government*. Two other studies are Painter, *The Reign of John*, and Warren, *King John*.

[3] Norgate, *John Lackland*, 289–93; Painter, *Reign of John*, 231–4; *Recueil*, xvii, 110 (for Salisbury).

[4] *CRR*, xi, no. 1195; xii, no. 2646; Painter, *Reign of John*, 330–6; Holt, *Magna Carta*, 253–4.

[5] *Walt. Cov.*, 225; *Ann. Mon.*, iii, 45; Holt, *Northerners*, 167, 171–2, 174; Carpenter, 'The personal rule of King Henry III', 54–5.

her sons as hostages to John on the grounds that his nephew Arthur, whom 'he should have kept honourably, he had wickedly murdered'. Matilda and William, her eldest son (married to a daughter of the earl of Hertford), ultimately suffered a similar fate. Both were starved to death in Windsor castle.[6] There could be no more potent illustration of the appalling consequences of John's unharnessed will.

John's reign, however, was far from being an orgy of mindless oppression. He was a king with clear political purposes, of which the paramount was the recovery of the Angevin empire: the continental fiefs that he had held from the king of France.[7] In 1202 these fiefs had been confiscated by the court of the French king and in 1204 King Philip had actually taken possession of Normandy and Anjou. John was left with a tenuous hold of Gascony and parts of Poitou. These provinces were large in area but limited in resources. Normandy was far more valuable than the rest of the Angevin empire put together. After 1204 John laboured to construct the diplomatic alliances which would enable him to mount a campaign to reverse the verdict of 1204. He also spent 'ten furious years' amassing the necessary resources. In the process, England was subjected to the personal presence of the king, as never before under the Angevins, who had spent much of their time overseas. The north, in particular, for the first time felt the weight of royal government: hence the central role played by 'the Northerners' in the ultimate revolt. Many of the financial grievances of the barons, therefore, arose not from senseless acts of greed or vengeance but from the king's desperate need to amass a treasure chest for war.

In thus 'much governing' England John was well placed. His predecessors had built up an administrative system whose range and power were almost unique in the medieval west.[8] The monarchy possessed extensive financial resources. The most traditional of all were the county farms and the proceeds of the manors of the royal demesne. Then there were the 'feudal sources' of revenue, the sources deriving from the tenurial relationship between the king and his baronial tenants-in-chief. Here the king could profit from scutages, reliefs, wardships and marriages of heirs and heiresses. Justice too was lucrative, especially criminal justice, with the king capitalizing on amercements and his entitlement to the chattels of outlaws and convicted criminals. In addition, the king taxed the Jews and exploited debts owed by Christians to Jews which had come into his hands. He made large sums from the royal forest and secured the occasional aid, or general tax, the most lucrative, a percentage levy on the value of movable property in 1207, raising £60,000.

[6] *F*, 107–8; *Chron. Maj.*, ii, 523–4; Norgate, *John Lackland*, 288.
[7] For the continental possessions of the Angevins, see Gillingham, *The Angevin Empire*.
[8] Warren, *The Governance of Norman and Angevin England*, is the most recent study.

To exploit these sources of revenue, as well as to maintain order and dispense justice, John's predecessors had constructed a formidable administrative apparatus. True, in the localities, magnates possessed extensive means of political and social control through their manorial and honourial courts, and through their share in royal jurisdiction: their private gallows and private hundreds. But cutting across or surrounding these areas of magnate power was the structure of royal administration. Here the basic unit was the county and within that the hundred, each with its own court. The king's chief local agent was the sheriff, who was appointed and dismissed at the royal will. The sheriff was responsible each year for a fixed money farm for his county and for collecting the numerous debts owed to the king by individuals. He also executed judicial decisions and a whole range of other orders. The chief agents for dispensing justice in the localities were the justices in eyre, who periodically visited the counties, sitting in the county courts, to hear 'all pleas': the pleas, that is, of the crown (pleas concerning serious crime) and the wide range of civil litigation brought before the king's judges by the petty and grand assizes, the legal measures introduced by Henry II. And then, alongside the sheriffs and the justices in eyre, there were quite separate officials for administering the royal forests.

At the centre the king had extensive means for monitoring and controlling the activities of his local agents. He retained by his side either the chancellor or his deputies, who were responsible for writing royal charters and letters. By John's reign both were precisely dated, and recorded, according to their type, on the chancery rolls, which show that almost every day, and frequently many times a day, the king was despatching letters to his sheriffs and other agents. For a period in John's reign there were also two institutions of government permanently resident at Westminster. The newest of these was a bench of justices which heard the same type of civil pleas as the eyres, together with cases referred to it from the county courts. However, between 1209 and 1212, John suspended the bench, as it was called, and its judges followed him round the country. The other institution at Westminster was far more important and of far longer standing: the exchequer. Its function was to exact and audit the money owed the king. It sent out twice a year to the sheriffs lists of all the debts which they were to collect and pay in to it. Each year the exchequer audited the accounts of the sheriffs and the other collectors of revenue, recording the results on an annual series of pipe rolls. The exchequer was, therefore, the main money-getting institution of the English kings. As such it was at the heart of their oppressive kingship.

It was these resources and this system which John drove forward with ferocious energy in the years after 1204. Individual barons suffered from the king's exploitation of his feudal sources of revenue and the debts which they owed to the Jews. They also resented the

increasingly narrow circle of men who came to enjoy John's patronage.
John was far from lacking the support of great barons; he retained the
loyalty of the earls of Pembroke, Chester and Derby as well as that of
many barons of the Welsh March. But often his closest servants were
new men, some of them foreigners, and their monopolization of office in
the later years of the reign created inevitable animosity.

Resentment at the pressures of John's government was not confined
to baronial ranks, however. The king's exactions affected a much wider
range of society. The issue of the forest touched knights, gentry and
ecclesiastical institutions just as much as it did great barons. Many
people in a county suffered when a sheriff was forced to raise money
above the county farm. Everyone over a minimal property qualification
had to pay the great tax on movables of 1207.

John could have escaped the consequences of his 'much government'
had he been successful. Instead, in 1214, his invasion of Anjou ran into
determined opposition, while further north his allies were decisively
defeated by King Philip at Bouvines. John returned home, his money
spent, his prestige in tatters. His enemies saw their chance. The road
from Bouvines to Runnymede was a short one.[9] Three-quarters of a
century before, in the civil war of Stephen's reign, the great barons had
extracted individual charters of concession from the king and the
empress. In 1215, although just as keen to satisfy individual aspirations, they were able to conceive a charter dealing with the general
grievances of themselves and others in society. The pressures of
Angevin government had made men aware of a common problem and
inspired them to find a common solution.

Magna Carta wasted no time on political theory.[10] The first clauses
declared that the English church should be 'free' and confirmed John's
existing promise of free elections. After that the Charter imposed a
series of restrictions on the operations of the king and his government.
Many of the initial clauses were concerned with money-getting. The
relief for an earldom and a barony was to be £100; for a knight's fee £5.
No reliefs were to be charged where there had been a minority; only
reasonable issues were to be extracted from land held in wardship; no
land was to be seized in satisfaction of debts if the chattels of the debtor
sufficed for payment. Debts to the Jews were not to gather interest
during minorities; scutages and aids, other than those taken on three
customary occasions, were only to be imposed 'by the common counsel
of the kingdom'; the counties were to be held at the 'ancient farm
without any increment'.

The Charter also regulated the operations of the judicial system and
attempted to make the king's justice both more available and more
equitable. Common, that is, broadly civil, pleas were to be heard in

[9] Holt, *Northerners*, 100.
[10] The charter is printed and translated in Holt, *Magna Carta*, 313–37.

'any certain place'. They were not, in other words, to follow the
vagaries of the king's movements around the country, as had happened, for the most part, between 1209 and 1212. Likewise, two judges
were to visit each county four times a year to hear the petty assizes, the
legal procedures developed by Henry II. The unharnessed and
sometimes vindictive operations of the king's will in the treatment of
individuals were also brought within bounds. Amercements were to be
related to the seriousness of the offence and the ability to pay. Earls and
barons were only to be amerced by their peers. The king was not to
deny, sell or delay right and justice (clause 40), and no free man was to
be taken, imprisoned, disseised, outlawed, exiled, or in any way
destroyed, nor would the king 'go against him' save 'by lawful
judgement of his peers or the law of the land' (clause 39).

The Charter had little to say about the personnel of government but
some of John's most notorious servants, notably Philip Mark and
Engelard de Cigogné (the sheriffs respectively of Nottinghamshire–
Derbyshire and Gloucestershire), were to be dismissed for ever from
office. Finally, under the so called 'security clause', the barons were to
choose twenty-five of their number who were empowered 'with the
commune of all the land' to force the king to keep the Charter if any
breach of it was complained of.

Some clauses of the Charter were highly specific; some were vague
and open to a variety of interpretations; some only touched the fringes
of problems. Nonetheless, the achievement of the Charter was immense. In detail, it imposed a large number of restrictions on the
operations of kingship. In general, it asserted a fundamental principle:
that the king's will was subject to the law. Like contemporary
chroniclers, the Charter sometimes implied that the law which it was
asserting was merely the law observed by previous kings but flouted by
the Angevins. This was largely fiction. Many of the clauses of Magna
Carta had no precise precedents. If Magna Carta brought the activities
of English kingship within the law, it was the law which Magna Carta
itself created.

In one sense the Charter was aimed not merely at King John but at
the administrative system created by his Norman and Angevin
predecessors. If John had got out the whip, they had supplied the horse.
The Charter, however, was far from condemning all the work of the
Angevins. It accepted the new legal procedures conceived by Henry II
and endeavoured to make them more readily available. As has been
mentioned, common pleas were to be heard in a 'certain' place (clause
17). Under clause 18, two judges were to visit the counties four times a
year to hear the petty assizes. These regulations showed that English
kingship had a future: for the only time in the Charter, the king was told
to expand his activities rather than contract them. Royal justice was in
demand. Thus there was no intention of reducing the king to a mere

feudal overlord. If Henry II was the author of the misfortunes of his house, he was also its saviour.

Clause 18 also showed something else about the Charter: it was far from being an exclusively 'baronial' document. The petty assizes which it sought to make more available were open to all free men. The two judges who were to visit the counties to hear the assizes were to sit with four knights of each county elected by the county court. This reflected both the ability and self-confidence of the knights and the general aspiration of local society to control its own affairs; an aspiration revealed equally by the proffers from individual counties in John's reign for the sheriff to be a local man. Thus the Charter reflected the political society with which the minority government had to deal. It would be concerned with the affairs of individual barons but it had also to respond to pressures from powerful groups in the counties. The politics of the minority, indeed, foreshadowed those of the revolutionary years between 1258 and 1265 when key importance attached to the demands of knights and gentry for the reform of local government.

Local or county society should not be seen as something distinct from lordship, however.[11] Barons, as much as knights, were part and parcel of it. It was barons too who hoped to control the petty assizes through having four knights sit with the judges, for those knights might well be their servants or clients. In the early thirteenth century there was nothing exclusively 'feudal' about the affinities of great barons. The latter might well obtain service and support from their knightly tenants, but they equally looked outside that circle and enlisted able men where they could be found, rewarding them with land, wardships and money fees. A great lord, like the king, was interested in efficient service and, in the search for it, could not afford to be confined to the tenants whom he had inherited. Likewise, many knights had a degree of independence derived from wealth, experience in local government and the fact that they often held land from several lords. An ambitious knight might enter the service of his tenurial lord if that seemed the best path to advancement, but, if it did not, he looked elsewhere. Thus in Oxfordshire, in John's reign, where the county's greatest baron, Henry de Oilly, was an ineffectual figure, his knightly tenants took service with Thomas Basset of Headington instead. McFarlane's dictum that 'lordship lasted so long as it was good lordship, or until it was ousted by better' applies as well to this period of history as it does to any later. In such a fluid situation the political structure of an English county was like the architectural structure of an Italian medieval city, a San

[11] This question will be clarified in Dr Crouch's forthcoming work. For an important recent article, see Waugh, 'From tenure to contract: lordship and clientage in thirteenth-century England', 811–39. For the knights in John's reign, see Holt, *Northerners*, ch. iv.

Gimignano for instance, where the towers of the nobility rose above the roofs of everyone else. But, just as those towers varied in height, and were frequently subject to destruction, so the dominance of the great varied between counties and between periods. Sometimes a baron might exercise a more or less stable rule; sometimes knights and gentry might have the independence to create their own harmony or discord. By the early thirteenth century, therefore, the business of politics was complex. Kings had to deal with towns and churchmen. They had to cope with the ambitions of individual barons. They had also to contain the aspirations of local groups, composed in varying degrees of barons, knights and freemen, groups which aspired to control the local government of their counties (as clause 18 of Magna Carta showed) and secure a large reduction in the bounds of the royal forest.

John sealed Magna Carta at Runnymede on 15 June 1215 with little intention of keeping to it. Distrust between the two sides was overwhelming and the demands of those who believed that they had been deprived of property and rights 'without judgement of their peers', and should have them restored under the terms of Magna Carta, created immediate disputes. Some time in July John asked the pope to annul the Charter. When the papal letter arrived in England at the end of September, the country was already at war. The rebels realized that John could never be restrained by Magna Carta. The only solution was his replacement. Consequently they offered the throne to Louis, the eldest son of the king of France. Louis based his claim on the argument that John had been deposed and that he was the rightful successor both by election of the barons and by hereditary succession, his wife being a granddaughter of Henry II.[12] Louis's attraction, however, lay not in the debatable merits of his claim but in the superabundant resources of the French monarchy. He seemed the one person who could bring victory. Louis landed at Thanet on 21 May 1216. Three of John's chief supporters, Hugh de Neville and the earls of Salisbury and Surrey, at once deserted to him. In his last days, 'brought down by a grave and incurable illness', John agonized over the future of his dynasty. Without divine and papal aid, he confessed to the pope, he could see no way to secure its 'perpetual hereditary succession'.[13] John died at Newark on the night of 27–28 October, as a great gale swept over the castle from the flat, empty valley of the Trent. At once the earl of Salisbury urged the defender of Dover, Hubert de Burgh, to surrender to Louis. The cause of King John's young son, he declared, was hopeless.[14]

---

[12] *Historiae Anglicanae*, 1868–70; Petit-Dutaillis, *Louis VIII*, 72–87. Louis may also have promised to return lands that English barons had lost in Normandy.

[13] *Ann. Eccles.*, 359: *Successionem nostram haereditariam perpetuam.*

[14] *Coggeshall*, 183–4; *Chron. Maj.*, 3–5.

Chapter 2

WINNING THE WAR, 1216–17

i. *The new government*

In the critical situation on John's death, the supporters of his nine-year-old son hesitated over how to proceed. One idea was to convoke an assembly at Northampton 'to elect' Henry king but since Louis also claimed to have been elected, this would merely place Henry on a par with his rival. Instead, therefore, it was decided to plunge ahead at once with the coronation and base Henry's title on what John called 'perpetual hereditary succession', Louis's claim 'by succession' – that he was married to a granddaughter of Henry II – being tenuous in the extreme.[1] The coronation took place, under the supervision of Guala, the papal legate, at Gloucester on 28 October.[2] That ultimate responsibility for the young king belonged to the pope and to Guala as his representative there could be no doubt. John had granted the kingdom to the papacy in 1213 and on 15 October 1216, just before his death, he had begged the pope to take his heir and his kingdom into papal protection.[3] At the coronation itself Henry did homage to the papacy. Four days later he placed himself further under the papal wing by taking the cross, not with any intention of going on crusade but, as a Peterborough chronicle put it, 'for the greater protection of himself and his kingdom'.[4] All these things, together with his tender years, made Henry peculiarly the pope's 'vassal and ward'. Pope Honorius recognized no bounds to the authority which he could exercise in England. As soon as he heard of John's death, he conceded to Guala full power without appeal to do what he thought expedient for the king and the kingdom. The loyalist magnates were ordered to submit to him 'humbly and devotedly'.[5]

[1] *Acts of the Parliament of Scotland*, 112; Duncan, *Scotland*, 523 and n.9; *Ann. Eccles.*, 359; *Historiae Anglicanae*, 1868–70; Petit-Dutaillis, *Louis VIII*, 74–87.
[2] The evidence for Henry's coronation is brought together in Norgate, *Minority*, 5 n. 1.
[3] *Ann. Eccles.*, 359.
[4] *Chron. Maj.*, 2; *Chron. Petroburgense*, 7; *Guisborough*, 158; see Lloyd, ' "Political Crusades" in England', 113–14; Lloyd, *The Crusade*, 208–9; Tyerman, *The Crusades*, 137.
[5] *Honorii III Opera*, 106; *Recueil*, xix, 625. For Honorius's dealings with England, see Sayers, *Honorius III*, ch. 5.

The links between the papacy and the English monarchy, thus forged, were to be of profound importance throughout Henry III's minority but, for the moment, they did nothing to solve the problem of who was immediately to control the government. Guala was not a military man and could not personally direct the war. Equally, he never aspired to manage affairs on a day-to-day basis. John himself had given thought to this problem. On his death-bed, he had appointed thirteen executors who, apart from actions for the benefit of his soul, were to assist his sons in the recovery and defence of their inheritance. At the same time he had begged his entourage to ensure that Henry himself was entrusted to the guardianship of William Marshal, earl of Pembroke, 'for he will never hold the land save through him'.[6] William Marshal had proceeded to conduct the young boy to Gloucester for his coronation but he had recognized at once that there was no point in standing on John's delegation. Any position that he held would be worthless unless it derived from the general will. In this appreciation he revealed what was to be a central feature of his rule: the way that it would depend on the convening of great councils and the conferral of common consent. Immediately after the coronation ceremony, therefore, far from making a vulgar grab for power, the Marshal had to be urged by the young king's supporters to assume the guardianship of the king and kingdom.[7] There were many good reasons for their choice.

William Marshal derived his surname from the office of marshal of the royal household which had been hereditary in his family since at least the reign of Henry I. The landed resources of the family were not particularly large, however, and William was a younger son with his own way to make in the world. He had served at the courts of all the Angevin kings and received from King Richard a splendid reward: the marriage to the heiress of Chepstow in Wales, Leinster in Ireland and Longueville in Normandy. To this John himself had added Pembroke, to which William, through his marriage, had an exiguous claim.[8] By 1216 William was an old man – he said, with some exaggeration, that he was over eighty[9] – but, vigorous in mind and body, he was an

---

[6] *Maréchal*, lines 15167–90, confirmed by *Normandie*, 180. John's executors were Guala; the bishops of Winchester, Chichester and Worcester; the master of the Templars; the earls of Pembroke, Chester and Derby; William Brewer; Walter de Lacy; John of Monmouth; Savari de Mauléon; and Falkes de Bréauté; *F*, 144. In fact, there is no evidence that they acted together as a political body.

[7] *Maréchal*, lines 15255–86, 15373–88.

[8] *Peerage*, x, Appendix G, 91–7. Biographies are Painter, *William Marshal* and Duby, *Guillaume le Maréchal*. William inherited the office and estates of his elder brother when the latter died without legitimate offspring in 1194. For the claim to Pembroke, see Flanagan, 'Strongbow, Henry II and Anglo-Norman intervention in Ireland', 63–4, 77.

[9] *Maréchal*, line 15510.

obvious person to shoulder the burden of the young king's cause. He commanded abundant material resources. He was also endowed with impressive personal qualities which were celebrated, if also simplified, in his biography, written around 1226 and based on the reminiscences of his squire, John of Earley.[10]

A principal theme of the biography was the unswerving fidelity which William had displayed to his lords. His fidelity to King John had certainly been remarkable. He disliked the king and, if he had gained much from him, he had also suffered at his hands. Moreover, after the loss of Normandy in 1204, William had done homage to King Philip for Longueville and thus, alone amongst the English barons, had retained his Norman lands. If, in 1216, William went over to Louis, his problem of owing allegiance to two kings was solved. There were, however, countervailing considerations, for defection might have repercussions on William's position in Wales, and even more in Ireland, where the rebellion had no footing. Perhaps William hedged his bets by conniving in the rebellion of his eldest son. But he himself remained firmly in the Angevin camp and ultimately there was surely more to this than a simple balance of self-interest. To William the dishonour of desertion, after long years of fidelity to the Angevins, outweighed any material pros and cons. 'I will never desert [King Henry] even if I have to beg my bread' he proclaimed.[11] William's loyalty, therefore, seemed to promise a rock on which King Henry's cause might be founded, a rock, moreover, which would attract rather than repel men found in the opposite camp. William had supped with King John but with a long spoon. In general he had made his reputation not as a local administrator or baron of the exchequer but as a boon-companion, knight and councillor. He was not associated with the unpopular processes of Angevin government and administration.

Even more than his loyalty, William's biography was concerned to extol his prowess as a knight. His reputation in this sphere was another factor of key importance in supporting his candidature in 1216. William had won fame as 'the greatest knight in the world' on the tournament field. Of course, the greatest knights could also be the greatest fools; the warrior 'vigorous in arms but in worldly affairs unwise and injudicious' was a common figure in twelfth- and thirteenth-century England.[12] William, however, was both vigorous and wise. Reading between the lines of the biography, it is clear that he had a shrewd head for the business of war. His experiences fighting for

[10] *Maréchal*, vol. iii, contains an extensive introduction by the editor, Paul Meyer, and an abridged translation into modern French. An English translation of this abridgement, covering the years 1216–19, is to be found in *EHD*, 81–103.

[11] Concern for his position in Ireland may equally have kept Walter de Lacy loyal.

[12] For one example, *Peerage*, v, 121 n.b.

the Angevins had grafted the sagacity of the calculating general on to the enthusiasms of the carefree knight. He was an ideal man to lead the young king's forces.[13]

William had another quality to which the biography draws attention, indirectly, in its stress upon the virtue of largesse and the value of material objects. Not surprisingly, for one who had carved out his own fortune, William understood the workings of patronage and with it the key to much contemporary politics. He would know how to use patronage both to bind the king's party together and tempt others to join it. His career had given him one final point of strength. His struggle to secure his wife's inheritance, particularly in Ireland, had set problems of allegiance and local control similar, if on a smaller scale, to those that he would face as regent of Henry III.[14]

William Marshal's material resources, fidelity to the Angevins, military expertise and political understanding, therefore, all recommended him as the young king's guardian. John himself had designated him for the position. Yet, asked to accept control on the day of the coronation, William still hesitated and postponed matters till the morrow. His own entourage gave conflicting advice, reflecting the mixture of idealism and self-interest within William himself. John Marshal, William's nephew, stressed the honour that could be won; John of Earley the material disadvantages: the king had no money and William himself would have to satisfy everyone's demands. Ralph Musard was more optimistic: William would be able to make his familiars 'rich men'.[15] William had hesitated partly because of his age, partly because he knew that he had an absent rival. This was the earl of Chester, who, as Alan Basset remarked, was the only possible alternative as the guardian of the king and kingdom.[16]

The earl of Chester was in his mid-forties. He too had a largely unblemished record of fidelity to the Angevins, while his material resources within England were greater than William Marshal's.[17] Chester could be magnanimous but he was also, like everyone else at this level of politics, highly ambitious and jealous of his rights and dignities. His demands and complaints were to cause William repeated difficulties. When Chester arrived on the day after the coronation, his

---

[13] For William and war, see Gillingham, 'War and chivalry in the *History of William Marshal*', 1–13.

[14] Crouch, 'Strategies of lordship in Angevin England and the career of William Marshal', 16–25.

[15] *Maréchal*, lines 15401–64. John Marshal was an illegitimate son of William's older brother.

[16] *Maréchal*, lines 15500–4.

[17] For Chester, see Harris, 'Ranulph, Earl of Chester'; Painter, *Reign of John*, 20, 25–9; Alexander, *Ranulf of Chester*.

entourage complained that the ceremony should have been delayed until his arrival. Chester, however, ignored these murmurings and urged William to accept control of the king, a decision that he may later have regretted.[18] Guala too added his persuasions, promising the old man 'remission and pardon of his sins'. It was the prospect of this spiritual reward, according to his biography, which finally induced William to shoulder the burden of the young king's cause. His hesitation had ensured that his position was indeed soundly based on general consent. As the Barnwell annalist put it, the king and kingdom were entrusted to his care 'by common counsel'.[19] William moved at once to broaden the base of his government. He could not, he said, personally look after the young king, for he needed to move about the kingdom. He entrusted him, therefore, to the care of his previous governor, Peter des Roches, bishop of Winchester, the armour-plated Touraigneau protégé of King John.[20]

Ralph Musard, in urging William to accept control of the kingdom, had hoped that he would make his familiars 'rich men'. William had, indeed, to grapple immediately with questions of patronage. The first enrolled letter of the new reign, issued on 30 October, conceded the castles of the Peak and Bolsover to William de Ferrers, earl of Derby, the brother-in-law of the earl of Chester, until completion of the king's fourteenth year. The aim was to bind Derby as tightly as possible to the cause of the young king by giving way to his most cherished ambition, one which his family was to pursue throughout the reign of Henry III, ultimately to its ruin. This was to secure the inheritance which Derby's grandfather, William II Peverel, had forfeited in 1154–55. In 1199 John had allowed Derby to obtain some manors by right of inheritance from William Peverel but had made him resign his claim to the greatest prize, the castles of Bolsover and the Peak, the latter the *caput* of the whole Peverel inheritance. The war had given Derby the chance to reverse this decision and in 1216 he had prised from John a grant (on unspecified terms) of the two castles.[21] In October 1216, therefore, William Marshal was confirming John's concession. But it was one thing to do this, another to actually get seisin of the castles for Derby. Part of the trouble was that the Peak was held by the great loyalist

---

[18] *Maréchal*, lines 15473–82, 15521–35. See below p. 36.

[19] *Maréchal*, lines 15547–58; *Walt. Cov.*, 233.

[20] *Maréchal*, lines 15580–610. The Barnwell chronicler (*Walt. Cov.*, 233) states that the care of the king and kingdom was entrusted 'by common counsel' to Guala and Bishop Peter as well as to William Marshal. William, however, was very clear that Peter owed his position solely to him: see below p. 106.

[21] *PR*, 1; *Peerage*, iv, 765–6; *RLP*, 188, 192b, 193. The earl of Derby's struggle to secure the Peverel inheritance is fully discussed in Golob, 'The Ferrers earls of Derby', 196–8, 201–5. The castle of the Peak is Peverel castle at Castleton in Derbyshire.

castellan, Brian de Lisle. Even John in his last days had failed to persuade Lisle to surrender it to Derby. Eventually he had authorized the latter to take the Peak by force, thus sanctioning, in the middle of a civil war, a private war within his own party.[22]

The grant to Derby also highlighted another of William's problems: he had to conjure up patronage with one hand tied behind his back. John, had he wished, could have granted Bolsover and the Peak to Derby in hereditary right, but William and his government felt disbarred from making grants in perpetuity, especially of a secular nature, while the king was under age.[23] This was not surprising. In Roman law the tutors who controlled children below the age of puberty (fourteen years) were prohibited from alienating the property of their wards.[24] Canon law was not directly concerned with the position of minors but ecclesiastics were particularly conscious of the rights of those under age. Indeed, Pope Alexander III had declared that it was unlawful for a bishop to cause loss to his church, and that it should always be kept unharmed, 'according to the [Roman] law relating to minors'.[25] Above all, in 1216, William Marshal and his colleagues had before them the example of English custom. Essentially they applied to the minority of the king the rule that already governed the minority of his subjects. As the lawbook *Glanvill* put it, during the minority of a tenant, a lord 'may not lawfully alienate any of the inheritance permanently'.[26] In one sense the application of this rule to the king showed the underlying strength of monarchy, for it indicated how closely interlinked were the rights of the king and his subjects. If those of the king were not maintained during a minority, those of his subjects might suffer the same fate. But, in the short term, the rule severely limited William's ability to reward the young king's supporters. Thus

[22] *RLP*, 188b; Holt, *Northerners*, 140. Bolsover was held by Gerard de Furnivall, who had joined the rebels by September 1216.

[23] For a grant, apparently in perpetuity, to the monks of Worcester cathedral on the day of John's burial there: *Worcester Cartulary*, nos 328, 328a.

[24] In cases of urgent necessity, however, tutors could seek permission to alienate from the praetor. The restrictions on tutors were increasingly extended to cover the curators who bore responsibility for the affairs of minors (those aged between fourteen and twenty-five); *Digest of Justinian*, ii, 808–12 (book XXVII, ix); Berger, *Dictionary of Roman Law*, 747–8, 611. See also *ibid.*, 421, 583, 682; *Institutes of Justinian*, 43–64 (book I, xiii–xxvi); *Digest of Justinian*, i, 125–38, 140–47 (book IV, iv, vi); ii, 745–812 (books XXVI, XXVII, i–ix); Lemosse, 'L'incapacité juridique comme protection de l'enfant en droit romain', 250; Buckland, *Text-Book of Roman Law*, 154, 170.

[25] Cheney, 'Inalienability in mid-twelfth-century England', 467, 468 n. 3; Metz, 'L'enfant dans le droit canonique medieval', 10–96. If he was using 'minor' in a technical Roman law sense, Alexander was referring to the protection afforded to those aged between fourteen and twenty-five; see above note 24 and the references cited there.

[26] *Glanvill*, 82; see *Bracton*, ii, 51–2.

the best that could be done for the earl of Derby was to grant him
Bolsover and the Peak until completion of the king's fourteenth year
when there was some implication that the latter might come of age.
This first concession of the reign thus encapsulated some of the major
issues of the early minority: the pressure to find patronage, the
difficulty of controlling the king's local agents and the obligation,
against the possibility of future victory, to safeguard the rights of the
young king.

ii. *The military situation*

On the night of 29 October, having accepted charge of the government,
William Marshal withdrew to his chamber and considered the
situation with John of Earley, Ralph Musard and John Marshal. It
seemed so bad that Earley contemplated an eventual withdrawal to
Ireland. The Marshal spoke bravely of how he would carry the king on
his shoulders from island to island and from land to land: 'I will never
desert him even if I have to beg my bread'. But it would be a marvel, he
said, if he could bring the young, penniless boy safely to port.[1]

There were reasons for apprehension. According to Painter's
calculations, at the time of John's death the holders of ninety-seven
baronies were in revolt, as against thirty-six who were loyal; of the
twenty-seven greatest barons, only eight remained loyal.[2] Louis
controlled London and virtually the whole of the eastern half of
England. He was in alliance with Alexander, king of Scotland, and with
Llywelyn, the prince of North Wales. Yet there were compensating
features. If Louis had more baronial support, he had virtually no
ecclesiastical; the excommunications launched by the pope against him
and his supporters had seen to that. In London, Louis's clerks Simon
Langton, Gervase of Heybridge, Elias of Dereham and Robert de St
Germain might preach that the excommunications were invalid but the
highest ecclesiastical post held between them was Dean of St Paul's, to
which Gervase had a doubtful title.[3] The abbot of St Albans steadfastly
refused to do homage to Louis unless first absolved from his homage to
the king of England, despite Louis's threats to burn the town.[4] At least
seven bishops were present at Henry's coronation and there were
eleven at the council convoked the next month at Bristol.[5] No bishop
supported Louis. Henry's coronation had been a makeshift affair, for

[1]   *Maréchal*, lines 15624–708.
[2]   Painter, *Reign of John*, 297.
[3]   Richardson, 'Letters of Guala', 252–4.
[4]   *Gesta Abbatum*, i, 259; see also *Historiae Anglicanae*, 1870.
[5]   Norgate, *Minority*, 5 n.1, to which list one can probably add the archbishop of
Dublin; *Melrose*, 66; *Ann. Mon.*, iv, 60; *Select Charters*, 336.

Westminster abbey, where it should have taken place, was in Louis's power and the archbishop of Canterbury, Stephen Langton, who should have officiated, was abroad at the papal court.[6] But Louis, despite holding the abbey, was never crowned at all, for the simple reason that there was no one to crown him.

There was equally little danger that Louis would immediately roll up the bases of Angevin power in the western half of England, bases which could derive some support from the resources of Ireland. True, the very coronation banquet had been disturbed by news of an attack, probably by Llywelyn or Reginald de Braose, on William Marshal's castle of Goodrich, less than eighteen miles away, but Llywelyn made no effort to move east into England.[7] His own priorities and the cordon of Marcher barons who remained loyal to the Angevin cause limited his activities to Wales. The Henrician position was also well protected from assault from the east. When the author of the *History of the Dukes of Normandy*, who was with Louis's army during the war, sketched the position at the time of Henry's accession, he reeled off a list of castles and their castellans: Peter de Maulay at Corfe; Hubert de Burgh at Dover; Engelard de Cigogné at Windsor; Falkes de Bréauté at Northampton, Oxford, Buckingham, Hertford, Bedford and Cambridge; Robert de Gaugi at Newark; Hugh de Balliol at Newcastle upon Tyne.[8] He could have added, amongst others, Philip Mark at Nottingham, Brian de Lisle at Knaresborough, Philip of Oldcoates at Bamburgh and Nicola de Hay at Lincoln. Many of these castellans commanded large sums of money extracted from ransoms and extorted from the local populations, and were quite able to survive for long periods on their own.[9] Several were foreigners of modest birth whom John had brought to England, men utterly dependent on the survival of the Angevin dynasty. Philip Mark, Engelard de Cigogné and Peter de Maulay, for example, were all from the Touraine, Maulay having begun his career as an usher in John's household.[10] Robert de Gaugi was a Flemish serjeant and Falkes de Bréauté, the greatest of the

---

[6] If, as seems likely, Guala ordered the bishop of Winchester actually to crown Henry, it was probably in deference to the claims of the archbishop of Canterbury; *Ann. Mon.*, iv, 60; Norgate, *Minority*, 5 n. 1. In November 1218 Guala assured Westminster abbey that the Gloucester coronation would not prejudice its rights; Westminster Abbey Muniments, no. 51111; Sayers, *Honorius III*, 168 and n. 30; see also the story in the Melrose chronicle: *Melrose*, 64.

[7] *Maréchal*, lines 15349–72 and p. 390. For Llywelyn, see Davies, *Wales*, 236–51.

[8] *Normandie*, 181. At Newcastle Balliol was the deputy of Philip of Oldcoates.

[9] Holt, *Northerners*, 228. For evidence of these wartime revenues, see, for example, *Pipe Roll 1215*, 45; *Pipe Roll 1221*, 95; E 372/67, r.3d, m.2; Holt, 'Philip Mark', 16; *Gesta Abbatum*, i, 295–8.

[10] *Normandie*, 180. For these men, see *Gloucester Pleas*, xiii–xvii; Holt, 'Philip Mark', 8–24; *Pipe Roll 1214*, xi–xii; Ballentyne, ' "Gerardus de Atyes" '.

castellans, the illegitimate son of a Norman knight who had made his name as a brutally efficient governor of Glamorgan. Falkes too had started out as a 'poor serjeant' of King John, known then only by his unusual first name which derived, so the story went, from the scythe – *falx* – with which he had killed a knight in his father's meadow in Normandy.[11] These men were as ruthless as any on the other side. The castles which they held formed an aggressive shield digging into territory held by Louis and defending the Angevin heartlands to the west. The Barnwell chronicler dates to the time of Henry's accession Louis's growing awareness that 'the royal castles were many and well fortified'.[12]

Before one castle, above all, Louis had suffered a decisive reverse. This was Dover, defended by Hubert de Burgh. Louis had begun the siege on 10 July 1216.[13] Personally directing the operations, he had taken the north-west barbican and undermined the gate behind it; but the breach was filled and on 14 October Louis conceded a truce. A few days later, when John's death was known, Hubert de Burgh rejected the earl of Salisbury's demand to surrender. Louis departed, as Roger of Wendover said, to besiege smaller castles.[14] Next year it was Dover, untaken in his rear, that forced Louis to split his army before the battle of Lincoln, with fatal results. Equally, it was Dover and the Cinque Ports which raised the fleet that destroyed Louis's reinforcements coming from Calais. In short, failure before Dover in 1216 laid the foundations for the defeats in 1217 which wrecked Louis's cause in England.

iii. *Magna Carta, 1216*

With both sides deeply entrenched, the first moves of the Henricians were diplomatic rather than military. A great council of the young king's supporters was summoned to Bristol early in November. Here, however, a difficulty arose over the position of William Marshal. He had, since his appointment, been calling himself 'justiciar'.[1] This was natural: the justiciar under the Angevins had controlled the

---

[11] *Normandie*, 172–3, 181; *RLP*, 68b; *Coggeshall*, 204.
[12] *Walt. Cov.*, 232.
[13] The siege is described in detail in *Normandie*, 177–80.
[14] *Coggeshall*, 182; *Chron. Maj.*, 5. *Normandie*, 180, asserts that John was upset by the truce. According to *Coggeshall*, 182, under its terms, Hubert agreed to surrender the castle if he did not receive help. That, however, Louis had been defeated is clear from his withdrawal from the castle and the fact that, although not relieved, it was never surrendered to him. The Barnwell chronicler simply says the truce was to last until the following Easter: *Walt. Cov.*, 232. That John, at the time of his death, had full confidence in Hubert is shown by orders on 18 October assigning him 500 marks: *RLP*, 199b.
[1] *PR*, 1–2; *RLC*, 293; see also *Recueil*, xix, 625.

government of England during the king's frequent absences overseas and thus held a position not so very different from that which William now occupied.[2] The problem was that John's last justiciar was very much alive in the person of Hubert de Burgh, who, with the truce in force at Dover, attended the Bristol council and protested at his apparent dismissal. The response was to devise a new title for William. He was now called by the king 'our ruler and the ruler of our kingdom' (*rector noster et regni nostri*).[3] Hubert, however, remained acutely aware that William Marshal was in effect doing his job. As he said later, 'all the time of the war he could not leave [Dover] castle and could not exercise the office of justiciar'.[4] Tension persisted between the two men throughout William Marshal's regency.[5]

With this matter on one side, the government moved to exploit what appeared its greatest asset – the death of King John and the succession of his young, blameless son. Henry shrugged and the weight of John's crimes fell from his shoulders. 'We hear', he declared in a royal letter, 'that a quarrel arose between our father and certain nobles of our kingdom, whether with justification or not we do not know. We wish to remove it for ever since it has nothing to do with us.'[6] That removal could be done, in part, by remedying the individual grievances which had pushed many into rebellion. Accordingly, in November and December, eighteen rebels were sent letters giving them safe-conducts to come to speak with the king or William Marshal.[7] On offer, at the very least, was the return of the lands which they had lost through their rebellion, King John's general practice having been to concede the lands of his enemies to his own supporters.[8] In some special cases more was attempted. Thus Hugh de Lacy, whom John had deprived of Ulster in 1210, was promised restoration of his rights and liberties through the counsel of the earls of Chester and Derby.[9]

The Henricians could also confront the more general cause of the war: John's rejection of Magna Carta. On 12 November 1216 at Bristol, a revised version of the Charter was issued by Henry III on the advice of Guala, eleven bishops, William Marshal, the earls of Chester and Derby, the count of Aumale, Hubert de Burgh, William Brewer and

---

[2] For a study of the office, see West, *Justiciarship*.
[3] *PR*, 3 onwards.
[4] *Chron. Maj.*, vi, 65.
[5] See below pp. 27, 53, 77–8.
[6] *F*, 145.
[7] *PR*, 2–16.
[8] These were the terms on which Warin fitz Gerald, one of those offered a safe-conduct, returned to the king's faith: *PR*, 3; *RLC*, 295; see also the terms offered to Gilbert de Laigle, *PR*, 17.
[9] *PR*, 4; Otway-Ruthven, *Medieval Ireland*, 80; Martin, 'John, lord of Ireland', 141–2; Lydon, 'The expansion and consolidation of the colony', 156.

eighteen other ministers and magnates. The document was sealed by the legate and William Marshal, here using for the first time his new title.[10]

This decision shaped the future of monarchy in England. In some ways it was extraordinary. The Charter, at King John's behest, had been condemned by the papacy and there was no possibility for Guala now to consult the pope about a reversal of policy. Equally, Henry was a minor and minors, according to both Roman law and English custom, could not make permanent gifts which diminished their patrimony. Yet here was Henry conceding fundamental liberties to his subjects, not until he was fourteen, or until he came of age, but for himself and his heirs in perpetuity. Responsibility for this change of course must ultimately have been Guala's. He must also have been responsible for particular changes in the new Charter, notably the omission of the clause in 1215 which promised the church free canonical elections.[11] On the face of it, this was a remarkable deletion since free canonical elections had been a central demand of the papacy since the twelfth century. But, in the context of 1216, it was an impossibility, for it might mean freedom to elect supporters of Louis, freedom not from a rapacious Angevin king but from a benevolent pope and legate.

In sanctioning the new Charter Guala was not, of course, acting alone. Probably all present saw the move as utterly necessary if the war was to be won and a stable peace secured thereafter. Beyond that, views may have differed. Some, perhaps, saw the concession as a distasteful expedient. William Brewer, for example, later asserted that the liberties in the Charter were invalid since they had been extorted by force.[12] But the majority of the magnates present probably supported the new Charter with enthusiasm. Now that King John was dead, 'they could at last express their real views'.[13] They had fought for John not in opposition to the Charter but for an amalgam of other political and personal reasons. The regent himself (as William Marshal will now be called) had quarrelled acrimoniously with John and later described him as a criminal ('felon').[14] The earl of Chester had already conceded a Charter of Liberties to Cheshire on the petition of his 'barons' there and can scarcely have objected to receiving liberties from the king when he was being forced to grant them to his men.[15] The clauses in the Charter which limited baronial relief to £100, prevented undue exploitation of

[10] *Select Charters*, 336–9.
[11] Conversely clause 5 on wardships was extended to cover ecclesiastical vacancies.
[12] See below p. 296.
[13] Holt, *Magna Carta*, 269.
[14] *Maréchal*, lines 18078–8. For William Marshal's attitude to the war, see also Holt, *Magna Carta*, 270, citing *Maréchal*, lines 14842–59, 15031–6.
[15] *Chartulary of St. Werburgh Chester*, 101–9; for a discussion of the date, see Harris, 'Ranulph Earl of Chester', 112.

wardships and forbad arbitrary arrest and disseisin would benefit the families of the Henrician magnates just as much as those of any rebel.

Those responsible for the 1216 Charter were not, however, utterly careless of the rights of the young king. Having boldly assumed that he could make permanent alienations while a minor, they at least diminished the effect by leaving out of the new Charter some of the clauses in the 1215 document which had impinged most closely on the rights and revenues of the crown.[16] Silently omitted, for example, was clause 25 which forbad the exaction of revenue above the old farm of the counties.[17] Likewise excised was clause 50 which compelled the king to dismiss such alien sheriffs as Philip Mark and Engelard de Cigogné, both of whom were now doing vital work as castellans. Another group of clauses the Charter frankly admitted had been put in abeyance as *gravia et dubitalia*. This frankness had a clear purpose. The clauses were being offered as subjects for negotiation, the king promising, when he had taken fuller counsel, to amend them in the interests of 'the common utility of all and the state and peace of ourselves and our kingdom'.[18] There was nothing disingenuous about this. The clauses were *dubitalia* in part because they were ambiguous, offering much to negotiate about. Did clauses 12 and 14, for example, mean that the king had to acquire common consent just for aids, or, a much greater encroachment on the customary rights of the crown, for scutages as well?[19] And what was to be done about the 'customs of the counties' and the forests into which special inquiries had been commissioned by the 1215 Charter?

The Charter of 1216, therefore, was a document put up for discussion, an offer to the rebels, an attempt to draw them into negotiation.[20] It endeavoured to strike a balance between the 'state of the king' and the 'common utility of all', thus suggesting a new basis for monarchy in England. In small ways the text was also clarified and improved, for example, by defining the size of a widow's dower and stating that heirs reached their majority at twenty-one. In bothering with such details, the officials who drafted the Charter showed 'remarkable confidence in the outcome of the war'.[21] That confidence, however, the events of the next few months were hardly to justify.

iv. *The period of stalemate, November 1216–February 1217*

Having granted a new version of the Charter, and put out feelers to individuals, the Henricians waited for results. Their hopes were shared

---

[16] Holt, *Magna Carta*, 271–2, for a discussion of the 1216 Charter.
[17] See below p. 114.
[18] *Select Charters*, 339.
[19] Scutages had customarily been levied at the king's will in place of military service.
[20] This point is also made by Stacey, *Politics*, 3–4.
[21] Holt, *Magna Carta*, 272.

by Pope Honorius who wondered, in a letter of 3 December, whether 'a pious and merciful God' might not 'convert the death of the king into good for his sons, and recall to their fealty those who persecuted the father, the cause of the hatred having been removed'.[1] Chroniclers and poets, writing after the war, believed that something like this had actually happened.[2] But in fact the initial harvest of the new reign was extremely disappointing. The rebels took oaths never to accept an heir of King John on the throne and, between Henry's coronation and Louis's departure for France to gather reinforcements around 27 February 1217, a period of four months, no one of consequence deserted Louis's cause.[3] Meanwhile, the military situation turned slowly against the Henricians.

On the day that the new version of Magna Carta was granted at Bristol, Louis began a siege of Hertford castle, forcing it to surrender some time between 30 November and 6 December.[4] Louis next attacked Berkhampstead castle (between 4 and 6 December) before agreeing to a general truce to last over Christmas. The regent accepted that this truce was in place on 15 December but it was purchased at a price, namely the surrender of Berkhampstead, which took place on 13 or perhaps 20 December.[5] The Christmas truce expired on 13 or 20 January. On the 13th the regent was at Oxford and discussions began with Louis at Cambridge. The English in Louis's party, however, refused to countenance any suggestion of a peace and all that was agreed was another truce, this one to last until 23 April. Again the Henricians paid a price – the surrender of the castles of Hedingham, Orford, Norwich and Colchester.[6]

---

[1] *Honorii III Opera*, 106.

[2] *Ann. Mon.*, iii, 48; *Political Songs*, 22.

[3] *Walt. Cov.*, 233. In November 1216 William de Albini, lord of Belvoir, who had defended Rochester against John in 1215, fined in 6,000 marks for the king's grace, gave his wife as a hostage for his faithful service and was released from prison. Next year he was given control of Sleaford castle: *Chron. Maj.*, 6; *PR*, 47, 68. The only other major baron to return to the king's faith was Warin fitz Gerald, who was probably not a man of much personal force: *RLC*, 295; Painter, *Reign of John*, 22.

[4] Only Roger of Wendover and the Southwark chronicle give dates for the events of November and December. They agree about the basic chronology but their precise dates sometimes differ by a week: *Chron. Maj.*, 5–6, 8; 'Southwark and Merton', 51–2; see also *Ann. Mon.*, ii, 287.

[5] *PR*, 12; *Walt. Cov.*, 234. It is impossible to reconcile the evidence bearing on the various truces of the winter of 1216–17 but the account given here is, I judge, the most likely version of events. Norgate's discussion, in which she postulated four separate truces (*Minority*, 18–19, 269–72), did not make use of all the evidence (for example, *PR*, 12), placed too much reliance on the very confused account given in *Maréchal*, lines 15717–43, and involved the redating of what seems a clear reference on 23 February 1217 to there having been two truces: *PR*, 109.

[6] *Walt. Cov.*, 235; *Maréchal*, lines 15735–48.

These depressing events puzzled William Marshal's biographer, who asserted that the truces were made without consulting him, which seems unlikely.[7] The fact was that the regent lacked the ability to take offensive action. For most of November and December he had remained at Gloucester or Bristol. It was not until early January that he ventured forth to Nottingham and took measures to succour the garrison holding out at Lincoln.[8] One restraining factor may well have been the threat to his rear posed by Llywelyn and Reginald de Braose. Another was that, as the regent lamented when he took up his job, 'the boy has no money'.[9] Thus knights were paid not with cash but with silks and jewels taken from the remains of John's treasure at Corfe and Devizes.[10] If supplies arrived intermittently from Ireland, within England such money as there was came not from regular revenues but from ransoms and extortions: on 8 December the regent threatened to burn Worcester unless it yielded up £100 which it had promised King John.[11] The problem was that revenue of this kind was usually absorbed by the local castellans. In December the regent tried urgently to secure £1,000 owed by the burgesses of Beverley but he never got it because the whole sum had been spent by Brian de Lisle on garrisoning Knaresborough castle.[12] Thus if the regent was quiescent, individual castellans were sometimes capable of aggressive action. In the dusk of 22 January 1217, with a force raised from his various castles, Falkes de Bréauté raided St Albans and extorted £100 from the abbot.[13]

The regent's task of co-ordinating such individual activity was not made easier by disputes within his own party. Brian de Lisle, for example, had still to surrender the Peak to the earl of Derby. He was enjoined to do so in a series of instructions issued between November and December 1216 and then, over Christmas, the king himself was produced to give verbal orders to Brian's deputy; all to no effect. Likewise there was a tussle between Derby and Philip Mark over possession of the royal manor of Melbourne in Derbyshire.[14] The regent was also having difficulties with the earl of Chester. The latter, infuriated by his failure to extract William of Lancaster (one of those captured at Rochester in 1215) from the custody of Peter de Maulay at Corfe, threatened to leave the kingdom *desolatum* and depart on

---

[7] *Maréchal*, lines 15735–44.
[8] *PR*, 20.
[9] *Maréchal*, line 15644; see also John of Earley's advice, lines 15453–9.
[10] *RLC*, 602b–3b; *Divers Accounts*, 34–7.
[11] *PR*, 10.
[12] *PR*, 8, 11; E 372/66, r.10d, m.1.
[13] *Chron. Maj.*, 12.
[14] *PR*, 4, 7–8, 15; *PR*, 20–1, 23, 29–30, 107. Melbourne had once been held by William Peverel, hence Derby's 'urgent demand' for its custody.

his crusade.[15] Meanwhile, the regent responded to Hubert's demands for help in munitioning Dover with the observation that he could perfectly well support the castle from the stock already in his possession.[16]

If, however, the regent was weighed down with difficulties, so was Louis. Since October 1216 he had gained Berkhampstead and tightened his hold on East Anglia but he had made no effort to move west against the main Henrician strongholds. His purpose in agreeing to the truce in January was to go to France to gather reinforcements.[17] Louis's journey to the coast, moreover, saw the first sign of a Henrician advance. The truces were broken, both sides blaming the other. The Henrician captain, Philip de Albini, established himself at Rye and managed, with the help of the Cinque Ports and the men from the Weald, under William of Kensham (nicknamed Willikin of the Weald), to shut Louis up in Winchelsea. Hearing the good news, the regent himself hurried up from Gloucester, only to be disappointed. On 28 February, when he had reached Chertsey or Dorking, he was met by Albini with the news that a French fleet had broken the blockade, that Rye had been retaken and Louis had sailed for France.[18]

v. *Louis in France, 27 February–23 April 1217: the movement to the young king*

The fortunes of the young king improved markedly during Louis's absence, which lasted until 23 April. On the morning of 5 March, as he left Shoreham-by-Sea, the regent was met on the road by his eldest son, William Marshal junior, and by the latter's bosom friend and ally, William Longespee, earl of Salisbury.[1] In the next few days a whole series of letters was issued, covering the two men's absolution from excommunication and the terms on which they entered the faith of the young king.[2] Nearly all contemporary chroniclers recognized that their desertion was a major blow to Louis. It was accompanied by the defection of a large number of lesser men; in March and early April over a hundred, mostly from Wiltshire (where the earl of Salisbury had substantial influence), Somerset, Dorset and Berkshire, joined the Henrician cause.[3] The young king also began to win castles. During March and April those of Rochester, Southampton, Portchester,

---

[15] *PR*, 19; *F*, 146, a letter which probably belongs to a period between February and April 1217, judging from its place on the close roll, *RLC*, 335b.

[16] *RLC*, 335b.

[17] *Walt. Cov.*, 235.

[18] *Normandie*, 182–7; *Maréchal*, lines 15761–869; *PR*, 108–9.

[1] *Maréchal*, lines 15873–88; *PR*, 35.

[2] *PR*, 109, 38; *RLC*, 299–299b.

[3] *RLC*, 300–4b; *Normandie*, 187; *Walt. Cov.*, 235; *Ann. Mon.*, iii, 47; *Chron. Maj.*, 13; *Coggeshall*, 185.

Farnham, Marlborough and Winchester (after a siege by the regent lasting several weeks) were all taken.[4]

Contemporary chroniclers provided two explanations for this winnowing out of Louis's party. The first, found in both Ralph of Coggeshall and the Barnwell chronicler, ascribed it to the extraordinary energy and activity of the legate.[5] Certainly, since the New Year, Guala had effected a substantial change in the position of the combatants. He had turned the war against Louis into a crusade. On 17 January Pope Honorius had granted Guala the power to suspend the crusading vows of those supporting the young king. On the strength of Honorius's somewhat ambiguous justification for doing this – that those siding with the king gained 'glory in the eyes of men and merit in the eyes of God' – Guala had not merely suspended existing vows; he had also granted the Henricians remission of their sins and signed them with the cross (whether or not they had taken it before), as though, in the words of the Barnwell chronicler, 'they were fighting against pagans'.[6] This new policy was in place by the end of February, when the royal host was said to contain a 'multitude of crusaders (crucesignatorum)', while Philip de Albini was described as 'the leader of the army of Christ (dux milicie Christi)'.[7]

A remarkable change had thus taken place. At the beginning of the war in 1215 the rebels themselves had taken the mantle of God and the church. Now, as the Barnwell chronicler observed, 'those who once called themselves the army of God, and boasted that they fought for the liberties of the church and the kingdom, were reputed to be the sons of Belial and compared to infidels'.[8] This new crusading element stimulated the morale of the Henricians but it confirmed and strengthened, rather than instigated, the decision to desert Louis. The

---

[4] Normandie, 187–8; Maréchal, lines 15889–16033.

[5] Walt. Cov., 235–6; Coggeshall, 185.

[6] RL, 527–9; Walt. Cov., 235–6.

[7] PR, 108; and see PR, 34, 57; F, 146. Drs Lloyd and Tyerman believe that the crusade had been proclaimed in England by 7 October 1216 since a papal letter of that date declared that 'Cum . . . S de Maloleone crucesignatus pro defensione regni anglie quod specialis iuris apostolice sedis existit carissimo in Christo filio J. regi anglorum illustri vassalo nostro existat fideliter et devote', his property should be protected: VL, Honorius III Regesta IX, f.8d (CPReg., 41); Lloyd, ' "Political Crusades" in England', 115, 119, n. 22; Tyerman, The Crusades, 137. In fact, the papal letter is ambiguous. In my view it means that Savari, 'having taken the cross [to go on crusade to the East], for the defence of the kingdom of England . . . stands for King John . . . faithfully and devotedly'. Compare the description of the earl of Chester as crucesignatus in F, 146. If Savari had indeed taken the cross specifically to defend the kingdom of England, it is strange that in November 1216 he went home to Poitou: Maréchal, lines 15713–16. The remaining evidence strongly suggests that the crusade was first proclaimed by Guala when the papal letters of January 1217 arrived in England.

[8] Walt. Cov., 236.

defections in March and April were highly regional and it is difficult to believe that the men of Berkshire and Wiltshire were simply more pious than those in the north.[9]

We should look, therefore, at the second explanation given for the desertions, that of the Dunstable annalist: 'the French became arrogant, repulsed the nobles of England from their counsels, began to call them traitors, and retained the castles which they took for themselves, and did not restore their rights to the English'. The Waverley annalist put this point slightly differently: both nobles and plebeians took the cross to fight against Louis, he said, 'preferring to have a king from their own land rather than from a foreign'.[10] These comments certainly got close to one of Louis's difficulties. He had been chosen to replace King John because he could back his candidature with the power and wealth of the French monarchy. The whole point, therefore, was for him to bring Frenchmen and French resources to England. This, however, was bound to create problems. Angevin apologists could paint the war as one fought to rescue the English people from the French invaders: thus the scutage imposed in 1217 was officially described as being 'to deliver England from the French'.[11] This propaganda may well have struck a chord amongst 'the plebeians', like those operating with William of Kensham in the Weald. It was propaganda, nonetheless, that was easily countered. Many of the great Angevin captains were aliens and the atrocities of the count of Nevers around Winchester can scarcely have been worse than those of Falkes around Bedford and Northampton.[12] Perhaps many English nobles shared the view of Gerald of Wales that Louis had come to free the *gens Anglorum* from the yoke of Angevin tyranny.[13] What created problems was less Louis's nationality *per se* than his difficulties, as the Dunstable annalist indicated, dividing influence and possessions between his English and French followers.

This is the background to the young Marshal's defection. In June 1216 he had complained to Louis over Adam de Beaumont acting as marshal of the army and demanded the office, hereditary so he said in his family, for himself. On this point Louis gave way.[14] The Marshal family also cherished a claim to the royal castle of Marlborough, which the regent's father had held from 1138 to 1158, making it the base for his

---

9 For a discussion which places more emphasis on the importance of the crusade in 1216–17, see Tyerman, *The Crusades*, 139–40.

10 *Ann. Mon.*, iii, 47; ii, 287.

11 *Pipe Roll 1215*, 14; see also *Coggeshall*, 185; *Ann. Mon.*, i, 62; *Political Songs*, 19.

12 *Ann. Mon.*, iii, 46.

13 Bartlett, *Gerald of Wales*, 96–8, 222–5.

14 *Normandie*, 174.

many exploits during the civil war of Stephen's reign.[15] But when Louis received the castle in July 1216 he infuriated the young Marshal by placing it under Robert count of Dreux, the brother of the duke of Brittany. Almost as soon as the young Marshal joined the Henrician cause, he went off to seize Marlborough. It remained in the hands first of his father and then himself until 1221.[16]

The earl of Salisbury's defection revealed another side of Louis's difficulties: that of dividing patronage between his English supporters. Salisbury was a bastard son of Henry II and thus was John's half-brother and Henry III's uncle. He had been a late-comer to Louis's cause, only joining up after the latter's landing in England. At the French court this change of sides was ascribed to a highly personal grievance: while Salisbury had languished in a French prison following his capture at Bouvines, John had seduced his wife.[17] If this was true, John's death removed one factor keeping Salisbury in Louis's camp. He remained, however, eminently buyable. Louis's problem was that he was unable to pay his price. Salisbury had gained his earldom through marriage to Ela, daughter and sole heiress of William fitz Patrick, earl of Salisbury. But the inheritance was comparatively small, leaving Salisbury as an earl without a castle; almost as bad as being a knight without a horse. Hence his driving ambition to increase his material power and resources. One way that he did so in John's reign was through securing the castle and honour of Trowbridge, which the great-great-grandfather of Salisbury's wife had given in frankmarriage to the Bohuns. John's seizure of Trowbridge from Henry de Bohun, earl of Hereford, and its conferral on Salisbury, however, constituted one of the disseisins committed 'unjustly and without judgement' *per volun-tatem regis*, which were redressed after the concession of Magna Carta.[18] Not surprisingly, the earl of Hereford became one of Louis's most ardent supporters and went to France, with the earl of Winchester, to offer him the throne.[19] Louis's difficulty, therefore, was that he could not possibly prefer Salisbury's claim to Trowbridge over that of the faithful Hereford. The regent, on the other hand, had no such difficulty.

---

[15] *Peerage*, x, Appendix G, 93–4; Painter, *William Marshal*, 4, 5, 8, 10; Norgate, *Minority*, 150. The Marshal family's interest in Marlborough was kept alive by its extensive private holdings in the vicinity, centring on such Berkshire and Wiltshire manors as Hamstead Marshal, Speen, Wexcombe and Great Bedwyn: Painter, *op. cit.*, 104. As Dr Crouch will show, many of William Marshal's knights were recruited from this area.

[16] *Normandie*, 175; *Maréchal*, 16028–33; see below pp. 185, 247.

[17] *Recueil*, xvi, 110 (the chronicle of William le Breton). Salisbury's wife was about twenty-three in 1214. John seems to have been in no hurry to secure Salisbury's release: *Peerage*, xi, 379; *RLP*, 140.

[18] *Peerage*, xi, 379–83; Painter, *Reign of John*, 40, 262, 330; Holt, *Magna Carta*, 121–2.

[19] *Normandie*, 160.

He provided, moreover, other material incentives. Salisbury was restored as sheriff of Wiltshire and castellan of Salisbury castle, custodies that he claimed to hold in hereditary right.[20] Even more, he was promised Sherborne castle and the counties of Somerset and Devon in return merely for 'homage and service'. How central this promise was in securing Salisbury's allegiance may be judged from the urgent letter sent to Peter de Maulay commanding him to surrender Sherborne and Somerset lest, the king warned, 'we lose the service of the earl. You have never done us as much good as you will have done us harm, if through you the earl leaves our service.'[21]

The damage done to Louis during his absence should not, however, be exaggerated. Salisbury and the junior Marshal were on the fringes of his cause, outer bark always likely to drop off. There were no similar problems with the inner core of Louis's party – with Robert fitz Walter, Saer de Quincy, earl of Winchester, and the Northerners, only two of whom (both tenants of loyalist lords) made their peace before the battle of Lincoln in May.[22] Louis landed with punctilious timing at Sandwich on 22 or 23 April just as the truce was about to expire.[23] The earls of Surrey and Arundel, who were waiting to see if he would return, decided to remain in his service.[24] Louis brought with him a small but powerful force and his fortunes immediately revived. He retook Farnham on 27 April and was joined next day by the earl of Winchester, 'with a great company of English chivalry'. By 4 May he had recovered Winchester, the regent withdrawing before his arrival. There were few indications that the war was about to turn decisively in the Henricians' favour.[25]

vi. *The nature of the civil war*

Why had the bulk of Louis's party held together so well? Why, alternatively, had the Henricians refused to abandon their young king? In answering these questions, men on both sides would have stressed concepts of fidelity and honour. The earl of Chester, declared the legate in 1217, 'serves and always has served kings of England well and faithfully'.[1] William Marshal, proclaimed a royal letter in December 1216 authorized by Guala and the bishop of Winchester, 'always stood

[20] There is no royal letter about this but Salisbury accounted for Wiltshire from the end of the war: *List of Sheriffs*, 152; *BNB*, no. 1235, for his hereditary claim.

[21] *PR*, 38, 86–7; *RLC*, 481b–2.

[22] Holt, *Northerners*, 141 and n. 1.

[23] 'Southwark and Merton', 52; *Walt. Cov.*, 236.

[24] *PR*, 110.

[25] *Normandie*, 189–90.

[1] *F*, 146.

faithfully by our father when alive, and now adheres to us and assists us with devotion and constancy so that we commend his service above that of all other magnates of our kingdom, since in our necessity he has proved himself like gold in the furnace'.[2] Fidelity, of course, brought fame. This was the theme with which John of Earley inspired the Marshal after he had assumed the regency; whatever the outcome 'no man will ever have acquired such honour on earth'.[3] This too was the theme of Pope Honorius. 'Your constancy, proved like gold in the furnace,' he told Henry's supporters in December 1216, 'will make you shine forth in the eyes of men and give you a great name.' Royal letters to the garrisons of Bedford and Northampton in January 1217 struck the same note: 'let your fidelity and constancy be commended for all time to the praise and glory of your name'.[4]

The same concepts were important on Louis's side. Even by forsaking King John, Louis's English adherents had behaved traitorously in some French eyes;[5] now it was impossible to desert the French prince without incurring a note of shame. Of course, there were different ways of doing this. The most honourable was that later adopted by the earl of Surrey: a formal announcement to Louis that he was abjuring his allegiance.[6] But William de Pont de L'Arche and John fitz Hugh, who simply left and went home, were hated 'even now' for their conduct. This observation comes from the regent's biography, which naturally glosses over the young Marshal's own change of sides. A London chronicle was less discreet, alleging that Louis thereafter refused to see him, 'calling him a perjurer and a breaker of faith because he deserted . . . against his oath'.[7]

Louis's own character and conduct helped to strengthen the oaths of allegiance taken to him.[8] He was everything John was not: pious, chaste and loyal to his followers. He returned to England in April 1217, as he had promised, on the expiry of the truce and later, in the negotiations for peace, refused to abandon his English supporters. But standards of right conduct, on both sides, were also underpinned, or undermined, by far more material considerations.[9] 'Note the fidelity of Hubert', wrote Matthew Paris, having narrated Hubert de Burgh's

---

[2] *PR*, 9–10.

[3] *Maréchal*, lines 15656–86.

[4] *Honorii III Opera*, 106; *PR*, 22.

[5] *Ann. Mon.*, iii, 47; *Chron. Maj.*, 6.

[6] *Normandie*, 199.

[7] *Maréchal*, lines 15823–33, 15878–88; *Liber de Antiquis Legibus*, 205.

[8] The pope specifically empowered Guala to grant dispensation from these oaths: *RL*, 528.

[9] For the regent himself, see above p. 15. The eulogy quoted above was written to persuade Meiler fitz Henry to perform the service that he owed him for land in Leinster: *PR*, 9; see also *PR*, 22.

refusal to surrender Dover. Hubert, Paris explained, had rejected Louis's promise to grant him Norfolk and Suffolk in hereditary right, and had scorned the argument, advanced by the earl of Salisbury, that oaths of fidelity had no force in a hopeless cause.[10] What Paris did not add was that, had Hubert changed sides, he could scarcely have retained the honour of Haughley in Suffolk, which King John had given him, for these were claimed by one of Louis's closest associates, the count of Perche.[11] The earl of Chester was in a similar position. In 1205 John had granted him nearly all the lands and fees of the honour of Richmond in Richmondshire. These were claimed by another French-man Louis brought to England, Peter de Dreux, duke of Brittany. In 1218 a compromise was reached whereby Peter was given the lands and fees of the honour south of the Humber, while Chester retained the substance, namely Richmondshire and indeed Richmond castle itself. Had the war gone the other way, the situations would have been reversed.[12]

English magnates had equally strong material reasons for remaining loyal to Louis. Many great men had hoped, through their rebellion, to realize deeply held claims to castles, lands and rights. In some cases those claims were the direct result of actions taken by King John, for example, his retention of Knaresborough and Boroughbridge as security for Nicholas de Stuteville's vast relief. In others, the families concerned had nursed the claims for generations. In that sense Professor Davis's remark that 'wherever we turn the politics of Stephen's reign seem to dissolve into family history' applies equally well to the civil war of 1215 to 1217.[13] Louis, whatever the Dunstable annalist thought, had done his best to satisfy the aspirations of his English (and Scottish) supporters. He accepted, for example, Robert fitz Walter's claim to Hertford castle,[14] King Alexander's to the northern counties,[15] and perhaps also, although here evidence is lacking, William de Mowbray's to York.[16] In the event of their capture Louis had surely promised the

---

[10] *Chron. Maj.*, 3–4.

[11] See below p. 244.

[12] *RLP*, 51; *Walt. Cov.*, 233; *PR*, 174; *RLC*, 385. In the partition Chester lost the lands and fees of the honour in Cambridgeshire, Norfolk, Suffolk and Lincolnshire. However, he had only been granted these in November 1217 and he received compensation: *RLC*, 340b, 350; *PR*, 120, 158. For the earl of Chester and the honour of Richmond under John, see Painter, *Reign of John*, 27–9; for Peter de Dreux and Richmond, see Painter, *Peter of Dreux, Duke of Brittany*, 10–17. John granted Chester Richmond castle on the rebellion of the hereditary castellan, Ruald fitz Alan, in 1216. Ruald had still to recover the castle in 1219: *RLP*, 163; *Yorkshire Eyre*, no. 29.

[13] Davis, 'What happened in Stephen's reign', 10.

[14] *Normandie*, 182, which is to be preferred to Wendover, who says exactly the reverse: *Chron. Maj.*, 5–6. For the comment of the Dunstable annalist, see above p. 29.

[15] *Melrose*, 66; Duncan, *Scotland*, 521–3; Holt, *Northerners*, 132.

[16] For this claim, see Holt, *Magna Carta*, 120, 158, 306, 346–7.

return of Knaresborough to Nicholas de Stuteville and Rockingham to William Mauduit.[17] There was no incentive for these men to desert Louis, for there was little prospect that the Henricians would satisfy their desires. When a very big and special fish, the earl of Salisbury, swam near the royal nets, the regent dug into the king's possessions to provide what seemed an alluring bait, but for most returning rebels all that was on offer was the restoration of their possessions as they had held them at the beginning of the war. Even someone as important as John de Lacy, the constable of Chester, was offered only that and 'concerning the other lands to which you say that you have a right' a promise of justice in the king's court. No wonder John took so long coming to terms![18]

In some cases the problem was that a rebel's demands, like fitz Walter's claim to Hertford or Mowbray's to York, impinged on the rights of the crown and could scarcely be settled until the young king came of age – whereas Louis could settle them immediately, or at least once he had won the war. More often the problem was even starker: the possessions coveted by a supporter of Louis were coveted equally by a Henrician. In such circumstances both parties had powerful reasons to remain true to their existing allegiances. Louis, for example, had conceded the castle of Mountsorrel to Saer de Quincy, earl of Winchester. Saer believed that this was the one part of his wife's inheritance that King John had denied him,[19] and not surprisingly he became one of Louis's most determined and energetic supporters. There was little prospect of retaining the castle if he went over to the young king: the earl of Chester was lord of part of Mountsorrel, had some claim to the castle and resented the way Saer's tenure there butted into the heart of his midlands interests, much as his grandfather had resented Beaumont control of Mountsorrel back in the reign of Stephen.[20]

Another great rebel in a similar situation was Gilbert de Gant. Louis had acceded to his claim to be earl of Lincoln, his uncle having been created earl by Stephen. But Stephen had earlier given the earldom to William de Roumare, half-brother of the earl of Chester's grandfather, and Chester claimed the earldom as heir to the Roumares.[21] Likewise,

---

[17] For Nicholas de Stuteville and Knaresborough, see Holt, *Magna Carta*, 208–9, 257–8. For the Mauduit claim to be castellans of Rockingham, see *Beauchamp Cartulary*, liv–lv.

[18] *PR*, 112 (23 May 1217). John returned to the king's faith on 9 August: *RLC*, 318.

[19] *Normandie*, 189; *Chron. Maj.*, 15; *RLC*, 24b–5. King John had, however, some justification for treating Mountsorrel as a royal castle: King, 'Mountsorrel', 9. He finally conceded it to Saer in June 1215 but it was in his hands again, following the latter's rebellion, in January 1216: *RLP*, 145b, 162b.

[20] King, 'Mountsorrel', 2–3, 6–9; Golob, 'The Ferrers earls of Derby', 209.

[21] *Chron. Maj.*, ii, 663; iii, 22; *Peerage*, vii, 667–75.

the king of Scotland knew that Robert de Vieuxpont had been granted Westmorland by King John in hereditary right; Nicholas de Stuteville that Brian de Lisle was determined to hold on to Knaresborough where John had placed him in 1205; and William Mauduit that the count of Aumale was busy installing himself in Rockingham.[22]

Those who did change sides in defiance of these realities rarely reaped much profit. It has been mentioned how the earl of Salisbury's position in Louis's camp was made uncomfortable by his dispute with the earl of Hereford over Trowbridge. Ironically, Salisbury was equally unable to swallow the bait which had lured him back into the Henrician camp, for Peter de Maulay steadfastly refused to surrender Sherborne and Somerset to him.[23] Reginald de Braose faced a similar problem when he finally deserted Louis for the young king. He was promised his father William's lands as the latter had best held them. The trouble was that, after his father's forfeiture, John had granted Totnes to Henry fitz Count and Barnstaple to Henry de Tracy; after the war the minority government was not prepared to simply disseise these loyalists and Reginald complained bitterly of the failure to fulfil the promises made to him.[24] Against this background one can understand why the rebels took oaths to accept no heir of King John as king; why it was precisely 'the English' amongst Louis's followers who advised him against making peace in January 1217; why Saer de Quincy, earl of Winchester, joined Louis in April 1217 'with a great company of English chivalry'; and why Winchester, Robert fitz Walter, the earl of Hereford, Gilbert de Gant, Nicholas de Stuteville and William Mauduit, all men with aspirations which Louis could satisfy and the young king could not, fought for the former at the battle of Lincoln.[25] Within the great struggle for the throne, therefore, a whole series of private struggles was waged between individuals over castles, lands and rights.[26] It was the private struggle over Mountsorrel which was to set the scene for Henrician victory.

vii. *Decision by battle: Lincoln and Sandwich*

Louis's return to England found the Henrician forces divided. In March and April 1217, while the regent had captured castles in the south, the earl of Chester had pursued his private campaign against the earl of Winchester and had laid siege to Mountsorrel. On Louis's

---

[22] Holt, *Northerners*, 220–2; *PR*, 13–14 and see below p. 72.
[23] See above p. 31 and below pp. 66, 71.
[24] See below p. 179.
[25] *Walt. Cov.*, 235; *Normandie*, 191; *Chron. Maj.*, 22; *Gervase*, 111.
[26] This theme is developed in Golob, 'The Ferrers earls of Derby', 209, 211.

arrival, both the regent and Chester had retreated: the former left Winchester to its fate, the latter abandoned the siege of Mountsorrel. Both imagined that they faced the whole of Louis's army but in fact Louis too had split his forces. The earl of Winchester and the count of Perche were sent to relieve Mountsorrel. Having done so, they proceeded to Lincoln to help the castellan of Arras and the Northerners in their siege of the castle, which was still being held for the king by Nicola de Hay. Louis himself, however, hesitated to commit all his forces to the north with Dover castle untaken in his rear and he restarted siege operations there on 12 May.[1]

Next day, at Northampton, the regent learnt of the division of Louis's power and saw his chance. He would unite the forces of the young king and bring the half of Louis's army at Lincoln to battle.[2] This was the greatest decision of William Marshal's career. Set-piece battles in the twelfth and thirteenth centuries were rare events but they could be utterly decisive, as Bouvines had shown only three years before. In 1216, on Louis's landing, William himself had advised John against offering battle and the king had withdrawn.[3] If those at Lincoln now accepted the challenge, the whole future of the Angevin dynasty would be at stake. The royal forces gathered at Newark on 17 to 18 May.[4] The process of co-ordination cannot have been easy, despite the brave speeches of the regent, the sermons of the legate and the white crusading crosses which the Henricians donned. It was probably around the time of the battle that the earl of Chester, or those in his circle, complained to the pope about the regent. He was too old for the job, they said. The pope should appoint Chester as his colleague, a request Honorius passed on to Guala, who wisely ignored it. Chester also caused trouble at Newark itself. When the Normans in the king's army came to the young Marshal, who had been born in the duchy, and asked him to assert their ancient right to strike the first blow, Chester threatened to depart unless he himself was allowed to start the action. But at least the siege of Mountsorrel had helped to bring the king's forces together, the earl of Derby, Philip Mark, Brian de Lisle, Robert de Vieuxpont, Robert de Gaugi and Falkes de Bréauté having all been present there.[5]

The regent's tactics before the battle were dictated by the nature of the terrain. Lincoln had grown up where the river Witham cuts east-west through the north-south ridge of oolitic limestone which rises 200 feet above the valley of the Trent, with the castle and cathedral

[1] *Normandie*, 191–2; *Maréchal*, lines 16034–114; *Chron. Maj.*, 15–18.
[2] *Maréchal*, lines 16153–81.
[3] *Ann. Mon.*, iii, 46.
[4] *Maréchal*, lines 16197–203. *Chron. Maj.*, 18, has a slightly different chronology.
[5] *RL*, 532; *Maréchal*, lines 16204–24; *Chron. Maj.*, 15.

perched on the northern edge of this ridge above the Witham.[6] The rest of the medieval town (still within the walls) ran southwards down the hill to the river, the height above sea-level dropping from 200 to 25 feet in less than 700 yards. In 1216 Louis's supporters had taken the town and, from within it, were laying siege to the castle. For the regent's army to attack from the south and fight up the hill was clearly impossible, as the Barnwell annalist recognized.[7] It was better to ascend the ridge (several miles wide) and approach from the north where there was a flat plain suitable for battle, the plain indeed where the battle of Lincoln had been fought in 1141.

Early in the morning of 20 May, therefore, with the rising sun glinting on their armour, the Henrician army drew up outside the north walls of Lincoln.[8] Their enemies accepted the challenge and came out of the town, only then to turn tail and go back into it. The fact was that the count of Perche and the Marshal of France, believing that their forces were outnumbered, had overruled the earl of Winchester and Robert fitz Walter and decided to decline battle.[9] Their tactics became to remain safely in the town, continue the siege of the castle, and wait for the arrival of Louis and the rest of his army.

The decisive moment had now arrived. It was vital for the Henricians to pursue their advantage before Louis's arrival transformed the situation. But what could they do with their opponents sheltering within the walls of the town? The answer was provided by the bishop of Winchester, who discovered, through a daring personal reconnaissance, that the town's western gateway, just beyond the north end of the castle, which had been blocked up at some point in the hostilities since 1215, could be opened.[10] The problem, of course, was one of surprise. To achieve it, a large part of the Henrician army under the earl of Chester, who thus began the action as he wished, assaulted

[6] For medieval Lincoln, see Hill, *Medieval Lincoln*.

[7] *Walt. Cov.*, 237.

[8] *Political Songs*, 25, for the sun. The author of *Maréchal* freely admitted his difficulty faced with conflicting accounts of the battle (lines 16401-9) and it is impossible to reconcile the contemporary evidence now. In what follows I have given what I think is the most likely version, without discussing all the problems of interpretation. For previous discussions, see Meyer, *Maréchal*, iii, 232 n. 3 and clix-x; Tout, 'The Fair of Lincoln', 240-65; Norgate, *Minority*, 35-45, 273-8; Brooks and Oakley, 'The battle of Lincoln', 295-312, where the version of events most differs from that which I have advanced; Hill, *Medieval Lincoln*, 201-5; Powicke, *Henry III*, 12-13, 736-9.

[9] *Maréchal*, lines 16243-400; *Walt. Cov.*, 237. According to Wendover, fitz Walter and the earl of Winchester wanted to attack the Henricians as they ascended the ridge up to Lincoln: *Chron. Maj.*, 20.

[10] *Maréchal*, 16500-20. The only problem in supposing that the blocked gate was the west gate of the town is the statement in *Maréchal* that it had been blocked 'anciently'. But, as Hill remarks (*Medieval Lincoln*, 204), 'the poet was not an archaeologist'.

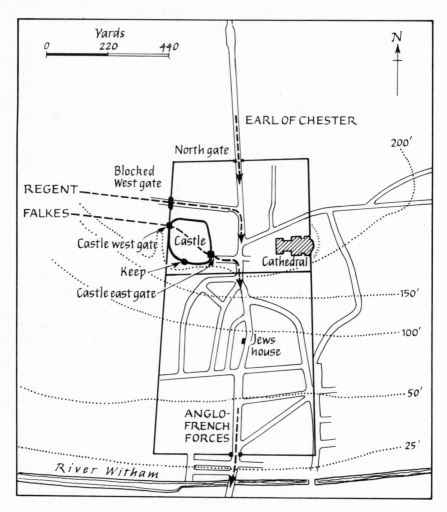

4. The battle of Lincoln, 20 May 1217

(based on the map of Lincoln in 1200 in Hill, *Medieval London*, 203)

the north gate.[11] Meanwhile, a force under Falkes de Bréauté was sent into the castle through the west gate in the castle walls, here coterminous with those of the town. Roger of Wendover says that the aim was for Falkes to open a gate.[12] More probably, it was to create a diversion so that the blocked gate could be opened. Falkes first placed his crossbow men on the castle walls, their arrows wreaking havoc amongst the enemy horses. He then sallied into the town itself, presumably through the main eastern gateway of the castle. That this was the first entry effected by the Henricians is clear from the remark of the Dunstable annalist that the barons left the walls in order to combat it.[13] The fight, in which Falkes was captured and then rescued, swung down the steep hill, away from the castle and cathedral, towards the lower town.[14]

This provided the opportunity. The blocked gateway was quickly opened, so quickly indeed that the regent spurred his horse and would have charged without his helmet if not restrained by a squire. The Henricians, led by the young Marshal and the earl of Salisbury, galloped down Westgate street and then wheeled right to meet their enemies, who were assaulting the eastern gateway and the keep by the castle's southern wall. The regent himself arrived with such force that he plunged three lances deep into the press, the bishop of Winchester behind him shouting over and over again in a high voice 'God helps the Marshal'. The surprise was complete. When the master-engineer of the Anglo-French party saw the Henricians approaching he actually thought that they were his own side, doubtless coming from the north gate to help finish off Falkes in the lower town. He placed a stone in his petrary to continue bombarding the castle and had his head cut off in mid-shout as he let it go. The fiercest fighting developed outside the front of the cathedral, in the shadow of the great Norman towers of Bishop Remigius, where the count of Perche stood his ground with a large number of followers. As the latter began to give way down the hill, the count was wounded by a spear jabbed through his vizor. He managed to bring three great blows down on the regent's helmet before falling dead from his horse.[15]

The battle, however, was not yet won. The French and English, having retreated down to the lower town, joined up there with a

---

[11] *Chron. Maj.*, 21; *Walt. Cov.*, 237; *Ann. Mon.*, iii, 49. That the attack on the north gate was led by the earl of Chester is my own speculation.

[12] *Chron. Maj.*, 21. It was, of course, the withdrawal of Louis's army within the town which enabled the Henricians to make use of the castle's west gate.

[13] *Ann. Mon.*, iii, 49. Equally, after Falkes's entry, *exinde* the Henricians entered the city *ex omni parte*: *ibid.*, 50.

[14] *Chron. Maj.*, 21; *Ann. Mon.*, iii, 49.

[15] *Maréchal*, lines 16577–768.

considerable contingent from their own party – perhaps that which had gone down in the fight against Falkes. Re-forming, they attempted to reclimb the hill but were met at the front by the Henricians coming from between the cathedral and the castle, were harried at the rear by Thomas and Alan Basset, and were charged from the right by the earl of Chester, who had at last effected an entry through the northern gateway.[16] Soon the French and English were streaming southwards out of the town. Many others, surprised on foot, or with their horses shot by Falkes's archers, or held up by a blockage at Lincoln's southern bar-gate, were taken prisoner. At the end of the day Robert fitz Walter, the earls of Winchester, Hereford and Hertford, and the Northerners Gilbert de Gant, William de Mowbray, Nicholas de Stuteville, Robert Grelley and William son of Robert de Ros were all prisoners.[17] The heart had been ripped from Louis's party in England. The battle of Lincoln, one of the most decisive in English history, meant that England would be ruled by the Angevin, not the Capetian, dynasty. No wonder the regent galloped off at once to bring the news of the victory to the king and legate at Nottingham.[18]

When the bishop of Winchester had returned to his men after discovering the blocked gateway, he had jokingly remarked that the bishop's house in Lincoln should be his prize for finding a way into the town.[19] After the battle the Henricians indeed received their rewards. Brian de Lisle was granted Knaresborough at its ancient farm until the completion of the king's fourteenth year and the earl of Salisbury was given custody of the city and county of Lincoln. Both these acts of patronage were made on the advice of the king's *fideles* and neither represented permanent alienations.[20] But something better was done for the earl of Chester: he was conceded the third penny and thus the earldom of the county of Lincoln. The problem of the king's minority was evaded by pretending that the earl was merely securing the inheritance of his father, though in fact Chester's fragile claim was not as heir to his father but as heir to William de Roumare (died 1198), the grandson of the William de Roumare whom Stephen had recognized for a time as earl of Lincoln.[21] Chester was also handed the castle of Mountsorrel, which he immediately razed to the ground, thus eliminating this threat to his midlands interests.[22]

[16] *Maréchal*, lines 16769–825. That an entry was made on the north of the city is plain from *Chron. Maj.*, 21; *Walt. Cov.*, 237.

[17] *Maréchal*, lines 16825–8, 16933–51; *Chron. Maj.*, 22–3; *Gervase*, 111.

[18] *Chron. Maj.*, 24.

[19] *Maréchal*, lines 16521–30.

[20] *PR*, 64, 65. For the significance of the grant of Lincoln to Salisbury, see below p. 66.

[21] *RLC*, 308b; *Peerage*, vii, 667–72, 675–6.

[22] *PR*, 64; *Ann. Mon.*, i, 224; iii, 50; compare *Chron. Maj.*, 24.

There were divided counsels among the Henricians about what they should do next. Some urged an immediate advance on London, some the relief of Dover. The regent, however, in tune with the personal ambitions of the combatants, allowed everyone to depart with their prisoners in order to make arrangements with them about ransoms – no one being keener to do this than the regent himself, having taken the great prize of Nicholas de Stuteville. A rendezvous was fixed for Chertsey, early in June.[23] This was missed by the earl of Derby, who was occupied by his private war for the Peverel inheritance. At long last he gained control of the Peak, Brian de Lisle being more amenable to its surrender now that he was confirmed in possession of Knaresborough. Derby then went on to besiege Bolsover, which was held by the rebels, taking the castle in the third week of June.[24] The young king's campaign was never to be so well co-ordinated again as it had been at Lincoln.

The delay in prosecuting the campaign was the less serious, however, because Louis was already prepared to give up. It was on 25 May at Dover that he heard the news of the Lincoln disaster. He abandoned the siege and went to London.[25] Negotiations for peace were opened under papal auspices and on 13 June the delegates from the two sides actually reached an agreement.[26] Louis was to release his English supporters from all oaths of homage and fealty, and restore the lands that he had taken. In return, he obtained good terms for his adherents. All, clerk and lay, were to be absolved from their sentences of excommunication and recover the lands and possessions which they had held at the beginning of the war. All prisoners taken after Louis's first arrival, and all who had been his supporters before, were to be released, their ransoms only to be paid up to the instalments due at the time of the peace. Magna Carta was also to be an integral part of the settlement. Louis's adherents were to enjoy 'all liberties and customs of the kingdom of England'. That these were to include the liberties in the Great Charter is shown by the next sentence, which stated that if 'improvements (*emendationes*) were made to the liberties' then they were to be enjoyed also. This clearly referred to 'the things to be improved (*emendanda*)' mentioned in the 1216 Charter.[27] Probably during the negotiations an actual text was given to Louis's delegation, which explains why one of the few copies to survive ended up in the French royal archives.[28]

[23] *Maréchal*, lines 17031–68.
[24] *Ann. Mon.*, iii, 50; *PR*, 69; Golob, 'The Ferrers earls of Derby', 210–11.
[25] *Normandie*, 195–6.
[26] *Receuil*, xix, 635–7; Smith, 'The treaty of Lambeth', 566–7.
[27] *Select Charters*, 339.
[28] *Layettes*, i, no. 1194.

The agreement reached soon collapsed. On the Henrician side, the legate insisted that Louis's ecclesiastical adherents, and in particular Simon Langton, Gervase of Heybridge, Elias of Dereham and Robert de St Germain, who had most blatantly defied the sentences of excommunication, be excluded from the settlement. Louis declared that 'there was no way he would make peace without them'.[29] These events revealed the power of the legate but he may well have received backing from those who thought the settlement as a whole was far too generous. Certainly some great Henricians, including the earl of Chester, shared his antipathy for Simon Langton.[30]

Louis had shown himself commendably loyal to his followers but many of them were no longer loyal to him. Kept in his camp by the prospect of an immediate settlement, they began to defect when this did not materialize. Between 15 June (when the failure of the negotiations was probably known) and 23 June, over sixty men returned to the allegiance of the young king. All told, between the end of May and the middle of August, there were over 150 submissions.[31] Of great men, the earl of Surrey had come in by 11 June; Reginald de Braose returned on 23 June, the earl of Arundel on 14 July and John de Lacy, constable of Chester, on 9 August.[32] To encourage this movement the Henricians put into effect what they could from the abortive settlement. Those returning were given their lands as they had held them at the beginning of the war. In addition, on 23 June, the sheriff of Worcestershire was ordered to read Magna Carta in his county court and cause it to be observed. Similar orders probably went out to other sheriffs.[33]

During all this period Louis sat tight in London, moving, for greater security, from the bishop's house to the Tower. Apart from *chevauchées* led by the viscount of Melun and the duke of Brittany, he was no longer capable of offensive action. There were more unsuccessful negotiations. The legate urged an advance on London but the regent demurred, as he had after the victory at Lincoln.[34] One reason, perhaps, was the situation in Wales. Reginald de Braose's return to the allegiance of the young king had infuriated his father-in-law and former ally, Llywelyn. In revenge, the Welsh prince had invaded Reginald's lands in south

---

[29] *Recueil*, xix, 636. I suspect that the text of the peace contained in Durand's *Thesaurus*, with its emphatic declaration that 'laymen only' were to recover their possessions as at the beginning of the war, contains Guala's proposals for a settlement in June. Note the reference to the *mandatum et dispositionem domini legati*: Smith, 'The treaty of Lambeth', 577, n. 15 and 567–9 for a full discussion.

[30] See below p. 228.

[31] *RLC*, 310b–18b.

[32] *RLC*, 310b, 311b, 312; *PR*, 72–3, 112–13; *RLC*, 314, 318.

[33] *RLC*, 336.

[34] *Normandie*, 198–9.

Wales and forced him to surrender Swansea castle and with it, in effect, the lordship of Gower. These Llywelyn entrusted to Rhys Gryg, a son of Lord Rhys of Deheubarth (d.1197). He then headed west, threatened the regent's castle at Haverford and took hostages from the latter's lordship of Pembroke.[35] This direct attack on his own territories brought the regent, in July, to his castles of Goodrich and Chepstow but he had neither time nor resources to advance further. Between 21–25 July and 7–13 August there were large assemblies at Oxford, where many submitted to the young king and the regent attempted both to discipline and reward the latter's supporters.[36] There seems to have been no clear plan as to what to do next, the regent intending on 13 August simply to hold another council at Oxford on the 25th. Instead, on that day he was at Sandwich sorting out the spoils following the final battle of the war.

The regent had arrived at Sandwich early in the morning of 24 August. The day was fine and one could see far out across the Channel. Advancing from Calais was the French fleet, bearing the reinforcements which had been raised by Louis's energetic wife. The regent was persuaded not to venture his own body and the English fleet was led out by Hubert de Burgh. It crossed in front of the French ships and seemed to be making for Calais. When Hubert's vessel went by, the French sailors yelled out in derision 'the hart! the hart!', as if it was a deer escaping from the hunt. The English, however, having got behind the French, turned and, with the wind now full in their sails, came up upon them.[37] The purpose of this tactic was to attack with the wind; the danger was that either the English would fail to cross the French line and be run down, or that having got behind it they would never catch up. To an extent the latter happened, several of the large French ships sailing on and escaping.[38] Behind them, however, the French flagship, commanded by Eustace the monk, and the bulk of the smaller vessels were caught, partly because they clewed up their sails eager for the fight.[39] Eustace's flagship, sitting low in the water with the weight of its trebuchet, treasure, horses and thirty-six knights and their retinues, was surrounded. From a cog standing high above it were hurled down on to its deck, in the words of Eustace's contemporary biography, 'finely pulverized lime in great pots . . . so that a great cloud arose. Then

<hr />

[35] *Brut*, 95–6.

[36] *PR*, 85, 86, 71, 81; *RLC*, 319. It was at this time that Hubert de Burgh was conceded the marriage of the countess of Gloucester and efforts were made to remove Robert de Gaugi from Newark castle.

[37] *Maréchal*, lines 17261–364; *Chron. Maj.*, 29, details that Matthew Paris may have got from Hubert himself.

[38] *Normandie*, 202; *Recueil*, xvii, 111.

[39] *Maréchal*, line 17336; *Recueil*, xvii, 111.

the French could no longer defend themselves for their eyes were full of powder; and since they were before the wind it caused them torment.'[40] The leaders of the French, Robert de Courtenay and William de Barres, were captured. Eustace the monk was discovered, after a long search, hiding in the ship's bilges. He offered a large sum for his life but was given only one choice, should his head be cut off on the side of the trebuchet or on the ship's rail?[41]

Louis heard the news of the disaster on the Saturday evening of 26 August. For a moment he seemed mad with rage and grief, then, 'destitute of present aid and despairing of the future', as the Dunstable annalist put it, he sued for peace.[42]

viii. *The peace of Kingston/Lambeth, 12/20 September 1217*

The peace negotiations opened on Monday, 28 August and they continued in fits and starts, while the regent began to blockade London, until 11 September when Louis received terms from the Henricians and decided to accept them, having taken advice from his remaining English supporters and the citizens of London.[1] Next day, Tuesday, 12 September, on an island in the Thames near Kingston, Louis met Guala, the regent, King Henry and his mother, and formally agreed to the peace. He was not absolved, however, for he refused to appear dressed only in his woollen underwear. A compromise was arranged and next day Louis reappeared on the island with a mantle over his underwear and received absolution from the ecclesiastics splendidly attired in copes and mitres.[2] The terms of the treaty ran from 12 September and from that date peace formally existed in England. However, on 20 September at Lambeth, the treaty was ratified by a larger and more formal assembly than had gathered on the island.[3] Three days later Louis began his journey back to France.[4]

The peace to which Louis had agreed differed, in one important respect, from the terms of 13 June 1217.[5] Guala now had his way. A clause firmly stated that 'laymen only' amongst Louis's adherents were

---

[40] Cannon, 'The battle of Sandwich', 664.
[41] *Maréchal*, lines 17365–462; *Normandie*, 200–2.
[42] *Normandie*, 202; *Ann. Mon.*, iii, 50.
[1] *Normandie*, 202–4, where the precise chronology of the negotations described is open to various interpretations: compare Petit-Dutaillis, *Louis VIII*, 169–71, with Norgate, *Minority*, 55–6. For the blockade, *PR*, 89; *Chron. Maj.*, 30. For Louis consulting his English followers, compare also *Liber de Antiquis Legibus*, 203, and *Maréchal*, lines 17683–8.
[2] *Normandie*, 204–5; *Maréchal*, lines 17704–16.
[3] Smith, 'Treaty of Lambeth', 562–75.
[4] 'Southwark and Merton', 53.
[5] For the texts of the peace, see Smith, 'Treaty of Lambeth', 575–9.

to have their lands and seisins as at the beginning of the war. Clerks could recover their lay fees but not their ecclesiastical offices and properties. Guala could deal with them, in their capacities as churchmen, as he thought fit. In the event, Simon Langton and his three colleagues were forced to leave England in order to seek absolution from the pope.[6]

For the rest, the June terms remained remarkably intact. The clauses on the recovery of lands, the release of prisoners and the payment of ransoms were virtually the same. There was still the clause on the enjoyment of the 'liberties and customs of the kingdom of England' and the mooted *emendationes* soon came to pass when a new version of the Great Charter was issued in November.[7] As the Barnwell annalist put it, describing the terms of the peace, the evil customs which had caused the war were to be abolished and the liberties sought by the magnates of England were to be observed. The settlement was equally generous when it came to Louis personally. As in June, debts owed to him were to be paid and he could retain the hostages taken in connection with them. Even more, by an arrangement which did not surface in the actual text of the treaty, he was promised 10,000 marks, nominally as compensation for the damage which he had suffered in England, actually to speed his exit from the country. The regent himself placed his Norman lands as surety for the payment and 4,000 marks were handed over at once.[8] Finally, Louis made a vague promise, which again was not in the text, that he would try to persuade his father to return the lost Angevin dominions or would do so himself once he became king.[9] The regent was later blamed for missing a great opportunity here, and blame was easy to lay.[10] Having, alone amongst the great English magnates, retained his lands in Normandy after King Philip had conquered the duchy in 1204, lands for which Louis might any day be his lord, he had every reason to want the latter's favour. On the other hand, he might plausibly claim that to hold Louis captive against the return of the empire might merely provoke a French invasion of what remained of it in Poitou and Gascony.

From the point of view of Louis's English followers, the attraction of the settlement should not be exaggerated. It did nothing for the personal grievances and ambitions of the former rebels: Robert fitz Walter did not gain Hertford castle, the earl of Winchester, Mountsorrel, the earl

[6] *Normandie*, 201; *Chron. Maj.*, 31–2; Richardson, 'Letters of Guala', 254–9.

[7] *Walt. Cov.*, 239. A London chronicle links the Great Charter of November 1217 directly with the peace treaty: *Liber de Antiquis Legibus*, 203–4.

[8] *DD*, nos 25, 26; *PR*, 284, 114–15, 168. The conflicting evidence as to how much was promised Louis is set out in Norgate, *Minority*, 83, n. 4. See also *Pipe Roll 1218*, xvii–xviii.

[9] *Chron. Maj.*, 31; *Ann. Mon.*, iii, 81; *Liber de Antiquis Legibus*, 204.

[10] *Chron. Maj.*, 25–6; iv, 157.

of Hereford, Trowbridge, William de Mowbray, York and William Mauduit, Rockingham. Gilbert de Gant did not become earl of Lincoln.

Likewise many former rebels remained oppressed by heavy ransoms. Here the terms of the peace treaty were quite narrowly drawn, or at least were narrowly interpreted by the government. They did not embrace men taken at Rochester in 1215, since they had not been adherents of Louis. Equally, they applied only to those who were still prisoners at the end of the war.[11] The latter no longer had to make ransom payments due later than 12 September 1217, the day that peace was agreed. Some important rebels, notably Robert fitz Walter and Gilbert de Gant, both detained by the count of Aumale until the conclusion of hostilities, could benefit from these terms but others, who had been released before the settlement and been absolved from excommunication, remained liable for all their ransoms. Thus the regent was perfectly within his rights in demanding the full ransom of Nicholas de Stuteville, including the payments due after the peace, since Nicholas had agreed the terms and presumably been released before the end of the war.[12]

As it was, whether or not in defiance of the terms of the treaty, many former rebels found themselves heavily burdened. The earl of Norfolk told Hubert de Burgh, in 1218 or 1219, that he had already paid 800 marks towards the ransom of his son, Ralph, 'whereby I am greatly damaged'.[13] By 1221 Peter de Maulay had received a total of 6,561 marks from sixteen prisoners (many of them taken at Rochester in 1215) who had been in his custody at Corfe.[14] In these circumstances some rebels had no alternative but to part with land. John fitz Hugh paid his ransom by giving John Marshal land in Cowley and Oxford; Simon of Kyme paid his by leasing five manors to the earl of Chester.[15] Under the terms of the agreement between the regent and Nicholas de Stuteville, unless the latter paid his 1,000 mark ransom by November 1218, then he was to surrender £200 worth of land in his manors of Kirby Moorside and Liddell.[16] Thus, as Professor Holt has remarked, if there was no formal policy of disinheritance, as there was to be after

[11] Smith, 'Treaty of Lambeth', 576 (clause 5 of the treaty); *RLC*, 358b, for the government's interpretation.

[12] *PR*, 97, 99. Nicholas de Stuteville died between his capture at Lincoln and the end of the war: *RLC*, 600b; *EYC*, ix, 15.

[13] SC 1/1, no. 60; *RLC*, 392b.

[14] *RLC*, 481b–2. For the difficulties of one of these prisoners, William of Lancaster, see below p. 197; for those of another, Reginald of Cornhill, see below p. 338.

[15] *Sandford Cartulary*, 99–100; *Gervase*, 111–12; *ERF*, 42, 44. For the financial difficulties of the Kymes, see Holt, *Northerners*, 248.

[16] C 60/9, m. 8; Holt, *Northerners*, 246–7.

the battle of Evesham in 1265, 'disinherited, nevertheless, some of [the rebels] were, at least of part of their estates'.[17]

Nonetheless, the rebels were lucky. Had John reached the position of the regent in September 1217, formal disinheritance would surely have been his aim. At the very least he would have imposed huge fines on the rebels for the redemption of their estates. He would equally have swept away the Great Charter – indeed those returning to his faith during the war had been made to forswear it.[18] In explaining why nothing like this happened, a London chronicler praised Louis himself. 'One should know that Louis could allowably and safely have left England with all his followers . . . had he been prepared to permit the king of England to take revenge on the English who stood against him and his father in the war. But he did not wish any of his adherents to be outside the peace.'[19] This, however, missed the point. By September 1217 Louis had little *power* to refuse anything. Had the Henricians persisted with the war, they could surely have forced him to surrender and then imposed a much harsher settlement.

There were probably elements, eager to retain the lands of the vanquished and profit fully from ransoms, who wished to do this. The Marshal's biography says that, after the battle of Sandwich, some loftily declared, 'we have only to pretend to treat with Louis . . . let us go and besiege London'. Matthew Paris later asserted that many were opposed to the clemency shown to Louis.[20] Divided counsels among the Henricians may well explain why the negotiations dragged on from 28 August to 11 September. On the Saturday evening of 9 September Louis was so frustrated at having heard nothing since 5 September that he was on the verge of sallying forth to fight, rather than remain cooped up any longer.[21] According to the *History of the Dukes of Normandy*, those most closely involved in the peace negotiations, apart from the regent and the queen, were the earls of Surrey, Arundel and Salisbury and the young Marshal.[22] Although not amongst Louis's most ardent supporters, all were former rebels. Perhaps more hard-line than the latter were the earls of Chester and Derby and the count of Aumale, who were apparently absent from the south at the time of the peace negotiations and thus not directly involved in them.[23] Aumale, as has been mentioned, stood to lose the ransoms of Robert fitz Walter and Gilbert

[17] Holt, *Northerners*, 248, and *ibid.*, 247–8, for a collection of examples.

[18] Holt, *Northerners*, 1.

[19] *Liber de Antiquis Legibus*, 203.

[20] *Maréchal*, lines 17651–4; *Chron. Maj.*, 30.

[21] *Normandie*, 203.

[22] *Normandie*, 204.

[23] *PR*, 91, 93. Neither the earl of Derby nor the count of Aumale sealed the final treaty: Smith, 'Treaty of Lambeth', 579 n. 1.

de Gant.[24] Chester sealed the final treaty when it was confirmed at Lambeth but the ransom that he imposed on Maurice de Gant, clearly in breach of its terms, shows that he was unhappy with it.[25] It may also be significant that the bishop of Winchester refused to agree to the first scutage of the reign which was designed to raise the money owed to Louis.[26]

That counsels of moderation prevailed was partly, as has been seen, because all the magnates would benefit from the Great Charter, irrespective of their allegiance in the war. Disinheritance, moreover, was no part of the legate's policy. His priorities were penance and absolution to wipe clean the stain of excommunication, and peace so that men could depart on crusade to the Holy Land. Roger of Wendover ascribed the lack of slaughter at the battle of Lincoln to the restraining force of family relationships and certainly these had always cut across the combatants. One of the regent's daughters was married to the rebel Hugh Bigod, heir to the earldom of Norfolk;[27] the earl of Winchester's brother was married to the earl of Chester's sister.[28] Such ties, however, might foment discord as much as cement alliances. More important in 1215–17 was that the war had not degenerated into feud and bitterness, as it was to do between 1263 and 1267. A key moment had come when John had been persuaded not to execute the garrison of Rochester castle on the grounds that this would lead to a vicious circle of tit for tat.[29] At the battle of Lincoln, the count of Perche was virtually the only person of note to be killed and everyone was very sorry about that.[30] In 1217 the chancery clerks headed their lists of those returning to the king's faith with derisive comments: *de perversis reversis, de eadem scola* or simply *cuccu*; but against the name of the earl of Winchester was placed an aphorism in a rather different vein: 'I will hate so long as I am able, if not, reluctantly I will love'.[31] When, in November 1217 itself, the earl's eldest son was tragically killed by his doctor, the king made a gift to the Hospitallers for the benefit of his soul.[32]

[24] *PR*, 97, 99.

[25] See below p. 82.

[26] *Pipe Roll 1221*, 95.

[27] *Chron. Maj.*, 22; *Normandie*, 171; *Peerage*, ix, 589–90. For a discussion of the role of family connections in politics, see Holt, 'Feudal society and the family in early medieval England: iii. Patronage and politics', 1–25, and pp. 21–2, more particularly, for the family connections of Robert fitz Walter. He and the earl of Winchester were 'first cousins in the half blood in the male line'.

[28] Painter, 'The house of Quency', 237–8.

[29] *Chron. Maj.*, ii, 626.

[30] *Maréchal*, lines 16761–8.

[31] *RLC*, 323, 323b; C 54/16, mm. 13, 7 (*Odero si potero si non invitus amabo*). I am grateful to Andrew Hershey for helping me to decipher this passage.

[32] *Giraldi Cambrensis Opera*, 174–5; *RLC*, 342b.

Of course, none of this stopped the Henricians extracting the last penny from ransoms; but then ransoms were part of chivalrous society and knights had to live. Nothing is more indicative of the spirit in which the regent himself closed the war than him greeting to Louis on Saturday, 9 September: he saluted him 'comme son damoisiel', as his lady-love.[33] The regent, in his private affairs, was soon ignoring the divisions of the war. At Lincoln he had captured Gilbert de Clare, heir to the earldoms of Hertford and Gloucester, and also to the great lordship of Glamorgan, strategically placed to the west of the Marshal lordship of Nether Went. On the coming of peace, the regent married Gilbert to his daughter Isabella.[34]

[33] *Normandie*, 203.

[34] This is the story preserved in a fourteenth-century chronicle, *Nicholai Triveti Annales*, 201. Its statement that, after the battle, Gilbert was imprisoned at Gloucester is confirmed by the record evidence: *PR*, 79. The Tewkesbury annals say the marriage took place on 9 October 1214 but this entry must have been made after the war because Gilbert is styled earl of Gloucester and Hertford: *Ann. Mon.*, i, 61.

Chapter 3

THE GOVERNMENT OF THE REGENT, 1217–19

i. *Government problems and structure after the war*

The war had determined that the king of England would be an Angevin not a Capetian. The question, on the coming of peace, was how effectively he would rule. The terms of the peace treaty had been moderate but it was vital to put them into effect, which meant returning men to the seisins that they had enjoyed before the war and deciding about the 'emendations' to be made to Magna Carta. Failure to make progress on these fronts might renew civil strife. As it was, 'the relics of former discord', as the Barnwell chronicler put it, 'still found an outlet in frequent tournaments': early in October 1217 one was prohibited at Blythe, 'since the tranquillity of our land is still tender and can easily be disturbed'.[1] The regent's second task was to recover the authority and rebuild the structure of the king's government, which had collapsed during the war, just as it had during the civil war of Stephen's reign. To what extent and within what limits the powers of kingship were to be restored became the central issue of the minority. The regent's tasks were connected. The return of seisin to former rebels required effective and controllable local agents to carry it out. Magna Carta sought to limit the king but also demanded that he make his justice widely available. If the government could succeed in conciliating former rebels and dispensing effective justice, it would more easily secure consent to the restoration of its authority and support for action against the disobedient.

In the localities there were a variety of obstacles to the reassertion of central control. The war of 1215–17, just like that of Stephen's reign, had produced a crop of newly constructed or reconstructed private castles. In many areas individuals and communities were determined to exploit the king's weakness and increase their own powers and liberties at his expense. In so doing they could claim to be implementing the terms of Magna Carta and its companion document issued in November 1217, the Charter of the Forest. In parts of eastern England, the focus of the rebellion, royal authority had almost disintegrated.

[1] *Walt. Cov.*, 240; *PR*, 116.

A tremendous responsibility, therefore, devolved on the king's local agents. They had to rebuild their castles and grip the peacetime administration of their sheriffdoms. Yet in some counties, where leading members of the regime were quarrelling amongst themselves over who should be the sheriff, it was not even clear who the king's local agents were. Elsewhere, the sheriffs of the war, with their power firmly based on the tenure of royal castles, had quickly asserted a peacetime rule over their counties, or at least over extensive areas within them. This was true, for example, of Philip of Oldcoates in Northumberland, Philip Mark in Nottinghamshire-Derbyshire, the earl of Chester in Lancashire, Shropshire and Staffordshire, the earl of Salisbury in Wiltshire and Falkes de Bréauté in Oxfordshire, Northampton-shire, Bedfordshire-Buckinghamshire and Cambridgeshire-Hunting-donshire. But, if the regent's authority depended on such men, it might also be threatened by them. During the war they had run their bailiwicks as they pleased, careless, if not contemptuous, of the king's orders, spending his revenues themselves rather than passing them to the exchequer. With the coming of peace these men had every intention of continuing in the same vein. Almost at once the regent was faced with the refusal of Philip of Oldcoates, Philip Mark, Robert de Gaugi, the count of Aumale and Hugh de Vivonne to surrender lands and castles either to former rebels or to the king. The politics of the minority frequently turned on the efforts of central government to vindicate its authority over these independent governors.

In the short term, however, the regent was under pressure to increase rather than diminish the power of the sheriffs and castellans. That was partly because they needed abundant resources to sustain their activities and authority; partly because, having won the war, they clamoured for reward. Here the regent's situation differed from that of Henry II. The latter, on his accession, owed few political debts and had no need 'to make concessions to win friends and buy support'.[2] Nor could the regent reward the victors by feeding them with the lands of disinherited former rebels as happened after the civil war of 1263–65. In 1217 the terms of the peace treaty ruled this out. The regent had no alternative but to find patronage from the king's own resources.

These resources, however, were limited in the extreme. The weakness of royal authority in the localities was both cause and consequence of the crown's poverty. At the end of the war it was necessary to borrow the money to get Louis out of the country. Virtually no regular revenue was coming into the centre. Indeed, there was nowhere for it to come, for the exchequer itself no longer functioned. Its very rolls had been in Louis's custody.[3] Likewise, the

---

[2] Warren, *Henry II*, 54.
[3] Smith, 'Treaty of Lambeth', 577 n. 11.

king's judges had ceased to visit the counties; nor were they holding pleas centrally on any regular basis. The only surviving institution of central government was the chancery. The civil war had equally seen the break-up of the king's military household, the nucleus of his army and the ultimate centre of his power. At times in his reign John had retained well over fifty household knights.[4] At Christmas 1217 Henry III gave robes to just seven.[5] Nor does the regent seem to have stepped in and taken over John's former knights. Instead, like Ralph fitz Nicholas who became steward of the earl of Derby, they scattered into the service of various great lords, thus encapsulating the passage of power from the king to the magnates.[6]

The power and institutions of central government, therefore, had atrophied but at least the regent remained in day-to-day control of what was left. Until a seal was made for the young king in November 1218, he continued to authenticate royal letters with his own seal and to attest the great majority of them. That his control was far from nominal is shown by the first exchequer memoranda roll of the new reign, that covering the period from Michaelmas 1217 to Trinity 1218. There a note was made to discuss with the regent the misdeeds of the count of Aumale, and sheriffs were given days to account 'by the Marshal' or 'by writ of the Marshal', which shows that he used his own letters as well as the king's to give executive orders.[7]

Although the regent thus sat in control of central government, his was not the first place. Above him there was still the legate Guala. After the war the latter was busy disciplining the clergy who had supported Louis and, against the background of the fourth Lateran council, furthering the cause of ecclesiastical reform. He acted against pluralism and inspired government measures banning Sunday markets.[8] Guala took no immediate responsibility for day-to-day political administration: he was associated with the issue of very few royal letters. But, until his departure in December 1218, he was closely involved with many of the major decisions of the government. He felt quite able to dictate orders to the regent in purely secular matters, telling him to act 'as you are bound to do for the honour of king and kingdom'.[9] Perhaps this irritated the regent but Guala's position

---

[4] A contemporary list of John's household knights (British Library Add. MS 41, 479) contains forty-seven names but it is clear that the total establishment was larger. This will be discussed by Stephen Church, who is writing a thesis on John's military household.

[5] *RLC*, 345b.

[6] *Rot. Lib.*, 125–6; *RLC*, 406.

[7] E 368/1, mm. 2d, 6, 6d, 7; for the regent's own letters, see also *RLC*, 343, 371, and (for two letters actually enrolled) West, *Justiciarship*, 234; E 368/3, m. 3d.

[8] Sayers, *Honorius III*, 171–3; Cate, 'The church and market reform', 51–3.

[9] *F*, 152; see also *DD*, no. 27, *RLC*, 367b, 368b.

unquestionably enhanced the authority of the government and ensured co-operation between church and state.[10] This had one disadvantage: since ecclesiastical vacancies were filled quickly, little or no revenue was available from them for the king.[11] But at least Guala and later his successor, Pandulf, ensured that those appointed to bishoprics were loyal to the king. Equally, bishops were encouraged to assume high government office. The barons of the exchequer after the war included the bishops of London, Coventry, Rochester and Winchester. Bishops were equally prominent among the justices in eyre appointed in November 1218.[12]

At the very centre of the regent's government, however, there was tension. His effective deputy was the king's tutor, Peter, bishop of Winchester. Peter was active at the exchequer and the only person, down to November 1218, to share, on any appreciable scale, in the attestation and authorization of royal letters.[13] The regent respected Peter and made him an executor of his will but more than once the two men found themselves sharply at odds.[14] The question of whether Peter owed his position as the king's tutor simply to the regent's delegation or whether he had independent authority deriving from King John or from 'common counsel' was perhaps always an underlying cause of friction between them. There were also difficulties with the justiciar, Hubert de Burgh. Hubert played little part in central government in the first year of peace. Indeed, until 1219, he hardly attested or authorized a single royal letter. Nor, unlike his predecessors before the war, did he preside at the exchequer and the bench.[15] Instead Hubert heard petty assizes in his sheriffdoms of Kent and Norfolk-Suffolk, thus attempting to restore order there and facilitate the process of settlement.[16]

The power of the regent's government was limited, therefore, by its internal divisions and the paucity of its resources. This situation encouraged men to pose basic questions about its authority. These questions were suggested in part by the concession of Magna Carta: quite apart from the detailed restrictions that it imposed on kingship, it

[10] The one area of dispute between church and state in this period was over the future of the Jews; see Richardson, *English Jewry*, 180–7.

[11] Howell, *Regalian Right*, 234 (where the revenue from Norwich in fact belongs to the period before the war); see *Handbook of British Chronology*, 212, 216, 223, 225, 229, 239, 251, 261 for the length of vacancies down to 1224.

[12] E 368/1, m. 4; E 159/3, m. 7; *PR*, 206–8.

[13] *RLC*, 344, 361, 361b, 363, 364, 364b; *PR*, 149, 151, 158, 160, 166; E 368/1, mm. 1, 2, 2d, 4d.

[14] *Maréchal*, lines 18334–42.

[15] West, *Justiciarship*, 116–17, 151–2, 168, 191, 253–4; *Dialogus de Scaccario*, 15–16; and below p. 65. For the writs with which Hubert was associated: *PR*, 151, 158.

[16] C 60/9, m. 4; *Pipe Roll 1218*, 26–8; *Pipe Roll 1220*, 169–70. Hubert was also involved in supervising the work of Dover Castle: *CPReg.*, 63.

encouraged the belief that obedience to the king was conditional. Thus the Dunstable abbey annalist liked to think that an oath of obedience, taken in 1218–19, was limited to the 'reasonable orders of the king'. Later, the regent's son declared his readiness 'to do [to the king] all the things which I ought to do as my lord' but added the saving clause 'according to the custom of the kingdom'.[17] Questions about the authority of the government were also raised by the fact that the king was a minor. Many sheriffs and castellans appointed by King John believed that the ministers of his son had no power to dismiss them. That could only be done once King Henry was of age. Even more limiting, and more significant constitutionally, was the view, power-fully expressed by the earl of Salisbury and Robert de Vieuxpont in 1220, that the only legitimate orders were those sanctioned by 'the magnates of England who are held to be and are of the chief council of the king'.[18] The sum of all this was that the regent, and his successors, could only govern with consent. Hence the increasing prominence of the body called the king's council.

Already in the war royal letters had averred that decisions had been taken on the advice of the council and, with the coming of peace, references to that body become more frequent. It plays a far larger role in the governance of England than it had ever done under John. The council was not a formal body. It could be a small group of ministers or a large assembly of ministers and magnates. The two are often difficult to distinguish since the term 'the council' was used to cover assemblies of both types. Decisions by large assemblies, or great councils as they will be called in this book, were sometimes described as taken 'by common counsel' but this was far from always the case. The first scutage of the reign, for example, was variously portrayed as imposed 'by common counsel of the earls and barons of England', 'by counsel of the magnates' and simply 'by the king's council'.[19] In fact, the special circumstances of the minority meant that those in charge at the centre had to take frequent counsel both from small groups of fellow ministers and from great gatherings of magnates. The role of the latter in the process of decision making is especially striking.

Clause 12 of Magna Carta 1215 had attempted to give great councils formal control over the granting of extraordinary taxation. Clause 14 had laid down how such bodies were to be convoked: the greater barons were to receive individual letters of summons; the other tenants in

[17] *Ann. Mon.*, iii, 53; *RL*, no. clii.
[18] See below p. 209.
[19] *PR*, 125, 171; C 60/9, m. 6. The same ambiguity in terminology was still found in the time of Edward I: Prestwich, *Edward I*, 441. For the council under John and in the minority, see Baldwin, 'The beginnings of the king's council', 27–59, and *The King's Council*, 12–22.

chief were to be summoned in general by the sheriffs. All letters of summons were to state the reasons for the assembly. These clauses, however, were omitted from the 1216 Charter and from its successors. There is little to show how the great councils of the minority were convened and their composition sometimes gave rise to disputes. Nonetheless, such gatherings were assembled with great frequency. They were involved, moreover, in a far wider range of decisions than the granting of taxation, important although that was. The regent, as has been seen, had effectively been appointed by a great council composed of the young king's supporters. During the war it was with the counsel and assent of the legate and the 'magnates of England' that he conceded, on the king's behalf, part of Worcester castle to the monks of Worcester cathedral. Likewise, it was by 'common counsel' of the king's *fideles* in May 1217 that the earl of Salisbury was given the city and sheriffdom of Lincoln.[20] The regent's authority and that of his successors depended, in practice, on securing such common consent from great councils and it is this which gives the minority much of its constitutional importance.

The period of his peacetime regency is the hardest part of William Marshal's career to evaluate. His biography was concerned with his gallantry and loyalty, not with his views about the future of England's polity. William had disliked King John and considered the civil war a tragedy. As a great baron he must have welcomed the concessions to his class in Magna Carta and was, therefore, well suited to preside over the process of resettlement. At the same time, however, as long serving *curialis*, defence of the king's rights came naturally to him: in 1214 he had enjoined the monks of Bury St Edmunds to 'preserve [the king's] privileges and liberties unhurt and unimpaired'.[21] He must have been aware of the customary oath taken by the king at the coronation to preserve and recover the rights of the crown.[22] Yet the regent was under intense pressure to find rewards for his supporters. He also wanted rewards for himself.[23] Thus his government took on a dual aspect. It did much to implement the terms of the peace treaty and restore the structure of royal administration, especially in the field of the dispensation of justice, but it also sanctioned the continuing passage of power and resources into the hands of the great men of the regime. With nothing else to give, it allowed them to draw off the revenues from the

[20] *Worcester Cartulary*, no. 328a; *PR*, 65.
[21] *Election of Abbot Hugh*, 84–5.
[22] Richardson, 'The coronation', 151–61.
[23] The close link between the regent's private affairs and those of the king is shown by the enrolment on the chancery fine rolls of his ransom treaty with Nicholas de Stuteville: C 60/9, m. 8. He also spent much time at his private manors, as well as at Marlborough, which he had taken over from his son.

king's escheats, wardships, demesne manors and sheriffdoms. On coming to the throne, Henry II had at once reined in the centrifugal forces which had thrived in the Anarchy.[24] After the civil war of 1215–17, such forces continued to flourish. The consequences for the future power of English kingship were potentially disastrous.

ii. Settlement, October–November 1217: individuals

With Louis safely out of the country, the regent's most vital task was to implement the treaty of peace. As far as individuals were concerned, its cornerstone was the restoration of former rebels to their lands. This was the clause under an emphatic 'first' (in primis) which was placed at the head of the treaty.[1] The procedure of implementation had already been established for the rebels who had entered the king's faith since April 1217. The latter had obtained writs ordering the sheriffs to put them back in seisin of the lands they had held when the war broke out or, alternatively, when they deserted King John. Similar writs were now obtained generally by former rebels, fully 1,000 being issued between September and November 1217.[2] Little is known of the procedures followed by the sheriffs. In one case, the sheriff of Lincolnshire sent a copy of the writ to his bailiff, who inquired through a jury what seisin the former rebel, William de Mortimer, had enjoyed at the beginning of the war and what he had lost as a result of it, and then gave him possession accordingly. But matters did not always run smoothly. Mortimer himself was promptly re-disseised by the Henrician who had gained his lands during the war.[3] In other cases, despite the best endeavours of sheriffs, former rebels were unable to recover seisin at all; sometimes it was the sheriffs themselves who held lands of former rebels and refused to surrender them.[4]

As the process of settlement got under way, a great council assembled at Westminster, remaining in session from c. 21 October until c. 8 November. Of former rebels, Robert fitz Walter, the earl of Winchester, Gilbert de Clare, Gilbert de Gant, Roger Bertram, Walter de Dunstanville and John fitz Alan were all expected to attend.[5] Indeed, during the council, London was full of former rebels 'doing fealty and homage [to the king]', as the Barnwell annalist put it, making out charters of faithful service, on pain of disinheritance, and

[24] Warren, Henry II, 54–63.
[1] Smith, 'Treaty of Lambeth', 576.
[2] Painter, William Marshal, 230.
[3] Lincs. Worcs. Eyre, lix, no. 297; see also no. 56.
[4] See the case of Roger de Vilers excluded by the sheriff of Dorset, Peter de Maulay, and his deputy, Peter de Rusceus: CRR, xii, no. 1145; xiii, nos 314, 333; RLC, 283b, 300.
[5] PR, 97, 99, 103–4; RLC, 325b, 336b.

obtaining writs of seisin from the chancery.[6] These men demanded and obtained the promised *emendationes* to the Great Charter, a new version of the document being issued around 6 November. They also brought pressure to bear in those cases where problems had occurred, or were expected to occur, in the process of re-seisin. As a result the major *causes célèbres* of the early minority were identified. The regent's response was immensely reassuring for former rebels. When the process of resettlement was being obstructed, he demonstrated a willingness to intervene, thus setting the pattern which was to be followed by his successors.

One of the most intractable problems was presented by the case of the great northern rebel, Roger Bertram, and his castle of Mitford, fourteen miles north of Newcastle upon Tyne. Mitford was being detained by a man who had done much to sustain Angevin interests in the north throughout the war, the sheriff of Northumberland, Philip of Oldcoates. Oldcoates, an Englishman of humble origins, had been in John's service since the 1190s; he had defended Chinon with Hubert de Burgh in 1204–5 and been sheriff of Northumberland since 1212. He had received custody of Mitford after its capture in January 1216, had defended it for a week against the king of Scotland and, judging from his later protestations, thought it monstrous that it should be returned at all to Bertram. He had already resisted at least one order to that effect. Both Oldcoates and Bertram were summoned to the October council and the former was once again instructed to give up the castle.[7]

A second case which was to become a *cause célèbre* was also considered at the council. This concerned William de Coleville's castle of Bytham, north of Stamford in Lincolnshire, and its surrounding lands. On Coleville's rebellion, King John had given the castle and lands to William de Fors, count of Aumale, who was Coleville's lord. William was a Poitevin who had come to England as a young man in 1213 and secured the rich inheritance of his mother, which included Holderness and Skipton in Yorkshire. It was doubtless these northern interests which explained his own flirtation with the rebellion but he had rejoined King John just prior to the latter's death and had retained possession of the properties of William de Coleville. At the end of the war the latter recovered his lands but not Bytham castle, for Aumale's constable defiantly closed its gates on the sheriff's approach. Soon afterwards Aumale resumed control of the lands as well. Further royal orders failed to remove him. As a result of the discussions at the council he was ordered once again to restore seisin to Coleville, 'all excuse and delay set aside', or come before the king on 26 November to explain himself.[8]

---

[6] *Walt. Cov.*, 240. Twenty-eight of these charters are preserved in C 47/34/8.

[7] RLC, 246b, 316, 321, 336b; *PR*, 122; *Melrose*, 68; Holt, *Northerners*, 222–3.

[8] *CRR*, viii, 163–4; *RLC*, 323b, 327; *PR*, 119.

In Nottinghamshire it was the sheriff himself, Philip Mark, who was causing the trouble. Having got control during the war of the manors of Oswaldbeck and North Wheatley, he was refusing to restore them to Roger de Montbegon, one of the twenty-five guarantors of Magna Carta in 1215. Mark was now ordered to give up the manors and pointedly informed that Roger held them under a charter of King John.[9]

The government also continued its struggle to get King John's Flemish serjeant, Robert de Gaugi, to surrender the castle of Newark. Here the lord of the castle was not a former rebel but the bishop of Lincoln, who had entrusted Newark to John merely for the duration of the political crisis. The question of Gaugi's tenure had already been considered by great councils during the war and as early as June 1217 he had been ordered to give up the castle 'by common counsel of the legate and the kingdom'. At the great council in October Gaugi at last appeared to comply and took an oath to deliver seisin to the bishop within forty days. Whether he would do so, however, was another matter. On 6 November orders went out to the sheriffs of Lincoln and Nottingham to force him to keep his promise.[10]

Of all these cases, only that of Newark was solved by the regent, the others rumbling on to torment his successors.[11] Nonetheless, he had demonstrated his willingness to help those unable to recover seisin. The government was on their side. True, special help might have to be paid for: in November 1217 Roger Bertram offered £100 for the writ which ordered Oldcoates to surrender Mitford but at least he was not expected to pay until he obtained seisin.[12] Some of the measures taken at the council, moreover, did have immediate effect. Kimbolton castle was returned to the earl of Essex and, if Oldcoates retained Mitford, his colleague, Hugh de Balliol, returned Prudhoe castle, just north of Newcastle upon Tyne, to Richard de Umfraville, Roger Bertram's uncle and political associate.[13]

In general, the process of resettlement was probably proceeding well. The writ of seisin was easy to obtain, hence its name, 'the common writ of seisin'.[14] Contemporary chroniclers relate the *causes célèbres* but do not suggest that there was any general failure to return lands. The

[9] *RLC*, 339.

[10] *PR*, 68, 71, 85, 121.

[11] The further history of all these cases will be followed in the ensuing pages. For the Mitford affair, see Holt, *Northerners*, 244–6, and below pp. 83, 85–8, 104, 130, 147, 162, 174–6, 197, 204–5, 208, 214. For the count of Aumale, see English, *The Lords of Holderness*, 37–49; Turner, 'William de Forz', 221–49; and (for Bytham) below pp. 86–7, 147, 166–7, 231.

[12] C 60/9, m. 8; E 372/66, r. 15d, m. 2.

[13] *PR*, 119, 120; *RLC*, 230, 379b; Roger Bertram's mother was Richard de Umfraville's sister: *Peerage*, ii, 160 n.a; Sanders, *Baronies*, 73, 131.

[14] For example, *CRR*, viii, 228.

Barnwell annalist indeed is more positive: 'and thus [the rebels] were reconciled to the king and recovered their lands. For this condition was understood, namely that no one should be disinherited on account of this war but all should be in the same state as at its beginning.'[15] Despite the grievances of individuals, there is no sign that disgruntled former rebels as a body became a factor in the politics of the minority, as 'the disinherited' were to do after the war of 1263–65.

There was one cardinal factor which facilitated the landed settlement. The rebellion had had a strong regional bias. After the war, if a rebel's lands were within an area dominated by a great Henrician sheriff and castellan, he might have difficulty recovering them. That was the situation, for example, of Roger de Montbegon to whom the Nottinghamshire county court, tightly controlled by the agents of the sheriff, Philip Mark, gave no support. But the majority of rebels were not in this position. In eastern England *they* had ruled in the shires. Thus the Lincolnshire county court stood vociferously behind Gilbert de Gant when he seemed to be unjustly deprived of his lands.[16] In the east it was the rebels who had committed disseisins and *multa mala*, and supporters of the Angevins who had been expropriated.[17] The clause in the peace treaty saying that the latter too should recover their possessions was no formality. The count of Aumale may have been secure at Bytham but elsewhere in Lincolnshire, as also in Kent, he had to be restored to his lands on the conclusion of the peace.[18]

Of course, the recovery of lands which former rebels had held in 1215 did nothing for their grievances of an earlier date. The government made no effort to reopen the most blatant examples of John's injustice: the earl of Salisbury, for example, continued to exclude the earl of Hereford from Trowbridge.[19] In some lesser cases, however, usually in return for money, grievances were remedied. During the council of November 1217 the rebel, Matilda de Cauz, fined in £40 for the return of her hereditary forestership of Nottinghamshire-Derbyshire which John had taken from her as long ago as 1202.[20] Later, probably in 1219, the regent, the justiciar, the bishop of Winchester and the council freed

---

[15] *Walt. Cov.*, 239.

[16] *RL*, nos lxxxvi, xvi. The control of local government by the rebels in Norfolk and Suffolk down to the time of the peace, only partly interrupted by Falkes's agents, is revealed by an enquiry at the exchequer: *Pipe Roll 1215*, 10.

[17] See Holt, *Northerners*, 249.

[18] *RLC*, 322b, 323b.

[19] In the case of Knaresborough and Boroughbridge, the situation was complicated by the death of Nicholas de Stuteville before the end of the war and the minority of his grandson: *EYC*, ix, 15–17.

[20] *PR*, 123; *RLC*, 316; *Pipe Roll 1219*, 98; Holt, *Northerners*, 30. The sheriff, Philip Mark, who controlled the forest in the counties, was still resisting its return to Matilda in 1220: see below p. 216.

Nicholas de Verdun from a debt which John had imposed on him 'by will and without judgement'.[21] Occasionally patronage was bestowed on former rebels. If the earl of Winchester did not recover Mountsorrel, in November 1217 he was granted, until the king came of age, the £31 10s annual farm which the canons of Barnwell owed for the manor of Chesterton, a manor which the earl claimed was his by hereditary right. At the same time, the northern rebel, Robert de Vaux of Gilsland in Cumbria, was granted, during the king's pleasure, the royal manor of Grimsby to sustain him in the king's service.[22] Former rebels were also rehabilitated into the political life of the country. During the November council the earl of Winchester in particular was clearly *persona grata* at the highest level, while two former rebels, John de Lacy and Robert de Ros, were ordered to conduct King Alexander into England.[23] Above all against their ransoms and their thwarted expectations, the former rebels could set one great victory, namely the concession of a new version of Magna Carta, accompanied this time by an entirely new document, a Charter of the Forest.

iii. *Magna Carta and the Charter of the Forest, November 1217*

At the great council of October–November 1217, according to the Barnwell annalist, 'there were frequent discussions about the governance of the kingdom, the stabilization of peace and the abolition of bad customs'.[1] Out of these debates emerged a new version of the Great Charter in what was to be virtually its final and definitive form.[2] As has been seen, the great magnates, whatever their allegiances during the

---

[21] *Pipe Roll 1218*, 42; *RLC*, 388; Holt, *Magna Carta*, 94; see also *Pipe Roll 1218*, 39.
[22] *RLC*, 342b.
[23] C 47/34/8 (charter of Nicholas fitz Theobald); see below p. 68; *PR*, 122–3. Ros was Alexander's brother-in-law of the half-blood, having married an illegitimate daughter of William the Lion.
[1] *Walt. Cov.*, 240.
[2] The date of the 1217 Charter has been the subject of debate, since the only surviving original was left without a dating clause: see Holt, *Magna Carta*, 273 n. 1 and (for the text) Stubbs, *Select Charters*, 341–4. There are three reasons for preferring a date around 6 November to the other alternatives, 12 and 23 September. i. The Charter's preamble is similar to that of the Charter of the Forest whose date is certainly 6 November. ii. A version of the Charter, preserved in the *Liber Niger* of Christ Church, Dublin, which conflates the texts of 1217 and 1225, concludes: *Datum per manum . . . R. Dunholmensis episcopi cancellarii nostri apud sanctum Paulum Londoniis vi die Novembris anno regni nostri secundo*. This cannot be borrowed entirely from the Charter of the Forest, which was 'given by the hands' of the legate and regent at St Paul's, rather than by the chancellor, and perhaps it preserves a genuine conclusion of Magna Carta 1217: see Lawlor, 'An unnoticed Charter of Henry III', 515, 517–18. iii. The council in session in late October–early November was by far the greatest gathering since the end of the war and a more likely forum for the issue of the Charter than meetings in September, which must have been preoccupied with the immediate conclusion of peace.

war, could agree upon the Charter's merits. Indeed, they now came together to assert, in several new clauses, their own interests against those of other sections of society.[3] Thus a new clause (39) forbad any free man from alienating land if that meant he was no longer able to provide the service owed 'to the lord of the fee'. Another (43) tried to prevent men evading the customs and services due to their lords by granting lands to religious houses and then receiving them back as the houses' tenants. Above all, immediately after the stipulation that everyone (which meant in practice the magnates) should observe towards their own men the liberties in the Charter, was inserted the qualification 'saving the liberties and free customs which they had before'.

As for matters omitted from the 1215 Charter which were offered for negotiation at the end of the Charter of 1216, the question of 'the river banks and their keepers' was dealt with in a new clause (20), somewhat tighter than that of 1215. The question of 'the customs of the counties' resulted in a great new clause (42), which regulated in detail the holding of the county and hundred courts. True, against this nothing was done about debts to the Jews, and little about scutages and aids. The 1215 Charter had stipulated that scutages, and aids other than those levied on three customary occasions, required the assent of a great council. It had also laid down detailed regulations as to how the great council was to be summoned. All that appeared in 1217, however, was the vague stipulation that scutages were to be taken as in the reign of Henry II, which implied that they should be levied less frequently and at lower rates than had been the case under King John. To later constitutional historians this seemed a serious diminution of the Charter. At the time, it appeared rather less so. The great council itself conceded an aid to the king, which it would scarcely have done had there been strong feelings about the omission of the clause. In practice, the minority government was dependent upon the support of great councils and it seemed highly unlikely that it could or would levy taxation without their consent.[4] In any case, the failure to make progress here was far outweighed in another area offered for negotiation, that of the forest. The result was not a new clause, it was an entirely new charter.

The royal forest played a central part in the politics of Angevin England for one reason above all. Its boundaries were not limited to the demesnes of the king but also encompassed large areas held by ecclesiastical institutions, barons, knights, gentry and freemen.

---

[3] For the changes in the 1217 Charter, see Holt, *Magna Carta*, 272-5.

[4] The clause may also have been omitted because it threatened to restrict the occasions when a lord could levy an aid from his own tenants: see Holt, *Magna Carta*, 204. Scutages differed from aids in that, levied in lieu of military service, they had not customarily required consent.

Anyone unfortunate enough to have lands within the forest was forbidden by forest law from creating waste and from making assarts and purprestures (that is, from converting land into arable and enclosing it with hedges and ditches). In a time of rising population and rising demand for corn, this gravely restricted the ability to exploit estates economically. In addition, forest law forbad the killing of deer and wild boar. In order to enforce this law, the Angevin kings had created a range of local officials and had staged regular visitations of special forest justices (the forest eyre). Punishment for committing waste, assarts and purprestures was usually financial (one paid an initial amercement and then an annual rent to maintain the encroachment) and was entirely a matter for the king's will. Not surprisingly, King John found the forest an extremely lucrative source of revenue.[5]

The Charter of the Forest, issued under the seal of the legate and the regent on 6 November, subjected the forest for the first time to a law other than that of the king's will and thus marked a radical new departure.[6] It had four main points. First, it pardoned past forest offences; all purprestures and assarts made in private woods within the forest since Henry II's accession were forgiven. This must have involved sacrificing a considerable income from the annual rents. Second, it regulated for the future the whole running of the forest administration, dealing with the holding of its courts, the activities of its officials and the level of punishments: no one henceforth (a concession particularly remarked on by contemporaries) was to lose life or limb for an offence against the protected beasts of the forest. Third, it gave privileges to those with private woods within the forest; and last and above all, it attempted to reduce the bounds of the forest itself. This was almost the only aspect of the forest which had been tackled in the 1215 Charter and two years later the solutions were more radical. In 1215 merely the areas afforested by King John were slated for immediate deforestation; in respect of the areas brought within the forest by Henry II and Richard I, John was granted the respite of a crusader. Since that meant a respite until he returned from his projected crusade, this was tantamount to postponing the matter indefinitely. In the Charter of 1217, by contrast, the afforestations of both John and Richard were to be subject to immediate deforestation. These, however, had not been large. The real prize related to the areas afforested by Henry II, for contemporaries believed that the expansion of the forest to include areas outside the royal demesne had been

[5] For the forest, see *Select Pleas of the Forest*, ix–cxxxiv; Young, *Royal Forests*. John's exploitation of the forest is discussed in Holt, *Northerners*, 159–63.
[6] For the text, Stubbs, *Select Charters*, 344–8.

essentially Henry's work. Under the Charter of 1217 Henry II's afforestations were to be established by 'good and law-worthy men' and then deforested.[7]

Thanks to the Charter of the Forest, the restrictions imposed on kingship in 1217 were far greater than two years before. From that point of view, former rebels, whatever their grievances over ransoms and so forth, could think that they had emerged victorious from the war. That was true, moreover, at various levels of society. In the Charter of 1217, as has been seen, great magnates protected themselves against their inferiors but the new clause 42, on the holding of the county and hundred courts, was prized by knights, gentry and a wide circle of local society. Equally, all sections of society might benefit from the Charter of the Forest.[8] Of course, it was one thing to receive concessions on paper; another for them actually to be implemented. And it was precisely here that the Charters of 1217 had a crucial defect. For a clause in Magna Carta 1215, left out both in 1216 and 1217, was that which had empowered twenty-five barons to force the king to keep the Charter. This was a clumsy device and a recipe for civil war but its omission left the Charters without means of enforcement. Almost immediately difficulties arose over implementing the Charter of the Forest. Later in the reign of Henry III, this weakness in the Charters was a key factor in generating more radical schemes of political reform.

Against these problems, however, the most important clause in the Great Charter, from the point of view of the barons, was immediately seen to be working. This was the clause on relief, the payment made by a baron to the king on succeeding to his estates. John and his predecessors had imposed reliefs of huge size: 1,300 marks on Eustace de Vesci in 1190; approaching 10,000 marks on Nicholas de Stuteville in 1205; 7,000 marks on John de Lacy in 1213.[9] Magna Carta, by contrast, fixed the relief for an earldom and barony at £100. At the end of the war this was put to the test immediately in respect of three earldoms to which the heirs were former rebels: those of Essex, where the heir was William de Mandeville, and Gloucester and Hertford, where the heir was Gilbert de Clare. In all three cases the relief was £100.[10] If, as seems likely, in October 1217 Gilbert de Clare married Isabella, the daughter of the regent, then the latter too reaped here his reward.

---

[7] For the bounds of the forest, see Bazeley, 'The extent of the forest', 140–72. Map 2, above p. xxii, gives a general impression of the extent of the royal forest as it was left after the minority and its immediate aftermath (see also below p. 392 n. 12).

[8] Maddicott, 'Magna Carta and the local community', 31–6. This clause may have been based on the returns of the inquiry into the malpractices of local officials ordered by Magna Carta 1215: Holt, *Magna Carta*, 274.

[9] Holt, *Northerners*, 177.

[10] *Pipe Roll 1218*, 76; *Peerage*, v, 129–31, 694.

iv. *The restoration of government, October–November 1217*

While the regent thus pressed ahead with implementing the peace treaty, he also faced the task of restoring the structure and authority of the king's government. At the centre, as has been seen, the war had terminated the sessions of both the bench and the exchequer. The restoration of the two offices to full efficiency and working order were not tasks of equivalent difficulty. The bench had to dispense civil justice to litigants many of whom positively wished their cases to be heard before the king's judges, while the exchequer had to extract money from the sheriffs and through them from the large numbers of sullen individuals who were in debt to the crown. Unless, however, the regent's government fulfilled the demand for justice, it would have neither the justification nor the power to insist that men meet the exchequer's demands and obey the mandates of the king. Unless it gave with one hand it could never take with the other.

Magna Carta itself had, in effect, called for the restoration of the bench when it stipulated that common, that is broadly civil, pleas be heard in 'any certain place', this demand having been prompted by the virtual suspension of both the bench and the eyres between 1209 and 1212, and the hearing of their pleas before John himself as he journeyed round the country.[1] After the war, the government clearly decided to revive the bench at once, for its legal experts inserted two new clauses (14 and 15) into the 1217 Charter which mentioned it by name and defined aspects of its jurisdiction: it was to hear all assizes of darrein presentment and all cases too difficult to be determined by the petty assize judges in the counties. As early as 18 November 1217 an order was addressed to the justices of the bench and some cases came before them in that Michaelmas term. From the Hilary term of 1218 they were in regular session at Westminster.[2] The chief problem was lack of trained judicial personnel, death having removed John's senior professional judge, Simon of Pattishall. However, a replacement was found in the person of his former clerk, Martin of Pattishall, while Ralph Harang and Stephen of Seagrave (a familiar of the earl of Chester) were brought in from local administration.[3] Significantly, an effort was made to reassure former rebels about the bench's impartiality or at least its political balance. The one pre-war justice to be reappointed for any length of time was John of Guestling, a former rebel and a familiar of one of King John's greatest opponents, Stephen

[1] Clanchy, 'Magna Carta and the common pleas', 219–32. Clanchy argues that 'any certain place' could also mean a place before itinerant justices.

[2] *RLC*, 344; *BNB*, iii, 305; i, 139. It was not till the Hilary term that final concords began to be made before the judges.

[3] Turner, *Judiciary*, 192, 194, 211, 213, 220–1.

Langton, archbishop of Canterbury.[4] Equally significant was the fact that in 1218 the justices were paid salaries, apparently for the first time, a measure almost certainly designed to reduce the temptation to accept gifts and bribes.[5] One figure, however, was missing from the sessions of the bench in 1218. The justiciar, Hubert de Burgh, did not preside as his predecessors had done before the war. In December 1217 a final concord was made before the regent, the justiciar and the new justices of the bench;[6] on 24 January 1218 concords were made before the same group of men when the bench reopened at Westminster. But thereafter Hubert's name was absent from the lists of judges until the end of the regency.[7]

Over the restoration of the exchequer, too, the government moved with speed. Its rolls were recovered, new chequered cloths purchased and in November 1217 the office was open for business. John's treasurer, William of Ely, had joined the rebellion so a successor was found in the king's clerk, Eustace de Faukenburg, while William Brewer, a senior baron of John's exchequer, also returned to harness.[8] Both the regent and the bishop of Winchester took an active part in proceedings. Once again, however, the justiciar, who should have presided, was conspicuous by his absence.[9] When the exchequer opened, the sheriffs were immediately summoned to account, presumably for the time of the war and the half year of peace before it. But in the period covered by the first exchequer memoranda roll of the reign (Michaelmas 1217–Trinity 1218), amidst a welter of 'summonses and resummonses, postponements and adjournments', not one did so. It was only from Michaelmas 1218 that the sheriffs began to account for the last half year of peace (Michaelmas 1214–Easter 1215), the exchequer abandoning any general effort to secure accounts for the war.[10]

---

[4] Turner, *Judiciary*, 192, 131, 145, 170, 182, 276. Langton himself finally returned to England in May 1218.

[5] *RLC*, 350, 365; Turner, *Judiciary*, 244–5; see *DBM*, 108–9.

[6] CP 25(1)/282/8, no. 5. This concord was made at Northampton whence the court and the judges had moved for the meeting with King Alexander.

[7] CP 25(1)/225/4, nos 1, 6; Meekings, 'Concords'; West, *Justiciarship*, 116–17, 151–2, 168, 191, 253–4. Final concords (records of agreement) made before the justices of the bench provide the chief evidence for its composition.

[8] *Pipe Roll 1215*, 20; Richardson, 'William of Ely', 55–6, 59; *RLC*, 340b. There is a study of Brewer's career in Turner, *Men Raised from the Dust*, 71–90.

[9] E 368/1, mm. 1, 2, 2d, 4d, 6, 6d, 7. The judgement cited in West, *Justiciarship*, 230 n. 6, is not stated to have been made at the exchequer. However, Hubert's name does appear in what was probably a list of the barons of the exchequer in November 1217. The names were as follows: the bishops of London, Winchester and Coventry, the regent, the justiciar, William Brewer, William de Cantilupe, Thomas of Erdington, Geoffrey of Buckland, E. the treasurer (Eustace de Faukenburg) and Robert de Neville: E 368/1, m. 4.

[10] *RLC*, 340b, 343, 343b; *Pipe Roll 1215*, 5–6; see also *Pipe Roll 1214*, xi–xii, 12.

Bringing the sheriffs to account, moreover, was as nothing compared with actually getting them to pay money into the exchequer. The first *Adventus Vicecomitum* of the new reign on 12 November (the occasion when sheriffs were supposed to appear at the exchequer with the money which they had collected) was a disaster. Only four sheriffs currently in office turned up and no money at all was proffered.[11]

Another problem immediately confronting the regent and the exchequer was conflict between leading members of the regime over the tenure of local office. Engelard de Cigogné and the earl of Surrey were contesting the sheriffdom of Surrey. Matthew fitz Herbert and Ralph Tirel disputed that of Sussex; Tirel, so the exchequer was informed, having 'made himself sheriff through the justiciar'. In the west country violent conflicts had arisen following the concession of Somerset and Devon to the earl of Salisbury in March 1217 on his entering the king's faith. The sheriff of Somerset, Peter de Maulay, had waged a private war to prevent Salisbury securing the county and was summoned to the October council to answer for the breaches of the truce between them. In Devon, Henry fitz Count and Henry de Tracy, probably on Salisbury's behalf, were trying to wrest the sheriffdom from Robert de Courtenay; the latter could not appear at the exchequer on 12 November because he was being besieged in Exeter castle.[12]

Salisbury was also striving to get control of the county and castle of Lincoln. He had been granted the sheriffdom, and the city of Lincoln, after the battle in May 1217 but had taken possession of the castle as well, thus ejecting Nicola de Hay, who had strong claims to enjoy its custody in hereditary right.[13] This was very much a family dispute. In 1216 King John had agreed that Salisbury's eldest son (who was a minor) could marry Idonea, daughter and sole heiress of Richard de Camville, who was himself the son and sole heir of Nicola de Hay. Camville had died some time between January and November 1217, which meant Idonea and Salisbury's son were certain, once Nicola de Hay was dead, to inherit the Hay barony in Lincolnshire and, if they could make good their claim, the custody of Lincoln castle. Equally, once Nicola was dead, Salisbury himself, during the long minority of his son, could expect to control this rich inheritance, including Lincoln castle, since (in November 1217) he had been conceded custody of Richard de Camville's lands. Unfortunately for Salisbury, Nicola de Hay would not die. Nor would she gracefully resign her rights to Salisbury as guardian of her granddaughter. Instead, she came before the October great council, protested at Salisbury's conduct and begged

---

[11] E 368/1, m. 4; *Pipe Roll 1215*, 4.

[12] E 368/1, m. 7; *PR*, 135, 103; *RLC*, 330b. See also *BNB*, no. 1331.

[13] *PR*, 65, 117–18, 130; *RLC*, ii, 5. For the Hay claim to the castellanship of Lincoln castle see Hill, *Medieval Lincoln*, 87–9; *RH*, i, 309, 315.

that her right to Lincoln castle be respected. As a result, Salisbury was ordered to surrender both the castle and the sheriffdom to her. That was not the end of the matter, however. In December, Salisbury recovered the sheriffdom and his efforts to secure the castle as well caused continuing trouble to the regent's successors.[14]

Not surprisingly, with no money coming in from the sheriffs, the government found it impossible to meet its most pressing obligation, the payment of the 6,000 marks still owed to Louis.[15] The regent, in desperation, turned to the great council and asked for an aid to raise the money. The fissures at the very centre of his government were immediately revealed by the reaction of the bishop of Winchester. As an entry in the pipe roll of 1221 put it, 'the bishop never conceded [that tax] nor furnished his assent but always spoke against [it] being given'. Why is unclear, although perhaps he had disagreed with the promise to Louis in the first place. Nonetheless, by 30 October, with the concession of Magna Carta and the Charter of the Forest already certain, the council had conceded a tax in the form of a scutage of two marks on the fee, half to be paid on 30 November when the first instalment to Louis was due, half on 2 February, the day of the second and final payment. In fact these terms proved unrealistic and virtually nothing was raised for Louis before August 1218.[16] Alongside the scutage a tallage was imposed on the royal demesne. Both the ravages of the war and the weakness of the king's authority were reflected in the sums imposed being much smaller than in previous years. The towns of Huntingdon, Bristol, Hereford, Worcester, Oxford and Northampton owed 1,580 marks for the tallage of 1214 and only 610 marks (and 10 tuns of wine) for that three years later.[17]

The levying of aids and tallages could only be occasional expedients. If the king's financial position was to be restored on a day-to-day basis, it was vital to regain control over his demesnes, escheats and wardships, which had fallen into many hands during the war. The struggle to achieve such a resumption dominated the politics of the early minority. There was a parallel here with the reign of Stephen, when the king's resources had equally been dispersed during a civil war; on his accession Henry II had moved at once to recover lost royal demesnes. With the coming of peace in 1217 the regent moved in the same way but with much less success. At the end of September 1217 the

[14] *RLP*, 178b; *RLC*, 265, 279b, 295b, 299, 337; *Pipe Roll 1218*, 45. For the earl of Salisbury and Lincoln, see below pp. 159, 175.

[15] *PR*, 114, 125, 168; *RLC*, 369, 369b.

[16] *Pipe Roll 1221*, 21; *PR*, 171; for the tax, see Mitchell, *Taxation*, 125–8. The tax had no connection with military service and was a scutage only in being levied on sees. In principle it was an aid which thus in custom needed consent.

[17] *PR*, 171; *Pipe Roll 1218*, xix.

sheriffs were ordered to establish and take into the king's hands the royal demesne in their counties, whoever held it. They were to return the results of their inquiries to the regent on 20 October, that is, at the beginning of the great council. At the end of the council a parallel initiative was taken over escheats.[18]

The financial benefits of these initiatives were, however, extremely limited. The pressure for patronage was so great that the properties resumed were simply returned to their previous holders.[19] The regent attempted to make a stand over the royal vill of Southampton but even here it took two years to shake it free from the earl of Salisbury's attentions.[20] The reality was that the regent was presiding over a steady stream of grants which confirmed men in possession of royal demesne, or conceded it to them *de novo*, either during the king's pleasure or until he came of age. Early in October 1217 the royal demesne manor of Writtle in Essex was granted to Philip de Albini. A month later, besides the grants to the earl of Winchester and Robert de Vaux, the vills of Derby, Edwinstowe and Carlton and Darlton in Nottinghamshire and Derbyshire were conceded, until the king came of age, to the sheriff Philip Mark, while Philip of Oldcoates was conceded, on the same terms, the farms of Newcastle upon Tyne, Bamburgh and Corbridge.[21] The regent also looked after his own. John Marshal became chief justice of the forests. He, Ralph Musard and John of Earley were also granted wardships.[22] In normal circumstances the king sold wardships at high prices but these, as far as the evidence goes, were all conceded free of charge. Guala himself begged not to be left out. Indeed, he did better than anyone else, since he secured a grant in perpetuity for the house of canons that he was founding at Vercelli. On 8 November, on the advice of eight bishops and five magnates, including the regent, the justiciar and the earl of Winchester, the king acceded to the 'prayers of Guala who has laboured long and hard for our peace and that of our kingdom' and granted the canons the advowson of Chesterton in Cambridgeshire.[23]

Thus in these early days of peace the regent was beset by warring local agents and the clamour for patronage. Both contributed to the utter poverty of the crown. It was a relief to turn to an area where an immediate solution was possible: relations with the king of Scotland.

[18] *RLC*, 336b; *PR*, 170–1; Warren, *Henry II*, 61–2, 274.

[19] Orders for restorations may be found from *RLC*, 330 onwards.

[20] *RLC*, 333, 345; *Pipe Roll 1219*, 25.

[21] *RLC*, 328, 342; *PR*, 123. For Oldcoates, see also below p. 72.

[22] *RLC*, 337, 341b, 342, 344; *PR*, 123–4, 127.

[23] Philadelfo Libico, *Gualae Vita et Gesta*, 100–1; Foster, 'Chesterton and Vercelli', 188–9. I owe these references to Nicholas Vincent.

v. *The settlement with the king of Scotland, December 1217*

The treaty of Kingston/Lambeth had laid down that if King Alexander of Scotland and Llywelyn, the prince of North Wales, wished to be included in the peace, they should restore the castles, lands and prisoners which they had taken during the war. In other words, the terms for them were to be the same as for everyone else: the return to the *status quo ante bellum*. It was easier to get Alexander to accept this than Llywelyn, however. The Scottish king's only tangible gain during the war had been Carlisle and its castle; he had been invested with the northern counties but had never enjoyed physical control over them.[1] Llywelyn, on the other hand, had taken actual possession of much of south-west Wales, as well as southern Powys and Montgomery.

Llywelyn, therefore, would have nothing of the *status quo ante bellum*. His allies in south Wales cheerfully continued the war, despite the peace of Kingston/Lambeth. At the end of the great council in November the regent set out for Gloucester for negotiations with the Welsh prince, hoping that, having been absolved from excommunication, he would come to Northampton to do homage to King Henry. Llywelyn, however, refused to come.[2]

Alexander, on the other hand, as soon as he heard of the peace of Kingston/Lambeth, sent his army home and waited at Jedburgh to see what would happen. He was right to be cautious for, on 23 September, the regent ordered a powerful group of northern magnates, including the former rebel Roger Bertram, to help Robert de Vieuxpont recover Carlisle. By 6 November, when letters of conduct were issued, Alexander had evidently agreed to come to England to see King Henry. The meeting took place at Northampton in the week before Christmas. Having already surrendered Carlisle and been absolved from excommunication, Alexander was received 'with reverence'. He did homage to the king for the earldom of Huntingdon (which was held from him by his uncle, Earl David) and 'the other lands which his predecessors had held from the king of England', as the chronicle of Melrose put it. Nothing was said about his claim to the northern counties. He had obtained nothing from the war.[3]

Despite this success, the ensuing Christmas court at Northampton revealed only too clearly the vacuum at the centre of government. The king appeared with the thirty-nine members of his household, including two trumpeters. Decked in their new Christmas robes, perhaps they looked well, but the presence of a nurse, and the small number of household knights (only seven), was a graphic reminder of both the

[1]   Duncan, *Scotland*, 523–4.
[2]   *Brut*, 96; *F*, 149.
[3]   *Melrose*, 69; *PR*, 122; *RLC*, 348.

infancy and poverty of the king.[4] The regent himself did not linger over the festivities. Leaving the king at Northampton, by 28 December he was at his castle of Usk. He had gone to oversee operations in his private war against Morgan, the lord of Caerleon, seven miles south of Usk. The latter had continued hostilities after the peace, swearing that he would fight on so long as the Marshal held a foot of his land. In response, some time after Michaelmas 1217, the Marshal's bailiffs had seized Caerleon itself. Having surveyed his new possession, the regent returned at once to Westminster, via Marlborough and his manors of Hamstead Marshal and Caversham, to grapple again with the problems of the king's government.[5]

vi. *Disputes over the sheriffdoms; the proclamation of Magna Carta; January–February 1218*

Back at Westminster in the middle of January, the regent presided, with the justiciar, over the opening sessions of the new judicial bench. Then, with these safely under way, he left the judges to continue on their own (as they did for the rest of his regency) and concentrated on finance. As a royal letter put it next month: 'it is very necessary for us and for the tranquillity of our kingdom that our *fideles* and bailiffs provide us with money with all their power'.[1] On 14 January the exchequer, unable to wait for the next customary *Adventus Vicecomitum* at Easter, opened with a special *Adventus*. The results were hardly reassuring. Only two sheriffs (or rather their deputies) turned up and they brought no money. The regent and the council discussed the situation with the barons of the exchequer, the latter expressing the fear that 'the sheriffs would retain for themselves the money coming in'. In particular there was concern that the sheriffs might spend the proceeds of the new scutage locally rather than pay it into the exchequer. The response to these problems was to prepare a list of summonses for the debts which the sheriffs were to collect and pay in. The principle was also stated that the scutage must come to the exchequer 'as anciently accustomed', even if it had then to be received back to fund local expenditure.[2]

The regent next tried to do something about the counties where there were disputes as to who exactly should be sheriff. In John's reign these would have been inconceivable, for he appointed and dismissed sheriffs at will. Now, however, the claimants clearly felt that they had some

4 *RLC*, 345b.
5 *RLC*, 349b; *Brut*, 96; *Maréchal*, lines 17748–86.
1 *RLC*, 376b–7.
2 E 368/1, m. 4; *Pipe Roll 1215*, 4; *RLC*, 352, 377b.

right to the sheriffdoms, either because of a promise made when they had entered the king's allegiance or because they had been appointed by King John and believed that they had an obligation to keep their custodies safe until his son came of age.

Early in February, therefore, William de Turri was appointed sheriff of Surrey until the dispute between Engelard de Cigogné and the earl of Surrey could be settled 'by the counsel of [the king's] *fideles*'. In fact, there is no evidence that the earl, who had probably gained the sheriffdom when he joined the young king in 1217, ever surrendered it.[3] Turri's abortive appointment took place while the regent was on his way to the west country: between 10 and 15 February he was at Exeter with the legate and a considerable assembly of magnates;[4] by 20 February he had turned back to Sherborne. The regent's purpose was to quell the private wars which had been raging over the possession of the sheriffdoms of Devon and Somerset. The attempt to install the earl of Salisbury in the two counties in accordance with the regent's promise of March 1217 was now abandoned: Robert de Courtenay was left in charge of Devonshire and Peter de Maulay of Somerset and Sherborne castle. Salisbury, however, received ample compensation. Maulay gave him £500, a settlement probably arranged by the bishop of Winchester, who had visited his manor of Downton in Hampshire early in January to arrange a 'concord' between Maulay and the earl.[5] The earl was also promised another £1,000 which the government attempted to pay in dribs and drabs over the next few years.[6] But the principal compensation took a different form, namely the custody (conceded on 26 January) of the lands of Eustace de Vesci, with the marriage of the heir. This would bring the earl an eight-year interest, for the heir did not come of age until 1226, in Alnwick castle and lands in the north worth over £400 a year.[7]

The government thus succeeded in ending the war in the west. But the result was merely to transfer disorder from Devon and Somerset to Northumberland. The trouble was that a large part of the Vesci lands had been entrusted by King John to the sheriff of Northumberland, Philip of Oldcoates. In November 1217 the regent had attempted to remove Oldcoates and install as keepers a knight and a clerk who were

---

3 *PR*, 135; *RLC*, 403b; *Pipe Roll 1219*, 206; for Engelard's appointment by John in April 1216: *RLP*, 178b.

4 *F*, 150.

5 HRO, Eccles II 159274, r.1. This evidence was drawn to my attention by Nicholas Vincent. In 1221 the £500 was allowed Maulay against money that he had received from the ransoms of various civil war prisoners held at Corfe: *RLC*, 481b–2; *Pipe Roll 1221*, 95.

6 *RLC*, 360, 370b, 381, 384, 387b, 388, 391b, 406b, 408b.

7 *RLC*, 350b; *PR*, 134; Holt, *Northerners*, 95 n. 4.

probably to account for the issues at the exchequer.[8] As compensation Oldcoates was promised lands worth £300 a year, a promise partly fulfilled by the concession, until the king came of age, of the farms from Newcastle upon Tyne, Bamburgh and Corbridge.[9] All this, however, was quite insufficient to persuade Oldcoates to surrender the Vesci lands either to the November keepers or, later, to Salisbury. In 1218 his deputy at Newcastle upon Tyne seized a cart containing £200 worth of Salisbury's possessions.[10] Nor in the west country did the exchequer assert much control over Peter de Maulay, for he cleared nothing from either the farms of Somerset-Dorset or from numerous other debts before his dismissal in 1221.[11] In that sense it was much the same as if Salisbury had indeed gained Somerset in return merely for 'homage and service' as promised in 1217.

At Exeter the regent strove to assert his authority in another area of England, with similar lack of success. This was in the vicinity of Rockingham castle where William de Fors, count of Aumale, had constructed a great power base for himself. In southern Lincolnshire, as has been seen, the count had been granted, during the war, the castle of Bytham and the other lands of William de Coleville. Less than twenty miles to the south-west, he had also been conceded the royal castles of Sauvey in Leicestershire and Rockingham on the northern boundary of Northamptonshire, specifically as compensation for his own possessions which had been appropriated by the rebels (not surprisingly, since many were situated in Yorkshire). Rockingham was the chief prize, standing on a splendid site above the fertile valley of the Welland and controlling the royal forest to the east. Aumale indeed took hold of much of Rockingham forest and also seized the neighbouring royal manors of Brigstock, King's Cliffe, Corby and Gretton. On 11 February 1218 the regent, already facing Aumale's refusal to surrender Bytham, tried to bring these presumptions to an end. The count was told in a royal letter that, since he had now recovered his own lands, he should surrender Sauvey, and Rockingham and the adjoining royal manors. Aumale, however, took no notice. It was not merely the king who suffered from his defiance, for Corby, Gretton and the Rockingham forest should have been returned, under the peace treaty, respectively to the former rebels Henry of Braybrooke, Walter of Preston and Hugh de Neville, who held them at fee farm from the king. Aumale was also occupying, in the same area, Nassington and Yarwell, the rich

[8]   *RLC*, 288, 295, 310b, 314b; *PR*, 122, 126–7; *RLC*, 326b, 343, 343b.
[9]   *PR*, 124. The promise may be deduced from *RLC*, 364b; C 60/12, mm. 8, 3d; *SC* 8/340, no. 16038.
[10]   *RLC*, 364b; *PR*, 192; *Yorks. Eyre*, no. 1111, and p. xxviii.
[11]   *Pipe Roll 1219*, 173, 183; *Pipe Roll 1221*, 93–5.

manors of another former rebel, Earl David of Huntingdon.[12] In effect, therefore, he was both depriving the king of castles and farms, and, just as he was at Bytham, obstructing the implementation of the treaty of Kingston/Lambeth.

If the regent could not enforce his will in Northamptonshire, it is not surprising that he was being defied further afield in Ireland. On the day after the order to Aumale, a letter was sent to the justiciar of Ireland, Geoffrey de Marsh. It stated that the king was astonished that he had disobeyed an order to come to England to do homage and report on Irish affairs. Now he was to come at Easter with all the money he could bring.[13] In fact, it was over two years before Geoffrey de Marsh came to England or the count of Aumale surrendered Rockingham.

After visiting Sherborne the regent moved on, with Guala and a considerable body of magnates, to his own manor of Sturminster (21–28 February). Here, with the consent of the council, the young Marshal was conceded the proceeds of the royal exchange in order to provide him with 1,000 marks a year and thus sustain him in the king's service.[14] Next day (22 February) the government addressed the problem of the king's finances. Recognizing that the scutage had not been paid as originally laid down by 2 February, the sheriffs were ordered to distrain all tenants-in-chief to have the outstanding money at the exchequer by 25 March. The barons of the exchequer were to report to the regent on how the money came in and were also to send to the sheriffs the writs of summonses prepared in January, 'in a form as strict as possible', the sheriffs being told to answer for the debts listed at the end of Easter (23 April).[15]

These measures had the sanction of the legate and the king's *fideles*. For the *fideles*, however, there was also a *quid pro quo*. Just as the original scutage had probably been linked in many minds with the issue of Magna Carta, so too were these measures to ensure that the scutage was actually paid. For, on the same day that the sheriffs were ordered to distrain for the tax, they were sent copies of Magna Carta and the Charter of the Forest and told to read them in the county court, 'having gathered together the barons, knights and all free tenants of the county'. The sheriffs were to see that the clauses in the charter were 'in

---

[12] *PR*, 136, 240; *Pipe Roll 1218*, 57–8; *Pipe Roll 1212*, 156; *RLC*, 423; Stringer, *Earl David of Huntingdon*, 115–17. E 32/253, a survey of the keepers of the royal forest in the early minority, states that the count of Aumale held the forests of King's Cliffe and Geddington, and Neville the rest of the Northamptonshire forest save for one wood held by Falkes. The Mauduit claim was to the constableship of Rockingham rather than the castle itself, which remained a royal one: *Beauchamp Cartulary*, liv–v.

[13] *RLC*, 376b–7.

[14] *PR*, 138–9; *RL*, no. lviii.

[15] *RLC*, 377b; Mitchell, *Taxation*, 126.

all things sworn to and observed'. They were also to take oaths of fealty to the king from the assembled barons, knights and freemen. In this way allegiance to the new king was inextricably linked with allegiance to the Charters.[16]

The broader reason for the proclamation of the Charters in February 1217 was to conciliate a country still far from at peace. Indeed, the sheriffs were specifically instructed to implement the last clause in the 1217 charter, placed there, they were told, by the counsel of Guala and the king's *fideles*. This commanded the destruction of all 'adulterine' castles, that is, private castles which had been built or rebuilt since the beginning of the war. In 1218–19 itself the government issued specific orders for the reduction of at least six castles and tried to insist that no new building should take place without its licence.[17] In March 1217 the sheriffs of the southern counties were also ordered to protect those who had been on the king's side during the war from molestation by former rebels. 'All things which were done in time of war', the sheriffs were informed, 'should be wholly remitted according to the form of peace between us and Louis.'[18] In fact, there had been no clause in the treaty specifically covering this point. Evidently the government wished that there had been.

vii. *The treaty of Worcester, March 1218*

At Exeter, in February 1218, negotiations had continued for a settlement with Llywelyn. 'By the counsel of the legate, regent and the magnates of England', a meeting was arranged with him at Worcester on 11 March. Amongst those appointed to conduct Llywelyn thither was the former rebel, John fitz Alan, while, at Worcester, the earl of Winchester attested the final settlement that was reached there.[1]

Llywelyn's ambition was to combine hegemony over the Welsh princes with a wide measure of independence from the king of England. That ambition dominated the politics of Wales during the minority and helped shape the course of affairs in England. Llywelyn abounded in self-confidence and force of character: 'whatever others may do', he later wrote, 'we will do nothing against our conscience. For we prefer to be excommunicated by man than do anything against God and be condemned by our conscience.'[2] When it was advantageous he resorted

---

[16] *RLC*, 377b.

[17] *RLC*, 350, 366b, 379b, 380, 383b; for references to the king's licence, see below p. 88 and *RL*, no. liii.

[18] *PR*, 140–1; for the impact of this pronouncement, see *CRR*, ix, 350. For other feuds arising from the war, see *Lincs. Worcs. Eyre*, no. 1111; *CRR*, ix, 348–50.

[1] *F*, 150–1.

[2] *RL*, no. cci.

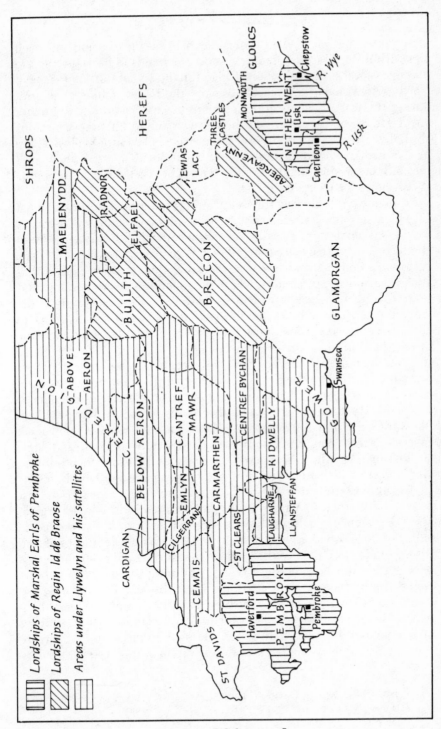

5. Southern Wales, 1218–23

to force; but he was also a master at exploiting the divisions between and within the Marcher families, using the hands of his daughters to purchase several crucial alliances. He usually styled himself prince of North Wales, and there certainly were the bases of his power, but during the war his chance had come to extend his authority further afield. He wrested control of southern Powys and Montgomery from his rival, Gwenwynwyn, and intervened decisively in south Wales. There he retained Cardigan for himself and partitioned (in 1216) the rest of the lands of the king and the English barons between descendants of the Welsh house of Deheubarth.[3]

From one point of view, the treaty of Worcester held the line against Llywelyn's pretensions. The prince left Wales and came to Worcester for the settlement; he agreed to receive no enemy of the king in Wales; and he promised to ensure that 'all the magnates of all Wales' did their customary homage and fealty to the king, thus acknowledging that Wales was not a principality where the magnates swore homage and fealty to him, and then only he himself swore homage and fealty to the king. In all these spheres, in the next few years, Llywelyn was to advance claims at variance with the treaty, which thus served to define rather than dull his vaulting ambition.[4]

From the material point of view, however, the treaty, from the first, was a humiliation for the English. While it affirmed the principle of the *status quo ante bellum*, it abandoned its substance. Llywelyn surrendered to Guala Montgomery and the other lands which he had taken in the war from John's ally, Gwenwynwyn, only to receive them back as custodian during the minority of Gwenwynwyn's son and heir. In the same way, he surrendered Cardigan and Carmarthen only for Guala to entrust them to him until the king came of age.[5] Technically, Llywelyn was the king's bailiff; in practice, the crown had lost control of Cardigan, which John had acquired early in his reign, and Carmarthen, 'for seventy years the centre of royal power in the valley of the Towy'.[6] Llywelyn also swore to do all he could to obtain the surrender to Guala of the lands and castles taken from the king's barons and supporters in south Wales. The implication was that Guala would restore them to their rightful owners. In fact, over the next few years, Llywelyn did little to disturb the partition of south Wales which he had effected in 1216–17. Thus the sons and grandsons of Lord Rhys of Deheubarth retained hold of the Marshals' Emlyn and Cilgerran, the fitz Martins' Cemais, the Brians' Laugharne, the Camvilles'

---

[3] Lloyd, *Wales*, 647–53; Davies, *Wales*, 244–51.
[4] *F*, 150–1; see below pp. 76, 192, 218–19.
[5] *F*, 150–1.
[6] Lloyd, *Wales*, 618, 648.

Llansteffan, the Londres's Kidwelly and the Braoses' St Clears and Gower.[7]

The regent's weakness at this time is most plainly displayed in his own exclusion from Emlyn and in Llywelyn's control of Cardigan and Carmarthen, custodies which before the war John had entrusted to the Marshal himself and from which Llywelyn was well placed to attack Pembroke, as indeed he did in 1220.[8] For the regent, however, the Worcester council brought some compensation. Llywelyn, together with the earl of Chester and the bishop of Winchester, begged the king to restore Morgan to Caerleon castle, which the Marshal had taken from him in the hostilities since the conclusion of the peace of Kingston/Lambeth. The council, however, if William Marshal's biography can be believed, decided against Morgan, on the grounds that he had been the aggressor, breaking a truce and ignoring the final peace.[9] Caerleon thenceforth, with a few intermissions, remained in the hands of the Marshal family. It was by far William's greatest gain from the civil war, providing a stronghold near the mouth of the river Usk, just as his castle of Chepstow, twelve miles to the east, guarded the mouth of the Wye.

The arguments over Morgan revealed differences between the regent, on the one side, and the bishop of Winchester and the earl of Chester on the other. At the same time tension was apparent with the justiciar. Hubert had not been on the tour of the west country in February. He was told by letter to give his assent to the committal of the mint (hitherto in his own hands) to the young Marshal and was lectured on the ancient custom of scutage being paid in at the exchequer.[10] Hubert was equally absent from the assembly at Worcester and was informed by letter that the council considered an order of

[7] For changes in Gower in 1220, see below p. 218. In 1216 or 1217 Llywelyn gave Maelgwn ap Rhys the castle and lordship of Carmarthen less the commote of Widigada in Cantref Mawr which went to the latter's brother, Rhys Gryg. In a partition presided over by Llywelyn in 1216, Maelgwn also received Cemais, Emlyn, Cilgerran and probably too St Clears, Laugharne and Llansteffan. Rhys Gryg was given Kidwelly, to which (see above p. 43) Llywelyn added Gower in 1217. However, Llywelyn retained Cardigan for himself, before and after the treaty of Worcester, having never implemented his promise to give it to Rhys Ieuanc and his brother, Owain ap Gruffud, the nephews of Maelgwn and Rhys Gryg. The division of south Wales in 1216 also involved the partition of the lands once of Lord Rhys in Ceredigion, Cantref Mawr and Cantref Bychan. After 1218 Llywelyn's kinsmen and vassals retained hold of the Mortimer lordship of Maelienydd. For all this see *Brut*, 92, 95, 98; *RL*, no. cv; Walker, 'Hubert de Burgh and Wales', 469–70; Lloyd, *Wales*, 649; Davies, *Wales*, 228; Walker, 'Anglo-Welsh Wars', 112–27; and the map, p. 75, and genealogical table, p. 423.

[8] *RLP*, 109b.

[9] *Maréchal*, lines 17788–872.

[10] *PR*, 96, 138–9; *RLC*, 352. However, 500 marks from the revenues of the mint were reserved for the sustenance of Dover castle.

December 1217, which put him in seisin of marshland south of King's Lynn, was 'less than reasonable'. The letter concluded with an admonition: 'since it is especially your task to favour and maintain justice, you should behave in this matter so that you are neither an example nor a cause of giving injury to others'.[11]

viii. *The failure to control wardships and sheriffdoms, March–May 1218*

After the conclusion of the treaty of Worcester, the regent returned to London. There he remained from April until July apart from brief visits to Worcester and Woodstock for Welsh magnates to do homage to the king in accordance with the new treaty.[1] During these months the centrifugal forces that he faced became even more apparent. He was unable to control important wardships; he attempted and failed to dismiss sheriffs; and he sanctioned the passage of county farms out of exchequer control.

Control over wardships and marriages was the most basic of the king's 'feudal' rights. Yet, in 1218, the regent failed to impose any significant penalty on Thomas of Moulton when he consolidated his interests in Cumberland by marrying the widow of Richard de Lucy of Egremont without the king's permission.[2] The regent was equally unable to install his own familiar, John of Earley, in the Avenel wardship, which included Bicknor castle. The Marcher baron, John of Monmouth, proved immovable despite all manner of threats.[3] Most costly of all, however, was the failure to gain hold of the castles and lands of the earl of Devon, who had died in 1216. In November 1217 the regent had tried to place these into the hands of officials who were to answer for the issues at the exchequer. He had experienced extreme difficulty, however, in removing the existing keepers: Robert de Courtenay and William Brewer junior.[4] At the end of March 1218 this attempt to exploit the lands directly was abandoned and instead they were conceded free of charge to Falkes de Bréauté. They came in two parts. Falkes was granted Plympton castle and all the lands of the earldom within Devon as his wife's dower, his wife (a marriage

---

[11] *RLC*, 355, 378, 345b, 144, 173, 177.

[1] *PR*, 142, 149–50, 155; *F*, 151; but see *Brut*, 96. The regent did not, therefore, attend the translation of St Wulfstan at Worcester on 7–8 June at which the king and bishop of Winchester were present: *Ann. Mon.*, iv, 409–10; *Walt. Cov.*, 240.

[2] *RF*, 474, 482; *RLC*, 354b, 358b, 366; *PR*, 165–6; *ERF*, 17; *Pipe Roll 1214*, 138–9; *Pipe Rolls Cumberland*, 8; E 372/67, r. 8, m. 1; Holt, *Magna Carta*, 213 and n. 4.

[3] *PR*, 127; *RLC*, 344, 357; C 60/9, m. 5; *Pipe Roll 1220*, 80; *Gloucester Pleas*, no. 193. However, John of Monmouth did eventually surrender the heir and account for Bicknor at the exchequer.

[4] *PR*, 90–2, 126, 136, 144; *RLC*, 342.

arranged by King John) being the widow of the son and heir of the late earl, the son having predeceased his father. This was far more than Falkes could legitimately expect as his wife's dower, since Plympton was the *caput* of the honour of Devon and it was against the custom of the realm for the *caput* to be included in the dower. Secondly, Falkes was conceded custody of the other lands of the earldom, together with the heir (his stepson), until the king came of age. It was, therefore, William Marshal, not King John, who made Falkes 'the equal of an earl', as the Barnwell annalist put it.[5]

The regent's decision was not an act of feckless generosity, however, since Falkes's services, as will be seen, were immense. But the price was great instability in the west country, where Falkes's intrusion into Devonshire was deeply resented by the great local magnate and sheriff of the county, Robert de Courtenay. Courtenay's wife was the daughter of the earl of Devon, who had died in 1216, and was thus the sister-in-law of Falkes's wife; Courtenay himself had been in seisin of Plympton castle and other lands of the earldom down to February 1218. Both he and Falkes were laying claim 'by reason of their wives' to the third penny of the earldom, which Falkes eventually obtained in 1219.[6] Courtenay, descendant of a great French noble house, thus found himself ousted from the wardship that he coveted by this 'poor serjeant' of King John. The result was to be virtual civil war in the west.

The fate of the Vesci and Devon lands, the two great wardships which had fallen in during the war, summed up the problems of the regent's government. In November 1217 it hoped to place both in the hands of keepers who would account at the exchequer: in both cases it failed to put the new keepers into seisin; in both it then cut its losses and conceded the wardships, absolutely free of charge, to great members of the regime, namely the earl of Salisbury and Falkes de Bréauté, only for the result to be violent local conflicts. Under John, by contrast, such wardships would have produced a steady annual revenue for the crown or been sold to the highest bidder.

Falkes knew at once that he would have trouble with Courtenay and on the day that he received custody of the Devon lands (30 March) he secured the latter's dismissal from the sheriffdom. The sequel, however, showed again the government's inability to command the sheriffs, for, within two months, the attempt to dismiss Courtenay had collapsed. On 8 May he recovered the county. At the same time, reflecting the anxieties about the probity of the sheriffs expressed at the

5   *PR*, 144–5, 430; *Walt. Cov.*, 253. See clause 7 of Magna Carta 1216, *Select Charters*, 337. Falkes's marriage also brought him control of the fitz Gerald chamberlainship of the exchequer. As Meekings pointed out to me, he is the 'F' in the writs of *Liberate* down to 1224.

6   *Peerage*, iv, 316–18; iii, 465 n.c; E 368/2, m. 20d; *RLC*, 393.

exchequer back in January, he pledged to 'answer well and faithfully for the debts and issues of the county for which he has the summons of the exchequer'.[7]

The exchequer in May 1218 was also attempting to deal with the desperate situation which had arisen in Yorkshire over the 'debts and issues of the county'. Here it was not a case, as in Devon, of a domineering but potentially disobedient sheriff but of a sheriff who seemed, in some places, to have no authority at all. On 3 May the count of Aumale, the earl of Surrey, John de Lacy, the constable of Tickhill (Robert de Vieuxpont), Robert de Ros and Hugh de Balliol were summoned before the barons of the exchequer to explain why they were preventing the sheriff of Yorkshire from 'holding pleas and doing those things which other [sheriffs] were bound and accustomed to do in the same county for the king's benefit so that he is the less able to pay his farm and answer for the debts of the king and other things for which he has the summons of the exchequer'. The consequences of this obstructionism, in which both former rebels and loyalists played an equal part, was that the sheriff, Geoffrey de Neville, was quite unable to pay any money at all into the exchequer from the farms of Yorkshire and from numerous other debts for the first two years after the war.[8]

Neville himself was not a bad choice as sheriff. Appointed by John in 1216, he was a royal chamberlain and a former seneschal of Poitou, very ready to act in a decisive fashion; he was to justify hanging men in Yorkshire without reference to the king's judges on the grounds that he had behaved like that in Gascony.[9] It was clearly vital, however, that he devote himself full-time to his task. Yet, at this very moment in May 1218, he was reappointed seneschal of Poitou, the current holder of the office, the archbishop of Bordeaux, being determined to depart on the crusade. This should have been the signal for his departure from Yorkshire but again the government found the dismissal of a sheriff quite beyond it. Instead, at the same time as his appointment as seneschal, Neville was confirmed in office as sheriff. Clearly he would go on no other terms. As a consequence, over the next two years, the situation in Yorkshire, run by Neville's under-sheriff, Simon of [Great] Hale in Lincolnshire, went from bad to worse.[10]

Another sheriff preparing to leave England at this time, although for the crusade, was the earl of Chester. Again there was no question of his resigning the sheriffdoms of Lancashire, Shropshire and Staffordshire to which John had appointed him during the war. Indeed, they were now so far removed from central control by rules laid down by the earl

[7] *PR*, 144; *RLC*, 361.
[8] C 60/9, m. 6; *Pipe Roll 1219*, 184, 204–5; see below p. 115.
[9] *RLP*, 165; *Yorks. Eyre*, no. 744 and pp. liv–lv.
[10] *BF*, 1033, 1068; see below p. 195.

that, if one of his under-sheriffs died while he was away, then another
was to be chosen not by the king but 'by counsel of the earl's *fideles*'.
Equally, the earl's bailiffs swore, in the event of their lord's death, 'to
keep his castles [apparently the royal ones in their custody] safe for the
use of the king until he comes of age and to hand them over to no one
save the king'.[11] In other words there was to be no question of the
regent's government, or its successor, laying hands on them. Courtenay
and Neville had at least been expected to account for the farms of their
counties, even if their willingness or ability to do so was doubted. There
was no such expectation with the earl of Chester. On 8 May, in
recompense for his expenses in keeping the royal castles in his charge,
he was given quittance of the farms of Lancashire, Shropshire and
Staffordshire until a term to be decided by the legate and the council.
He continued to draw off their revenues until the summer of 1221. Nor
was this concession exactly justified by the threat from Llywelyn, since
before leaving on his crusade Chester had prudently reached an
agreement with him.[12]

ix. *The great council of May 1218*

While the regent thus struggled to control the sheriffdoms, or allowed
their revenues to be used to support great *curiales*, he was equally
concerned to secure peace and order by acts of conciliation. There was
an element of such conciliation, indeed, in the abortive dismissal of
Robert de Courtenay as sheriff of Devon, for Devon was a county with a
strong desire to have a local man as sheriff and the new appointee,
Robert de Albemarle, was a local knight. When Courtenay recovered
the office he promised the council and the exchequer, so Albemarle was
told, to 'act in a moderate fashion towards the knights and others of the
county by your counsel and that of the other *fideles* of the county'.[1] The
government was also adopting wider measures of appeasement. On
2 April the chief justice of the forest, John Marshal, and the sheriffs of
various counties were ordered to cause the Charter of the Forest 'to be
sworn to . . . and firmly observed'. Later in the month the sheriffs were
instructed to proclaim that all those who felt that ransoms were being
demanded from them, against the form of the peace, were to come
before the king's council at Westminster on 9 May.[2] The gathering at
Westminster was in fact a great council. The range of its decisions

---

[11] E 368/1, m. 1d.
[12] C 60/9, m. 6; *Pipe Roll 1220*, 69–70, 72–3, 171–6; *Pipe Roll 1221*, 59, 96, 139–40;
Ann. Cest., 50; see below p. 253 The farms conceded were both those of the counties and
of the royal demesne manors within them.
[1] *RLC*, 361; PR, 216, 554; *BF*, 183; Holt, *Magna Carta*, 53.
[2] *RLC*, 378, 358b.

shows clearly how far the government of the regent was dependent on the counsel and consent of such great assemblies.

One ransom case considered by the great council was that of Maurice de Gant. Captured by the earl of Chester at the battle of Lincoln, he had agreed that, in default of paying his ransom of over 1,500 marks by Easter 1218, the earl could have hereditary possession of his manors of Leeds and Bingley. In due course Chester had indeed taken possession of them. This would have been perfectly legitimate had Gant been released before the conclusion of the peace of Kingston/ Lambeth and thus been unable to benefit from its terms. But, in fact, at the end of the war, he was still in Chester's prison and should have been exempted from any ransom payments due later than 12 September 1217.[3] Both men now came before the May council. If, as seems likely, Gant complained about the breach of the peace treaty, it did not surface in the recorded pleadings. There, he merely claimed that he had made the agreement 'through the compulsion of imprisonment'. The decision of 'the council of the king and the magnates of the land' was that Chester should remain in seisin.[4] Doubtless this was largely political. In May 1218 Chester was being asked to surrender part of the honour of Richmond to the duke of Brittany. He was also preparing to depart on a crusade. This was not the time to offend him.[5]

The verdict in the Gant case can scarcely have pleased former rebels but at least it had been taken by a great council and Gant was told that he could bring a legal action against the earl, if he wished; something he proceeded to do.[6] Other decisions of the council showed the extent to which it influenced or controlled matters of high policy. Thus Geoffrey de Neville was appointed as the new seneschal of Poitou by the counsel of the king's 'magnates and *fideles*'.[7]

The great council also sanctioned important steps in relation to the Jews. This was a highly sensitive area. The legislation of the fourth Lateran council had demanded that a series of restrictions be placed on the Jews. The latter were also extremely unpopular with the many laymen who owed money to them. The regent's duty, however, was to protect the Jews. They formed part of the 'demesne' of the crown; taxation imposed on them had been highly lucrative under the Angevins and so had debts owed by Christians to Jews (the *debita*

[3] *RLC*, ii, 87–87b; E 372/69, r. 7d, m. 2.

[4] *Yorks. Eyre*, nos 315, 1133. For Louis's later complaint about the extraction of ransoms, contrary to the terms of the peace, from those taken at the battle of Lincoln, see *Chron. Maj.*, 77.

[5] *PR*, 174; *RLC*, 361b.

[6] *Yorks. Eyre*, nos 315, 1133; see below p. 129. For measures to enforce the payment of ransoms, see *RLC*, 356; *PR*, 148.

[7] *PR*, 152–3.

Judeorum), for these came into the king's hands on the death or forfeiture of the Jewish creditors. In 1218 a compromise was arrived at. In March, as a concession to ecclesiastical feeling, the Jews were ordered to wear a mark of distinction, the *tabula*, but, for the rest, it was decided 'by common counsel' that the Jews should enjoy the same privileges as before. In return, however, the council of May 1218 obtained an important safeguard. When the exchequer of the Jews, the institution which dealt with the *debita Judeorum*, restarted in that month, its justices were appointed 'by common counsel'.[8] The aim was plainly to ensure that they were acceptable men who would act in a moderate fashion. Significantly, the Paper Constitution, the radical scheme of reform propounded in 1244, was to demand a return to the method of appointment of 1218, laying down that at least one justice of the Jews be chosen by a great council.[9]

Other decisions taken by the great council of May 1218 were reassuring for former rebels. The king, on its advice, confirmed the package of properties outside Bristol, known as the Barton, to the earl of Gloucester as appurtenant to his earldom, a concession which the castellan of Bristol, Hugh de Vivonne, was obstinately resisting.[10] Gloucester, of course, if a former rebel, was also the regent's son-in-law. But in May 1218 Roger Bertram, too, seemed near success: at long last the guillotine had come down on Philip of Oldcoates over his detention of Mitford. Early in April he had been instructed, 'as many times before', to return the castle to Bertram, failing which his lands would be taken into the king's hands. Oldcoates did fail and on 17 May the orders went out for his lands to be seized.[11]

There were other indications that the divisions of the war were healing. In January 1218, when John de Braose and his brothers, the sons of the William de Braose whom King John had murdered, were released from prison, the earls of Chester, Derby, Salisbury, Surrey, Arundel, Winchester, Gloucester and Essex, and Robert fitz Walter, amongst others, stood surety for their faithful service.[12] This was a group which reflected virtually every shade of political conduct during

---

[8]   *RLC*, 378b; *PR*, 157, 154; Richardson, *English Jewry*, 180–3; Meekings, 'Justices of the Jews', iv, 179. The plea roll of the exchequer of Jews for 3 and 4 Henry III is printed in *Documents of English History*, 285–332. The exchequer also dealt with the debts which the Jews themselves owed the king.

[9]   *Chron. Maj.*, iv, 367.

[10]   *RLC*, 344, 360b; Altschul, *The Clares*, 27–8. For the Barton, and the wood of Furches and the chase of Keynsham with which it was always associated, see *Accounts of Bristol Castle*, xxxvi–liii. For Vivonne's continued refusal to surrender the Barton, see below p. 105.

[11]   *RLC*, 357b; C 60/9, m. 5.

[12]   *PR*, 134. See 'Neath Cartulary', 152, where the release of the brothers is ascribed to the influence of their uncle, the earl of Gloucester.

the war. In the summer of 1218 two great loyalist earls, those of Chester and Derby, left England for the crusade. They took with them John de Lacy, constable of Chester, who was one of the earl of Chester's greatest tenants but who had also been a principal rebel.[13] Evidently the differences between the two men had been settled.

x. *The siege of Newark, July 1218*

By the summer of 1218 the problems confronting the regent's government were starkly apparent. They derived, in part, from the very men who had carried the young king's cause through to victory and who, as Roger of Wendover observed, now defied the king's orders and refused to restore the castles and lands which they had obtained during the war.[1] Thus Philip of Oldcoates was excluding both Roger Bertram from his castle of Mitford and the earl of Salisbury from the lands of Eustace de Vesci; the count of Aumale was refusing to restore Bytham to William de Coleville and Rockingham to the king; Hugh de Vivonne was preventing the earl of Gloucester obtaining the Barton at Bristol; Robert de Gaugi was holding on to Newark at the expense of the bishop of Lincoln. In other areas, especially in Yorkshire, heartland of the rebellion, the sheriff was struggling to assert his authority against magnates determined to increase their local power at the king's expense. At the same time, the government was finding it difficult to dismiss sheriffs and was presiding over a steady depletion of royal resources as wardships and shrieval and manorial farms were granted away to sustain the great men of the regime. The result of this patronage was to destabilize both the north and the west, creating conflict between Philip of Oldcoates and the earl of Salisbury over the Vesci lands and between Falkes and Robert de Courtenay over the lands of the earl of Devon.

The regent faced these problems with an empty treasury and with limited power to take independent action, hence the great councils which were summoned throughout his regency. Nonetheless, in the summer of 1218, his government acted with decision against one recalcitrant castellan: Robert de Gaugi. The latter's refusal to surrender Newark had been discussed at the Worcester council in March 1218, when Guala and the five bishops present had doubtless procured the order instructing the sheriff of Nottinghamshire, Philip Mark, to help the bishop of Lincoln recover the castle, if necessary by force.[2] That assistance, however, if it was supplied, had proved

---

[13] *Ann. Cest.*, 50; *Walt. Cov.*, 240–1; *Ann. Mon.*, ii, 289; iii, 54; Lloyd, *The Crusade*, 82.
[1] *Chron. Maj.*, 33.
[2] *RLC*, 355, 378; *F*, 150.

insufficient. Consequently, the regent turned to other measures and summoned an army to muster at Stamford in Lincolnshire, some thirty miles south of Newark, on 15 July. Taking the king with him, the regent was at Newark by 19 July and four days later, when he left for Nottingham, the siege was evidently over. On 27 July, at Wallingford, Gaugi formally surrendered the castle to the king and it was returned, with Guala's agreement, to the bishop of Lincoln. Although one of the bishop's knights had been killed during the siege, Gaugi was not punished. He received £100 from the bishop for the stock in the castle and recovered the manor of Catthorpe in Leicestershire of which he had been deprived the previous February. There he immediately set about building an unlicensed castle, a project brought abruptly to an end when, later in the year, he was struck dead by lightning.[3]

Thus the regent had overcome his weakness and asserted his authority. Would he continue in the same vein? There were several men in the army of Newark who must have pressed him to do so: William de Beauchamp, for example, deprived by Falkes de Bréauté of Bedford castle; Reginald de Braose, excluded by Henry fitz Count and Henry de Tracy from, respectively, Totnes and Barnstaple; and William de Coleville and Hugh de Neville, denied respectively Bytham castle and Rockingham forest by the count of Aumale.[4] On the way from Stamford to Newark the king's army had indeed passed by Bytham. Faced, at the start of his reign, with comparable problems posed by disobedient castellans, Henry II had acted decisively. He had marched to the north and forced the then count of Aumale to surrender Scarborough castle and other royal properties. He had besieged and taken the royal castle of Bridgenorth, detained by Hugh de Mortimer. The earl of Hereford had submitted and surrendered the castles of Hereford and Gloucester. As a result of these and other measures, before the first year of his reign was over, Henry II, in Professor Warren's words, 'had mastered the barons'.[5]

In the regent's case, however, his action at Newark stood alone. The orders issued in May 1218 to seize Philip of Oldcoates's lands for failing to surrender Mitford were never executed. Instead, at the end of June, Oldcoates was politely asked merely to give up the Vesci lands to the earl of Salisbury, which he in any case refused to do.[6] Mitford for the moment was quietly forgotten. Thus the regent bequeathed a series of

---

[3] Sanders, *Military Service*, 110; *RLC*, 365, 352b, 380; *Chron. Maj.*, 33–4; *PR*, 164; *Ann. Mon.*, iii, 54.

[4] *RLC*, 379b.

[5] Warren, *Henry II*, 60–1.

[6] *RLC*, 364b. However, for firm measures around this time (on paper at least) against Robert of Cockfield, the bishop of Durham and John of Monmouth, see C 60/9, m. 4; *ERF*, 15, 8; *PR*, 127.

unresolved problems to his successors. It was they who had to prize Mitford and the Vesci lands from Philip of Oldcoates and lay siege to Rockingham in 1220, Bytham in 1221 and Bedford in 1224.

The fundamental reason for the regent's inaction was his poverty and the consequent paucity of the military forces of the king's household. Thus his power of independent action was limited. To take military measures he needed to mobilize support. That was the more difficult because there was evident sympathy for Gaugi within the regime. In August 1217 a royal letter had told him that, although he deserved 'the severest judgement' for his disobedience, the king 'preferred clemency to severity . . . because you have served us and our father for a long time'.[7] In the event, as has been seen, clemency prevailed after Newark was taken. Faced, therefore, with reluctance within the regime to move against Gaugi, the regent looked to support from outside, looked, in fact, to former rebels. In this he set a pattern for the minority government in its dealings with mutinous castellans. In July 1218 many former rebels were thus summoned to Stamford with their service, including fifteen of the twenty-five guarantors of the 1215 Magna Carta.[8] Equally, Guala and the church were full-square behind the regent's action, which the bishop of Lincoln encouraged by a private gift of £100. Ecclesiastics were expected to supply 194 of the 470 knights summoned to Stamford.[9]

It was one thing, however, to mobilize support against Robert de Gaugi, quite another to enlist it against some of the other disobedient castellans. The fact was that Gaugi was an easy nut to crack. He was only a serjeant and Newark was his only castle. There was no comparison between him and Philip of Oldcoates controlling Northumberland, the Vesci lands and the castles of Newcastle upon Tyne, Bamburgh and Mitford in the far north. The issue at Newark, moreover, was clear-cut. The bishop was not a former rebel. He had given the castle to the king merely during the war; failure to return it might mean, as Gaugi was reminded, that magnates would be unwilling to entrust castles to the king in future emergencies. Gaugi, on receiving custody of the castle, moreover, had taken an oath to surrender it, in the event of King John's death, to no one save the bishop of Lincoln: exactly what in 1217–18 he was asked to do.[10]

Gaugi, therefore, had none of the justifications which some great loyalists could use for keeping former rebels from their lands. The count of Aumale, for example, could complain that Bytham had been granted

   [7] PR, 85.
   [8] Sanders, *Military Service*, 109 and n. 3; *RLC*, 602.
   [9] RLC, 602; Sanders, *Military Service*, 108–14, where a contemporary list of those summoned to the army is printed.
   [10] PR, 81; RLP, 193b.

to William de Coleville by his (Aumale's) mother's first husband, although the latter 'had no rights in Bytham save through his wife, [and] should never have alienated part of his wife's demesne, let alone the *caput*', as Bytham was.[11] Likewise, Henry de Tracy had grounds for keeping Reginald de Braose out of the Braose share of Barnstaple, having been granted it, so he claimed, in hereditary right by King John, after the fall of Reginald's father, William de Braose.[12] Falkes de Bréauté also claimed to hold Bedford castle under a charter of King John. William de Beauchamp constantly demanded its return in accordance with the terms of the treaty of Kingston/Lambeth. But if Bedford, before the war, had been a royal castle, of which the Beauchamps had merely some claim to be hereditary constables, then that constableship, at most, was what they were entitled to recover under the treaty. John's grant of the actual castle to Falkes might be perfectly lawful.[13] Cases like this, therefore, scarcely justified, at least in 1218, the type of action taken at Newark. Essentially they needed to be sorted out by legal actions. Indeed, Reginald de Braose later brought actions for the recovery of Totnes and Barnstaple, as, in all probability, did William de Coleville for Bytham castle.[14]

Both the count of Aumale and Philip of Oldcoates had other grievances which tended to stay the government's hand. Aumale might have chopped and changed sides in 1215–16 but he had rejoined John just before his death and had remained loyal to his son; loyal, moreover, at great personal cost, for his extensive lands in the north had been overrun by the rebels. He had then lost the ransoms of Robert fitz Walter and Gilbert de Gant under the terms of the treaty of peace.[15] The government itself acknowledged that Oldcoates had grounds for discontent, since it had failed to compensate him sufficiently for the prospective loss of the Vesci custody. At the end of June 1218, when ordered to give up the latter to Salisbury, he was promised speedy

[11] English, *Holderness*, 42–3.
[12] *RLP*, 101; *RLC*, 137; *CRR*, viii, 365; Sanders, *Baronies*, 104–5. Since the 1130s the honour of Barnstaple had been split into two halfs, one (including apparently the castle – *PR*, 72) held by the Braose family, one by the Tracy. John's gift thus made Henry de Tracy lord of the whole honour. For John's gift of the Braose share of Totnes to Henry fitz Count during pleasure in 1209, see *RLP*, 89; Sanders, *Baronies*, 90.
[13] *Coggeshall*, 205–6. Norgate, *Minority*, 293–6, discusses Falkes's claim to Bedford castle, setting out the relevant evidence. See also *VCH Bedfordshire*, iii, 9–10; Stenton, *English Feudalism*, 237–8.
[14] For Coleville, see below p. 231. For Reginald de Braose's actions for the recovery of Barnstaple and Totnes: *RLC*, 376b; *CRR*, viii, 226, 323, 365; ix, 111–12, 143; and below p. 179.
[15] *Normandie*, 174, 179; *Walt. Cov.*, 231; *RLC*, 322b, 323b; *PR*, 136; Turner, 'William de Forz', 229–32.

satisfaction from the king's council. The government was also mindful that Salisbury himself was excluding Oldcoates's associate, Hugh de Balliol, from the manor of Mere in Wiltshire, despite numerous attempts to remove him. In June 1218 another effort was made to place Balliol in seisin.[16]

In the Mitford issue, there was another complicating factor. The whole question had become caught up in the intricate family politics of the north of England, where alliances of kin and neighbourhood were already cutting across the divisions of the war. The more convoluted the Mitford affair became, however, the harder it was to solve, Oldcoates's feeling that he was facing a range of enemies making him all the more unwilling to surrender the castle to Roger Bertram. Not surprisingly, the latter found one ally in the earl of Salisbury, whom Oldcoates was excluding from the Vesci custody.[17] Another appeared in the person of the great northern loyalist, Robert de Vieuxpont, who was sheriff of Cumberland and hereditary sheriff of Westmorland, and who regarded Roger Bertram as his 'nephew'. Equally, both men were kinsmen and political allies of the important northern rebel, Richard de Umfraville.[18] Umfraville too had a grievance against Oldcoates, since the latter was building a castle at Nafferton in Ovingham which threatened Umfraville's castle less than a mile away across the Tyne at Prudhoe. These enemies of Oldcoates struck against him during the siege of Newark. On 19 July, at Umfraville's instigation, a royal letter ordered Oldcoates to pull down his castle at Nafferton since it menaced Prudhoe and was being constructed without the king's licence. Vieuxpont, too, probably had a hand in this order since he was confirmed in office as sheriff of Cumberland on the day that it was issued. Oldcoates, of course, took no notice and two years later, as will be seen, had his revenge.[19]

The action against Robert de Gaugi, therefore, stood alone. Indeed, it made no difference to the continuing movement of manors and sheriffdoms out of exchequer control. At Newark, no doubt as a pay-off for his support in the siege, measures were taken to provide the earl of Salisbury with the £500 worth of land promised him, so it was said, by King John. In June he had been given the royal manors of Writtle (Essex) and Finedon (Northamptonshire), and these were

---

[16] *RLC*, 364b; C 60/9, m. 4; *RLC*, 230, 314b, 340.

[17] See below p. 205.

[18] *RL*, no. xxxi. Robert de Vieuxpont's mother was a sister of Roger Bertram's grandmother, both being daughters of Hugh de Morville I. Richard de Umfraville was Bertram's uncle, being the brother of Bertram's mother: Stringer, 'The early lords of Lauderdale', 47; Stringer, *Earl David of Huntingdon*, 128, 201; *Peerage*, ii, 160 n.a; Sanders, *Baronies*, 73, 131.

[19] *RLC*, 379b, 455b, 459b; Holt, *Northerners*, 243; *PR*, 161; and see below p. 202.

now followed by the gifts of Cheltenham, Awre and Newnham in Gloucestershire.[20]

Also at Newark an expensive bargain was struck which restored Tickhill to Ralph de Lusignan, at the cost of losing Cumberland for the king. King John had granted the castle and honour of Tickhill to Ralph, one of the great nobles of Poitou, in right of his wife Alice, countess of Eu in Normandy. During the war, however, Tickhill had come into the hands of Robert de Vieuxpont, who subsequently refused to surrender it, on the grounds of a title which he claimed in right of his own wife.[21] Since Ralph's disaffection could have serious consequences in Poitou, it became vital to restore Tickhill to him. This was now done but, in return, at Newark on 19 July, Vieuxpont was confirmed in office as sheriff of Cumberland on terms, defined a few days later, which absolved him from accounting at the exchequer for the farm or profit of the county until the king's court had done him justice in the right that he claimed to Tickhill. The consequence was that Vieuxpont answered neither for Cumberland's farm nor its private debts during his tenure of the sheriffdom, which lasted until February 1222, and the county simply disappeared from the pipe rolls.[22]

xi. *The problem of the forest, July 1218*

While in Nottinghamshire for the siege of Newark, the regent was brought face to face with another of the centrifugal forces pressing on the government after the war: the intense determination of the counties to exploit the Charter of the Forest and achieve a large measure of deforestation. Here the regent's obligation to maintain the rights of the king conflicted directly with his desire to further the process of conciliation.

In April 1218 the Charter of the Forest had been sent to the counties with orders that it be upheld. The Charter had laid down two stages for the process of deforestation: the areas brought within the forest by Richard I and John were to be 'immediately' deforested, while the much larger areas made forest by Henry II were to be deforested once they had been established by 'good and law-worthy men'. The government, however, had provided no procedures for all this to take place and in Nottinghamshire and Huntingdonshire the counties had

---

[20] *RLC*, 365b, 364, 364b.

[21] Holt, *Northerners*, 233 n. 4. Robert had been custodian of Tickhill for a time in John's reign: *ibid.*, 226–7.

[22] *PR*, 95, 161; E 368/4, m. 3d (Madox, *Exchequer*, ii, 68 n.t); for the date of the concession to Vieuxpont, see Dr Crook's introduction to *Pipe Roll 1221*.

pressed ahead on their own with perambulations of the areas afforested by Henry II.

The aim of these and other perambulations in the early minority was radical in the extreme. It was to remove the royal forest virtually entirely from the counties concerned. Their starting point was that there had been no royal forest at all in the counties when Henry II had come to the throne, or at least none outside the royal demesne. The perambulations then defined the area afforested by Henry II and now to be deforested under the terms of the Charter. Thus in Huntingdon-shire, the unauthorized perambulation of 3 July 1218 stated that Henry II had afforested 'all Huntingdonshire' save three demesne woods, a conclusion which the Marshal's government greeted with indignation since it meant that, apart from the three woods, the whole county should now be deforested.[1] The Nottinghamshire perambula-tion was even more extreme.[2] It made no allowances for demesne woods and claimed that Henry II had afforested what was basically the area of Sherwood forest. The implication was that the rest of the forest in the county (and it was with the fertile areas beyond the core of Sherwood that the perambulators were most concerned) had been afforested by Richard and John and should be immediately deforested, with Sherwood itself, as defined by the perambulation, to follow.[3] Thus the royal forest was to vanish from the county.

The government had every reason to be indignant. In Nottingham-shire, the afforestation of the areas beyond Sherwood had certainly taken place earlier than the reigns of Richard and John, while Sherwood itself and the area to the east, known as The Clay, had been forest under Henry I.[4] It was quite possible that Henry II had simply restored them to the forest after their loss under Stephen. Here, however, there was an ambiguity at the heart of the Charter. It made no distinction between areas afforested by Henry II de novo and areas that he had merely returned to the forest after their loss in Stephen's time. If, as the government came to insist, deforestation was confined to the former, the areas to be deforested would be greatly reduced. After the king assumed power in 1227 the perambulators in Huntingdonshire admitted that Henry II had merely put the situation back to what it

---

[1] E 32/38, r. 2. The perambulation is here stated to have been made on the orders of the chief justice of the forest, John Marshal, and Hugh de Neville, the forester of Huntingdonshire. But in January 1219 the king described it as having been made without his orders: *RLC*, 386.

[2] C 47/11/1, no. 6. It was claimed that this perambulation (of 21 May 1218) was made on the king's orders.

[3] Crook, 'The forest boundaries in Nottinghamshire', 35-6. For maps of the parts of Sherwood forest which it was claimed Henry II had afforested, see *The Sherwood Forest Book*, 35, 36, modified by Crook, *op. cit.*, 42.

[4] Crook, 'The forest boundaries in Nottinghamshire', 36; *Regesta*, iii, no. 831.

had been under Henry I. Consequently all the county remained within the forest instead of escaping from it.[5]

At Leicester on 24 July 1218, therefore, the regent tried to get hold of the process of deforestation before it ran wild. The men of Huntingdonshire were made to fine in 40 marks for deforestation, according to the terms of the Charter of the Forest, and a new perambulation was ordered. At the same time perambulations by 'twelve law-worthy and prudent knights' to establish what should be deforested according to the Charter were ordered to take place in every county under the supervision of the chief justice of the forests, John Marshal.[6] The results were to be sent to the king. The implication was that they would be implemented if he found them acceptable. This was a sensible measure of the regent's. It displayed a willingness to implement the Charter of the Forest provided the king was not short-changed in the process. In this it set a pattern for the future conduct of the government.

The regent spent the rest of the summer at his manors of Hamstead Marshal, Long Crendon and Caversham, and also at Marlborough. In September, before visiting Chepstow, he was at his manor of Bosham in Sussex and also at Reginald de Braose's castle of Bramber. Perhaps it was at this time that he arranged a marriage between his daughter, Eva, and Reginald's son and heir, William. Like the earlier marriage between Gilbert de Clare and the regent's daughter, Isabella, this alliance was suggested by mutual interests in south Wales where both the regent and Reginald de Braose were threatened by the ambitions of Llywelyn. It also represented, again like the marriage between Gilbert and Isabella, a stage in bridging the political gulf created by the war.[7] During the summer the regent was involved in advancing his private affairs on another front. It has been seen that, in September and October 1217, he had launched inquiries into the king's demesnes and escheats and attempted to take them into the king's hands. He had equally provided patronage by granting demesnes and escheats to magnates and *curiales*. In this scramble he was determined not to be left

---

[5] *RLC*, ii, 169b, 206–206b. Similar admissions were made in other counties. See Bazeley, 'The extent of the forest', 149–50. In Nottinghamshire the area claimed, in 1218, as afforested by Henry II, together with all the royal demesne in the county north of the Trent, was equally retained as forest after 1227: Crook, 'The forest boundaries in Nottinghamshire', 39–40. See the map below, p. 391.

[6] C 60/9, m. 4; *PR*, 162. In fact it seems that the new perambulation in Huntingdonshire only took place following a second commission in July 1219: *PR*, 197; E 32/38, r. 2.

[7] No date for the marriage is known save that it had taken place by the time of the regent's death: *Maréchal*, lines 14941–3. It is unlikely to have been arranged before Reginald's succession to his father's estates. In 1218 Reginald granted William immediate possession of the honours of Bramber and Knepp, and this may have been part of the marriage agreement: *PR*, 165; *CRR*, ix, 306–7.

out. Indeed, whatever happened to others, he clearly intended a group of escheats and a royal demesne manor to be one day his family's in hereditary right.

The manors in question had been held by Geoffrey, count of Perche, down to his death in 1202 and, after the loss of Normandy in 1204, were controlled by the king, who thus excluded Geoffrey's son Thomas, the count of Perche killed at the battle of Lincoln in 1217. After the battle four of these manors, Aldbourne and Wanborough (Wiltshire), Newbury (Berkshire) and Toddington (Buckinghamshire), were granted to the earl of Salisbury, who recovered them following the attempted act of resumption in 1217.[8] Salisbury, however, then struck a bargain with the regent and they partitioned the lands between them. Salisbury kept Aldbourne and Wanborough, while the regent acquired Newbury and Toddington. All this had happened by August 1218 when the latter established markets and fairs at Toddington.[9] The regent and the earl were also moving to secure the royal demesne manor which the count of Perche had held at Shrivenham in Berkshire. After 1204 John had retained this in his own hands. In October 1217 it was granted to Robert count of Dreux, brother of the duke of Brittany, to sustain him in the king's service, but some time in the next year the regent and Salisbury gained possession, probably by some private agreement with Robert.[10] They also underpinned their tenure of all the Perche manors by buying out the claims of the late count's uncle and heir, the bishop of Chalons, who came to England in December 1217.[11] Nothing could show more clearly the intention of the regent and Salisbury to hold on to the lands, which combined ideally with their existing interests in Berkshire and Wiltshire. Their hope, clearly, was that when the king came of age he would concede the manors to them or their descendants in hereditary right. Eventually, in 1229, that precisely came to pass.[12]

[8] RLP, 7, 9b, 66b; RLC, 3b, 311b, 333.
[9] RLC, 368, 466; CChR, 102. Salisbury also retained £5 worth of land in both Newbury and Toddington. The affair of the lands of the count of Perche is discussed in Painter, William Marshal, 271–2. For possible encroachments by the regent on the forest of Dean, see Bazeley, 'The forest of Dean', 160–1.
[10] RLC, 3b, 339; Pipe Roll 1218, 31; Pipe Roll 1219, 158; RH, i, 13. In 1221–22 when the question of Shrivenham was discussed at the exchequer it was noted that the earl of Salisbury held part and the earl of Pembroke part: E 159/4, m. 12.
[11] BF, 1146, 1154; PR, 129.
[12] CChR, 102. Wanborough became the earl of Salisbury's chief seat in Wiltshire: BF, 708, 719. As Dr Crouch has pointed out to me, these links of neighbourhood were at the heart of the longstanding connection between the Marshal family and the earls of Salisbury. The regent's mother was the sister of Patrick earl of Salisbury and thus the regent was the first cousin once removed of Ela, William Longespee's wife: see Painter, William Marshal, 9, 13, and above p. 30 n. 15.

xii. *The inauguration of the king's seal and the revival of the general eyre, November 1218*

In the autumn of 1218, while advancing his private affairs, the regent remained painfully aware that the authority of his government was weak and the peace of the country far from assured. In August the earl of Salisbury was told not to tourney, much as he had been in October 1217, 'until the state of peace of the kingdom of England has been made firmer and more secure'.[1] The pope, in September 1218, when he finally gave way to Guala's request, 'worn out by his labours', to resign his legation, had no doubt that a successor was necessary, 'to preserve the king and kingdom in tranquillity'.[2] The regent was cripplingly short of money. The 6,000 marks due to Louis should have been paid by 2 February 1218 but at the end of August the debt had only been reduced by 389 marks; 3,461 marks were then scraped together, of which 1,300 marks came from the exchequer, 521 marks from loans and 900 marks from the regent himself. Although he received a writ of *liberate* for this sum, it had not been paid by the time of his death.[3]

When the exchequer opened in October the situation was better than the year before but still fairly desperate. At least fifteen sheriffs or their deputies turned up at the initial *Adventus*, as against only four in 1217, but the money brought by them and other bailiffs was probably not much more than £216.[4] The first pipe roll of the new reign, covering the accounts of the sheriffs since the war, vividly reflects the state of disorganization. Those for nine of the sheriffdoms were missing, presumably not heard, while several which were included were severely truncated.[5] As will be seen, the king's cash revenue from ordinary sources was probably running, at this time, at *c.* £4,500 a year, a sum more than four times smaller than in John's reign. In this situation the importance of the first scutage, which provided some £1,400 of the cash revenue recorded in pipe rolls of 1218 and 1219, is obvious but according to Mitchell's calculations, of the £7,398 13s 4d owed for the tax, only £2,818 were eventually collected, a mere thirty-eight per cent of the whole.[6] The fact was that the minority government lacked the power to get great men to pay the scutage. In the Easter term of 1218 exchequer writs ordered the sheriffs to distrain the earls of Gloucester, Essex and Winchester to pay it but not a penny was received from

---

[1] *PR*, 174.

[2] *Ann. Eccles.*, 405 (*CPReg.*, 58).

[3] *RLC*, 369, 369b; *Divers Accounts*, 34. In August 1218 740 marks came from Ireland.

[4] See Appendix, p. 415.

[5] *Pipe Roll 1218*, xi.

[6] Mitchell, *Taxation*, 128; *Pipe Roll 1218*, xviii. I have calculated myself the sum received from the scutage in the rolls of 1218 and 1219.

them. A total exemption, meanwhile, was granted to Robert fitz Walter. There was also dissension within the heart of the government itself, where the bishop of Winchester's continued opposition to the scutage forced the regent and the council to concede him the whole sum that he owed.[7]

Early in November 1218, therefore, uncertain whether there were 40 marks in the treasury, the king wrote to the pope apologizing for his inability to pay the annual tribute of 1,000 marks. 'Our bailiffs', he explained, 'with their districts impoverished by war, are less able than is customary to answer at our exchequer.' Five days later (11 November) the government, rather than wait till the following Easter, decided to hold a special *Adventus* at Hilary 1219. The sheriffs were to distrain for the debts owed the king, so that they could answer 'sufficiently at the Hilary exchequer' both for their farms and summonses.[8] It was, however, to more general remedies that the great council which gathered at Westminster in the first week of November turned.

One major decision of this council, attended by Stephen Langton, archbishop of Canterbury, who had returned to England the previous May, was to give the king a seal of his own. Henceforth all royal letters were authenticated by Henry III's seal, which showed him, in the customary fashion, enthroned on one side and on horse-back in full armour on the other, in both cases as a fully grown man. In fact, the inauguration of the seal did not mean that Henry himself, now eleven years old, assumed any part of his regal powers. Although he appeared at great councils, he spent much of his time, separated from the regent and the seal, at royal castles or manors like Wallingford, Guildford and Havering. Although his seal authenticated royal letters, they were still attested by the regent or the bishop of Winchester, who thus continued to shoulder the responsibility for them. Nonetheless, the introduction of the king's seal was commented on by nearly all the chroniclers and clearly enhanced the authority of his government.[9]

The great council entrusted the new seal to the keeping of the chancery clerk, Ralph de Neville, in whose custody it was to remain for the next twenty years.[10] This was a striking demonstration of the control which great councils could exercise over major appointments. It made a deep impact on Neville, who was later to declare that, since he had been appointed by a great council, only a great council could

---

[7] *RLC*, 349b; E 368/1, m. 2d; C 60/9, m. 5; *Pipe Roll 1218*, 64; *Pipe Roll 1220*, 119–20, 35; *Pipe Roll 1221*, 21.

[8] *RLC*, 381; *DD*, no. 25; C 60/11, m. 11.

[9] *PR*, 177; *CPReg.*, 47–8; *Ann. Mon.*, i, 64; ii, 291; *Coggeshall*, 187; *Chron. Maj.*, iii, 43.

[10] *Chron. Maj.*, 74, 364; iv, 367; Powicke, 'The chancery during the minority', 228. The titular chancellor down to his death in 1226 was the bishop of Durham, Richard de Marsh, but he never exercised day-to-day control over the seal.

dismiss him, an argument which was echoed in the Paper Constitution of 1244. Neville's immediate sense of responsibility in November 1218 is reflected in the large numbers of notes which suddenly appear in the chancery rolls recording on whose authority royal letters were issued.[11]

The first letters patent promulgated under the new seal announced regulations governing its use. No charter or letter patent was to be issued which conferred anything in perpetuity until the king came of age. The letter embodying this pronouncement was witnessed by the legate, the archbishops of Canterbury and York, the regent and the justiciar, in the presence of twelve bishops, eight abbots, eight earls and fifteen other named magnates. Probably those present took an oath before Guala to the same effect.[12]

Considerable importance attached to this assertion of principle. True, the maxim that the king could not make permanent alienations until he came of age had been honoured in large part since the beginning of the reign. As has been seen, it was founded on English custom and had antecedents in Roman law.[13] Ecclesiastics could appreciate its force given the restrictions in canon law on the alienability of church property. Lay magnates could see that, if the rule was breached during the minority of the king, then it might equally be violated during the minority of a baron. In the short term, however, the prohibition limited the freedom of the government and frustrated the widespread desire for permanent rewards. The government had certainly broken the rule when it came to Magna Carta and the Charter of the Forest. It had also sanctioned several gifts 'in pure and perpetual alms' to religious houses for the benefit of John's soul. It had found a way of making Ranulf of Chester earl of Lincoln and had given the advowsen of Chesterton to Guala's foundation at Vercelli. If Guala, as a reward for his services in the war, could be exempted from the rule, why not everyone else?[14] There was, therefore, every reason for a clear statement of principle to save the rights of the king from further erosion and the legate, the regent and the clamorous magnates around them from themselves. Quite probably the new policy was accompanied by the formal destruction of the Charter Roll which was being kept in 1218.[15] Another was not started until the king assumed full powers in 1227.

The restriction placed upon the king's ability to make grants was limited in its application, however. It prevented fresh grants in

[11] *RLC*, 381–3b.
[12] *PR*, 177; *F*, 163; *RLC*, ii, 75b. Guala did not leave England until mid-December 1218: *RLC*, 384.
[13] See above p. 18.
[14] *PR*, 123, 173; and see *Worcester Cartulary*, nos 328, 328a.
[15] *PR*, 173; C 60/9, m. 6.

perpetuity but did not require the resumption of alienations made since the start of the war, although there was clearly some feeling that it should have done this. 'We ought rightfully to have the forests and lands of which . . . our father was seized at the beginning of the war' the king had declared in December 1217, when explaining an action in respect of the forests of Ombersley and Horwell in Worcestershire. Later, in 1220, the government interpreted the oath of November 1218 in just this sense: it was an oath to keep the king in seisin 'of all the lands which were in the hands of King John on the day that war first broke out'. Yet, in fact, the government spoke with a forked tongue. In March 1218 it accepted an offer of 700 marks for a charter deforesting Ombersley and Horwell.[16] The assertions of November 1218 did not lead to fresh attempts at resumption. Indeed, grants continued. In November 1218 itself Engelard de Cigogné came before the council and demanded that 'he might be sufficiently rewarded for his great service so that he might be better sustained in the king's service'. He was conceded, by Guala, the bishops of Winchester and Worcester, the regent, William Brewer and Falkes de Bréauté, the royal demesne manors of Benson and Henley, and promised either the county of Surrey (over which he was still in dispute with the earl of Surrey) or £100 a year from the first escheats to fall in. Next month, 'by common counsel', Philip of Oldcoates was conceded £90 a year from the farms of Collingham and Bardsey, two royal demesne manors in Yorkshire.[17]

At the same time as the king's seal was inaugurated, another measure was taken whose importance is impossible to exaggerate, a measure which would enable the government both to dispense justice and increase its revenues. This was the revival of the general eyre. If the king's government was to recover authority, it was vital to fulfil expectations in the sphere where Magna Carta called for more government action, not less: the sphere of justice. The revival of the bench had already gone some way to meet the demand for justice, helping to fulfil in particular the Charter's stipulation that common, that is, broadly civil, pleas be heard in a 'fixed place'. The demand for justice could also be fulfilled by sending judges to hear civil pleas in the counties.[18] Indeed, clause 18 of the 1215 Charter had demanded that two judges visit the counties four times a year to hear the petty assizes. The main vehicle of royal justice in the localities before the war, the general eyre, had, however, been on an altogether different scale from the petty assize eyres envisaged in the Great Charter.

The general eyre was an eyre not merely for petty assizes but for *all*

[16] *RLC*, 347; *F*, 163; C 60/9, mm. 6, 5; *Pipe Roll 1218*, 30; *Ann. Mon.*, i, 64.

[17] *RLC*, 403–403b, 384b; *PR*, 184. Engelard was to receive a £50 annual fee until he obtained the escheats or the county of Surrey.

[18] As argued by Dr Clanchy, 'Magna Carta and the Common Pleas', 219–32.

pleas both criminal and civil. Its judges also carried out detailed investigations into royal rights. It was general, moreover, not merely in the scope of its authority but also in the geographical area that it covered, the usual practice being for the judges, divided into a number of groups, to cover all or a large part of the country in their visitations. The general eyre was not popular, however, for financially it was extremely burdensome, largely through the variety of amercements which the judges imposed on local communities in the course of hearing criminal pleas. Conceivably, some radicals in 1215 hoped that the general eyre might come to an end, as, towards the end of the thirteenth century, it was indeed to do. Its criminal work could be hived off to justices of gaol delivery, who were already appearing in John's reign; its civil business could be taken by justices for civil pleas like those envisaged in the Charter.[19] After the war, it was vital for the minority government to resist any suggestions of this kind. Indeed, perhaps one reason why clause 18 of the 1215 Charter was altered in 1217, so that the petty assize judges were to visit the counties once a year rather than four times, was because the more frequent visitations might interfere with the general eyre and imply that it was unnecessary.[20] The fact was that the minority government stood urgently in need of the revenue which the general eyre would produce. It must also have recognized that, in the anarchic situation following the war, gaol delivery and petty assize judges would simply lack the authority to dispense effective justice. Even the justiciar, Hubert de Burgh, when he heard petty assizes in Norfolk and Suffolk in the summer of 1218, had been unable to get men to accept the verdicts of the juries, large numbers of which were challenged by the process of attaint.[21]

What was needed in 1218, therefore, was a great, nationwide general eyre. Only that could dispense effective justice, generate substantial revenue, investigate the rights of the king and impress the authority of his government on the kingdom. Concern with just these points was revealed by additions in 1218 to the questions (the articles of the eyre) put by the judges to the juries of presentment which appeared before them. Thus the jurors were to say who had failed to pursue outlaws or burglars, who had held new markets without royal permission and who had heard pleas of gaol delivery or of approvers without warrant from the king or his justiciar. The further clause asking who had introduced new customs was intended both to defend the rights of the crown and

---

[19] See Crook, 'The later eyres', 244–8. Dr Crook's *General Eyre* is the chief source for the subject.

[20] The more obvious reason for the change is the administrative burden such visitations would have imposed at a time when there was a scarcity of trained judicial personnel.

[21] *Pipe Roll 1219*, xvii–xviii. The proffers for these writs may be found in C 60/11.

protect people in the counties from the impositions of both sheriffs and magnates. In a sense, the eyre enshrined the political balance which the government had to strike. On the one hand, it must give the kingdom justice and order. On the other, it needed to defend the king's rights and increase his revenues. If it could do the former it was more likely to secure acceptance for the latter, as well as win support for the assertion of royal authority against the refractory. The necessity for that support was very much in the government's mind in November 1218. It was almost certainly when the king's seal was inaugurated that the 'magnates of England' swore before Guala to preserve and promote 'the royal honours and rights', obey and assist the regent and the king's councillors in doing the same, and repress violators of the peace. A very similar oath was administered to the counties by the justices in eyre.[22]

On 4 November 1218, therefore, the whole of England, apart from the west midlands, was divided between eight groups of judges. They were to start work on 25 November and hear all pleas, both criminal and civil. Everything was done to make the visitation of 1218 as impressive as possible. In terms of the area to be covered, it was the most comprehensive eyre since that of 1176. The commissioning writs, among the first to be sealed with the king's new seal, were attested by the regent in the presence of the archbishop of Canterbury and the bishops of Winchester and Durham. The groups of justices were usually headed by a bishop or an abbot and included a justice of the bench and one or more local magnates.[23] The justices were equipped with an oath to administer to the knights and free tenants of each county, which bound them to keep the peace, obey the king's orders, preserve his rights and maintain the laws and customs of the kingdom. They were also to assemble on the king's orders and those of his council to coerce the disobedient; a striking effort to secure military support from outside the regime for some future assertion of royal power.[24]

The impressive display with which the eyre was launched reflected the government's anxiety as to how far the authority of the judges would be accepted. It was careful to reserve the amercement of barons for the king's council, thus upholding the stipulation in the Great Charter that barons should be amerced by 'their peers'.[25] Likewise, the judges were ordered to refer all demands for liberties and 'difficult'

---

[22] VL, Honorius III Regesta X, f. 83–83v (*CPReg.*, 65, where the summary is slightly misleading); *DD*, no. 27. For the articles of the 1218 eyre, see C 47/34/1, no. 14A; *Wiltshire Eyre*, 30.

[23] *PR*, 206–9; Crook, *General Eyre*, 71–6. In late 1218 and early 1219 sessions of the bench were suspended to enable concentration on the eyre.

[24] *Ann. Mon.*, iii, 53; *DD*, no. 27.

[25] *RLC*, 383b, 387b. For later practice, see *Bracton*, ii, 330; Holt, *Magna Carta*, 232; Harcourt, 'The amercement of barons by their peers', 737.

pleas to the council. On the Yorkshire eyre such pleas were set down on a separate roll and it is evident that the 'difficulties' were often as much political as legal, the cases involved touching the susceptibilities of great magnates.[26]

These apprehensions were not unjustified. The Dunstable annalist, in recording the oath administered by the judges, believed that it only enjoined obedience to the '*reasonable* orders of the king'. On the eyre itself many challenged the verdicts of juries through the process of attaint, just as they had on Hubert de Burgh's visitation of Norfolk and Suffolk earlier in 1218.[27] Some great men, for example, Falkes de Bréauté and Robert de Ros, simply prevented the execution of judgements which went against them.[28] Both Hugh de Neville and Fulk d'Oyry, on behalf of his lord, the count of Aumale, impugned the honesty of the judges on the Lincolnshire and Nottinghamshire circuit.[29] There were other, more purely administrative problems: on the civil side, what to do about writs which had been lost, a not uncommon occurrence given the time since the last eyres; and on the criminal side, how to replace trial by ordeal now that it had been forbidden by the fourth Lateran council, a question the king's council left to the discretion of the judges.[30]

Despite these difficulties, there can be no doubt that the first eyre of the reign was a great success. It was completed in all the designated counties by the end of 1219, the west midlands being covered by a circuit in 1221–22.[31] It brought a vital injection of cash into the exchequer, the total recorded receipts in the pipe rolls of 1219, 1220, 1221 and 1222 being respectively £990, £645, £1,050 and £560; and this when the king's annual cash income from ordinary sources around 1220 was little more than £5,000. The eyre also inquired into the king's rights, producing, county by county, lists of land to which he was entitled by wardship or escheat.[32] The judges took a high view of their honesty and authority. Those in Lincolnshire, in a letter to the regent, justiciar and bishop of Winchester, forcefully rebutted Fulk d'Oyry's strictures: they had been appointed 'to this eyre, for the peace of the king and the kingdom, to give justice to each and everyone, poor as well as rich'. They had done nothing save 'by the counsel and judgement of all of the county court, and nothing contrary to right . . . or opposed to

[26] *RLC*, 383b; *Yorks. Eyre*, nos 1096–1153 and pp. xxvi–xl for Lady Stenton's analysis of the roll.

[27] *Pipe Roll 1219*, xvii–xviii. The proffers for these writs may be found in C 60/9.

[28] *CRR*, viii, 198–9; xi, no. 2002; C 60/11, m. 8 (*Pipe Roll 1219*, 149); *RLC*, 619, 633.

[29] *RL*, nos xvi, lvi; *Lincs. Worcs. Eyre*, lv–lvii, no. 712.

[30] *PR*, 210, 186; Bartlett, *Trial by Fire and Water*, 127, 138.

[31] Crook, *General Eyre*, 71–8.

[32] *BF*, 244–88.

the approved custom of the kingdom'.[33] The Waverley annals, not generally favourable to the king's government, took the judges at their own valuation: 'in this year peace returned and was stabilized in England, and the justices, who are popularly called itinerant, went through all of England after Christmas [1218], reviving the laws and causing them to be observed in the pleas before them according to the Charter of King John'.[34]

The eyres, therefore, together with the revival of the bench, went a long way to meet the demand for royal justice which had been expressed in the Great Charter, a demand seen after the war in the 130 fines, recorded in the pipe rolls of 1218 and 1219, for the writ *pone*, which moved cases from the county court to the bench.[35] On the Lincolnshire eyre the press of civil business was so great that the judges held concurrent sessions for assizes (cases heard with juries) and pleas (cases heard without).[36] The rolls of the Lincolnshire and Yorkshire eyres in 1218–19, although incomplete, record 1,340 separate items of business in their civil pleas section.[37] Equally striking was the number of cases settled before the justices by final concords – 1,037 in the twenty-six counties visited in 1218–19, some 280 more than when the justices had last visited the same counties in John's reign.[38]

To some extent the judges do seem to have fulfilled their boast 'to give justice to each and everyone, poor as well as rich'. Falkes de Bréauté, described at this time by the Tewkesbury annalist as *plusquam rex in Anglia*, was convicted of disseisins on the Kent, Somerset and Oxfordshire eyres, at least two of the successful litigants being no more than small freemen. If Falkes went on to defy the verdicts, the judges were not always so easily brushed aside.[39] At the end of the Lincolnshire eyre they lost patience with William de Ros of Tydd 'for refusing to obey the demands of the king and his justices touching the novel disseisins which he has done and of other evil suspicions whereof he was accused', and they brought him to heel by ordering his arrest and the seizure of his lands.[40] Robert de Percy came before the Yorkshire justices to answer the charge of murdering the carter of Robert de

---

[33] *RL*, no. xvi. For the bishop of Bath's sense of his reputation as a justice in eyre, see *CRR*, viii, 80–1; Powicke, *Henry III*, 39.

[34] *Ann. Mon.*, ii, 291.

[35] *Pipe Roll 1218*, xxi; *Pipe Roll 1219*, xvii.

[36] *Lincs. Worcs. Eyre*, xxxviii, xlii.

[37] *Lincs. Worcs. Eyre*, nos 1–912; *Yorks. Eyre*, nos 1–428. The numeration is that of the editor, Lady Stenton.

[38] Crook, *General Eyre*, 63–76.

[39] The remark of the Tewkesbury annalist was itself made while recording the abbot's victory against Falkes in a grand assize case: *Ann. Mon.*, i, 64; C 60/11, m.8 (*Pipe Roll 1219*, 149); *CRR*, xi, no. 2002; *RLC*, 619, 633.

[40] *Lincs. Worcs. Eyre*, nos 911, 24–6, 29, 33, 98; *RLC*, 408b; *CRR*, viii, 116.

Vieuxpont and was placed in custody.[41] In Oxfordshire, in the heart of Falkes de Bréauté's sheriffdoms, one of his local agents, Richard Foliot of Warpsgrove, released a man 'for fear of the justices itinerant who were coming into those parts'.[42]

The great council of November 1218, and the eyre which it launched, marked an important phase in the process of reconciliation after the war. The council saw the return of Archbishop Langton to the political stage, following his period of exile at the papal court. Langton had been suspended from office by the pope in 1215 for failing to take action against John's opponents. He had helped negotiate the terms of the Great Charter and strongly believed in its merits; his presence in England served almost as its guarantee. Yet, within the confines of the Charter, Langton was ready to work for the recovery of royal authority, even if his role was overshadowed by that of the papal legate. Thus he attested both the royal letters which set out the rules governing the use of the seal and those which launched the general eyre. He attested the former in the presence of such erstwhile rebels as the earls of Arundel, Gloucester, Hereford, Essex and Oxford, and Robert fitz Walter, Peter fitz Herbert and William de Beauchamp. At the beginning of October, moreover, an appointment took place which was probably designed to reassure former rebels about the political neutrality of the judicial process.[43] During nearly all the Michaelmas term of 1218 the earl of Arundel sat as the senior justice of the bench, joining there another sometime rebel and familiar of Archbishop Langton, John of Guestling. Four ex-rebels were also appointed as justices of eyre.[44]

A belief in the utility of the judicial process is revealed by the number of former rebels who brought legal actions in an attempt to solve problems arising from the war. Admittedly, the government devised no specific action for anyone denied the return of his lands and the usual response in such circumstances was simply to try again with another writ of common seisin: 'and since he could not have seisin he sought another writ, and a third'.[45] The assize of novel disseisin, however, could be employed by those ejected after they had, or alleged they had, recovered seisin. It was also used by those, like Maurice de Gant and Henry Bek, who had lost lands as a result of ransom agreements.[46]

---

[41] *Yorks. Eyre*, nos 1079, 1140; Holt, *Northerners*, 249.

[42] *CRR*, xi, no. 1956.

[43] *PR*, 177; Meekings, 'Concords'.

[44] William of Trumpington, Thomas of Moulton, John of Guestling, William de Albini: Crook, *General Eyre*, 71, 73, 74–5. For a fuller discussion of Archbishop Langton's attitude, see below pp. 263–5. Arundel had deserted to Louis in June 1216.

[45] *Lincs. Worcs. Eyre*, no. 299; *CRR*, ix, 380; xii, no. 1145; xiii, no. 315.

[46] *Yorks. Eyre*, nos 315, 1133, 251, 383, 1125 and pp. xxii, xxxiii–iv; *Lincs. Worcs. Eyre*, no. 712, and p. lv.

Some of these cases came very definitely under the heading of 'difficult' and were tossed, like hot coals, between the justices of eyre, the bench and great councils. Ultimately, former rebels enjoyed mixed success. Maurice de Gant, Henry Bek, Robert de Percy and Nicholas de Chavencurt all lost their actions.[47] On the other hand, Gilbert de Gant, William de Coleville, William de Mortimer, Robert de Girros and Thomas de Costentin were victorious.[48] The balance was sufficient to prevent former rebels developing a contemptuous disregard for the judicial process. Robert de Percy had committed *multa mala* in Richmondshire during the war and had murdered Robert de Vieux-pont's carter after it. In 1219 he lost the case he was bringing against the bishop of Durham for the return of Osmotherley. Yet, in 1224, he brought an action at the bench when his mill at Hornington was pulled down 'wickedly and feloniously and in breach of the king's peace' by William de Percy.[49] By this time Robert himself was being commissioned as a judge to hear petty assizes. Likewise, if Robert de Ros prevented by force of arms the execution of a judgement which went against him on the 1219 eyre, and was convicted of numerous disseisins, he also made use of both the eyre and the bench to reach peaceful agreements settling his private disputes.[50]

On the Lincolnshire eyre of 1219 one case above all was of key importance in demonstrating to the former rebels that well-connected loyalists would not ride roughshod over them. This was the action of novel disseisin brought by Gilbert de Gant, Louis's earl of Lincoln, against his wartime captor, the count of Aumale. Probably Aumale had entered the property in question, Edenham, five miles north-east of Castle Bytham, during the hostilities and had disseised Gant after the latter recovered possession on the conclusion of the peace. When the case came before the eyre, the jurors gave their verdict in Gant's favour. The judges ordered him to be put back in seisin and sentenced Aumale to pay damages of 5 marks. So far so good. But then Fulk d'Oyry, Aumale's steward, intervened at court and obtained a royal letter which apparently returned seisin to Aumale, despite the judgement passed at the eyre. This caused an explosion. Gilbert de Gant came before the judges with 'the whole shire assisting him and acclaiming with him and for him, and indeed for themselves, and, as they say, for the common liberty of the whole kingdom granted and sworn'. Gant and his supporters demanded that there should be no change 'without

[47] *Yorks. Eyre*, nos 1133, 1125; *Lincs. Worcs. Eyre*, nos 299, 898; *CRR*, viii, 307.

[48] *Lincs. Worcs. Eyre*, no. 297 (the Mortimer case). For the other cases, see below pp. 165–6, 255.

[49] *Yorks. Eyre*. nos 1079, 1125; *CRR*, xi, nos 1483, 2037; *PR*, 485, 489; Holt, *Northerners*, 56, 179, 243; see below p. 129 n. 6.

[50] *Yorks. Eyre*, no. 304; *Yorks. Fines*, 33; *CRR*, ix, 275; see below p. 195.

judgement in the state of his possession which he had acquired by judgement of the king's court in accordance with the due custom of the kingdom'. The judges took his part and sent the letter of protest, mentioned above, to the regent, the justiciar and the bishop of Winchester. As a result Gilbert de Gant remained in seisin and Aumale had to proceed against him by the process of attaint like everyone else, ultimately without success.[51]

In their reference to 'the common liberty of the kingdom granted and sworn', 'the whole shire' of Lincolnshire was clearly thinking of the Great Charter and in particular of the clause which had laid down that no freeman was to be deprived of his possessions 'save by the lawful judgement of his peers or by the law of the land'. In siding with the shire, the justices seemed indeed, in the words of the Waverley annalist, to be going 'through all of England . . . reviving the laws and causing them to be observed in the pleas before them according to the Charter of King John'.

In the spring of 1219, as the justices in eyre bent to their work, two of the most prominent of all the rebels, Robert fitz Walter and the earl of Winchester, left England for the crusade. They were accompanied by another former rebel, the earl of Arundel, who thus forsook his position at the bench. There could be no better demonstration that the process of settlement, in the eyes of such men, was proceeding in acceptable fashion. In the East the earl of Winchester must have met the earl of Chester and John de Lacy, who had gone out in the summer of 1218. During the war Winchester and Chester had been at each other's throats over Mountsorrel. On the crusade their differences were composed, for it was probably then that a marriage was arranged between Margaret de Quincy, the niece of the two earls, and John de Lacy, Chester's tenant; a marriage that ultimately, thanks to Chester's good offices, brought John de Lacy the earldom of Lincoln.[52]

xiii. *The end of the regent's government, December 1218–April 1219*

After the great council of November 1218 the structure of the regent's government began to change. The effect of the replacement, in December 1218, of Guala as legate by Pandulf, the papal chamberlain, is hard to gauge; but after the inauguration of the young king's seal, although the majority of letters were still attested by the regent, the bishop of Winchester began to take a more pronounced share in their

---

[51] *Lincs. Worcs. Eyre*, no. 151, and pp. li–liii; *RL*, no. xvi; and see below pp. 165–6. For Fulk, see Major, *The D'Oyrys*.

[52] *Ann. Mon.*, ii, 292; iii, 56; *PR*, 185; Lloyd, *The Crusade*, 82; *Peerage*, vii, 675–88; Eales, 'Henry III and the end of the Norman earldom of Chester', 104. For Margaret's father, see Painter, 'The house of Quency', 235, 237–8.

attestation and authorization. A more prominent role at the centre was also acquired by the justiciar, Hubert de Burgh. Although still not attesting royal letters, from January 1219 onwards he sometimes acted as their authorizor in company with the bishop of Winchester.[1] In some ways, indeed, the government was taking on the appearance of a triumvirate. Thus the justices in Lincolnshire, as has been seen, sent their letter of protest (written between 25 November 1218 and 16 February 1219) jointly to the bishop of Winchester, the regent and the justiciar.[2]

The regent had returned to Westminster from Marlborough, which had already become a favourite residence, in mid-January 1219, probably for the opening of the Hilary exchequer. According to his biography, he fell ill around Candlemas (2 February).[3] A date around this time is confirmed by the record evidence: on 26 January royal letters were attested both by the regent and the bishop of Winchester, then, between 27 January and 5 February, the bishop attested seventeen letters enrolled on the close and patent rolls and the regent only two.[4] The regent's illness was long: it was three and a half months before he died. He was subjected to sudden sharp internal pains and ultimately could scarcely eat, being kept alive for the last fifteen days of his life on mushrooms and sodden bread.[5] However, while the body decayed, the mind and personality remained intact. Hence his biography reaches its climax in the most detailed and moving of death-bed scenes to survive from the middle ages.

Having got over the initial impact of his illness, the regent resumed the attestation of royal letters, a task he continued to share with the bishop of Winchester until his resignation on 9 April. He was, however, too ill to attend a great council convoked at Rochester early in March almost certainly to meet two envoys who had arrived from the king of France. These, to the relief of the English government, brought a letter from King Philip which signalled his readiness to accede to the request of the pope and renew the truce, which was due to expire at Easter 1220.[6]

The regent's illness did not lead to any slackening of the government's activity. On 11 March the bishop of Winchester and Hubert de Burgh took joint responsibility for the safe-conduct issued to Philip of

---

[1] *PR*, 185 onwards; *RLC*, 386 onwards.
[2] *RL*, no. xvi; for the date, Crook, *General Eyre*, 75. I suspect that Guala's letter to the three ministers – *DD*, no. 27 – comes from late in his legation. See also *Pipe Roll 1218*, 42, where the date is suggested by *RLC*, 388.
[3] *Maréchal*, lines 17880–3.
[4] *RLC*, 386b–7; *PR*, 186–7.
[5] *Maréchal*, lines 18443–56.
[6] *RLC*, 387b; *PR*, 188; *DD*, no. 29.

Oldcoates so that he could come to London to see the king's council 'about his affairs'. Four days earlier the bishop had returned to another old problem, that of the Barton outside Bristol which the castellan, Hugh de Vivonne, was still refusing to surrender to the earl of Gloucester, despite orders in November 1217, May 1218 and January 1219. Hugh was now warned that, unless he delivered the Barton to the earl, 'as ordered many times before', then all his lands would be taken into the king's hands.[7]

Vivonne's reply to this mandate highlighted the problems of the government in controlling its local agents. He reminded the king that he had 'told your council at the exchequer' that 'I would never surrender [the Barton] to the earl unless you made provision so that I could sustain the castle of Bristol'. Although he had then been promised 100 marks and £100 worth of rents, he had received nothing. Vivonne was merely the deputy at Bristol of his fellow Poitevin, Savari de Mauléon, who had left England in 1216, yet he clearly felt perfectly able to defy orders from the centre and form his own opinion of what was in the best interests of the king. What gave his stand all the more force was that, in some ways, he was quite right. After his resignation in 1221, when accounts began to be rendered by the constable, the costs of maintaining Bristol castle absorbed all the revenues from the Barton and more besides.[8] Nor, in the end, was the Barton surrendered to the earl of Gloucester, the minority government preferring to compensate him in other ways.[9] As for the threat to seize his lands, Vivonne pulled out all the stops of the loyal and much tried servant: 'you can easily do that', he told the king, 'but I certainly do not think I deserve it. For my family and I, in the service of King John . . . and yourself, have lost across the seas more fruitful and richer lands than I will ever have in England, and I have faithfully served King John . . . while he lived, and you after his death, and still I serve you and will all the days of my life, so long as it pleases you.'[10]

The regent, who would have applauded these sentiments, decided to die not at the Tower but at his own manor of Caversham near Reading. The journey by river was taken gently, the regent in one boat, his countess following in another. They left the Tower on or soon after 16 March; by 18 March they had reached Cookham just beyond Maidenhead and two days later they were at Caversham. While he went slowly up river, the seal had remained behind at Westminster, the treasurer, Eustace de Faukenburg, attesting a letter there on 19 March.

[7] *PR*, 189; *RLC*, 405b, 387, 360b, 344b, 344; see above p. 83.
[8] *RL*, no. lxxv; *PR*, 99; *Accounts of Bristol castle*, 1–4.
[9] See below p. 147 n. 6.
[10] *RL*, no. lxxv.

But next day the chancery was at Caversham, and the regent well enough to attest and authorize a royal letter.[11] Between 20 March and 9 April, the bishop of Winchester was associated with only six of the twenty-six letters enrolled on the chancery rolls, the remainder being the sole responsibility of the regent. In these last days, in his own house, surrounded by his friends and *familia*, he exercised closer control over the issue of royal letters than at any time since the making of the king's seal.[12]

In these circumstances the regent took thought for the future of the kingdom. He summoned a council to Reading and on two successive days, 8 April (Easter Monday) and 9 April, king, legate and nobles came to Caversham and sat around his bed. The regent's original intention was to choose someone 'to guard [the king] and the kingdom', in other words, a successor to himself. On the first day, however, the bishop of Winchester stood up and protested at this proposal. The king, he asserted, had been entrusted to his care, only the kingdom to the regent's. The regent denied this. At Gloucester, at the start of the reign, he reminded the assembly, he himself had been made 'guardian and master of the king and kingdom together'. Subsequently he had merely 'bailed' the king to the bishop.[13] This argument seems to have altered the regent's mind, however. As he remarked to his *familia* next morning, 'no people in any land are of such diverse opinions as they are in England. And if I bailed the king to one I have no doubt that the others would be jealous.'[14] On 9 April, therefore, at the second gathering round his bed, the regent raised himself on his elbow, took the king by the hand and entrusted him to God and the pope and to the legate Pandulf as his 'master in their place'. The dying man had a last word for the king. He prayed that, if he followed the example of a 'certain criminal ancestor' (*alcun felon ancestre*), God would not give him a long life; a prayer which showed at the last William's view of King John and pointed the way forward for the reign of Henry III.[15]

The august delegation departed but William Marshal, remembering the central role of great councils during his regency, had a last doubt. Might men impugn his decision because it had been made in private?

[11] *Maréchal*, lines 17914–36; C 60/11, m. 7; *RLC*, 405b.

[12] C 60/11, m. 7; *RLC*, 389b–90; *PR*, 189–90. On 24 March, however, Bishop Peter attested a letter at Reading which was not enrolled on the chancery rolls: *RL*, no. xi (where misdated). There may have been others.

[13] *Maréchal*, lines 17949–18028; but see *Walt. Cov.*, 233. The last day on which the regent attested letters was 9 April. The bishop of Winchester's attestations commence on the 10th: *RLC*, 390. This suggests the first meeting was on 8 April and the second, at which the regent resigned, on 9 April; see Painter, *William Marshal*, 276 n. 9.

[14] *Maréchal*, lines 18038–46.

[15] *Maréchal*, lines 18063–90.

So, just as at the beginning of his regency he had ensured general assent
to his assumption of power, so now at its end he did the same about the
choice of his successor. He sent instructions to his son telling him to
present the king to the legate in the presence of 'the baronage'. As this
was being done, probably back at Reading, the bishop of Winchester
attempted once again to assert his rights over the king. He stepped
forward and seized the boy by the head, only to be sharply reprimanded
by Pandulf and the young Marshal.[16]

After his resignation on 9 April, over a month of life remained to
William Marshal. He retained his dignity and common sense. 'Shut up!
people would think I had gone mad!', he snapped at John of Earley,
when the latter urged him to sing in the hope that it might make him
feel better. But when his daughter, Jean, sang before him in a weak, shy
voice, he soon broke in, 'don't have a shameful air when you sing; you
will never sing well that way', and he showed her how it should be
done.[17] Pandulf dreamt of William just before his death and, with all
the authority of the pope's legate, absolved him from his sins. William
learnt of this supreme absolution on the final day of his life (14 May)
and was confessed and absolved for the last time by Pandulf's
messenger, the abbot of Reading.[18] This, however, was no case of
'between the stirrup and the ground, I mercy asked, I mercy found'.
Rather, William Marshal would willingly have said with Dr Johnson,
'as the tree leans, so let it fall'. Few laymen can have met death with
more confidence that their earthly values would secure them salvation
in the next world. Thus when Henry fitz Gerald, supporting him as he
lay in bed, begged William to think of his salvation and the church's
teaching that no one could be saved who does not return what he has
taken, the reply was robust: 'Listen, Henry! the clerks are too hard on
us. They shave us too close. I have taken 500 knights and appropriated
their arms, horses and equipment. If, for that reason, I am forbidden
the kingdom of God, there is nothing I can do, for I cannot return what
I have taken. I can do no more than present myself to God repenting of
all my faults. . . . But the argument of the clerks must be false or else
nobody would be saved.'[19] Likewise, when his clerk Philip, in a strident
voice, reminded him of his robes and furs which could be sold 'for
money to acquit your sins', the reply was equally firm: 'I have had
enough of your advice. . . . It will soon be Pentecost. My knights need
their robes. This will be the last time that I give them to them.'[20] Thus
died the Marshal. 'We believe that his soul is in the company of God

[16] *Maréchal*, lines 18091–118.
[17] *Maréchal*, lines 18528–80.
[18] *Maréchal*, lines 18910–66; *Ann. Mon.*, ii. 291.
[19] *Maréchal*, lines 18468–96.
[20] *Maréchal*, lines 18685–706.

because he was good in this life and in his death', declared the biography.[21]

xiv. *The crisis facing English kingship*

The regent's services to the Angevin dynasty had been immense. In the direst of situations in the war, he had shouldered the young king's cause and brought it through to victory. His courage had provided the will to fight a decisive battle and his generalship had discerned the ideal moment at which to do so. He had also shown considerable political skill, beating off challenges to his own position, understanding the importance of patronage and basing his government firmly on consent expressed in numerous great councils. His government had also done much to heal the wounds of the war. It had pushed ahead with restoring former rebels to the seisins that they had enjoyed at the outbreak of hostilities. It had accepted a version of the Great Charter and promulgated the Charter of the Forest, decisions which shaped the future of England's polity. Fittingly, the regent's funeral cortège was conducted from Caversham to the Temple Church in London not by the legate, justiciar or bishop of Winchester but by former rebels, namely the earls of Surrey, Essex, Oxford and Gloucester.[1]

The regent had equally set about rebuilding the structure of Angevin administration. He had restored the exchequer and attempted to preserve the rights of the crown. He had refused to sanction the deforestations demanded under the Charter of the Forest and had attempted (if with scant success) an act of resumption of the king's demesnes and escheats. In November 1218, when the royal seal was inaugurated, a clear statement had been made that the king could not make permanent alienations until he came of age. Above all, the regent had moved to meet the demand for royal justice expressed in the Great Charter, thus demonstrating the positive benefits that flowed from kingship. He had restored the bench at Westminster, placed former rebels on it and paid the justices salaries to reduce corruption. He had also initiated a great general eyre which, while increasing the king's revenues, also dispensed justice on a wide and impressive scale.

Thus the regent conciliated the enemies of King John and the critics of Angevin government. He showed how it might be possible to win support for the assertion of royal authority, support which the oaths taken by the magnates of England in November 1218 and by the knights and free tenants before the justices in eyre had been designed to consolidate. Already the success in removing Robert de Gaugi from

[21] *Maréchal*, lines 18979–82.
[1] *Maréchal*, lines 19005–11.

Newark castle had depended on many former rebels rallying to the king's army.

Yet, for all this, the regent bequeathed massive problems to his successors. His government had accepted Llywelyn's extraordinary advances in Wales and the Marches, had failed to discipline its justiciar in Ireland and had been a mere spectator as Hugh de Lusignan and the magnates in Poitou treated its officials with contempt. Well might King Philip of France remark in 1219 that 'the children of King John have neither as much money nor as much power to defend themselves as had their father'.[2] There was one basic reason for the powerlessness of the government outside England: its weakness and poverty within England itself. If the limbs were feeble, the trouble was with the heart.

The task of rebuilding the king's authority and resources within England was immense. The centrifugal forces encountered by central government were diverse and powerful. In many counties there was fierce resistance to the activities of the king's local agents. To combat that situation, those agents needed to be strong, but that raised the spectre of such men becoming over-mighty and impossible to control. Thus the regent had totally failed to prize the Barton outside Bristol from Hugh de Vivonne and Bicknor castle from John of Monmouth. He had been unable to remove Philip of Oldcoates from either the castle of Mitford or the Vesci custody and been equally unsuccessful in his attempts to extract the count of Aumale from Castle Bytham and from Rockingham and its surrounding forest and manors. At the centre itself authority was fragmented. Ministers were frequently at odds; little could be done without the consent of great councils; and overshadowing everything was the poverty of the crown. To understand the depth of the crisis facing English kingship at the time of the regent's resignation, a crisis in many ways comparable to that facing Henry II after the civil war of Stephen's reign, that poverty and its causes must be analysed in more detail.

A calculation of the king's financial resources in the years after the war, given the only partial survival of receipt rolls, depends very largely on the pipe rolls: the annual records of the exchequer on which the accounts of the sheriffs and other local officials were recorded. These must be used with care.[3] They are concerned only with what might be called the king's ordinary revenue. They do not include revenue received from Ireland, revenue accounted for at the separate exchequer dealing with Jewish affairs, and revenue from some extraordinary

---

[2] *Recueil*, xix, 680.
[3] What follows is a detailed discussion of exchequer procedure and of the problems of using the pipe rolls to estimate current income. Readers who would prefer merely to consult the conclusion should turn to p. 112. For an important discussion of the whole subject, see also Stacey, *Politics*, 201-5.

taxation (notably the carucage of 1220 and the fifteenth of 1225). Equally, distortions can occur when an important county, like Yorkshire, accounts in a particular pipe roll not for one year but for two.[4] The rolls of the early minority also present special problems. It is necessary, if trying to estimate current revenue from them, to make allowances for income and expenditure which clearly date back to the war or before, for the way debts were written off as part of political bargains and for the expenditure, particularly belonging to the years 1218–20, which is only recorded in later rolls.[5]

There is also a more technical problem connected with the timescale of the revenue recorded in the pipe rolls. According to the great book written about the exchequer in 1178, the *Dialogus de Scaccario*, the exchequer held two sessions each year, the first at Easter, the second at Michaelmas. It summoned the sheriffs to appear at the start of both these sessions to pay over the farms of their counties and numerous specified private debts. These biannual appearances were called the *Adventi Vicecomitum*. The revenue proffered at them was recorded on receipt rolls, one for the Easter term and one for the Michaelmas. As proof that they had paid over their money, the sheriffs were given tallies, normally one for each individual debt. Then, in the Michaelmas term, the exchequer audited the accounts of the sheriffs in turn, by going through the list of the debts (called the summonses) which it had ordered them to pay in at Easter and Michaelmas, the sheriffs presenting their tallies as proof that payment had been made. At the same time the sheriffs were given allowances for revenue which they had expended locally on the king's orders. These shrieval accounts were recorded on the pipe rolls which were drawn up each Michaelmas term.[6] It might seem, therefore, that each pipe roll will record the revenue from the *Adventus Vicecomitum* of each Easter and Michaelmas, together with the money which the sheriffs had expended locally since their account the previous year. If allowance is made for various distortions, a pipe roll should thus reflect fairly accurately the king's ordinary annual revenue.

Unfortunately, this picture in the *Dialogus* did not correspond to practice, at least by the thirteenth century. Although most of the king's revenue probably came in fairly early in the Easter and Michaelmas terms, it was not all received on the nail at the biannual *Adventi*

---

[4] Another problem is that occasionally debts were only cleared on the pipe rolls years after they had been paid. For the Jewish exchequer, see Jenkinson, 'The records of exchequer receipts from the English Jewry', 18–54.

[5] The failure of Sir James Ramsay (*Revenues*, i, 262–82) to make such distinctions led him to grossly inflate the revenue received during the early minority.

[6] *Dialogus de Scaccario*, 69–70, 72–3, 81–2 and (for the whole process of account) 84–126.

Vicecomitum. Indeed, the exchequer both summoned sheriffs to pay revenue in at times other than the two customary *Adventi* and remained open for its receipt throughout much of the year. Thus the Michaelmas receipt roll ran on to record revenue received until the beginning of the Easter term and the Easter roll contained revenue received down to the beginning of the Michaelmas.[7] Equally, due to pressure of business, the exchequer no longer audited all the accounts of the sheriffs in the Michaelmas term. For example, eleven sheriffs accounted in the Michaelmas term of 1221 and the rest in 1222, four in the Hilary term, seven in the Easter term and four in the Trinity. The exchequer, therefore, now opened at Hilary and Trinity as well as at Easter and Michaelmas, and the pipe roll was completed not in the Michaelmas term but in or after the following Trinity term when the last accounts were heard.[8]

Had the exchequer, when hearing accounts in the Hilary, Easter and Trinity terms, only audited money paid in by the conclusion of the *Adventus Vicecomitum* of the previous Michaelmas, each pipe roll might have neatly recorded the revenue received between Michaelmas and Michaelmas. This, however, was not its practice. Instead, comparison between the few surviving receipt rolls of the early minority and the pipe rolls shows that the procedure was to audit money paid in down to the actual date of the account. The same was true of money expended locally on the king's orders.[9] What this means, therefore, is that the pipe roll of, say, 1221 records in some counties money paid into the treasury and expended locally down to the Trinity term of 1222 when the accounts of those counties were heard. The *terminus a quo* of the roll equally varies from county to county, depending on the date of each sheriff's previous account.[10] The roll of 1221, therefore, records revenue received in the Michaelmas term of 1221 but it also stretches

[7] These statements are based on the *Adventi Vicecomitum* and the receipt rolls of the early minority, for which see Appendix, p. 413, where figures extracted from the pipe rolls are also set out.

[8] *Pipe Roll 1221*, introduction; see also *Pipe Roll 1219*, xii–xiii, xxiv–v; *Pipe Roll 1220*, v–vii. Much of this already applied in John's reign: see *Memoranda Roll 1208*, 20–1. The exchequer had two departments: the lower exchequer, which was the exchequer of receipt where the money was paid in, and the upper exchequer, which was the exchequer of audit.

[9] Dr Harris deduced that this was likely from studying the dates of fines and writs of allowance recorded on the pipe roll of 1219: *Pipe Roll 1219*, xii–xiii, xxiv–v; see also his introduction to *Pipe Roll 1220*, viii, and Dr Crook's introduction to *Pipe Roll 1221*. There is further valuable discussion in Knight, 'The Pipe Roll of 6 Henry III', 77–93, which shows that the pipe roll on a few occasions might even include receipts and expenditure (not apparently as later additions) after the date of the account.

[10] For the receipt rolls on which these conclusions are based, see Appendix, p. 414. My analysis of them has been far from exhaustive, however, and much new light will be shed when they are properly edited.

forward to include some of the revenue received down to Trinity 1222 and back to grasp revenue perhaps as early as the Michaelmas term of 1220.[11] In the early minority, therefore, the revenue of any particular financial year, if that is taken to be the revenue recorded on the two annual receipt rolls, may be split between three pipe rolls.

These facts inevitably nullify Sir James Ramsay's simplistic attempt to relate the politics of each year to its revenue as revealed in the pipe roll, an exercise not helped by Sir James associating, throughout the reign of Henry III, the politics of each year with the pipe roll of its predecessor.[12] There is no need, however, to despair altogether. In broad terms, a pipe roll of the minority does reflect a year's revenue but it is the revenue from Easter to Easter, rather than from Michaelmas to Michaelmas. Although the pipe roll of 1224, to take another example, may record revenue received as early as Michaelmas 1223 and as late as Trinity 1225, the amounts drawn from these extremes cannot have been large. The effective limits of the roll are rather the revenues received during the Easter terms of 1224 and 1225, revenues which the roll divides probably fairly evenly with the pipe rolls of 1223 and 1225.[13] Meanwhile, the great bulk of the revenue recorded on the Michaelmas receipt roll of 1224 (the only Michaelmas one to survive from the minority) is recorded on the 1224 pipe roll. This alone means that a high proportion of the king's annual income appears on the pipe roll since the amount found on the Michaelmas receipt roll was always much greater than that found on the Easter. A pipe roll can, therefore, provided one makes adjustments for doubled and missing accounts and for the distortions peculiar to the period after the war, give at least an impression of the king's annual revenue. The rolls can be employed even more usefully to show broad changes in the king's revenue over a period of years.

If, then, one looks at the first two pipe rolls of the reign, which thus include the ordinary revenues from the Easter and Michaelmas terms of 1218 and 1219, and some revenue stretching into the Easter term of 1220, the picture they reveal is catastrophic. The revenue recorded in the first roll as paid into the exchequer is a bare £2,800. As has been seen, this roll has the accounts for only twenty sheriffdoms and some of

---

[11] When a county account was audited early in the Michaelmas term, payments later in the term would miss the audit and appear on the pipe roll for the following year. For this happening in respect of payments recorded on a surviving Michaelmas receipt roll in the reign of Henry II, see Richardson, 'The exchequer year', 177–8.

[12] Ramsay, Revenues, i, 270 onwards. Ramsay's mistake originated in making the roll for 2 Henry III that for 3 Henry III.

[13] The receipt rolls for the Easter terms of 1224 and 1225 are missing. These remarks are based on comparisons between the surviving Easter receipt rolls and the relevant pipe rolls.

these are truncated. But even in the roll for the next year, 1219, where twenty-six sheriffdoms accounted, six of them for both 1219 and the previous year, the amount recorded as paid in was only £5,880. The total cash revenue in the two rolls, therefore, amounted to £8,680, an average between them of £4,340. If an allowance is made for one sheriffdom which accounted for 1219 in the roll of the following year, and for accounts belonging to 1219 which are placed on separate rolls, then the total reached is only some £9,030, an average of £4,515.[14] This was not, of course, the king's total cash revenue. £493 6s 8d were received in 1218 from Ireland;[15] the citizens of London probably made payments towards their 2,000 mark fine for lifting the interdict imposed on them in the war;[16] and a limited amount of revenue was paid directly to the regent rather than to the exchequer.[17] But none of this decisively altered the situation. How little money the government had to play with is confirmed in another way: by the total value of the writs of *liberate* which ordered payments out of the exchequer. Not all these writs were actually honoured but even if they had been, the total disbursed between Michaelmas 1217 and Michaelmas 1219 was under £7,000, or less than £3,500 a year. For the following year, Michaelmas 1219 to Michaelmas 1220, the sum was still a mere £5,295. Comparison with the pipe roll income of John's reign shows how comprehensive was the collapse of the king's revenue. In the roll of 1203 total cash receipts amounted to £20,830.[18] In the first years after the war, therefore, King Henry III's ordinary cash income, running at c.£4,500 a year, was less than a quarter of what it had been before the war.

There was also a marked drop in the amount of money spent on the king's orders as opposed to being paid into the exchequer. In the pipe rolls of 1218 and 1219 the total thus expended was £3,860. A search through later rolls, however, reveals expenditure datable roughly to the years 1218 and 1219, and amounting to at least £3,460, making a

[14] Here and elsewhere, in making adjustments for missing and doubled county accounts, I have simply halved the sums involved and distributed them equally between the two rolls: see Appendix, p. 413. For the sums on the separate rolls, see below p. 414 n. 3. Since there is no roll for 1217, the sums in the rolls of 1218 and 1219 are correspondingly inflated but probably by no very large amount.

[15] *RLC*, 369.

[16] By the Hilary term of 1223 the Londoners, in seven separate instalments, had paid £675 of their fine into the exchequer: E 368/5, m. 13(1)d.

[17] The total sum accounted for by the regent's executors was £1,624. Within this amount it is impossible entirely to disentangle money actually received during his peacetime regency from receipts before and during the war and debts owed by the regent to the king for various manorial and other farms which he may or may not have collected. The regent's executors did not account until 1224: *Divers Accounts*, 32–7.

[18] Holt, 'The loss of Normandy and royal finance', 97.

notional total for the two rolls of £7,320 and an average between them of £3,660.[19] This compares with expenditure valued at £13,797 in the roll of 1203. The total revenue, cash and expenditure, in the pipe rolls of 1218 and 1219 was £12,540, while the notional total, with the various adjustments made above, is £16,350; an average of £8,175. The total revenue in the roll of 1203, at £34,627, was four times as much.[20] The contrast with the situation before the war was made starkly clear at the very moment of the regent's resignation. The initial *Adventus Vicecomitum* at the exchequer at Easter 1219 produced a meagre £65, as against £2,320 for the one recorded Easter *Adventus* of John's reign.[21]

The individual components of the collapse of royal revenue are easy to discern. Compared with before the war, the exchequer was receiving little money from a whole range of private debts. It was obtaining around £2,000 less from the manors of the royal demesne, virtually nothing from wardships and virtually nothing again from the county farms. In respect of the last, the annual 'ancient' farms of the counties were nominally worth, in the years after the war, about £2,000.[22] It had long been known, however, that the revenues which the sheriffs had to make up their farms – various fixed dues, the proceeds of the county and hundred courts, and the issues of some royal demesne manors – came (at least in normal times) to a great deal more than the farms. The exchequer had devised two methods of tapping the surplus. One was to demand that the sheriffs account for fixed annual increments above the farm; the other, developed in John's reign, was to make the sheriffs 'custodians', who cleared their farms and then accounted for all the revenue which they had left above them, that extra revenue being called 'profits'. In some years of John's reign the profits had been worth over £1,500, nearly all of which was paid into the exchequer. The total value of farms and profits, therefore, approached £4,000, an important slice of the king's annual income. John, however, had been forced to dismantle the custodian system before the war and the extraction of increments by name, and profits by implication, was forbidden by clause 25 of Magna Carta in 1215.[23] That clause, as has been seen, was omitted from the Charters of 1216 and 1217 but the government simply lacked the strength to take advantage of the fact. The failure to secure

---

[19] There is additional expenditure in the early minority which it is impossible to date exactly. In particular, by the Hilary term of 1223, the citizens of London, in clearance of their fine for the lifting of the interdict and one other debt, had made payments totalling £791 to Flemish merchants and others: E 368/5, m. 13(1)d.

[20] Holt, 'The loss of Normandy and royal finance', 97.

[21] E 159/2, m. 1; *Memoranda Roll 1208*, 31–3; and see Appendix, p. 415.

[22] *Pipe Roll 1220*, xiii. My own calculations coincide with this estimate of Dr Harris.

[23] Harris, 'King John and the sheriffs' farms', 532–42; Carpenter, 'Decline of the curial sheriff', 2–10.

revenue above the ancient farms, therefore, itself reduced the king's visible income by over £1,500 as compared with the best years of John's reign. Equally serious was the tiny size of the cash revenue received from the ancient farms themselves, potentially worth, as has been said, some £2,000 a year. In the rolls of 1218 and 1219 combined, the total amount reaching the exchequer from this source was a bare £123. In the roll of 1214, by contrast, the amount had been some £1,330.

In 1218 the government had given two explanations for its poverty. One was that the country had been so impoverished by the war that the sheriffs could not account properly at the exchequer. In some areas the physical damage done by the war was indeed extensive and may well be reflected in the low sums imposed on the royal demesne for the tallage of 1217.[24] The war had also, of course, shaken the king's local power in many parts of England, making it impossible to exploit traditional sources of revenue. Thus, apart from the bishop of Worcester's fine for the deforestation of Ombersley and Horwell, virtually no money was obtained from the forest in the early minority. The sheriffs also found difficulty in collecting both the first scutage of the reign and a whole range of other private debts. Resistance to their authority was likewise reflected in the struggles of the men of Cumberland, Nottinghamshire and Shropshire, in this period, to limit the number of shrieval officials.[25] The situation was particularly critical in the eastern counties, which had contained the centre of the rebellion. It has already been noted how the exchequer believed that the obstruction of local magnates was preventing the sheriff of Yorkshire answering properly for the revenues of the county, and its apprehension was well justified.[26] The debts of the sheriff, Geoffrey de Neville, in the pipe roll of 1219, already amounted to £904, including £414 owed from the farms of the county and various manors, and £223 from the amercements of the eyre of 1218–19. All this money was still owed in 1222, when Geoffrey was allowed against it £200 for his expenses going to Poitou in 1218. The remainder of the debt had virtually to be written off.[27] Shrieval authority was also uncertain in Essex-Hertfordshire where investigations at the exchequer showed that the regent's under-sheriff and successor, Walter de Verdun, had failed to collect farms from the

---

[24] *DD*, no. 25; *Pipe Roll 1218*, xix; for damage in the war, see *Historiae Anglicanae*, 1870–1.

[25] See below pp. 150, 181, 235 n. 1.

[26] See above p. 80.

[27] *Pipe Roll 1219*, 204–5; *Pipe Roll 1221*, 138–9; E 372/66, r. 11, m. 2; *RLC*, 361. In the pipe roll of 1225, Geoffrey's son, John, was allowed 1,000 marks for his father's expenses in King John's service, notably in maintaining the castles of Scarborough and Pickering, and then permitted to pay off his remaining debts, which still amounted to £991, at an annual rate of £5: E 372/69, r. 13d, m. 2; see *RLC*, ii, 116b.

hundreds as well as other debts. There were also problems in Norfolk where Hubert de Burgh's under-sheriff was ordered in 1219 to maintain and defend the king's liberties as they had existed in John's reign before the war.[28]

The government, in 1218, also identified a second reason for its poverty, or more exactly for its lack of ready cash, namely that the sheriffs were retaining 'for themselves' the money which they collected rather than paying it in to the exchequer. Up to a point this was a natural and necessary development both for fighting the war and securing the peace. In both periods the king had an absolute need for strong local agents with plenty of money. In Yorkshire in 1218 the government acknowledged that Geoffrey de Neville would require all that he could raise above the farm, and perhaps more, to sustain the royal castles of Scarborough and Pickering.[29] There were indeed no more vital tasks than the garrisoning and repair of the king's castles, for which large sums were necessary. Falkes after the war spent £312 on works at Northampton castle and Hubert, down to 1221, used up to £2,604 munitioning and rebuilding Dover. The works at Dover indeed – the three solid beaked towers, which blocked off the north-west gateway undermined by Louis's mining operations, and the new Constable's gateway to the west which has remained the chief entrance to the castle – were amongst the greatest achievements of the minority.[30] The castellans naturally drew on the resources of their sheriffdoms to support their castle expenditures; for those at Dover, Hubert, down to Michaelmas 1220, devoted up to £1,656 from the farms and judicial issues of his sheriffdoms of Kent and Norfolk-Suffolk. They equally drew on these revenues to finance other activities. The bishop of Winchester employed the issues of Hampshire to pay the wages of seven serjeants retained in the king's service, as well as to finance other expenses of the king's household. Falkes used the revenues from his sheriffdoms to fund the king's stay at Northampton after the Christmas of 1218, while the regent used the farms of Essex-Hertfordshire, in so far as he could collect them, to support his multifarious activities in the king's service.[31]

Against the fragility of shrieval authority in the eastern counties,

[28] *RLC*, 402b; *Pipe Roll 1220*, 106; E 159/3, m. 8; E 372/66, r. 8, m. 1. How far the regent collected the farm of Essex-Hertfordshire as sheriff down to his death may also be questioned: see *Divers Accounts*, 34.

[29] *RLC*, 377b; *PR*, 145–6.

[30] *Pipe Roll 1218*, 57; *Pipe Roll 1219*, 78; *RLC*, 459; *Pipe Roll 1220*, 59. Brown, Colvin, Taylor, *King's Works*, ii, 633 n. 6, gives a larger amount but by adding together overlapping sums.

[31] *Pipe Roll 1220*, 59, 122; *Pipe Roll 1218*, 56–7; *RLC*, 352, 357b, 459; *Divers Accounts*, 34. Down to Easter 1221 Hubert also received for Dover £604 from Isaac the Jew of Norwich.

the regent had reason to be grateful for the power exercised by the great governors in the midlands: the power of Philip Mark, for example, keeping tight control over Nottinghamshire-Derbyshire, and of Falkes de Bréauté.[32] Falkes's achievement in particular was remarkable. His responsibility was unique, for he held the sheriffdoms of Northamptonshire, Oxfordshire, Bedfordshire-Buckinghamshire and Cambridgeshire-Huntingdonshire, together with the great castles of Northampton, Oxford, Bedford and Hertford. He had no previous experience of peacetime administration in England; it was for his abilities as a soldier that he had acquired his English castles and sheriffdoms. 'Little he was in stature but very valiant', commented the *History of the Dukes of Normandy*.[33] Yet Falkes adapted to the requirements of peace with flexibility and vigour. Completely emancipated as he was from feudal ties, he recruited an exceptional staff to run his sheriffdoms. Ralph de Bray, who accounted for them at the exchequer down to 1220, was a former steward and under-sheriff of another hard and unpopular man, William Brewer; later, after Falkes's fall, he became steward of the earl of Chester. John of Hulcote, who was Falkes's under-sheriff in Cambridgeshire-Huntingdonshire, was a former under-sheriff of Walter of Preston in Northamptonshire and later sheriff in his own right of Oxfordshire and Norfolk-Suffolk. Hugh of Bath, the under-sheriff in Bedfordshire-Buckinghamshire, was a former king's clerk and steward of Queen Isabella and later became a justice at the exchequer of the Jews. Another former king's clerk in Falkes's employ, later to have a long and celebrated career in the king's service, was Robert Passelewe. It was typical of Falkes that he should make the most experienced professional attorney of the day, the *miles literatus* Matthew of Bigstrup, a member of his *familia*. Before the war, Matthew had worked for a large number of clients; after it, he worked almost exclusively for Falkes.[34]

Falkes and his officials dominated their sheriffdoms and laboured to recover the rights of the king within them. Not surprisingly, it was on Falkes's strength that the government, after the war, frequently relied in moments of crisis; the regent must have felt fully justified in conferring upon him the lands of the earldom of Devon. And, in general, the regent can scarcely be blamed for failing to staunch the haemorrhage of gifts and concessions, many of which were sanctioned by the council. Sometimes, indeed, they fulfilled promises made by King John who, for reasons of utter necessity, had given away, on various terms, numbers of demesne manors during the war.[35] The need

32 For Philip, see Holt, 'Philip Mark', 8–24.
33 *Normandie*, 173. Falkes was also sheriff of Rutland from 1218 to 1221.
34 C 60/20, m. 4; Carpenter, 'Sheriffs of Oxfordshire', 159–60.
35 *RLC*, 364–364b, 365b; *RCh*, 216b; *RLC*, 223b, 282b; *RLP*, 154.

to reward and sustain loyal servants was just as great in the years of tenuous peace.

There were, however, still profound dangers to the present and future power of English kingship in the way its resources had fallen into the hands of great men during and after the war. At the end of the regent's period of office, the papacy itself sounded the alarm. In April 1219 it ordered Pandulf to work towards the resumption of 'the castles, demesnes and possessions and all other things rightfully belonging to the king', thus outlining the battleground of English politics down to 1224.[36] This clarion call can have come as no surprise. The exchequer, as has been seen, was worried as early as January 1218 about the sheriffs retaining revenue for themselves and the next year Pandulf spoke openly of 'the malice' of the sheriffs.[37] The great local governors were doing vital work, or were they? It was impossible for the centre always to be sure. Hugh de Vivonne asserted that he needed the revenue from the Barton outside Bristol to maintain the castle but just how he was spending its revenues the exchequer never knew since he never accounted for them. As early as 1218 the regent and the exchequer would have preferred a system whereby the king's local agents paid their revenues into the exchequer and local works were funded, as and when necessary, by cash received from the centre via writs of *liberate*. Hence the regent's insistence that Hubert de Burgh pay the scutage of Kent into the exchequer, 'as anciently accustomed', before receiving it back to fund the work at Dover.[38] In that way the exchequer attained far more oversight of the king's revenues. If, on the other hand, the great local governors simply drew off the revenues from the royal demesne and the shrieval farms, central government was left powerless, without control and without resources. That, in effect, was the situation of the regent. In and after the war, with a highly limited central income to draw on, he could act only through painfully constructed coalitions with the local governors who had the money. In short, there were good grounds for the pope's complaint in 1220: the great men of England were, he wrote, 'revelling on the royal goods while the king begs'.[39]

It is the scale with which revenue from the royal demesne and the county farms had passed from exchequer control which needs to be appreciated. In respect of the demesne, a comparison between the pipe rolls of 1214 and 1219 makes this starkly apparent. Over fifty manors

---

[36] VL, Honorius III Regesta X, f. 88 (*CPReg.*, 65). For Powicke's view of the threats to the power of kingship after the war, see *Henry III*, 49–51. For more recent discussions, see Stacey, *Politics*, 9–12; Eales, 'Castles and politics', 31–2.

[37] *RL*, no. xxviii.

[38] *RLC*, 352.

[39] *RL*, 535.

and boroughs, which had produced a revenue of around £2,000 in the roll of 1214, produced virtually nothing for the exchequer in the roll of five years later. The reason was that the manors had been used to provide patronage for sheriffs, castellans and other servants of the king. The catalogue of alienated manors, moving from north to south, gives some impression of the extent of the dispersal – in Northumberland: Newcastle upon Tyne, Bamburgh and Corbridge; in Yorkshire, Driffield, Knaresborough, Boroughbridge, Collingham and Bardsey; in Nottinghamshire and Derbyshire: Derby, Edwinstowe, Melbourne, Bolsover, the Peak, Mansfield, Sneinton and Chesterfield; in Lincolnshire: Grimsby; in Shropshire: Edgmond; in Staffordshire: Newcastle-under-Lyme; in Worcestershire: Droitwich, Bromsgrove and Feckenham; in Gloucestershire: Dymock, Awre, Newnham, Cheltenham and Westall; in Northamptonshire: Corby, Gretton, King's Cliffe, Brigstock, Apethorpe, Geddington and Finedon; in Oxfordshire: Bloxham and Benson; in Huntingdonshire: Godmanchester; in Cambridgeshire: Chesterton; in Essex: Writtle; in Hertfordshire: Hertford, Essendon and Bayford; in Berkshire: Cookham, Bray, Windsor and Shrivenham; in Hampshire: Odiham and Andover; in Wiltshire: Marlborough, Devizes and Rowde; in Somerset: Chewton, Pitney and Wearne.[40]

The alienation of the demesne depleted the king's potential revenue but acts of patronage had equally affected the revenue from the county farms. In Lancashire, Shropshire, Staffordshire and Cumberland, the government had allowed the sheriffs, the earl of Chester and Robert de Vieuxpont, to retain the farms for periods as yet undetermined.[41] Vieuxpont, moreover, went further than the letter of the concession, with the result that no accounts at all were rendered for Cumberland until his departure in 1222.[42] Thus no record was ever made of what happened to the issues of the 1218–19 eyre in the county.

Elsewhere the 'malice' of the sheriffs were even more blatant. Some time in 1218–19 the earl of Salisbury equipped his deputy in Lincolnshire with the following remarkable letter. 'Everyone is to know that we have prohibited William fitz Warin, our sheriff of Lincoln, from paying anything to the king's exchequer from the issues of the county of Lincoln, until the king's council has satisfied us concerning the lands

[40] Although escheats rather than royal demesne, I have included Bolsover and the Peak here since they had been in the king's hands since 1154–55. Although regularly used to supply patronage, the demesne had always provided an important part of the king's revenue. Between 1240 and 1245, according to Dr Stacey's calculations, it yielded about 20 per cent of the king's annual cash income: Stacey, *Politics*, 206, 211. For studies of the royal demesne, see Hoyt, *The Royal Demesne*, and Wolffe, *The Royal Demesne*.

[41] See above pp. 80–1, 89.

[42] E 368/4, m. 3d; *Pipe Roll 1221*, introduction.

and the promises made to us by the king and his council, and I have received the issues from the foresaid sheriff and will acquit him towards the king at the exchequer.'[43] This act of defiance was tamely tolerated by the government and Salisbury cleared virtually nothing from the farm of Lincolnshire until he resigned the sheriffdom in 1222. By then he had run up debts totalling £1,307, a sum still outstanding in 1224. He had also failed to clear £115 worth of amercements imposed by the eyre of 1218–19. In Wiltshire, too, Salisbury's performance in respect of the farm was hardly commendable. He paid no revenue from it into the exchequer, received only one substantial allowance for expenditure and, when the pipe roll for 1222 was closed, owed £217, again a sum still outstanding in 1224.[44] The exchequer was equally unable to oversee Peter de Maulay's handling of the revenues from Somerset-Dorset. At the time of his removal in 1221 he owed over £800 from back farms of the counties and had failed to clear debts, totalling £224, from the eyre of 1218–19. His total debts as sheriff for the years 1217 to 1222 amounted to £1,537 6s 8d.[45] Further west, in Cornwall, exchequer authority was even weaker, for the sheriff, Henry fitz Count, rendered no account at all. Perhaps these men justified their retention of revenue on the grounds that they were owed money by the king for expenditures during the war. But then they had equally received revenue during the war for which the exchequer was not asking them to account. In short they were attempting to secure the best of both worlds.[46]

The annual loss to the exchequer from the farms of Lincolnshire, Wiltshire, Lancashire, Shropshire, Staffordshire, Cumberland and Cornwall was in the region of £900, while the total annual loss from these counties, given that no revenue at all was obtained from either Cumberland or Cornwall (with its lucrative tin mines), was over £2,000.[47] The passage of power and resources to the great regional governors had, therefore, taken place on a large scale. Nor was it easy to change. The danger, indeed, was that such governors would prove almost impossible for the regent's successors either to control or remove. These men were not, after all, simply shouldering vast burdens happy in the knowledge that the revival of centralized kingship would

[43] E 159/2, m. 5d.

[44] *Divers Accounts*, 44–5; *Pipe Roll 1221*, 163; E 372/66, r. 14, m. 1, r. 15d, m. 1.

[45] *Pipe Roll 1221*, 95. The sum was to some extent notional. Had Maulay accounted properly he would have received various allowances (especially involving *terrae datae*) which would have reduced the amount owed in respect of the county farm.

[46] When wartime expenditure was set against peacetime revenue it was usually the result of some political bargain: see below pp. 256, 376–7, and E 372/68, r. 9d, m. 2 (William de Cantilupe).

[47] In addition, the concession to the earl of Chester meant he was allowed manorial and other farms of an annual value of £97: *Pipe Roll 1220*, 70, 73, 172, 174–5.

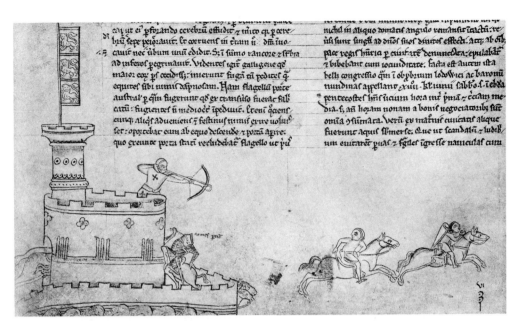

1. *above* Matthew Paris's drawing of the battle of Lincoln, May 1217. The royal standard flies over the tower of the castle, while under the castle's walls the count of Perche dies, stabbed through the eye-hole of his helm, as described in the life of William Marshal.

2. *left* The eastern gateway of Lincoln castle as rebuilt in the minority of Henry III after damage during the civil war. The upper storey and battlements have been lost.

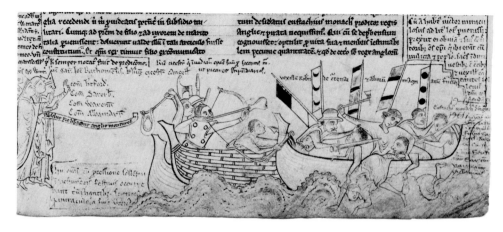

3. Matthew Paris's drawing of the sea battle off Sandwich, August 1217. On the left, the bishops of Winchester, Salisbury and Bath absolve those who will die for 'the liberation of England'. On the extreme right, Eustace the Monk is beheaded.

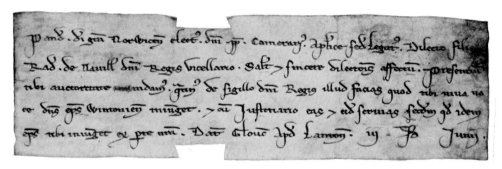

4. Pandulf's letter of 11 June 1219 in which he instructs Ralph de Neville, in respect of the king's seal, to do what the bishop of Winchester enjoins him *viva voce* and to follow those things with the justiciar and serve the latter. It was these instructions which placed Hubert de Burgh in charge of the attestation of royal letters.

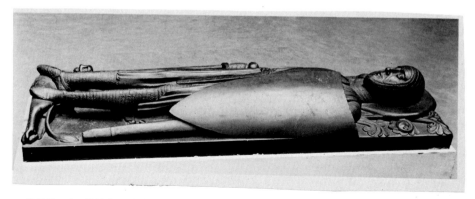

5. Effigy (c. 1230s) probably representing the regent, William Marshal, earl of Pembroke, in the Temple Church, London, as restored by the Victorians but before bomb damage in the Second World War.

6. Dover castle from the north-west. This was the angle from which Louis attacked the castle in 1216-17. Left of centre (beyond the later brickwork in the foreground) is the trinity of towers with which Hubert de Burgh blocked up the gateway brought down by Louis's mining operations. On the right is Hubert's new gateway, the Constable's Tower.

7. Newark castle from across the Trent. King John died here in 1216. The regent besieged the castle in 1218 when Robert de Gaugi refused to surrender it to its lord, the bishop of Lincoln. The right-hand tower is twelfth-century; the other tower and most of the wall are late thirteenth-century.

8. The only surviving example of Magna Carta 1217, now in the Bodleian Library. The seals are those of the legate Guala (left) and the regent William Marshal. Although almost certainly conceded in November 1217, copies of the Charter were despatched to the counties in February 1218. If the Bodleian charter is one of these (it was preserved at Gloucester abbey), it may explain why it was left without its dating clause, plans to provide a new February dating clause having been abandoned. But why has the clerk omitted the word *Cartam* in the last line?

enable them one day to lay them down. Nothing is more indicative of the fact that great men, in the circumstances of this period, positively desired to run sheriffdoms with little interference from the centre than the grant, albeit abortive thanks to the resistance of Robert de Courtenay and Peter de Maulay, of the counties of Devon and Somerset to the earl of Salisbury, merely for his 'homage and service'.[48] Indeed, since he cleared nothing from their farms, it was on something approaching these terms that the earl of Salisbury held Lincolnshire and Wiltshire. He was also successful in keeping the justices in eyre out of Wiltshire, for, although one was twice planned, no visitation took place in the county until after his death in 1226.[49] When, in 1219, a writ deprived Salisbury, as sheriff, of the forests of Melksham and Devizes in favour of the constable of Devizes, he simply joined forces with the bishops of Bath and Salisbury and issued a contrary order in the king's name.[50] Within Wiltshire *he* would decide what was in the king's interests, not whoever was in charge of the exchequer and the chancery: hence his steadfast refusal to surrender Mere to Hugh de Balliol and his disregard of a stream of royal orders to distrain those in the county owing debts to the Jews. It comes equally as no surprise to find the justices of the bench making sarcastic comments about the 'negligence' of Salisbury or his deputy in prosecuting the king's affairs as sheriff of Lincolnshire.[51]

A similar situation to that in the earl of Salisbury's sheriffdoms, although even more extreme, had developed in Cornwall under Henry fitz Count. Quite apart from not accounting at the exchequer, he too aimed to shut out the justices in eyre. To that end, in 1219, he appointed judges on his own authority to hear petty assizes in the county. No wonder the government after the war was concerned about its loss of control over justice in the localities and, in 1218, added to the articles of the eyre a question about those who had heard pleas of gaol delivery or approvers without warrant. In 1221 it went further and included an article about sheriffs and bailiffs who had heard pleas of the crown (instead of reserving them for the king or his justices).[52]

The model to which the earl of Salisbury and Henry fitz Count

---

[48] *PR*, 38, 86–7. The concession to Salisbury was *salvo regali nostro* but what this constituted was not specified. The earls, barons, knights and freemen of the counties were to swear homage and fealty to him saving their fealty to the king and to answer to him henceforth as their lord.

[49] Crook, *General Eyre*, 71, 81.

[50] *RLC*, 395, 413.

[51] E 159/3, m. 3; *CRR*, ix, 232.

[52] *PR*, 202–3; *Wiltshire Eyre*, 29–30. An eyre was commissioned in Cornwall in 1218 but did not take place: Crook, *General Eyre*, 71. Dr Harris discusses Henry's position in *Pipe Roll 1220*, xi. The hearing of pleas of the crown by sheriffs was forbidden by Magna Carta (clause 24 in 1215).

aspired was exemplified in Ranulf earl of Chester's position in Chester. There he and his predecessors had never answered for a farm and controlled the whole running of criminal and civil justice. In Chester the petty assize writs ran in the earl's name, not the king's. Ranulf himself spoke naturally of 'my' writ of mort d'ancestor. The civil war had enabled Ranulf to expand his power base by the acquisition of the sheriffdoms of Lancashire, Shropshire and Staffordshire. As has been seen, he did not account for the farms of these counties and in Shropshire, like his predecessor, he heard pleas of the crown.[53] Under the arrangements made in 1218, if one of his under-sheriffs died while Ranulf was on crusade, it was not central government which was to appoint a successor but the earl's *fideles*.[54] Likewise, within Yorkshire, Ranulf was determined to maintain and develop Richmondshire as a self-contained administrative unit under his own control. His exclusion of the sheriff gave rise to anxious discussions at the exchequer about the 'many debts' in the shire which could not be collected. In defiance of the treaty of Kingston/Lambeth Ranulf also held on to Richmond castle at the expense of its hereditary constable, the former rebel Ruald fitz Alan.[55]

Compared to the earl of Salisbury and Henry fitz Count, Falkes was almost a model sheriff. But the rule he exercised in his shires enabled him to commit numerous disseisins, to defy verdicts which went against him on the eyres of 1218–19, to force former rebels to purchase at high prices the restoration of their lands and to protect his under-sheriffs in Oxfordshire as they intimidated and expropriated some of the chief county knights.[56] In 1219 Falkes was described by the annals of Tewkesbury abbey as *plusquam rex in Anglia*.[57]

The fact was, of course, that castellanships and sheriffdoms were not simply offices. They were highly coveted items of patronage. Hubert de Burgh was offered the counties of Norfolk and Suffolk in hereditary right to desert to Louis in 1216; a year later the earl of Salisbury accepted Devon and Somerset as the price for returning to the young king; in 1218 Engelard de Cigogné was guaranteed either the county of Surrey or £100 a year in escheats to sustain him in his 'great service'; in 1221 Hugh de Vivonne was promised that he could recover Bristol

---

[53] Harris, 'Ranulf, Earl of Chester', 110–13; Bodleian Library MS, Dodsworth 31, f. 88 (a reference I owe to Dr Crouch); *Gloucs. Warw. Eyre*, no. 1262. Note that the article of the eyre about pleas of the crown was an addition in 1221: *Wiltshire Eyre*, 29; *Gloucester Pleas*, xvii.

[54] E 368/1, m. 1d. See above pp. 80–1.

[55] E 368/4, m. 11; *Yorks. Eyre*, nos 1145, 29; *CRR*, x, 188.

[56] *CRR*, xi, nos 1914–34, 1935–63, 2002; *RLC*, 633; C 60/22, m. 7; *CRR*, xiii, no. 2014; *Beds. Fines*, 232. The activities of Falkes's officials in Oxfordshire are discussed in Carpenter, 'Sheriffs of Oxfordshire', 165–98.

[57] *Ann. Mon.*, i, 64.

castle or a custody of equivalent value when he returned from the seneschalship of Poitou.[58] It is not surprising, therefore, that men were highly reluctant to surrender such custodies. In 1219, moreover, they could claim that their tenure had still many years to run. Many of the castellans and sheriffs, appointed as they had been by King John, believed that they had a duty to retain their custodies until the king came of age. The evidence for this, although sometimes disputed, is overwhelming.[59] In 1225 it was specifically stated that Peter de Maulay had taken an oath to King John not to surrender the castles in his care 'until the king was of legitimate age'. The earl of Chester may well have taken a similar oath; at any rate, before setting out on his crusade in 1218, he made his bailiffs swear that they would 'keep his castles safe for the king's use until he comes of age'.[60] In 1220 the pope wrote bitterly of those who detained the king's castles and other possessions, 'putting forward the frivolous excuse that they wish to keep these safe until the king comes of full age'.[61]

In April 1219 the king was eleven and a half. There was no more vital question than when he would attain his majority, for that was the moment when the tenure of offices and custodies would come up for cancellation or renewal. In 1219, however, there were reasons for thinking that the moment might still be far distant. There were no precedents for a royal minority in England to settle the matter and much would depend on the decision of the king's overlord, the pope. Canon law, on the subject of children, as systematized and clarified by the decretalists, was heavily influenced by Roman law. Here the age of majority was not attained until twenty–five but an important change of status took place earlier at the age of puberty, which was fixed at fourteen years. Henry III would be fourteen in October 1221. Concessions made early in his reign until the conclusion of his fourteenth year suggested that he might then come of age, as, for example, Frederick II had done in the kingdom of Sicily, which was also a papal fief.[62] On the other hand, the determining factor in Sicily was probably local feudal law and in England barons attained their majority when they were twenty-one, a point stated specifically in a new passage inserted into clause 3 of Magna Carta in 1216. The general consensus of opinion was that this rule should also apply to the king.

[58] *Chron. Maj.*, 4; *RLC*, 403–403b; *PR*, 306.

[59] For discussion, see Turner, 'The minority of Henry III (part i)', 270–6; Norgate, *Minority*, 280–6.

[60] *Walt. Cov.*, 260; E 368/1, m. 1d; for Chester's appointment by King John, see *RLP*, 164, 176b, 175b, 193b.

[61] *RL*, 535.

[62] Metz, 'L'enfant dans le droit canonique medieval', 11–23; Van Cleve, *Frederick II*, 57. The last concession made by Henry III with fourteen as its *terminus ad quem* was in September 1219: *RLC*, 400b.

Thus, although Henry assumed full regal powers in January 1227, when he was aged nineteen years and three months, he later complained that this had occurred 'before he was of full age'. The view was shared by Henry's subjects. The abbot of Dore renewed charters granted after January 1227 on the grounds that they had been conceded 'while the king was of minor age'; the bishop of Bath did likewise on the grounds that his charters had been granted 'before the completion of the [king's] twenty-first year'.[63]

If, therefore, the king was indeed to come of age when he was twenty-one, that gave many of the governors a life in their custodies down to October 1228. Their tenure had thus more than nine years to run at the time of the regent's resignation. Some custodians, moreover, believed that their positions should rightfully last much longer than that, for there was often some vestige of hereditary claim behind the tenure of manors, castles and sheriffdoms. That was true of the regent's own tenure of the castle and manor of Marlborough, in which indeed his son succeeded him on his death in 1219.[64] The earl of Winchester, likewise, nourished a hereditary claim to Chesterton, which he had held briefly from King Richard in the 1190s. In 1217 he was merely granted the farm which Barnwell priory owed the king for the manor. Nonetheless, he took physical possession of the property and then granted the priory a considerable slice of land from it, a grant confirmed by his son.[65]

The earl of Derby treated the old Peverel castles and honours of Bolsover and the Peak in exactly the same way. Officially he held these only until the king was fourteen, but he behaved, as Dr Golob has shown, as though the Peverel inheritance was already his in hereditary right. In Bolsover and the Peak, he both made grants *de novo* and confirmed those made by his ancestor, William Peverel. As far as he was concerned, Bolsover was 'my castle' where the canons of Darley were supposed to celebrate mass 'to me and my heirs according to ancient custom'. In the forest of the Peak, according to a jury verdict in 1251, Derby (between 1217 and 1222) took for himself more than 2,000 deer and over 10,000 oak trees worth £567 15s.[66]

The sheriffdoms and county castles were equally threatened by hereditary claims. The Angevins had always recognized that the occasional acceptance of a hereditary sheriffdom might serve a useful purpose but in general they had resisted such concessions.[67] John had

---

[63] *Chron. Maj.*, vi, 69; C 60/28, m. 13d; C 60/32, m. 9.

[64] See above pp. 29–30.

[65] *Pipe Roll 1194*, 76; *RLC*, 342b; *Bernewelle*, 75; E 159/4, m. 8.

[66] Golob, 'The Ferrers earls of Derby', 213–19; *CRR*, xvi, no. 1704.

[67] For John's acceptance of Robert de Vieuxpont's claim to Westmorland, see Holt, *Northerners*, 221, 226.

bought out the Bohun title to Gloucester castle and the sheriffdom of Herefordshire. He had also resisted the claims of Walter de Beauchamp to Worcestershire, of the earl of Salisbury (in right of his wife) to Salisbury castle and Wiltshire, and of Henry fitz Count to Cornwall.[68] The conditions of the war and the minority revived the aspirations of all three men. In August 1215 John, angling for support, had made Walter de Beauchamp sheriff of Worcester but only during royal pleasure. Walter did better than this in March 1217, following his return to the faith of the young king, when he was conceded the sheriffdom until completion of the king's fourteenth year. In fact, Walter remained in office, with one short break, until his death in 1235 and was succeeded by his son.[69] Salisbury, likewise, recovered Salisbury castle and the sheriffdom of Wiltshire on his return to the king's faith in 1217 and held them until his death, after which the claim to a hereditary title was pursued by his son. Salisbury, as has been seen, was also sheriff of Lincolnshire and engaged in a long struggle to profit from his daughter-in-law's claim to hold in hereditary right the constableship of Lincoln castle.[70] Henry fitz Count was conceded the county of Cornwall in 1217 'as his father Reginald earl of Cornwall held it so that he shall not be disseised save by consideration and judgement of our court'. In rendering no accounts for the county, Henry, who styled himself earl of Cornwall in his charters without any sanction from the king, was only following his father's example.[71] The earl of Chester, meanwhile, had claims of his own to Lincoln castle and to the castle and county of Stafford. The earl's hopes of turning these into reality were doubtless encouraged by John's grant to him, during the war, of the castle and manor of Newcastle-under-Lyme in hereditary right.[72]

The parallels between the minority of Henry III and the anarchy of Stephen's reign should not be overstressed. The legal measures of Henry II's reign meant that the English monarchy in 1217 had far more to offer than in 1154 and for that reason was more soundly based. Hence the supreme importance of the revival of the bench and the eyres in 1217–18. Nonetheless, the parallels were marked. In Stephen's reign central authority had foundered as power passed from the king to the

---

[68] *RCh*, 53; *BNB*, no. 1235.

[69] *Beauchamp Cartulary*, xlviii–xlix, xxii; *RLP*, 153b; Madox, *Exchequer*, ii, 150n, although see *PR*, 37–8, 40, which may indicate some disagreement over the terms of Walter's tenure.

[70] *BNB*, no. 1235; *Peerage*, xi, 382–3; Hill, *Medieval Lincoln*, 87–9; see above p. 66.

[71] *PR*, 30; *Lists of Sheriffs*, 21; *Peerage*, iii, 429; Painter, *English Feudal Barony*, 110, 112.

[72] *RCh*, 216b; *F*, 16. In all these cases, of course, tenure of public office both supported and was supported by extensive private interests in the counties concerned. For the earl of Salisbury's fees in Wiltshire and those that his son would inherit in Lincolnshire, see *BF*, 719–22, 1072–3.

great magnates. The latter ruled, or attempted to rule, the localities through their possession both of private and royal castles, through their tenure of earldoms and through sheriffdoms held in hereditary right. Sheriffs were eager to limit the amount of revenue which they paid into the exchequer and exclude the justices in eyre from their counties.[73] The eyres indeed virtually ceased. The exchequer withered and royal revenue collapsed. The total for receipts and expenditure in the pipe roll of 1130 was around £24,000. In the first two years of Henry II's reign it averaged just over £10,000.[74] On Henry II's accession, as Professor Warren has commented, 'it was more than likely that the realm of England would, as Germany did after a civil war, disintegrate into principalities.'[75] The same possibility was present in 1219.

This does not mean that those holding local office in 1219 were opposed to the recovery of centralized kingship. They were *curiales*. They could appreciate that there would be benefits from a strong and wealthy king. They had joined together in 1218 to safeguard the king's rights and prevent permanent alienations until he came of age. For the old Marshal perhaps that seemed enough; let the king sort matters out in due time. Yet within the career of every *curialis* there was a paradox: each wished to escape himself the burdens which, in the king's name, he was imposing on everyone else. If one day there was to be a resumption of the king's demesnes, sheriffdoms and castles, every individual hoped that *his* faithful service might exempt *him* from it. The earl of Derby might have promised to surrender the Peverel inheritance once the king was fourteen but the emphasis was very much on 'if' the king wanted him to do so. If the young king lacked ability or resolution, if the political situation that he faced was unstable, then the day that he came of age might easily be the day when widespread permanent alienations would begin.

The young king's position when he attained his majority would certainly be alleviated if the regent's successors could carry through a resumption themselves, as the papacy was urging. Such a course would equally bring immediate relief to the finances of the minority government. But did that government have the authority, let alone the will, to pursue such a policy? Its situation contrasted sharply with that of Henry II. The latter was a young ambitious king. No one doubted his right to resume his castles and demesnes. In 1219, by contrast, the right of central government to remove sheriffs and castellans before the king

[73] Davis, *King Stephen*, 32–3, 129–45; Cronne, *The Reign of Stephen*, 226–9; *Regesta*, iii, nos 68, 273–6. But for a different perspective, see King, 'King Stephen and the Anglo-Norman aristocracy', 180–94; Prestwich, 'The treason of Geoffrey de Mandeville', 303–10.

[74] Green, 'The earliest surviving pipe roll', 16; Ramsay, *Revenues*, i, 66–9.

[75] Warren, *Henry II*, 362.

came of age was very much open to challenge. At the same time, the Dunstable annalist, reflecting doubtless a widespread view, thought that only the 'reasonable' orders of the king should be obeyed; and some magnates believed that the only legitimate decisions were those authorized by great councils. This view was to be stated explicitly by the earl of Salisbury and Robert de Vieuxpont in 1220.

If the long-term threat to the monarchy was that of the permanent passage of power in parts of England to great sheriffs and castellans, there were also far more immediate dangers. The first was simply that the country would collapse into anarchy, with central authority impotent in the face of disobedient sheriffs and castellans, unlicensed tournaments, escalating private wars and magnates, knights and gentry usurping the rights of the king. As will be seen, in 1219 and 1220 such anarchy seemed very close. The other danger was that in attempting to pursue the policy of resumption the government would provoke civil war. A resumption would disturb a host of vested interests; if it was mishandled, if it was carried through on a party basis, armed conflict might well be the result. Here too the danger nearly materialized. There were three castle sieges between 1220 and 1224, while at the end of 1223 the country hovered on the brink of civil war.

Two related questions, therefore, had to be answered by the regent's successors. Would they emulate his success in conciliating former rebels and bridging the fissures of the war? Would they also reverse his failure and carry through the programme of resumption which the papacy was demanding? Before either question could be addressed, however, there was another problem to be solved. The regent's resignation had added a void at the centre to the weakness of royal authority in the provinces. Entrusting the king to Pandulf had simply postponed the issue of who was to be in day-to-day charge of the administration. The first decision to be made in 1219, therefore, was the form that the new government itself should take.

Chapter 4

THE TRIUMVIRATE, 1219–20: THE VERGE OF ANARCHY

i. *The establishment of the triumvirate, April–June 1219*

By the middle of June 1219 a new structure of government had emerged to replace the regency. The justiciar, the bishop of Winchester and the legate took control at the centre, a triumvirate which, with changes in the balance of power within it, remained in being until 1221. There are two notable features about the creation of the triumvirate. The first is that it was not put together by a few ministers in a chamber, the medieval equivalent of the smoke-filled rooms, but was fashioned (as the regent saw it must be) out in the open by great councils at Reading, Oxford and Gloucester. Here again, therefore, great councils exercised a decisive role in appointing the king's chief ministers. The second feature is the way that the triumvirate nearly foundered at birth through disagreements between Pandulf and his colleagues. Although these were never repeated in so acute a form, they reflected a central fact about the new government: its structure did not facilitate quick and clear decisions. Even over minor matters, which John would have settled in a moment, the ministers had laboriously to co-operate; misunderstandings were inevitable. Since, moreover, the three ministers were often separated geographically, they had to keep in touch by letter. It is this correspondence, together with other letters addressed to the justiciar, that gives the politics of this period its unique illumination.

Pandulf had received the king from the young Marshal 'in the presence of all', presumably at Reading, and it was presumably the great council assembled there which confirmed his position. As the king later remarked, Pandulf was made 'first counsellor and chief of all the kingdom of England . . . by common consent and provision of all the kingdom'. No decision was taken, however, about the day-to-day running of the government. Instead, another great council was summoned to Oxford on 17 April to consider the matter.[1] Meanwhile, royal letters were attested by the bishop of Winchester, who pushed on with the task of bringing Philip of Oldcoates to heel. The latter,

[1] *Maréchal*, lines 18091–102; *Chron. Maj.*, vi, 64, where, by a slip, Guala's name is given rather than Pandulf's; *RLC*, 405b; E 159/2, m. 1.

complaining that he could not come south because of 'ambushes laid by certain people who plot harm against [me]', had spurned the ordinary safe-conduct offered him in March. Now the bishop of Durham and the archbishop of York were ordered to conduct him to the king, Pandulf and the council.[2]

At the Oxford council a decision was reached about the organization of central government: the justiciar was given charge of the attestation of royal letters, thus replacing the bishop of Winchester. The bishop remained, however, at the justiciar's elbow. Between 18 April and the end of the month he only attested four letters, as opposed to thirty-five attested by Hubert, but, while the two ministers authorized no letters alone, they authorized seventeen together.[3]

The Oxford council, therefore, seemed to have settled the future structure of government, with the justiciar taking responsibility for the attestation of royal letters. That the new regime would pursue much the same line as the old in the sensitive area of the forest was shown by the acceptance, on 22 April, of a fine of £100 from the men of Somerset and Dorset for deforestation according to the terms of the Charter of the Forest, only for this to be qualified by the stipulation (for which both Hubert and Peter took responsibility) that the results of the ensuing perambulation were first to be sent to the council 'so that then it may be decided . . . what seems to be expedient'.[4] Perhaps the council envisaged here was a small gathering of ministers but other contentious issues continued to be dealt with by great councils. At Oxford itself, 'before the king's council and the magnates', consideration was given to the case, adjourned from the Yorkshire eyre, in which Maurice de Gant was seeking recovery of the manors of Leeds and Bingley which the earl of Chester had entered in 1218 under their ransom agreement. It was decided to uphold the previous verdict in Chester's favour, given by the great council of May 1218, although Maurice, who had been proceeding via an assize of novel disseisin, was told sympathetically 'that if he wished to implead [Chester] concerning right, it is certainly (bene) permissible for him to do so'.[5]

After the Oxford council broke up around 22 April, Pandulf set out westwards. By 30 April he was at Cirencester, where he fell ill and remained until at least 14 May. Hubert and Peter, meanwhile, with the seal, headed back to Westminster, which they reached on 27 April.[6]

---

[2] PR, 190; see above p. 104.

[3] PR, 191–3; RLC, 390–1b, 406; C 60/11, m. 6.

[4] C 60/11, m. 6; PR, 190–1.

[5] Yorks. Eyre, nos 315, 1133, and see above p. 82. Lady Stenton (ibid., pp. xxxiv, 415) is wrong in stating that these proceedings took place at Westminster.

[6] However, it was at this point that judgement was given in another case adjourned from the Yorkshire eyre, the former rebel Robert de Percy failing to recover Osmotherley from the bishop of Durham: Yorks. Eyre, no. 1125, p. xxii.

They were immediately faced with a demonstration of how insignificant their sole authority was considered to be compared with that of great councils. The proffered ecclesiastical conduct had brought Philip of Oldcoates as far south as Nottingham. He had then returned to the north, declaring that 'the day decided for holding the next council was [10 June] and that it was irksome to him to have to go to court at present, and then wait for that day, since he did not believe he would find [the king's] council gathered together [before then]'. However, he added that if he received a safe-conduct he would undoubtedly come to the June council. Clearly, for Oldcoates, 'the council' was a gathering of some size and indeed the decisions of the assembly that he eventually attended were described as taken 'by common counsel'. Only such a body, in Oldcoates's view, had the authority to deal with his affairs. Hubert and Peter took him at his word and on 27 April issued the required letters of conduct to the council which was to be held at Reading. At the same time they left Oldcoates in no doubts as to what was expected once he got there. He was to obey the king's orders relating to Mitford castle and render account for the lands, illicitly in his hands, of Roger Bertram and Eustace de Vesci. Meanwhile, he was immediately to surrender these lands for delivery to Bertram and the earl of Salisbury.[7]

The new government seemed, therefore, firmly in the saddle and moving forward with despatch. Yet the arrangements made at Oxford were about to collapse. The origin of the crisis which engulfed the government may be found in a writ, authorized by Peter and Hubert on 23 April, which instructed the sheriff of Yorkshire, 'as he loves himself', to hand the issues of the county to 'no-one in the world by any letter, order or instruction, save to the king at the exchequer, through the hands of the barons of the exchequer'. This was almost certainly a measure to prevent Pandulf drawing directly on the king's revenues for his own and papal purposes.[8] His reaction was immediate: he restricted the justiciar's ability to control the seal and placed a block on the disbursement of the king's revenues. In seven urgent letters, written between 30 April and 26 May, two under all the panoply of his legatine authority, Pandulf ordered the vice-chancellor and keeper of the seal, Ralph de Neville, to deposit the king's revenues at the New Temple, to distribute nothing from them without 'our special mandate and

---

[7] *RL*, no. xxi (a letter from the archbishop of York which reported to the king Oldcoates's statement): *PR*, 191–2. For the council Oldcoates attended, see below n. 12 and pp. 146–8.

[8] C 60/11, m. 6. In October the revenues from Yorkshire were assigned to pay debts to the pope, although nothing seems to have come of the arrangement: C 60/11, m. 2.

licence', and not to depart from the exchequer with the seal 'on the order of anybody'.[9]

The repercussions of this *démarche* on Hubert's authority are plain. Between 6 and 18 May he ceased to attest royal letters, the task being taken over at Westminster by the treasurer, Eustace de Faukenburg, and the bishop of Coventry, who was a baron of the exchequer.[10] On 15 May Hubert, who was then near Windsor, received messengers from Pandulf. They told him of their master's desire for a meeting and of his wish 'to work in all things through [Hubert's] counsel for the honour of God and the benefit of the king'. Hubert's response to this attempt at conciliation was lukewarm. As he informed Neville and Faukenburg in a letter, 'we told [Pandulf] . . . that if he wished to agree with your counsel, we would diligently agree with his for the honour of God and the benefit of the king and kingdom'. Meanwhile, Hubert announced that he was setting out for London, although the legate's envoys had said that their lord would come to the Windsor area to speak with him.[11]

The crisis at the heart of the government was resolved at the great council which had been planned for the second week of June, although in the event, perhaps for the convenience of Pandulf, it met at Gloucester rather than at Reading.[12] Pandulf communicated the results of the settlement to Ralph de Neville, who had remained in London with the seal, in a letter of 11 June. In respect of the seal, he was 'to do what the bishop of Winchester enjoins you by word of mouth, and with the justiciar you are to be obedient to those things and to him [the justiciar?] as the bishop enjoins you on our behalf'.[13]

The effect of Pandulf's injunction was to place Hubert once more in charge of the seal. He resumed as the normal attestor of royal letters and the seal henceforth usually followed his movements about the country; from now onwards the chief responsibility for day-to-day government was his. Hubert's control was not limited to the chancery,

9 *RL*, nos xciii, xciv, xcviii, c–ciii; for the dating of these letters, see Powicke, 'The chancery during the minority', 229–31. I suspect that a mistake was made in the dating clause of *RL* no. xxii: compare no. ci and see Powicke, *ibid.*, 230 n. 80. Pandulf's intervention is discussed in Cazel, 'The legates Guala and Pandulf', 19–20.

10 *RLC*, 391b; *PR*, 194; *ERF*, 31; C 60/11, m. 6.

11 *RL*, no. xcvii.

12 *RL*, no. xxi; *PR*, 191–2; *RLC*, 393. Hubert warranted the earl of Gloucester's absence from the exchequer as he was at Gloucester *per preceptum regis . . . coram legato nobis et aliis magnatibus de consilio regis in octabis Trinitatis*: E 159/2, m. 2; see also *Lincs. Worcs. Eyre*, no. 712.

13 *Presencium tibi auctoritate mandamus quatinus de sigillo domini regis illud facias quod tibi viva voce dominus episcopus Wintoniensis iniunget, et cum justiciario eas et eidem servias, secundum quod idem episcopus tibi iniunget ex parte nostra*: SC 1/6, no. 37.

however. Taking a close interest in financial matters, he sat, and probably presided, from the Michaelmas term of 1219 onwards, at the exchequer. He was equally head of the judicial administration of the country. He presided over some sessions of the bench in every year between 1219 and 1223.[14] If he is not recorded as ever present in the manner of his predecessors, that may reflect less a change in status or activity than a decision to record the justiciar's real rather than his fictional presence. Hubert's control over the judicial system was equally clear in the letters asking him to postpone or hasten the hearing of law cases. In other matters, by contrast, in the months after June 1219, men wrote to Hubert and Peter jointly.

Peter had been demoted but he retained an important role. He was still the guardian of the king, a position which might easily metamorphose one day into that of chief minister. He continued to be active in government. He sat at the exchequer and, although the number of royal letters he now attested was tiny compared to Hubert, he stood in whenever the latter was separated from the seal. Sometimes, when Hubert was available, Peter would be responsible for a run of royal letters, often when one at least was concerned with the affairs of the royal household.[15] In the months immediately after June 1219, moreover, the two men worked closely together. It was Peter who conveyed to Neville, on Pandulf's behalf, the instructions about the seal and, thereafter, between July and October 1219 inclusive, by far the largest number of authorized letters were authorized by them jointly. Also in this period they both wrote letters in their joint names and received letters addressed to them jointly.[16]

Above Peter and Hubert remained the legate. Until his resignation in 1221 there seems little doubt that his claim to be in ultimate control of king and kingdom was accepted. Pandulf had, after all, demon-strated his authority in the crisis of May 1219: his orders had been accepted by Neville and his letter had given the instructions about the new arrangements for keeping the seal. Pandulf's authority differed from Guala's in that it depended, in part, on the Marshal's death-bed committal of the king to his care and its confirmation by a great council. But it also derived, like Guala's, from the legatine authority given him by the pope, which was clearly intended to be as embracing in secular as it was in ecclesiastical affairs. In the letters announcing his appointment in September 1218, the pope conferred on him full power

---

[14] Hubert presided over some sessions in the Trinity and Michaelmas terms of 1219, the Easter term of 1220, the Michaelmas term of 1221 (though here only for one case), the Hilary term of 1222 and the Easter term of 1223: Meekings, 'Concords'.

[15] For example, RLC, 401–401b; PR, 204–5.

[16] I suspect that RL, no. viii, belongs to this period.

(*plenariam potestatem*) and ordered ecclesiastics and laymen to carry out his instructions.[17]

In discharging his authority Pandulf had certain advantages. A papal chamberlain, the only title used in his letters apart from legate, he was close to Pope Honorius, the two men having enjoyed similar careers at the curia. 'In his wisdom and faith we have unshakeable confidence' wrote the pope in his letter of appointment. Honorius's letter also referred to Pandulf's love of England and certainly he knew the country well, having spent much of 1215 there as a papal envoy, following previous missions in 1211 and 1213. He was also bishop-elect of Norwich.[18] Pandulf, moreover, like Guala, had the personality to go with his post. Stories abounded of how he had stood up to John's threats of physical violence during a stormy interview in 1211.[19] His letters show him confident and determined but also diplomatic. This was just as well, because his position in England was difficult. In 1215 Pandulf had pronounced Stephen Langton's suspension. Now, as legate, his authority over the church was bound to reflect on Langton's as archbishop. Honorius, indeed, had carefully exempted Pandulf, until he was consecrated as bishop of Norwich, from his obedience to Langton as his metropolitan.[20] The clergy, more generally, resented the cost of Pandulf's legation and the taxation for the crusade which he imposed. The precentor and treasurer of Lichfield complained of both and several of the canons refused to contribute to Pandulf's entertainment when he stayed there briefly in July 1219. The proceeds of the taxation, however, gave Pandulf one final point of strength. They meant that he was not merely the overall director of the king's government but also, through a series of loans, its paymaster.[21]

Until 1221, therefore, when Bishop Peter ceased to be the king's guardian and Pandulf resigned his legateship, the government of England was something of a triumvirate, although, as will be seen, Hubert rapidly strengthened his position within it at Peter's expense. Of course, other ministers were also important at the centre, most notably Ralph de Neville as keeper of the seal, William Brewer as a baron of the exchequer and Martin of Pattishall as the senior professional justice. In June 1219, for example, Peter and Hubert sent

[17] VL, Honorius III Regesta X, f. 13; *Ann. Eccles.*, 405 (*CPReg.*, 58). However, for the possibility that a great council gave some sanction to Guala's position, see *Walt. Cov.*, 233.

[18] *Ann. Eccles.*, 405 (*CPReg.*, 58); Sayers, *Honorius III*, 173–5.

[19] *Ann. Mon.*, i, 209–17; ii, 268–71; for discussion of the episode, see Holt, *Magna Carta and Medieval Kingship*, 6–8; Mason, 'St Wulfstan's staff', 159–60.

[20] *Chron. Maj.*, ii, 629–30; *RL*, 533; Powicke, *Langton*, 132, 145–6; Sayers, *Honorius III*, 174–5.

[21] SC 1/6, no. 20.

their advice to Neville about the framing of a judicial writ but told him to do what he thought 'most just and best', having taken the counsel of Martin of Pattishall.[22]

The essential feature of a government thus structured was its difficulty in reaching rapid and decisive decisions. At the centre, power was in the hands of several individuals, individuals, moreover, who were often in different parts of the county. Pandulf met with Hubert, Peter and the other members of the government at great councils and at these times he occasionally authorized important royal letters. But he also spent a good deal of time away from the seal, partly, at least so William Brewer thought, because he disliked the *taedium* and expense of London where Hubert and the seal often resided.[23] In these periods of separation he occasionally wrote directly to Ralph de Neville[24] and to other royal agents, but in general he seems to have worked through Hubert, or Hubert and Peter, issuing his instructions and advice in a steady flow of letters. Although there was no repetition of the crisis at the time of the triumvirate's birth, Pandulf's instructions were not always obeyed. Indeed, it is clear that decisions emerged as the result of a continuous process of discussion between the chief members of the government, a discussion which ranged from minor matters of patronage to major issues of state.[25] In respect of the latter, of course, the chief ministers could not act alone. Pandulf himself was very aware of the accusation that he acted autocratically. He was anxious to demonstrate his willingness to take advice and was wise to do so. The government of the triumvirate, just like that of the regent, had to secure support for its actions at great councils. It could only govern with consent.

ii. *The triumvirate: attitudes and ambitions*

The questions awaiting resolution by the new government were, as has been seen, related. Would it continue the process of settlement after the war with the regent's success? Would it equally have more success than the regent in rebuilding the king's authority and resources? The triumvirate's approach to these problems was shaped by the circumstances of its creation. That creation had been by great councils, whose chief decision had been to elevate Hubert over Bishop Peter's head, to put him, in effect, in Peter's place as the man in immediate charge of

[22] SC 1/6, no. 26. For discussion of writs with which Pattishall was associated in the minority, see *Registers of Writs*, lxxix–xxx.

[23] *RL*, no. lxix.

[24] SC 1/6, no. 38; *RLC*, 396b, for the ensuing writ authorized by Hubert and Peter.

[25] This aspect of Pandulf's legation is stressed by Cazel, 'The legates Guala and Pandulf', 19–21.

the administration. The reason for the decision is clear. The magnates trusted Hubert to provide a form of amenable, moderate government; they did not trust Peter to do so. In large measure Hubert fulfilled these expectations. That, ultimately, was the reason why he and his allies were able, within the limits set by the Charters, to reassert the authority of the king's government.

In 1219 Hubert doubtless argued that he was merely entering his own but in fact there was nothing automatic about his promotion. It was true that previous justiciars had presided over the exchequer and the bench, and supervised the general running of the administration.[1] Not unnaturally, therefore, the Marshal, in the days immediately after his appointment, thought of styling himself justiciar.[2] But whatever Hubert's claims *ex officio*, they had helped him not a bit during the Marshal's regency. During that time he had played little part at the exchequer and had never attested a royal letter. He had begun to authorize letters only from January 1219 and then always in company with the bishop of Winchester, to whom he was clearly the junior partner. Not for nothing did the Waverley annalist date Hubert's appointment as justiciar to 1219.[3] In 1219, however, there was another alternative to Hubert's elevation: to retain him in his subordinate role and to appoint someone else to take the regent's place. One obvious candidate, the earl of Chester, was away on crusade. There was, of course, another, namely Bishop Peter, and Peter was very ready to stake his claim, if his violent reaction to the regent placing the king in Pandulf's custody is any guide. Peter, unlike Hubert, had been prominent at the exchequer during the regent's time and had taken an increasingly major role in both attesting and authorizing royal letters. It was he who had, in effect, replaced the regent during his illness and in the days between the latter's resignation and the Oxford council. To understand why the great councils of April and June 1219 preferred Hubert to Peter it is necessary to look more closely at the background and careers of the two men.

Hubert de Burgh was a Norfolk man, from Burgh next Aylesham, not far from Norwich, where he built an elegant chancel to the parish church.[4] The St Albans' chroniclers with loose geography and abusive intent, stated that Peter des Roches was a Poitevin, and this has been accepted by later historians;[5] but in fact, as Nicholas Vincent has

[1] *Dialogus de Scaccario*, 15; West, *Justiciarship, passim*.

[2] See also Falkes's comment on Hubert's position after 1219: *Walt. Cov.*, 259.

[3] *Ann. Mon.*, ii, 291.

[4] Johnston, 'Lands of Hubert de Burgh', 418–32; Ellis, *Hubert de Burgh*, 189–90. Ellis's work is a competent biography based on printed primary sources. See also Cazel, 'Religious motivation in the biography of Hubert de Burgh', 109–19.

[5] *Flores Hist.*, ii, 129; *Chron. Maj.*, 220, 240. It was abusive intent because the Poitevins were traditionally notorious for their treachery.

recently shown, his homeland was further north, in the Touraine. Both Hubert and Peter, as far as the evidence goes, had begun their careers in the 1190s: Hubert in John's household, Peter in King Richard's. Both in the early 1200s had been in John's chamber, possibly as rivals.[6] In 1205, while Hubert vainly held out in Chinon against the army of King Philip, John made Peter bishop of Winchester. Both men could claim heroic records during the 1215–17 civil war: the one at the battle of Lincoln, the other at Dover and then in the sea-fight off Sandwich. Both in 1219 were probably aged between forty and fifty. Yet, if their careers had in some ways run parallel, in terms of background, experience and outlook the two ministers were very different.

A pivotal moment in highlighting and accentuating the differences came in 1215 when King John replaced Peter as justiciar with Hubert. The fact that this took place at Runnymede in the presence of Stephen Langton, archbishop of Canterbury, and other magnates shows that it was an act of conciliation.[7] Hubert, it would seem, was far more acceptable as justiciar than Peter. The same feeling clearly prevailed, again in the presence of Langton and the magnates, four years later. It is not difficult to see why. Peter des Roches was 'as hard as rock', the monks of Winchester complained after his death, making an obvious but apposite pun upon his name.[8] Peter's military expertise and loyalty to King John made him an exceptional churchman. He had been the only bishop to remain with the king during the interdict and he had suspended Langton from office in 1215. His relations with the archbishop cannot have been easy. Nor was the archbishop alone in taking a jaundiced view of Bishop Peter, for the latter, sitting at the exchequer, had been at the heart of the unpopular process of John's money-getting, as the anonymous satire ran:

> 'The warrior of Winchester, up at the Exchequer,
> Sharp at accounting, slack at Scripture,
> Revolving the royal roll . . .'[9]

During his time as justiciar between 1213 and 1215 Peter had fired off arrogant letters to great magnates and implemented some of John's most controversial measures: the imposition of the Poitevin scutage, for example, and the exaction of the huge fine on Geoffrey de Mandeville for the hand of the countess of Gloucester.[10] The Waverley annalist,

---

[6] Weiss, 'The early career of Hubert de Burgh', 237 and n. 13.
[7] *Chron. Maj.*, vi, 65; ii, 489, 629–30.
[8] *Ann. Mon.*, i, 110.
[9] *Political Songs*, 10–11. The translation is that of Dr Clanchy, *England and its Rulers*, 183.
[10] Holt, *King John*, 9–10. For a study of Peter as justiciar, see West, *Justiciarship*, 179–211.

writing almost certainly in 1219 itself, believed that Peter had been made justiciar 'so that little by little he might subject the powerful men of the land to the will of the king'. The fury aroused by his conduct, the chronicler added, 'is not sedated even now'.[11] That might well be taken as the verdict passed on Peter's career at the Oxford and Gloucester councils in 1219.

The probability is that Peter did little to distance himself from the taint of John's aggressive kingship. The opportunities to act in that spirit during the minority were limited but Peter made the best of them. Thus in November 1218, together with William Brewer, he imposed highly extortionate terms on some Lincolnshire gentry who owed debts to the Jews.[12] It would be interesting to know what Peter said after the war about the Charters. As bishop of Winchester, he was certainly prepared to benefit from the Charter of the Forest. It was in accordance with the latter's terms that William Brewer, as a forest official in Hampshire, made concessions to the bishop in 1218. Likewise, as a minister, Peter accepted proffers (with Hubert) for deforestations under the Charter's terms.[13] Later, however, in 1232, having at last ousted Hubert from office, Peter scoffed at the fundamental clause in the Great Charter which laid down that no free man was to be deprived of his property, exiled, outlawed or otherwise proceeded against save by judgement of his peers or by the law of the land. There were, he declared, no peers in England as there were in France, referring here, Powicke suggests, 'with deliberate perversity' to the 'small privileged group known as the peers in France'. It was permissible for the king, Peter continued, to have anyone in the kingdom exiled and condemned by the judgement of such judges as 'he wished to appoint'.[14] Nor did Peter confine himself to words. During his brief government between 1232 and 1234 he encouraged the king in a series of disseisins *per voluntatem regis* and justified them in the light of the 'plenitude of royal power'.[15] Yet no clause in the Great Chapter was more deeply ingrained in the minds of Englishmen than that which forbad such conduct. Between 1218 and 1220 the men of Lincolnshire, the abbot of St Augustine's, Bristol, and the great northern baron, Richard de Umfraville, all complained of its breach. The importance of kings

[11] *Ann. Mon.*, ii, 281, xxxi.

[12] *PR*, 179–80; Holt, *Magna Carta*, 276–7.

[13] Winchester Cathedral MS Alchin Scrapbook I, nos 2, 3 (a reference I have from Mr Vincent); *Winchester Chartulary*, no. 329. Brewer held the forestership of Bere in Hampshire by hereditary right: Turner, *Men Raised from the Dust*, 71.

[14] *Chron. Maj.*, 252; Powicke, *Henry III*, 76; for further discussion, see Clanchy, *England and its Rulers*, 220–1.

[15] *BNB*, no. 857; *CRR*, xv, nos 131, 1026, 1047, 1308, 1426–7, 1475, 1895; *CR 1231–34*, 401; *CChR*, 114; *RL*, no. ccc/xxxix.

proceeding by judgement was also fundamental to Archbishop Langton's thinking.[16] If Peter gave any hint of these views after the war, his
rejection in 1219 becomes all the more understandable.

Hubert's reputation and outlook were very different. If Peter was the
Touraingeau in England, Hubert had been the Englishman in the
Touraine and Poitou. He had spent much of John's reign overseas and
only returned to England, after a three-year absence culminating as
seneschal of Poitou, just before Magna Carta. He had, therefore, no
opportunity to become associated with John's unpopular policies.[17] He
may also have positively disassociated himself from some aspects of
John's conduct.

In later life Hubert conversed lengthily with the St Albans'
chronicler, Matthew Paris. He highlighted the heroic and dramatic
episodes in his career: the scene outside the postern gate of Dover castle
in 1217 when he spurned Louis's overtures and the moment before the
battle of Sandwich when he enjoined his followers, if he was captured,
to allow his execution rather than to surrender the castle 'for it is the key
to England'.[18] Hubert may well have spoken much earlier to another
chronicler, Abbot Ralph of Coggeshall. At any rate, Coggeshall
preserves two stories of Hubert's early career. One is in the heroic
mould familiar from Paris. When the fall of Chinon, which he had
defended bravely for a year, became inevitable in 1205, he had sallied
out with his troops to do battle and was only captured when seriously
wounded. The other story concerned the fate of Arthur, John's nephew
and rival, who had been in Hubert's custody at Falaise in 1202. Hubert
had refused (a scene famous from Shakespeare's play) to implement
John's order for Arthur's blinding and castration, believing that it
stemmed more from the king's 'sudden fury than from the rule of equity
and justice'. Thus Hubert distanced himself in the clearest possible
way from Arthur's murder, John's most horrendous act. He may also
have underlined the difference between himself and Bishop Peter, for,
according to one story, it was the latter's familiar, Peter de Maulay,
who had been Arthur's executioner.[19]

Hubert also had a more personal grievance against King John. In
1201 the king had given him the Three Castles in Gwent: Grosmont,
Skenfrith and Whitecastle. Four years later, while Hubert was in
captivity, John had granted them in hereditary right to William de
Braose to hold with all appurtenances 'as Hubert de Burgh held them'.

---

[16] See below p. 264.
[17] Weiss, 'The early career of Hubert de Burgh', 247–50; West, *Justiciarship*,
221.
[18] *Chron. Maj.*, 3–4, 28–9; *Hist. Angl.*, ii, 359 n. 1; Vaughan, *Matthew Paris*, 13.
[19] *Coggeshall*, 139–40, 146, 154–5. The story about Maulay was current at the end of
the century in the area of the family's northern estates: *Guisborough*, 144, xxvii–viii.

In 1218 Hubert had demanded that William's son, Reginald de Braose, return the Three Castles to him, claiming them 'as his right and for which he has a charter of King John and of which King John disseised him by his will (*per voluntatem suam*) and without judgement as he says'. Thus, at a special session of the king's court, in the presence of Archbishop Langton himself, Hubert accused John of precisely the type of conduct that Magna Carta sought to prevent when it stated that the king should deprive no free man of property save by the law of the land or by judgement of his peers: the very clause that Peter was later to ridicule.[20] The dissimilarity between the two men could hardly be more sharply drawn.

Underlying these contrasts between Peter and Hubert were important differences in their social and material positions. As bishop of Winchester Peter enjoyed a power base and an independence which Hubert in 1219, as will be seen, completely lacked. Peter was also a foreigner. One did not need to inspect a medieval *Who's Who* to discover that, for he retained a warm affection for his homeland in the Touraine. He especially asked the poet, Henry of Avranches, to write about St Martin of Tours, the 'saint of his native country' (*natalis patrie*), and he left money in his will for the foundation of a Cistercian house, a house established at Clarté Dieu, north of Tours.[21] Further south in Poitou, of which early in his career he had been treasurer, Peter maintained close connections with the great local magnates, notably Savari de Mauléone and the vicomte of Thouars.[22] He also had links with Normandy, where his son or nephew, Peter des Rivaux, had apparently been born.[23]

It is conceivable that Peter's nationality encouraged his cavalier approach to Magna Carta. It certainly influenced the composition of his friends and associates in England. A large proportion of Peter's *familia*, as Nicholas Vincent has shown, were foreigners, his clerks and officials coming from the Touraine, Poitou and above all from Normandy. In 1220 Peter promised to send home (*partes nostrae*) his knights and nephews so that they could not tourney in England.[24] Among the bishop's closest associates before and after the war were Peter de Maulay and Engelard de Cigogné, both from the Touraine.[25]

---

[20] *Rot. Lib.*, 19; *RCh*, 160b; *BNB*, no. 1330; *RLC*, 404, 386b. For another comparable grievance of Hubert against John: *CRR*, xiii, no. 59.

[21] *Henry of Avranches*, 125; information from Mr Vincent.

[22] *Rot. Norm.*, 34; *Winchester Pipe Roll 1208–9*, 2, 39, 68, 70.

[23] This, as Mr Vincent will show, is indicated primarily by Peter's name, which is often rendered de Orivall in contemporary sources.

[24] *F*, 162–3.

[25] *Melsa*, i, 105–6; *Gloucester Pleas*, xiii–xv; *Winchester Pipe Roll 1209–10*, 65, 68; Winchester College Muniments, 15237, 15238, a reference which I owe to Mr Vincent.

By 1219 Peter had also drawn the Poitevin William de Fors, count of Aumale, and perhaps the Norman, Falkes de Bréauté, into his circle: in 1218 Falkes and Peter de Maulay were entertained together at the bishop's manor of Taunton.[26] The impression that Peter was the head of a party of aliens in England was reinforced by the politics of the early 1220s. In 1219 matters were less clear-cut: Hubert was also close to Falkes. Nonetheless, Peter's foreign friends and foreign connections inspired as little confidence as did his record under John that he would treat English magnates and English customs with respect. When Ralph of Coggeshall looked back from the minority at Peter's appointment as justiciar in 1213, he averred that 'the great men of all the kingdom murmured at an alien being placed over them'.[27] They did not want the same again in 1219.

Hubert, by contrast, could not afford to treat either the Great Charter or individual magnates in a high-handed fashion. Indeed, it may be suspected that he made the most of his differences with King John precisely so as to indicate that he would not do so. The key point to grasp about Hubert's situation is its material insecurity; his fortune was still all to make. In other circumstances that insecurity might have made him a loyal and ruthless servant of the king, which, no doubt, had been the intention behind the paucity of the permanent rewards which King John had given to him, as to many other of his servants. But in 1219 it would be many years before the king would come of age. If Hubert's conduct provoked widespread opposition, he would simply not survive that long.

Hubert was a younger son of a gentry family.[28] Perhaps initially he had been educated for the church, which explains why he could read: a talent which must have helped him master the apparatus of government after 1219.[29] He probably entered John's service through his elder brother, William de Burgh, who went to Ireland with John in the 1180s and established himself in Munster.[30] Hubert's first wife, who died before the end of 1214, was a Warenne, the heiress of the junior, Wormegay, line. William de Warenne, earl of Surrey (1202–40), a neighbour in Norfolk, was very conscious that the marriage made Hubert part of the Warenne kin; he borrowed money from him and remained a political ally throughout the minority. But the marriage brought Hubert little in the way of hereditable land: since his wife had

[26] HRO, Eccles II 159274, r. 11d, 12d (under Taunton); and see below p. 166.
[27] *Coggeshall*, 168.
[28] In 1234 the manors of Burgh, Beeston, Newton (in Norfolk) and Sotherton in Suffolk were said to be of Hubert's inheritance: *CR 1231–34*, 443; Johnston, 'Lands of Hubert de Burgh', 419–20.
[29] *CR 1231–34*, 161.
[30] Otway-Ruthven, *Medieval Ireland*, 69.

a son by her previous marriage to Doun Bardolf, Hubert had only a life interest in the castle and honour of Wormegay. Hubert's second wife, the countess of Gloucester, had died in 1217, a few days after their marriage, and he had gained nothing from it.[31] John's chief gift to Hubert had been the honours of Haughley in Suffolk and Rayleigh in Essex but these were held only during the king's pleasure, and neither had a castle in being.[32] Early in 1219 the king's court gave Hubert seisin of the Three Castles but this was simply because of Reginald de Braose's default. The court had made no judgement about who had the better right.[33]

After the war Hubert exploited ransoms like anyone else, in the process extracting the manor of Banstead from William de Mowbray.[34] But, remembering his material insecurity, he could not risk giving offence to the great men of the land. His relations with the earl of Chester, moreover, were already difficult. The latter's long-standing antipathy had begun, according to Matthew Paris, when John preferred Hubert as surety for money owed the French for the truce of 1214.[35] Hubert, therefore, had to keep in, as far as possible, with all sides, wheel, deal and compromise, rather than move straight ahead. His relations with Reginald de Braose illustrate the point. Early in 1219 armed force had been necessary to implement the court's decision to give Hubert possession of the Three Castles. But Hubert did not leave it there. Probably he recognized that Reginald's claim was more soundly based than his own. At any rate, he quickly came to an agreement whereby, it would seem, he held the Three Castles from Reginald in return for minimal services.[36] On his part, Reginald must have hoped for Hubert's support in the cases that he was bringing for the recovery of Totnes and Barnstaple. He needed that support even more in the suit which was being started against him by his nephew John, son of his elder brother murdered by King John, for possession of the whole Braose inheritance. Since Hubert now held the Three Castles from Reginald, both had an interest in defending the case. That Reginald

[31] *Peerage*, vii, 140–1, 141 n.b; *RL*, nos xxxiv, xii (a letter one can almost hear Warenne dictating to the clerk). For Hubert's possessions, see Johnston, 'Lands of Hubert de Burgh', 418–32, and Ellis, *Hubert de Burgh*, 203–28. Hubert's first wife had borne him a son, which entitled Hubert to hold her inheritance for life.
[32] *RLP*, 153; *RBE*, 596; *RLC*, 316b–17; *BF*, 278, 282. Haughley and Rayleigh had escheated to the crown following the treason of Henry of Essex in 1154–5.
[33] *RLC*, 404, 386b.
[34] *The Coucher Book of Furness*, II, ii, 291; *Pipe Roll 1218*, 61. Mowbray's ransom arose from his capture at Lincoln; presumably he was then sold to Hubert.
[35] *Hist. Angl.*, iii, 231; *RLP*, 140b.
[36] This may be deduced from *CRR*, xi, nos 1894, 2418, 2788; xii, nos 59, 307; CP 25(1)/80/5, no. 59.

was not entirely disappointed in these hopes will be seen in due course.[37]

Hubert, then, was preferred as the regent's successor because he seemed to promise, as Peter did not, a form of open and moderate government acceptable to the magnates. This did not mean, however, that the triumvirate had no wider objectives. Far from it. The cardinal fact to appreciate about English politics after 1219 is that the government was committed to a very clear programme of action, a programme for the recovery of royal power. The immediate objectives were set forth in letters which Pope Honorius addressed to Pandulf in March and April 1219. Pandulf was enjoined to compel the justiciar of Ireland, Geoffrey de Marsh, to come to England to account. He was likewise to constrain Llywelyn to fulfil the promises that he had made in the treaty of Worcester. Within England, he was to ensure that the adulterine castles constructed in the war were destroyed, an objective which touched on one of Pandulf's recurrent themes: the necessity for firm action to maintain the peace of the realm.[38]

The most significant of the papal letters, however, were those which faced up to the problems analysed in the last chapter and called for the recovery of the rights of the king and the restructuring of political power in the localities of England. Pandulf was to ensure that the magnates upheld their oath (clearly that taken in November 1218) to preserve the king's honours and rights. More important, he was to 'strive to recall to the demesne of the king the castles, demesnes and possessions, and all things rightfully belonging to the king'.[39] These letters were almost certainly issued at Pandulf's request and reflect his assessment of the situation in England. They marked a new beginning. Guala's own position on the question of resumption had been prejudiced by his extraction of the advowson of Chesterton for Vercelli. Although men were well aware of the concept that the king's rights should be maintained and recovered, the practice had often run contrary to it. The programme of resumption was now set out in a clear and unequivocal manner, and was reiterated in further papal letters in May 1220 and April 1221.[40] Its achievement became the central aim of the king's government.

The papal reaction to Pandulf's suggestions is easy to explain, for the importance of maintaining and recovering rights was part of a familiar background. The rights of those under age, moreover, struck an especial chord. In the twelfth century Pope Alexander III had drawn a parallel between the protection of these under Roman law and the way

---

[37] *RLC*, 405b. See below pp. 168, 216.
[38] VL, Honorius III Regesta X, ff. 82d, 83 (*CPReg.*, 64).
[39] VL, Honorius III Regesta X, f. 88 (*CPReg.*, 65).
[40] See below pp. 189–90, 248.

that church property too should be kept from harm.[41] The popes also knew that kings were under a special obligation to maintain royal rights. In 1220 itself Pope Honorius declared that the King of Hungary was obliged by his coronation oath to resume those that had been alienated. Honorius was almost certainly aware too of the equivalent clause in the English coronation oath, introduced perhaps in 1154, by which the king swore to preserve the rights of the crown and recover those which had been lost. The concept of such an oath was grasped the more readily because it was probably modelled on an undertaking which bishops, since the early twelfth century, had given at their consecrations to preserve and recover the rights of their sees.[42] Quite apart from these general considerations, Pope Honorius had more particular reasons for being concerned with the situation in England. As he explained in numerous letters, the king was both a crusader and a ward in his custody. He, therefore, 'exists under our protection, and thus his rights cannot be usurped by anyone without injury to our rights, and thus it behoves us to attend, as if prosecuting our own cause, to the recall of those rights to his hands'.[43]

For Honorius, there were no half measures in this. One ironic consequence was that he became as concerned as any Angevin king to uphold royal rights over the church, ordering cathedral chapters 'above all things reverently to preserve the royal right and honour' and elect pastors 'faithful to the king'. As a result, there was continuing harmony over episcopal elections, with those chosen often being *curiales*: in 1221 the treasurer of the exchequer, Eustace de Faukenburg, was elected to the bishopric of London and next year the keeper of the seal, Ralph de Neville, became bishop-elect of Chichester. Pandulf was equally concerned to preserve the king's rights to the revenues of ecclesiastical vacancies. If he protected a vacant see or monastery from rapacious royal officials by securing the custody of the temporalities himself, he stressed that he held them as the king's representative. In the only case, that of the bishopric of Ely, where he retained the temporalities for any length of time, he either paid the revenue into the exchequer or spent it in the king's service.[44]

There is no reason to think that Hubert or Peter disagreed with the objectives of Pandulf and the papacy. True, Powicke believed that

[41] Cheney, 'Inalienability in mid-twelfth century England', 467. See above p. 18 and notes 24, 25.

[42] Cheney, 'Inalienability in mid-twelfth century England', 468, 470; Richardson, 'The coronation', 151–61; Kantorowicz, 'Inalienability', 490, 499.

[43] VL, Honorius III Regesta X, f. 88 (*CPReg.*, 65). The papacy at this time was confronting similar problems of a minority and the collapse of royal power in Aragon, another kingdom that was a papal fief: see Bisson, *Aragon*, 38–9, 58–9.

[44] *Historiae Anglicanae*, 1871–2; *Divers Accounts*, 46. See also 'Cerne Cartulary', 200–1.

Hubert essentially lived from day to day. In respect of the dispersal of the king's sheriffdoms and castles, 'his own tendency, probably his own inclination, was to accept it, and to take a hand in the game'.[45] Both Hubert and Peter were certainly deeply entrenched in local power, the former as castellan of Dover and sheriff of Kent and Norfolk-Suffolk, the latter as castellan of Winchester and sheriff of Hampshire. Peter, indeed, used his power as sheriff of Hampshire and keeper of the New Forest to diminish rather than defend the rights of the king, for in the course of hugely increasing the arable land on his episcopal estates, he made sizeable encroachments on the royal forest.[46] Yet whatever the two ministers hoped to get away with in their own bailiwicks, that did not lessen their determination to enforce the rights of the crown against everyone else, or at least everyone outside their (increasingly different) political constituencies.

Hubert himself was well aware of the political implications, not least for himself, of pushing through precipitous changes but he was not content simply to leave things as they were. The key to Hubert's approach lay in his office. As justiciar his duty was twofold. He must uphold and dispense justice: 'it is especially your task to favour and maintain justice', the regent had reminded him in 1218; and he must also, as other letters to him stressed, maintain the rights of the crown.[47] Hubert's view of his responsibilities was in full accord with these sentiments. Thus a royal letter that he attested informed the justiciar of Ireland that 'we [the king] have appointed you in our place to preserve our rights and dispense justice to everyone'.[48] There was nothing incompatible between these obligations and the wheeling and dealing described above. The art was to combine the two. Justice unleavened by politics was simply unworkable but politics without justice, concessions without thought for the rights of the crown, would quickly blast Hubert's reputation and secure his ejection from office. It was not by going down that road that he held on to power for thirteen years. Hubert's view, moreover, became increasingly exchequer-centred. The exchequer was the operations room where the battle for control of the king's manors and sheriffdoms was fought out. It was there that Hubert presided, hearing many of the individual county accounts and seeing, in the counters on the exchequer cloth, the paltry size of the king's cash revenue.

[45] Powicke, *Henry III*, 31, 51. Powicke, *The Thirteenth Century*, 23, however, contains a highly perceptive discussion of Hubert's approach and position.
[46] *RLC*, 633; E 32/253; Titow, 'The Bishop of Winchester's Estates', 21, 73–92. According to Dr Titow's figures (p. 21), the demesne under seed rose from 11,189 acres in 1214 to 13,532 in 1227.
[47] *RLC*, 378; *RL*, nos v, cxi; SC 1/1, no. 209. For discussion of Hubert as justiciar, see West, *Justiciarship*, 213–65, and Warren, *Governance*, 176.
[48] *RLC*, 570–570b.

Hubert's task, therefore, was to preserve and recover the rights of the crown. At the same time he was expected to dispense justice and provide a form of government acceptable to the realm. Up to a point the two tasks were perfectly compatible. Acceptability to former rebels meant forcing Philip of Oldcoates to disgorge Mitford and the count of Aumale to relinquish Bytham; both ambitions were integral to the reassertion of royal authority, the more especially as Aumale was also depriving the king of Rockingham and various manorial farms. On the other hand, an acceptable government was also one which gave way to the intense pressure from the counties to implement (as they thought) the Charter of the Forest. Here the process of conciliation was incompatible with the recovery of kingship. Somehow the new government had to find a middle way. It had to show that the restoration of royal authority would be in the general interest and would not mean a return to the evil practices of King John. Unless this message could be put across, the government would always lack the support necessary to tackle the dispersal of the royal demesne, the loss of control over the sheriffdoms, the poverty of the crown and the consequent repercussions further afield in Wales, Ireland and Poitou.

The early months of the triumvirate were immensely important for Hubert personally. He had to show that he could do his job: could gain control of the chancery, bench and exchequer, cope with a mass of conflicting petitions for justice and favour, and command continuing consent for his actions from great councils. It was in this critical period that he laid the foundations for his thirteen years of power. More generally, the new government, in its first year, continued the policies of the regent in attempting to enforce the peace settlement and conciliate former rebels. Yet in terms of bringing recalcitrant castellans to heel and prosecuting Pandulf's more general programme of resumption, it achieved little. Its very structure, as has been said, precluded clarity and efficiency. The ministers had to co-operate laboriously amongst themselves and seek consent from great councils. The private correspondence of the period gives a graphic picture of the problems which crowded in upon them. In Poitou, the powerlessness of the king's agents became starkly apparent. Within England, attempts to solve the problem of the forest proved abortive. Philip of Oldcoates and the count of Aumale continued their defiance. Unlicensed tournaments, the young Marshal's retention of Fotheringhay, Oldcoates's conflict with the bishop of Durham, Henry fitz Count's pretensions in Cornwall, the activities of the constable of Tickhill and private wars in Lincolnshire and the west country added new centres of disruption. England seemed at times to be on the verge of anarchy.

iii. *Abortive initiatives, June–July 1219*

The great council which met at Gloucester in June 1219, therefore, established the justiciar in control of the seal. It is possible that Pandulf may also have hoped to realize more general changes. By this time he must have possessed the papal letter of 23 April urging resumption of the king's castles and demesnes. Perhaps it was in anticipation of its arrival that on 10 May he had asked Ralph de Neville to send him 'the form under which Guala entrusted the keeping of castles'.[1] As it was, however, the initiatives taken at the Gloucester council were limited both in their intention and their effect.

The most original measure, conceived 'by common counsel', was to circumvent the 'malice of the sheriffs', as Pandulf put it, by giving them coadjutors to assist in collecting the amercements from the recent eyres. The sequel illustrates the problems caused by the lack of contact between Pandulf and his colleagues, as well as the governor's general lack of information about what was going on in the localities. On 22 June, after his return to London, Hubert authorized a royal letter implementing this decision: two knights in each county were to be appointed by the justices in eyre as coadjutors of the sheriffs. Yet, as late as 7 July, Pandulf remained ignorant of this, for on that date he wrote to Peter and Hubert expressing astonishment that nothing had been done in the matter.[2] The sheriffs and the knights, according to the 22 June order, were to bring the amercements to the exchequer in two stages, on 1 August and 29 September. The sheriff of Devon, however, wrote to Hubert to say that he could not meet this deadline since he had only received the list of amercements from the justices on 23 July, this despite the fact that the eyre had finished in the county on 27 June.[3] On the other hand, the bishop of Durham, the senior justice in Yorkshire and Northumberland, wrote to explain that the new timetable was actually laxer than that which he had himself imposed, with the result that the 22 June order retarded rather than accelerated the collection of the amercements in these counties.[4]

In the event, the financial proceeds of the eyres were considerable, although how far this was due to the knights who assisted the sheriffs is unclear. The knights failed to ensure effective collection of the amercements in Yorkshire, Lincolnshire and Somerset-Dorset, where the sheriffs, respectively Geoffrey de Neville, the earl of Salisbury and Peter de Maulay, were left owing a total of over £550.[5]

---

[1] *RL*, no. xcviii.
[2] C 60/11, m. 5; *RL*, no. xxviii.
[3] *RL*, no. xxxiii; Crook, *General Eyre*, 73.
[4] *RL*, no. xxiii.
[5] *Pipe Roll 1219*, 183, 200, 205, 131; *Pipe Roll 1221*, 138–9, 155, 94; *Divers Accounts*, 45.

The Gloucester council also turned its attention, with mixed success, to some of the problems which had plagued the regent. A temporary settlement was reached with the earl of Gloucester over his claim to the Barton outside Bristol. Hugh de Vivonne was left in possession and the earl was given compensation.[6] Vivonne's victory hardly suggested that the government would make much progress in its trench warfare against the count of Aumale. Although the latter had been ordered in November 1217 to return Bytham castle and its surrounding lands to William de Coleville, in accordance with the peace settlement, he had not complied. Coleville had briefly gained possession of the lands after the war, only for Aumale to eject him. He was able, therefore, to bring an assize of novel disseisin for their recovery before the Lincolnshire eyre. This case was adjourned, by order of the council, to the great council meeting at Gloucester. It was still, however, too hot to handle and Hubert, as justiciar, in what was to become a characteristic act of temporization, simply ordered that it be transferred from there to the bench at Westminster.[7] Equally, nothing came of the attempt on 20 June, after Hubert's return to London, to prise the Northampton-shire forest from Aumale and return it to the former rebel, Hugh de Neville.[8]

The letters of safe-conduct, issued to him in May, produced Philip of Oldcoates at the Gloucester council. This may have been the occasion when he agreed to surrender the Vesci lands to the earl of Salisbury and compensate the latter for the revenue that he had lost. Although 190 marks of that compensation remained unpaid nearly two years later, the silence of the sources suggests that Salisbury did now gain possession.[9] This, then, was a victory for the government, bringing to an end the conflict which had begun when Oldcoates was first ordered to give the Vesci custody to Salisbury in January 1218. In respect of Oldcoates's exclusion of Roger Bertram from Mitford, however, much less was achieved. All that seems to have happened was the stationing within the castle of the knights and serjeants of Hugh de Balliol. Probably the government saw this as a step towards the eventual restoration of the castle to Bertram but since Hugh resented his own failure to wrest Mere in Wiltshire from the earl of Salisbury and since he was an ally of Oldcoates, the only result was to add a new element of complexity to the whole affair.[10]

[6] The agreement over compensation in June 1219 lasted until August 1220 when another spate of orders commanding the resignation of the Barton to the earl began. Eventually the agreement was renewed until November 1222: E 372/66, r. 15d, m. 2; *RLC*, 426, 429b, 448. For later evidence, see Altschul, *The Clares*, 27–8.

[7] *Lincs. Worcs. Eyre*, nos 439, 708, 712, 732, p. lv; see above p. 57 and below pp. 165–7.

[8] *RLC*, 393, 423, 496.

[9] *RLC*, 456b.

[10] See below p. 162.

Proceedings at the Gloucester council were wrapped up by a sentence of excommunication promulgated against those who disturbed the peace of the king and kingdom. It was not long, however, before Oldcoates was writing, in furious complaint, to the king about the bishop of Durham. In defiance of the sentence, and despite Oldcoates's offer to accept justice at the king's or the bishop's court, the bishop had sent an armed band which set fire to one of Oldcoates's houses, seized his men and incarcerated them 'like thieves' at Durham. Oldcoates declared his own reluctance to do anything to disturb the peace of the king and kingdom, and begged the king himself to take action against the bishop 'lest by his example, others have less fear about disturbing and breaking the peace of your kingdom'.[11] In the next few months it sometimes appeared that Pandulf, Peter and Hubert were doing nothing else but fight fires lit by potential violators of the peace.

After the Gloucester council Hubert and Peter returned to London. There, as has been seen, Hubert took charge of the seal. He also moved at once to assert control over the judicial administration of the country and presided for the first time over sessions of the bench.[12] However, the two ministers were soon hurrying back to the Welsh Marches, this time to Hereford (28 June–3 July), probably to bring influence to bear at the election of the new bishop of Hereford.[13] On the way at Oxford, on 24 June, news came of the death of Earl David of Huntingdon. This at once created a new centre of disturbance. The government's duty was to take the earl's lands into the king's hands. That, however, was no easy task. Earl David had rebelled during the war and his lands had been granted to William Marshal junior. In 1218 orders had been issued for them to be returned to David but William had held on to Fotheringhay castle and probably some of the lands as well. Meanwhile, the count of Aumale was still occupying David's manors of Nassington and Yarwell near Rockingham.[14]

When, therefore, on 24 June Falkes de Bréauté, as sheriff of the counties in which most of the lands lay, was ordered to take them into the king's hands and seize anyone offering opposition, the opposition in question was clearly that anticipated from the young Marshal, now earl of Pembroke, and the count of Aumale. Indeed, on or soon after

[11] SC 1/5, no. 69. Oldcoates held land from the bishopric and had been its custodian before the election of the bishop, Richard de Marsh. These were the seeds of the conflict.

[12] Meekings, 'Concords'. In the five concords dated 16 and 17 June, Peter's name was placed second to Hubert's in the list of judges.

[13] PR, 195.

[14] ERF, 33; RLC, 305b, 354b, 397, 428b; Stringer, Earl David of Huntingdon, 53, 48, 115–17.

26 June, Falkes reported that Pembroke's men from Fotheringhay had seized David's manor at Yardley (Hastings), south of Northampton, and had defied orders from Falkes's under-sheriff to leave. Falkes himself, already embroiled in private quarrels with the Marshal, felt, probably to Hubert's relief, that strong action by himself would only make matters worse. Instead, he reminded Hubert of his position 'in the presence of the legate and the high council of the king', stressed his duty as justiciar of England to do justice to everyone and urged him to come personally to 'correct these presumptions'.[15]

This letter, at the beginning of his active justiciarship, put Hubert on the spot. The very fact that Falkes lectured him on his duties shows the uncertainty of his position as well as its opportunities. It was vital now for Hubert to demonstrate that he could do his job, could dispense justice and uphold the rights of the king. But equally the last thing he wanted to do was antagonize Pembroke. So he tried to steer a middle course. Falkes's invitation to visit Northamptonshire was declined but a sharp letter of reprimand was sent, in the king's name, to Pembroke. The latter's reaction revealed only too clearly the dangers facing Hubert: dangers which would soon have swept a less careful man from office. The earl was furious. 'My soul', he told the king in a letter, 'is astonished beyond what is possible to be believed in that you have chosen to think that I have transgressed against your excellence and dignity, since I would never do anything or order anything to be done against [them] from which it might be possible to derive any evil suspicion.' For the rest, William disclaimed knowledge of the activities of his officials and offered to correct their excesses, 'according to the law and custom of the kingdom'.[16] But a month or so later Falkes wrote again to inform Peter and Hubert that these officials were now seizing the dower lands of Earl David's widow.[17] It was another year before Pembroke eventually surrendered Fotheringhay and the count of Aumale gave up Nassington and Yarwell.

At Hereford, between 28 June and 3 July, Hubert, Peter and Pandulf met once more with the king's council.[18] Hubert made use of his new power at the exchequer to give 'good hope' to Walter de Lacy that his account as sheriff of Herefordshire might be respited until Michaelmas. He also secured a gift from the king of 100 oaks for Walter's wife.[19] At

[15] *ERF*, 33; *RL*, no. v (where misdated 1217). On 30 June a tournament was prohibited at Northampton: *PR*, 194–5.

[16] *RL*, no. xli.

[17] *RL*, no. xl; *RLC*, 395b.

[18] C 60/11, m. 4d.

[19] *RLC*, 394b; SC 1/1, no. 213 (*CACW*, 8); *RL*, no. xxxv. Walter was lord of Ewias Lacy as well as sheriff of Hereford. His support would help secure Hubert's installation in the Three Castles.

the same time Hubert and Peter accepted a fine of 100 marks from the knights and freemen of Cumberland for deforestation according to the terms of the 1217 Charter of the Forest and for the limitation of the number of serjeants employed by the sheriff (Robert de Vieuxpont) to keep both forest and county.[20] These were acts of conciliation but the triumvirate did not shy away from launching a general initiative which was bound to be unpopular, a general initiative, however, which was soon dragged down to earth. On 4 July royal letters, authorized by Hubert and Peter, appointed in each county commissioners, who were local knights or magnates, to inquire into the unauthorized assarts, sown or unsown, made since the king's coronation, both in his demesne woods 'and in the woods of others'. All these assarts were to be taken into the king's hands and their perpetrators were to appear before the justiciar and the council on 16 August to show by what warrant they had made them.[21]

This was a bold measure, which Pandulf later described as taken by his 'provision and counsel' and that of Hubert and Peter.[22] While avoiding the opprobrium of staging a full forest eyre, its aim was to make money both by amercing those guilty of assarting and by imposing fines for the recovery of their corn sown in the assarts. The initiative immediately ran into difficulties. The commissioners in Hampshire, writing to Peter and Hubert, drew attention to one fundamental problem: 'We are not distinctly and clearly told in which woods we ought to inquire about assarts since in the king's letters which we have received . . . no distinction is made between assarts made within and without the regard [that is, in effect, within or without the boundary of the forest] or within and without liberties'.[23] This, of course, was perfectly true. The commissioners had been told to inquire into assarts in the king's demesne woods and 'the woods of others'. The implication was that the latter were private woods within the bounds of the royal forest but this was not stated specifically and for a very good reason: the government was trying to gloss over the fact that no one knew exactly what the bounds of the royal forest were.

It has been seen that, in July 1218, John Marshal had been commissioned to perambulate the forests under the terms of the 1217 Charter. In 1219 the government continued to accept proffers from individual counties for perambulations likewise according to the Charter's terms. But in general, both in 1218 and 1219, it had stalled over implementing the results, probably because the deforestations demanded appeared too extreme. The 1219 perambulation in Huntingdonshire, for example,

[20] C 60/11, mm. 5, 4.
[21] *PR*, 211–20.
[22] *RL*, no. cxix.
[23] SC 1/2, no. 70.

was exactly the same as that of 1218, which had been rejected for putting the whole county, apart from three demesne woods, outside the forest's bounds.[24] Not surprisingly, therefore, the government could give little guidance to the Hampshire commissioners. They were merely told that the inquiry was to be made 'concerning the woods in which the verderers and foresters of fee have power', a reply which settled nothing since the woods over which the verderers and foresters had power were precisely what was in dispute.[25]

The extent and manner in which the forest initiative was implemented, therefore, depended very much on the local situation. In Gloucestershire the commissioners wrote to the justiciar complaining that the bailiffs of Savari de Mauléone and Hugh de Vivonne prevented them making inquiries in the forest of Alveston.[26] In other counties, notably Yorkshire, the inquiry and seizures were probably not carried out at all.[27] In Nottinghamshire and Derbyshire, on the other hand, where the forest was still under the control of Philip Mark, attempts to carry through the seizures provoked a storm of protest, partly no doubt because Mark had no intention of respecting the demands for extensive deforestation in the two counties. When Pandulf was at Darley abbey in Derbyshire later in July, the men of the two counties came before him and begged him to 'save for them their corn in the assarts' which had been taken into the king's hands. Pandulf, clearly under intense pressure, thought it wise to advise Peter and Hubert 'saving the right and interest of the king ... to further [the men's] indemnity and that of others who have a similar cause, as you think most expedient for the king and for them'. How the government beat a progressive retreat over the measure will be seen in due course.[28]

iv. *Pandulf and Scotland, July–August 1219*

Pandulf was writing to Peter and Hubert from Derbyshire because, after meeting early in July at Hereford, the triumvirate had separated. Peter and Hubert had returned to London, where they remained until 10 August. Pandulf, charged by the pope with ensuring that Llywelyn conserved the king's rights and possessions, had gone to Shrewsbury.

---

[24] See above, p. 90; E 32/38, r. 2; *PR*, 197. This perambulation was commissioned by Hubert and Peter on 20 July and held ten days later.

[25] *PR*, 212.

[26] SC 1/1, no. 160.

[27] *PR*, 219, where there is no mention of returns to the inquiry being received from Yorkshire.

[28] *RL*, no. cxix; see below pp. 159, 163–4. For the demands for deforestation in Nottinghamshire and Derbyshire, see the map below p. 391. I am grateful to Dr Crook for allowing me to see his forthcoming article on the Derbyshire forest.

There he made various complaints, on the king's behalf, against the Welsh prince, who responded with complaints of his own against the Marcher barons.[1] Pandulf then journeyed north, passing through Derbyshire, to Norham, where on, or soon after, 2 August he met King Alexander of Scotland. Pandulf had been commissioned by the pope to sit in judgement on the Anglo-Scottish treaties of 1209 and 1212. The request for this papal intervention had come from Alexander himself, and not surprisingly. His father had paid King John 10,050 marks and surrendered his claims to the three northern counties in return for nothing. Alexander's eldest sister had not married the heir to the English throne as promised. No marriage had been found for Alexander's second sister, although both girls remained in English custody, nor for Alexander himself.[2] The English government was equally keen to escape from an entanglement which would involve the king in a hardly advantageous marriage. At Norham matters were adjourned until 3 November, with Pandulf hoping that he could then achieve a 'peace' or political settlement, rather than have to pronounce a formal legal judgement, a settlement which was ultimately reached in June 1220.[3]

It was not until mid-September that Pandulf was back in London and once more in direct contact with Hubert and Peter. In this period of separation he consulted and, where necessary, endeavoured to control his colleagues through a string of letters. On a purely judicial matter, he wrote, from Shrewsbury, to Hubert asking him to postpone the plea between Reginald de Braose and his nephew John over the Braose inheritance which had now started at the bench.[4] On more general matters, however, he wrote jointly to Peter and Hubert, seven letters to them surviving from this period. Thus when Philip of Orby came before him at Shrewsbury, and asked for custody of the lands of the recently deceased Turstin Banaster, Pandulf ordered Peter and Hubert 'after diligent debate to do what you judge expedient for the king's honour and utility'. Only four days after Pandulf's letter they acceded to Orby's request in return for a fine of 50 marks.[5] This was characteristic of Pandulf's dealings with his colleagues. He left much to their

---

[1]   CPReg., 64; RL, no. cxvii; Lloyd, Wales, 656.
[2]   F, 157. The treaties of 1209 and 1212 are discussed in Anglo-Scottish Relations, xlv–viii; Duncan, Scotland, 244–52. (I cannot follow Duncan in thinking that under the 1212 treaty the three northern counties were to be part of an appanage for the heir to the Scottish throne. Alexander did homage to John for 'all the rights for which his father had done homage to Henry II', which was at most Tynedale and lordship over the honour of Huntingdon.)
[3]   F, 157; see below p. 196.
[4]   RL, no. cxvii.
[5]   SC 1/1, no. 47; ERF, 35; see also SC 1/1, no. 206. Philip was the earl of Chester's justiciar of Chester.

judgement and was constantly asking their advice, for example, about letters received from the king of Scotland.[6] Likewise, it was after taking advice that he proposed to place restrictions on the Jews in accordance with the decrees of the fourth Lateran council. But Pandulf was also ready to chastise and command. He expressed astonishment that the two ministers had failed to implement the decision over the collection of amercements and had not protected the chamberlain of London from harassment. He ordered them to attend to both matters and to avenge the injury done to one of his own servants 'against the peace of the king and kingdom ... so that no one else follows that example and commits worse deeds, and so that you are seen to wish to procure the peace and tranquillity of the king and kingdom'.[7]

v. *Poitou, July 1219*

Having arrived back at Westminster from Hereford on 12 July, Hubert and Peter were faced with the problem of Poitou. From the towns, the seneschal and Queen Isabella, who had returned to her county of Angoulême in 1218, came the cry for military and financial help. Unless it arrived they all warned that the land would be lost.

One anxiety was over what would happen when the truce of 1214 with the king of France expired at Easter 1220. In 1204 King Philip had briefly subjected nearly all Poitou, outside La Rochelle. He remained installed in Poitiers and further north was firmly in control of Anjou. Since King John, in the French view, had forfeited all his continental lands, his son had no right at all to hold Poitou or Gascony.[1] A more immediate threat in 1219 was posed by Louis's reappearance as the leader of a crusade to uproot the Albigensian heretics in the county of Toulouse. There was a widespread fear, expressed in a papal letter of 15–17 May, that under the pretext of this venture, Louis intended to subjugate the lands of the king of England in Poitou and Gascony.[2] Indeed, later in the month, when he passed near La Réole, on the Garonne, a party in the town wished to surrender it to him. The council

---

[6] *RL*, no. xxvii.

[7] *RL*, nos xxviii, xxvii, cxviii; Richardson, *English Jewry*, 183–4. Pandulf's other letter belonging to this period is *RL*, no. cxix.

[1] *DD*, nos 52; *Recueil*, xix, 760; Gillingham, *Angevin Empire*, 67, 70–1, 80. For the argument that Gascony was not involved in the forfeiture of 1202 because it was an allod, rather than a fief held from the king of France, see Chaplais, 'Le Traité de Paris de 1259 et l'Inféodation de la Gascogne Allodiale', 121–37, especially pp. 133–5. There appears, however, to be no reference to Gascony's allodial status in either the voluminous diplomatic correspondence of the minority or any other source, although King Henry's government had every reason to emphasize it, had they known of its existence.

[2] *DD*, no. 34; *CPReg.*, 67, from where the date may be deduced.

and 'faithful' burgesses thus begged the king for aid to fortify La Réole 'so that, although at present sited at the extremity of your land, your enemies will find there a firm obstacle'.[3] Meanwhile, Geoffrey de Neville, having leapt from the frying pan, as sheriff of Yorkshire, into the fire, as seneschal of Poitou and Gascony, informed the government of the plight of Elyas Ridel, the lord of Bergerac, who 'holds the March of your land towards the Agenais and Périgueux against your enemies'. Neville cautioned the king that, when Louis returned from Toulouse, Ridel would 'lose his land completely unless you help him'.[4]

On top of these external threats, there was another problem, and that the most insuperable: the almost total collapse of authority within Poitou itself. The letters of Geoffrey de Neville became increasingly strident and despairing. 'We have often told you', he wrote to the king and his council, 'that you should take counsel how to defend the land of Poitou and Gascony not against the king of France but against your barons who devastate your land and capture and ransom your burgesses, and so behave towards you that it appears (and we believe it) that they have no liking for your service.' Geoffrey went on to identify the cause of his powerlessness: he had no money. 'We, however, because of our poverty are unable either to defend the land or subjugate [the barons] nor', Neville continued, breaking into the first person under the force of his indignation, 'do they rate me any higher than if I was a little boy.' Unless measures were quickly taken, Neville threatened to return to England, 'and don't say that *we* lost the land of the king because you yourselves, through lack of counsel (*consilium*), are casting it away'.[5] In late May the situation further deteriorated when Hugh de Lusignan began to molest the town of Niort and generally disturb the king's 'land' in an attempt to force the English government to grant him the properties of his uncle, Ralph de Lusignan, the count of Eu, who had died on 1 May. Of Geoffrey he took no notice 'since he and others see that we are so feeble both in troops and money'. Geoffrey thus warned the king that 'unless quick and effective measures are taken to defend your land . . . Hugh and the magnates of your land will take possession themselves of your lands and towns, and subject them to an alien dominion'. If nothing was done, Geoffrey threated that on 24 June he would set out for the Holy Land, 'since in no way will we remain here to your shame and damage and mine'.[6]

---

[3] *DD*, nos 48–50. These details come from a letter of the autumn of 1219 when the burgesses put on record the events of the summer. La Réole's envoy, Merlet de Frigido Monte, probably told the same story when he was in England in July: *RLC*, 395b.

[4] *DD*, no. 38. A messenger from Ridel himself was in England in July: *RLC*, 397b.

[5] *DD*, no. 43. The tone of this letter suggests it is near in time but perhaps a little earlier than *DD*, no. 33, which belongs to late May.

[6] *DD*, no. 33. For other problems, see *F*, 156.

Queen Isabella was having an equally hard time asserting her authority in Angoulême. 'Although there may be no need to fear about the king of France', she wrote to her son, 'we have neighbours who should be feared just as much as the king.' Several times, she complained, she had asked her son for help but had received nothing. Henceforth, she warned him, 'do not feed us with words'; unless speedy measures were taken, 'we cannot rule and defend our land . . . and will lose it'.[7]

This then was the situation that the government was facing by July 1219. But its solutions were diplomatic and political rather than financial and military. In March envoys from the king of France had indicated their master's readiness to renew the truce.[8] By 7 July another ambassador was in England, whom Pandulf demanded to see, although he also wanted to know what Peter and Hubert had discussed with him and what they thought 'expedient for the royal honour'. The result was that, on 24 July, a royal letter was sent to Philip which expressed King Henry's readiness to renew the truce for four years and tried to expedite the arrangements for its confirmation.[9]

As for the threat from Louis, the government relied on papal protection. In letters to the cities and magnates of Poitou and Gascony, on 24 July, for which Peter and Hubert were jointly responsible, the king expressed his confidence that there was nothing to fear from Louis because 'the pope has taken ourselves, our lands and our fees under his special protection'.[10] For the rest, despite the complaints of Geoffrey de Neville, the government threw in its lot with Hugh de Lusignan. There was no alternative to this. With his father's death on crusade in 1219, Hugh became lord of Lusignan and count of La Marche. He was also betrothed to Henry's sister, whom he held in custody. As Neville's letters showed, there was nothing that could be done against him. Perhaps, however, something might be done with him. Thus a royal letter of 24 July made a virtue of necessity and reflected, in flowery phrases, on how the alliance between Hugh and King Henry was confirmed by a double tie: that of fealty and fraternal affection. Hugh was then informed that the seneschal, towns and magnates of Poitou and Gascony had been ordered to obey him in the king's affairs. If an invasion did occur, Hugh was urged to protect the towns and the land, and informed that he could draw on 2,000 marks which the king hoped to borrow from Bordeaux and La Rochelle, a sum for which Peter and Hubert stood as surety. As for the lands of the count of Eu, Hugh was assured that they were being entrusted to the earl of Surrey, as the

---

[7] *DD*, no. 39.
[8] *PR*, 188; *DD*, no. 29.
[9] *DD*, no. 41; *F*, 156; see *Recueil*, xix, 680, 684.
[10] *F*, 154, 155; *DD*, no. 34.

countess of Eu had requested, to be kept safe for the use of herself and her children; the future of the lands would be settled with Hugh's counsel.[11]

In the short term, these measures were enough. King Philip did renew the truce and Louis did not invade. Poitou, nonetheless, had been fed with words. The envoy from La Réole took back a confirmation of the town's liberties, not material aid to assist with its fortification.[12] The alliance with Hugh de Lusignan merely gave him added scope to do as he pleased. The fact was that, within Poitou, as Dr Hajdu has shown, developments over the last thirty years had undermined the king of England's power as count. In 1189 Richard I's control of fifteen castellanies had made him the dominant power in Poitou; the families of Lusignan, Thoaurs and Mauléone combined held only one more. By 1216, however, the number of comital castellanies had dropped to five and those of the families of Lusignan, Thouars and Mauléon had risen to thirty-six. In the same period the lords of Lusignan had also become counts of La Marche.[13] A consequence of these changes was that, as Geoffrey de Neville made clear, the seneschal had virtually no regular revenues. Indeed, later in 1219, on his return to England, Neville could leave his deputy only the 'rents' from the ports of Poitou and Gascony, and these came to a bare £50.[14] The customs of Bordeaux, at the time, were assigned for the repayment of loans but they were worth, at most, a few hundred pounds a year.[15] Fundamentally, Poitou was dominated by a small number of great families and by the towns of Niort, St Jean d'Angély and, above all, La Rochelle. The most the seneschal could hope to do was mediate in their quarrels and filter their demands through to the government in England.

The only way to assert the king's authority in Poitou, and to defend the province from attack, was to establish a loyal and efficient seneschal with ample supplies of men and money. But there was no prospect of doing that from Poitevin and Gascon resources. Essentially the problems of Poitou had to be solved, if solved they could be, in England. Only when the king had restored his authority there would he have the resources to recover his position overseas.

[11] F, 155–6.
[12] RLC, 395b; see DD, nos 48–50.
[13] Hajdu, 'The structure of politics in Poitou', 34; Gillingham, Angevin Empire, 78.
[14] RL, no. xlvi.
[15] PR, 243, 203, 232. In 1236 the customs and provostship of Bordeaux were farmed at around £400 a year: CPR 1232–47, 137; Stacey, Politics, 175.

vi. *Alarms and excursions: Staines, Northampton, Lincoln and Tickhill, July–August 1219*

In July 1219 the prospects of reasserting royal power in England seemed remote. Whilst trying to concert policy over Poitou, the triumvirate was faced with a series of immediate challenges to its authority arising from an unlicensed tournament at Staines, the detention of Earl David's lands in Northamptonshire, an attempt to seize Lincoln castle and the depredations of the constable of Tickhill.

In the midst of all this, Hubert de Burgh's private correspondence shows that he was coping with a steady stream of petitions which gave him the opportunity to uphold the rights of the crown, dispense justice and win favour. Robert de Vieuxpont, for example, in his capacity as castellan of Carlisle, wrote complaining that Hugh de Balliol was interfering with a mine in Tynedale which belonged to Carlisle castle: 'and so', he continued, lecturing Hubert on his duties in a manner reminiscent of Falkes de Bréauté, 'I earnestly beg you, as he to whom the emendation of such matters belongs and for love of me, to cause that offence to the king to be remedied . . . acting in such a way that the king does not suffer a severe loss and I owe you the more copiously deeds of thanks'.[1] Hubert, therefore, was invited to uphold the rights of the crown as Vieuxpont saw them. The only problem was that Hugh de Balliol might have a different view of what these were. More straightforward was Robert de Courtenay's letter announcing his mother's death. Robert had already done homage to King John for her lands and paid his relief but, so he said, he did not wish to have entry into her lands in Devon without Hubert's consent. Hubert here went through the motions of maintaining the rights of the king. A royal letter in August ordered Courtenay, as sheriff, to take his mother's lands into the king's hands, and it was another two months before he obtained private seisin of them.[2]

Courtenay's letter also asked Hubert, 'if you think it right', to issue a writ of prohibition in a law case and informed him of the difficulties already mentioned in collecting the eyre amercements. It thus ran the gamut of the financial, judicial and administrative business that Hubert was beginning to handle. Around this time Hubert also received letters from the earl of Pembroke and the archbishop of Canterbury. Both recognized Hubert's special responsibility for the dispensation of justice: on other matters at this time Langton, like Pandulf, was writing jointly to Hubert and Peter. To both petitions

[1] SC 1/1, no. 209. This letter cannot be dated exactly but Vieuxpont says that he forgot to mention the matter when he last saw Hubert. Vieuxpont had been at the Gloucester council early in July: C 60/11, m. 4d.

[2] *RL*, no. xxxiii; *ERF*, 36, 38.

Hubert responded in the way requested, thus demonstrating to the greatest lay and ecclesiastical magnates in England his efficiency and utility. Pembroke's letter, however, while demanding justice, also made it clear, as had Vieuxpont's, that it was a question of favour. He begged Hubert 'as my dearest friend for love of me', to give full justice to his serjeant William de Bricheville 'and, if you please, cause his land to be repledged to him, acting in such a way that he may feel that he has benefited from my prayers proffered to you and so that I owe you on his behalf deeds of thanks.[3]

Hubert took sole responsibility for the letter issued in Bricheville's favour on 19 July but he could not always act by himself.[4] Although Langton, amongst other things, asked him to secure the return of the crusader Geoffrey de Lucy's chattels, the decision to do so was actually taken by the king's council, with the ensuing writ (on 21 July) being authorized by both Hubert and Peter.[5] In the matter of the tournament at Staines, Langton wrote to Hubert and Peter jointly. Planned for 28 July, it had been forbidden by royal letter five days before. With Langton and the bishop of London on the spot to stop it, the tourneyers had abandoned their plans, declaring that they would meet again at Michaelmas and get permission first from Pandulf. But, as Langton informed Hubert and Peter, 'they say that neither for the legate nor for anyone else will they forgo it, and they add that they have pledged together that if anyone presumes to injure, in however small a way, one of their number on account of it, all together will unanimously rise up against him who does the injury'.[6]

Despite this alarm, Hubert and Peter attempted to push ahead on another front, that of getting Earl David's lands into the king's hands. On 22 July they issued a writ which ordered the constables of Fotheringhay and Rockingham (in effect the earl of Pembroke and the count of Aumale) to surrender the manors of Fotheringhay, Nassington and Yarwell.[7] This sidestepped the main issue, the detention of the castles of Fotheringhay and Rockingham themselves. But it was followed in August by Hubert and Peter moving from London to Northampton, an acceptance, in effect, of the invitation Falkes had offered back in June. Were they about to reassert royal authority in the county? Certainly they seem at this time to have been clearing the way for action against one particular individual, perhaps the count of Aumale. Late in July the archbishop of York promised Hubert and Peter, 'in the truth in which God is', counsel and aid in the matter

[3] SC 1/1, no. 148.
[4] RLC, 396b.
[5] Acta Stephani Langton, no. 61; RLC, 397, 391.
[6] PR, 198; Acta Stephani Langton, no. 62.
[7] RLC, 397.

which has been explained to him by their envoy. 'Be certain', he continued, in a passage whose conclusion is indecipherable, 'that neither you nor anyone else who loves the honour of the king can have joy or happiness . . . until he of whom you tell us, who struggles to disturb the peace of the king and kingdom . . . .'.[8]

At Northampton, however, Peter and Hubert had also to decide what to do about the measure over forest assarts launched back in July. The returns were due before the justiciar and council on 16 August and, by then, those from at least seventeen counties had indeed been received. An attempt was now made to fulfil the original purpose of the measure and make some money from it. The sheriffs, on 17 August, were ordered to return the corn in the assarts to those who had sown it. This was to comply with the demand made to Pandulf by the men of Nottinghamshire and Derbyshire. But, at the same time, security was to be taken that the assarters would appear before the council at the end of October to answer both for their transgressions and for the value of the corn which they had sown. What actually happened in October will be seen in due course.[9]

If the government meant next to address the situation in Northamptonshire, it was prevented by a sudden crisis further afield. News arrived that the earl of Salisbury was trying to force his way into Lincoln castle and expel Nicola de Hay. Immediate action was concerted. Hubert, Peter and Falkes de Bréauté took the king with them and covered the seventy-odd miles from Northampton in under two days. They were at Lincoln by 19 August. There the garrison of the castle was increased by a force under Falkes's command, and the knights and free men of the county, by an order authorized by Hubert and Peter, were instructed to assist Falkes 'in the affairs of the king, which he will explain to them, for the conservation of the peace of the kingdom of England'.[10]

In one sense the government had scored a success, yet the whole episode revealed its extraordinary weakness. Here, after all, was Salisbury, the sheriff of Lincolnshire, trying to seize Lincoln castle. He was also refusing to answer for the county farm at the exchequer. Yet no attempt was made to remove him from office. The paradox of the situation was seen in the order to Salisbury, as sheriff, and his colleagues collecting the eyre amercements to give 250 marks to Falkes

---

[8] *RL*, no. xxxii; *RLC*, 396b.

[9] *PR*, 219; *RLC*, 398; see below pp. 163–4.

[10] *PR*, 200–1; *Pipe Roll 1219*, 78. It is possible that the count of Aumale accompanied the king to Lincoln, for it was there that he fined for a writ of attaint against the jury which had given the verdict in favour of Gilbert de Gant on the Lincolnshire eyre: C 60/11, m. 3; *Pipe Roll 1219*, 129.

to 'sustain' Lincoln castle: sustain it, that is, against Salisbury himself.[11]

Having staved off the crisis at Lincoln, the king and Peter returned to Northampton, while Hubert visited his castle at Wormegay, went on to Norwich, Yarmouth and perhaps Burgh itself, and then returned to London. This was the first occasion on which Hubert controlled the seal without Peter at his side. At Yarmouth he authorized a writ which ordered the men of the Cinque Ports to 'preserve [the king's] peace and rights unharmed' in the fairs there, 'as you wish your liberties and rights to be preserved in their integrity', a concept of reciprocity which was to feature in many writs in the minority.[12] Hubert also dealt in measured fashion with another request from Robert de Vieuxpont. The latter wanted a writ empowering him as sheriff of Cumberland to distrain Robert de Ros to return munitions to Carlisle castle where Ros himself had been castellan before the war. The royal letters issued from Wormegay on 30 August, however, were addressed to Ros himself and, while ordering him to return the munitions to Vieuxpont, made no mention of distraint.[13]

As he journeyed south Hubert learnt that matters were getting out of hand in another area of dispute – Tickhill, which, as has been mentioned, had been restored to Ralph de Lusignan, count of Eu, in 1218. When the count died on 1 May 1219 his lands were entrusted to the earl of Surrey as representative of his cousin, the widowed countess and her children.[14] Surrey, in the presence of Pandulf, Hubert and the king's council, perhaps at Gloucester in June, had pledged to restore to Brian de Lisle, who was absent on crusade, the manor of Laughton en le Morthen from which the constable of Tickhill had ejected him. Between 4 July and 17 August, however, Hubert received letters from Brian's steward, William Basset, and his ally, Philip Mark. Hubert was thanked for 'so kindly' sending royal letters to Surrey on Lisle's affairs but informed that the earl's own letters to the constable of Tickhill had been ineffective. The latter had refused to do anything for Basset and continued to waste and destroy the land at Laughton.[15]

It was into this violent situation that Pandulf butted on his way south from Norham. On 29 August, from Doncaster, some six miles north of Tickhill, he despatched a letter to Hubert and Peter. The constable and men of Tickhill were daily committing worse iniquities 'and by way of derision they call the king not a king but a boy'. Pandulf, therefore, invoking his legatine authority for the first time in his correspondence

---

[11] RLC, 398b.
[12] PR, 201–2.
[13] RL, no. xxxi; RLC, 399b.
[14] Peerage, v, 158–63; F, 155–6; Powicke, Loss of Normandy, 255.
[15] SC 1/1, nos 57, 130; Yorks. Eyre, nos 519, 1100; RLC, 219.

with the two ministers, forbad them 'to proceed in the affair of the countess of Eu, if she should come, until we have spoken and deliberated together and taken counsel how such great excesses may be severely corrected for the honour of God, the church and the king and for the peace of the kingdom'.[16]

The countess had indeed now arrived in England. She and the earl of Surrey had seen the king, who received them 'most attentively and warmly' and appointed 15 September as the day to deal with the countess's business. Surrey, who told Hubert all this in a letter, went on to remind him of their joint relationship with the countess, 'our niece, your kinswoman', and begged him 'with all possible affection, to be present on that day, since I believe that the affairs of the king and ourselves may be brought to a happy and prosperous conclusion by means of your counsel and aid. And this, as you love us and the countess, omit on no account.'[17] When, therefore, the triumvirate met once more, at the New Temple in London in the middle of September, the business of Tickhill was the first item on the agenda.

vii. *The Michaelmas term of 1219: exchequer and bench*

In reality there was no alternative to granting the countess of Eu seisin of her lands and she received them on 19 September. To refuse to do so was to risk further antagonizing her kinsman, Hugh de Lusignan, in Poitou. As far as the evidence goes, the countess made no payment for her seisin, although it was entirely a matter of the king's grace, given that she also held the county of Eu from the king of France. King Philip by contrast imposed a relief on the countess of over £8,000.[1]

Meanwhile, the triumvirate grappled with other problems. The justiciar of Ireland, Geoffrey de Marsh, was ordered once again to come to England and to keep proper accounts of his receipts. Ireland in the interim was to be placed in the care of the archbishop of Dublin.[2] The sheriff of Cornwall, Henry fitz Count, was instructed in a letter dated 17 September, for which Hubert, Peter and Pandulf all took responsibility, to cease his presumptions 'against the honour of the king's dignity'. Earlier in the year Hubert and Peter had complained about Henry's failure to obey the king's orders. Now the council had learnt that, without any authorization, he had appointed his own judges to

---

[16] SC 1/1, no. 39: *non regem sed puerum nominant deridendo.*

[17] *RL*, no. xxxiv, where *neptis vestrae, cognatae nostrae* is probably a scribal error for *neptis nostrae, cognatae vestrae.* Hubert's first wife was the great-granddaughter of the William de Warenne earl of Surrey who died in 1138. The countess of Eu was his great-great-granddaughter: Sanders, *Baronies*, 101, 119–20.

[1] *PR*, 203; *Layettes*, i, no. 1360; Baldwin, *Philip Augustus*, 242, 342.

[2] *RLC*, 400b; SC 1/6, no. 26.

hear petty assizes, an alarming indication of the position of independence that he was seeking to achieve in Cornwall.[3]

The struggle was also continued over Mitford. As has been seen, in
June 1219 an attempt had probably been made to ease Oldcoates out of
the castle by installing within it some knights of Hugh de Balliol. The
only result was that the government had now to buy out both men. On
21 September letters issued by Hubert, Peter and Pandulf assigned £60
worth of land to Oldcoates during the king's pleasure, while Hugh was
granted once again the royal manor of Mere in Wiltshire, this time until
the completion of the king's fourteenth year.[4] It may well have been at
this juncture that the king was produced to personally order Oldcoates
to surrender the castle and Oldcoates, before Pandulf and the council,
agreed to do so. The agreement, however, soon collapsed. At the end of
October another letter, authorized by Hubert and the council in
Pandulf's presence, was sent to Oldcoates ordering him to give up
Mitford. This was combined with further attempts both to give him the
£60 worth of land and to get the earl of Salisbury to vacate Mere in
Hugh de Balliol's favour. Evidently the government had not fulfilled its
side of the bargain.[5]

At Tickhill, in September, King Henry had been derided as 'not a
king but a boy'. His personal intervention had failed to shift Philip of
Oldcoates from Mitford. Clearly measures were desperately needed
to enhance his authority and that of his government. This was the
background to the decision taken at the end of October to send Robert,
quondam abbot of Thorney, to the papal court. His mission was to seek
papal sanction for a second coronation ceremony.[6] In 1216 Henry had
been crowned at the wrong place and by the wrong person – at
Gloucester rather than at Westminster abbey, and by Guala or the
bishop of Winchester rather than the archbishop of Canterbury. A new
coronation, putting this right, would enhance the king's prestige and
please the abbey and the archbishop.

Hubert stayed in London until 15 November. He was closely
involved with the Michaelmas session of the exchequer, the first over
which he could preside as justiciar. Peter remained active at the
exchequer, working both alone and in conjunction with Hubert: the
two there together ordered Hubert's under-sheriff in Norfolk to
maintain the king's rights in the county as they had existed before the
war.[7] But Hubert's jurisdiction over the office is plain. He fixed the day
for his under-sheriff in Kent to account and when Walter de Lacy, the

  3   *PR*, 202.
  4   *RLC*, 400b. See above p. 147.
  5   *PR*, 221; *RLC*, 407, 408, 408b.
  6   *RLC*, 402; *Walt. Cov.*, 244; *PR*, 221; C 60/12, m. 9.
  7   *RLC*, 402b; for Peter at the exchequer, see E 159/3, m. 1.

sheriff of Herefordshire, renewed his request for the postponement of his account for 1217–18, Hubert attested a royal letter to the desired effect. Walter then thanked Hubert for his kindness and asked him to concede respites for various debts which he owed the king.[8] Hubert may well have been responsible for a significant development at the *Adventus Vicecomitum* on 30 September. Eight of the sheriffs who did not appear in person had their deputies closely questioned as to the whereabouts of their masters and the replies were entered on the Memoranda Roll. Thus William de Cantilupe, the sheriff of Warwick-shire-Leicestershire, was revealed as being with the king at Walling-ford; Simon of Hale, Geoffrey de Neville's under-sheriff in Yorkshire, more encouragingly, was on his way with money.[9] This was all part of the exchequer's growing control. Six sheriffs who had not accounted at all in the pipe roll of 1218 accounted in the 1219 roll for the whole period since the war. Altogether twenty-six sheriffs accounted, only those for Cumberland and Cornwall being absent without excuse. Consequently the pipe roll of 1219 is a far more impressive document than its predecessor, running to 211 printed pages as opposed to 94.

Success in terms of accounting was not, however, matched by the actual generation of revenue. True, it was probably at this time that Hubert struck a bargain with the earl of Salisbury which at last shook Southampton and its £200 annual farm free from the latter's control. Thus the government indicated its desire to resume the royal demesne, although it made no further progress in that direction and the cost over Southampton was the concession to the earl of Salisbury of most of its revenues since the war. Equally, many sheriffs continued to retain for themselves the money from their county farms and other sources of income. Salisbury himself was still refusing to pay anything in from the farm of Lincolnshire.[10] The *Adventus Vicecomitum* of Michaelmas 1219 produced £334; that was £118 better than the year before but still an insignificant sum compared with the thousands of pounds which must have come in at the Michaelmas *Adventi* of John's reign. The diminutive revenue revealed by the pipe roll of 1219 has already been analysed.[11]

As Hubert and Peter struggled with the king's finances, the difficulty of exploiting traditional sources of revenue in the face of local opposi-tion was thrown into sharp relief. This takes us back to the forest. 28 October was the day that those convicted by the July inquiry of

[8] E 159/3, m. 3; *RL*, no. xxxv; *RLC*, 400b; SC 1/1, no. 110.

[9] E 368/2, m. 8. Such examinations had taken place before but not on the same scale: compare E 368/1, m. 4; E 159/2, mm. 15, 1.

[10] *Pipe Roll 1219*, 25; *RLC*, 333, 345. Salisbury's defiance continued despite the payment to him from October 1219 of a £300 annual pension until he was provided with £300 a year in escheats: *RLC*, 406b, 411, 416, 441.

[11] See Appendix, p. 415, and above pp. 112–14.

making assarts were to come before the king's council, ready to pay over the price of the corn sown in them and to answer for the transgression of assarting. That a large number of angry men from the forest districts now appeared at Westminster seems clear. Whether they paid over any money is doubtful. What they certainly did was lay complaints before Hubert and the council about the whole administration of the forest. The initiative over assarts thus collapsed and was replaced by an impressive measure of appeasement. On 8 November strongly worded royal letters, attested by Hubert, ordered the implementation of the clauses in the Charter of the Forest which controlled the lawing of dogs and limited the numbers of the foresters. The letters concluded with the general injunction that those in charge of the forests were to desist from other breaches of the Charter and 'treat those [within the forests] so amicably that they no longer, through the oppressions of you and yours, have grounds for complaint'.[12]

Hubert certainly wished to recover the rights and revenues of the king but he was equally concerned to maintain the peace and tranquillity of the realm, which was impossible without regard to the interests and liberties of the king's subjects. Perhaps there was a middle way. In September Hubert had stressed the necessary coexistence of the rights of the men of the Cinque Ports and those of the king. Likewise, the order of 8 November declared that the king's forests 'can be more effectively and securely kept . . . with a moderate number of foresters . . . preserving for us everything which belongs to our forests and not damaging the men living in them'.[13]

At the same time as the exchequer was in session at Westminster, so was the bench. Hubert presided over the initial sessions and intervened to adjourn cases or bring them to judgement.[14] Just as Walter de Lacy wrote to him about postponing his account at the exchequer, so the earl of Surrey demanded that Hubert adjourn a case in which he was the defendant and prevent his land being taken into the king's hands 'for my default when I have never had any summons.[15] During this term several important cases between great men involved Hubert and the government in difficult choices and balances between justice and politics.

In the first of these cases the earl of Pembroke impleaded Falkes de

---

[12] *RLC*, 433b–4.

[13] *RLC*, 433b–4; *PR*, 201–2, compare *ibid.*, p. 200.

[14] Meekings, 'Concords'. Hubert's name headed the list of judges before whom all nineteen concords were made on 13 and 20 October. In the single concord made on 6 October, Peter's name preceded Hubert's. Peter, however, was present at the making of only one more concord during the minority (in 1221).

[15] SC 1/1, no. 216; see *CRR*, viii, 35, for a reference to the case.

Bréauté for the manors of Luton in Bedfordshire and of Brabourne, Sutton and Kemsing in Kent. The case turned on whether Pembroke, after the war, had granted these manors to Falkes in perpetuity or merely during his pleasure. This in turn involved the question of whether the charters which appeared to do the former were genuine, or forged by Falkes 'wickedly to disinherit us', as Pembroke put it.[16] This was a dispute of extraordinary importance because, together with the frequent clashes within Falkes's sheriffdoms, it opened up a sore between the two men which influenced the course of politics down to 1224.

Pembroke's case got off to an inauspicious start when the bench decided against him on the question of whether or not the land should be viewed.[17] Around the same time, on 29 October, a letter authorized by Hubert and Peter ordered the earl to surrender Fotheringhay castle to the king of Scotland. It was explained that since Earl David had held the honour of Huntingdon and thus the castle from the Scottish king the wardship belonged to the latter.[18] This decision was part of the settlement with the king of Scotland that Pandulf was now trying to construct. Pembroke, however, took no notice of the injunction and was still holding Fotheringhay a year later. He aired his own grievances in a letter written to Hubert between 20 October and 12 November: 'I ask you as my dearest friend not to permit my knight and man [William de Ros] to be treated and molested unjustly [by Falkes de Bréauté], although I myself, my concerns and my affairs, through the will of certain people, which I deplore, are so treated.'[19] Like others in this period, therefore, Pembroke made no criticism of Hubert, who took steps to appease him, on 12 November authorizing a writ which restored William de Ros to his lands and chattels.[20] A few days earlier the mistake of accusing Pembroke of misconduct, which had led to his astonished protest in June 1219, was avoided. A writ, which had charged him with unjustly deforcing someone of a mill at Marlborough, was altered; the mill was now merely 'in your hands as it is said'.[21]

Two other important cases at the bench in this Michaelmas term had begun on the Lincolnshire eyre and concerned the count of Aumale in suits against former rebels. One of them was the case brought against the count by Gilbert de Gant for tenements at Edenham near Bytham, the case where, on the eyre, the intervention of the government in

[16] The lands in question had come to William Marshal through his first wife. King John had given them to Falkes on William's rebellion: *CRR*, viii, 77–8, 248–52; *RLP*, 199b.
[17] *CRR*, viii, 77–8.
[18] *PR*, 222; see *CRR*, xvii, no. 18.
[19] SC 1/1, no. 149.
[20] *RLC*, 408b; see *CRR*, viii, 116, and for William de Ros, above p. 100.
[21] *RLC*, 407.

Aumale's favour had provoked the storm in the county court and the remonstrance of the judges. In the event the verdict of the jury in Gant's favour had been allowed to stand, as the county and the judges had demanded, and Aumale had begun proceedings to overturn it by fining for a writ of attaint against the original trial jury. Significantly, his pledge for this fine was Peter, bishop of Winchester.[22] When the case came before the bench between 18 and 25 November, Aumale had been excommunicated and Gant argued that therefore he had no need to answer him. By this time Hubert and Pandulf had left Westminster for a meeting with Llywelyn, leaving Peter to mind the bench and exchequer. It was Peter, therefore, with the bishop of London, who decided that the Aumale *v* Gant case should proceed 'notwithstanding the excommunication'. This decision flew in the face of the 'custom', recorded at the bench only the next year, 'that excommunicates shall not be heard in any plea'.[23] One suspects that Peter had been behind the original government intervention in Aumale's favour which had sparked off the protest in the Lincolnshire county court. That was a protest against the attempt to disseise Gant 'without judgement', in contravention of 'the common liberty of all the kingdom', in contravention, that is, of the very clause in the Great Charter which Peter was later to ridicule.[24]

In the event, after Peter's decision, the case was merely adjourned for lack of jurors and the next year Aumale abandoned it.[25] If Gant was angered by Peter's dubious support for Aumale, the same week saw another former rebel score a resounding success against the count. This was William de Coleville in the assize of novel disseisin which he was bringing against Aumale for lands around Bytham castle. It has been seen how Hubert had adjourned this case to the bench from the great council at Gloucester in June 1219. There he continued to watch over its progress, ordering an initial postponement until 18 November because of lack of jurors. However, between 18 and 25 November the jurors turned up and gave their verdict in Coleville's favour.[26] By this time Aumale had been excommunicated by Pandulf for taking part in a prohibited tournament at Brackley. He was also ignoring a further demand that he restore Rockingham and Sauvey to the king and was fortifying both castles. He was virtually in open revolt. On 30 November royal letters denounced the count's misdemeanours and forbad anyone to give him assistance.[27] The government, however, failed to

[22] C 60/11, m. 3; *Pipe Roll 1219*, 129; see above pp. 102–3.
[23] *CRR*, viii, 158; ix, 52–3; Turner, *The King and his Courts*, 113–14.
[24] See above p. 137.
[25] *CRR*, viii, 158, 235, 367; ix, 102, 258.
[26] *CRR*, viii, 30–1, 163–4. See above p. 147.
[27] *PR*, 257–8; *CRR*, viii, 158; see also *RLC*, 403.

follow this up. Aumale made his peace with Pandulf and apparently agreed to go on a crusade.[28] He retained Sauvey and Rockingham with its surrounding manors. In that respect the government had totally failed to assert its authority over him. On the other hand, although Coleville had still to recover his castle, he had won his case for the lands around Bytham. Even against a great noble, with a friend at the very centre of government, a case could be brought to a victorious conclusion by a former rebel and the peace of 1217 upheld.

viii. *Poitou; the forest; November–December 1219*

While the government thus struggled to vindicate its authority in England, its difficulties multiplied further afield. Late in the evening of 1 November 1219 the seneschal of Poitou, Geoffrey de Neville, landed at Dover. He wrote at once to Pandulf, announcing that he would be in London on 4 November with 'much to discuss with you about the affairs of the king'.[1] The tidings he brought were scarcely reassuring. True, Louis had now returned to France and Hugh de Lusignan was making a show of co-operating with the king's government in Poitou. But that government had virtually no power, and Neville had come home to resign his office.

One problem was the increasing disaffection of the queen. In the late summer she had written to Pandulf complaining bitterly of the enmity of Hugh de Lusignan and Geoffrey de Neville, and accusing her son's council of supporting the former seneschal of Angoulême, Bartholomew de Puy, against her. Unless things improved, the queen threatened to 'remove ourselves from the counsel and affairs of our son'. She also observed rather ominously that Bartholomew de Puy had appealed for the restoration of his lands to the king of France on the grounds that 'our land belongs to [the king's] fee'.[2]

Neville himself, early in August 1219, had been on the point of returning to England, 'compelled by great want of money, which I was needing and do need'. However, considering the 'tribulation' of the king's land and the 'damage' which would be done by his departure, he had taken a loan of 160 marks, for which Hugh de Lusignan was pledge, and had stayed put, warning that unless the money was repaid 'you will find no one henceforth who will lend you anything'.[3] At least this had showed that Neville was now reconciled with Hugh de Lusignan, but his departure had only been postponed. Perhaps the last straw was the decision in September, for which Pandulf, Hubert and Peter were all

[28] *PR*, 240.
[1] *RL*, no. xlii.
[2] *DD*, no. 58.
[3] *DD*, nos 36, 37.

responsible, to assign to Gerard Brochard, master of the Templars in Aquitaine, all the rents of the city of Bordeaux until 1,157 marks owed him by King John had been paid. Neville, in fact, had already pledged half the revenues of Bordeaux in return for a loan of 560 marks. Now he was deprived of one of his few remaining sources of revenue. He left his deputy, William Gualer, as Gualer informed Hubert, no revenues 'save those from the ports, which are only worth £50 from all the things from Poitou or Bordeaux'.[4]

A fortnight after Neville's return to England, Pandulf and Hubert had left Peter at Westminster and were on their way with the great seal to Hereford. There, early in December, Pandulf, on the advice of Archbishop Langton, the bishop of Hereford, Hubert and the Marcher barons, gave Llywelyn a day for the settlement of outstanding grievances: 7 January at Worcester. Measures were also taken to help Reginald de Braose fortify his castle of Builth against the king's enemies.[5] Around this time Reginald wrote to Hubert noting that the king's council had conceded to him the honour of Kington, which formed part of the Braose inheritance in Herefordshire, 'through you and by your grace'.[6] Although John de Braose continued his suit for the honour of Bramber in Sussex, Reginald's statement may reflect a decision in his favour in respect of the rest of the Braose inheritance.[7] He thus reaped some reward for his grant of the Three Castles to Hubert.

Reunited at Winchester in mid-December, the triumvirate returned to the question of Mitford. Philip of Oldcoates was given various allowances and was promised that, from the first suitable escheats, he would be given an exchange 'for the farms which he has in his hands from the demesnes of the king': the farms, that is, which he had been conceded in part-exchange for the Vesci lands back in November 1217. On the other hand, he was told to surrender Mitford to Roger Bertram without delay or Pandulf would excommunicate him and lay an interdict on his lands. Oldcoates's insolent response to these favours and threats will be seen in due course.[8]

The government also endeavoured to reach a settlement over the vexed question of the forest. There was every reason to do so. The perambulations carried out since July 1218 had proved completely unacceptable. Huntingdonshire's in July 1219 repeated word for word the verdict of the year before which the government had scornfully rejected.[9] The uncertainty was good for neither side. The government

[4] PR, 203, 232, 243; RL, no. xlvi.
[5] RLC, 409, 434.
[6] RL, no. lxxvi.
[7] CRR, viii, 10–12; ix, 9, 306–7; Walker, 'Hubert de Burgh and Wales', 471.
[8] C 60/12, m. 8; ERF, 40; PR, 224. See below p. 174.
[9] E 32/38, r. 2; PR, 197; RLC, 386; see above pp. 90–1.

could not exploit the forest effectively, as the failure of the measure over assarts had shown, and the counties had made no secure gains from the Charter. What was needed was a compromise which would concede a degree of deforestation without stripping the king of all the forest that he possessed outside his demesne. This was now attempted. On 13 December groups of important *curiales* were appointed in each county to inquire, the following January, through panels of twenty-four knights and freemen, into the boundaries of the forest. The commissioners were empowered to deforest John's afforestations. Those made by Henry II were to be shown to the justiciar and the council 'and if the inquiry pleases them, then immediately forests of this kind will be deforested on the word of the justiciar and the council'.[10]

The insistence on seeing the results of the perambulations before their implementation followed the example of the regent's government. But the perambulations of 1219 were far more elaborately planned than those of the year before, when John Marshal had been given no set programme. They suggest a real effort to achieve a settlement. Doubtless the hope was that the combination of *curiales* as commissioners and the stress on pleasing the justiciar and the council would lead to perambulations less radical than those of 1218–19. This hope, however, proved vain.

Alongside this major initiative, Hubert continued to cope with a flow of petitions and complaints. On 14 December, for example, he issued a royal letter in response to another complaint from Robert de Vieuxpont about encroachment on mines belonging to Carlisle castle, Robert having urged him to act in such a way that 'the honour and profit of the king are maintained and in no respect impeded or diminished'. It is indicative of the influence which Vieuxpont conceived Hubert to possess that his letter was especially altered in order to request Hubert to send his own letters, as well as those of the king, on the matter.[11]

ix. *The triumvirate apart, December 1219–January 1220*

Having been together at Winchester in mid-December, the triumvirate separated until early February, when they were reunited at Westminster. In this period apart, their activities can be traced in no less than twenty-two private letters.[1] The king, Pandulf, Peter and several magnates remained in the Winchester area until after Christmas.

---

[10] *PR*, 258–9; *RLC*, 434b, 435.

[11] SC 1/1, no. 210; *RLC*, 409b; *PR*, 224.

[1] Pandulf's letters to Hubert in chronological order are: SC 1/1, no. 185; *RL*, no. xlviii; SC 1/1, nos 184, 166; *DD*, nos 59, 62; *RL*, no. lxv; *DD*, nos 63–5; *F*, 158; *RL*, no. lxx. Other letters are *DD*, nos 61, 68; *RL*, nos lxi, lxiii, lxvi, lxix; SC 1/1, nos 73, 76, 106, 198.

Pandulf then travelled to Wells for an ecclesiastical council and stayed in the west until the end of the month prior to the meeting with Llywelyn at Worcester, which had been adjourned until 9 February. The king and Peter were together at Salisbury on 31 December. The former then went to Wallingford and thence (10 January) to Northampton. Peter, by contrast, acted as one of the commissioners for the perambulation of the forest in Hampshire before going to West-minster at the end of the month.[2] Hubert, meanwhile, with charge of the seal, was at Westminster in early January for the opening of the Hilary exchequer.

During this period Hubert was concerned with maintaining the rights of the crown and remedying grievances arising from the 1217 peace. Thus, on 24 January, a royal letter reminded the archbishop of Dublin that he had been given the office of legate by the pope 'especially so that you may preserve our rights unharmed and you will defend them all the more strongly the more you brandish the sword', a rebuke which so angered the archbishop that he decided to come to England to clear his name.[3] Hubert also moved to protect one of the great rebels, Roger de Montbegon, from the harassment of the sheriff of Nottinghamshire-Derbyshire, Philip Mark. Philip was ordered to give Montbegon seisin of the manors of North Wheatley and Clayworth for which the latter had a charter of King John. This was to continue the struggle, which the regent had begun in 1217, to implement the terms of the peace settlement on Montbegon's behalf.[4]

The writ in Montbegon's favour was authorized by Hubert and the council, a formula which was becoming increasingly common and which, to some extent, reflected Peter's eclipse. In February 1220 it was, for example, Hubert and the council which made a decision at the exchequer.[5] Hubert's authority over the latter office was also very clear. In December 1219 William Brewer had asked whether he should perambulate the forest in Hampshire or sit with him at the exchequer. Hubert decided, against Brewer's advice, on the former, perhaps so that Brewer could keep an eye on the bishop of Winchester's performance as a commissioner in a county where he would benefit considerably from extensive deforestation.[6] When the Hilary term of the exchequer opened, presumably on 14 January, Hubert was able to preside for the first time without Peter's presence. In May 1219, Pandulf had written to Ralph de Neville about the working of the

---

[2] SC 1/1, nos 184, 198, 106; *RL*, nos lxi, lxiii; *RLC*, 434b, 410b.

[3] *RLC*, 435; see *RLC*, 404, 494; *RL*, nos lxxiv, lxxxiv.

[4] *RLC*, 410; see above p. 58 and below p. 179.

[5] E 159/3, m. 13.

[6] SC 1/1, no. 76; *RLC*, 434b. That William was not with Hubert in January 1220 is evident from *RL*, no. lxix.

exchequer. Now he told Hubert to 'order the exchequer as you think most expedient' and sought the advice of Hubert 'and the others' who were there.[7]

If Hubert, in control of the seal and the exchequer, formed one centre of power at this time, another was very clearly with Pandulf. It was he who dealt with the problem of the date and location of the next meeting with Llywelyn. The latter had informed Pandulf of his refusal to come to the council arranged for Worcester in January. Amongst other things, he alleged that he had a 'good and authentic' document from King John exempting him from attending any *colloquium* outside his own boundaries.[8] Pandulf would have none of this. He agreed to postpone the meeting until 9 February but fixed it once again for Worcester. Hubert did not participate in this decision but Pandulf, in informing him about it by letter, stressed that he had acted on the advice of the bishops of Winchester and Salisbury, the earl of Salisbury, William Brewer, Philip de Albini and Geoffrey de Neville.[9] On other occasions Pandulf was careful to involve Hubert in decisions. It was probably at this time that Hugh de Vivonne wrote to Hubert, 'as my greatest hope for consolation', begging that a particular marriage be conceded to his nephew, Hugh Chaceporc, 'so that I and mine can stay in England (*in partibus anglicanis*)'. He had, he declared, already spoken to Pandulf and Peter, who declared that 'if it pleased you, it pleased them'.[10] On 29 December Pandulf himself wrote to Hubert to say that those around him agreed that a wardship should be given to William Brewer but the letter was altered to include the clauses 'if your counsel coincides with this' and 'if you judge it expedient'. On 2 January Hubert issued the required letter in Brewer's favour, doubtless grateful for Brewer's own letters at this time which were keeping him in touch with Pandulf's proceedings.[11]

In these matters there was no disagreement between the triumvirate but equally, with authority thus fragmented, there were bound to be misunderstandings and delays. On 3 January, for example, from Stanley in Wiltshire, Pandulf told Hubert of the death of John de Neville and ordered that his lands be taken into the king's hands. He was ignorant of the fact that, as long ago as 14 December, John's brother and heir had done homage to the king and been given seisin of the inheritance.[12] When a prisoner escaped from Winchester gaol, the

[7] *RL*, no. lxv; *F*, 158. See above pp. 129–30.
[8] SC 1/1, no. 73 (*CACW*, 2).
[9] *RL*, no. xlviii.
[10] SC 1/1, no. 211.
[11] SC 1/1, nos 184, 73 (*CACW*, 2); *ERF*, 41. For Brewer thanking Hubert, *RL*, no. lxix.
[12] SC 1/1, no. 166; *RLC*, 409b.

gaoler made his excuses first to Peter and the king, and then returned to Hampshire to explain matters to William Brewer, who equipped him with a sympathetic letter to Hubert.[13] In this case Pandulf was not consulted. In another, in January 1220, there was concern that Pandulf had failed to consult his colleagues. On 16 January Pandulf sent the king the new bishop-elect of Ely and asked him to take his fealty. The bishop-elect found the king at Wallingford but, as the latter informed Hubert and Peter in a letter authenticated by the seal of his steward, William de Cantilupe, 'since we do not have your counsel, with the assent and advice of the elect, we send him to you, ordering you to send him speedily back to us, with a letter [about what is] to be done'.[14]

The issue which must have given rise to most tension between the ministers was that of patronage. Peter and Hubert each had their own followers and supporters to satisfy and their strength and prestige depended on being able to do so. 'My sole hope is in God and in you', Ralph de Trubleville informed Hubert around 1220. Unless Hubert provided him with patronage there were 'no way' he could stay any longer with the king.[15] At the end of 1219, when the king's falconer, Walter de Hauvill, died, Hubert wrote to Peter suggesting that his lands be entrusted to Geoffrey and Gilbert de Hauvill. Peter, however, entertained his own ideas. At Salisbury, on 31 December, he had got the king to write to Pandulf asking 'for the lands to be committed with your council' (as he told Hubert) to Henry de Hauvill. He now advised Hubert to postpone the whole matter until it could be discussed with Pandulf, averring, at the end of the letter, 'we desire very much to speak with you'. Hubert took Peter's advice but got his way, on 12 February, the Hauvill lands being given to Geoffrey and Gilbert de Hauvill.[16]

A government in which even minor questions of patronage went to and fro in this way would always find it difficult to move with force and despatch. Yet in one matter, in January 1220, speed seemed essential. This was the business of renewing the truce with the king of France, which was due to expire at Easter. On 17 January Hubert was told by Pandulf to delay no further over sending envoys to the king. They were not to return without securing a definite reply from King Philip.[17] Pandulf had also sent Hubert a draft of a possible letter to the king, although he acknowledged that, with Peter and William Brewer, to whom he wrote separately, he might be able to devise a better.[18] There

[13] SC 1/1, no. 75.
[14] RL, no. lxiii; SC 1/1, no. 106. Note that the letter, announcing the king's assent to the election, was authorized by Hubert and the council, rather than Hubert and Peter: PR, 224–5.
[15] SC 1/1, no. 202.
[16] SC 1/1, no. 198; RLC, 411; West, Justiciarship, 245.
[17] DD, no. 62.
[18] DD, nos 59, 60, 61. For Peter's ensuing letter to Hubert, see no. 68.

were indeed reasons for speed and anxiety. The process of renewal had begun smoothly enough in the early part of 1219 but since then there had been delays. In September 1219 an envoy had been sent to King Philip with a draft treaty but no reply had been vouchsafed, despite, as Pandulf complained, the despatch of further envoys.[19] Meanwhile, late in 1219, the mayor and burgesses of La Rochelle warned Hubert of intelligence that, when the truce expired, 'the king of France has decided to descend on us first at La Rochelle with arms . . . remembering that last time [in 1204], he had all the land of Poitou in his power save La Rochelle . . . and realizing that if he can subdue it in any way, he will easily possess the rest of the land of Poitou'.[20] Equally alarming were the rumours that King Philip was trying to tempt Hugh de Lusignan into his allegiance by the offer of the county of Eu and that Hugh himself was about to throw over King Henry's sister and marry the daughter of King Philip's seneschal of Anjou.[21] Meanwhile, just before Christmas 1219, despite the existing truces, a dispute had broken out on the border of Anjou and Poitou, between Philip's seneschal of Anjou and the Angevin loyalist, Guy de la Possonnière, lord of Rochefort-sur-Loire. This forced Guy, as he told Hubert in a letter, to fortify the king's castle at Rochefort against assault.[22]

Not surprisingly, therefore, the burgesses of La Rochelle 'on bended knees, with floods of tears', begged for troops and money to fortify their town and other towns in Poitou. Likewise, Guy de la Possonnière demanded help to defend Rochefort. He also urged the despatch of a new seneschal, otherwise 'I fear very much that the king will suffer great damage'.[23] The urgent need to choose a new seneschal was indeed another theme of Pandulf's letters to Hubert. On 17 January the latter was instructed not to 'wait for counsel on these matters, since we wish it and advise it in every way in good faith'.[24]

There was nothing, of course, that the government could do to meet these demands for material help and the despatch of a new seneschal was, for various reasons, delayed for another year. But, in respect of the negotiations with the king of France, Hubert did move with speed, envoys having been appointed by 25 January.[25] Meanwhile, Pandulf endeavoured to stiffen Hubert's nerve in the face of impending trouble at home. 'Since', he wrote on 24 January, 'as several have told us, many people are coming to London in a spirit not of devotion but

[19] PR, 205–6; DD, nos 46, 60.
[20] DD, no. 52.
[21] F, 159; DD no. 70.
[22] DD nos 69, 70.
[23] DD, nos 52, 70.
[24] DD, no. 62.
[25] RLC, 410b.

disturbance, we advise and order you, deferring to no-one against justice, to place your hope in the Author of salvation, since we fear nothing, whatever men say against us.'[26] There was no question of Hubert resenting Pandulf's interference. Quite the reverse: in the face of the rumours, he himself urged Pandulf to return to London. This, however, the latter was reluctant to do: it would mean 'labouring' to London and then back to the west to Worcester for the meeting with Llywelyn, a meeting that Pandulf ordered Hubert to attend.[27] Hubert, however, stuck to his point and got William Brewer, who blamed Pandulf's attitude on his dislike of London, to write as well urging the legate's return.[28]

On 30 January Pandulf at last gave way and postponed the meeting with Llywelyn, 'since', he wrote to Hubert, 'we have not come to do our will but what is expedient for the honour of the church and the utility of the king and kingdom'. 'I hope', he concluded, 'that your counsel is sound and our labour useful and fruitful.' The next day he wrote again in a more sympathetic vein. He was hastening to London 'for the urgent affairs of the king and kingdom'.[29]

x. *The triumvirate in London; Philip of Oldcoates; February 1220*

Pandulf, as he said, was brought back to London by 'many necessities'. One of these was Philip of Oldcoates's continued defiance over Mitford. The threats delivered in mid-December, of excommunication by Pandulf and the seizure of his lands, had fallen on deaf ears.[1] Instead, Philip, in a letter to Hubert, vented all the feelings of loyalists who had won the war and seemed to be losing the peace. 'You should not allow us to be everywhere trampled upon, nor do we wonder that those things which we justly possess, we are unwilling to relinquish into the hands of your enemies since up till now we have been the loser in all things and thus we have become opprobrious to our enemies and an object of derision in our own circle.'[2] Philip, however, like the earl of Pembroke earlier, did not blame Hubert for what was going wrong. Indeed, he thanked him for 'the great diligence which you placed in the expedition of my affairs at Winchester', a reference to the various concessions made to him in mid-December. He also assumed that Hubert too would regard Bertram as an enemy. The real culprit was

[26] *DD*, no. 63.
[27] *DD*, no. 59; *RL*, no. lxv; *DD*, no. 63.
[28] *RL*, no. lxix.
[29] *F*, 158; *RL*, no. lxx.
[1] See above p. 168.
[2] *RL*, no. x. It is possible that the clerk got this phrase the wrong way round and meant to say that Philip had been made *opprobrium* in his own circle and *derisio* to his enemies.

elsewhere: 'you should not, we are sorry to say, for fear of one single man, allow such people [presumably Bertram and his like] to be promoted beyond their merits, people who deserve to go under rather than to flourish'.

The 'single man' stigmatized here was clearly Pandulf and it was to Pandulf that Hubert forwarded Philip's letter, asking him what to do. Pandulf's reply, from Malmesbury on 25 January, was robust: 'an excess of this kind cannot be left unpunished . . . these offences are seen to touch all the kingdom'. However, he was unwilling to proceed without the counsel of Hubert and others of the king's *fideles*, 'lest it be said by our enemies that we have acted rashly and unwisely, even if our sole counsel is perfectly good'. At this stage Pandulf still intended to go to Worcester. It was with the advice of those there that he would decide what was for 'the honour of the king and to the confusion of the unfaithful and our decisions will hold fast with due firmness'.[3] What ultimately changed his mind were perhaps the rumours of those coming to London 'in a spirit not of devotion but of disturbance'. Amongst the latter were probably Falkes and the earls of Salisbury and Pembroke.

Between 3 and 7 February the potentially explosive case between Falkes and the earl of Pembroke was to reopen at the bench.[4] There was also tension between Falkes and Salisbury over Lincoln castle, where the former was providing part of the garrison. On 9 January messengers from Nicola de Hay had come before Falkes and the king at Northampton warning them that Salisbury, offering bribes and hostages, was doing all he could to gain entry into the castle.[5] Hubert tried to hold the balance between the parties. In November he had protected Pembroke's knight, William de Ros, from Falkes's bailiffs. Now, in January, when he wrote to Pandulf about the church of Combe, he almost certainly asked for it to be bestowed on one of Falkes's clerks, something the latter had requested 'so that from one devoted to you I might become still more so.'[6]

With Pandulf in London, the main pleadings between Falkes and Pembroke went ahead, with the earl accusing Falkes of 'wickedly' forging his charters. Judgement was postponed until the Easter term.[7] A response was also concerted in the Oldcoates affair. He was given another chance. His contempt for royal orders, as a royal letter to him on 6 February observed, merited severe punishment but, thanks to the king's 'sincere love', he was given fifteen days in which to surrender

---

[3] *F*, 158.

[4] *CRR*, viii, 248–52.

[5] *RL*, no. lxi.

[6] *RL*, no. lxvi; *DD*, no. 65. Pandulf wrote back to say that he had already given the church to the son of the count of Savoy.

[7] *CRR*, viii, 248–52. For the settlement of the case, see below p. 203.

Mitford to Pandulf's almoner. If he failed to do so, he would be excommunicated and his lands taken into the king's hands.[8]

Thus Oldcoates escaped immediate punishment, despite Pandulf's threats. Perhaps Hubert pleaded for his old comrade (they had defended Chinon together in 1204–5); but the basic fact was that, with the danger hanging over Lincoln castle, with the case between Falkes and the earl of Pembroke in session at the bench and with the court tied to London anxiously awaiting the arrival of envoys from the king of France, this was no time to set the north in flames. So, although Pandulf had dismissed Oldcoates's excuses as 'frivolous', the letter of 6 February went on calmly, but firmly, to reason with him about them.[9] Oldcoates alleged that he was both unable and unwilling to vacate Mitford until the earl of Salisbury had surrendered Mere to Hugh de Balliol, Balliol's men now being installed in the castle. On this question Oldcoates offered to stand by the testimony of Philip Mark, who had carried messages between himself and the council. The *majores* of the council, however, now declared that there was no connection between Mere and Mitford, although full justice was promised Hugh over his claims to the manor.

Oldcoates's further assertion that Hubert and Peter had promised him compensation for his expenditure on Mitford was also dismissed on the grounds that such an undertaking could not bind the king. Perhaps Hubert and Peter resented being disowned in this way. At any rate, another royal letter sent to Oldcoates, with or without Pandulf's knowledge, promised that in compensation for his works on the castle he could have 50 marks owed to the king by Roger Bertram, *once* the latter had gained seisin of Mitford.[10] Thus the government, torn by different views as to how to proceed, reacted with a mixture of threats and arguments, tinged with conciliation. The mixture had no effect on Oldcoates. He had some grounds for thinking that promises made to him had been unfulfilled, for the issues of Mitford and Mere had certainly been linked in the past.[11] Once again he called the government's bluff and got away with it. He did not surrender Mitford and was neither excommunicated nor deprived of his lands.[12]

xi. *The renewal of the truce with the king of France, March 1220*

If the Oldcoates affair was a humiliating failure for the government, and in particular for Pandulf, it was redeemed by one great success: the

---

[8] *PR*, 225–6.

[9] *PR*, 225–6; *F*, 158.

[10] C 60/12, m. 7; *Pipe Roll 1220*, 194.

[11] See above pp. 88, 162.

[12] For the sequel, see below p. 197.

renewal of the truce with the king of France. By 25 February the envoys despatched in January had returned with ambassadors from King Philip, who bore with them a draft of the treaty.[1] It is not impossible that the delays over the New Year, about which Pandulf had complained, reflected divisions at the French court. That Louis himself coveted Poitou is clear from subsequent events. In the end, however, King Philip's counsels prevailed. His priority had always been the retention of Normandy, contiguous as it was to the French royal demesne and yielding far more revenue than Anjou, Poitou and Gascony put together.[2] He had no wish, late in life, to risk Normandy for dubious advantages further south.

When Philip's envoys arrived, Pandulf convoked a council of lay and ecclesiastical magnates.[3] Bishop Peter now felt sufficiently confident to pay King Philip back for his delays. The writ he attested, summoning the earl of Pembroke to the council, concluded: 'the sooner you care to come the more wearisome the delay will be for the envoys of the king [of France] . . . if we defer bringing the matter to a conclusion'. This letter reached the earl at Cirencester as he was hastening to his mother, who was grievously ill at Chepstow, in fact on her death-bed. The piece of diplomatic gamesmanship was either above his head or beneath his contempt. Whilst characteristically assuring the king that 'always and everywhere I am prepared to obey your orders as my dearest lord', he simply returned the writ of summons with the request that he be given an exact date to be in London, since the writ did not mention one.[4]

In fact, at Westminster more cautious counsels prevailed and matters were concluded as quickly as possible. On 3 March King Henry issued letters patent which confirmed the continuation of the existing truce for four years from Easter 1220.[5]

The renewal of the truce afforded the government a breathing space. On the face of it, the moment was ideal for appointing a new seneschal for Poitou and Gascony, as Pandulf and Guy de La Possonnière were urging; a seneschal who, under cover of the truce, might set about restoring the king's authority in those provinces. The problem, however, was less one of personality than of resources. Geoffrey de Neville was a hard, energetic man, yet as seneschal he had been treated 'like a little boy'. The financial resources available in Poitou and Gascony were negligible and there was little prospect of them being

[1] *DD*, no. 71; *F*, 159.
[2] Holt, 'The loss of Normandy and royal finance', 95–6, 104–5, although see Mr Gillingam's discussion of the revenues of Anjou and Aquitaine in *Angevin Empire*, 42–4, 73.
[3] *Walt. Cov.*, 243.
[4] *DD*, no. 71; SC 1/4, no. 74.
[5] *F*, 158–9; *Layettes*, i, nos 1387–9.

supplemented from England. While the king was staying at the Tower of London during Lent, Pandulf had to lend 200 marks towards his expenses.[6] The most that Hubert and the council hoped to give Geoffrey de Neville in mid-February, when there was a scheme (in fact postponed) to send him back to Poitou as a stop-gap measure, was 300 marks, a sum far inferior to the debts that he had left behind there.[7]

In these circumstances, if the government sent someone out from England as seneschal he would be utterly powerless, but if it turned to a great Poitevin magnate he might prove impossible to control. One name canvassed for the post around this time by Pandulf and the council was that of the count of Aumale. This proposal was not as far-fetched as it seemed. It had the advantage of removing a trouble-maker from England and it would mean appointing a native of Poitou whose main interests nonetheless were in England, thus giving the government a means of disciplining him.[8] The earl of Salisbury, however, did not see it like this. There had been an agreement for Salisbury's younger son to marry Aumale's daughter. When Aumale called this off, Salisbury had written to Hubert, whom he had just seen at the exchequer, to say that, if the count misbehaved in future, it would be nothing to do with him. Now he wrote to Pandulf to say that Aumale's appointment as seneschal would not go forward with his consent, 'since it seems to me that the count, in respect of the things which he now keeps in England, which are small, is less obedient than he should be to the orders of the king; so I have no doubt that if he had the seneschalship and dominion of Poitou which is great, he would be even less obedient to the king's orders'.[9] Clearly Salisbury viewed his own acts of disobedience in a very different light.

All that was done at this time, therefore, was to send out a succession of special envoys to Poitou.[10] These crossed with ambassadors from Hugh himself who put some pointed questions about what exactly their lord could expect from his marriage to Joan, the king's sister. The replies, contained in a royal letter of 10 March, were extraordinarily frank. In respect of John's promise, under the terms of the marriage alliance in 1214, to increase Hugh's lands, the king reminded Hugh that, until it was fulfilled, John had granted him Saintes, the Saintonge and the isle of Oléron. King Henry then said that, with Hugh's counsel and aid, he would try to put the promise into effect. But, since this

[6]   *RLC*, 415 and 414b for another loan from the citizens of London.
[7]   *RLC*, 411b.
[8]   For Aumale's family background in Poitou, see Turner, 'William de Forz', 222–4. Fors is twelve kilometres south of Niort. However, the chief holdings of the family may have been in the isle of Oléron.
[9]   *RL* nos xv, cx.
[10]   *RLC*, 411; *DD*, no. 76.

involved obtaining for Hugh £2,000 worth of land in Anjou and the
Touraine, counties controlled by the king of France, the prospects of
doing so were, in fact, remote. What Hugh was really after was a
permanent grant of Saintes, the Saintonge and Oléron instead, but this
was not forthcoming. As for the fees promised by John to various of
Hugh's knights, 'we wish you to know', King Henry confessed, 'that we
have not the wherewithal to fulfil all that our father promised'.[11]

The English government was telling nothing but the truth, although
in doing so it certainly displayed a remarkable complacency. It could
surely have scraped together the 160 marks of Geoffrey de Neville's
debts for which Hugh had stood surety back in 1219, instead of merely
promising to speak to Neville about them when he got back from
Scotland.[12] The fact was that, now the truce with the king of France
had been renewed, Hugh had missed the bus, or so the English
government thought. In reality, he could hardly have been shown more
plainly how little he could expect from his marriage to Joan and how
little he had to fear from throwing her over.

xii. *The process of conciliation, April 1220*

During the Easter term of 1220, in the course of his case at the bench
against Henry de Tracy, Reginald de Braose complained bitterly of the
council's failure to fulfil the promises made to him when he had entered
the king's faith in 1217.[1] His complaints were not entirely in vain; if he
never wrested Barnstaple from Tracy, he was soon to recover Totnes
from Henry fitz Count.[2] Other former rebels, in April 1220, demonstrated considerable confidence in the government. On 6 April a
dramatic scene took place in the Nottinghamshire county court. Roger
de Montbegon, despite Hubert's intervention the previous January,
was still finding the peaceful seisin of his lands obstructed by the sheriff,
Philip Mark, and when the county court, manipulated by Mark's
agents, denied him the return of corn seized from those lands,
Montbegon stormed out of the meeting shouting, 'if you don't want to
return the corn to me I will seek it as I am able'. But Montbegon did not
cut loose in Nottinghamshire. Instead, he hurried to Westminster and
secured a writ (dated 11 April) which ordered the sheriff of Nottingham
to return his corn and allow him peaceful possession of his lands.[3] A
fortnight later Hubert and Peter took responsibility for the first
appointment of a former rebel to a sheriffdom. This was Robert

---

[11] *F*, 159. For the marriage contract with Hugh: *RCh*, 197b-8.
[12] *F*, 159; *DD*, nos 36, 37.
[1] *CRR*, viii, 365.
[2] *CRR*, ix, 111-12; Sanders, *Baronies*, 104-5; *PR*, 206-7; see below p. 216.
[3] *RL*, no. lxxxvi; *RLC*, 415; see above p. 170.

Mantell, who fined in 100 marks for the sheriffdom of Essex-Hertford-shire, counties over which the government had free disposal, thanks to the death of the regent. Six of the thirteen pledges for Robert's fine were former rebels, including the earl of Oxford.[4]

The earl of Oxford's credentials as a pledge were unimpeachable, for he had just been elevated to one of the highest positions in the government. During April 1220 Hubert presided over several sessions of the bench. While he did so, Oxford was introduced as one of the judges and thereafter, down to the Easter term of 1221 (a period when Hubert did not sit), the earl presided at the bench as the senior judge.[5] Oxford's nomination had a precedent in the appointment of the earl of Arundel to the bench in the Michaelmas term of 1218 but it was much more significant, for Oxford was not merely a former rebel. He was also one of the twenty-five barons of Magna Carta's security clause and had actually attested the letters which implemented the twenty-five's judgements on John's disseisins and malpractices.[6] It would be hard to think of a more emphatic measure of reconciliation than his promotion after the war to be the senior justice of the bench. Reginald de Braose and other rebels with cases before the court could at least have no complaints about the political bias of their judges.

A far more difficult task was to reach an acceptable settlement in the question of the forest. Here the government continued to tread a difficult path between the rights of the king and the demands of the counties. By April 1220 it had digested the returns of the perambula-tions carried out the previous January.[7] The hope that these would achieve a workable compromise proved false. The new perambulations were just as radical as the old. In Oxfordshire and Buckinghamshire, for example, the perambulators, who were twenty-four knights from each county, asserted that Henry II had placed within the regard, that is, within the forest, all the woods of the knights which were now within the forest in the counties. Before his time there had 'never' been either regard or regarderers save in the demesne woods of the king, the 'never' being an emphatic rejection of the argument that Henry had merely recovered what had been lost under Stephen. In effect the perambu-lators were demanding that, outside the demesne woods, both counties should be completely deforested.[8] The twenty-four knights and free tenants who made the perambulation in Huntingdonshire were even more vehement. They repeated the assertion of the perambulations of

---

[4] C 60/12, m.6; *PR*, 231; *RLC*, 326. Robert's under-sheriff was to be appointed with the consent of Hubert and the council.

[5] Meekings, 'Concords'.

[6] Holt, *Magna Carta*, 349.

[7] See above pp. 168–9.

[8] C 47/11/1, nos 19, 14.

1218 and 1219 that, apart from the demesne woods, it was Henry II who had 'created' the forest in the county and they went on to complain about the burden of the forest officials and the multiplication 'until the present day' of innumerable evil customs: 'to such a degree', they concluded, have 'the evils in England multiplied'. They then turned to the immediate past, reminding the government of the two previous perambulations of the Huntingdonshire forest and the fact that they had fined in 40 marks (in 1218) to have seisin according to the results. They had then been deprived of seisin, having enjoyed it for nearly a year, why they did not know. 'All in the county' sought its return.[9]

The Huntingdonshire remonstrance reveals, more forcefully than any other document in this period, the frustration felt in the counties at the failure to implement the Charter of the Forest or, as the government would have claimed, at the failure to pervert it. The perambulations equally reveal how strong feelings were over the issue amongst the knightly class. In both Oxfordshire and Buckinghamshire the twenty-four knights who carried out the perambulations were concerned to deforest the woods of 'the knights' now within the regard. Grievances over the forest were not confined to knights, however. In Huntingdonshire, where the forest covered all the county, the perambulators were knights and free tenants, and they associated 'all in the county' with their demands.

Once again, however, the government did not give way before this pressure. Towards the end of April it ordered the Yorkshire forest between the Ouse and the Derwent to be kept as in John's time 'until we have been certified whether the perambulation of the forest was justly done . . . and whether the knights sworn to do that perambulation have robbed us in that perambulation or not'. Two days later the men of Berkshire were forbidden to take advantage of their perambulation until it was accepted by the council.[10]

The rejection of the perambulations, however, was balanced by acts of conciliation. On 27 April, in response to complaints brought before the king by the men of Nottinghamshire, Derbyshire and elsewhere, Philip Mark and other foresters were ordered to limit the number of their officials appointed to keep the king's forest. In addition, as in November 1219, they were ordered to 'treat [those within the forests] . . . in so friendly a fashion that they no longer have reason to complain of the oppressions of you and yours'. Philip Mark, in his capacity as sheriff, was also instructed to reduce the number of serjeants he was employing to administer his two counties. The government, in the order of 27 April, equally repeated the sentiments expressed in

---

[9] E 32/38, r. 2; and see above pp. 90–1, 150–1.
[10] *RLC*, 417.

November 1219 about there being a middle way. A moderate number of foresters, it asserted, would both preserve the king's rights better and offend those living in the forests less.[11] Here, perhaps, was a way forward for the kingdom.

xiii. *The justiciar and the council, October 1219–May 1220*

By the end of April 1220 the triumvirate had been in power for approaching a year. The most impressive achievement of this time had been Hubert de Burgh's. He had, as will be seen, found a way of demonstrating that his government worked with counsel and consent. He had also established himself at the centre and secured control over 'the three things in particular' by which, as King Henry later put it, England was governed: 'that is to say the law of the land, the great seal, and the exchequer'.[1] In this pivotal position Hubert had dealt with a mass of petitions for the postponement of law cases, the redress of grievances, the respite of debts, the concession of patronage and the maintenance of the rights of the crown. The opportunities for winning favour, but also for giving offence, had been immense. Hubert had retained his balance. He had kept in with Falkes de Bréauté and the earl of Pembroke, and with Robert de Vieuxpont and Philip of Oldcoates. He had moved to uphold the rights of the crown, yet had also stressed that local officials must act moderately in accordance with the Charter of the Forest. Hubert's willingness to conciliate former rebels had been demonstrated in the case of Roger de Montbegon and in the elevation of the earl of Oxford to the bench.

If the private letters written to Peter had survived a better idea would be obtained of the business with which he was dealing. But that Peter had lost ground within the central administration there can be no doubt. From July to October 1219 inclusive, ninety-two royal letters were authorized jointly by Hubert and Peter, as against twenty by Hubert and sixteen by Peter acting alone.[2] There was also one letter authorized by Hubert and the council. The most usual formula almost implies Peter's watchful presence at Hubert's elbow, letters being authorized by Hubert 'in the presence' of Peter. But from November 1219 to January 1220 inclusive, only eleven letters were authorized jointly by the two ministers. Hubert acted as sole authorizor of twenty-six letters and took responsibility for another four acting with the council. Peter alone authorized only four letters. This reduction in Peter's role was partly because, for some of the period, he was separated

---

[11] *RLC*, 436–436b; and see above p. 164.

[1] *DBM*, 236–9.

[2] The following figures for authorizations are derived from the printed close and patent rolls and the unprinted fine rolls (C 60/11, 12).

from Hubert and the seal. But even when the two men were reunited at the end of January 1220, the old form of co-operation never completely reasserted itself. In February 1220 twelve letters were authorized by Hubert alone and four by Hubert and the council. Only four were authorized by Peter and Hubert, while Peter authorised not a single letter by himself.[3] In March and April the number of letters authorized jointly by the two ministers outnumbered for the last time (and here only by a small margin) those authorized by Hubert alone or by Hubert and the council.[4] March 1220 is also the last month for which a letter survives written jointly to Peter and Hubert.[5]

Hubert, therefore, had strengthened his grip on the central administration. He had also devised a method of showing that his government acted with the consent of the council, although leaving open what the precise nature of this council was. Increasingly, royal letters were authorised not by Hubert and Peter but by Hubert and the council. Councils, in particular great councils, had played a central role in major decisions under the regent, as has been seen, but the formula 'by the regent and the council' was never appended as a note of authorization to royal letters. From October 1219, by contrast, increasing numbers of letters, often ones which embodied important decisions, were specifically stated to have received authorization from the justiciar and the council. In March 1220 six royal letters were thus authorized; in May 1220 eleven. Since such notes were appended to the actual letters, as well as being inscribed on the chancery rolls, the recipients were plainly informed of the council's role.[6]

How far the new formula reflected a new role for 'the council', whatever that was, as opposed to simply a change in diplomatic practice, is impossible to say. In one sense Hubert's need to demonstrate that he had acted with consent was a sign of his weakness but the phrase, 'the justiciar and the council', also revealed his supremacy over the other anonymous counsellors. It was, moreover, in 1219 and 1220 always 'the justiciar and the council', never 'the bishop of Winchester and the council'. Indeed, in October 1219 a note of authorization which had read 'by the same [Hubert], the bishop of Winchester and the king's council in the presence of the legate' was carefully altered by the deletion of the bishop's name.[7] The formula 'by the justiciar and the

---

[3] Taking all letters, authorized and unauthorized, Hubert attested fifty-five letters in February and Peter five. Martin of Pattishall attested one letter.

[4] Peter only attested two letters in these months, as against 112 attested by Hubert. Martin of Pattishall attested four letters.

[5] *RL*, no. lxxxiii; *RLC*, 414. It should be noted, however, that fewer private letters survive after January 1220.

[6] That the notes of authorization were appended to the letters themselves is clear, for example, from *Ann. Mon.*, iii, 121; *CR 1227–31*, 321.

[7] C 60/12, m.9.

council' left open, of course, whether the council in question was a large gathering of magnates or a small one of ministers. Either might be the case since the term 'the great council' or 'parliament' was not used to distinguish the former. There was, therefore, in the formula a degree of ambiguity, perhaps deliberate, which was to be exposed later in 1220.[8] But it was hardly in Hubert's interests to define matters more closely. He had acted with consent. With luck that consent would be judged wide and sufficient.

xiv. *The frustration of the triumvirate, April 1219–April 1220*

For all Hubert de Burgh's personal achievements, the triumvirate's first year had been a period of immense frustration. It continued to be defied by Philip of Oldcoates at Mitford, by the count of Aumale at Rockingham, by the earl of Pembroke at Fotheringhay and by Henry fitz Count in Cornwall. If William de Coleville had recovered his lands around Bytham from Aumale, he was still excluded from the castle. What was worse, in March and April 1220, private wars seemed to be threatening in Devonshire and Lincolnshire.[1]

In Devonshire this was the consequence of Falkes's installation in the county back in 1218. In March 1220 Falkes informed Hubert that Robert de Courtenay, William Brewer junior and other magnates of Devon and Cornwall had met at Exeter on 9 March, planning to raid and despoil his land, and were only restrained by letters from the earl of Salisbury which forbad them to move until his own truce with Falkes expired on 13 April. This truce the earl wished to make use of in Lincolnshire, a reflection of his continuing conflict there with Falkes over the custody of Lincoln castle. Despite Salisbury's prohibition, Courtenay, who was sheriff of Devon, had forcibly prevented Falkes's men from munitioning Plympton castle. The matter of fact way in which Falkes passed all this on to Hubert strongly suggests that private wars and truces at this time were tolerated by the government and second nature to the magnates. At no point did Falkes complain that either Courtenay's action or the planned descent on his lands was, or would be, in breach of the king's peace. Indeed, the king's peace was not mentioned in the letter. Plainly, in Devonshire, for practical purposes, it did not exist. Falkes's desire for Hubert's intervention was also qualified: his immediate reason for writing was simply Courtenay's claim to have acted on royal orders. Falkes addressed Hubert frankly as a friend who would 'have joy in his success and should grieve at his injuries' but warned that 'although you hold me beloved and

---

[8] See below p. 209.
[1] For the anarchic situation in Yorkshire, see below p. 195.

intimate, do not be precipitate or hasten beyond justice for I do not wish the transgressions done to me and mine to be broadcast to everyone'.[2] There was little danger of Hubert being precipitate but his reaction made a point. In response to Falkes's request for advice about what to do, he apparently counselled him to bring a legal action against Courtenay. This began at the bench later in the year. It was an action for breach of the king's peace.[3]

Early in April 1220 Hubert passed on to Pandulf another piece of alarming intelligence: the earl of Pembroke was strengthening Marlborough castle. Pandulf's response was to order Hubert to issue royal letters 'as strict as you can make them', forbidding such proceedings.[4] Pembroke's tenure of Marlborough highlighted the need to resume the king's castles, counties and manors. But since April 1219 virtually nothing had been achieved in terms of implementing the programme laid out by Pandulf and the papacy. Little progress had been made towards a resumption of the royal demesne; likewise, the county farms of Shropshire, Staffordshire, Lancashire, Cumberland, Cornwall, Lincolnshire and Somerset-Dorset were still outside the control of the exchequer. At the end of April 1220 another effort was made to reassert royal authority over Cornwall. The men of the county were told no longer to obey the sheriff, Henry fitz Count, who had left court without licence, unwilling to obey the king's orders.[5] But it remained to be seen whether Henry's dismissal could be made a reality. The question mark over the government's authority, while the king was under age, to remove sheriffs and castellans appointed by King John was demonstrated in another transaction. On the day of Henry fitz Count's 'dismissal', Richard fitz Regis, John's bastard by the sister of the earl of Surrey, surrendered Wallingford castle. Richard was about to depart overseas. He had done less well than the earl of Chester and Geoffrey de Neville, men of much greater influence, who had retained their custodies in similar circumstances. Nonetheless, the government's victory was qualified by an agreement that Richard should recover the castle if he returned before the king came of age. He also remained as sheriff of Berkshire.[6]

Behind the government's weakness, of course, lay the sickly state

---

[2] *RL*, no. cxlix. For Falkes's installation in Devonshire, see above pp. 78–9.

[3] *CRR*, ix, 322. Falkes's legal action shows that the episode belongs to 1220 and not as usually supposed to 1221. The royal letter to the sheriff of Devon of March 1221 which has been taken to prove the latter date (*RLC*, 451) is different in content from the one referred to in Falkes's letter to Hubert: *RL*, no. cxlix. For the substantive pleadings in Falkes's case, see *CRR*, x, 115–16.

[4] *RL*, no. lxxxv.

[5] *PR*, 231.

[6] *PR*, 231–2; E 159/3, m.13.

of the royal finances. Early in April 1220 there was no money at all in the treasury.[7] When the Easter session of the exchequer opened on 6 April, the initial *Adventus* produced a pitiable £52, actually less than the year before.[8] The total proceeds from the counties for the whole Easter term (for which a receipt roll survives)were only £1,733, a sum which suggests that the king's annual cash income was still around £5,000. Jewish debts were making no decisive difference to the situation. The receipt roll, providing evidence of these for the first time, shows that they amounted to £186 19s ½d. At the end of the Easter term the exchequer anxiously balanced income and expenditure, and noted, with relief, that there were still £133 14s 5d in the treasury![9] By contrast, a surviving budget of the French monarchy for one of the three financial terms of 1221 reveals a surplus of revenue over expenditure of more than £9,000.[10]

There were, nonetheless, some achievements to set against the triumvirate's failures. The truce had been renewed with the king of France. At home, the exchequer had been much more successful, in 1219–20, in securing accounts from the sheriffs than it had been the year before. If there had been no general resumption of the king's castles and demesnes, at least new concessions of county and manorial farms to members of the regime had been virtually halted.[11] The earl of Salisbury, moreover, had surrendered the farm of Southampton and been kept out of Lincoln castle. Philip of Oldcoates had vacated the Vesci custody, while William de Coleville had won his assize of novel disseisin against the count of Aumale. Above all, perhaps, Hubert's role at the centre and the measures to conciliate former rebels had given the government a broad basis of support. For all its failures and humiliations, it had never given up the struggle to assert royal authority. Like a lifeboat in heavy seas, after each buffet of the waves its rudder had turned it back on to course and its engine had pushed it slowly forward on its way. In the next ten months many of the particular problems which had frustrated the government would be brought to a solution.

[7] Whitwell, 'Revenue and expenditure under Henry III', 710 n. 1.
[8] See Appendix, p. 415.
[9] Appendix, p. 414; Whitwell, 'Revenue and expenditure under Henry III', 710, n. 1.
[10] Baldwin, *Philip Augustus*, 352.
[11] The royal manor of Easingwold was conceded to Robert, *quondam* abbot of Thorney, in October 1219 when he was sent on his mission to the pope but he was expected to answer for its farm at the exchequer: C 60/12, m.9; *PR*, 221.

Chapter 5

THE TRIUMVIRATE, 1220–21: SUCCESS

i. *The king's second coronation, May 1220*

On 3 April 1220 Pandulf wrote to Hubert from Merton in Surrey. He had, he said, already heard Hubert's news from another source; he would decide nothing until he had discussed with Hubert and other *fideles* what was expedient for 'the royal honour and utility'.[1] Hubert's news was almost certainly the return from Rome of Robert, *quondam* abbot of Thorney, with papal letters authorizing the king's second coronation. The decision, taken at a council in London, was to proceed with the ceremony without delay. Pandulf and Langton appointed the feast of Pentecost, 17 May, as the day, the place, of course, being Westminster abbey.[2]

The king's second coronation marked a turning point in the political history of the minority. Admittedly, within a few months Llywelyn had forcefully affirmed his power in south Wales, while at home the king's finances remained precarious. Another attempt to resume the royal demesne came to nothing and although a general tax was conceded, its proceeds proved highly disappointing. In addition, the government's authority to act without proper counsel and consent was directly challenged. Nonetheless, the coronation was followed in quick succession by Philip of Oldcoates's surrender of Mitford, the count of Aumale's ejection from Rockingham, Henry fitz Count's removal from Cornwall and the earl of Pembroke's resignation of Fotheringhay. Early in the next year the count of Aumale was also expelled from Bytham.

There was little in the immediate situation around the time of the coronation to suggest that this transformation was about to take place. On 26 April Pandulf, writing to Hubert from Dunstable, agreed that 'the times are evil and the malice of men and the times grows daily'. Consequently he accepted Hubert's suggestion that judgement should be postponed in the case which Robert de Vieuxpont was bringing at the bench against the countess of Eu, represented by the earl of Surrey, for the castle and honour of Tickhill. When Vieuxpont, who was in

[1] *RL*, no. lxxxv.
[2] *Walt. Cov.*, 244.

the north, heard this on 10 May, he refused to accept the suggested adjournment and demanded justice on the appointed day. He equally refused, as the bishop of Durham told Hubert by letter, to remain in the north in order to conduct the king of Scotland into England for a meeting planned with King Henry in June. Instead, he intended to be present at the coronation; then, after the hearing of his case, which was due at the bench in early June, he would hurry back to the north to meet the king. When the case, nonetheless, was adjourned, Vieuxpont, present at the bench, challenged the ostensible grounds: 'he did not believe that the earl [of Surrey] had journeyed in the king's service to Scotland'.[3]

Given Vieuxpont's reaction to the mere postponement of the case, Hubert had good grounds for deferring the verdict, which would probably have been in the countess's favour.[4] In that sense, if he privately supported his kinswoman, the countess of Eu, as the earl of Surrey hoped, then he put the tranquillity of the realm first. But, until a verdict was delivered, or a settlement reached, Vieuxpont, under the agreement made in 1218, continued as sheriff of Cumberland without accounting at the exchequer.

The coronation, therefore, went ahead in 'evil days'. There was a multitude of threats to the king's peace and authority in England, while in Wales and Poitou, as will be seen, the situation was even worse. On 17 May Langton crowned the king in Westminster abbey. The *regalia* included a gold crown studded with diverse stones, a gold sceptre and silver gilt staff, and a tunic with a dalmatic of red samite. Much of this was probably new, John's *regalia* having been either lost in the Wash or, more likely perhaps, sold in the war.[5] At least £760 were spent on the ceremony and the celebrations, thus exhausting a good proportion of the revenues from the exchequer's Easter term.[6] The annals of Dunstable, drawn up under the auspices of the prior, who was probably present, averred that 'a greater celebration has not been seen in our days'.[7]

The money was well spent, for the coronation was a turning point in more than a merely chronological sense. Part of its purpose was to enhance the authority of the king and his government, a king dismissed the year before as 'not a king but a boy' and a government which lacked the authority to carry through a resumption of the king's castles,

---

[3] *RL*, nos xcii, xcix; *CRR*, ix, 1–2; for the substantive pleadings in the case, see *ibid.*, 212–13.

[4] For Vieuxpont's eventual abandonment of his claim in return for compensation: *Yorks. Fines*, 42–3.

[5] *Walt. Cov.*, 244; E 401/3B, r.1; Jenkinson, 'The jewels lost in the Wash', 163–6. See also Holt, 'King John's disaster in the Wash', 75–86, and Warren, *King John*, 278–85.

[6] E 401/3B, r.1d.

[7] *Ann. Mon.*, iii, 57

demesnes and possessions. Since Henry II's accession, in all probability, kings of England had taken an oath at their coronations to preserve and recover the rights of the crown.[8] In 1220 it may well be that, under the direction of Pandulf and the papacy, this oath was a focal point of the ceremony. Certainly, the importance of such a clause in the coronation oath was very much in the pope's mind, for later in the year he instructed the king of Hungary to revoke certain alienations because 'at his coronation he had sworn to maintain undiminished the rights of his kingdom and the honor of his crown'.[9]

The oath of the king was combined, on the day after the coronation, with an oath taken by the barons. According to the Dunstable annalist, they swore that they would resign the royal castles and wards in their hands at the king's will and render faithful account for their farms at the exchequer.[10] This oath got to the heart of the government's difficulties. At the time of the coronation Philip of Oldcoates, the count of Aumale and the earl of Pembroke were refusing to surrender the castles of Mitford, Rockingham and Fotheringhay. In addition, Pembroke's tenure of Marlborough was creating anxiety, while Henry fitz Count was ignoring his dismissal as sheriff of Cornwall. Likewise, the sheriffs of Lancashire, Shropshire, Staffordshire, Cumberland, Lincolnshire, Somerset-Dorset and Cornwall, some with the king's licence and some without, were not accounting properly for their farms at the exchequer, while numerous royal manors, instead of producing revenue for the king, were being used to support *curiales* in his service.

The baronial oath of 18 May 1220 was part of a wider programme, which was set out in a series of papal letters sent to England in the month of the coronation. In these, the pope returned to the subject of his letter of April 1219, when he had ordered Pandulf to try to recover, for the king, his castles, demesnes and possessions. But the pope's tone was now far more strident, reflecting Pandulf's frustrations at a year in which nothing had been achieved. The chief consequence of that failure was also specified: the king's poverty. It was, Honorius declared, 'vain and ridiculous to maintain fidelity where the evidence of works contradicts it'. Whereas former kings of England had been wealthy, King Henry, although 'a minor who spends much less than his predecessors, labours ... under such great need that he rarely or never has enough to provide for royal magnificence, wherefore great harm can come to him and such a kingdom'. The pope was clear what had caused this situation: 'speaking openly', it was that lay and ecclesiastical magnates 'have dishonestly usurped and detain usurped ... the castles, manors and vills and other demesnes of the king ... putting forward the

8 *Historiae Anglicanae*, 1869; Richardson, 'The coronation', 153–61; *RL*, 551; *F*, 229.
9 Kantorowicz, 'Inalienability', 490, 499; *Regesta Pontificum*, i, no. 6318.
10 *Ann. Mon.*, iii, 57.

frivolous excuse that they wish to keep these safe until the king comes of full age'. Thus, 'grasping what is not theirs, they feast on the royal goods, while the king begs'. Honorius therefore laid down a three-point programme: the king's castles, manors, vills and other demensnes were to be restored to him; full satisfaction was to be given for the issues received from them since the war; and henceforth no one, however faithful, was to hold more than two royal castles. If the lay and ecclesiastical magnates did not obey these orders, Pandulf was to coerce them with spiritual penalties.[11]

There can be little doubt that the initiative behind the despatch of these letters came from Pandulf himself. Honorius acknowledged as much when, in the last of the letters dated 30 May, he observed that he had responded 'to the diverse articles' which Pandulf, through clerks and messengers, had put forward.[12] Pandulf's attitude in the summer of 1220 was made very plain when consulted by the justices of the bench about a clash between the jurisdictional claims of the king and the church. 'He wished that the royal rights should be preserved', was his reply.[13] Honorius, indeed, as he had done before with Guala, thought it as well to add a note of caution, counselling Pandulf, in the letter of 30 May, to proceed carefully 'concerning the royal castles', lest the barons were given 'material for stirring up trouble in the kingdom'.[14]

It was one thing to lay down a programme of action, another to have the power to execute it. Here, too, the coronation was important. The oath taken by the barons the day afterwards had a second clause. Having sworn to surrender their castles and wards and account faithfully for their farms, they also undertook to wage war against any 'rebel' who resisted the king and, having been excommunicated by Pandulf, made no satisfaction within forty days. The rebel was then to be disinherited. This clause had parallels in the oaths taken in 1218–19 by the 'magnates of England' and by the knights and free tenants in the counties to give assistance to the regent or to the king and his council.[15] It was clearly designed to ensure military support from the barons for the assertion of royal authority against the disobedient castellans. It thus revealed the magnitude of the problem facing the government and the necessity for enlisting help from outside the regime in order to solve it.

The coronation facilitated the mobilization of support in another

---

[11] RL, 535–6; Prynne, An Exact Chronological Vindication, iii, 43 (a parallel letter to that in RL, 535–6, but mentioning 'earls, barons, castellans and other nobles' as the usurpers rather than ecclesiastical lords); F, 160.
[12] VL, Honorius III Regesta X, f. 186d (CPReg.,71).
[13] CRR, ix, 119.
[14] VL, Honorius III Regesta X, f. 186d (CPReg., 71).
[15] Ann. Mon., iii, 57; see above p. 98.

way, for it furthered the rapprochement between the king's government
and former rebels. The key to this process was the establishment of
mutual confidence. It was not enough for former rebels to be ready to
fight for the government. The government had to feel that it was safe to
allow them to do so. It had to be sure that once such men had licence to
draw their swords, they would sheathe them again when bidden. Large
numbers of erstwhile rebels must have been present at the coronation
ceremony. Roger de Montbegon was certainly there, for he received a
concession from the king on the following day. That these men met in a
spirit of harmony is attested by the Barnwell annalist. Old men at the
coronation, he reported, declared that none of Henry's predecessors
had been crowned in circumstances of such concord and tranquillity.[16]
This soothing atmosphere was the result of both the general approach
of the government since the war and the immediate measures of
conciliation in April 1220, which were analysed in the last chapter: the
intervention in favour of Roger de Montbegon; the appointment of
Robert Mantel as sheriff of Essex; the instructions to the forest officials
to behave 'amicably'; and, perhaps above all, the promotion of the earl
of Oxford to the bench. Indeed, these steps, like the postponement of
Robert de Vieuxpont's law case, may well have been designed to secure
harmony at the time of the coronation. Immediately after the ceremony
the earl of Pembroke, his mother having died, did homage for her lands
and fined in £100 for his relief, a potent demonstration to the great
assembly of Magna Carta's value.[17] Five days later, on 22 May, writs
were despatched to all the sheriffs ordering them to eradicate the abuse
of scotale, that is, ale made by officials and sold compulsorily at high
prices, an abuse from which the king and council had learnt that 'a
great deal of evil arises'.[18] This was to take further clause 7 of the
Charter of the Forest which forbad the making of scotale by any forester
or beadle. Thus the coronation marked an important stage in the
course of reconciliation after the war and, in so doing, made government action against refractory castellans the more feasible, as events
were soon to show.

ii *Wales and Poitou, May 1220*

Threats to the king's authority in England around the time of the
coronation were abundantly apparent. So, in even greater measure,
was the weakness of that authority in Wales and Poitou. Just before the
coronation, Hubert, Peter, Pandulf and Archbishop Langton had met
Llywelyn at Shrewsbury. There, on 5 May, an agreement was reached

[16] *Walt. Cov.*, 244.
[17] E 159/3, m.8; E 372/69, r.15d, m.1.
[18] *RLC*, 436b.

whereby Llywelyn had Dafydd, his son by his wife Joan, King John's illegitimate daughter, recognized as his heir by the king of England, thus excluding the claims of his older but illegitimate son, Gruffud. This concession facilitated the realization of one of Llywelyn's chief ambitions: to ensure that his principality of Gwynedd and his overlordship throughout the rest of native Wales should pass intact to Dafydd, instead of being divided between him and his half-brother.[1] At Shrewsbury another concession was made to Llywelyn. His ally, Morgan, was allowed to reopen his case for Caerleon against the earl of Pembroke. (Morgan's attorney, significantly enough, was Falkes's knight, Henry de Frankesney.)[2] In return for all this, Llywelyn agreed, or so the government thought, to surrender Maelienydd, which he had occupied in the war, so that the king could transfer it back to its lord, Hugh de Mortimer. Meanwhile a meeting at Oxford on 2 August was fixed to hear disputes between Llywelyn and the Marcher barons, particularly the earl of Pembroke, and truces were arranged to last until Michaelmas.[3]

This settlement seemed at least to promise peace around the time of the coronation but the court had hardly returned to London before it began to disintegrate. To the formal demand to give up Maelienydd, issued on 10 May, Llywelyn replied that he had only agreed to surrender the homage of the nobles there. He then went on to claim that, in fact, 'their homage belongs to us and our princedom', although he agreed not to raise the question until the king came of age. Meanwhile, neither he nor the king should have 'dominion'. The treaty of Worcester had made it clear that the homages of the Welsh princes belonged to the king, not to Llywelyn. In Maelienydd, and probably throughout the rest of native Wales, Llywelyn was now claiming that they belonged to his princedom, an ambition which would formally bring the whole of native Wales under his lordship. Llywelyn also cautioned the government that if Hugh de Mortimer tried to dispossess the princes in Maelienydd, he would take no responsibility for the 'scandal and disturbance' which would arise, 'especially since we are barely admitted to the king's counsels in these matters'.[4] This gave the government due warning of the disturbances which would arise, although not in Maelienydd, later in the summer.

The extent of the trouble in Wales had yet to be revealed by the time of the coronation but the parlous situation which had arisen in Poitou was all too apparent. The towns had greeted the renewal of the truce in

---

[1] F, 159; Davies, Wales, 249.
[2] RLC, 436b; PR, 463.
[3] F, 164; RLC, 418, 418b; Walker, 'Hubert de Burgh and Wales', 471.
[4] RL, no.cv. For Llywelyn's refusal to surrender Knighton (on the western fringe of Maelienydd) to Mortimer, see RCh, 229; RLC, 85b; PR, 149; RL, no. xlix.

March 1220 with relief but envoys from La Rochelle and La Réole brought news that William L'Archevêque, the lord of Parthenay, and Robert de Rancon were making war on Niort and St Jean d'Angély, while other local magnates were molesting La Rochelle itself. They begged the king to send a seneschal who could secure his rights and 'defend . . . the land from the attacks of your enemies since those who were there formerly were too weak in the face of your enemies'.[5] The response was minimal. In letters of 21 and 22 May Niort, in effect, was told to defend itself, while, as for a seneschal, it was still a case of 'we are going to send him shortly to your parts'.[6]

Perhaps the government was too astonished to do anything else, for it had just received extraordinary news. Hugh de Lusignan had married. He had thrown over the daughter in favour of the mother and had married Queen Isabella herself. From the point of view of the two participants, the union had everything to recommend it. Only King John's appearance as a suitor had prevented Hugh's father from marrying Isabella in 1200. The marriage was not without advantages for the English government. Indeed Isabella, in her letter of explanation, argued that she had acted wholly in her son's interests: she had rescued Hugh from some French marriage 'by which, if it had happened, all your land in Poitou and Gascony, and our land too, would have been lost'.[7] The problem was that, controlling now the counties of both La Marche and Angoulême, Hugh had almost total dominance in Poitou and the queen warned her son that he should 'behave in such a way towards [Hugh], who is so powerful, that it will not be your fault if he does not serve you well'. That immediately raised the question of whether the government should give way on two issues. The first was mentioned by Isabella herself. She demanded that Hugh be given Niort in Poitou and Exeter castle and Rockingham in England: that is, the portions of her dower of which she had never obtained seisin. The second question was what was to happen to the marriage portion, comprising Saintes, the Saintonge and the isle of Oléron, which Hugh had received with the now discarded Joan. His dominant ambition over the next few years was to retain it, to get, that is, two marriage portions for the price of one marriage.

Faced with these dilemmas, the government prevaricated. On 22 May a royal letter congratulated Hugh on his marriage and, while making no mention of her *maritagium*, asked for the release of the rejected Joan. For the rest, the government invited Hugh to attend England's latest tourist attraction, the translation of the body of Thomas Becket in Canterbury cathedral on 7 July, and promised that

[5] *DD*, nos 78, 79; *RLC*, 418b, 419.
[6] *PR*, 232–3.
[7] *DD*, no. 84.

then all matters would be settled to his satisfaction.[8] This was *not* what Hugh wanted and he was soon spreading disturbance throughout Poitou.

iii *The settlement with the king of Scotland; the surrender of Mitford; June 1220*

Whatever the situation in Poitou, within England the coronation was followed by a series of swift advances by the government, the first being the removal of Mitford from the clutches of Philip of Oldcoates. There was little sign of a change of fortune, however, as Hubert and his colleagues made their way to York, late in May, for a meeting with King Alexander of Scotland. Indeed, a fresh challenge to royal authority was developing at Berkeley castle in Gloucestershire.

On the death of Robert of Berkeley, the sheriff, Ralph Musard, had been ordered to take his castle and lands into the king's hands. In late May or early June, however, Musard had found the earl of Salisbury installed at Berkeley. On demanding that he surrender the castle, together with Robert's lands and chattels, Salisbury had promised obedience to the orders of the king, Hubert and the council. 'But', Musard reported to Hubert by letter, 'you should know that he did not then hand over seisin.' Salisbury had two reasons for this disobedience: he had been owed money by Robert of Berkeley and, more important, he maintained that the latter's widow, who was his 'niece', was pregnant.[1] In effect, therefore, Salisbury was making a pre-emptive bid for the custody of the possessions of the forthcoming heir. Hubert, however, was determined to resist the earl's pretensions. At York, on 12 June, he and the council authorized a letter which ordered Salisbury to surrender the castle. Musard was to go to ensure that he did so, although initially the instruction was more realistic. He was merely to go to see *whether* he did so, which, of course, he did not.[2]

Hubert, here, was apparently acting against the earl of Salisbury, who was still, indeed, refusing to account for the farm of Lincolnshire where he was sheriff. Yet a letter written by Salisbury around this time shows that he was thinking of Hubert in the warmest terms. Salisbury thanked Hubert for what he had said in his letters, explained that illness prevented him coming to York and asked for news of what happened there. He said nothing about Berkeley castle but assured Hubert that he 'could be confident that we will always be prompt and prepared to follow your will in all things for the honour of the king and kingdom'. This was much what he had told Musard but the earl now continued: 'by your grace there is and should be between us so much

---

[8] *DD*, no. 85.

[1] SC 1/1, no. 156; *Peerage*, ii, 126. For the debt, see *Gloucs. Warw. Eyre*, no. 301.

[2] *RLC*, 420; *PR*, 234.

integrity and sincerity of love in which there should be no doubts, that we consider your honour to be ours, and thus, through the help of God, we will be one heart and one will, as is fitting for those once brought up together [*de antiquo nutrimento*]'.[3] These words go far beyond conventional phrases. They indicate that an alliance was forming or had formed between the two men, an alliance which was to be of fundamental importance in the politics of England down to 1225.

Salisbury's reference to his upbringing with Hubert is obscure. What is certain is that, after the war, he had two powerful motives for cultivating friendship with the justiciar. The first, concerning the future of the lands of the count of Perche, will be considered later.[4] The second turned on Salisbury's continued exclusion of the earl of Hereford from the castle and honour of Trowbridge. Salisbury's original installation in place of Hereford had been one of John's arbitrary disseisins which the twenty-five had attempted to reverse in 1215. In 1226 the then earl of Hereford commenced an action at the bench against Salisbury's widow, which eventually led to a partition of the honour between the two families.[5] In holding on to Trowbridge throughout his own lifetime, despite his highly dubious legal title, Salisbury must have felt that nothing was more important than a close relationship with the justiciar.

The earl of Salisbury's tenure of Berkeley castle was not the only problem to confront the government on its way north to York. Anarchy in Yorkshire itself seemed to be reaching a new pitch. In the Hilary term of 1220 the sheriff of the county told the bench that an armed band had prevented him from executing a judgement of the justices in eyre against Robert de Ros. On 5 June Pandulf wrote to Hubert from Lincoln about the sheriff's actual arrest and urged him to secure his release 'according to justice and the law of the land . . . since you are bound to observe this to everyone, acting in such a way that the honour of the king may be preserved unharmed'.[6] The sequel to Pandulf's request is unknown but Hubert certainly took steps to dispense justice on this northern journey. At Leicester he heard all outstanding cases of novel disseisin from the counties of Warwick and Leicester. He did the same at York for the Yorkshire cases and Robert de Ros was convicted of no less than nine disseisins and amerced 200 marks.[7] As the

[3] *RL*, no. cxvi.

[4] See below p. 244.

[5] *CRR*, xii, no. 2646; xiv, no. 751; Sanders, *Baronies*, 91–2; Holt, *Magna Carta*, 121–2, 254, 346.

[6] *CRR*, viii, 198–9; *RL*, no. cxi. Probably 'the sheriff' in these episodes was the under-sheriff of Geoffrey de Neville rather than Neville himself. I cannot follow Norgate, *Minority*, 159 n.3, where Pandulf's letter is dated to January 1221. In the original MS (SC 1/1, no. 347) *Junii* is clearly not a contraction of *Januarii*.

[7] *RLC*, 436b; *Pipe Roll 1220*, 36–7; *Pipe Roll 1221*, 133–4, 137; see *RL*, no. cxiii.

government moved north, moreover, it built on the oaths taken at the coronation by checking, according to the Barnwell annalist, that the castellans of castles appointed by King John were prepared to deliver them peacefully to the king 'as their lord'.[8]

At York the settlement with the king of Scotland, for which Pandulf had been striving since August 1219, was reached. Alexander was to marry Henry's eldest sister, Joan, if she could be recovered from the hands of Hugh de Lusignan in Poitou. If not, he would marry Henry's second sister, Isabella, who was brought to York for inspection. Henry also promised that, within a year from October 1220, husbands would be found 'in his land' for Alexander's sisters, Margaret and Isabella.[9]

Pandulf had certainly achieved a settlement that was favourable to the king of England.[10] Alexander accepted Joan without a *maritagium*; much later he complained that, according to King John's original promise, he should have received Northumbria with her. Equally, his eldest sister, instead of marrying the king of England, was to marry one of his subjects. The only *quid pro quo* was that Alexander was once again promised Fotheringhay and was forgiven the 5,000 marks outstanding from his father's fine of 15,000 marks for the agreement of 1209.[11] How far the English government would be able to fulfil its side of the agreement remained to be seen. It had to rescue Joan from Poitou and prize Fotheringhay from the earl of Pembroke. On 18 June a writ, authorized by the justiciar and council, instructed Pembroke to surrender the castle without delay 'as he wishes there to be love and friendship between the king and the king of Scotland'.[12]

The visit to York in June 1220 was the government's first appearance in the north since the end of the civil war, apart from Pandulf's visit to Norham in 1219. The occasion demonstrated the political rehabilitation of the great northern rebels and thus consolidated the harmony achieved at the coronation. As in November 1217 Robert de Ros was commissioned to conduct King Alexander to England and, despite his convictions before Hubert for disseisin, he was one of those who swore to uphold the eventual treaty. So too did Roger Bertram, Robert de

---

[8] *Walt. Cov.*, 244.

[9] *PR*, 234–5; *F*, 160–1.

[10] Duncan, *Scotland*, 526.

[11] Thus I interpret the 5,000 marks mentioned by the Dunstable annalist (*Ann. Mon.*, iii, 58). Norgate (*Minority*, 140 n.3) has a different interpretation. Duncan (*Scotland*, 246) shows that Alexander's father paid 10,050 marks of the 15,000 mark debt.

[12] *PR*, 236. At this time Pembroke was at the French court arranging for the Norman side of the Marshal inheritance to be conferred on his brother, Richard: *Layettes*, i, no. 1397.

Vaux and William of Lancaster.[13] Not long before, Lancaster and his father, Gilbert fitz Reinfrey, had written to Hubert and the council claiming that there was no way in which they could pay the 2,000 marks outstanding from their ransom, even if 'all our land was sold, or mortgaged for all our lives'. They begged them, 'for love of God and moved by mercy for our great poverty and impotence', to persuade Peter de Maulay, who was collecting the money, to accept payment by instalments.[14] On 8 May 1220, soon after his father's death, William met the bishop of Durham in Richmondshire. He was destitute of horses and equipment and wholly incapable of coming south to see the king, so the bishop, in a letter on his behalf, begged Hubert to allow him to do homage and fine for his relief when the king came to York.[15]

But, if Lancaster was poor in material possessions, he was still rich in status, as his participation in the agreement with Alexander shows. At York, as the bishop requested, he did homage to the king and fined in £100 for his relief, in accordance with the terms of Magna Carta. His pledges for this fine included the northern rebels Peter de Brus, Roger Bertram and Richard de Umfraville, the count of Aumale, who had switched sides during the war, and the northern loyalists Geoffrey de Neville and Hugh de Bolebec.[16]

The great gathering at York provided an ideal forum for Roger Bertram to pressurize the government over Philip of Oldcoates's detention of Mitford. Oldcoates had conducted Alexander through Northumberland but had not come on to York. On 18 June letters authorized by Hubert and the council replaced him as sheriff of Northumberland by Hugh de Bolebec.[17] At long last Oldcoates saw the end of the road. He surrendered Mitford to Bolebec and, in return, was allowed to keep Northumberland.[18] Bertram did not immediately obtain the castle, for Hubert was determined to obtain guarantees from him first. Oldcoates himself may have believed that the fortress would remain in the king's hands.[19] The government, however, had scored a tremendous victory. Since 1217 it had been attempting to get Oldcoates to surrender Mitford. Now it had succeeded. It had enforced its will in the remotest reaches of the realm.

[13] PR, 235.

[14] SC 1/1, no. 92. By November 1221 Maulay had received £1,850 from William: RLC, 481b.

[15] SC 1/1, no. 135.

[16] ERF, 48–9; C 60/12, m.4.

[17] RLC, 421; PR, 236.

[18] Hence Philip accounted for the farm of the county down to Michaelmas 1220 and on his death in November 1220 was described as 'lord' of the county's [under-]sheriff: Pipe Roll 1220, 191; ERF, 56.

[19] See below p. 214.

Oldcoates had eventually succumbed to a mixture of threats and blandishments, a combination that he had resisted well enough in the past. The difference was that the government was in the north surrounded by a large body of magnates. It had the power to implement its menaces, if necessary by military force. The immediate background here was the oath taken by the barons the day after the coronation both to surrender castles to the king and to wage war against those who proved rebellious, an oath which fitted exactly with the Mitford situation. A longer-term background was the reconciliation between the government and former rebels, a reconciliation affirmed at York itself. For just as the army which removed Robert de Gaugi from Newark in 1218 contained many erstwhile rebels, so did the potential army mustered at York. Of course, Oldcoates's enemies would have taken action against him whatever they thought of the government. What was new was that the government was prepared to trust them to do so. In that sense the reconciliation after the war was a two-way affair.

iv. *The siege of Rockingham, June 1220*

Having completed its business at York on 18 or 19 June, the government moved south. Time was short before the second great ceremonial event of the year, the translation of Thomas Becket to his new shrine in Canterbury cathedral, which was due to take place on 7 July. Hubert and Peter were at Nottingham on 20 June, Leicester on the 23rd and Northampton on the 25th. But next day they suddenly doubled back, hurried fifteen miles to the north and arrived at Rockingham. Surprise was total. The count of Aumale was not in the castle and his garrison, according to Roger of Wendover, had only three loaves of bread. After a brief siege, on which Falkes spent £100, the garrison surrendered on 28 June. Possession was also taken of Sauvey castle and the manors that Aumale was detaining in Northampton-shire.[1]

The Barnwell chronicler, in explaining the background to the siege of Rockingham, accused the count of Aumale of a unique act of defiance. After the coronation, he alleged, the king went through the kingdom finding out whether those entrusted with castles by King John would deliver them peacefully to him 'as their lord'. In all the kingdom no castle denied him entry save Rockingham.[2] But was it really like this? The truth seems rather that the count was the victim, not without cause, of a unique act of governmental pressure. The king's perambulation through his kingdom, mentioned by the chronicler, was, in fact,

---

[1] *Chron. Maj.*, 59; *Walt. Cov.*, 245; *RLC*, 439b; *Pipe Roll 1220*, 14; *PR*, 240.
[2] *Walt. Cov.*, 245.

merely his journey to and from York. The king may well have taken the opportunity to receive assurances from Philip Mark at Nottingham and Falkes at Northampton that they would surrender their castles at his order but these places were on the direct route to and from York. The only occasion when the king deviated from that route was when he doubled back from Northampton to Rockingham on 26 June.

The government, therefore, made a positive decision to bring Aumale's defiance to an end, apparently on the spur of the moment, unless its failure to move directly on Rockingham from Leicester was a blind. Probably it suddenly appreciated that the castle was there for the taking. Since Pandulf seems to have made his own way south, the initiative came from Hubert and Bishop Peter, who authorized letters together both at Northampton and Rockingham on 26 June.[3] Perhaps a particular spur to action was supplied by Hugh de Lusignan's demand for Rockingham as part of his wife's dower, although the need to secure Fotheringhay, only twelve miles to the east, for King Alexander was even more urgent. It was one thing, however, to take on the count of Aumale, quite another to engage the earl of Pembroke.

If Peter acted in this way against Aumale, whose cause he had supported the year before, perhaps he also ensured that he saved face and escaped punishment. On 29 June letters patent announced that Aumale had surrendered Rockingham and Sauvey freely and spontaneously. At the same time the king, in a letter authorized by Hubert and Peter, forgave Aumale all the revenue that he owed for the manors and forests which he had been occupying since the war, thus writing off debts worth £335 15s.[4] This, of course, violated the papal injunction of May 1220 that magnates should give full satisfaction for manorial and other issues which they had received since the war. At long last, however, the government had liquidated Aumale's Northamptonshire fiefdom. The peace of 1217 could be implemented in the county: Henry of Braybrooke recovered Corby, Walter of Preston, Gretton, and Hugh de Neville the Northamptonshire forest. The king himself took possession of Earl David's manors of Nassington and Yarwell. He also regained his demesne manors of King's Cliffe and Brigstock, and the fee farms from Corby and Gretton, thus taking a step towards the resumption of the royal demesne. For the financial year 1220–21, these changes were worth an extra £102 to the king, of which £84 were paid into the exchequer.[5]

3 *PR*, 239; *RLC*, 422.
4 *PR*, 240; *Pipe Roll 1220*, 15; *Pipe Roll 1221*, 146.
5 *Pipe Roll 1220*, 15–16, 120–1; *Pipe Roll 1221*, 187–8; *RLC*, 423. In addition, Hugh de Neville henceforth accounted for all the farm of the Northamptonshire forest: *Pipe Roll 1220*, 120–1; E 372/66, r.9, m.2.

v. *Philip of Oldcoates and Poitou, July 1220*

Thomas Becket's translation on 7 July 1220 was a splendid international occasion, presided over by Stephen Langton as archbishop of Canterbury and attended by an archbishop from Hungary, the archbishop of Rheims and three of his suffragans. The earl of Pembroke kept order in Canterbury during the celebrations, from which there was one conspicuous absentee: Hugh de Lusignan himself.[1] Far from accepting the invitation to the translation, he was refusing to release the king's sister and oppressing the Poitevin towns. His aim was to force the government to concede him both Isabella's dower and Joan's *maritagium*.[2] Indeed, if Hugh himself was absent, his messengers and those of Queen Isabella were in Canterbury demanding, as the government put it, 'many and great things in the name of the queen's dower'. Also present were messengers from Aimery, vicomte of Thouars, equally demanding 'many things promised and agreed' by King John. And, if that was not enough, the translation was attended by one unwelcome guest, Richard I's widow, Queen Berengar of Navarre, who likewise demanded 'many things' under the agreement John had made over *her* dower. Not surprisingly, the government decided to postpone a great council due to meet in London while it tried to sort matters out.[3]

Queen Berengar was demanding payment of £1,000 a year and £4,500 worth of arrears. Given the threat posed by Navarre to the southern frontier of Gascony, it was important to satisfy her.[4] Responsibility for the settlement, reached in London in July, was taken by Pandulf, Hubert and a wider body of magnates, including the earl of Oxford, Reginald de Braose and the count of Aumale, who was clearly back in the fold after the siege of Rockingham. The queen immediately received 1,000 marks, which the king had to borrow from Pandulf; for the rest, she was to have 2,000 marks a year until the arrears had been cleared. This money was to come from the proceeds of the exchange and from the tin mines of Devon and Cornwall. The earl of Pembroke had been granted the exchange in 1218, although perhaps only until he succeeded to his father's estates. While still hanging on to Fotheringhay, he now proclaimed his willingness to surrender it, wishing, as he told the king, 'to place the profit of my lord above my own'.[5] Getting

---

[1] *Walt. Cov.*, 245; *Ann. Mon.*, iii, 58; *Normandie*, 208–9.

[2] *DD*, no. 92; *PR*, 261.

[3] SC 1/2, no. 92 (*CACW*, 12).

[4] The considerations which underlay Richard's marriage to Berengar are discussed in Gillingham, 'Richard I and Berengaria of Navarre', 157–73.

[5] *PR*, 243–5, 265; *RLC*, 442; E 368/3, m.2; *RL*, no. lviii. For an agreement with Berengar in 1218 which had not been fulfilled, see *PR*, 179.

control of the Cornish tin mines was another matter, however, for they were occupied by Henry fitz Count.

The ambitions of Hugh de Lusignan in Poitou presented problems on an altogether different scale. When the king's envoys had arrived there in June 1220 they had managed to secure a truce for seven weeks. Nonetheless, Hugh was still threatening La Rochelle and virtually blockading Niort.[6] Letters of expostulation and reproach from these towns reached England with every fair wind, five from Niort surviving from June and July 1220 alone.[7] The burden of advice was much the same as before. 'Send us such a governor, as you have promised many times, who will have the strength to preserve us and your land of Poitou from such great and imminent danger', pleaded the mayor and commune of Niort.[8] The towns also had strong views about the type of man they wanted. For the mayor and commune of Bordeaux, it must be a seneschal from England 'against whom the king may have recourse if he offends against him'.[9] Likewise the men of Niort warned Hubert against appointing anyone 'from our parts, lest [the land] is committed to such a one who will retain it and appropriate it for himself, as you know in time gone by some imprudently have done'. When they heard a rumour that Aimery, vicomte of Thouars, might be chosen, they warned the king that he was their mortal enemy and that in John's time he had been in league with the king of France.[10]

The government's solution in this perplexing situation was to turn to Philip of Oldcoates. Having at last extracted him from Mitford, it decided to send him, as seneschal, to Poitou.[11] Pandulf later alleged, rather critically, that this was Hubert's idea.[12] In fact, it had much to recommend it. Oldcoates fitted the bill of someone sent from England against whom the government could act if he misbehaved. He had no Poitevin interests but was familiar with the Angevin empire, having defended Chinon with Hubert in 1204–5. Also, of course, the appointment, like that proposed earlier of the count of Aumale, removed a turbulent figure from English politics. His talents could be put to better use in Poitou.

There were, however, two problems. The first lay with Oldcoates himself, who did not want to go. He was fully occupied with his quarrels in the north of England. Indeed, when he came to London in July,

---

[6] *DD*, nos 86, 87, 88.

[7] *DD*, nos 86, 87, 90, 106; *RL*, no. cxx.

[8] *DD*, no. 87.

[9] SC 1/1, no. 61; *RL*, no. cvii.

[10] *RL*, no. cxx; *DD*, no. 90.

[11] For an offer at this time from Reginald de Pons junior to accept the seneschalship (at a considerable price): *DD*, nos 81, 82.

[12] See below p. 214.

which was probably when his appointment was first suggested, he aimed a shrewd blow at his northern enemies. He accused Richard de Umfraville, Roger Bertram's uncle and ally, of strengthening his castle at Harbottle, near the Anglo-Scottish border, contrary to a royal prohibition.[13] This was retaliation for Umfraville's similar accusation in 1218 about the castle which Oldcoates had been building at Nafferton in Northumberland, less than two miles from Umfraville's castle at Prudhoe.[14] The government, however, swallowed Oldcoates's bait. On 25 July a writ, authorized by Hubert and the council but for which Pandulf was later blamed, was addressed to the sheriff of Northumberland, that is, to Oldcoates himself: he was to instruct Umfraville to reduce Harbottle to its size before the war. Hubert may have sensed danger here. If Umfraville refused to obey the instruction, the sheriff was merely to report back. Nonetheless, when the order arrived in the north it caused an explosion of indignation, as will be seen.[15]

The second problem with Oldcoates's appointment was again that of resources. Without them no amount of personality or experience could turn someone into the strong seneschal for whom the towns were clamouring. In Poitou and Gascony resources remained almost non-existent. In June or July the men of Niort warned the king that he had no more than £25 worth of rents in the town. If the concession of the revenues of Bordeaux, which were largely the customs, to the burgess Rostand de Columb and the master of the Templars, Gerard Brochard, was coming to an end in the summer of 1220, there was no prospect of them, or other revenues, becoming available to Oldcoates.[16] As the latter informed Pandulf in August, 'the burgesses of La Rochelle, Bordeaux and Gascony have told me that if I go to their parts they will in no way answer to me for the revenues of the king until they have been properly satisfied for the debt which Geoffrey de Neville . . . owes them'.[17]

It was vital, therefore, for a new seneschal to be provided with substantial resources from England. But in July 1220, following the expenses of the coronation and the promises to Queen Berengar, the king was virtually penniless. When the receipt roll for the Easter term of 1220 was closed, there were only £133 remaining in the treasury. The government, therefore, decided on a new approach. Early in August a council was due to meet at Oxford to deal with the quarrels of Llywelyn

[13] PR, 265; SC 1/2, no. 10.
[14] See above p. 88.
[15] RLC, 436b–7. See below p. 208.
[16] DD, no. 90; PR, 203, 232, 243.
[17] SC 1/2, no. 15. Since this letter was written in mid-August, Oldcoates's appointment must have been proposed at the latest in early July.

and the Marchers. At Canterbury it was decided to make this the setting both for a general discussion of the affairs of the kingdom and for a demand for extraordinary taxation which would clear the king's debts and support his government in Poitou.[18]

vi. The great council of August 1220

When the great council met at Oxford, Llywelyn was conspicuous by his absence. All that was done was to give him another day at Westminster on 30 September.[1] The assembly was able, therefore, to concentrate on the question of taxation for Poitou and a variety of other issues, in the short term with apparent success. A new tax was indeed conceded and an inquiry was set up which was intended to lead to the resumption of the royal demesne: the first attempt to realize on any general scale part of the programme enjoined by the papal letters of April 1219 and May 1220. In addition, an agreement was reached with the justiciar of Ireland, Mitford was at last returned to Roger Bertram and disputes were settled between competing magnates. Later, however, both the tax and the resumption ran into difficulties and the limits of the government's power were again revealed.

One of the private disputes considered at Oxford was the rancorous case that the earl of Pembroke was bringing against Falkes de Bréauté for the manors of Luton, Sutton, Brabourne and Kemsing. This was now concluded by Falkes buying out the rights of Pembroke and his heirs for 1,000 marks. The settlement did not, however, establish good relations between the two men or reconcile Pembroke to the loss of the manors, which he recovered after Falkes's fall.[2]

A second dispute in which Pembroke was involved was concluded more harmoniously. This was with none other than the earl of Salisbury, previously Pembroke's bosom friend. Indeed, during the summer of 1220 it looked as though the Pembroke-Salisbury alliance was about to be removed from the political landscape. The bone of contention was the future of the Berkeley inheritance which Salisbury had been occupying, in whole or part, since the death of Robert of Berkeley in May 1220. His justification for doing so, as has been seen, was that Robert had owed him money. He also asserted that his 'niece', Robert's widow, was pregnant.[3] Thomas of Berkeley, Robert's brother, clearly believed, however, that this pregnancy was a fiction; he was thus being excluded from the Berkeley inheritance to which he was the heir. To remove Salisbury's obstruction, he secured powerful help: he

---

[18] SC 1/2, no. 92 (CACW, 12).
[1] RL, no. cxxiv; F, 164.
[2] CRR, ix, 205; Ann. Mon., iii, 92.
[3] See above p. 194.

married the earl of Pembroke's niece. In return, Pembroke undertook to get his homage accepted by the king as Robert of Berkeley's heir and to acquit him in all things against the earl of Salisbury. Some time, probably late in July, Pembroke had written to Hubert complaining that Salisbury was still deforcing Thomas of his castle and inheritance 'against justice, the custom of the kingdom and the law of the land'. He had manifestly transgressed an undertaking made in Hubert and Pembroke's presence 'that he would in no way injure anyone to the disturbance of the kingdom, but that he, more than we ourselves, would preserve the tranquillity of the king and kingdom'. Pembroke now begged Hubert 'to attend diligently to putting right all this, and do not suffer Thomas . . . who is so closely tied to us that we are neither able nor willing to fail him, to be any longer maltreated so injuriously in respect of his inheritance by the earl of Salisbury'. Hubert should act so that 'we, who are always yours, henceforth may be bound all the nearer and more devotedly to you and yours all [our] days'.[4]

In devising a settlement, Hubert wished to retain the love of Salisbury and Pembroke while furthering the interests of the crown. This he did with some finesse. Pembroke gave Salisbury 60 marks in settlement of the debts that Thomas owed him.[5] Salisbury presumably admitted that his niece was not pregnant and this cleared the way for Thomas to do homage for his inheritance, fine in £100 for his relief and receive seisin of his lands.[6] He did not, however, recover Berkeley castle, which Salisbury surrendered not to Thomas but to the king, who retained it until 1224.[7] On these terms Salisbury and Pembroke buried their differences and soon blamed their dispute on the general unreliability of Thomas of Berkeley, against whom they both brought law cases.[8] The following month a royal letter, authorized by Hubert, expressed certainty that Salisbury 'does nothing and wishes to do nothing . . . against our peace'.[9]

When Thomas of Berkeley finally recovered his castle in 1224, he gave hostages for his faithful service.[10] In 1220 Hubert was determined to extract similar safeguards from Roger Bertram, a determination which may reflect both the strategic importance of Mitford and a distrust of Bertram himself. Perhaps Hubert's attitude to him was not so different from that of Philip of Oldcoates. After Oldcoates had surrendered Mitford to Hugh de Bolebec, Hubert had intervened,

---

[4] Gloucs. Warw. Eyre, no. 301 and pp. li–lii; RL, no. clv; Peerage, ii, 126–7.
[5] Gloucs. Warw. Eyre, no. 301.
[6] ERF, 52; C 60/12, m.12.
[7] RLC, 630b.
[8] Gloucs. Warw. Eyre, no. 301; CRR, x, 132, 182, 248; CRR, xi, nos 50, 69.
[9] PR, 247.
[10] RLC, 630b.

through the archbishop of York, to prevent Bolebec passing the castle on to Bertram.[11] This brought Bertram south to the August council. He had powerful supporters, his pledges for a debt on 9 August being William Brewer and the earl of Salisbury, whom Oldcoates, of course, had excluded from the Vesci wardship.[12] Above all, however, Pandulf himself, at least in Oldcoates's later view, intervened on Bertram's side.[13] Bertram was made to give a charter for his faithful service and promise delivery of his son as a hostage to the bishop of Durham. He then obtained a writ which ordered Bolebec to give him seisin of Mitford.[14] What happened when he got back to the north will be seen in due course.

Bertram's backers throughout the Mitford affair had included men who had fought on either side in the civil war. At the Oxford council another indication that the divisions of the war were losing their significance lay in those who stood pledge for William de Albini's faithful service now that his hostages were being released. Apart from the archbishop of Canterbury, they included die-hard Angevins, like William Brewer and Geoffrey de Neville, trimmers like the earls of Pembroke and Salisbury, and such staunch rebels as the earls of Oxford, Essex and Roger Bertram. If, moreover, there was a lingering suspicion about Bertram, there was no denying his high place in the counsels of the king. Both Bertram and Reginald de Braose were amongst those at Oxford on whose advice a settlement was reached with Geoffrey de Marsh, the justiciar of Ireland.[15]

The government had been struggling to get Marsh to England since 1218. Having got him there, it was determined to make the most of the opportunity and lay down exact rules for the governance of Ireland. Geoffrey's failure had been largely financial. As the king put it later, after John's death 'we received absolutely nothing from our demesnes, assessed rents and escheats of Ireland'.[16] Geoffrey now fined in at least £1,300 for these arrears. As for the future, he was to have the 'assessed rents' to meet the costs of keeping 'the land' and the king's castles, and was to answer at the exchequer of Ireland for all other revenues and for anything left over from the rents. These issues were to be delivered to the king at his order. To ensure that Geoffrey complied with all this, he was loaded down with a formidable array of checks and sanctions. The solemnity of the agreement was emphasized by it being made in the

[11] *RL*, no. cxxxii.
[12] C 60/12, m.3. His other pledge was William de Beauchamp, whom Falkes was excluding from Bedford castle.
[13] SC 1/2, no. 15.
[14] *PR*, 246–7.
[15] *PR*, 246–7, 263–5.
[16] *RLC*, 476b.

presence of Pandulf, the archbishop of Dublin, Peter, Hubert, the earl of Salisbury, William Brewer, Falkes, Walter de Lacy, Reginald de Braose, Roger Bertram and seven other magnates and ministers.[17] From one point of view these arrangements were a triumph for the government, from another they revealed its extraordinary weakness. An Angevin king of full power, distrusting Geoffrey so much, would surely have dismissed him from office. In the event, Geoffrey, once back in Ireland, continued much as before.[18]

The main purpose of the agreement with Geoffrey was to secure a better financial return from Ireland. During the council important steps were likewise taken to improve the king's finances in England, one being to set in train a resumption of the royal demesne, something the papacy had urged with increasing stridency in its letters of April 1219 and May 1220. On 9 August all the sheriffs were ordered to inquire, in full county court, what demesnes had been in King John's hands at the beginning of the war and who held them now. In addition, they were to inquire about escheats which had come into the king's hands before, during or after the war. The current holders of these lands were to come before the king and his council on 30 September to show warrant for their tenure. If they could not do so, the lands would be taken into the king's hands. The close connection between this measure and finance was emphasized by the conclusion of the order, which told the sheriffs to be at the exchequer on 30 September to answer fully for everything which belonged to their offices, failing which they would be dismissed.[19]

The resumption of the demesne had been attempted unsuccessfully immediately after the war and was a highly sensitive issue, which explains why the initiative in 1220 was so tentative, envisaging no immediate seizures. A second financial measure taken at the council, however, promised altogether more immediate rewards. This was the tax designed to provide a treasure for Poitou and liquidate debts like those owed to the pope, Pandulf and Queen Berengar. As a royal letter, again of 9 August, stated, the tax had been conceded 'in common by all the magnates and *fideles* of our kingdom . . . for our great need and because of the pressing urgency of our debts and for the preservation of our land of Poitou'. The tax was a carucage: a levy at the rate of 2s on every 'yoked plough' (*caruca . . . juncta*). The money was to be paid in at the New Temple on 30 September. Only the demesnes of the archbishops, bishops and their *rustici*, together with the demesnes of the Cistercians and Premonstratensians, were to be exempt. The sheriffs were to collect the tax with two knights of their counties elected 'by the

[17] *PR*, 263–5.
[18] Norgate, *Minority*, 125; see below p. 253.
[19] *RLC*, 437.

will and counsel of all of the county in full county court'.[20] This was another attempt, like the knights appointed to collect the eyre amercements in 1219, to circumvent the 'malice' of the sheriffs.

The form of the 1220 tax was a compromise between a levy on movable property on the one hand and a scutage on the other. Everyone at the Oxford assembly knew that a tax on movable property was by far the most lucrative and burdensome that could be imposed. The last such tax in 1207 had brought in more than £60,000. The scutage of 1217, on the other hand, produced merely £2,818.[21] The carucage was a middle way. It had been levied before, in 1198 and 1200, and had raised much less than the tax on movables of 1207. Just to make sure, the rate in 1220, at 2s a plough, compared with 5s a plough in 1198 and 3s in 1200.[22] But a carucage seemed better than a scutage, for, as it was levied on ploughs rather than knights' fees, it was related to the real wealth of the kingdom.[23] Equally, the process of assessment and collection cut through the paraphernalia of the honours, the sheriffs and knights being responsible directly for all lay ploughs.

Already at Oxford, however, there were signs that there might be difficulties over raising the tax. Alan Martel, deputy master of the Templars in England, asked Hubert to exempt the order from it. 'You told us', Martel recalled later, 'that you were unable to exempt other religious men completely . . . but that you would place the exaction and vexation of the carucage owed by us in respite until Michaelmas.' Thus Hubert stood firm while preparing to retreat. In the event the proceeds of the carucage were to prove highly disappointing,[24] partly because in the north there was fierce opposition to the levying of the tax at all.

vii. *The north of England: counsel, consent and dissent, August–September 1220*

In August 1220 the government was faced with implementing several important decisions relating to the north: the reduction of Richard de Umfraville's castle at Harbottle, the return of Mitford to Roger Bertram and the levying of the carucage conceded by the Oxford council. Over all three the government ran into difficulties. In the ensuing disputes over Harbottle and the tax its critics enunciated

[20] *RLC*, 437.
[21] Mitchell, *Taxation*, 91, 126.
[22] Mitchell, *Taxation*, 7–8, 32–4. In both years it is unclear how far the tax was actually levied as opposed to being bought off.
[23] The aim was clearly to assess the tax on ploughs (*caruca sicut juncta*) but it seems that sometimes it was ploughlands which were assessed: Mitchell, *Taxation*, 133–4; *BF*, 289–90; Tomkinson, 'The carucage of 1220 in an Oxfordshire hundred', 212–16.
[24] SC 1/1, no. 150; see below pp. 223–5.

fundamental beliefs about the need for counsel and consent, beliefs which underlay the politics of the minority and shaped future programmes of political reform.

In Roger Bertram's case the difficulty was soon resolved. After the Oxford council he had hurried north. He reached Durham to find a council in session there, attended, amongst others, by the archbishop of York, the bishop of Durham and the custodian of Mitford, Hugh de Bolebec. Bertram 'vehemently' demanded that Bolebec surrender Mitford to him, only for the archbishop, acting on previous orders from Hubert, to intervene and prevent it. One can only suppose that Hubert had failed to apprise the archbishop of the agreement reached with Bertram at Oxford. Perhaps Bertram had out-galloped the royal messengers. In any case the result, as the archbishop informed Hubert by letter, was that he (the archbishop) 'incurred the indignation not only of Roger but also of his relations, friends and associates'. Fortunately, other business then led to the archbishop's departure and the bishop of Durham, now informed of the arrangements reached at the Oxford council, received Bertram's son as hostage and sanctioned the delivery of the castle.[1] The Mitford affair was over.

The indignation of Bertram and his associates was scarcely surprising: they had waited nearly three years for the restoration of the castle. But at least the government had been on their side. Indeed, it had the grace to forgive Bertram the £100 fine he had made back in 1217 for seisin of the castle 'since he did not have nor was he able to have that for which he promised it'.[2] The delay in restoring Mitford was not, however, the only reason for the reaction of Bertram and his associates. They were also boiling with anger over Philip of Oldcoates's parting shot: the order to Bertram's uncle and ally, Richard de Umfraville, to dismantle his castle of Harbottle. This order had been authorized by Hubert and the council.[3] Nonetheless, Umfraville's letter of protest to Hubert was a sparkler compared to the flame-throwers which he and his friends directed at Pandulf. It was Pandulf whom they held responsible for the decision and whom they deemed to have the power to alter it. To Hubert, Umfraville simply set out why his castle was not adulterine (unauthorized) and asked him to explain this to the king's council. It was to Pandulf that he expressed his 'astonishment', begging him 'to cause the execution of that mandate to be suspended until I, my friends and peers have spoken to you'.[4] Robert de Vieuxpont and the earl of Salisbury, in separate letters to Pandulf, made the same request, Vieuxpont adding that, if the king's council did not cease from such

[1] *RL*, no. cxxxii; *PR*, 246–7.
[2] E 372/66, r.15d, m.2; and see *RLC*, ii, 101.
[3] *RLC*, 436b–7. See above p. 202.
[4] *RL*, no. cxxii; SC 1/2, no. 16.

presumptions, then men 'will not be so obedient . . . to you, your orders and the orders of the king as hitherto, and so a great discord may arise'.[5]

What made the injury all the worse in Umfraville's view was that, as he said to Pandulf, it was 'contrary to the form of justice to do injury unjustly to those demanding justice', for he had 'often demanded from you . . . and still do demand judgement of the court of the king by consideration of my peers' as to whether the castle was adulterine or not. The echo of the clause in Magna Carta which laid down that no freeman was to be deprived of his possessions 'save by the lawful judgement of his peers, or by the law of the land' was here unmistakable.[6]

Vieuxpont and Salisbury also challenged the legitimacy of the decision in another essential manner. The relevant writ had been authorized, like an increasing number in this period, by the justiciar and the council. The purpose of this formula, as has been seen, was to confer added authority on decisions by showing that Hubert had acted with the consent of some wider body. But here there was an element of bluff, for was the council in question a small assembly of ministers or a large gathering of magnates? It was this bluff which Vieuxpont and Salisbury called, revealing in the process their view that it was only the wider council of magnates, the great council, which could sanction important decisions. The order over Harbottle, Vieuxpont informed Pandulf, had 'emanated from a certain part of the king's council, without the common counsel and assent of the magnates of England who are held to be and are of the chief council of the king'.[7] The reaction of Salisbury, as befitted his status, was even more personal and extreme. After accusing the council of having been misled by the 'false accusation' of Philip of Oldcoates, he continued: 'such an order is not held to be done rightfully without our assent and counsel, who are and are held to be of the chief council of the king, with other chief men'.[8] No doubt here are the grounds on which Salisbury frequently justified his disobedience to government orders in the early minority. The earl considered himself something of a constitutional expert. On one occasion he informed Archbishop Langton that 'it is not permissible for any sheriff to expel forceful intruders, according to the custom of England, unless within three or four days of the intrusion'.[9]

---

[5] SC 1/2, nos 17, 10.

[6] SC 1/2, no. 16; Holt, *Magna Carta*, 279.

[7] *absque commune consilio et assensu magnatum Angliae qui tenentur esse et sunt de capitali consilio domini regis*: SC 1/2, no. 17.

[8] *absque nostro assensu et consilio qui sumus et tenemur esse de capitali consilio domini regis cum aliis capitalibus tale preceptum fieri de iure non tenetur*: SC 1/2, no. 10.

[9] SC 1/11, no. 59.

Clearly theories were equally forming in his mind about the rights and powers of great councils.

Vieuxpont made one final point about the order over Harbottle: the injustice seemed a poor repayment when the king's petitions for an aid had been heard 'so favourably'. That they had been heard 'favourably' was not, however, a universal view in the north. Indeed attempts to impose the carucage in Yorkshire raised questions of counsel and consent similar to those in the Harbottle episode. On receipt of his instructions about the tax, the sheriff, Geoffrey de Neville, as he informed Hubert and the council by letter, had summoned an assembly of earls, barons and free men to York on 14 September. In fact only the stewards of the magnates had turned up and they had declared unanimously that 'their lords knew nothing about giving this aid and tallage to the king, and had not been asked about it . . . They also said that the magnates of these parts, like others of England, should have been consulted about doing this by the king, either *viva voce* or by letters.'[10] There was some truth in this complaint. Although the government claimed that the carucage had been granted by 'all the magnates and *fideles* of the kingdom', the only northerner present at Oxford had been Roger Bertram.[11]

The Yorkshire protest was rooted in Magna Carta, clause 12 of the 1215 Charter having stipulated that extraordinary taxation could only be levied by 'common counsel' of the kingdom and clause 14 having laid down rules for the summoning of the necessary assembly. According to these rules, all major barons were to receive individual letters of summons, a requirement perhaps echoed in the Yorkshire reference to royal letters. These clauses of the 1215 Charter were deleted from the Charters of 1216 and 1217 but the trouble in 1220 was not caused by a deliberate attempt to take advantage of the omission. The magnates *had* been summoned to the assembly at Oxford and been informed of the financial pressures on the government. Perhaps the letters had not got through in time, or perhaps confusion was caused by the cancellation of a previous assembly at London.[12] Whatever the explanation, the Yorkshire protest revealed that the principles of the Great Charter, even the abortive one of 1215, were too deeply

[10] *RL*, no. cxxx.

[11] *PR*, 263. Also present was the earl of Salisbury who had extensive lands in the north as a result of holding the Vesci wardship.

[12] SC 1/2, no. 92. Sir Goronwy Edwards (*CACW*, 12) believed that this summons, which only survives in draft form, was addressed to Falkes and the earls of Salisbury, Pembroke, Surrey and Gloucester, whose names appear at its foot. But also at the foot of the letter is the word *Universis*, which suggests that the letter was widely distributed. *Universis* appears to have been written at the same time as the text of the letter, whereas the list of names is in a different hand or at least a different ink. For writs of summons and their time-scale, see Holt, 'The prehistory of parliament', 1–28.

impregnated in the counties to be overridden by the government, whether by accident or design. The government appreciated this and retreated. Geoffrey de Neville's courageous but unrealistic offer to impose the carucage in Yorkshire, if Hubert and the council ordered, was declined. Instead, it seems likely that the government took its cue from Neville's observation that the Yorkshire magnates would agree to the tax if the king summoned them before him when he came to York in October for another meeting with King Alexander.[13] Thus the government acted in the spirit of the Great Charter of 1215.

viii. *The king's recovery of Cornwall; the despatch of Philip of Oldcoates to Poitou; August–September 1220*

Since the king's second coronation in May 1220, the government had scored a series of individual successes. It had extracted Philip of Oldcoates from Mitford and restored the castle to Roger Bertram. It had ejected the count of Aumale from Rockingham and returned the surrounding forest and manors to the former rebels, who had held them before the war. At the great council of August 1220 an agreement had been reached with the justiciar of Ireland; an attempt to resume the royal demesne had been launched; and a carucage tax had been conceded. At the same time, the reaction to the tax in the north, and the protests over the dismantling of Harbottle castle, had revealed the fragility of central authority and the necessity to move with counsel and consent. Between September 1220 and February 1221 the pattern was much the same. Henry fitz Count was expelled from Cornwall and the earl of Pembroke surrendered Fotheringhay. The count of Aumale was prized from Bytham and the castle at last returned to its lord, the former rebel William de Coleville. The government even succeeded in packing Philip of Oldcoates off to Poitou and recovering Joan from Hugh de Lusignan. Hubert himself continued to be closely concerned both with justice, finance and the maintenance of the rights of the crown, on the one hand, and appeasing erstwhile rebels on the other. But the government's successes were marred by the failure of the attempted resumption and the paucity of the proceeds from the carucage. At the same time, it could only look on as Llywelyn staged a remarkable invasion of south Wales, an invasion which had bearing on the issues of both Cornwall and Fotheringhay.

The question of Cornwall had been discussed at Oxford in August. A delegation from the county, led by the bishop of Exeter, had come before Hubert and the council, and offered 500 marks to have a local

---

[13] *RL*, no. cxxii. The £200 which Yorkshire eventually paid for the carucage looks very much like a lump sum agreed with the government: *Divers Accounts*, 16.

man as sheriff, as conceded in the charter they had obtained from
King John. This proffer was, in effect, a request for the forceful removal
of Henry fitz Count, who had already been nominally dismissed as
sheriff both in April and in July 1220. It plainly revealed Henry's
unpopularity in Cornwall, with its strong traditions of local autonomy,
and suggested it would be easy to eject him.[1] There were other reasons
for acting against him. The government had long worried about
Henry's disobedience and pretensions to autonomy. He was appointing his own judges to hear petty assizes and failing to account at the
exchequer. His detention of the county's tin mines meant that Queen
Berengar's money had to be found from other sources. In addition,
envoys were now in England demanding Cornwall for Guy, vicomte of
Limoges, and his brother, the grandsons of Reginald, earl of Cornwall.
Nonetheless, at the Oxford council, a decision over the proffer was
postponed until Michaelmas.[2]

The reason for the postponement was anxiety over Llywelyn's
intentions in Wales. The prince, as has been seen, had neglected to
attend the Oxford council. Instead, he had gone to meet Ranulf, earl of
Chester. Ranulf had returned to England from his crusade in July but
rather than join the king at Oxford he had gone straight to Chester,
where he was received on 16 August 'with the greatest veneration'. The
government signalled its displeasure by granting to someone else the
custody of two manors of Earl David which Ranulf coveted. On the day
of his arrival at Chester the earl had a meeting with Llywelyn and
reaffirmed their understanding of 1218.[3] The two men had much in
common. Llywelyn felt that the government hardly consulted him
about Welsh affairs. Chester now found Hubert, a man of low status
whose position he had resented since 1214, taking the role for which he
himself had been proposed in 1216 and 1217.[4] The alliance between
Chester and Llywelyn was to become a major factor in the politics of the
next few years. For the moment it left the Welsh prince free to intervene
in south Wales.

After the Oxford council, therefore, it was for Wales that Hubert set
out. Stopping at Berkeley on the way, he arranged about the custody of
the castle and then took ship over the Severn estuary. He checked on his
former Braose castles at Skenfrith and Whitecastle, and returned down
the Wye valley to Chepstow, where he presumably conferred with the
earl of Pembroke. From Chepstow, on 21 August, royal letters warned
the sheriffs of the Marcher counties that Llywelyn was gathering an

---

[1]   C 60/15, m.9; *PR*, 231, 241; *Pipe Roll 1208*, 183; Holt, *Magna Carta*, 54. For Henry's
depredations in Cornwall, see *RLC*, 429.

[2]   SC 1/1, no. 117.

[3]   *Ann. Mon.*, iii, 60; *Ann. Cest.*, 50–1; *RLC*, 426b, 443b.

[4]   *RL*, no. cv; *Hist. Angl.*, iii, 231.

army to march against Reginald de Braose 'or another of our *fideles*, we still do not know whom'.[5]

Despite the threat from Llywelyn, during this visit to Wales Hubert was constantly concerned with the day-to-day maintenance of law and order and the protection of the rights of the king. On 16 August, at Berkeley, the abbot of Malmesbury was ordered to deliver an approver 'who appeals several of the county of Gloucester of being members of a gang of thieves' to the sheriff, Ralph Musard. Five days later, from Chepstow, another royal letter informed the abbot 'that all approvers, wherever taken in our land, and whoever they may be, ought to come to our court or elsewhere at our order'. Unless the abbot delivered the one in his custody, 'you do not wish to preserve our liberties, and we will not preserve your liberties'. This threat had the desired effect and Musard was soon writing direct to Hubert: 'know that I have by me the approver who was at Malmesbury, and he talks a great deal and says he will clear our country (*patria*) of malefactors and freely promises that he will do that'. Musard went on to ask for instructions and assured Hubert that he would 'hold no duel between [the approver] and those he accuses unless you order me'. Hubert decided not to issue such an order. Instead, Musard was told to bring both accuser and accused before the justices at Westminster at Michaelmas.[6]

The original intention when the Oxford council broke up was for Hubert, Peter and Pandulf to reassemble at Winchester at the end of August.[7] However, there was now a change of plan. Hubert evidently considered that nothing more was to be done for the security of south Wales. Perhaps he imagined that the danger had passed. In any event, he and Pandulf, although only in contact through letter, decided on a bold move: they would go to the west country and turn Henry fitz Count out of Cornwall. Peter was informed of this decision but not apparently involved in making it.

It was not easy to co-ordinate action when the three leading members of the government were separated. On 25 August Pandulf, who was at Castle Cary, told Hubert by letter 'we have waited for you to come to the Dorchester area where we are now, in order that we might consider the matter of Cornwall, and we are astonished that you

[5] *RLC*, 428.

[6] *RLC*, 427, 428; SC 1/1, no. 158; *RLC*, 429. While Hubert was at Whitecastle he also commissioned Martin of Pattishall to deliver Hereford gaol: *RLC*, 427b, and (for the roll of the proceedings) *CRR*, ix, 198–201. There is a great deal of other evidence in the close rolls of his interest in approvers. Note also the new article of the eyre in 1218 enquiring into those who had held pleas of approvers without warrant from the king or justiciar: *Wiltshire Eyre*, 30.

[7] *F*, 162.

have not come'. In fact, Hubert had overtaken Pandulf, for the following day, when the latter was at Sherborne, he was at South Petherton, about ten miles further west. Pandulf, therefore, wrote again to Hubert, arranging to see him early the next morning at Ilchester, mid-way between them.[8] Meanwhile, Peter was still expecting to meet Hubert at Winchester and indeed urged Pandulf to join them there. Only having written did he receive a letter from Hubert summoning him to the west to meet Pandulf and to help deal 'both with the question [of Poitou] and Henry fitz Count'. This, Peter complained, was highly inconvenient, for, with the great annual fair due at Winchester, his presence was necessary both to guard his own liberties and the peace of the kingdom. Nonetheless, as he informed Pandulf by letter, lest the affairs of the king should suffer through his absence, he would hurry to meet him.[9]

The question of Poitou had indeed taken a turn for the worse, for the complex patchwork of Philip of Oldcoates's appointment seemed about to come apart. Oldcoates had learnt that the Poitevin and Gascon towns would answer to him for none of their revenues until the debts owed by Geoffrey de Neville had been paid. 'Wherefore I tell you', he wrote to Pandulf, 'that I much hate going to those parts where I believe I will receive shame and disgrace, and where I will be unable to undertake the king's service in an honourable fashion.' 'And in addition', he continued, 'I do not consider myself well served in that the castle of Mitford, which I committed into the king's hands, you have caused to be restored to Roger Bertram, by which you have not put me in the frame of mind to render good service. So I signify to your lordship that you can have no faith in me making the journey to those parts or undertaking the work there and you should provide for another seneschal to be sent.' 'I do not wish', Oldcoates concluded, in familiar vein, 'to leave alone and unprotected the lands and castles which I keep amongst my enemies'; enemies doubtless made all the more implacable since the Harbottle castle episode.[10] On receipt of this missive, Pandulf wrote to Peter urging him to be 'solicitous' in the matter of Poitou. But he sent (on 25 August) the letter itself and some pointed criticism of his own to Hubert. 'We had no confidence that Philip of Oldcoates ought to go there, although you seemed very certain about the matter, travelling always over seas and mountains and seeking those things which are not to be had. As a consequence, the whole matter has been delayed until now, not without great damage.'[11]

When the triumvirate with the young king reached Exeter on

[8] F, 162; SC 1/1, no. 182.
[9] F, 162–3; RL, no. cxxxiii.
[10] SC 1/2, no. 15.
[11] F, 162–3; SC 1/1, no. 182.

1 September, therefore, it faced both uncertainty in Wales and the collapse of its schemes for Poitou. Pandulf was also worried about a tournament planned in defiance of the year's ban which he had imposed and he ordered Hubert to issue royal letters prohibiting it.[12] At Exeter itself, by the counsel of the king's *fideles*, the government had to widen the exemptions from the carucage to include the demesnes of all ecclesiastics. These problems and setbacks, however, were balanced by total success in Cornwall itself. The knights of the western counties were summoned but they were scarcely needed, for Henry fitz Count came in and made terms.[13] He surrendered the county, and the castle of Launceston, 'absolutely' to the king. In return he received a meaning-less promise that, when the king came of age, Pandulf, Peter, the bishop of Exeter, Hubert, William Brewer and Falkes would use their influence so that he would receive justice in the king's court.[14] The real compensation was financial, Henry being given 500 marks cash down (a sum borrowed from Pandulf) and promised at least another 600 marks in the future.[15] Having achieved this success, the government was in no mood to throw it away by giving the county to the Limoges brothers. Here the oath taken by the magnates in November 1218 at the time of the inauguration of the king's seal came to the rescue. The king, so the brothers were informed, was to be kept in seisin of the land which King John had held at the beginning of the war and was barred from making permanent alienations until he came of age.[16]

The danger of Cornwall, under someone outside the royal family, becoming a county virtually exempt from the king's government had thus been terminated. The money given to Henry was well spent or, rather, well borrowed. In November Hubert and the council were able to commit the Cornish tin mines to local custodians for 1,000 marks a year and, the following month, they accepted the 500 mark offer from the bishop of Exeter and the men of the county for a local man as sheriff.[17] In the Pipe Roll of 1222, which for Cornwall covered the two years from October 1220, the total sum recorded as paid into the treasury from the tin mines, the shrieval farm and the fines made by the county was no less than £1,645, while another £333 were received direct from the revenues of the mines by Queen Berengar.[18]

[12] *F*, 162–3; *Ann. Mon.*, iii, 60.

[13] *PR*, 247; *RLC*, 437–437b.

[14] *PR*, 266–7.

[15] *RLC*, 442, 457b.

[16] *F*, 163; however, a manor once held by his mother was conceded to the vicomte: *RLC*, 429, 437, 171; SC 1/1, no. 117.

[17] C 60/15, m.9. The county's fine was also for quittance of the carucage. Having paid it, the county was also to clear, at 300 marks a year, the 1,300 mark fine that it had made with King John (*Pipe Roll 1208*, 183) for deforestation and other liberties.

[18] E 372/66, r.9d, m.2.

Henry fitz Count's fall also enabled the government to fulfil part of the promise made to Reginald de Braose on his return to the king's faith in 1217. This was to return to him, or rather to his son William, the castle and honour of Totnes which fitz Count had been occupying since the war.[19] At Exeter itself Hubert dealt with the case of another former rebel, William de Marsh, a Somerset magnate and the lord of Lundy island. William had written complaining that, despite numerous royal letters, Philip de Albini and his men, operating from Devizes, were still preventing him enjoying peaceful seisin of his lands; indeed, they asserted that it would please Hubert and the council if William was subjected to harsh imprisonment. Consequently he dared not come and see Hubert personally. Meanwhile, he had sold nearly all his chattels to raise 300 marks to ransom his wife and some of his children, and still needed 180 marks to free four more children detained in Poitou in contravention of the peace between the king and Louis. Hubert's reaction to this letter was much the same as it had been in the case of Roger de Montbegon earlier in the year. As far as the issuing of writs was concerned, he would help, even though he was acting against Philip Mark or, in this case, Philip de Albini. Thus on 7 September he instructed the sheriff of Somerset to maintain William in peaceful possession of his lands free from molestation.[20] In the same way, later in the month, Hubert tried once again to place Matilda de Cauz in charge of the Nottinghamshire forest, something first attempted back in 1217. In the process he neatly sidestepped the findings of an inquiry staged by Philip Mark which showed that Mark, as sheriff, had the right to appoint 'superior serjeants' over the forest.[21]

Hubert's chief concern in September, once the Cornwall crisis was over, was to salvage Philip of Oldcoates's posting to Poitou. Here he was successful. On 16 September, with the government now at Winchester, Oldcoates's appointment was at last announced and, on the same day, before he could change his mind, ships were provided for his passage.[22] Something was done to meet his grievances and objections. He was allowed to remain as sheriff of Northumberland and constable of Newcastle upon Tyne and Bamburgh; surely sufficient protection against his northern enemies. The promise of £300 in land from escheats in place of the £300 he presently held from the royal demesne was reaffirmed.[23] As for resources, with the proceeds from the carucage not yet due, Pandulf came to the rescue, dipping into the money from the crusading twentieth and loaning the government

[19] PR, 296-7. This took place in 1221.
[20] SC 1/1, no. 219; RLC, 429; see PR, 122 and (for William), Powicke, Henry III, 748.
[21] RLC, 431; PR, 272, 123.
[22] PR, 249-52; RLC, 430.
[23] C 60/12, m.3d.

2,007½ marks. Hubert and Peter pledged that this would be repaid from the first money to arrive at the Michaelmas exchequer. Of this loan, however, 1,000 marks were absorbed by Queen Berengar and, in the end, only 500 marks were given to Oldcoates, although another 200 marks went to the men of Niort to help them fortify their town. Not surprisingly, Oldcoates had to be equipped with letters asking for a loan of 500 marks from the men of La Rochelle or Bordeaux.[24] Oldcoates's immediate instructions were probably no more than to get possession of Joan and patch up a truce with Hugh de Lusignan. But this did not mean that the government was ready to give in entirely. Rather it hoped to achieve something through papal pressure: a letter from Honorius, on 25 September, threatened Hugh with spiritual penalties if he did not surrender both Joan *and* her *maritagium* of Saintes and Oléron.[25] In attempting to send Oldcoates to Poitou, Hubert had been accused by Pandulf of 'travelling always over seas and mountains and seeking those things which are not to be had'. This was an astute appreciation of the patient labour with which the justiciar tackled his problems. It was erroneous only in prophesying failure. In the end, Hubert had attained his objective, as he was to do in much else during the course of the minority.

ix. *Llywelyn's campaign in south Wales; the earl of Pembroke's surrender of Fotheringhay; Hugh de Lusignan's delivery of the king's sister; August–November 1220*

While the government was moving to evict Henry fitz Count from Cornwall, Llywelyn had struck in Wales, although not in the manner expected. In July 1220 the king had ordered Rhys Gryg to surrender to Llywelyn, as the king's representative, the lands and castles that he had gained during the war. These were chiefly the castle and lordship of Kidwelly and Swansea castle with the lordship of Gower, all of which Rhys in practice owed to Llywelyn himself. In 1220 the government's aim was probably to return these to their rightful holders, respectively the heiress of Thomas de Londres, who was the ward of William Crassus, and Reginald de Braose. Llywelyn's role was that demanded of him under the treaty of Worcester in 1218, namely to secure the surrender of the lands which had been taken during the war from 'the barons of England and the March'.[1]

It was in fact precisely against Rhys Gryg, acting ostensibly as the king's agent, that Llywelyn marched the army about which Hubert had

[24] *PR*, 253, 249–50; *RLC*, 442.
[25] *PR*, 250; *RL*, 536–7.
[1] *RLC*, 423; Walker, 'Hubert de Burgh and Wales', 470–1; *ERF*, 40, 50; see above p. 76.

been worrying on 21 August. Rhys's resistance was quickly overcome. On 29 August he surrendered Kidwelly and Gower, and gave hostages as security that he would do homage to the king. This, however, was no more than a cover to keep the English government happy. Essentially, Llywelyn had acted in his own interests, not the king's.[2] The real object of his campaign was soon revealed: to take revenge on the earl of Pembroke. There had been constant conflict between Llywelyn and the earl, which was perhaps inevitable with the former installed in Cardigan and maintaining Maelgwyn ap Rhys both in Carmarthen and the Marshal lordships of Emlyn and Cilgerran. Llywelyn had complained bitterly of the breach of the truce promulgated at Shrewsbury in May. He also believed that Pembroke was refusing to pay a ransom for men whom he, Llywelyn, had taken during the war, presumably during his attack on south-west Wales in 1217.[3] Having brought Rhys into line, therefore, Llywelyn invaded Pembrokeshire. On the first day of the campaign (29 or 30 August), he took and razed Narberth. On the second day he seized Wiston and on the third he burned Haverford to the castle gate 'and so throughout the week he . . . inflicted immense slaughter on the people every day', as the Welsh chronicle, *The Brut*, put it. Ultimately, the knights and men of the lordship bought a truce until the following May by giving Llywelyn £100 and agreeing not to rebuild the castles that had been destroyed.[4]

The events of August and September 1220 were a stunning affirmation of Llywelyn's power. He had humiliated the earl of Pembroke and could settle the future of south Wales as he pleased. Thus he returned Kidwelly not to William Crassus, a familiar of the earl, but to a chastened Rhys Gryg. Likewise he gave Gower not to Reginald de Braose, whose eldest son had married Pembroke's sister, but to Reginald's nephew and rival, John. In 1219 and 1220 Llywelyn had been expected to attack Reginald de Braose, the son-in-law who had deserted him during the war. Establishing John de Braose in Gower, and making him too a son-in-law, was both a more subtle and a more effective riposte.[5] Llywelyn had claimed, in May 1220, that the homages of the nobles of Maelienydd belonged to his princedom, not to the king, and in south Wales he had put that ambition into practice. Under the treaty of Worcester he should have ensured that the nobles

---

[2] *RL*, no. cliii; Walker, 'Hubert de Burgh and Wales', 470–1. Conceivably Llywelyn detected unwanted signs of independence in Rhys, who in 1219 had married a daughter of 'the earl of Clare'; *Brut*, 97.

[3] *RL*, nos cxxiii, cliii; *Ann. Mon.*, iii, 61–2.

[4] *Brut*, 97–8; *RL*, nos cxxiv, cxxv.

[5] *RLC*, 459b; *Brut*, 99; 'Neath Cartulary', 152–3; Walker, 'Hubert de Burgh and Wales', 470–1. Davies, *Wales*, 244, 248, gives a somewhat different account. For the government's unavailing instruction to Llywelyn to surrender what he had taken from Rhys, see *RLC*, 431b.

of Wales did homage to the king of England but in the south he had allowed only Rhys Ieuanc to do so.[6] Rhys Gryg in Kidwelly, John de Braose in Gower and Maelgwyn ap Rhys in Cemais, Cilgerran, Emlyn, St Clears, Laugharne, Llansteffan and Carmarthen all owed their lordships to him and presumably had done him homage for them.[7] The extent to which Llywelyn aspired to create an independent principality under himself was revealed, a few years later, in his claim, in direct contravention of the treaty of Worcester, that he had 'no less liberty' than the king of Scotland, who could receive outlaws from England 'with impunity'.[8]

The earl of Pembroke in 1220 had been caught totally unprepared. He had spent part of the summer in France, was burdened with debt and had yet to rally his forces in Ireland.[9] He also appreciated that the government lacked the resources to fight on his behalf. Writing to Hubert early in September about the outrages, he asked not for a task force but a letter. The king should inform the men of Pembrokeshire that their agreement with Llywelyn was null and void, and that the latter had no authority from the king (as he claimed) for his actions. In addition, Pembroke asked that justice be given him on 30 September, that is, the day appointed by the Oxford council.[10]

From one point of view Pembroke's plight gave the government its chance, for, in return for its intervention against Llywelyn, it could demand an obvious price: the surrender of Fotheringhay. The need to secure Fotheringhay, indeed, was becoming increasingly pressing as the meeting with King Alexander, arranged for York in October, loomed closer. On 11 September, therefore, a royal letter was despatched from Shaftesbury couched in rather different terms from the one Pembroke had requested. It expressed the king's anger and astonishment that he had not surrendered Fotheringhay. He was now to vacate it immediately 'lest the whole business of the marriage [between Alexander and the king's sister] remains incompleted to our great damage and shame'. As for Llywelyn, all that Pembroke got was a promise of justice on 30 September, linked with an injunction from the king and Pandulf to refrain meanwhile from retaliation.[11]

This injunction Pembroke agreed to obey, while indicating that he expected the government's full support. He firmly believed, he said, that Hubert grieved at the injuries that he had suffered at the hands of

---

[6] *RL*, no. cv; *Brut*, 96. Llywelyn had never fulfilled his promise of 1216 to give Cardigan to Rhys: *Brut*, 92, 98.

[7] See the map above p. 75, and genealogical table below p. 423.

[8] *RL*, no. cci.

[9] *RL*, no. lviii.

[10] *RL*, nos cxxv, cxxiv.

[11] *RLC*, 429b; *RL*, no. cxxix.

Llywelyn. He would obey the king and Pandulf provided they gave him justice. As for Fotheringhay, he remained non-committal: he wished to promote the interests of the king and his sister, he would answer for the castle on 30 September and was prepared to do the will of Hubert and the king as far as he could and should.[12] In fact, when Pembroke arrived at Westminster he got what he demanded and gave little concrete in return. On 5 October royal letters, authorized by Hubert and the council, were addressed to Llywelyn and the men of Pembrokeshire exactly on the lines that Pembroke had requested.[13] In return, Pembroke made some promise about Fotheringhay and on 11 October was informed that Henry Foliot was being sent to receive its surrender. Pembroke, however, then wrote to say that, not wishing to impede the negotiations with the king of Scotland, he had instructed John Marshal to give up the castle to *the king's council*, which in effect was a refusal to surrender it to Henry Foliot. Fotheringhay was still in Pembroke's hands in the last week of November.[14]

By 13 October the king, Pandulf and Hubert were in York, having left Bishop Peter behind in London with the seal to look after the Michaelmas sessions of bench and exchequer.[15] The magnates of Yorkshire may well have gathered before the king at York and granted him the modest sum of £200 in place of the carucage.[16] King Alexander agreed to be patient. He was doubtless informed of the earl of Pembroke's willingness to surrender Fotheringhay and regaled with the prospect that Joan would soon be released by Hugh de Lusignan. By the end of the year the government was indeed in a position to fulfil its assurances on both counts.

In respect of Fotheringhay it took one last push. On 23 November Pembroke was informed that Gregory de Turri was being sent to receive the castle and on the same day letters authorized by Hubert and Peter removed Pembroke's familiar, Ralph Musard, from the sheriffdom of Gloucester. This was a variant of the threat which had worked so well earlier in the year when Philip of Oldcoates's dismissal from Northumberland had persuaded him to surrender Mitford. It worked again. Pembroke gave up Fotheringhay and on 3 December Ralph Musard was restored to Gloucestershire.[17]

---

[12] *RL*, no. cxxix.

[13] *F*, 164; *PR*, 254–5.

[14] *PR*, 257; SC 1/62, no. 9.

[15] *RLC*, 439.

[16] *RL*, no. cxxx; *Divers Accounts*, 16.

[17] *PR*, 272–4; *RLC*, 442, 442b. Also at this time orders were issued, although apparently not implemented, for the seizure into the king's hands of the manors of Hintlesham and Hingham which were held, during the king's pleasure, by respectively the earl of Salisbury's familiar, William Talbot, and John Marshal: E 368/3, m.9d; *Pipe Roll 1221*, 32–3.

Around this time the government also received glad tidings about Joan. The story here had begun with a great meeting at Angoulême early in September between Hugh de Lusignan and representatives of the Poitevin and Gascon towns. Hugh had agreed, before moving to war against the towns, to lay his grievances before the king and his councillors. Envoys from Hugh and the towns were accordingly in England early in October.[18] Faced with war in Poitou, and the coming meeting with Alexander, the government now abandoned the attempt to withhold Isabella's dower in England against the return of Joan's *maritagium*. On 5 October, by a decision of Hubert and the council, the dower, including Berkhampstead castle and probably also Rockingham, was delivered to one of Hugh's knights. In return, Hugh was asked either to bring Joan to England himself or surrender her at La Rochelle.[19]

Hugh gave a cordial reception to King Henry's envoys on their arrival. He delivered Joan to them and regretted that illness, which the envoys thought was genuine enough, prevented him from coming to England to do homage to the king. 'As far as I could judge from the count's words', one of the reports home concluded, 'he wants very much to serve you and assist you faithfully.'[20] The caution was justified. The English government had swopped Isabella's dower in England for Joan's return but nothing had been agreed about the parts of her dower in Poitou (notably Niort) of which she had been denied possession.[21] Equally, the English government continued to press through the pope for the return of Joan's *maritagium* of Oléron, Saintes and the Saintonge. Here were the seeds of future conflict.[22]

One person was absent from the meeting with Hugh de Lusignan: Philip of Oldcoates himself. Oldcoates had left England in no very tranquil state of mind. He had submitted a petition containing a whole list of demands, including the suspension of legal actions brought against him by the bishop of Durham and a guarantee that his promised £300 worth of land should come from the *first* escheats.[23] He travelled through France, perhaps intending to see King Philip, and died at Étampes, thirty miles south of Paris. The government had learnt of his demise by the end of October and hastened to get hold of Bamburgh and Newcastle upon Tyne.[24] It was left once again with the problem of finding a seneschal for Poitou and Gascony.

---

[18] *DD*, no. 93; *RLC*, 431b.
[19] *PR*, 254–5; *RLC*, 432b.
[20] *DD*, nos 96–8.
[21] Niort was controlled by its citizens: *DD*, no. 90.
[22] *PR*, 257, 267–8; *Ann. Mon.*, iii, 75; *F*, 169.
[23] SC 8/340, no. 16038; compare C 60/12, m.3d.
[24] *Ann. Mon.*, iii, 64–5; *PR*, 269; *RLC*, 473.

x. *The Michaelmas exchequer of 1220 and the proceeds of the carucage*

The task of finding someone to replace Philip of Oldcoates was not helped by the limited success of the measures launched at the Oxford council in August to improve the king's financial situation. It was on 30 September that the inquiry into the king's demesnes and escheats was due to be delivered to the government. Those who held them were to come before the king and show warrant for their seisin or be dispossessed. Falkes, indeed, now surrendered the royal demesne manor of Godmanchester in Huntingdonshire which he had received in 1217 to sustain him in the king's service.[1] But, for the rest, there is little evidence of dispossession. In some cases, of course, seisin had been granted until the king was fourteen, which was still a year away, or until he came of age; but, in others, property was simply held during the king's pleasure and was quite open to resumption. Although the inquiry may have prompted some individual investigations at the exchequer, it looks as though the government backed away from this unpopular initiative. If, however, it was unable to realize a general resumption, it took every opportunity to take individual manors and farms into the king's hands. The year before, it had bought the earl of Salisbury out of Southampton; in June 1220 it had recovered the Northamptonshire manors on the fall of the count of Aumale; and in August it repossessed Chesterton in Cambridgeshire as soon as it heard of the earl of Winchester's death on crusade. Once in the king's hands, moreover, the manors were usually retained, in contrast to the practice in 1217 and 1218.[2]

The sheriffs had also been threatened in August 1220 with dismissal if they failed to be at the exchequer on 30 September to answer fully for all the things belonging to their sheriffdoms. In fact, sheriffs or their deputies from eighteen of the twenty-nine sheriffdoms appeared on 30 September, much as the year before. None of the absentees was dismissed. The total revenue proffered, £301, was actually less than at Michaelmas 1219. The individual who brought most (£100) was Hubert's deputy as sheriff of Norfolk–Suffolk.[3] If the pipe roll of 1220 is taken as reflecting the revenue from the Michaelmas term of 1220, together with some of that from the Easter terms of 1220 and 1221, the results appear equally disappointing. The total recorded as paid into the exchequer was £4,560. If adjustments are made for the sheriffdoms

---

[1] *Pipe Roll 1220*, 137–9; *Pipe Roll 1221*, 170–1; *RLC*, 319b.

[2] *Pipe Roll 1219*, 25; *Pipe Roll 1220*, 14–16, 132–3, 137, 139; *Pipe Roll 1221*, 170–1; *RLC*, 342b; *ERF*, 50–1; E 159/4, m.8. The farm of Godmanchester was assigned to repay a debt to the Templars: *RLC*, 479.

[3] See Appendix, p. 415. However, the representatives of some boroughs in 1220 brought their farms without the amount being specified.

which accounted for 1220 in the roll of the following year, then the sum rises to a notional £5,350. That the king's ordinary cash revenue at this time was indeed running at around £5,000 a year is also suggested by the income recorded in the receipt roll of the Easter term of 1220, which was £1,733; the issues of the Easter roll, on later evidence, being perhaps a third of those recorded on the roll for the Michaelmas term.[4] Meanwhile, the adjusted total for expenditure from the pipe roll of 1220 is £2,040. Thus the grand total for receipts and expenditure, on the adjusted figures, is £7,390, £785 *less* than the averaged total of the adjusted figures derived from the rolls of 1218 and 1219. In short, with the benefits from the recovery of Cornwall not yet apparent, the level of the king's ordinary revenue seemed at a standstill.

Equally disappointing were the proceeds of the carucage, likewise due in London on 30 September. When the collectors closed their accounts some time in 1221 their receipts came to only £2,671 1s 8½d, although more dribbled in later with much huffing and puffing from the exchequer.[5] Perhaps another couple of thousand pounds came from the aid imposed on the church, after it secured exemption from the tax.[6] Thus the proceeds from the taxation of 1220 and from the king's ordinary annual revenue, both around £5,000, help to explain the sums which writs of *liberate* ordered the exchequer to disburse between Michaelmas 1220 and Michaelmas 1221. At £10,785 these were more than double the year before. The £2,671 from the carucage, together with the proceeds from the clerical aid, took the total yield from the taxation of 1220 above the £2,818 eventually acquired from the scutage of 1217.[7] Nonetheless, the 1220 carucage and aid produced far less than the taxation for the crusade which Pandulf was levying on the church in England. By July 1220 this had raised £12,000.[8] Even more, the yield in 1220–21 was dwarfed by the £60,000 obtained from the 1207 tax on movable property.

The taxation of 1220 failed, in fact, to restore the king's position either in England or Poitou. Of the initial 3,000 marks (£2,000) from the carucage, which had arrived by 25 November, 1,000 marks were given to Queen Berengar, arrangements to pay her from the tin mines

---

[4] Whitwell, 'Revenue and expenditure under Henry III', 710–11. There were, however, considerable variations in the balance of revenue between the terms.

[5] The accounts of the receivers and collectors of the carucage are printed both in *Divers Accounts*, 16–19, 20–6, and *BF*, 1437–45. *BF*, 292–334, has some of the more detailed rolls compiled in the course of the assessment and collection and *BF*, 1446–56, a later inquiry.

[6] The contribution of Dunstable priory to the aid was 3 marks: *Ann. Mon.*, iii, 60; see also *RL*, no. cxxx.

[7] Mitchell, *Taxation*, 126.

[8] *CPReg.*, 74.

of Cornwall and the exchange having yet to get off the ground. Another 1,500 marks went to Pandulf to repay the money that he had lent for the settlements with Queen Berengar in July and Henry fitz Count in September. That left for Poitou a bare 500 marks, which seems to have been given to an envoy of the vicomte of Thouars.[9]

That the government did not make more money was partly the fault of the carucage itself. Even if it was paid in full, with the rate set at only 2s, the number of ploughs or plough lands on which it was assessed in each county meant the yields would never be particularly large. In a medium-sized county like Northamptonshire, for example, the total of lay *carucae* assessed was 2,613, which meant that the county owed £261. This may be compared with £1,211 received from lay property in the county from the tax on movables of 1225.[10] But what was equally evident to the government, apart from its steady retreat on the question of clerical liability, was the failure to get the tax assessed at all in some counties, while in others, where it was assessed, it was only partially paid. In that sense, the fate of the carucage showed how far the government still had to go in reasserting its authority in the counties of England.

That authority, at least when it came to collecting the carucage, stood highest in several of Falkes's sheriffdoms, where virtually all the sums assessed were paid. On the other hand, the exchequer was deeply suspicious about the yield from Bedfordshire-Buckinghamshire, where Falkes's under-sheriffs refused to co-operate with the knights chosen to assess and collect the tax.[11] Even worse was the situation in some of the former rebel-held counties of eastern England. In Essex and Norfolk–Suffolk, half or more of the assessed sums remained outstanding when the receivers closed their accounts.[12] Further north the tax was not assessed at all. How the Yorkshire magnates refused to pay it since they had not been consulted has already been seen, and ultimately a lump sum of £200 was obtained from the county. (For the 1225 tax, by contrast, £2,369 were received from Yorkshire.)[13] Perhaps there were similar protests in Lincolnshire, where the lump sum agreed, or at least received, was a mere £40.[14] Nothing at all was obtained from Northumberland until 1223.[15] There may have been

---

[9] *RLC*, 442. There appears to be no precise evidence as to how the clerical aid was spent.

[10] *BF*, 326; *Divers Accounts*, 55, 60; Cazel, 'The fifteenth of 1225', 71.

[11] *Divers Accounts*, 23–4; E 368/7, r.15(14), m.21; *BF*, 1446–56.

[12] *Divers Accounts*, 23–5.

[13] *Divers Accounts*, 56, 60; Cazel, 'The fifteenth of 1225', 71.

[14] *Divers Accounts*, 16.

[15] *Divers Accounts*, 22, where the sheriff who accounts (William Brewer junior) was appointed in February 1223: *PR*, 365.

problems with consent elsewhere. Nothing was ever obtained from the earl of Chester's sheriffdoms of Lancashire, Shropshire and Stafford-shire. In 1224 Chester's succesor as sheriff reported that 'the barons of Lancaster do not wish to give the carucage'.[16] Chester's own demesnes and fees may have been formally exempted from the tax. Robert fitz Walter certainly secured exemption, just as he had from the scutage of 1217.[17]

Chester and fitz Walter had just returned from their crusade and were absent from the Oxford assembly but a much wider circle of magnates, some of whom had certainly been at Oxford, caused difficulties over paying the tax. In several counties the earls of Pembroke, Salisbury, Gloucester, Surrey and Arundel either prevented the tax being assessed at all on their lands or insisted on answering for it themselves apart from the normal system of collection.[18] Although Engelard de Cigogné was told in a royal letter attested by Hubert that the sheriff and knights of Berkshire must collect the carucage within his bailiwick of Windsor, Engelard told Hubert flatly that he and the knights of the Windsor hundreds would collect it themselves and they did so.[19]

The government's sense of the carucage's failure was still spawning inquiries in the 1230s.[20] Hubert himself had equally seen the dis-appointing performance of the sheriffs at the beginning of the Michaelmas term, for he was presiding then at the exchequer. Hence Geoffrey de Neville wrote to him to explain that 'my sheriff of Yorkshire, detained on the king's business, cannot appear before you and the barons of the exchequer on the day after Michaelmas'.[21] Later in the month, however, when Hubert, Pandulf and the king went to York to see Alexander, Bishop Peter was left in charge of the exchequer and the great seal. Peter appears to have made somewhat autocratic use of his independence. He put his two colleagues in an awkward situation by announcing that, provided they agreed, the king would accept a proffer of 1,000 marks a year for the tin mines of Cornwall.[22] More remarkable still, he issued a letter in his own name declaring that, having inspected a royal charter, it was clear to him that the manor of Newburn should be exempt from tallage and thus 'he ordered' the

[16] E 368/6, mm.9d, 17. For these and other difficulties of collection, see Mitchell, *Taxation*, 132 n.58.

[17] *RLC*, 430b, 442; *BF*, 298, 312, 326, 327, 1453; *Divers Accounts*, 20.

[18] *Divers Accounts*, 20–1; *BF*, 298, 311–12, 326, 1446–56.

[19] *RL*, no. cxxxix; *Divers Accounts*, 16; *BF*, 302–6.

[20] *BF*, 1446–56.

[21] SC 1/1, no. 162. See also *RLC*, 429, where the sheriff of Somerset–Dorset was ordered to return an inquiry to Hubert 'at your account at Westminster on the day after Michaelmas'.

[22] C 60/12, m.2. In the event the proffer was accepted: *PR*, 272.

sheriff not to levy it. This decision should surely have been left to Pandulf, Hubert and the council.[23]

Hubert's concern with what had happened at the exchequer in his absence, and a desire to keep a check on its activities in the future, may well be the background to a significant change which, as Dr Crook has shown, took place at this time in the exchequer memoranda rolls. Hubert was back at Westminster by 1 November. Two days later the hearing of the account of the sheriff of Essex–Hertfordshire began at the exchequer. This is known because the date is given at the head of the account in the exchequer memoranda roll. The introduction of a date into the heading was an innovation and one which had come to stay; from this point onwards the dates on which all the sheriffs accounted are known. The coincidence of the change with Hubert's return to Westminster makes it highly likely, as Dr Crook has argued, that he was responsible for it. Although Hubert was frequently present in person at the hearing of shrieval accounts, indeed they were sometimes held up until he could attend, he might equally be drawn away by other business. The innovation in the memoranda rolls enabled him to see, at a glance, what accounts had been heard in his absence.[24]

This change in the form of the memoranda rolls was followed by an advance of more substance which was also a pointer to the direction that the government wished to take. Philip of Oldcoates's death cleared the way for the break-up of his northern fiefdom. The revenues from the royal demesne manors of Newcastle upon Tyne, Bamburgh and Corbridge, worth £115 a year, were recovered and retained in the king's hands.[25] Then in January 1221 Hubert and the council placed the county and forest of Northumberland and the castles of Newcastle upon Tyne and Bamburgh under four separate keepers.[26] The new sheriff of the county, moreover, was appointed as a custodian answering for the issues above the farm. Around the same time, with his lord, Richard fitz Regis, absent abroad, the under-sheriff of Berkshire, Henry de Scaccario, was also made to answer as a custodian. The government therefore took advantage, for the first time, of the omission of clause 25 of Magna Carta 1215, which effectively prohibited the exaction of revenue above the farm, from the Charters of 1216 and 1217. For the year 1220–21 the two sheriffs accounted for profits above

---

[23] E 368/4, m.2d; printed in West, *Justiciarship*, 240 n.4.

[24] *Pipe Roll 1221*, introduction; *Pipe Roll 1220*, vi–vii.

[25] *Pipe Roll 1221*, 9; *Pipe Roll 1220*, 191–2. Bamburgh was henceforth accounted for within the county farm. Oldcoates's death also released the £90 annual farm from the manors of Collingham and Bardsey in Yorkshire. This was soon assigned by Hubert and the council to fund the works at Beaulieu abbey: *PR*, 184, 278, 280–1.

[26] *PR* 278–9.

the farm of some £67.[27] The amount was comparatively small but Hubert and the exchequer had signalled very clearly their desire to impose stricter financial terms on the sheriffs. In Northumberland and Berkshire the new policy was only possible thanks to the departure of Oldcoates and Richard fitz Regis. The implication was that a wholesale removal of the sheriffs would be necessary before it could be given general application.

Another change of practice in the last quarter of 1220 signalled the new spirit in the government. Since the war it had given permission, in the king's name, for the establishment of markets and fairs, often charging for the privilege. Between September and November 1220 it was decided that such concessions should be valid only until the king came of age and this limitation was inserted in all subsequent grants.[28] Thus the government demonstrated clearly its determination to protect the rights of the king.

xi. *The count of Aumale and the siege of Bytham, December 1220–January 1221*

The Christmas court at Oxford was celebrated with a magnificence which impressed Roger of Wendover. The clerks of the king's chapel sang the *Laudes Regiae*, the celebratory hymns in praise of kingship, as they were henceforth to do at the great festivals of Easter, Pentecost and Christmas. Robes were distributed to twenty-five household knights, eighteen more than at Christmas 1217.[1] According to Wendover, the king was surrounded by 'the earls and barons of the kingdom'. The count of Aumale, however, did not stay till the end of the festivities; instead, he left Oxford in the middle of the night without the king's permission. This was the prelude to his brief revolt, which culminated in the siege of Bytham castle. The government's success in suppressing the count's insurrection was an important step towards the reassertion of its authority, for the detention of Bytham was the last case outstanding where a great man was defying orders to surrender a castle obtained during the war. The return of Bytham, after the siege, to its lord, William de Coleville, fulfilled the peace treaty of 1217 and confirmed the reconciliation between the government and former rebels. Indeed, like the removal of Robert de Gaugi from Newark in 1218 and of Philip of Oldcoates from Mitford in 1220, the government's victory depended in some measure on its willingness and ability to utilize its former enemies' military power.

---

[27] *Pipe Roll 1221*, 1, 3, 8, 9.

[28] The change took place between 18 September and 7 November. Its novelty is shown by the way some of the early limitation clauses are interlineations in the text of the concessions: C 60/12, m.2; C 60/15, mm. 10, 9; *RLC*, 444b.

[1] *Chron. Maj.*, 60; *RLC*, 345b, 409; Kantorowicz, *Laudes Regiae*, 174–7. At Christmas 1219 there were seventeen household knights: *RLC*, 444.

The political base for the government's triumph lay partly, therefore, in its relations with former rebels. But equally important was a change within the regime itself. Since August 1220 a rapprochement had taken place between the government and the earl of Chester. Chester had been pointedly absent from the Oxford council in August but next month he was restored to the Montfort half of the honour of Leicester;[2] and in December, reversing a decision taken at the Oxford council, he received the wardship of various manors of Earl David. He then attended the Christmas court at Oxford.[3] It was probably around this time that Hubert himself co-operated with Chester in a remarkable fashion. The two men, together with Falkes, Philip de Albini, William de Cantilupe, Geoffrey de Neville, Brian de Lisle, Engelard de Cigogné and Hugh de Vivonne, addressed a letter to the pope in which they warned him against restoring to England a person whom he had earlier excluded 'for his immense malice . . . and the crime of lese-majesty, and for disturbing the whole kingdom'; a person who gloried in being a cause of King John's death and who thirsted for the blood of his son and his *fideles*.[4] The subject of this diatribe was almost certainly Master Simon Langton, Louis's chancellor and Archbishop Stephen's brother, whom the pope had exiled from England after the war. In October 1220 Archbishop Langton had set out for the papal court. One of his aims in visiting Rome was to secure the recall of Pandulf, whose position as legate inevitably reflected on his own authority as archbishop,[5] but clearly rumours had reached England that he also hoped to effect the return of his brother Simon, perhaps indeed in some position of authority. That Hubert was involved in the furious response hardly suggests that he was, at this stage, close to Langton. It also reflects his efforts to avoid becoming boxed in politically, for here he was co-operating with the very men, Chester, Falkes, Cantilupe, Lisle and Engelard, who three years later, in concert with Aumale, were to plot his downfall.

Hubert, therefore, with timing that was lucky or inspired, had come to terms with Aumale's potential allies within the regime just before the latter's revolt. The government had also demonstrated its strength elsewhere. After Christmas it returned to London, where a great

---

[2] *PR*, 254; *RLC*, 431b. Chester had held the lands of the earldom *ad opus* Simon de Montfort: *RLP*, 150. After Chester's departure on his crusade news arrived of Montfort's death and his lands were taken into the king's hands, although as no accounts for them appear on the pipe rolls, it is likely that the revenues were reserved for Chester: *PR*, 161–3, 184–5.

[3] *RLC*, 443b, 426b, 455. The manors given to Chester included Nassington and Yarwell. They were in the king's gift as Earl David had held them in chief.

[4] *F*, 171. For the date of the letter and speculation as to its background and purpose, see Denholm-Young, 'A letter from the council to Pope Honorius', 88–96.

[5] *Ann. Mon.*, iii, 62, 74; Powicke, *Langton*, 145–6.

council was held. News must have arrived about Aumale's activities but this did not impede steps to remove another castellan who had proved awkward in the past. Early in January Pandulf, Hubert and Peter were all involved in appointing the castellan of Bristol, Hugh de Vivonne, in place of Philip of Oldcoates as seneschal of Poitou.[6] There were some grounds for this choice. Although a Poitevin, Vivonne had lost most of his lands in the province, while he had acquired significant properties in England through marriage.[7] He could thus be punished if he misbehaved. Vivonne's appointment raised immediately, as perhaps was intended, the question of Bristol castle, where, as castellan, he had defied the government over the return of the Barton to the earl of Gloucester. In 1221 he clearly wanted to retain the castle, just as Oldcoates, on his appointment as seneschal, had retained his northern custodies. But Vivonne's position was much weaker. Beginning as the deputy at Bristol of the great Poitevin magnate, Savari de Mauléon, he had been appointed in his own right merely in 1219, and then quite specifically during the king's pleasure. Vivonne, therefore, was made to surrender Bristol to Pandulf, although, in return, Hubert, the earls of Chester and Salisbury, Falkes, William Brewer, Geoffrey de Neville and Philip de Albini all pledged that, if he was recalled or compelled to return to England, he might either recover the castle or custodies of equivalent value.[8]

In January 1221, therefore, the government had seen off one castellan and was in no mood to be challenged by another. Having left the Christmas court during the night, Aumale had gone to Bytham, where he munitioned the castle and despoiled the neighbouring villages of Edenham and Deeping. He then struck north, attempting unsuccessfully to take the castles of Newark and Sleaford, before returning south to suffer a further check at the castle of Kimbolton.[9] When news of these outrages reached London, Aumale was excommunicated in St Paul's cathedral by Pandulf and at least half a dozen bishops, both the earls of Salisbury and Chester taking part in the ceremony. Chester later observed that Aumale had been excommunicated 'by the common counsel of the prelates and magnates of all the kingdom'.[10] This spiritual penalty, however, was combined with a measure of conciliation. On 22 January Aumale was instructed to give credence to what

[6] *PR*, 275–7, 308.

[7] *RL*, no. lxxv; SC 1/1, no. 211; *RLP*, 161b; *ERF*, 109; *BF*, 378, 751. When seneschal for a second time in the 1230s, Vivonne expanded his private interests in Gascony: Stacey, *Politics*, 174.

[8] *PR*, 277, 281, 306–7; *Ann. Mon.*, iii, 64–5; Norgate, *Minority*, 282–3.

[9] The details of Aumale's revolt may be pieced together from *Chron. Maj.*, 60–1; *Walt. Cov.*, 247–8; *Ann. Mon.*, iii, 63–4.

[10] *Walt. Cov.*, 247; *Ann. Mon.*, iii, 63–4; C 47/34, no. 8.

Robert de Vieuxpont and Geoffrey de Neville told him on the king's behalf and was given letters of safe-conduct lasting until 2 February.[11] The next day, however, attempts at compromise were swept away. Neville and other magnates were summoned to Northampton with all the armed forces that they could raise. The reason was that, from making vain demonstrations in front of castles, Aumale had now succeeded in taking one. He had, as a royal letter put it, 'furtively and seditiously seized the castle of Fotheringhay . . . devastating and plundering our land and violently disturbing and infringing our peace and that of our kingdom'.[12]

Various suggestions have been made to explain Aumale's sudden mutiny.[13] Was he provoked by being passed over as Oldcoates's successor as seneschal of Poitou or by being refused some part of Oldcoates's northern custodies? It is impossible to say. What seems more certain, as Dr Crook has argued, is that part of the trail lies through the royal demesne manor of Driffield in Yorkshire. Driffield was worth at least £72 a year and was situated eleven miles west of the count's castle of Skipsea. A previous count of Aumale had held it from 1154 until his death in 1179; it had then remained in the king's hands until 1215 when John had conceded to Aumale 'the right which he [Aumale] has in the manor of Driffield'.[14] Aumale thereafter retained unchallenged possession until 23 November 1220, when an order was issued for the manor's seizure into the king's hands.[15]

Dr Crook connects the government's action in seizing Driffield with the inquiry into the royal demesne inaugurated at the Oxford council in August 1220. But it is strange that Driffield virtually alone should be singled out for resumption and then returned to Aumale after his revolt.[16] It is more likely that the manor's seizure was designed as a punishment or a warning to Aumale, just as on the same day Ralph Musard was removed from Gloucestershire in order to get the earl of Pembroke out of Fotheringhay. But as a punishment or warning for what? One possibility lies in Aumale's failure to implement the

---

[11] *RLC*, 446; *PR*, 278; *Walt. Cov.*, 248.

[12] *RL*, no. cxlv. The indication in this letter that the initial excommunication took place *before* the seizure of Fotheringhay outweighs the statement in the Dunstable annals that one reason for the excommunication was the seizure of a royal castle. The annals are also wrong in saying that the excommunication took place on 25 January: *Ann. Mon.*, iii, 63–4.

[13] Turner, 'The minority of Henry III (part II)', 248–9; Turner (R.V.), 'William de Forz', 238; English, *Holderness*, 44.

[14] Crook, 'Pipe Roll 5 Henry III', 25–7; *RLP*, 154; C 60/18, m.10.

[15] C 60/15, m.9.

[16] Crook, 'Pipe Roll 5 Henry III', 25–7; *RLC*, 458.

settlement made with Pandulf after his excommunication in 1219;[17] another in his refusal to surrender the castle of Bytham.

Bytham castle lies at the centre of Aumale's revolt. It was there that he went after leaving the Christmas festivities at Oxford; there that he returned having taken Fotheringhay; and there that the king's forces, as early as 28 January, were directed.[18] The conflict between Aumale and William de Coleville over possession of Bytham, as has been seen, raised complex issues of right, which were best settled by a law case. A verdict in just such a case was indeed delivered, for the Dunstable annalist gives as a reason for Aumale's excommunication in January 1221 the fact that he 'scorned to obey the judgement of the kingdom concerning the castle of Bytham which was adjudged to William de Coleville'.[19] Perhaps it was Aumale's defiance which provoked the order over Driffield in November or perhaps the final 'judgement of the kingdom' was delivered at the Christmas court itself. If so, Aumale's departure, unlicensed and in the middle of the night, is readily understandable. It was all too much. In June 1220, despite his sacrifices in the war, he had been ejected from Rockingham castle and the surrounding manors; in November he had been deprived of Driffield, despite John's recognition of his right; and now he was to lose Bytham castle to William de Coleville, who had acquired it unjustly from his (Aumale's) mother's first husband.

Was there any pattern to Aumale's subsequent conduct? Dr Stacey suggests that there was and that, in particular, his attack on Fotheringhay was an attempt to bring the earl of Chester in on his side. The key piece of evidence here is the statement by the Barnwell chronicler that, at the time of Aumale's assault, Fotheringhay was in Hubert's custody. Dr Stacey argues that, with the earl of Pembroke finally out of the castle, the king of Scotland had given it to Hubert as part of an agreement by which the latter would marry his sister; a marriage which took place later in 1221. What the king of Scotland was actually giving Hubert, of course, was the custody of Fotheringhay during the minority of Earl David's heir, an heir who was the nephew of the earl of Chester. Dr Stacey suggests, therefore, that Chester resented Hubert's acquisition of Fotheringhay, coveting it for himself. By ejecting Hubert from the castle Aumale thus hoped to win Chester's sympathy and support.[20]

If, however, this was Aumale's plan, it 'backfired', as Dr Stacey observes, because one reason why Chester was infuriated by Aumale's conduct, according to the Barnwell chronicler, was precisely the

---

[17] PR, 240; Ann. Mon., iii, 64.
[18] Chron. Maj., 60–1; RLC, 448.
[19] Ann. Mon., iii, 64.
[20] Stacey, Politics, 21–3.

seizure of Fotheringhay, 'the inheritance of his nephew'.[21] His fury was all the more understandable if, as seems likely, far from resenting Hubert's tenure, he was already confident of securing Fotheringhay and the rest of the inheritance for himself. Although Hubert had custody of Fotheringhay, it was only as the king's representative, for the royal letter of 23 January states specifically that the castle was in the king's hands.[22] (Clearly it had yet to be delivered to the king of Scotland.) That, moreover, the English government already intended Chester to receive custody of David's inheritance from the king of Scotland, as he did later in 1221, is suggested by the fact that it had already granted him the manors of David which were in its gift.[23]

On the whole, it seems likely that when Aumale left Oxford he had no plan of campaign other than to capture castles and strengthen his position to the north and south of Bytham. Who actually held the castles seems to have been of no consequence: the lord of Newark and Sleaford was the bishop of Lincoln, of Kimbolton, the earl of Essex. Fotheringhay, attacked last, assumed importance only because, the moat having frozen over, it was the one castle that Aumale was able to take.[24] Of course, in the broadest terms the count must have hoped that his demonstration would persuade his friends to rally to his side. How close that came to happening cannot be known. The Barnwell chronicler recorded that Aumale acted 'as it is said by the counsel of certain magnates of England, both natives and aliens'. Roger of Wendover named names, all aliens, like Aumale himself: Falkes, Philip Mark, Peter de Maulay and Engelard de Cigogné.[25] Earlier, in 1219, Aumale had enjoyed the support of another foreigner, the bishop of Winchester. In 1221 there was certainly a lot of sympathy for Aumale, as there had been before for Robert de Gaugi, and, like Robert, he was treated with great leniency after his submission. But the testimony of both the Barnwell annalist and Roger of Wendover was probably influenced by the events of 1223–24.[26] Just before Aumale's revolt, as has been seen, Hubert was able to co-operate with Falkes and Engelard

[21] Stacey, *Politics*, 23; *Walt. Cov.*, 248.

[22] *RL*, no. cxlv. It is also possible that Hubert's marriage was not mooted until later in 1221: see below p. 245. Gregory de Turri who was sent to take possession of Fotheringhay in November 1220 (*PR*, 272) may well have been one of Hubert's knights since he featured in Hubert's *constabularia* in the army of 1223: C 72/3, m.1.

[23] *RLC*, 443; *PR*, 285.

[24] *Ann. Mon.*, iii, 63.

[25] *Chron. Maj.*, 60–1; *Walt. Cov.*, 247.

[26] The Barnwell chronicler (*Walt. Cov.*, 247) says that Aumale's supporters remained hidden and it was only subsequent events which brought them to light. Wendover's judgement (*Chron. Maj.*, 61) that the leniency shown to the garrison after the siege set the worst possible example was probably made in the light of the siege of Bedford in 1224.

over Simon Langton and both Falkes and Philip Mark played their part in Aumale's suppression.

The government, therefore, was able to move with speed. Pandulf lent £200 towards the expenses of the campaign and the earl of Pembroke expressed his eagerness to join the army with as many knights as the king wished, despite having set out for 'remote parts'.[27] By the time that the royal army gathered at Northampton on 2 February, Fotheringhay had already been evacuated and Aumale himself was in headlong flight. On the night of 31 January he passed through Nottingham and next day, as Robert of Laxton, who had a spy in his entourage, reported to Hubert, he 'rushed' over thirty miles further north to Stainton, between Conisbrough and Tickhill. There he armed himself and told his wife that he would neither eat again nor rest until he reached his castle at Skipton in Craven. He had, however, only five horses and those were 'weak and feeble'. The government reacted to this intelligence by summoning northern magnates to lay siege to Skipton and to Aumale's castles at Skipsea and Cockermouth.[28] Three days later, on 6 February, the royal army closed around Bytham itself, while Aumale took refuge not at Skipton in Craven but twenty miles to the north-east at Fountains abbey. The garrison of Bytham, some thirteen strong, resisted the king's mangonels and petraries, provided amongst others by Falkes and Philip Mark, for between two and six days. Then they came out of the castle and surrendered to the king. Aumale himself was brought from Fountains abbey under conduct of the archbishop of York.[29]

The siege of Bytham was a larger military operation than that of Rockingham had been the year before but Aumale escaped just as lightly. Some of Bytham's garrison were imprisoned and perhaps sent into exile, but that was all.[30] Four years later the bishop of Bath remarked, after the siege of Bedford castle, that 'if those taken at Bytham had been hung', then the Bedford garrison would not have defied the king.[31] No doubt Aumale's foreign friends rallied to his aid but the count had other supporters. Pandulf himself, before he would lift the excommunication, demanded some security that Aumale would obey his orders rather better than after his last excommunication was lifted in 1219. This security was provided by the earls of Chester, Salisbury, Gloucester, Surrey and Pembroke, together with John de

[27] PR, 283-4; RL, no. cxlvii. For accounts covering the cost of the siege, see Divers Accounts, 17-19; RLC, 453-4.

[28] Ann. Mon., iii, 64; RL, no. cxlviii; RLC, 474b.

[29] Ann. Mon., iii, 64; Chron. Maj., 61; RLC, 448b, 452b; Pipe Roll 1220, 14; and for the garrison, RLC, 450b, 451, 456.

[30] Walt. Cov., 249; Coggeshall, 188; RLC, 450b, 451, 456.

[31] Walt. Cov., 268; see also Chron. Maj., 61.

Lacy, Falkes, Robert fitz Walter, Gilbert de Laigle and Brian de Lisle. Each agreed to give Pandulf 100 marks if Aumale proved to be disobedient in the future. Pandulf himself then interceded for Aumale's forgiveness, mindful, so Roger of Wendover said, of his great services in the war. There may have been a reckless element in the count of Aumale. A year later, in a similar situation, the earl of Derby behaved with more restraint. Nonetheless, the count had remained loyal to King Henry throughout the war, at considerable cost, and could feel genuinely hard done by in the subsequent peace.[32]

One reason for the government's victory in 1221 was Hubert's reconciliation with the earl of Chester and his relations with Aumale's other potential allies within the regime. But the government equally relied on a much wider circle of support, support which must itself have discouraged the count's potential allies from showing their colours. Aumale was excommunicated by the 'common counsel of the . . . magnates of all the kingdom' and many former rebels were involved in the military operations against him. All the knights of Lincolnshire were at the siege of Bytham, while Roger de Montbegon, William of Lancaster, Roger Bertram, Richard de Umfraville, Robert de Vaux, Robert de Ros, Nicholas de Stuteville II, Peter de Brus, William de Mowbray, John de Lacy and Richard de Percy were involved in the operations against Aumale's northern castles.[33] Such men may well have enjoyed punishing Aumale for his desertion in the war, although after his submission, it should be noted, both John de Lacy and Robert fitz Walter were amongst his pledges. Former rebels were also encouraged by the nature of the cause. The origins of the count's revolt lay in his refusal to restore Bytham to William de Coleville under the terms of the peace of 1217. Ultimately Coleville had secured a 'judgement of the kingdom' in his favour and that judgement was consistent with the line the government had taken throughout 1220. It had supported Roger de Montbegon against Philip Mark and William de Marsh against Philip de Albini. It had restored Hugh de Neville to the Northamptonshire forest and Roger Bertram to Mitford. Such actions had all helped to give the government a broad basis of support.

xii. *The achievement of the triumvirate, May 1220–January 1221*

With the conclusion of the siege of Bytham in February 1221, Pandulf, Hubert and Peter had been in control of affairs for some twenty-two months. Their first year together, from April 1219 until April 1220, had

---

[32] C 47/34, no. 8; *Chron. Maj.*, 61.

[33] E 372/66, r. 14d, m. 2; *RLC*, 474b. Because so many were involved in the military operations, the scutage of Bytham was levied on only a small number of fees: Mitchell, *Taxation*, 136–40.

been full of setbacks and England had stood at times on the verge of anarchy. Thereafter, the government still experienced weakness and failure. The proceeds of the carucage and the clerical aid conceded in August 1220 only temporarily alleviated the king's poverty. Ordinary royal revenue remained small. The papal letters of May 1220 had set out a grand scheme of resumption but the result had been simply a tentative and unproductive effort to recover the royal demesne, while a general resumption of the castles and sheriffdoms had not even been attempted.

Nonetheless, since the king's second coronation in May 1220, the log-jam had begun to move. A whole series of long-standing problems centring on the custody of Mitford, Rockingham, Cornwall, Fothering-hay and Bytham had been brought to solution. In the process the peace treaty of 1217 had been upheld and former rebels appeased. Mitford had been given back to Roger Bertram, the Rockingham forest and surrounding manors returned to Hugh de Neville, Walter of Preston and Henry of Braybrooke, and Bytham restored to William de Coleville. Later in 1221 some of the promises made to Reginald de Braose on his return to the king's faith were fulfilled with his son's installation at Totnes. In the course of all this, the government had vindicated its authority over such recalcitrant sheriffs and castellans as Philip of Oldcoates, the count of Aumale, Henry fitz Count and Hugh de Vivonne. By securing the castles of Rockingham and Bristol, and the county of Cornwall, it had taken a step towards the resumption of the king's castles and sheriffdoms. The death of Philip of Oldcoates had equally made possible renewed control over the county and castles of Northumberland and the extraction of profits above the shrieval farm. If the general resumption of the king's demesne had failed, the fall of the count of Aumale and the deaths of Oldcoates and the earl of Winchester had brought manors and manorial farms back into the king's hands. These, moreover, had usually been retained to produce revenue rather than granted out again to provide patronage.

If the government thus addressed the problems posed by the power and independence of the great castellans, it had equally faced up to the second of the centrifugal forces rampant after the war: the determination in the counties to secure both deforestation and a general relaxation of the pressures of shrieval administration. Here the government had held a difficult balance between maintaining the rights of the king and conciliating the men in the counties.[1] The government wanted the support of the knights and gentry, yet

[1] For the way the government wavered back and forth in 1220 over whether to accede to the request of the knights and free tenants of Shropshire for the complete removal of the serjeants appointed to keep the peace in the county, see *PR*, 240–1; *RLC*, 422, 423b.

distrusted them. It called them in to collect the eyre amercements
and the carucage, thus combating the 'malice' of the sheriffs, but
threatened them with punishment and an inquiry by *fideles* sent from
the king's court if they failed in their task.[2] The balance between the
rights of the king and the aspirations of the counties was most difficult
to strike in the sphere of the forest. Here the government refused to
implement the results of the perambulations laid down by the Charter
of 1217, yet, on other matters, ordered the Charter to be upheld.
Equally, it intervened within individual counties, on the petition of
their men, to limit the number of shrieval officials. In the spring of 1221,
a measure of how far its strength had increased, the government
commissioned a forest eyre in Yorkshire under the new chief justice of
the forest, Brian de Lisle; eyres were comissioned later in 1221 in Essex,
Nottinghamshire, Derbyshire, Northamptonshire and Huntingdonshire. But when these visitations encountered opposition, they were
postponed, as will be seen.[3]

This careful approach was a necessity for a government whose
actions had to be founded on consent. The dangers of proceeding
without it had been highlighted in Robert de Vieuxpont's warning to
Pandulf during the Harbottle castle episode: if, he declared, orders
continued to emanate from a 'certain part of the king's council, without
any counsel and assent of the magnates of England who are held to be
and are of the chief council of the king', then men 'will not be so
obedient to you, your orders and the orders of the king as hitherto, and
so a great discord may arise'.[4] By and large the government had heeded
this warning. The close association that Hubert forged with the
council, nebulous body although that was, facilitated the acceptance of
decisions, even if not in the Harbottle castle case. The government was
continually convening great councils. It had attempted to summon all
the magnates to Oxford in August 1220, even if not all had appeared,
and there was sufficient consensus at the assembly for a grant of general
taxation to be conceded. Likewise a 'judgement of the kingdom'
removing Bytham from the count of Aumale had been followed by the
latter's excommunication 'by the common counsel of the prelates and
magnates of all the kingdom'.

The coronation, as has been suggested, was a turning point in more
than a chronological sense. The king's own coronation oath, the oath of
the barons the next day and the accompanying papal letters put the
restoration of the king's authority and the resumption of his possessions
at the forefront of the political agenda. The oath of the barons was also

---

[2] *RLC*, 437. Note how this threat was added in place of an expression of thanks.
[3] *RLC*, 475b; *PR*, 282, 285. Brian replaced John Marshal in February 1221. For the
postponement of the eyres see below p. 252.
[4] SC 1/2, no. 17.

designed to secure their support for the coercion of the disobedient. Against the count of Aumale that support had been forthcoming from many former rebels, in part because they were eager to settle old scores, but also because the government of the triumvirate had proved acceptable. The king's coronation oath bound him to maintain peace and dispense justice as well as uphold his rights. It stressed, therefore, the benefits which flowed from kingship. The government had provided those benefits. It had dispensed justice, upheld the peace treaty of 1217 and met such aspirations of the counties as were compatible with the rights of the king.

Between the rights of the king and those of his subjects there was a necessary inter-relationship. That had been emphasized in writs of 1219 and 1220 which Hubert had attested. The men of the Cinque Ports and the abbot of Malmesbury were told that, if they did not preserve the king's liberties, they could not expect the king to preserve their own.[5] Such sentiments had all the more force for being obvious and commonplace. If the king's rights were not preserved, he would simply lack the power to preserve the rights of his subjects. The problem was one of finding a workable balance between the two. The government's task was to reassert the rights of the crown without threatening a return to the practices of John and provoking dangerous discontent. Hubert had indicated that somewhere there was a middle way. After protests had come before him and the council, he attested letters which asserted that the forests could be run in a manner which would both maintain the rights of the king *and* preserve those living within them from oppression. Such a balance was also in the minds of the king's subjects. Some time in 1219 or 1220 the abbot of St Augustine's, Bristol, wrote to Hubert to complain about the castellans of Bristol who were seizing his goods 'without judgement against the statutes of the kingdom', a clear reference to the Great Charter. But the abbot also vigorously denied that he had attempted anything against 'the dignity and profit of the king'.[6] In fact, the middle way was never easy to discover and the reassertion of royal power, in such matters as the forest, wavered back and forth depending on the situation. Thus the government mixed pragmatism with its propaganda as it strove, in the aftermath of the war, to re-establish the relationship between the king and his subjects and find a new basis for English monarchy. One measure of its success was the confidence with which it turned to former rebels to liquidate the resistance of Philip of Oldcoates and the count of Aumale.

Mention has been made above to 'the government' but since the

---

[5] See above pp. 160, 213.
[6] SC 1/1, no. 71; see *Pipe Roll 1220*, 79. The abbot was one of the regent's executors.

coronation the shift in the balance of power within it had continued. Hubert's star waxed as Peter's waned. True, in November 1220, when the monks of St Augustine's, Canterbury, came to Westminster about the election of a new abbot, they still dealt with Hubert, Peter and Pandulf.[7] But the days when the bishop and the justiciar worked closely together, taking joint responsibility for large numbers of royal letters, were over. The last month in which the greatest number of letters were authorized by them jointly was April 1220.[8] Increasingly, Hubert either acted alone or, when a decision needed extra authority, acted with the council. Given his ability to settle the quarrels and win the support of great men (like the earl of Salisbury), he had less and less need for the bishop of Winchester. Peter still stepped in to control the seal and the exchequer during Hubert's absences, most notably when the latter went to York in October 1220,[9] and he attested and authorized occasional letters outside such periods, often when they were connected with the royal household.[10] But, in the business of government, he was very much the deputy or junior partner. A note of authorization to a writ issued during the Oxford council in August 1220 – 'by the bishop of Winchester, the justiciar and William Brewer' – was carefully altered to place the justiciar's name before the bishop's.[11]

Peter, however, was still the king's guardian. How crucial that position was to his power and prestige is clear from the St Augustine's account of the election of its new abbot. The monks wrote to Peter about the vacancy precisely 'because the king was being educated in [his] custody'.[12] No wonder Peter had seized the king by the head when he thought that he was about to lose control of him in 1219. What broke the triumvirate up in 1221 was Pandulf's resignation as legate and Peter's removal as the king's guardian.

---

[7] *Historiae Anglicanae*, 1873.

[8] See above pp. 182–3.

[9] Peter was left with the seal again in November 1220, perhaps while Hubert went to deal with a threatened tournament at Staines: *RLC*, 439b–40b.

[10] For writs from May 1219, with which Peter was involved, dealing with the affairs of the royal household: *RLC*, 391b, 393, 393b, 397, 397b, 401, 401b, 403, 409, 410b, 412, 414, 422, 422b, 439b–40, 441b, 443, 444, 446, 448. For writs dealing with the household with which only the justiciar was associated: *RLC*, 412b, 414b, 431b.

[11] C 60/12, m.3.

[12] *Historiae Anglicanae*, 1871.

Chapter 6

THE TRIUMVIRATE: DISSOLUTION

i. *The tensions within the triumvirate*

During the spring and summer of 1221 Hubert and Pandulf struggled on towards achieving a resumption of the king's 'castles, demesnes and possessions'. They scored some individual victories: Marlborough was surrendered by the earl of Pembroke and Corfe by Peter de Maulay; the earl of Chester began to account for the farms of Lancashire, Shropshire and Staffordshire; several royal demesne manors were taken into the king's hands. In addition, the government succeeded in dismissing Geoffrey de Marsh from the justiciarship of Ireland. The chief events of the period, however, were political. In April 1220 Bishop Peter left England on a pilgrimage to Santiago. While he was away Pandulf and Hubert constructed an alliance with the earl of Pembroke, which tied the latter to their regime and furthered the policy of resumption by removing him from Marlborough castle. Shortly afterwards both Bishop Peter and his familiar, Peter de Maulay, were accused of treason, Maulay being removed from the castellanship of Corfe. Then, following his return to England in July (the month Pandulf resigned as legate), Bishop Peter ceased to be the king's guardian. These events constituted a watershed in English politics. They opened factional divisions which ultimately determined both the timing and manner in which the king assumed regal powers and took possession of his castles and sheriffdoms.

Underlying these developments were tensions within the triumvirate. There can be little doubt that Bishop Peter resented Hubert's growing ascendancy, analysed in the last chapter, and that by the early months of 1221 the two men were bitter rivals. True, there seem to have been no differences between them on major issues of policy. They had worked together to get Philip of Oldcoates out of Mitford and the earl of Pembroke out of Fotheringhay. If Peter was friendly with the count of Aumale, he had been at the sieges of both Rockingham and Bytham; indeed, he had brought his mangonels and petraries to the latter.[1] Peter was more than a one-dimensional political figure. He founded religious houses, issued statutes for his diocese, prosecuted a campaign against

---

[1] *PR*, 284; HRO, Eccles II 159277, r.3.

Sunday markets and, of course, went on pilgrimages.[2] But he must have found his political situation after 1219 immensely frustrating. One senses this in his behaviour when he enjoyed some freedom of action. Then, like a tiger given a run outside the cage, he fixed harsh terms for repayment of debts to the Jews; gave permission, in defiance of the custom of the kingdom, for the count of Aumale's case to proceed at the bench; tried to annoy the envoys of the king of France by delaying the ratification of the truce; and gave judgement on the Newburn charter without waiting for Hubert and the council. Peter was a proud, arrogant man. In two of his three surviving letters to Hubert, in 1219–20, he placed his own name first, whereas the usual custom with bishops and earls was to do the reverse.[3] Peter no doubt wished to treat Hubert as a minister to whom he could rap out peremptory advice about the issue of royal letters;[4] but the reality was that he was first passed over as the regent's successor and then demoted from Hubert's partner to deputy. Given the powers inherent in the office of justiciar and the political skill with which Hubert wielded them, the contest between the two men was always likely to be unequal.[5]

Early in 1221 an event of immense significance was approaching which added fresh fuel to this conflict. The king's fourteenth birthday on 1 October 1221 inevitably prompted questions about the future of Peter's guardianship of the king, the most precious jewel, as it were, in his episcopal mitre. The age of fourteen had long been invested with educational significance as the dividing line between *pueritia* and *adolescentia*. In Roman law, moreover, it was precisely the moment at which the tutor's authority over his 'pupil' ceased.[6] Significantly, the only account of the cessation of Peter's guardianship indicates that it occurred once the king had 'exceeded the age of a pupil'.[7] There was, however, nothing automatic about Peter's removal. His control of the king could easily have continued after October 1221[8] but the king's fourteenth birthday certainly provided his enemies with powerful arguments with which to attack his position.

---

[2] *Chron. Maj.*, 490; *Councils and Synods*, ii, part i, 125; Cate, 'The church and market reform', 51.

[3] *F*, 164; SC 1/1, no.198; *DD*, no.68. Compare *RL*, nos cxxxii, cxliv, ccxvii; SC 1/1, no.192 (letters from the archbishop of York and the bishops of Salisbury and Carlisle). Significantly, the bishop of Durham, a man who also stood on his dignity, placed his name before Hubert's: *RL*, nos xxiii, xcix, clvii. The significance of these points of diplomatic is discussed in Stones and Stones, 'Ralph Neville', 251–2.

[4] See his letter in *F*, 164.

[5] See Stacey, *Politics*, 17, which particularly stresses Hubert's advantages as head of the judicial system.

[6] Orme, *From Childhood to Chivalry*, 6; for Roman law see above p. 18 and n. 23.

[7] *Walt. Cov.*, 260.

[8] See below p. 258.

That attack seemed all the more important because the king's fourteenth birthday might also have a bearing on his assumption of regal power. The general consensus in England, as has been seen, was that the king should come of age when he was twenty-one. But the concessions made early in the minority until the completion of the king's fourteenth year implied that some alteration in his political status could take place then.[9] The decision ultimately would be the pope's and men were bound to wonder whether he might indeed decide on fourteen as the age of majority or, alternatively, if he was reluctant to override local feeling, decree that the king could exercise regal powers before he technically came of age.

The pope's decision would depend to a large extent on the reports that he received about the progress of the king's education, a subject on which Pandulf could give him first-hand information. Little is known about the course of King Henry's studies. His tutor, Master Henry of Avranches, prepared an elaborate grammar for the king but, running to some 2,200 lines, perhaps this served more to impress the court than to educate his pupil.[10] What was true, however, was that the king's education in the business of politics was considerable. In the long periods when he was separated from the government, he had presided over his own court at Wallingford or Havering, received a stream of letters and visitors, and dealt with their demands and requests. He had communicated his will to the government, or sought its advice, in letters of his own authenticated by the seal of his steward, William de Cantilupe.[11] In September 1220 the earl of Pembroke had written separate letters to Hubert and to the king about the misdeeds of Llywelyn. He reminded the king, 'as was made sufficiently clear to you at [the council in August] at Oxford', of Llywelyn's transgressions and demanded justice from the king 'in your own person . . . so that I have no grounds for thinking that you have consented [to what Llywelyn has done] but rather consider him a liar, and so that it does not appear that you do not wish to assist me in my right'.[12] A letter like this must have been considered by the king. It gave him a very clear idea of the political realities of the situation. The king was also pressurized in smaller matters. Some time before June 1221 Peter de Maulay wrote separate letters to the king, Hubert and Pandulph about Roger of Acaster, tutor to Henry's brother Richard. Having explained the facts of the case, he begged the king, 'moved by divine piety, and for love of Richard your brother and me, to speak to your council and so actively involve yourself that [Roger] may be able either to recover his land or to

---

[9] See above p. 123.
[10] *Henry of Avranches*, 56–9.
[11] *CRR*, viii, 323; *RL*, no. lxxxvii; *RLC*, 414b; SC 1/2, no. 18.
[12] *RL*, nos cxxiv, cxxv.

have such an exchange for it that it will give honour to you and be of value to him. And be pleased to inform me (who are yours) of your pleasure'.[13]

None of this shows that the king had a large input into the government's policy or that he was becoming impatient about the restrictions placed upon him. But it does indicate that men already treated him as an independent force, separate from Hubert, Pandulf and Peter. His emergence was also reflected in the increasing sums of money spent on and by his household. In the year 1218–19 (Michaelmas to Michaelmas) the total revenue assigned to meet the expenses of the household was roughly £680; in 1219–20 it was £1,240; by 1220–21, £2,350. This money was spent on food, drink, clothing and a whole series of miscellaneous gifts and fees.[14] The amount was still a great deal smaller than later in the 1220s when the household receipts averaged around £7,700 a year. Nonetheless, the rising sums reflected the growing size of the king's establishment. At Christmas 1220 robes had been distributed to ninety-eight members of his household, comprising knights, serjeants, valets, boys and messengers. At Christmas 1217 the number had been only thirty-nine. The household knights themselves had increased from seven to twenty-five.[15]

Both the progress of the king's education and the expansion of his household, therefore, increased the possibility of his being declared of age in October 1221 or at least of his being allowed then, or soon afterwards, to assume part of his regal powers. The political significance of such an event was momentous whenever it occurred. It would be the hour when numerous grants of land and office would come up for cancellation or renewal and when the personal relationship which everyone had built up with the king would be put to the test. Of that men had long been aware. Act now so that 'you will deserve all the more the special grace of the royal *serenitas* when [the king] arrives at mature years' warned a royal letter, attested by Hubert, in January 1220.[16] If the king was indeed to acquire power in October 1221, or in the foreseeable future thereafter, then it was vital for those fearful or distrustful of Peter to bring the latter's guardianship to an end. The longer Peter had to win the king's special grace, the longer he presided

---

[13] SC 1/4, no. 74; SC 1/2, no. 11; *RL*, no. clvi.

[14] These sums are calculated from the writs of *liberate* and *computate* assigning money for the king's expenses, matched, in the case of the latter, where possible and necessary, with evidence from the pipe rolls. I have excluded expenditure on the coronation. The great bulk of the money came direct from the exchequer to Peter des Rivaux, William de Cantilupe and other household officials. It is impossible to know exactly how it was spent. For a rather different set of figures, see Tout, *Chapters*, i, 191–2.

[15] *Divers Accounts*, 52–3; *RLC*, 345b, 444.

[16] *RLC*, 435–435b.

over a household expanding in size and power, the more certain was the ultimate fall of his enemies.

The approach of the king's fourteenth birthday in October 1221, therefore, both provided a justification for Bishop Peter's removal and increased the necessity for it. No one can have been keener to effect such a change than Hubert himself but it seems highly likely that he found an ally in Pandulf. The latter had, in effect, obtained authority to change the king's governor as early as May 1220 when a papal letter ordered him to 'cause the king to be kept by prudent and honest men, not distrusted either by him or his kingdom, who will instruct him in good morals and teach him to fear God and love his vassals'.[17] The reflection on the king's existing guardian is obvious. There was no criticism of Henry's immediate, 'master and tutor', Philip de Albini, since the pope was later anxious to retain him in office.[18] It was Peter who was 'distrusted' by the kingdom and hated by the vassals, being indelibly associated with the excesses of John's kingship. Might he not encourage the young king to follow the same disastrous path? If so, Pandulf was bound to be concerned. He wished to preserve and recover the rights of the king but not at the cost of renewing civil strife.

In the early months of 1221, therefore, the whole future of Bishop Peter's guardianship must have been the subject of question and debate. It is possible that Philip de Albini, who presumably owed his position to Peter, was allowed to leave on a crusade in April 1221 so as to prepare the way for further changes in the royal household. Perhaps too the bishop's own departure on pilgrimage in the same month was connected with his defeat in the contests at court.[19] At the very least it reflected his dispensability. His absence and the suspicions it aroused underlay the remarkable political events which quickly followed.

ii. *The alliance with the earl of Pembroke, May 1221*

Bishop Peter departed on his pilgrimage to Santiago soon after Easter 1221, which the court celebrated at Woodstock on 11 April.[1] In the same month the earl of Pembroke returned to England after his visit to 'remote parts', presumably Wales and Ireland. He was in a sour mood, for his lands in Bedfordshire had been seized by Falkes de Bréauté, probably in the attempt to enforce various shrieval rights. To Pembroke this was astonishing because, as he informed Hubert by letter, 'I was with the king and spoke to him' (probably at Gloucester after Easter) 'and I am always . . . prepared, according to the custom

---

[17] VL, Honorius III Regesta X, f.186 (*CPReg.*, 71).

[18] *Chron. Maj.*, 67; VL, Honorius III Regesta X, f.117.

[19] *PR*, 286–7; *Chron. Maj.*, 67.

[1] *PR*, 286; *RLC*, 454.

of the kingdom, to do towards him everything which I ought to do as my lord'. Pembroke, therefore, demanded that his lands be left in peace and told Hubert, who was at Westminster for the sessions of the Easter exchequer, to expect him by 25 April. In fact, a deputation was sent to meet the earl, headed by none other than Falkes himself, a deputation which carried a message from the king about Marlborough castle.[2] This was the opening shot in negotiations which concluded with an agreement that Pembroke was to marry Eleanor, the king's youngest sister.

The prime movers behind this marriage alliance were Pandulf and Hubert. It was they, as Pembroke recalled the following year, who 'earnestly and diligently persuaded [me] . . . to take one of the king's sisters as [my] wife'.[3] Hubert was already bound to the earl of Pembroke, as also to the latter's friend and ally, the earl of Salisbury, by one very clear material interest: their mutual concern with the lands of the count of Perche. In 1218, as has been seen, Salisbury and the regent had divided some of the count's former manors between them. In 1219 the young Marshal had succeeded to his father's share. Another former possession of the count of Perche was the honour of Haughley, in Suffolk, and this was held by Hubert de Burgh.[4] The tenure enjoyed by Hubert and the two earls was, however, far from secure. Although Salisbury had been granted the count of Perche's manors by the king, the latter had never sanctioned their subsequent division with the regent. Even more, neither Salisbury nor the regent had any warrant for the possession which they had obtained of the royal demesne manor once held by the count of Perche, namely Shrivenham in Berkshire.[5] Hubert for his part had been granted the honour of Haughley by King John but he held it only during the king's pleasure.[6] The lands of the count of Perche, therefore, were escheats *par excellence* which could be resumed by the king at any time. The earls of Pembroke and Salisbury and Hubert de Burgh had the strongest possible mutual interest in seeing that never happened.

If the marriage agreement built on this existing link between Hubert and the earl of Pembroke, it also had more immediate purposes.[7] One was to block a proposal that Pembroke should marry a sister of

---

[2] *RL*, no. clii; *RLC*, 454b; *PR*, 287.

[3] VL, Honorius III Regesta XI, f.258 (*CPReg.*, 88).

[4] See above p. 141.

[5] After 1218, in the *terrae datae* section of the pipe roll, while an allowance was made for Shrivenham, it was never stated who actually possessed it, a blank space being left instead: *Pipe Roll 1218*, 31; *Pipe Roll 1219*, 158; *Pipe Roll 1221*, 1; E 368/4, m. 12; see above p. 92.

[6] *RBE*, 596; *RLC*, 316b–17; *BF*, 282.

[7] The reasons for the proposed marriage were set out, in a letter to the pope, after it had finally taken place in 1224: *DD*, no. 140.

Robert count of Dreux: 'a confederation with aliens' which would make it easier for *extranii* to enter the kingdom. Hubert and Pandulf also wished, as Pembroke himself put it, 'to bind [me] more fully and more firmly in the royal service'. In 1224 the king explained why: there had been 'magnates in England who were struggling to turn the heart of [Pembroke] from us by malicious confederations'.[8] Almost certainly, part of the background here lay in the antagonisms at court, which have just been analysed. Bishop Peter had left on his pilgrimage sourly at odds with his colleagues. His official destination was Santiago but, once out of the country, there was no knowing what he would actually get up to. There were a variety of rumours about his activities. One was that he was plotting with the king of France, another that he was visiting the pope.[9] The implications of such a visit, with the king's fourteenth birthday approaching, were considerable. Might not the bishop return armed with papal authorization for the continuation of his guardianship or alternatively for the declaration that the king was now of age? Might he not also lure into his camp those, like the earl of Pembroke, disaffected with the current state of affairs? Against these possibilities, certainly it was wise to take precautions, especially when the bishop's temporary absence provided the ideal opportunity to do so. Thus the agreement with the earl of Pembroke was pushed through quickly so as to be in place by the time of Peter's homecoming. As a consequence, many barons, the earl of Chester amongst them, were not consulted and the marriage was made conditional on Hubert and Pandulf securing their consent.[10]

There may have been another reason why the agreement over the Pembroke marriage was made at this time; it ensured Pembroke's assent to Hubert's own intended marriage to Margaret, the sister of Alexander, king of Scotland. This marriage took place later in 1221, perhaps in October, but it was probably agreed with Alexander in June 1221 when the English court went to York for the latter's marriage to King Henry's sister.[11] Hubert must have considered very carefully

---

[8]   VL, Honorius III Regesta XI, f.258 (*CPReg.*, 88); *DD*, no. 140.

[9]   *PR*, 286; *Walt. Cov.*, 260; *Ann. Mon.*, iii, 68. According to the bishop's own pipe roll, his journey was to Santiago: HRO, Eccles II 159277, rr.6d,7. The Dunstable annals state that he left England in company with the bishop of Hereford: *Ann. Mon.*, iii, 68.

[10]   *DD*, no. 140.

[11]   Matthew Paris (*Chron. Maj.*, 66–7) indicates that Hubert's marriage took place in York at the same time as Alexander's and this has been accepted by most historians. But Paris later changed his mind and placed the marriage, still in 1221, in London and in the presence of the archbishop of Canterbury, who did not return to England until July: *Flores. Hist.*, ii, 173; for the chronology of Paris's works, see Vaughan, *Matthew Paris*, 92, 100, 102–3. For Langton's involvement, see also *Chron. Maj.*, vi, 71; and note where the marriage is placed chronologically in *Ann. Mon.*, iii, 69, 76, and *Walt. Cov.*, 250.

the merits of this prospective marriage. It brought him little in the way of a *maritagium* and thus did nothing to alleviate his material insecurity. On the other hand, it carried tremendous prestige. From being the younger son of a gentry family, who had made good in royal service, he became the brother-in-law of a king and tied himself into the royal families of England and Scotland. He also became earl-worthy: the earldom of Kent, which Hubert received in 1227, was entailed on his and Margaret's joint issue. No wonder Robert de Courtenay, whom Hubert sent to Scotland to negotiate with Alexander, reported in triumph: 'the king received your palfrey with pleasure and praised it a great deal, about which I was happy and joyful, since I know that the relationship with the king can be worth a great deal to you'.[12]

Hubert later claimed that he was married 'by the counsel of the magnates'. It may be that the various concessions that were made in May 1220 to the earls of Surrey and Salisbury and to the count of Aumale, who was restored to Driffield, were designed to secure their consent to Hubert's as well as Pembroke's marriage.[13] In another way, too, Hubert moved to strengthen his position and appease a potentially dangerous enemy. At the bench, in May 1221, a settlement was arranged between Reginald and John de Braose. John's suit against his uncle for the Braose inheritance had been blocked by the *casus regis*. Such cases, *Bracton* implied, were best settled by agreement between the parties.[14] This is what now happened. Reginald surrendered Bramber to John and his heirs, in return for what was probably a quitclaim of the rest of the Braose inheritance, outside Gower. Since Reginald had actually conceded Bramber to his son William, the latter was compensated by the concession of Totnes.[15] For Hubert, this settlement removed John's challenge to his tenure of the Three Castles, which he held under a grant from Reginald. He could go into the

---

[12] *RL*, no. cxxxvii. The marriage helped fulfil the promise made to Alexander in June 1220 to find husbands in England for his two sisters. For Hubert's close relationship with Alexander, see *CRR*, xvi, no. 18.

[13] *Chron. Maj.*, vi, 71; *RLC*, 457b–9b; *PR*, 287–8; C 60/15, m.6.

[14] When an inheritance was disputed between a younger son and the son of an older brother, a verdict could not be given in favour of the latter because it would reflect on the king's claim to the throne, John having become king instead of Arthur, the son of his older brother Geoffrey: *Bracton*, ii, 189–90; iii, 284; iv, 46; Pollock and Maitland, *History of English Law*, ii, 285.

[15] *CRR*, x, 127, 195; *PR*, 296–7. In fact the agreement quickly collapsed and war erupted between Reginald and John, probably in Gower. A second agreement was reached, apparently on the same lines as the first, in 1226; whether John gained seisin of Bramber before then is doubtful: *BNB*, no. 167; *Brut*, 99; 'Neath Cartulary', 152–3; *CRR*, xi, nos 390, 1969; xii, no. 2672. In 1226 Reginald also compensated William with a grant of his land in Gwent and Abergavenny.

negotiations for his marriage more confident in the security of these most prized possessions.[16]

It was Falkes, of course, who had most to fear from a close alliance between Hubert and Pembroke. Indeed, on 18 May a writ, authorized by Hubert, protected Pembroke's lands from Falkes and his under-sheriffs in the way that the earl had demanded in April.[17] But this did not mean that Hubert had necessarily taken sides against Falkes. He may rather have hoped to reconcile the two men. That, at any rate, would seem to be the most natural interpretation of Falkes leading the deputation which opened the marriage negotiations with Pembroke.

Falkes brought a message to Pembroke about Marlborough castle whose liberation was indeed the final purpose of the suggested marriage to the king's sister. A royal letter of 1224 began its explanation of the union by stating that, when it was proposed, Pembroke 'still had the castles of Marlborough and Ludgershall'. Under the terms of the marriage contract, the explanation continued, he surrendered them to Pandulf, although they were to be returned if the marriage was not celebrated within a certain time. The surrender of the castles, the letter continued, was 'very expedient for us, for thus other magnates might be more easily induced to similarly resign our castles which they held'. The Dunstable annals, indeed, believed that, unless others surrendered the castles committed to them, Marlborough was to be returned to Pembroke.[18] The aim of the marriage, therefore, was to further a political programme as much as to establish a political alliance. Pembroke, as has been seen, had captured Marlborough in 1217 and in company at first with his father he had remained there ever since. No doubt the Marshals hoped that one day the king would recognize their tenuous, if long-standing, claims to hold the castle in hereditary right: fitting reward for the regent's monumental service in the war. The narrow aim of binding Pembroke to the king's government could have been better secured by allowing him to remain in control of Marl-borough, indeed by promising that, when the king came of age, Marlborough might become Eleanor's *maritagium*. That the reverse happened is that plainest possible proof that the government in 1221,

---

[16] In 1224 Hubert complained that Reginald was distraining him to perform services for the Three Castles in contravention of their original agreement. The result was a second agreement under which Reginald recognized the right of Hubert and his wife and their heirs to hold the Three Castles from the king: *CRR*, xi, nos 1894, 2418; xii, no. 307; CP 25(1)/80/5, no. 59. Hubert, however, remained worried about John de Braose's claim and in 1228 (after Reginald's death) he arranged for the king to grant the castles to John in hereditary right. John then granted them to Hubert and his heirs: *CChR*, 74, 83; *CRR*, xiii, no. 592; CP 25(1)/80/5, no. 119.

[17] *RLC*, 458b.

[18] *DD*, no. 140; *RLC*, 465b; *Ann. Mon.*, iii, 68. The custody of Ludgershall was usually linked with that of Marlborough.

far from living from day to day, was striving to realize the programme which Pandulf, sanctioned by papal letters, had been urging since 1219: the programme for the resumption of the king's castles and possessions.

That this general programme was at the top of the political agenda in 1221 is equally shown by a papal letter which was addressed to Peter, Hubert, the earl of Chester, William Brewer and other, unnamed, councillors of the king on 29 April. It stated that, since the king was under the pope's special protection, 'it is unworthy and wholly absurd ... if we suffer him to be defrauded of his rights. Since, therefore, as has been intimated to us on his behalf, the wards and escheats belonging to the king are detained and occupied by several people, who enjoy these against God's will', Peter, Hubert and the others were to recover these for the king, using their power to coerce the recalcitrant. The parallel between this papal letter and those written the year before, at the time of the king's coronation, is obvious and probably it was Pandulf again who secured it.[19]

The need to prosecute the programme of resumption was equally clear to Hubert as he surveyed the state of the king's finances. After Easter 1221 he had remained at Westminster for the whole period from 22 April to 26 May, during which time the accounts for Falkes's sheriffdoms were heard at the exchequer. By contrast, when Hubert was absent from Westminster in the Hilary, Easter and Trinity terms of 1221, no accounts were heard. Indeed, those in the Trinity term, despite the presence at the exchequer of the treasurer and William Brewer, were held up until Hubert's appearance.[20] The siege of Bytham had mopped up much of what remained from the carucage. The revenue of the Easter term of 1221 was better, but hardly decisively better, than the year before. The initial *Adventus* at Easter 1221 produced £145, £93 more than in 1220. The total proceeds from the counties, as recorded on the receipt roll for the Easter term of 1221, were £2,332, £599 better than in the roll for the previous year. Some additional assistance was obtained in 1221 by a tallage on the Jews, which produced £654, of which perhaps half came in during the Easter term, but until the arrival of £1,693 of Irish treasure in July the king was desperately short of ready cash.[21] Repayment of loans from Pandulf of £461 and £533, although secured against the first monies arriving at the exchequer, were postponed again and again.[22]

The need to realize the papal programme, therefore, was urgent. The

[19] *F*, 167.
[20] *Pipe Roll 1220*, vi–viii; E 159/4, m.8.
[21] *Divers Accounts*, 16–19; *PR*, 296; 'A Jewish Aid to marry', 92–111; and see Appendix, pp. 414–15.
[22] *RLC*, 445; *PR*, 283–4; *RLC*, 465b.

resumption of Marlborough was a step in that direction but whether it would encourage similar resignations was problematic. Pembroke, after all, had been bought out, and not everyone could be given a king's sister for a castle. The earl, moreover, could not claim, like some other castellans, that he owed his appointment to King John and was under an obligation to keep the castle safe until King Henry came of age. The cause of resumption, however, could now receive powerful assistance from Pembroke himself. After his surrender of Marlborough, he was left without a royal castle in his custody. Like a great cog thrown out of the works, he was no longer involved in the current machinery of local power and could contemplate its dismantling with equanimity. Indeed, since Falkes, his principal enemy, held five royal castles and four sheriffdoms, Pembroke had everything to gain, and nothing to lose, from a general resumption.

There was, however, a more immediate test for Pembroke's alliance with Hubert. While the marriage agreement was being negotiated at Westminster rumours arrived of a plot aimed at the heart of the king and his government.

iii. *The fall of Peter de Maulay, June 1221*

The allegations of conspiracy centred on Peter de Maulay, the castellan of Corfe, and were brought to Westminster by Richard Mucegros, of whom more later. The details are known from Falkes's *querimonia*, the great complaint he addressed to the pope in 1225, following his exile, which gives a detailed but highly partial account of English politics between 1221 and 1224. According to this source, Maulay was accused, 'as a traitor to the king', of agreeing to hand over to the king of France the great state prisoner in his custody at Corfe, Eleanor of Brittany. In this murky pool there was also swimming a much bigger fish, Bishop Peter himself. The reason that he had gone abroad, it was suggested, was precisely to plot the whole affair with the king of France and to provide the ship which would spirit Eleanor away.[1] The Dunstable annalist and Ralph of Coggeshall add that Engelard de Cigogné, the castellan of Windsor, was also accused of being involved in the conspiracy.[2]

Faced with these charges, the government acted with stealth and decision. The great court, which was customary at Whitsun, was switched at the last moment from Oxford to Winchester, the cathedral city of the great conspirator and within striking distance of Corfe.[3]

---

[1]   *Walt. Cov.*, 260. The Dunstable annalist names Mucegros: *Ann. Mon.*, iii, 75.
[2]   *Ann. Mon.*, iii, 68; *Coggeshall*, 190.
[3]   *RLC*, 459b, 460b.

Maulay arrived at Winchester for the Whitsun celebrations at the king's summons 'as a true man should'. He suspected nothing, although measures to remove him from Corfe were already afoot. Having eaten the solemn Whitsun feast on 30 May, he was called into the king's chamber 'as if secret matters were to be discussed there'. Instead, Hubert and his accomplices accused him of treason, tearing his clothes, subjecting him to injuries and insults, and at last throwing him into chains. Perhaps Engelard de Cigogné was put through the same ordeal, which was designed, of course, to force a confession. Certainly, he too was imprisoned.[4]

In the event, both the accused were soon freed, but on conditions. On 4 June Hubert moved to Wareham, four miles from Corfe, and Maulay formally surrendered the castle to the king's representatives, namely Hubert himself, the earls of Salisbury and Pembroke, and William Brewer; a clear indication of the men who had masterminded the government's action.[5] Salisbury was thus revenged for being kept out of Sherborne and Somerset by Maulay in 1217. In return for his surrender, Maulay was released and allowed to remain as sheriff of Somerset–Dorset. Engelard de Cigogné also remained as castellan of Windsor but after giving hostages, according to the Dunstable annalist, as security for its surrender when the king wished. The Dunstable annalist goes on to say, as though part of the same story, that the king, making his way to York for his sister's marriage with Alexander, while not removing the constables of Oxford, Northampton and Nottingham, left household knights in the castles for their greater security. If this is true, and the king certainly went through these towns on his journey north, then the government was taking precautions against Falkes and Philip Mark.[6]

What then lay behind all this? Richard Mucegros was either the father or, less likely perhaps, the eldest son, of Robert Mucegros whose marriage had brought him considerable lands in Somerset, including some near Corfe castle. When, however, Robert failed to meet the payment, due at Easter 1221, for having married his wife without the king's permission, Peter de Maulay, as sheriff, had seized his lands into the king's hands.[7] The accusations against Maulay, therefore, may have had their roots in this local quarrel, one of many between him and those in his sheriffdom.[8] The Mucegros family was well placed to make its charges heard, for the elder Richard had been a justice under King

[4] Walt. Cov., 260; Ann. Mon., iii, 68; Coggeshall, 190.
[5] PR, 321.
[6] Ann. Mon., iii, 68.
[7] C 60/15, m.4; ERF, 61; BF, 425; RLC, 470; CRR, x, 108; Turner, Judiciary, 132–3, 145, 188.
[8] For example, CRR, xii, no. 1145.

John and the family retained many links with the court.[9] That Hubert and his allies quickly realized that the accusations were false is clear from Maulay and Cigogné's release and continuation in office. It is possible that Hubert was engaged from start to finish in a cynical plot to discredit Bishop Peter and dismiss Peter de Maulay. On the other hand, the very tensions which would have encouraged Hubert to make a pre-emptive strike against the bishop meant that extraordinary accusations against him might be believed.

As Falkes's *querimonia* admitted, there was circumstantial evidence to give credence to the charges. For a start, the conspiracy held together in terms of personnel. Maulay and Cigogné had long been close associates of Bishop Peter, sharing with him a common homeland in the Touraine.[10] Eleanor of Brittany herself, the sister of the murdered Arthur and the daughter of Geoffrey, King John's elder brother, was bound to be a source of anxiety to the government, a focus of flitting conspiracy and ambiguous intrigue. She was still featuring towards the end of the century in romantic stories as 'the true heir to England' to whom indeed, according to one tale, a conscience-stricken King Henry had briefly resigned his crown. Not surprisingly, until her death in 1241, she was kept in frustrating if comfortable confinement in the great castles of Corfe, Bristol and Gloucester, a true Lady of Shalott.[11]

Above all, behind the whole conspiracy stood the sinister figure of Bishop Peter. Had he really gone to Santiago? The story that he was conspiring with the king of France was not the only alternative version, for there was also a rumour that he was visiting the pope.[12] And certainly, with the odds stacked so heavily against him in England, Peter had, it might seem, every reason to look to French or papal intervention to transform the situation in his favour.

Hubert, therefore, seized the opportunity provided by Bishop Peter's absence and his new alliance with the earl of Pembroke to move against one of the bishop's principal lieutenants. Maulay's removal from Corfe weakened Peter's power, while prosecuting the general policy of resuming the king's castles and possessions. In this context the resumption of Corfe had greater significance than that of Rockingham, Bristol and Marlborough, where tenure dated only from Henry's reign. Corfe was taken from Maulay, as Falkes's *querimonia* put it, 'against the pristine oath which he had made to the [the king's] father not to surrender his castles until the king came of legitimate age'.[13] The

---

[9] Turner, *Judiciary*, 132–3, 145, 188. Richard Mucegros senior had also been connected with the elder William Marshal.

[10] See above p. 139.

[11] *Lanercost*, 12–13 (the chronicle of the friar, Richard of Durham).

[12] *Ann. Mon.*, iii, 68.

[13] *Walt. Cov.*, 260.

episode increased the government's authority and injected the poison of faction into English politics.

iv. *Retreat and advance, summer 1221*

The surrender of Marlborough and the seizure of Corfe were triumphs for the government upon which it quickly built. Nonetheless, in the summer of 1221, its weakness in the localities, faced with determined opposition, was once more revealed as the forest eyres, commissioned in the spring of the year, were progressively suspended or abandoned.[1]

Given the rejection of the perambulations of 1220, the intention in 1221 was presumably to hold the eyres within largely unrevised boundaries. Opposition to such a plan was scarcely surprising. The only county where the eyre may have taken place in the summer of 1221 was Essex. This itself must have created considerable resentment, for the perambulations of the minority demanded large deforestations in the county, attempting to restrict the royal forest to its south-west corner.[2] As a result the government shied away from making the Essex eyre too burdensome financially. The debts arising from it totalled around £50, some £135 less than from King John's forest eyre in the county in 1212.[3] For the rest, none of the eyres planned down to October 1221 was held before the spring of 1222. The Yorkshire eyre was postponed from 24 May to 21 June 1221 and then to some later date. The same thing happened in Nottinghamshire and Derbyshire where the eyre was due to open in June 1221 and in Northamptonshire where it was scheduled for October. In all, the counties offered a total of £160 for the postponements. In addition, in May 1221 the knights and free tenants of Berkshire fined in £133 6s 8d for the suspension of the eyre in the county until the king came of age. All this money had, however, a deceiving glint. Of the £293 promised in 1221, only £58 were cleared in the pipe rolls of 1221 and 1222. Nothing at all was obtained from Yorkshire's fine of £66 13s 4d.[4]

Despite these setbacks, the government quickly consolidated its success over Marlborough and Corfe. Indeed, in so far as it conciliated the counties by giving way over the forest eyres, it was better placed to do so. After receiving the surrender of Corfe, Hubert and the king

---

[1] See above p. 236.
[2] Fisher, *The Forest of Essex*, 20–4; see also Liddell, 'The bounds of the forest of Essex', 110–13.
[3] E 372/67, r.3, m.1; *Pipe Roll 1212*, 57–8.
[4] *RLC*, 475b; *PR*, 288–9; C 60/13, m.6; *Pipe Roll 1221*, 6, 82, 137, 193; E 372/66, r.3d, m.1; r.6d, m.1; r.11, m.1; r.13, m.1; see Crook, 'The forest boundaries in Nottinghamshire', 37.

hurried north to York for Alexander's marriage to the king's sister. Then they headed for Shrewsbury and a great council (27 June–3 July) attended amongst others by Llywelyn. On the way to Shrewsbury, Pandulf received the surrender of Devizes castle from Philip de Albini junior, who was about to leave England as custodian of the Channel Islands.[5] Around this time Pandulf also took an important decision which finally restored the farms of Lancashire, Shropshire and Staffordshire to exchequer control. In 1218 these had been conceded to the earl of Chester until a date to be decided by the legate and the council. Since Chester began to account for the farms from the last quarter of the 1220–21 financial year, it seems highly probable that the termination of the concession was decided by Pandulf at the Shrewsbury council, which Chester attended.[6] Thus the government exacted a *quid pro quo* for the favours, culminating in the wardship of the honour of Huntingdon, which Chester had received since his return from crusade.[7] Indeed, in May 1221 he had already vacated the royal demesne manor of Geddington, despite its concession to him (in 1217) until completion of the king's fourteenth year. The month before, the government had likewise promoted the policy of resumption by buying Philip de Albini senior out of the royal manors of Grimsby and Torksey on his departure for his crusade.[8]

At Shrewsbury the government also exercised some glimmerings of authority over Llywelyn. In respect of his conflicts with the earl of Pembroke and Reginald de Braose, nothing was done save patch up a truce but at least the council settled the dispute which had arisen between Llywelyn and Rhys Ieuanc, the Welsh prince giving Cardigan to the latter in fulfilment of his promise made in 1216.[9] More striking were measures with regard to Ireland. Early in July £1,693 had arrived 'from the aids and promises of Ireland' but so had unsatisfactory reports about Geoffrey de Marsh's performance as justiciar.[10] He had not kept the agreement of August 1220: the issues of Ireland were still being received in his own chamber rather than at the exchequer. So, on 3 July, by a writ authorized by Hubert and the council, Geoffrey was dismissed and replaced by the archbishop of Dublin, a decision

[5] *PR*, 196, 293. Albini's tenure was only during the king's pleasure.

[6] *Pipe Roll 1221*, 59–60, 96–7, 139–40 and introduction; see above p. 81.

[7] *PR*, 285. Chester received further concessions at Shrewsbury itself: *RLC*, 463b–4. These may also have induced him to give his support to the earl of Pembroke's marriage: *DD*, no. 140.

[8] C 60/15, m.6; *RLC*, 319, 511; *Pipe Roll 1221*, 144–6, 188.

[9] *PR*, 294, 331–2; *Brut*, 98. Rhys had appealed for help in his quarrel to the earl of Pembroke.

[10] The sum included a £580 payment *de promisso* of Geoffrey, probably a contribution towards the fine he had made in 1220 to be quit of arrears. The rest of the money came *de secundo auxilio Hiberniae*: E 401/4, r.1d; *PR*, 296, 316.

described a fortnight later as having been made 'by the common counsel and with the assent of the magnates and *fideles* of England'. The government realized, however, that its power to actually enforce this decision was limited. Consequently, it offered Geoffrey an inducement. In return for relinquishing the justiciarship, he would be pardoned the 1,800 marks outstanding from his fine of August 1220 for his transgressions up to that date and forgiven all accounts and complaints for his time as justiciar. In other words, he could pocket all he had made. Geoffrey accepted this at once and vacated his post.[11] In effect, like the earls of Pembroke and Chester, he too had been bought out.

At the end of the Shrewsbury council Hubert journeyed back to Westminster, the hearing of the account for Lincolnshire at the exchequer on 13 July coinciding exactly with his arrival. Two very different churchmen, Archbishop Langton and Bishop Peter, were about to return to England with wide-ranging consequences for both the structure of government and the state of politics.[12]

v. *Pandulf's resignation and achievement*

Archbishop Langton arrived back in England in July 1221. His return spelt the end of Pandulf's legation. No doubt pointing to the increasing strength of the king's government, and the impossibility of his own position during a legation, Langton had persuaded the pope both to withdraw his legate and put no one in his place. At Westminster, therefore, on 26 July, in the presence of the bishops of Salisbury, Winchester and London, Pandulf resigned his office.[1]

Looking back from the 1250s, Matthew Paris, not in general a friend of papal legates, gave Pandulf fitting praise: 'by virtue of the authority given to him in the time of his legation, he vigorously repressed many warlike tumults'.[2] The importance of Pandulf's role, since the regent's resignation in 1219, had been immense. He had stiffened and energized the government, come to its rescue with frequent loans and kept before its eyes the ultimate objective: the resumption of the king's castles, demesnes and possessions. That objective had not been achieved. The government had lacked the power and authority to attempt wholesale removals of the great castellans and sheriffs, and had backed down from a proposed resumption of the demesne. The frailty of its authority in the localities was revealed at the time of Pandulf's own resignation by the withdrawal of the forest eyres. Nonetheless, since the king's

---

[11] *PR*, 295, 315–17; *RLC*, 476b, 477.
[12] *Pipe Roll 1220*, vi–viii.
[1] *Nicholai Triveti Annales*, 209; *Walt. Cov.*, 250; *Ann. Mon.*, iii, 74; *Flores. Hist.*, ii, 172–3; *PR*, 310–11; Powicke, *Langton*, 145–6.
[2] *Flores Hist.*, ii, 173.

second coronation in May 1220, the government had scored a whole series of successes. Pandulf himself had taken a key role in Philip of Oldcoates's removal from Mitford, Henry fitz Count's expulsion from Cornwall and the Pembroke marriage treaty which brought the release of Marlborough. He had taken personal control of Bristol and Devizes when Hugh de Vivonne and Philip de Albini junior went abroad and had terminated the agreement whereby the earl of Chester enjoyed the farms of Lancashire, Shropshire and Staffordshire. If a general resumption had failed, many individual manors had been taken into the king's hands.

The growing assurance of the government around the time of Pandulf's resignation was revealed by the judicial eyre in the west midlands which opened in July 1221. When Lady Stenton edited the surviving rolls, she was impressed by the confidence displayed by the judges (one of whom was the earl of Pembroke) in their dealings with great magnates, as compared to their wariness on the eyres in Yorkshire and Lincolnshire in 1218 and 1219. And certainly, on the Shropshire eyre in 1221, the great loyalist Marcher baron, Hugh de Mortimer, was convicted of disseising two of his knightly tenants, Robert de Girros and Thomas de Costentin, both former rebels, while in Gloucestershire Thomas of Berkeley disclaimed the practices 'in the time of his brother' and promised to hand prisoners over to the sheriff without making difficulties.[3]

The new eyres also brought a welcome injection of cash. In the pipe roll of 1220, when only the dwindling proceeds from the visitations of 1218–19 were available, the sum recorded as reaching the exchequer from the eyres was £645. In the roll of 1221 the issues from the new visitations had boosted this to £1,050. The rise in the king's income is indeed the final measure of Pandulf's achievement. The cash revenue recorded in the pipe roll of 1221 is £7,600. The adjusted total, allowing for the fact that sheriffs of Cornwall and Essex–Hertfordshire accounted in the roll of the following year, is £8,280, nearly £3,000 more than the equivalent figure derived from the pipe roll of 1220. The increase in the government's cash resources is equally reflected in the amounts which writs of *liberate* ordered to be disbursed: some £9,835 between Michaelmas 1221 and Michaelmas 1222, as opposed to £5,295 between the same terms in 1219 and 1220. Pandulf's last act as legate was of a piece with the rest of his career. He publicly disavowed an

---

[3] *Lincs. Worcs. Eyre*, l; *Gloucs. Warw. Eyre*, xliv–vi and nos 1131, 1132; *Gloucester Pleas*, no. 294. For Girros and Costentin, see *Gloucs. Warw. Eyre*, no. 981; *RLC*, 260, 373b, 554b; *BF*, 962–3. Girros complained that he had recovered seisin after the war by 'the common writ' and had then been disseised by Mortimer. For the response to the new clause in the articles of the eyre about sheriffs and others holding pleas of the crown, see *Gloucs. Warw. Eyre*, no. 1262; *Gloucester Pleas*, xvii.

attempt by the prior and canons of St Frideswide's to obtain an advowson through an action in the church rather than in the king's courts.[4] As Pandulf had told the justices of the bench in 1220, in a similar type of case, 'the royal rights are to be preserved'.[5] That had been the leit-motif of his career in England. Appropriately, when the new abbot of St Augustine's, Canterbury swore fealty to the king in November 1220, he swore it on Pandulf's cross.[6]

vi. *The end of the king's pupillage and the watershed in English politics*

In July 1221, at the same time as Archbishop Langton's arrival brought an end to Pandulf's legation, Bishop Peter too came back to England. By a superb *coup de théâtre* he returned in company with the first friars to reach the country and went with them to Canterbury; so much for the charges that he had been dabbling abroad in treason. Peter then proceeded to Westminster, which he had reached by 20 July.[1] Quite apart from Pandulf's imminent resignation, he was faced with an extraordinary *bouleversement* in the political situation: the accusations of treason against himself and his closest associates; Peter de Maulay's ejection from Corfe; and the marriages proposed for Hubert and the earl of Pembroke.

For himself Peter extracted at once some compensation. At the end of July Hubert permitted 400 marks of the bishop's wartime expenditures to be set against his peacetime revenues as sheriff of Hampshire.[2] Peter did even better for Peter de Maulay. He was unable to restore him to Corfe but, late in July, he secured his formal acquittal at a great council.[3] Around the same time, on 29 July, Hubert and the council pardoned Maulay the 7,000 marks which he owed King John for his marriage to the heiress of the Fossard barony in Yorkshire, a barony worth over £400 a year. Formally this pardon was in return for Maulay's various expenditures at Corfe; in reality its concession, without question or inquiry, was compensation for Maulay's removal from the castle.[4] In that sense it was similar to the financial settlements that had been offered to the count of Aumale after his loss of Rockingham and to Geoffrey de Marsh after his removal from the justiciarship of Ireland. Maulay himself no longer ruled one of the kingdom's key castles but he had secured the future of his family as a great northern magnate house.

[4] *PR*, 310–11; for the case see *CPReg.*, 60; *CRR*, x, 141–2; *PR*, 274.
[5] *CRR*, ix, 118–19; see also *CRR*, ix, 52–3.
[6] *Historiae Anglicanae*, 1873.
[1] *Nicholai Triveti Annales*, 209; *PR*, 310–11.
[2] *RLC*, 467, 317b; *Pipe Roll 1220*, 122.
[3] *Walt. Cov.*, 250–1; *Ann. Mon.*, iii, 75.
[4] *RLC*, 481b–2; *Pipe Roll 1221*, 95 and introduction; *Pipe Roll 1212*, 5–6.

Bishop Peter may also have reacted to the Pembroke marriage agreement, conceived as it had been without his cognizance or consent. The royal letter of 1224 stated that, after the initial agreement, certain people opposed the marriage, 'asserting that we had no greater treasure than our marriage and that of our sisters, whence it behoved us to marry our sisters so that we gained a great alliance in foreign parts'.[5] One piece of evidence suggests that this was Peter's attitude. On 21 July, the day after he reappeared at court, he attested a writ of *liberate* giving the abbot of Stratford, an experienced diplomat, 20 marks for his expenses 'going on a mission [of the king] to Germany'. This was the first writ which Peter had attested since November 1220. He did not attest another until May 1222. It looks as though he was taking a very personal initiative. Was the abbot's task to investigate the possibility of marrying the king's sister in foreign parts?[6]

It was not long, however, before Peter had to face another blow to his position, a blow which he had probably anticipated but which, nonetheless, was far worse than any that had gone before. This was the removal of the king from his custody. The only direct reference to the event comes in Falkes's *querimonia*. According to its story, 'when the bishop of Winchester had returned from Spain, and the king himself, having exceeded the age of a pupil, was recognized as being free from his custody', the bishop could not prevent the king adhering to the counsels of the justiciar.[7] Since the bishop returned to England in July 1221, a plausible date for the change might seem to be 1 October 1221, when the king completed his fourteenth year. In educational theory, the age of fourteen marked the division between *pueritia* and *adolescentia*, while in Roman law it was precisely the moment at which a tutor's authority over his pupil ceased.[8]

It may well be, therefore, that Peter's tutorship came formally to an end in October 1221. On the other hand, there is some evidence that, in practice, his connection with the king had been severed somewhat earlier. The last writ connected with the royal household which Peter attested or authorized was in January 1221. In April, just before he left on his pilgrimage, he made a loan towards the household's expenses. This is the last evidence of his connection with it.[9] After Peter's return, the two writs concerned with the royal household enrolled before the end of September were the sole concern of Hubert, as they generally

---

[5] *DD*, no. 140.

[6] *RLC*, 465b, 495b. In October and December envoys from Germany were in England: *RLC*, 471, 483b.

[7] *Walt. Cov.*, 260.

[8] *PR*, 310–11; Orme, *From Childhood to Chivalry*, 6. See above p. 241.

[9] *RLC*, 448, 454, 452b.

continued to be thereafter.[10] On 19 September 1221 Bishop Peter took the cross, determined to leave England on crusade.[11] It seems likely, therefore, that the bishop never recovered effective control over the king after his return from his pilgrimage. At the very least, his taking the cross in September suggests that he knew that his guardianship was coming to an end.

The termination of Peter's tutorship could certainly be justified by the king's advancing years but it was also highly political. Although in Roman law the powers of tutors ceased when their pupils became fourteen, comparable authority was then assumed by curators, who oversaw the affairs of minors (those aged between fourteen and twenty-five). Equally, although the age of fourteen could mark a division in the educational process, it did not signal its end. Later in the century Giles of Rome assigned the years from seven to fourteen, or thereabouts depending on individuals, as the period for study and 'moderate exercise', and the period thereafter for learning how to ride and fight.[12] In April 1221 the pope himself considered Henry's training to be incomplete, for he tried to prevent Philip de Albini from leaving the king 'before he has been perfectly educated'.[13] The king's emancipation from Peter, moreover, brought no change in his general lifestyle. In 1221 and 1222 he still spent a good deal of time apart from the government, staying at places like Havering, Guildford and Wallingford.[14] There was no reason why Peter should not have continued after October 1221 as the head of his household with continuing responsibility for his education.

That this did not happen is testimony to the deep suspicions that Peter had long evoked, suspicions reflected in the papal letter of May 1220, which had ordered Pandulf to 'cause the king to be kept by prudent and honest men, not distrusted either by himself or his kingdom, who will instruct him in good morals and teach him to fear God and love his vassals'.[15] Such concerns were probably shared by Archbishop Langton, whose return to England had coincided with Peter's own. The latter's enemies, therefore, were well placed to rally support for his removal, just as they had been to block his succession to the regent in 1219.

For Hubert himself, of course, the purpose in discontinuing the tutorship was to prevent Peter establishing his sway over the king, a sway which would become all the more dangerous as Henry moved

[10] *RLC*, 466b, 468; for later writs, *RLC*, 471–471b; 478, 481, 482, 482b.
[11] *Ann. Mon.*, ii, 295.
[12] Orme, *From Childhood to Chivalry*, 6; for Roman law, see above p. 18 and n. 24.
[13] VL, Honorius III Regesta X, f.117.
[14] *RLC*, 458b, 464b, 466b, 486b, 487b, 489, 522b.
[15] VL, Honorius III Regesta X, f.186 (*CPReg.*, 71). See above p. 241.

towards his fourteenth birthday and the possible assumption of regal powers. In this objective, Hubert achieved a resounding success. Peter's son or nephew, Peter des Rivaux, remained as one of the senior clerks and, in effect, treasurer of the royal household until the end of 1223 but his political influence was negligible.[16] Peter's own connection with the household was severed almost entirely. Consequently, as Falkes's *querimonia* remarked, he was unable to prevent the king cleaving to the counsels of Hubert and his accomplices.[17] The bishop, however, had scarcely made the best use of his opportunities. For over five years, as Dr Clanchy has remarked, he 'was . . . in a position to exercise more personal influence than anyone else over the growing king', a king whose father was dead and mother was abroad, and whose warm-hearted and affectionate nature is sufficiently attested by his later career.[18] Yet, when it came to it between 1221 and 1223, this counted for nothing at all. What had gone wrong in the relationship between the boy and the bishop can only be guessed. Perhaps Peter was by turns remote and overbearing. Although the bishop's pipe rolls show that the king spent some of his time on Winchester episcopal manors,[19] for the most part he seems to have lived at royal residences and castles like Hertford, Havering and, above all, Wallingford.[20] 'In the expenses of the bishop's *familia* when it came to visit the king at Wallingford' ran one entry in the episcopal pipe roll.[21] Perhaps such descents were not altogether welcome; perhaps the occasion at Reading in April 1219 when Peter pulled the king by the head did not stand alone. Whatever the reasons, Peter's failure to win the king's affection and loyalty was to have serious consequences for the course of English politics.

After Peter's return from Spain he continued to sit at the exchequer and to attest and authorize occasional writs, although these dealt largely with foreign affairs or with matters arising from his sheriffdom of Hampshire.[22] He was still prepared to work with Hubert. He attested the writs dealing with the latter's annual fee as justiciar and his expenditures at Dover. At times, notably in May 1222, the two men

---

[16] Tout, *Chapters*, i, 190–1; *Chron. Maj.*, iii, 220. The close relationship between Peter and Peter des Rivaux is evident in the bishop's pipe rolls which in most years record small payments towards the latter's expenses, for example HRO, Eccles II 159274, rr.3,5d,6,7d; 159276, r.6; 159277, rr.2,2d.

[17] *Walt. Cov.*, 260.

[18] Clanchy, *England and its Rulers*, 184.

[19] HRO, Eccles II 159274, r.4d; 159275, r.9; 159276, rr.7d, 9,10; 159277, rr.2, 2d, 5, 7.

[20] *RLC*, 362, 370–1, 386, 387, 391, 391b, 393, 393b, 396, 397b, 403, 412, 431b, 440b, 441b, 443, 444, 446.

[21] HRO, Eccles II 159277, r.2d.

[22] *RLC*, 486, 494, 494b, 498b, 499b, 500b, 501, 522b, 525b; *PR*, 331.

seemed to have reached a *modus vivendi*.[23] But the events of 1221 were a watershed in English politics. Peter's association with the royal household had been broken.[24] He and his closest associates had been accused of treason. Whatever the proffered explanations, apologies and compensations, these were events which could be never be forgiven or forgotten. From now onwards, Peter was determined to pull down Hubert de Burgh. It is no accident that Falkes's *querimonia* begins its explanation of the crisis of 1223–24 with the accusations against Peter de Maulay in 1221 and termination of Bishop Peter's custody of the king.[25]

Peter, therefore, was the natural ally of others disaffected with what was soon to be, with Pandulf's resignation, Hubert's government. The greatest of these men was the earl of Chester. Since his return to England, in July 1220, Chester had received a string of concessions from the king but he had also to endure the sight of Hubert, whom he had long disliked, in control of government, a position for which Chester himself had been proposed in 1216 and 1217. Hubert, moreover, was now closely linked with the earl of Pembroke, while Chester was an ally of Llywelyn, Pembroke's greatest enemy. This alliance was consummated in 1222 by the marriage of Chester's ward and eventual heir, John le Scot, the son of Earl David, to Llywelyn's daughter 'for the purpose of effecting a lasting peace', as the annals of Chester put it.[26]

Hubert's alliance with Pembroke had other factional consequences, placing him, whatever his intentions, under mounting pressure to break with Falkes de Bréauté. His relationship with the earl of Salisbury, who had run up against Falkes at Lincoln, worked in the same direction. Falkes, perhaps for this reason, became increasingly close to Peter. Already in 1218 Peter had entertained him and Peter de Maulay at his manor of Taunton. In the autumn of 1221 all three decided to go on crusade together.[27] It is significant that, after the crisis at Corfe, as has been seen, precautionary measures were taken against Falkes and Philip Mark, the latter another natural ally of Peter since he was a kinsman of Engelard from the Touraine. What was opening up in 1221, therefore, was a political divide between Hubert and the earls

---

[23] *RLC*, 495b, 515b, 526b, 573. See below pp. 280–1.

[24] Of the twenty or so writs dealing with the expenses of the royal household in 1222, Peter was only associated with two: *RLC*, 499b–500, 522b.

[25] *Walt. Cov.*, 260.

[26] *Ann. Cest.*, 50–3; British Library, Cotton Ch. xxiv, 17 (the marriage agreement). It was probably as a consequence of this alliance that Chester became a supporter of John de Braose in his conflict with his uncle Reginald, who was in turn supported by the earl of Pembroke: *BNB*, no. 167; *CRR*, xi, no. 1969.

[27] HRO, Eccles II 159274, rr. 11d, 12d; *Ann. Mon.*, iii, 75; *PR*, 321.

of Pembroke and Salisbury on one side, and Peter, Chester, Falkes, Engelard and Peter de Maulay on the other.

At the heart of this divide were struggles for central and local power but it was given an extra dimension by the question of nationality.[28] There were essentially two elements to being English: that of being *naturalis*, native-born, and that of regarding England as one's homeland, *partes nostrae*. In the twelfth century the knightly class, the bedrock of local society, was English in both these senses. Above them there remained the great Anglo-Norman magnates with lands both in England and in Normandy. Whether these men were born in England or, like the earl of Pembroke, in Normandy was partly a matter of chance. What they regarded as their homeland depended on where their greatest estates lay and where they spent the bulk of their time, especially perhaps in their early years. Many may well have felt that they had homelands both in England and Normandy. Certainly, there was no difficulty in these men being regarded as English. William de Warenne, earl of Surrey (1202–40), for example, was lord of Lewes and Conisbrough but his birthplace is unknown and he lost extensive lands in Normandy in 1204.[29] His niece was the countess of Eu; his father, Hamelin, was an Angevin *par excellence*, the bastard son of Geoffrey of Anjou. Nonetheless, King John could confidently tell the Cinque Ports in 1216 that he was making Surrey their warden 'because we do not wish to place any alien (*alienigenam*) as head or master over you'.[30] This Englishness of the arisocracy was obviously increased by the loss of Normandy in 1204. It is true, as Dr Stevenson has shown, that family and tenurial connections between the kingdom and the duchy remained extensive.[31] Thus the countess of Eu was allowed to keep the honour of Tickhill. But the fact remains that no great magnate involved in English politics after 1219 personally held lands in Normandy. Unless Normandy could be recovered, and the chances of that became increasingly remote, the children of great barons henceforth would always be native-born and England their only homeland.

In the civil war natives and aliens fought on both sides. Thereafter, there were never hard and fast political divisions between them. The Poitevin count of Aumale was able to find sureties from amongst the chief English magnates. Peter's greatest ally became the earl of Chester. If the earl of Pembroke regarded England as one of his homelands, he was acutely aware that he had been born in Normandy,

---

[28] Clanchy, *England and its Rulers*, 241–4, discusses the development of national feeling in the reign of Henry III.

[29] *Peerage*, xii, i, 499–503; Powicke, *Loss of Normandy*, 506, 225.

[30] *RLP*, 184.

[31] Stevenson, 'England and Normandy, 1204–1259', ch. iii and pp. 379–485.

ironically just like Falkes, his greatest enemy.[32] But, as the divisions of the war healed, the issue of the aliens seemed to come more and more to the fore. It was clear in the localities, where aliens were so often found at the focal points of trouble: Robert de Gaugi at Newark, the count of Aumale at Rockingham and Bytham, and Peter de Maulay at Corfe. The manner, moreover, in which some of these aliens wielded their local power, power which in Falkes's case was uniquely wide, branded them as brutal oppressors of their English subjects. 'Here is the scourge of the earth! here the affliction of the natives, to whom the people of England were so often given over as booty', was the way Archbishop Langton described Falkes, according to the latter's own *querimonia*.[33] The conflict between aliens and natives was equally clear at the centre where Bishop Peter jousted with Hubert. The majority of those with whom Peter was most closely associated, notably Peter de Maulay, Engelard, Falkes and the count of Aumale, were aliens like himself, men who were neither native-born nor able to regard England as *partes nostrae*. Bishop Peter was very clear that he was a Touraingeau not an Englishman. He had a warm affection for, and maintained close links with, his homeland.[34] However much these first generation imports saw their future in England, nothing, in their own eyes or those of others, could make them part of the *gens Anglicana*. The Poitevin, Hugh de Vivonne, for example, had made a good English marriage, while his family had lost most of its lands in Poitou, yet Vivonne could still ask for patronage so that he could stay 'in English parts' (*in partibus Anglicanis*).[35] He clearly did not regard these as *partes nostrae*. Whether Falkes maintained any connections with Normandy may be doubted. His loyalty was more to a dynasty than to a place.[36] But he was only too clear about the distinction between *naturales*, on the one hand, and aliens, like himself, on the other. By the end of 1221, as will be seen, these distinctions were being felt and proclaimed at the very highest level of English politics.[37]

[32] *Maréchal*, lines 16208-9.

[33] *Walt. Cov.*, 268-9.

[34] See above p. 139.

[35] SC 1/1, no. 211.

[36] Essentially, men like Falkes and Hugh de Vivonne, having lost their lands in their native country, became homeless until they or their descendants were accepted in England. Vivonne referred to the loss of his family lands *in partibus transmarinis* rather than *in partibus nostris: RL*, no. lxxv.

[37] See below p. 272.

Chapter 7

THE GOVERNMENT OF THE
JUSTICIAR, 1221–23

i. *Archbishop Langton and Hubert's government*

Pandulf had resigned but he had left a clear programme of action behind him: the general resumption of the king's castles, demesnes and possessions. As far as the castles and sheriffdoms were concerned, this was still a remote prospect. It had never been attempted during Pandulf's legateship. A much more immediate objective was a general resumption of the royal demesne. *That* had been tried in the autumn of 1220 without success but the resumption of individual manors had kept the issue alive. A related problem was that posed by the counties – Cumberland, Lincolnshire and Somerset–Dorset – where the sheriffs were still not answering properly for the farms at the exchequer. If, however, Pandulf's programme was to be realized, that raised another issue, an issue already apparent in the widespread resistance to the forest eyres: if the king's government was recovering its strength, what were to be the limits or, to put it another way, what was to be the future of the Charters?

The new government's approach to these questions remained to be seen. Pandulf's departure and Peter's eclipse left Hubert with pre-eminent but not sole authority. He continued to co-operate with the council when taking major decisions over patronage, appointments and expenditure. He had also to establish a working relationship with Archbishop Langton. Even during Pandulf's constricting legateship, Langton had taken an important part in the kingdom's political life. He had been involved in launching the first eyres, adjudging the Three Castles to Hubert, preventing tournaments and negotiating with Llywelyn. After his return to England in 1221 there is no sign that he aspired, like Pandulf, to counsel and control the day-to-day running of government, but his participation in the crucial decisions helped shape the course of politics. His influence was exercised in three directions: to guarantee the government's adherence to the Charters; to support its prosecution of the programme of resumption; and to maintain the peace and tranquillity of the realm.

Langton was an Englishman and an academic, who had made his

name as a master at the university of Paris.[1] He was, therefore, an intellectual in politics, though whether the politics of the minority taxed his intellect, as opposed to his judgement, may be doubted. Central to Langton's political ideas was a contemporary commonplace: the distinction between the lawful and the tyrannical king. Langton had taught at Paris that it was legitimate to resist the latter, to resist, that is, kings who proceeded by their own will, *proprio motu*, without judgement.[2] In John's reign Langton had put his principles into practice. He had warned the king not to act, without judgement, against the Northerners and had refused, without judgement, to surrender Rochester castle.[3] The insistence on the king proceeding by judgement or by the law of the land was enshrined, of course, in Magna Carta, which Langton had played a key role in negotiating. He was fully committed to its principles and was determined to ensure that it was upheld in the minority. Indeed, insofar as ecclesiastical liberties were concerned, he hoped apparently to see its provisions extended.[4]

Within these limits, however, Langton was ready to support the recovery of royal power. This was not simply because the papacy urged him to uphold Pandulf's programme, although it may well have done so. Even during the interdict Langton had sought, so he claimed, nothing to the 'prejudice of the king and his crown'.[5] In 1214, practical man that he was, he had even profited from one of John's most notorious exactions: the 20,000 mark fine imposed on Geoffrey de Mandeville for the marriage of the countess of Gloucester. Half of this was assigned to the archbishop in recompense for his losses during the interdict.[6] In Langton's view the church had created kings to act as its defence, its 'arms'.[7] Clearly, unless English kingship recovered from its enfeebled state after the war, it could not perform this basic task. It was easy, moreover, for Langton as a bishop, sworn to protect the rights of his see, to support the government when it tried to uphold a similar principle on behalf of the king, the more especially when the king was a

---

[1] Powicke, *Langton*, is the chief study of the archbishop.

[2] Powicke, *Langton*, 94–5; Holt, *Magna Carta*, 188.

[3] *Chron. Maj.*, ii, 551; *Coggeshall*, 173; Rowlands, 'King John, Stephen Langton and Rochester castle', 267–79.

[4] Holt, *Magna Carta*, 187–8; *Councils and Synods*, ii, part i, 162, a reference I owe to Professor R. L. Storey.

[5] *Gervase*, lxxxiii; Holt, *Magna Carta*, 188.

[6] *RLC*, ii, 110b; E 372/69, r.8 m.2, which states that Langton actually received the 10,000 marks while Peter des Roches was justiciar, although it is more likely that Mandeville simply made arrangements whereby the money could be paid from assigned lands: see *CR 1227–31*, 67.

[7] 'An unpublished document on the great interdict', 418 (a sermon of Langton's from 1213).

minor. Langton's personal affection for the young boy made the task all the more congenial.[8]

This does not mean, however, as Powicke implied, that Langton was the driving force behind the government in the years after his return; that he propelled forward the programme of resumption while Hubert remained content with the status quo.[9] It is true that Langton placed his weight behind the resumption of the demesne in 1222 and of the castles and sheriffdoms in the following year but this, as will be seen, was a case of supporting initiatives of others rather than of originating them himself. Indeed, in the politics of the years 1221 to 1224, just as in 1215, Langton frequently appears 'as a mediator and a moderator, rather than an originator'.[10]

In respect of the resumption of the demesne and, ultimately of the castles and sheriffdoms, there seems little doubt that Hubert was ready to move forward himself. His duty as justiciar was to maintain the rights of the crown. That duty, moreover, was given added force and direction by his increasingly 'exchequer-centred' outlook. Essentially, Hubert wished to create as large a cash revenue as possible at the exchequer, where, of course, he sat in control. This concern is reflected in the way that he ran his own sheriffdoms. Immediately after the war, with the regent and the bishop of Winchester in charge at the exchequer, Hubert had been as keen as any other local official to spend the money from his counties with as little surveillance as possible. In January 1218 a writ had to insist that he pay the proceeds of the first scutage into the exchequer, rather than spend them immediately on the work at Dover castle. As it was, down to Michaelmas 1220, Hubert drew off £1,656 from the farms and judicial issues of Kent and Norfolk-Suffolk to support Dover's garrison and building works, the sums reaching the exchequer being correspondingly reduced.[11] Thereafter, everything changed. The revenues from his counties were payed into the exchequer and he was granted a money fee of £1,000 a year to maintain the castle. In addition, between 1221 and 1224, the exchequer funded the operations there to the tune of £883.[12] If Hubert treated his own sheriffdoms in this way, bringing their money to the exchequer

---

[8] Walt. Cov., 244.

[9] Powicke, Henry III, 47–8, 50–1, 57.

[10] Holt, Magna Carta, 188.

[11] RLC, 352; Pipe Roll 1220, 58–9. In addition, between September 1218 and Easter 1221 Hubert received £604 from Isaac the Jew of Norwich. This too was allowed him for the support of Dover.

[12] RLC, 479b, 495b, 515b, 573; Divers Accounts, 13. In 1222 Hubert was also conceded £300 a year at the exchequer to sustain him as justiciar. This sum was paid partly in cash and partly set against the the £100 annual increment which he owed as sheriff of Norfolk–Suffolk: RLC, 526b, 599b.

rather than spending it locally, he must have been even keener to apply the same regimen to everyone else. Tighter discipline over the sheriffs, however, was difficult to achieve without removing the men currently in office, something that Hubert knew was beyond his power. A much more immediate way of increasing the king's revenue was by resuming the royal demesne.

In pursuing his objectives, Hubert moved with the slow and cautious labour which had sometimes exasperated Pandulf. He was like a man making his way across a treacherous marsh. He tested the ground as he went. If it was firm he advanced, if it gave way, he retreated. Hence the various compromises over the staging of the forest eyres. Hubert was equally careful when it came to dealing with individuals. In July 1221, for example, when the exchequer asked what it should do about Roger de Quincy, the son of the late earl of Winchester, who had failed to appear to prosecute his suit to Chesterton, Hubert's reply, patient and unprovocative, was simply that he should be summoned again 'through letters of the king sealed by the exchequer seal'.[13] The fact was that men did not voluntarily surrender manors, castles and offices, as the cases of the earls of Pembroke, Chester and Geoffrey de Marsh in 1221 had demonstrated. They had to be bargained with and put under pressure. All Hubert's political skills would be necessary to make possible his forward policy.

That policy, in the year and a half after Pandulf's resignation, achieved one notable success. After a false start, Hubert's government achieved a resumption of the royal demesne. It also demonstrated where it stood in respect of the Charters, for, in January 1223, King Henry proffered a verbal confirmation of them. In both the resumption and the confirmation Langton's hand is clear. The resumption was achieved in relative political harmony. But the period also saw the growth of faction and one major political crisis. It thus paved the way for the highly divisive manner in which the king at the end of 1223 ultimately recovered control over his castles and sheriffdoms.

ii. *The conflict in Poitou*

Pandulf had resigned his legation at the end of July 1221 but he did not leave England until October and then on a mission of the king to Poitou. As Norgate commented, nothing shows better the extent to which he had taken King Henry's cause to heart.[1]

The government had appointed Hugh de Vivonne as seneschal of Poitou and Gascony in January 1221. It had commissioned him to

[13] E 159/4, m.8.
[1] Norgate, *Minority*, 177–8.

recover the king's rights and had envisaged a term of office which would last at least three years. Hugh himself was less sanguine, fearing 'some misfortune' which might compel his return to England, and his forebodings proved only too justified.[2] Throughout the summer of 1221 he was at loggerheads with Hugh de Lusignan, who refused to surrender Joan's *maritagium*, despite pressure from the pope. Until he did so the English government withheld Niort, which Isabella claimed as part of her dower. At the end of September it went further and confiscated the possessions she held as dower in England.[3] A few days later, on 6 October, Hubert and the council, apparently here composed of Langton, Bishop Peter, the earls of Chester and Salisbury and William Brewer, sent out Engelard de Cigogné and Emery de Sacy 'to keep and defend our land of Poitou'. This, however, was a stop-gap measure. For the long term, a new seneschal was appointed in place of Hugh de Vivonne: none other than his former master, Savari de Mauléon.[4] Savari was lord of Talmont and head of a family which controlled nine castellanies in Poitou.[5] He was, therefore, exactly the type of seneschal the towns had warned against in 1220: a great local magnate, who might pursue his own interests and prove impossible to discipline. He was also a famous troubadour, a man, in Powicke's words, whose 'fluctuating loyalty was a boon to be sought rather than a duty to be demanded'.[6] On the other hand, if the boon was granted, he was the one man who might be able to stand up to Hugh and Isabella.

The trouble was that Savari had not actually agreed to take up the post. His appointment was like casting a fly at a trout and hoping that it would rise. In this difficult situation the government turned to Pandulf. At the *magnam instanciam* of the king and council, he agreed to go out to Poitou to look after the king's affairs and persuade Savari to become seneschal.[7] After his departure matters became even more complex. Envoys of Savari arrived in England with various petitions from their lord. The government also learnt that open war had broken out in Poitou. Hugh was besieging the castle of Merpins in Angoulême, which he considered was part of Isabella's inheritance. In fact, the English government had tried to transfer Merpins from Reginald de Pons to Isabella back in 1217. Now Reginald, ostensibly holding the castle for the king, was transformed from villain to hero. Messengers, therefore,

  [2] *PR*, 306-7.
  [3] *F*, 169; *Ann. Mon.*, iii, 75; *PR*, 302.
  [4] *PR*, 303-4; *RLC*, 470b.
  [5] Hajdu, 'The structure of politics in Poitou', 34. Chaytor, *Savaric de Mauléon*, is a short biography.
  [6] Powicke, *Henry III*, 3.
  [7] *PR*, 304; *DD*, no. 108; *CRR*, x, 209.

were sent after Pandulf with fresh instructions. He was to try to arrange as long a truce as possible with Hugh so that Savari could come to England and negotiate the terms of his appointment.[8]

When these measures concerning Poitou were taken in October, there was a considerable gathering of magnates at Westminster, including Archbishop Langton. Perhaps this was the moment of Hubert's marriage to Margaret of Scotland, at which Langton officiated.[9] Having attested a writ on 6 October, the justiciar did not attest again until 19 October, responsibility for royal letters being assumed in the meantime by William Brewer.[10] This was a busy time for Hubert to be absent from court but even a justiciar needed a honeymoon.

iii. *The resumption of the demesne, October 1221: failure*

On 1 October 1221 King Henry celebrated his fourteenth birthday. He did so amidst rumours of unrest, for the exchequer, early in the Michaelmas term, had to assure the sheriff of Yorkshire that 'there is no dissension between the barons and so he can come securely with money and cross through Lincoln'.[1] One reason for tension was the whole question of whether the king's fourteenth birthday should bring a change in his status. This was evidently discussed by the magnates present at Westminster in October. They may have agreed that Bishop Peter's tutorship should formally end but for the rest they decided that there should be no alteration in the king's position. Hence, early in November, the king wrote to the pope asking him 'not to change the state of our land' until envoys had informed him of its 'state and of our doings'.[2] Although the pope agreed to make no change, that did not secure a tranquil breathing space of seven years until the king was twenty-one, for, as the letter of November implied, the pope might always decide that the king should attain his majority earlier or, alternatively, should take over the reins of government before he was formally of age. The pope was most likely to do this in response to a request from England. The prospect that someone, or some party, would make that request, thus pulling the lever that would transform the structure of central and local power, injected a constant note of uncertainty into political life.

---

[8] *Ann. Mon.*, iii, 75; *PR*, 315, 327; *RLC*, 477b, 478; *DD*, no. 108; for Merpins, see *RCh*, 196; *PR*, 85–6, 152–3; *F*, 156.

[9] *RLC*, 470b; *Flores Hist.*, ii, 173.

[10] *RLC*, 472–472b; *PR*, 303–5.

[1] E 368/4, m.5. Neither the sheriff of Yorkshire nor Lincolnshire appeared at the 1221 Michaelmas *Adventus*: E 159/5, m.7.

[2] *DD*, no. 108.

Another potential source of discontent was an important government initiative launched just before the king's fourteenth birthday. This concerned the king's demesnes and escheats. On 30 September writs were issued to all the sheriffs and to between two and four coadjutors in each county, mostly local knights, ordering them to take into the king's hands all the demesnes of which King John had been seized at the beginning of the war, and all escheats which had been in his hands and those of his son. They were to instruct the former holders of these lands to be *coram rege* at the end of October to show if they had 'sufficient warrant' for their tenure.[3]

This was a far more radical measure than the comparable initiative of August 1220.[4] In 1220 the commissioners were merely ordered to discover who held the demesnes and escheats. In 1221 they were to seize them into the king's hands. In 1220 the holders came to Westminster to retain their seisin, in 1221 to recover it. They were guilty until they could prove their innocence. Much preparation went into the 1221 measure, particularly in drawing up the list of seventy-three men who were to act as the sheriffs' coadjutors. This can only have taken place on Hubert's instructions, and it was he who attested the writs of 30 September, but, apart from that, the measure was curiously fatherless. There was no indication that the king's council had sanctioned it. Perhaps the measure had been prepared in anticipation of general consent which was not forthcoming. That Hubert went ahead anyway shows his continuing commitment to the policy of resumption after Pandulf's departure.

The failure to secure general consent to the initiative ensured its failure, however. In November and December writs were issued in favour of twenty-seven individuals, instructing the sheriffs to re-seize them of land taken into the king's hands as a result of the order.[5] In some cases the sheriffs had simply taken the chance to pursue local feuds. Robert de Courtenay deprived Falkes of the lands of the earldom of Devon. Falkes deprived Henry of Braybrooke of Corby and Philip Mark evicted Roger de Montbegon from Oswaldbeck.[6] Usually those who recovered their lands proved their right to them through the production of a royal charter but this did not mean that tenure less well protected was now lost. No major royal manor or escheat returned to the king's hands as a result of the measure, even where tenure was specifically limited to the king's fourteenth year.[7] Thus the earl of Derby continued to hold Melbourne, as well as Bolsover and the Peak.

[3] C 60/15, m.1d; see *Pipe Roll 1221*, introduction.
[4] See above pp. 206, 222.
[5] *RLC*, 477b–85b.
[6] *RLC*, 478b–9.
[7] *PR*, 315, 64.

On 1 November Brian de Lisle, by counsel of the king's *fideles*, was conceded the castle and vill of Knaresborough during the king's pleasure at the same £50 annual farm that he had previously been allowed to enjoy until the king's fourteenth year. Others who continued to hold substantial portions of royal demesne, or to draw off its revenues, although their tenure had always been during the king's pleasure, included the earl of Salisbury, Falkes, Engelard de Cigogné, William de Cantilupe, Godfrey of Crowcombe, Walter de Verdun and Thomas Basset.

Early in November a large number of great men were present at court, the formal resignation of Geoffrey de Marsh as justiciar of Ireland taking place in the presence of the earls of Chester, Salisbury, Pembroke, Gloucester and Derby, William Brewer, Falkes and Brian de Lisle.[8] It was doubtless this body of men which ensured that the act of resumption was still-born. The atmosphere in which they did so was probably highly rancorous. Rumours of dissensions between the barons had been abroad early in October and by Christmas the government was in the middle of a major crisis.

iv. *Crisis, December 1221–January 1222*

On 19 September 1221, during a solemn mass in his cathedral, the bishop of Winchester had taken the cross. He was to be accompanied on his crusade by both Peter de Maulay and Falkes de Bréauté. No doubt the bishop and Maulay were encouraged to leave England by their political eclipse but Peter was also responding to an invitation which paid tribute to his international reputation. According to the chronicler, Ralph of Coggeshall, he had been elected to the archbishop-ric of Damietta. Peter was still intending to depart as late as 7 December but once the implications of the fall of Damietta on 10 September had sunk in, the crusade was postponed.[1]

Thus the Christmas court at Winchester digested Peter's obtrusive hospitality without the consolation of his early departure. The celebrations were also marred by an atmosphere of crisis. The king had instructed the sheriff of Yorkshire to spend Christmas at York in order to fortify the city against the fear of disturbance in the kingdom.[2] Some flesh is put on these bones by the Barnwell chronicler. According to his story, dissensions had arisen between the earl of Chester on the one side

[8] *PR*, 316.
[1] *Walt. Cov.*, 250; *Coggeshall*, 190; *Ann. Mon.*, ii, 84, 295; iii, 75; *PR*, 320–1; note the concessions at the same time to Falkes and Maulay in November 1221: *RLC*, 481b–2.
[2] *Chron. Maj.*, 67; *RLC*, ii, 90. Failure to enrol royal letters between 7 and 20 January may also reflect the crisis, a point I owe to Professor Cazel.

and the earl of Salisbury and Hubert de Burgh on the other, 'for it was said, and several suspecting this preached it through England, that aliens, who coveted the disturbance of the kingdom more than peace, tried to induce the earl of Chester to harass the king and disturb the kingdom. But the earl of Salisbury and the justiciar, rulers of the king and kingdom, vigorously prepared themselves with their followers to resist'. At this point Langton had intervened. He had summoned a great council to meet in London after 13 January and threatened potential troublemakers with spiritual penalties. Eventually, 'at his instance and that of the bishops both sides were recalled to peace and concord'.[3]

The alliance between Hubert and the earl of Salisbury had been in formation, if not in place, since June 1220. In December 1221 they were almost certainly standing shoulder to shoulder with the earl of Pembroke, who received a large gift of game from the king on 28 December and whose knight, Thomas Basset, was confirmed in possession of the royal manor of Slaughter.[4] It was always on the cards that Chester would quarrel with Hubert's government, the more especially once that government was closely linked with Pembroke. If he did, his natural allies were Peter and Falkes, the 'aliens', perhaps, of the Barnwell chronicler's story. It may be significant that Peter and Chester were acting together in October 1221 in the affairs of Hugh de Lacy, while, in November, Chester and Falkes were the two pledges for a fine of William of Hartshill.[5]

An immediate focus of the crisis was clearly in the north, at York, and also perhaps at Lincoln where Falkes and the earls of Salisbury and Chester had been in contention over custody of the castle.[6] Early in October 1221, as has been seen, the sheriff of Yorkshire had to be assured that 'there is no dissension between the barons and so he can come securely with money and cross through Lincoln'.[7] It may be significant that, in the aftermath of the crisis, Salisbury at last resigned as sheriff of Lincolnshire, having until the end maintained his refusal to answer for the county farm.

Another strand in the rising tension was probably Pembroke's promised marriage to Henry's sister. In the spring of 1221 Pembroke complained to the pope about the 'enemies' who were blocking the completion of the marriage. Quite probably one of these was Chester. That he came to oppose the union is suggested by the stress placed,

---

[3] *Walt. Cov.*, 251.
[4] *RLC*, 485.
[5] *PR*, 301; C 60/16, m.9.
[6] For Chester's claim to Lincoln castle, which had been held by his grandfather in Stephen's reign, see *PR*, 117–18; Stenton, *First Century of English Feudalism*, 241.
[7] E 368/4, m.5.

in a royal letter to the pope, on his agreement when first consulted about it.[8]

The divisions of this period are also revealed in two letters to Hubert. One was from the earl of Salisbury, passing on information which he had received from John Marshal. John had obtained royal letters, which ordered Falkes, as sheriff, to let him have his wood of Norton [Greens] in Northamptonshire in peace. Falkes, however, had declared 'that if [John] sent him thirty pairs of the king's letters he should not have peace in respect of the wood nor of other things in his sheriffdom. And, in the presence of the servant whom [John] had sent, he called John himself and all native-born men of England (*omnes naturales homines Angliae*) traitors, saying also that all we native-born men of England wished and desired war, and that he would find such a great war for us that all England would be too small for us.' Falkes was only too happy for this to be put on the record. 'He freely ordered the servant of John Marshal', Salisbury continued, 'to narrate these words to his lord, and for his lord to relay them to us and to others.' Clearly John Marshal did just that, for the second letter to Hubert was from the earl of Pembroke. He retold Falkes's outburst almost word for word, added that he himself had given the wood at Norton to John Marshal and concluded: 'therefore we ask you most earnestly to correct for us the excesses of this man, so capricious and mendacious (*tam inconstantis et mendacis viri excessus*), knowing for certain that we will never withdraw from the court of the king unless your power, *quod absit*, denies us justice'.[9]

This episode probably occurred between Michaelmas 1221 and Trinity 1222.[10] That it was connected to the crisis around Christmas 1221 is strongly suggested by the Barnwell chronicler's story, which related, as has been seen, how certain people preached throughout England that aliens desired the disturbance of the kingdom more than peace. That, of course, was exactly what the earls of Pembroke and Salisbury were doing. Their picture of Falkes, disdainful of royal letters, threatening a war which would make England too small for native-born men, suggested that the country was on the brink of hostilities. Equally, it would not be surprising if Falkes at this time had turned to the earl of Chester for help, hence the further allegation that the aliens tried to induce Chester to harass and disturb the kingdom.

The clash between Falkes and John Marshal, like some disputes between the former and the earl of Pembroke, arose from Falkes's determination to uphold what he considered to be the rights of the king in his sheriffdoms. Hence he had imprisoned John's bailiff at Norton and refused to free him until, as Salisbury put it, John 'finds safe

---

[8] VL, Honorius III Regesta XI, f.258 (*CPReg.*, 88); *DD*, no. 140.

[9] *RL*, nos cxcvi, cxcvii.

[10] See below note 15.

pledges to render to [Falkes] all the customs and undue demands which he claims from the land of Norton'.[11] The incident had, however, a wider significance. It provides by far the most important evidence there is that tensions between *naturales* and aliens in the politics of these years were deeply felt by the chief actors themselves. They were not the preserve of poets and monastic chroniclers. Falkes's outburst was the reaction of an alien infuriated by accusations, like those made against Bishop Peter, Peter de Maulay and Engelard de Cigogné in June 1221, that aliens were traitors. He replied by throwing the accusation back against the *naturales*, as well he might, remembering their conduct in the war. Falkes clearly intended to lump John Marshal and his family and associates together as native-born, and the earl of Salisbury explicitly accepted this designation, speaking of 'all we native-born men of England (*nos omnes naturales homines Angliae*)'.[12] Pembroke did not associate himself with the native-born so directly. He had, after all, been born in Normandy.[13] Nevertheless, both earls were eager to pass Falkes's words on to Hubert. They clearly expected him to see the threat to make war on *omnes naturales homines Angliae* as a threat aimed directly at himself.

In the event, as has been seen, Langton intervened to sedate the conflicts. Falkes was not always so disobedient as his enemies made out. Indeed, he obeyed a writ of November 1221 ordering him to return lands which he had taken *per voluntatem suam* from the burgesses of Bedford.[14] Whether Hubert himself had broken decisively with Falkes may be doubted since they were to co-operate closely later in 1222. In the Norton affair itself Hubert kept his balance, for he seems to have referred the demands that Falkes was making of John Marshal to an inquiry. Thus in the Trinity term of 1222 a jury from Northampton-shire was summoned to the bench to recognize 'what rights and customs King John had before the war in the hundreds of Sutton and Norton', the first being held by the earl of Salisbury and the second by John Marshal from the earl of Pembroke.[15]

Elements in the settlement of the crisis can be glimpsed in a series of changes in the custody of castles, counties and manors, although the precise give and take is impossible to sort out. At the end of January

---

[11] *RL*, no. cxcvi.
[12] *RL*, no. cxcvi.
[13] *Maréchal*, lines 16208–9.
[14] *RLC*, 480; *Ann. Mon.*, iii, 75.
[15] *CRR*, x, 333. For Sutton and Norton, see *Pipe Roll 1221*, 186; *BF*, 326; *CRR*, ix, 205. There is no sign of the inquiry in the bench's rolls for the Michaelmas term of 1221. The rolls for the Hilary and Easter terms of 1222 are lost: *CRR*, x, 261 n.1. If, therefore, I am right in thinking that the inquiry was the sequel to the dispute, the latter probably took place between Michaelmas 1221 and Trinity 1222.

Peter de Maulay was deprived by Hubert and the council of Sherborne castle and the forests of Somerset and Dorset,[16] his last remaining custodies. But equally, next month, after his deputy had accounted for Lincolnshire at the exchequer, Salisbury gave up the sheriffdom of Lincolnshire. His replacement, Stephen of Seagrave, was a justice of the bench but also a tenant and familiar of the earl of Chester.[17] The result was that the exchequer had at long last recovered control of Lincolnshire's farm which Salisbury since the war had been pocketing for himself.

v. *The recovery of the county farms, November 1221–February 1222*

Despite the failure of the resumption and the subsequent political crisis, the government had indeed persevered with efforts to improve the king's financial position. In November 1221 it had made one significant advance. It accepted a fine of £2,228 from the widowed countess of Oxford for the custody of the lands of her son until he came of age. In the pipe roll of 1222 she paid £667 towards the fine and her late husband's debts into the exchequer. This was the first major wardship to fall in since the end of the war. Its treatment was in marked contrast to the concessions, in 1218, of the lands of Eustace de Vesci and the earl of Devon to the earl of Salisbury and Falkes de Bréauté completely free of charge.[1]

The exchequer was also eager to resume control over the county farms which still remained beyond its supervision. Cornwall's had been recovered after the fall of Henry fitz Count in September 1220 and those of Lancashire, Shropshire and Staffordshire when the earl of Chester's tenure was terminated by Pandulf some time in the summer of 1221.[2] That still left, in October 1221, the farms of Somerset–Dorset, Lincolnshire and Cumberland, where the recalcitrant sheriffs were, respectively, Peter de Maulay, the earl of Salisbury and Robert de Vieuxpont.[3] Maulay's prospective departure on his crusade made him amenable to a bargain which removed him from Somerset–Dorset. On 20 November 1221 the government accepted a 200 mark offer, 'in the name of all of the counties' of Somerset and Dorset, for Maulay's replacement by Roger of Ford, his former under-sheriff.[4] In return for

---

[16] *PR*, 324–5.

[17] *PR*, 327. For other changes and concessions, see *RLC*, 487b. (It was at this point that the earl of Salisbury's knight, William Talbot, finally vacated the manor of Mere.) For the dates of shrieval accounts in 1221–22, see *Pipe Roll 1221*, introduction.

[1] *ERF*, 75; E 372/66, r.8, m.1.

[2] See above pp. 215, 253.

[3] See above pp. 119–20, 89.

[4] C 60/16, m.9; *PR*, 320; *CRR*, x, 106–8.

his resignation, Maulay was given quittance by Hubert and the council, comprising here the bishops of Winchester, Durham and London, William Brewer and Falkes, of the 6,561 marks which he had received from ransoms of prisoners kept at Corfe during the war, and of the 2,306 marks outstanding from the issues of Somerset–Dorset. This sum embraced the farm of the counties since the war, the issues of the 1219 eyre, virtually none of which Maulay had cleared, and numerous private debts which he had collected but not paid into the exchequer. Officially, Maulay was allowed these 8,867 marks against the 750 marks which he had given the earl of Salisbury in 1218 and the 1,500 marks which he had spent on Sherborne castle. These two sums, however, only amounted to 2,250 marks, so the balance of 6,617 marks was spirited away by saying that this was the sum that Maulay had spent on knights and serjeants during the war.[5] In effect, as Dr Crook has said, Maulay's debts were simply written off.[6] Having shed debts totalling 15,867 marks during the year, Maulay's fall certainly had a silver lining. For the government, however, there was some compensation: £122 were paid into the exchequer from the farm of the counties for the financial year 1221–22 and another £65 were spent locally on the king's orders.[7]

The aftermath of the Christmas crisis of 1221, as has been seen, brought about Salisbury's departure from Lincolnshire and the exchequer's recovery of control over the farm. The new sheriff, Stephen of Seagrave, paid £268 into the treasury for the three-quarter year between February and Michaelmas 1222.[8] February 1222 also saw the exchequer recover control over the county of Cumberland. In that month Hubert permitted, and perhaps masterminded, a settlement of the case which Robert de Vieuxpont had brought against the countess of Eu for the honour of Tickhill, the case Hubert had adjourned, due to the evil of the times, in May 1220. Vieuxpont now abandoned his claim to the honour in return for £100 and the grant of six and a half of its fees. Hubert, meanwhile, reserved the claims of the king to the honour's demesnes and services. Under the terms of the agreement of 1218, Vieuxpont's tenure of the sheriffdom of Cumberland was to last until his claim to Tickhill had been settled.[9] Since this had now happened the government could regain control of the sheriffdom. It did so on 13 February, entrusting Cumberland and Carlisle castle to the clerk Walter Mauclerc and Pembroke's representative at court, William de

5   RLC, 481b–2; Pipe Roll 1219, 173, 183; Pipe Roll 1221, 95.
6   Pipe Roll 1221, introduction.
7   E 372/66, r.4, m.1.
8   E 372/66, r.14, m.1.
9   BNB, no. 127; Yorks. Fines, 42–3. See above p. 89.

Rughedon.[10] Since Vieuxpont had answered neither for the farm nor, going here far beyond the terms of the agreement, for the rest of the issues of the county, the financial gain from the change was considerable: £289 reached the treasury from Mauclerc's first full year as sheriff.[11]

After the crisis of Christmas 1221, therefore, the government had picked off the last two counties where the sheriffs were not answering for their farms at the exchequer. Since September 1220, Cornwall, Lancashire, Shropshire, Staffordshire, Somerset, Dorset, Lincolnshire and Cumberland had all been brought back within exchequer control. The exchequer failed to get Vieuxpont to account for the back issues of Cumberland and the proceeds of the first eyre vanished into his coffers.[12] Likewise, the exchequer never extracted a penny from Salisbury for Lincolnshire's back farms and eyre issues, which together totalled some £1,420.[13] Nonetheless, a huge transformation had taken place since 1220 in the revenue received from the county farms. In the pipe roll of that year £133 were recorded as reaching the exchequer from that source. In the pipe roll of 1222 the sum was £1,657.[14]

This improvement in the king's financial situation was equally apparent at the Easter exchequer of 1222. Hubert's return to Westminster, after visiting his castle at Skenfrith and spending Easter with the king at Wallingford, coincided exactly with the start of the exchequer's term. The *Adventus Vicecomitum*, on the opening day, produced £558, £413 more than the year before.[15] The total proceeds from the counties, which were recorded on the Easter term's receipt roll, were £3,440, more than £1,000 better than in 1221. Against this background, the government felt strong enough to proceed with the forest eyres which had been abandoned the year before. It was soon to discover that it had overreached itself.

vi. *The Yorkshire protest over the forest eyre, May–June 1222*

In 1221 forest eyres had been commissioned in Yorkshire, Essex, Nottinghamshire, Derbyshire, Northamptonshire and Huntingdonshire but only those in Essex and Huntingdonshire had taken place by April 1222. The Essex eyre, which was held perhaps in the summer of 1221, was, in deference to local feelings, a comparatively restrained

---

[10] *PR*, 326.
[11] *Pipe Rolls of Cumberland*, 6–11.
[12] E 368/4, m.3d; Crook, *General Eyre*, 73.
[13] *Divers Accounts*, 44–6.
[14] The adjusted sum derived from the 1222 roll is £1,473.
[15] *Pipe Roll 1221*, introduction and see Appendix, p. 415.

affair.[1] Feelings were just as strong in Huntingdonshire, where the county had drawn up the great remonstrance in 1220 over the failure to implement the perambulations of 1218 and 1219.[2] On his Huntingdonshire eyre, however, which was scheduled to start in November 1221, Brian de Lisle had gone to work with a will, shielded, no doubt, by Falkes and his under-sheriff. An amercement of 20 marks was imposed on the county for its unlicensed perambulation of 1218 and the amercements as a whole totalled £80 15s 10d, which was two thirds of the sum achieved by the eyre of 1212.[3]

This success encouraged the government to try again with the forest eyres which had been postponed in 1221. On, or soon after, 11 April 1222 Brian de Lisle began his eyre in Northamptonshire, another county where Falkes was sheriff. The amercements assessed totalled some £209, over £20 more than those imposed on the eyre of 1212.[4] Demands for a measure of deforestation were clearly ignored and there were disturbances in the county.[5] Brian next moved on to Yorkshire, intending to start his eyre at the end of May.[6] But the shire was ready for him, or rather not ready, for an important group of barons and knights, most of them former rebels, refused to come to York for the pleas. Those who did come were greeted in the county court by the steward of Nicholas de Stuteville II, the knight Walter of Sowerby, who ordered everyone to depart and appealed to the pope against the attempt to hold the eyre.[7] Stuteville was clearly one leader of the opposition, while others who stayed away included William de Mowbray, Richard de Percy and William de Albini, all members of the committee of twenty-five barons appointed to enforce Magna Carta in 1215. Their protest was understandable. The knights and free tenants who had perambulated Yorkshire's forest in 1220 had included Walter of

[1]   See above p. 252.
[2]   See above pp. 89–90.
[3]   *RLC*, 475b; E 372/66, r.2d, m.2; *Pipe Roll 1212*, 81–2. The eyre had certainly taken place by January 1223 (*PR*, 403) and since the only recorded commission is one for November 1221, it may have gone ahead at that time or soon after, the forest eyres being suspended for a year in June 1222.
[4]   *RLC*, 516, 492; E 372/66, r.6d, m.2; *Pipe Roll 1212*, 134–5.
[5]   *RLC*, 503b.
[6]   *RLC*, 516, 492. Proffers were again accepted for the postponement of the eyre in Nottinghamshire and Derbyshire: Crook, 'The forest boundaries in Nottinghamshire', 37.
[7]   E 372/67, r. 11d, m.2; for Sowerby, see Holt, *Northerners*, 45. His fine was for the contempt of not coming to the pleas of the forest at York and *quia venit in pleno Comitatu apud Eboracum praecipiens omnibus de predicto comitatu quod omnes inde recederent scilicet de placitis forestae ibidem per brevem regis summonitis ubi insuper appellavit ad papam contra libertates Regis*. Nicholas de Stuteville was the younger son of the Nicholas de Stuteville who had died in the war but he inherited some of his father's lands and controlled those of his nephew during the latter's minority: *EYC*, ix, 17–21.

Sowerby himself. They had asserted that Henry II had afforested large parts both of Galtres forest and the forest between the Ouse and the Derwent.[8] Virtually identical claims were made by the perambulators of 1225.[9] These areas, therefore, were due for deforestation under the terms of the Charter of the Forest. But Brian de Lisle ignored all this. Amercements were imposed for hunting between the Ouse and the Derwent and in the forest of Galtres. Robert de Ros and his son were amongst those thus penalized.[10] Probably Brian de Lisle argued that these parts were 'ancient forest', dating back before Henry II's time. Perhaps he was right, but to the men of Yorkshire he seemed to be defying the Charter of the Forest. Indeed, by merely summoning to the pleas those who lived outside the forest, Brian was in breach of the clause in the Charter which confined attendance at the eyre to those living within the forest's bounds. In essence, therefore, Sowerby was appealing for papal help to uphold the Charter of the Forest, an extraordinary turn-about since the time when King John had appealed to Innocent III to quash the Great Charter, but understandable, considering that the legate, Guala, had sealed the Charter of the Forest in company with the regent in 1217.

The protest in the county court of Yorkshire in 1222 over the forest eyre parallels that made there two years before over the levy of the carucage.[11] In both cases the spokesmen were knights, the stewards of the great magnates themselves having refused to appear.[12] In both cases the issue turned on breaches of the Charters: the clause in Magna Carta 1215 stipulating that extraordinary taxation needed consent and the clause in the Charter of the Forest promising deforestation. Both episodes show how deeply rooted the Charters had become amongst the barons and knights who formed the bedrock of English local society.

In Yorkshire the protest over the forest eyre stopped Brian de Lisle almost in his tracks. True, a 50 mark amercement was slapped on Sowerby and one of 40 marks on Stuteville, while amercements of 110 marks were imposed on twelve others involved in the boycott. The men of the wapentakes of Gilling, Hang and Hallikeld, who had also not attended the pleas, were amerced a total of £58 8s 8d. But the rest of the amercements, as recorded in the pipe rolls of 1223, 1224 and 1225,

---

[8]   C 47/11/1, no. 10. See the map below, p. 391.

[9]   C 47/11/1, nos 20, 21. In 1225 deforestation was also demanded in Farndale: see CR 1227-31, 225.

[10]   E 368/5, m.12(1)d; West, Justiciarship, 262, n.1; E 372/67, r. 11d, m.2. The Ros's amercements were also for other unspecified offences.

[11]   See above p. 210.

[12]   Knights and stewards in the early thirteenth-century county court were often one and the same: see Coss, 'Knighthood and the early thirteenth-century county court', 45-57.

totalled only £73 12s 9d, a far cry from the £1,250 imposed on the county by the eyre of 1212.[13]

The reverberations of the crisis in Yorkshire were soon felt at a great council which had gathered in London. The result was an impressive measure of conciliation. Some time in June it was 'provided and conceded *de communi consilio nostro*' to suspend the forest eyres altogether for a year from 24 June.[14]

vii. *The resumption of the demesne, June 1222: success*

The postponement of the forest eyres in June 1222 was part of a process of conciliation which was designed to clear the way for the first general government advance since the end of the war: the resumption of the royal demesne. The resumption succeeded in June 1222 partly because of ideas about the inalienability of the royal demesne, although those ideas had been insufficient to carry through resumptions when they had been attempted before in September 1217, August 1220 and October 1221. The difference in 1222 was that the act was much more carefully set up through a whole series of bargains and concessions. Many of these were designed to mollify the potential losers from the resumption but the postponement of the forest eyres had a wider purpose. Its aim was to conciliate a broad spectrum of magnate and gentry opinion in the counties and thus win support for Hubert's regime, a regime which in other ways too had shown itself acceptable. Hence, at a great council in June 1222, Hubert was able to mobilize Archbishop Langton and the bishops and the magnates of the land behind the act of resumption and thus overcome opposition to it.

During the spring and summer of 1222 the government could concentrate on preparing the way for the resumption undisturbed by troubles further afield. With the consent of the earl of Pembroke and Reginald de Braose, Llywelyn was informed, in April 1222, of the council's determination that the truce should be renewed for another year.[1] From Poitou news arrived that Pandulf had secured a truce with Hugh de Lusignan. This had not been easy. Hugh had succeeded in taking Merpins from Reginald de Pons, while Hugh's ally, William l'Archevêque, the lord of Parthenay, had attacked the persons and properties of the burgesses of Niort. The latter, as visual testimony to their sufferings, sent to England Robert Dent de Fer, whom William had blinded. Hubert, 'moved by God', provided him with a pension of a

---

[13] E 372/67, r.11d, m.2; E 372/68, r.13d, m.2; *RLC.*, ii, 66b; E 372/69, r.9d, m.1; Holt, *Northerners*, 159. Hang, Hallikeld and Gilling were the wapentakes of Richmondshire.

[14] *RLC*, 507b.

[1] *PR*, 331–2.

penny a day and a place in the hospital of St Leonard at York.[2] In
Poitou it was the pope who eventually came to the rescue, excommuni-
cating Hugh and placing his lands under an interdict. These penalties
were lifted when Hugh, probably in March, agreed to the truce and
submitted the matters in dispute to the pope. When news of this
reached England, Hubert and the council, on 13 April, restored Hugh
to his wife's dower.[3]

Free from distraction, therefore, the government strove to create the
political conditions where an act of resumption was possible. How far
the aftermath of the Christmas crisis helped or hindered here is difficult
to say. Conceivably, Langton's intervention and the various bargains
of January and February 1222 (if such they were) had engendered a
spirit of reconciliation. On the other hand, there is evidence that in
March 1222 Bishop Peter planned to dislodge Hubert by having the
pope declare the king capable of rule. Master William de Sancto
Albino, who left England for the papal court soon after 25 March, may
have been charged with such a mission.[4] In the event Bishop Peter's
plans came to nothing for the moment because the papacy ignored his
suggestion or request, but it may be that the bishop's evident
co-operation with Hubert in the early summer of 1222 was designed to
lure the latter into a false sense of security. On the surface, however, by
May 1222 Hubert had achieved a working relationship with his
enemies and created the atmosphere in which an act of resumption
might proceed.

Hubert had remained in London for the whole period from 12 April
to early July, save for a few days in May when he hurried to Wallingford
to celebrate Whitsun with the king. He clearly carried the main burden
of day-to-day government, in May and June acting as sole authorizor
for some 117 letters close and patent, as well as sitting at the exchequer
and intervening at the bench.[5] But he also co-operated closely with the
council, with which he authorized around thirty royal letters, many of
them involving important acts of patronage. The earl of Chester was
involved with four letters in this period and Peter with no less than
twenty, authorizing fifteen in company with Hubert, the last time that
the two ministers acted together in this way on any scale.[6]

It was Peter, indeed, on 7 May, who attested and authorized, with
the council (virtually the only time that this formula appears), the writ
of *liberate* which gave Hubert his £1,000 a year for the keeping of Dover

---

[2] F, 169; DD, no. 109; RLC, 492b–3, 509b; *Pipe Roll 1230*, 55.

[3] *F 169;* PR, 329–31; RLC, 492b.

[4] See below pp. 303–4.

[5] RLC, 498b; E 368/4, m.2(2)d for Hubert at the exchequer. For the bench, see
below p. 281.

[6] RLC, 494b–503b, 516–516b; PR, 332–5, 344.

9. The castle of Montgomery. Roger of Wendover records that the site found for the new castle in 1223 'seemed impregnable to everyone'.

10. The keep of Skenfrith castle. Hubert de Burgh gained possession of the castles of Skenfrith, Whitecastle and Grosmont (The Three Castles) in 1219. He visited Skenfrith on several occasions during the minority and probably built the keep during these years.

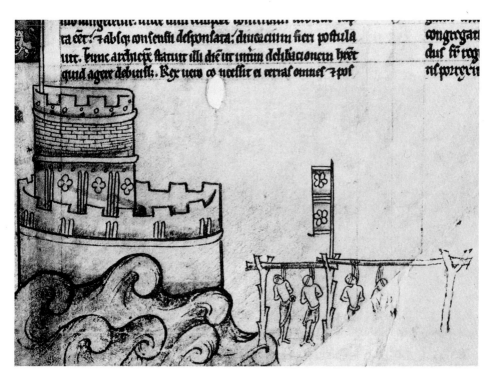

ta ēēr̄ : ꝶ ablệ conſenſu deſponſata : diuuacium̄ fier̄ poſtula
uit. hunc archieꝓ ſtatuit illi die ur̄ inim̄ deliberacionem̄ hr̄ē
quid agere debuiſti. Rex uero co n̄ceſſit et ceteraſ omneſ ꝶ poſ

11. Matthew Paris's drawing of the hanging of the garrison of Bedford castle in 1224. Falkes de Bréauté's coat of arms flies over the gallows.

12. The Close Roll for December 1223 at the point where the king took over the attestation of royal letters. The relevant line, three from the bottom, reads (with abbreviations expanded): *Teste me ipso* (attested or witnessed by myself) *apud Westmonasterium decimo die Decembris anno eodem coram* (in the presence of) *domino Archiepiscopo Cantuariensi et H. de Burgo Justiciario nostro et R. Sarresburiensi et J. Bathoniensi Episcopis*. This may be compared with the earlier form, three lines above, where a letter is *T[este] H. [de Burgo]* (attested by Hubert de Burgh) at the Tower of London on 9 December.

The attestor was the person who took ultimate responsibility for the letter. Frequently a further note stated that a letter was *per* (through) some named individual, thus indicating who had given immediate authorisation for its issue.

13. Effigy (c. 1230s) in Salisbury cathedral of William Longespee,
earl of Salisbury (d. 1226).

14. Matthew Paris's drawing of Falkes de Bréauté's death in 1226. The devil (his head lost through a trimming of the MS) feeds him a poisoned fish. Falkes's shield, upturned, is shown in the left margin.

15. Magna Carta 1225. This is the copy sent to Wiltshire which was ultimately deposited by the knights of the county in Lacock Abbey. It is now in the British Library. The Charter is authenticated with Henry III's great seal, which was made for him in 1218.

castle.[7] This was part, moreover, of a more general settlement. On or around the same day, important concessions were made to Brian de Lisle, Geoffrey de Neville, the earls of Chester and Pembroke and the count of Aumale; the relevant royal letter, in the last case, being authorized by Hubert, Peter and the council, a unique formula. A week later, Hubert, Peter, the earl of Chester, William Brewer and 'others of the council' authorized the writ which quitclaimed Engelard de Cigogné of a large number of debts.[8]

Hubert's return from the Whitsun celebrations at Wallingford coincided with the opening of the Trinity exchequer.[9] On 12 June, acting with the council, he removed Robert de Courtenay from the sheriffdom of Devon, a major victory for Falkes, who had tried, and failed, to oust Courtenay in 1218.[10] At the same time Hubert watched carefully over the case at the bench which had arisen from Falkes's attempt to enforce what he thought were the rights of the king in his sheriffdoms against the earls of Pembroke and Gloucester. On 19 June Hubert and the council authorized a writ respiting the shrieval demands against the earls until the end of October and, when the case appeared at the bench ten days later, it was likewise postponed until Michaelmas 'through default of the jurors and by order of the chief justiciar'.[11]

By the middle of June a large body of lay and ecclesiastical magnates had assembled at Westminster. They secured the postponement of the forest eyres discussed above and sanctioned the levy of a poll tax, carefully related to ability to pay, to succour the king of Jerusalem.[12] It was in this setting of individual bargains, concessions to the kingdom and co-operation over the Holy Land that the act of resumption proceeded.

On 24 June the king explained, in a royal letter, that it had been 'provided by the counsel of the archbishop of Canterbury and the bishops of England and Hubert de Burgh, our justiciar, and our earls and barons that all our demesnes should be taken into our hands as from 11 June last'. By 24 June the earl of Salisbury had already come before the king's council and surrendered the manors of Writtle, Finedon, Cheltenham, Awre and Newnham. His example was followed by Engelard de Cigogné, who surrendered the manors of Windsor, Cookham and Bray, Odiham, Benson and Henley; by Philip Mark,

---

[7] *RLC*, 495b.

[8] *RLC*, 495b, 496, 497.

[9] *Pipe Roll 1221*, introduction.

[10] *PR*, 333; *RLC*, 499. See above p. 79.

[11] *RLC*, 500; *CRR*, x, 333.

[12] *RLC*, 516b. Each earl was to pay three marks, each baron one mark, each knight one shilling, each free tenant one penny and the landless, who had chattels worth half a mark, also a penny. The tax was to be paid over three years. It does not seem to have raised a large sum: see Mitchell, *Taxation*, 141–2.

who gave up Derby, Edwinstowe, Ragnall and Carlton; the earl of Derby, who vacated Melbourne; and John d'Athée, who resigned Kingston upon Thames. On 24 June itself the sheriffs were given a specific list of the demesnes which they should take into the king's hands. Including the lands that had already been formally surrendered, this embraced forty-nine properties held by thirty-seven separate individuals or institutions. Apart from those involved in the formal surrender between 12 and 24 June, the victims included the earl of Pembroke and the count of Aumale (who was deprived once again of Driffield), Falkes, Robert de Courtenay, Geoffrey de Neville, Walter de Lacy, Walter de Verdun, Godfrey of Crowcombe and Thomas Basset. This was not, therefore, a resumption carried out on any party basis.[13]

The aim behind the act was clearly to keep the resumed lands in the king's hands and make money from them. The sheriffs were to account at the exchequer and inform it 'how much the land can be worth, and what improvements can be made for our benefit'.[14] In general this aim was achieved, although not in so sweeping a style as the act had seemed to promise. In at least fifteen cases the properties nominated for resumption remained with, or were quickly recovered by, the previous tenants on terms which brought no financial benefit to the crown. In seven cases this seems to have been after some formal inspection of title.[15] In others, royal servants managed to hold on to properties on the grounds that they needed their revenues to support castles or other legitimate activities. Thus Falkes quickly recovered Hertford and was conceded its farm to sustain the castle; Henry de Hauvill continued to enjoy the revenues of Brigstock in order to maintain the king's falcons;[16] and Engelard de Cigogné, after a struggle, recovered all the properties that he had surrendered and paid not a penny for them into the exchequer.[17]

[13] C 60/16, m.4, printed in *Pipe Roll 1221*, appendix.

[14] C 60/16, m.4.

[15] The mill of Marden (Heref.), William fitz William; the wood of Marden, Nicholas Seculer; Fawsley (Northants.), Hugh Russell; Burton (in Fordington, Dorset), Hamo of Burton; Whitwell (a member of Fordington), Robert Chauntemerle; Sutton (in Woking, Surrey), Gilbert Basset; Brokehampton (in Kineton, Warw.), Ralph de Trubleville: *RLC*, 518, 527; C 60/16, m.2; *RLC*, 503b–4b, 511, 505. Most of these tenants produced charters of John, although Gilbert Basset only held from him *de ballio*.

[16] *RLC*, 504b; *RLC*, ii, 31b.

[17] See below p. 293. Other cases where the effects of the act were nullified were: Shrivenham (Berks.), the earls of Pembroke and Salisbury and their tenants, discussed below; Bere Regis (Dorset), the earl of Pembroke: *RLC*, 506; Marden and Lugwardine (Heref.), Walter de Lacy (these manors seem to have been within the county farm both before and after the act; perhaps the intention was for Walter de Lacy, who was sheriff, to account for them outside the farm; see also *RLC*, 575b); Rugeley and Cannock (Staffs.), bishop of Coventry. See also *RLC*, 506, for land in Waltham (Lincs.) not specifically mentioned in the writ of 24 June.

In other cases, however, the act of resumption had more edge. In all, twenty-four properties covered by its scythe produced revenue for the king for the financial year Michaelmas 1222 to Michaelmas 1223 in the pipe roll of 1223. Of this revenue £536 was received directly by the exchequer and £68 was expended locally.[18] Another £49 were apparently contributed within the county farms.[19] Thus the act of resumption had increased the king's annual income by some £600. At the same time, in the pipe roll for 1223, demesnes resumed piecemeal since 1219 contributed around £290 to the exchequer for the year 1222–23,[20] while those within the county farm may have been worth some £117.[21] The total cash revenue from the demesnes outside the county farms recorded in the pipe rolls of 1218 and 1219 was £2,419, an average between the rolls of £1,210. Thereafter, if one takes the figures adjusted for doubled and missing accounts, the cash revenue increased in the rolls as follows: £1,805 for 1220; £2,370 for 1221; £2,694 for 1222; £3,668 for 1223. The cash revenue from the demesne had, therefore, increased threefold since the first years after the war.

In 1222 some of the properties embraced by the resumption were eventually allowed to remain in the hands of their previous tenants, who now paid money into the exchequer. This was the case with Falkes in respect of Essendon and Bayford; Philip Mark in respect of Carlton and Edwinstowe; and William de Cantilupe in respect of Calne. The earl of Salisbury, however, vacated entirely the properties which he had

[18] The manors and their tenants were: Newport, Ralph de Toeny (Essex); Writtle, the earl of Salisbury (Essex); Essendon and Bayford (Herts.), Falkes; Cheltenham and Westall, Newnham, Awre (Gloucs.), the earl of Salisbury; Dymock (Gloucs.), Walter of Clifford; Slaughter (Gloucs.), Thomas Basset; Apethorpe (Northants.), Baldwin de Gisnes; Finedon (Northants.), the earl of Salisbury; Carlton, Edwinstowe (Notts.), Philip Mark; Carlton in Lindrick (Notts.), Gerard de la Barre; Mansfield (Notts.), Adam de St Martin; Bolsover and the Peak, Melbourne (Derby), the earl of Derby; Derby, Philip Mark; Kingston upon Thames (Surrey), John d'Athée; Calne (Wilts.), William de Cantilupe; Driffield (Yorks.), the count of Aumale. I have included Bolsover and the Peak (as one property) and Calne here, although they were not specifically mentioned in the writ of 24 June.

[19] Selborne (Hants.), Robert de Bareville; Bloxham (Oxon.), Walter de Verdun; [Pitney and Wearne in] Somerton (Som.), Godfrey of Crowcombe; Bere Regis (Dorset), Geoffrey de Neville.

[20] Chesterton (Cambs.); Grimsby (Lincs.); Corby, Gretton, King's Cliffe, Geddington (Northants.); Newcastle upon Tyne, Corbridge (Northumb.); Westhall (Suff.). See above pp. 222, 253, 199, 226. For Westhall (where I have made some adjustment of the figures since it accounted in the 1223 roll for more than one year), see RLC, 443b; E 372/67, r.6, m.1. The money figure would have been larger, perhaps by some £250, had there been an account for Hampshire and thus for Basingstoke, Portsmouth and Southampton in the 1223 roll: see Pipe Roll 1219, 24, 35–6; Pipe Roll 1221, 16, 26, 28; E 372/66, r.7d, m.1; E 372/68, r.1, mm.1, 2; C 60/12, m.6; RLC, 424, 455b, 472, 478, 482b, 523b.

[21] Torksey, Caistor (Lincs.); Bamburgh (Northumb.); Marlborough (Wilts.). See above pp. 253, 226, 247 and for Caistor, see RLC, ii, 5; RLC, 423b, 487b, 515.

surrendered. So did many other lords; for example, the earl of Derby (Melbourne), John d'Athée (Kingston upon Thames), Geoffrey de Neville (Bere), Godfrey of Crowcombe (Pitney and Wearne), Ralph de Toeny (Newport Pagnell), Baldwin de Gisnes (Apethorpe), Thomas Basset (Slaughter), Gerard de la Barre (Carlton in Lindrick), Walter de Verdun (Bloxham), the count of Aumale (Driffield), Adam de St Martin (Mansfield) and Walter of Clifford (Dymock). Some of the manors thus liberated, as well as others which had come earlier into the king's hands, were committed in the course of 1222–23 to their men at farm: for example, Cheltenham, Finedon, Dymock, Bulwell, Driffield, Havering and Marlborough. The justiciar was closely involved in this, for he frequently authorized the writs setting the terms of such tenancies.[22]

The financial gains from the new policy were to some extent illusory. Although John d'Athée, for example, no longer drew his annual £50 from the farm of Kingston upon Thames, he was given writs of *liberate* for the same sum to be paid to him from the exchequer.[23] The farms which the men of Derby and Edwinstowe paid into the exchequer at Michaelmas 1222 and Easter 1223 were given, in whole or part, to Philip Mark, although thereafter Mark had to be content with an annual £5 received from the men of Bulwell.[24] The essential point was that the government had broken the grip which great men had held on the royal demesne since the war. It could now manage the demesne as it wished and control far more closely than before how the revenue from it was spent.

The person who was hardest hit by the act of resumption was undoubtedly the earl of Derby, who was asked to give up, in June 1222, not merely the manor of Melbourne but also the castles of Bolsover and the Peak. In one sense Derby had little cause for complaint since these properties had been conceded to him until the completion of the king's fourteenth year but the earl's driving ambition was to secure Bolsover and the Peak, the heart of the Peverel inheritance, in hereditary right. Between 1217 and 1222 he had indeed behaved as though he held them in perpetuity.[25] In June 1222 Derby surrendered the royal manor of Melbourne with as much grace as he could muster but the pill of Bolsover and the Peak he could not swallow. Shortly before 27 June he appeared before the king in the chapel of St Katherine at Westminster, the twelfth-century infirmary chapel of the monks which was frequently used for important meetings. Derby begged for delay. He would return

[22] C 60/18, mm. 6, 7, 8, 10.

[23] *RLC*, 520b, 544b, 565, 610.

[24] *RLC*, 531b, 546; C 60/18, m.5. For compensation received by Luke de Drumare and Adam de St Martin, see *RLC*, 487b, 504.

[25] See above p. 124.

home to speak to his men and then surrender the castles. This request, however, was refused and he was told to appear again next day before the king and the council. Instead, early the next morning Derby left London without speaking to the king.[26] The parallels with the count of Aumale's unlicensed departure from the Christmas court of 1221 are obvious. Both men had been ordered to give up castles to which they cherished deeply felt claims of right. Derby, however, did not go on the rampage. Like the earl of Chester, his brother-in-law and ally, his whole career had been based on loyal service to the Angevins. His gains had been considerable, even if he could not keep Bolsover and the Peak.[27] The government did not panic. Letters, one of which was authorized by Hubert, were sent after him, expressing the king's displeasure and insisting he surrender the castles.[28] Gradually Derby was reeled in. By February 1223 the government was able to commit the castles and honours of Bolsover and the Peak to Brian de Lisle (from whom the Peak had been prized for Derby in 1217) at an annual farm of £100.[29]

Derby's lot was particularly severe because he alone, in June 1222, had been ordered to surrender castles. But others caught by the act might well have claimed that their tenure, in different ways, was soundly based. Engelard de Cigogné, for example, had been granted Benson and Henley in 1218 by the regent, the legate, Bishop Peter, the bishop of Worcester, Falkes and William Brewer, to sustain him in the 'great service' that he was giving the king.[30] The manors surrendered by the earl of Salisbury had been assigned to him in 1218 in fulfilment, so it was said, of King John's promise to give him £500 worth of land.[31] Even harder was the lot of Philip Mark, since he had been granted Derby, Carlton and Edwinstowe until the king came of age, which had certainly not happened in June 1222.[32] And then there was the count of Aumale, deprived once more of Driffield where John, in August 1215, had rendered him 'the right which he has' (whatever that was) in the manor and taken his homage for it.[33]

The forces moving behind the resumption of June 1222 must have been very great in order to overturn, as well as they did, tenure entrenched in this way. One force was clearly the nature of the royal demesne itself. There was a growing sense, in the early thirteenth

[26] *RLC*, 502–502b.
[27] Golob, 'The Ferrers earls of Derby', 191–8.
[28] *RLC*, 502–502b.
[29] *PR*, 365; C 60/18, m.8.
[30] *RLC*, 403–403b.
[31] *RLC*, 364–364b, 365b.
[32] *PR*, 21; *RLC*, 342; see above p. 68.
[33] *RLP*, 154.

century, that the royal demesne manors formed a *corpus* of land peculiarly attached to the crown.[34] Thus the Great Charter of 1215 exempted the king's 'demesne manors' from the requirement that counties and hundreds should be held at the ancient farm without any increment. There was as yet no hard and fast rule that the royal demesne was inalienable. King Henry, between 1227 and 1234, granted away several royal demesne manors in hereditary right in return for various services.[35] But the idea of inalienability was gaining ground.[36] It could be embraced within the clause in the coronation oath, which enjoined the king to maintain the rights of the crown and recover those which had been lost.[37] A quite specific statement of the concept had already appeared in a legal treatise, which was put together in John's reign: 'the king ought rightfully to preserve and defend . . . all lands of the crown of the kingdom in all integrity and without diminution'.[38] That the royal demesne had a continuing and unextinguishable life was implied in the law book *Bracton*, which was being drafted in the 1220s. This stated that the peasants (*glebae ascripticii*) of the royal demesne retained their special privileges, 'no matter in whose hands the king's demesne may come'.[39] The same idea was given added force by John's practice, for, although he made permanent alienations of the demesne, he usually did so in return for money farms. This meant that the manors were still, in a sense, part of the demesne, contributing revenue to the king and remaining liable to tallage.[40] Although the demesne had always been used as a source of patronage, there was clearly also a feeling that it should provide for the king's support. This view was powerfully expressed by the pope in 1220. It was precisely the detention of the king's 'castles, manors, vills and other demesnes' which meant that he 'laboured under such great need' that he could 'scarcely or never provide for royal magnificence'. Those detaining the king's possessions were 'revelling on the royal goods while the king begs'.[41]

Against the background of these ideas, the use of the demesne to support not the king but great men in his service, however valuable that

---

[34] For the royal demesne in the twelfth and thirteenth centuries, see Hoyt, *Royal Demesne*, chs iv, v, vi; Wolffe, *Royal Demesne*, chs i, ii; Hallam, *Domesday Book*, 74–7, 95–7.

[35] Examples include Pitney and Wearne; Finedon; Wrockwardine; Apethorpe: *CChR*, 115, 116, 119, 132, 134.

[36] This is discussed in Hoyt, *Royal Demesne*, 140–8; Wolffe, *Royal Demesne* 40–51; Harriss, *King, Parliament and Public Finance*, 134–43.

[37] Richardson, 'The coronation', 151–61.

[38] *Die Gesetz*, 635; for the date, see Harriss, *King, Parliament and Public Finance*, 135 n.1.

[39] *Bracton*, ii, 37.

[40] Hoyt, *Royal Demesne*, 147. See, for example, the cases of Headington and High Wycombe: *RCh*, 109b.

[41] *RL*, 535.

service might be, was increasingly hard to justify. That must have seemed especially so for Langton and the bishops, sworn as they were to uphold the inalienability of their own episcopal properties.[42] Laymen too appreciated that it might be difficult to secure permanent hold of royal demesne. This was why Philip of Oldcoates was so anxious to exchange the £300 worth of land which he held from the demesne for £300 worth of escheats.[43] It cannot be said, however, that the clarity of the issue carried through the resumption *nem con*. After all, the issue had been exactly the same in 1217, 1220 and 1221, when acts of resumption had sunk without trace. In 1222 there were other factors which kept it afloat.

One was quite clearly the whole series of concessions and bargains which had continued from January to June 1222. These had created a climate in which an act of resumption might be agreed. In effect the count of Aumale was bought out of Driffield by the confirmation of King John's pardon of the £2,333 6s 8d outstanding from his mother's fine to have her inheritance and by the quittance, arranged by Peter and Hubert, of £350 owed for Driffield's back farms since the war.[44] There was also a major concession implicit in the act itself. Unlike the acts of 1220 and 1221, which had lumped demesnes and escheats together, it was concerned solely with the royal demesne. This naturally enhanced the clarity of the issue and reduced the number of potential losers. In particular it left virtually intact the ring which the earls of Pembroke and Salisbury and Hubert de Burgh had formed around that great escheat, the lands and the honour of the count of Perche. Hubert himself, with no royal demesne manors held during the king's pleasure, had thus nothing to lose from the act. The one former Perche property which came within its scope was the royal demesne manor of Shrivenham, which the earls of Pembroke and Salisbury had by 1222 granted to Reginald de Blancmuster, Eudo fitz Warin and Warin de Munchensy, the last having married Pembroke's youngest sister.[45] These three men were the tenants mentioned in the writ of 24 June. But here the act was simply not implemented, the sheriff of Berkshire either never taking possession of Shrivenham or returning it immediately to the earls' tenants.[46] Ultimately, with the rest of the Perche lands, it was granted by the king to Pembroke and to Salisbury's son in hereditary right.[47]

[42] Kantorowicz, 'Inalienability', 488–502; Richardson, 'The coronation', 151–3.

[43] C 60/12, m.8.

[44] E 372/66, r.10, m.1. Although Aumale did not have the writ in *RLC*, 496, the pardon of his mother's fine is recorded in *Pipe Roll 1221*, 125.

[45] *RH*, i, 13b; *VCH Berks*, iv, 532.

[46] I deduce this from the pipe rolls where there is no evidence of Shrivenham coming into the king's hands.

[47] *CChR*, 102.

Even confined to the royal demesne, the act was carefully targeted. The manors to be seized were individually specified. There was no attempt to resume manors which former kings had conceded in hereditary right. There was equally no attempt, as there had been in September 1221, to achieve a general resumption of the demesne which had been in King John's hands at the beginning of the war. The act thus made concessions to the feeling that John's grants had some continuing validity, even though they had been made during the king's pleasure. (When John Marshal learnt that his tenure of Feckenham was under threat in 1221 he told Hubert at once that it had been granted him by King John to sustain him in the king's service.)[48] Even in respect of manors conceded by King Henry, on which the act was centred, there was some selectivity. Thus the earl of Chester's familiar, Henry of Audley, retained Edgmond unchallenged, although he held it merely during the king's pleasure under a writ of 1220. Audley was protected in 1222 to good purpose. Five years later, the king granted him Edgmond in hereditary right in return for a mewed sparrow hawk a year.[49]

Even with these compromises, however, the act was scarcely unresisted, as Engelard de Cigogné's successful evasions show. Essentially men surrendered the demesne because they were made to by the pressure exerted on them by the great council of June 1222. Those enjoying the royal demesne, it needs to be remembered, were comparatively small in number. A much larger group of barons and bishops held no demesne at all and doubtless they made up the majority of those attending the council. Many present were probably former rebels from the north, hence the successful pressure to suspend the forest eyres after the protest in Yorkshire, a concession which must have done much to enlist support for the regime over the resumption. The emphatic endorsement of the great council met, of course, one of the chief excuses that men had adduced for disobeying the king's orders, namely that only measures sanctioned by great councils of magnates had authority. But the great council also revealed the

[48] SC 1/1, no. 140. The act embraced only three properties which John had given away, in two cases during the war and one in 1213–14: the victims here were respectively the count of Aumale (Driffield), Walter of Clifford junior (Dymock) and Gerard de la Barre (Carlton in Lindrick). By contrast, John Marshal and the earl of Salisbury's familiar, William Talbot, remained untouched in respectively Hingham and Hintlesham, which John had granted them during the king's pleasure in 1213. Salisbury himself kept Andover, Droitwich, Bromsgrove and Braunton, which John had given him in August 1215: *RLP*, 154; *RLC*, 282b; *Pipe Roll 1214*, 156, 168; *RLC*, 223b, 224b. Likewise, Philip de Albini held on to Chewton Mendip which John had granted him during pleasure in the same month: *RLC*, 226.

[49] E 368/3, m.2(3); *Pipe Roll 1220*, 176; *CChR*, 55. In 1213–14 Edgmond had been within the county farm.

potential physical force which could be brought to bear on recalcit-
rants, rather in the same way as had the coronation of 1220 through the
oath taken by the barons to wage war against those who refused to
surrender the king's 'castles and wards'. Thus the resumption had the
same pattern as the assertions of government authority over Newark,
Mitford and Bytham, where the centre had rallied forces from outside
the regime in order to assert its will over Robert de Gaugi, Philip of
Oldcoates and the count of Aumale.

Langton and the bishops had prepared the way for the resumption
by defusing the Christmas crisis of 1221 and had given vital support to
its actual realization in June 1222. That the act was Langton's
initiative, however, is less clear. Resumption of the demesne had been
on the government's agenda since the end of the war. There had been
attempts to achieve it in 1217, 1220 and 1221. On the last occasion the
initiative was probably Hubert's. Equally, Hubert must have been at
the heart of the detailed bargains and concessions which were made in
April and May 1222. In a wider sense, moreover, the act succeeded
because of the nature of Hubert's rule. The dispensation of justice, the
conciliation of former rebels and the readiness to withdraw unpopular
measures created a form of government that men were prepared to
support.

viii. *The emergence of the king and the London riots, July 1222*

With the resumption of the royal demesne under way, a considerable
part of the programme set out in the papal letters of 1219, 1220 and
1221 had been achieved. The most intractable problem of all, however,
that of the resumption of the castles and sheriffdoms, remained.
Conferring power on an altogether different scale from demesne
manors, men were far less ready to give them up. Many of the great
governors of the minority, moreover, had been been appointed by
King John and believed that they were obliged to keep their custodies
safe until the king came of age. The resumption of the castles
and sheriffdoms, therefore, could scarcely be tackled until the king
was either declared of age or, in some other way, had assumed
power.

Hubert himself took no initiative to change the *status quo* in this area.
That was not surprising. The king's coming of age might be like the
explosion of a bomb, demolishing the whole structure of local and
central government. Unless Hubert could drop the bomb on his
enemies, or alternatively see that it was exploded safely, he might find
himself amongst the wreckage. The circumstances of the explosion
needed to be very carefully set up. Hubert made his preparations by
strengthening his hold over the king. Meanwhile, he was fully occupied

following through the resumption of the demesne, maintaining the peace of the kingdom and protecting the rights of the crown.

After the resumption of the demesne in June 1222, Hubert visited his castle of Skenfrith and met the earl of Pembroke at St Briavels. He probably tried to sort out the latter's dispute with the earl of Gloucester over the castle of Dinas Powys in Glamorgan.[1] There is no sign that Hubert had Bishop Peter with him on this visit to Wales but he *was* accompanied by the king. Indeed, the tour marked an important stage in the king's political emergence and probably also in his relationship with his justiciar, for, under the aegis of Hubert, who authorized all the relevant writs, Henry began, for the first time in his reign, to dispense the gifts of wine, timber and game so central to the largesse of medieval kingship. Thus at Wimborne Minster, on 24 July, Henry gave a cask of wine to the household official, Adam of Stowell, and, later on the same day at Corfe, two deer to William de Cantilupe junior, the son of his steward. At Devizes on 27 July he presented fifty oaks to William Brewer and, the following day at Malmesbury, gave firewood to the abbot of Stanley and timber, towards a new roof for her church, to the prioress of Kington. Over the Bristol channel at St Briavels, on 5 August, he gave five deer to the earl of Pembroke and, two days later, back at Gloucester, two deer to Walter of Clifford, who was in the process of evacuating the royal manor of Dymock.[2]

The king could also admire Hubert's determination to dispense justice and maintain the rights of the crown against the greatest in the land. Thus, on 28 July, Hubert authorized a writ which expressed the king's astonishment that the bishop of Salisbury had been hunting in the royal forest of La Rugge. He was to desist 'until you have shown us in all haste . . . whatever reason or warrant you have, and then we will do to you what is just. Meanwhile, however, you are on no account to hunt there.'[3]

When Hubert was at Oxford, on his way back from Wales, disturbing news arrived from London. A riot had occurred between the citizens and the men of the abbot of Westminster. What was particularly alarming, according to Matthew Paris's later account which perhaps came from Hubert himself, was that the leader of the Londoners, Constantine fitz Athulf, 'a great man in the city', had raised memories of the civil war by shouting in a loud voice the French battle cry 'Mountjoy, Mountjoy' and, even more provokingly, 'Let God and our Lord Louis help us'.[4] This Francophile feeling was understandable. Louis's behaviour had won golden opinions from the Londoners,

---

[1] *PR*, 346.

[2] *RLC*, 506–507b; C 60/18, m.7.

[3] *RLC*, 517.

[4] *Chron. Maj.*, 71–3; *Ann. Mon.*, iii, 78–9 for what follows.

while the king's government had forced them to pay a 2,000 mark fine for lifting the interdict imposed during the war.[5]

On hearing of the disorders, Hubert moved with speed. Leaving Oxford on 11 August, he was at the Tower of London two days later. He summoned the mayor and citizens before him and demanded to know who was responsible for the outrages. When Constantine arrogantly stood forward and boasted of his exploits, Hubert had him arrested on the spot 'without any tumult'. The following day Falkes, on Hubert's orders, took Constantine up river and thence to execution at Tyburn. Hubert and Falkes then entered the city in force and made a series of arrests. Eventually the mayor was deposed, hostages were taken for London's good behaviour and the citizens were reconciled to the king on the payment of a large fine.[6] 'Constantine fitz Athulf was hanged and without judgement' complained a London chronicle. The element of arbitrariness in Hubert's behaviour long rankled in the city.[7] Hubert's own view is probably reflected in Matthew Paris's final comment on the episode: 'Constantine was a criminal and deserved to be hung'.[8]

Having settled matters in London, Hubert set out on a tour of his possessions in the eastern counties, spending 26–28 August at Rayleigh. Bishop Peter accompanied him and the two ministers co-operated together over the question of Hugh de Lusignan. In June 1222 Pope Honorius, acting under the terms of the settlement which Pandulf had reached with Hugh, had told the latter to return the *maritagium* of Henry's sister to the king and surrender the castle of Merpins. If he failed to do this before 30 November the sentence of excommunication would be reimposed. At the same time, the government had issued letters of safe-conduct for Hugh to come to England to do homage to the king and reach a general settlement.[9] By August Hugh's reply had arrived, borne by Bartholomew de Puy. A mere letter of safe-conduct was far from enough. As though he was some pope or emperor, he demanded that Peter and the earl of Chester come to Gascony and meet him at St Macaire. If this was intended to be a refusal to come at all, Hubert and Peter called Hugh's bluff: a measure of the importance that they attached to reaching a settlement with him. Thus, although it was 'disagreeable' to the king, Hugh was told that, in the last resort, Peter would come to St Macaire. The king's letter to

[5] *Liber de Antiquis Legibus*, 203–4. By the Hilary term of 1223 payments by the Londoners had more than cleared the 2,000 mark fine: E 368/5, m.13(1)d.

[6] I can find no record evidence of the fine, which may consequently have been paid cash down. For the hostages, see *RLC*, 569.

[7] *Liber de Antiquis Legibus*, 5, 205; see also *Ann. Mon.*, ii, 297; *Chron. Maj.*, 223.

[8] *Flores Hist.*, ii, 176.

[9] *F*, 169; *PR*, 334.

Hugh concluded: 'united in sincere love, and thus made the stronger, we will be able to resist the more firmly those who strive to attack us, than if, which God avert, we are parted by discord'.[10] The events of the next two years were to prove this rather obvious assertion only too true.

ix. *The Michaelmas exchequer of 1222; Wales; Poitou*

Hubert returned to London from the eastern counties in time for the Michaelmas bench and exchequer. This was one of the most important sessions of the exchequer since the end of the war, for it consolidated the recent advances in bringing the sheriffdoms and the royal demesne under the king's control. The accounts for Cumberland, Lincolnshire and Cornwall, counties for which the sheriffs had not previously answered at all since the war, or had not answered for the farm, were taken in succession in October. Discussions took place at all the county audits about manors whose seizure had been ordered in the summer, or which had so far escaped seizure. As a result, the exchequer memoranda rolls for 1222–23 have a very different appearance from those earlier in the reign. At the Yorkshire account, for example, which began on 31 October, the future of Driffield was considered and on 13 November the king, by a writ which Hubert authorized, accepted a proffer of 20 marks from the men of the manor to hold it at a farm of £72.[1] During the Cumberland account, Hubert moved to protect the men of the royal demesne manors in the county from the burdens imposed by the far too numerous officials of Thomas of Moulton, who was custodian of the Cumberland forest in right of his wife. In so doing, he indicated once again how the interests of the king should go hand in hand with just and moderate government. Moulton was told, in a letter authorized by Hubert, that his activities brought profit to himself but damage to the king. Henceforth, he was to oppress neither the men from the royal demesne nor those from elsewhere in his bailiwick. His 'great and unjust exactions' must cease.[2]

The government's increasing grip over its sheriffdoms and manors was reflected in the pipe roll for 1222, where the cash revenue recorded, if the figures are adjusted for doubled and missing accounts, was £10,340, over £2,000 more than the year before and nearly £5,000 more than the roll of 1220. Particularly striking was the improvement in the cash revenue from the county farms. On an adjusted basis, this totalled

---

[10] *F*, 167–8; *PR*, 339.

[1] E 368/5, m.6; C 60/18, m.10. Knight, 'Pipe Roll 6 Henry III', 200, sets out the dates for the county accounts in 1222–23. The Cornwall account is headed in the memoranda roll 'the first after the war'.

[2] *RLC*, 513. This letter is dated 16 October. The hearing of the account for Cumberland began the day before.

£1,473 in the roll of 1222, as against £563 in the roll of 1221 and only £133 in that of 1220. Nor was this transformation achieved simply because the sheriffs were spending less of their farms in the localities, the amount thus spent in the roll of 1222, to take the adjusted figures, being only some £150 less than the year before.

During the busy months of October and November Hubert authorized alone some 200 letters close and patent but he co-operated with the council over appointments and patronage, and secured Bishop Peter's consent to the concession of his annual fees as castellan of Dover and justiciar.[3] In this period, however, Peter was involved in the attestation or authorization of a bare five writs.[4] That there was friction between him and Hubert is suggested by their conflicting decisions over the future of Odiham manor, which Engelard de Cigogné was supposed to have surrendered under the act of resumption. On 21 October Hubert authorized a writ which conceded Odiham to the men of the manor at an annual farm of £50.[5] The following month this decision was reversed. A writ attested by Hubert, but authorized significantly by Peter and William Brewer, returned the manor to Engelard, while stipulating that he should answer for the annual £50 farm. But although the men of Odiham complained of his oppression, Engelard failed to account for the manor and was finally pardoned the outstanding farm in 1227.[6] Engelard equally managed to retain or recover the manors of Benson, Windsor, and Cookham and Bray which he had surrendered on or soon after 12 June 1222. Although, by a decision of Hubert and the council, he was supposed to account for the last three, he never did so. Accounts for Windsor, and Cookham and Bray, as for Odiham, had to wait until they came into Hubert's hands in 1224.[7]

The influence that Peter, Chester and Falkes could still wield is equally seen in three decisions over Welsh affairs which were implemented in writs of 11 November. All impinged on the interests of the earl of Pembroke, who was absent at this time in Ireland. The first writ, which Hubert authorized, ordered Llywelyn to give Falkes custody of Cemais under the terms of the treaty of Worcester, Falkes being the custodian of the lordship during the minority of the fitz Martin heir, who was his nephew. This was all fairly academic since there was little chance of Llywelyn complying, but Pembroke cannot have welcomed

---

[3] *RLC*, 515b, 526b; for the council, see for example *RLC*, 515, 518, 520b, 521b; *PR*, 341, 349, 350, 352; C 60/18, m.10 (grant of a wardship to Henry of Audley).

[4] *RLC*, 515b, 518b, 522b.

[5] C 60/16, m.2; C 60/18, m.10.

[6] *RLC*, 521b–2; *CR 1227–31*, 1; E 372/70, r.5, m.1.

[7] C 60/16, m.3; E 372/67, r.7, m.1; r.12, m.1; E 372/68, r. 14d, mm. 1, 2; E 372/70, r.15, mm. 1, 2.

any move to install Falkes next door to his own lordships in south-west Wales. Indeed, believing that the fitz Martin wardship should have been in his gift rather than the king's, he presumably thought that Falkes had no right to hold it in the first place.[8] The second order offered Llywelyn what was probably a quid pro quo for the surrender of Cemais. It instructed his ally, the earl of Chester, to go personally to the castle of Whittington in Shropshire, only five miles from Llywelyn's manor at Ellesmere, and, if it was sufficiently strong to be defended against the Welsh, to prevent any further building operations there. Next year Llywelyn took matters into his own hands and destroyed Whittington for himself.[9] The lord of the castle was Fulk fitz Warin whose exploits acquiring Whittington in John's reign were to be celebrated in the famous 'Legend of Fulk fitz Warin'.[10] More to the point in 1222 was the fact that Fulk was a familiar of the earl of Pembroke.[11]

It was the order embodied in the third writ of 11 November which was most damaging to Pembroke, however. Attested but not authorized by Hubert, this informed the earl of a decision taken by 'common counsel': he was to surrender Caerleon to the king 'without delay'. The latter would then give full justice both to him and to anyone else who came forward. This was to strike at the great Marshal gain from the civil war and to return to the battleground of 1218, when both Peter and the earl of Chester had tried to have Caerleon returned to its Welsh lord, Morgan.[12]

In November 1222 the government was also grappling with the affairs of Poitou. The safe-conduct offered to Hugh de Lusignan in September had not brought him to England. Instead, in November, Hubert and the council sent out the abbot of Boxley and Philip de Albini to negotiate a peace with him. Hugh was to be given until 1 August 1223, a wisely long term, 'to do to [the king] what he ought to do', which presumably meant perform homage and return Joan's *maritagium*. In the meantime, while negotiations were pending, the government sought to obtain the suspension of the papal excommunication which was due to be pronounced against Hugh on 30 November.[13]

---

[8] *PR*, 351–2; *Peerage*, viii, 533; *RLC*, ii, 140. The custody had been granted Falkes by King John. Since 1216 Maelgwn ap Rhys had been in actual possession of Cemais.

[9] *RLC*, 520b; see below p. 298.

[10] The legend is printed in *Fouke le fitz Waryn*. For the family, see Meisel, *Barons of the Welsh Frontier*.

[11] Fulk was granted Wantage in Berkshire by William Marshal junior before the latter succeeded his father (*PQW*, 81) and (my information here is from Dr Crouch) attests several of his charters. See also E 368/2, m.9, where the earls of Pembroke and Salisbury act as Fulk's pledges in June 1219.

[12] *PR*, 352.

[13] *PR*, 389. See above p. 291.

In November the new seneschal of Poitou, Savari de Mauléon, at last arrived in England, a visit with which Peter was closely involved. Savari's various petitions were settled by a gift of 500 marks; the writ, which was issued on 2 December, being authorized by Hubert and Peter in the presence of William Brewer and Falkes.[14] The government now determined to exploit the advantages of a great local magnate as seneschal. On 4 December the citizens of Bordeaux were upbraided for making unlicensed alliances with local magnates and neighbouring towns, and Savari was ordered to discover and recover the 'lands, castles, rents and possessions . . . in Poitou and Gascony' taken without warrant from the king and his ancestors. But the other side of Savari's power was precisely the offence that he gave to the towns. In November envoys were also present in England from Bordeaux, bearing numerous complaints about Savari's exactions and overbearing conduct. Meanwhile, the men of La Réole had refused to receive him and had expelled the Piis family, the chief supporters of the king of England, from the town. So, alongside its critical letter of 4 December to the citizens of Bordeaux, Hubert and the council simultaneously authorized one that was very different in tone. This explained that Geoffrey de Neville was being sent out to check on the situation, an appointment which was bound to detract from Savari's authority.[15]

On the whole, the situation in Poitou and Gascony was far better than it had been earlier in the year. Hugh de Lusignan seemed to have been held in check by the truce arranged by Pandulf. Savari, whatever offence he gave to the towns, had clearly taken vigorous hold of the seneschalship. He styled himself 'seneschal of Poitou and Gascony by special mandate of the king of England'.[16] The government also had more money to play with. Apart from the 500 marks given to Savari, orders were issued in November and December for 200 marks to be given to Peter on behalf of the vicomte of Thouars, while 100 marks were assigned to help with the fortifications of St Jean d'Angély and Niort.[17]

x. *The confirmation of Magna Carta, January 1223*

In the summer of 1222 the government had both resumed the royal demesne and withdrawn the forest eyres. That balance between the exercise of authority and its limitation was revealed even more clearly early in 1223, when unpopular initiatives were palliated by the king's verbal confirmation of the Charters.

After celebrating Christmas at Oxford, Hubert and the king had

---

[14] *RLC*, 524b; for the bishop and Savari, see also *RLC*, 525b.
[15] *PR*, 353–7.
[16] Bibliothèque Nationale, Paris, MS 5480, f.462.
[17] *RLC*, 520, 525.

arrived at Westminster after the beginning of the exchequer's Hilary term. They had been delayed by a visit to the west country, probably to deal with the situation created by the sudden death of the sheriff of Somerset–Dorset.[1] At Westminster Hubert attended to the future of the royal demesne, on 29 January authorizing the writ which committed the manor of Marlborough to its men at an annual farm of £50.[2] He also conceived a series of measures designed to increase the king's revenues and reassert his authority in the localities. A tallage was imposed on the royal demesne; commissioners, most of whom were local knights, were appointed to sell the windfalls in the royal forests; and orders were issued for the holding of regards prior to the start of the forest eyres. This last move drew attention once again to the failure to implement the clauses in the Charter of the Forest over deforestation and raised the suspicion that the government intended to breach the promise, made by 'common counsel' back in June 1222, to suspend the eyres for a year.[3] More provocative still was the instruction which went out to all the sheriffs on 30 January. They were to inquire in full county court, by the oaths of twelve knights of their counties, 'what customs and liberties' King John had had at the beginning of the war 'in lands, forests, and other things both inside boroughs and without'. The sheriffs were not merely to return the inquiry to the king at Easter. They were also to ensure that the rights and customs it revealed were proclaimed and observed.[4] This measure was prompted by the government's recognition of how much the king had lost in terms of rights and revenues since the beginning of the war, but it was easily regarded in the counties as an attempt to return to the evil practices of John's reign.

While these measures were being conceived, a great council was in session at Westminster. The proposed inquiry into the king's rights raised widespread concern. It was Langton who led the protest and voiced perhaps the conditions on which the measure might proceed. According to Roger of Wendover, he demanded a confirmation of the Charters by the king, pointing out that the latter had promulgated them with general consent after the peace with Louis. At this William Brewer objected: 'the liberties you seek', he growled, 'since they were violently extorted ought not rightfully to be observed'. Langton hurried him out of sight: 'William, if you love the king you should not impede the peace of the kingdom.' At this point the king himself intervened, how spontaneously cannot be known: 'seeing the archbishop moved to anger, he said "we have sworn to all those liberties and we are bound to

---

[1] *PR*, 364.
[2] C 60/18, m.8.
[3] *PR*, 403–4; 399–402; *F*, 168; Mitchell, *Taxation*, 148. See above p. 279.
[4] *F*, 168.

them for that we have sworn we will observe" ' . Thereafter the writs (of 30 January) commissioning the inquiry and its implementation were 'immediately' despatched.[5]

The confirmation of the Charters did not secure general agreement to the inquiry. Unlike the innocuous commission for the selling of the windfalls, there was no indication that it had obtained conciliar consent.[6] Nonetheless, the confirmation was, in reality, the price for the inquiry's launch. The government had indicated where it stood. Whatever rights it recovered for the king, it did so within the limits set by the Charters.

In February good news arrived from Poitou. The abbot of Boxley

[5] *Chron. Maj.*, 75–6. Norgate, *Minority*, 215 n.3, has argued that Henry's confirmation of Magna Carta was misdated by Roger of Wendover (the only source) and that the episode took place in January 1224 not January 1223. Norgate has been followed by Professor Holt (*Magna Carta*, 282). It is quite true that Wendover on a few occasions, in his narrative of the minority, places events in the wrong year (for example, *Chron. Maj.*, 64, 94). Henry's confirmation of the Charters, however, is not one of them. Wendover's account of the confirmation is embedded in narrative which manifestly belongs to December 1222 and January 1223. Wendover has the king spending Christmas of 1222 quite correctly at Oxford before coming to London for the *colloquium*. Having confirmed the Charters he says that the king immediately (*protinus*) commissioned an inquiry into the liberties in England in the time of Henry II. Although described in somewhat different terms, this is clearly, as Norgate accepted, the inquiry ordered in January 1223 (*F*, 168). Norgate's arguments for January 1224 are two-pronged. i. Wendover says that the king came to London for the *colloquium* at which he confirmed the Charters 'on the octave of Epiphany', that is, on 13 January. But in fact in 1223 Hubert and the king did not reach London until 20 or 21 January, whereas in 1224 the king was certainly in London on the appropriate date. A mistake of a few days, however, hardly seems very significant and is scarcely sufficient grounds for positing in its place a mistake of a whole year. ii. Norgate suggests that in 1223 there were 'no circumstances likely to suggest such a demand' (for the confirmation of the Charter), whereas such a demand was natural in 1224 when the king had just entered into part of his regal powers. This is a questionable observation given that the inquiry launched on 30 January 1223 was clearly very unpopular and in April 1223 the attempt to implement its findings was relinquished. As the writ explaining this admitted (*RLC*, 569), the measure had raised fears that the government intended to revive the malpractices of John's reign. It is not at all unlikely, therefore, that its initial launch provoked demands for the confirmation of the Charters. It can scarcely have still provoked them in January 1224 since the inquiry had been withdrawn ten months before. If 1224 is the correct date, it is strange that Roger of Wendover was mistaken about it since the additional significance given to the whole episode by the fact that the king was now in control of his own government would surely have imprinted the timing on his mind. For the same reason the silence of other chroniclers concerning the whole episode, had it taken place in January 1224, is also less explicable. In short, while there is positive evidence, in the shape of Wendover's linkage of the confirmation with the inquiry, to place the confirmation in January 1223, the case for a year later rests on mere surmise.

[6] *PR*, 399. However, Wendover does say that the king sent the letters ordering the inquiry, *habito super hoc consilio*: *Chron. Maj.*, 76.

and Philip de Albini had managed to secure a truce with Hugh de Lusignan until 1 August. This was ratified by Hubert and the council on 13 February.[7] Hubert and the king then set out for the north, leaving Bishop Peter in charge at Westminster to complete the Hilary session of the exchequer.[8] The tension between the two ministers may be reflected in the writ which Hubert authorized in Lincolnshire on 19 February. The barons of the exchequer were informed that the king was sending them William de Cantilupe 'in order that he may sit at the exchequer and attend with you to our affairs there'.[9]

What drew Hubert and the king to the north at this time is not clear. It may have been problems with the Anglo-Scottish border.[10] In any case, when they were at Nottingham on 1 March, news arrived which entailed a rapid change of plan. Llywelyn had lost patience. He had seized Fulk fitz Warin's castle at Whittington and the neighbouring castle of Kinnerley, which belonged to Baldwin de Hodenet. Perhaps the last straw had been Fulk's plan to marry his son to a daughter of his Welsh neighbour, Madoc ap Gruffyd, a match to which Llywelyn was opposed. Hubert and the king, therefore, hurried to the Welsh Marches and were at Shrewsbury by 7 March. There, the earl of Chester, Llywelyn's 'friend and familiar', as the Dunstable annalist put it, came to the king and promised that Llywelyn would give satisfaction within a specified time.[11]

With matters thus settled Hubert spent a week at Gloucester, where he committed the manors of Cheltenham and Dymock, recovered in the previous year's resumption, to their men at farm.[12] He then returned to Westminster where a final surrender was made over the 30 January inquiry, which had clearly provoked much hostility in the counties. On 9 April the king, by the counsel of his *fideles*, ordered the sheriffs neither to proclaim nor cause to be observed the liberties and customs which the inquiry revealed. 'You are to know', concluded the king's letter, which was to be read in full county court, 'that it was not our intention to raise or have observed evil customs in our kingdom.' After encountering resistance, the justiciar had retreated, a response utterly characteristic of his administration down to its end in 1232. In 1223 itself he also drew back, just as he had in 1221 and 1222, from the holding of burdensome forest eyres.[13]

---

[7] *PR*, 366.

[8] E 368/5, m.13(1)d. Peter was assigned 500 marks by the king 'to do the things which we have ordered him': *RLC*, 534b.

[9] E 368/5, m.13(1)d. Cantilupe, however, sided with Peter rather than Hubert later in the year.

[10] For the border, see *RLC*, 496b; *RL*, no. clxiii.

[11] *RLC*, 537; *Ann. Mon.*, iii, 82.

[12] C 60/18, m.6.

[13] *RLC*, 569. For the forest eyres of 1223, see below p. 337.

Hubert's achievements since Pandulf's resignation had been considerable. In Wales and Poitou his government had attempted little more than maintain uneasy truces. But at home it had reasserted exchequer control over the county farms and resumed the royal demesne. The issues of the Easter term of 1223 confirmed his achievement.[14] The total proceeds from the counties were £4,275, nearly £1,000 greater than the year before and £2,542 more than in 1220. In addition, the Easter receipts in 1223 were swelled by a tallage on the Jews, which produced £1,690, while £254 more came from ordinary Jewish debts, making a grand total of £6,219. The pattern of rising revenue is also reflected in the pipe roll for 1223. The total cash revenue in the roll, to take the adjusted figures, was £12,180, as against £10,340 in the roll of 1222.[15] The adjusted total of receipts and expenditure in the 1223 roll, at £13,980, was nearly double that for the roll of 1220. Again the writs of *liberate* reveal the same pattern. Between Michaelmas 1222 and Michaelmas 1223 they ordered the exchequer to disburse £11,480, as against £9,835 the year before and only £5,295 in 1219–20. There was more money, therefore, to spend on gifts, fees, wages, the sustenance of Poitou and the maintenance of the royal household. The total revenue assigned to the latter, between Michaelmas 1222 and Michaelmas 1223, was £3,785, as opposed to £2,345 two years before.

Hubert, therefore, since Pandulf's resignation, had succeeded in reasserting the king's rights and increasing his revenues. In the process he had shown himself a master of politics. He had acted with swift brutality against the Londoners but had also known when to compromise and give way over the forest eyres and the implementation of the 30 January inquiry. In addition, the king had proffered a verbal confirmation of the Charters. Thus Hubert's government remained acceptable to a wide body of opinion and was able to secure the backing of Archbishop Langton and a great council for the resumption of the royal demesne. Hubert had held the first place in the administration and had maintained vital alliances with the earls of Salisbury and Pembroke but he had also worked with his enemies and bowed sometimes to their influence. In January 1223 itself a fresh attempt to remove the earl of Pembroke from Caerleon testified to Peter and Chester's continuing power.[16] In fact, since Peter's humiliation in 1221 Hubert's supremacy had always been under threat, as the Christmas crisis of 1221 had

[14] For the figures which follow, see Appendix, pp. 413–17.

[15] In the roll of 1223 around £1,200 was contributed by the new tallage on the royal demesne. Another aspect of the exchequer's growing control around this time is seen in the increasing number of attermined debts in the pipe rolls: see the discussion in Knight, 'Pipe Roll 6 Henry III', 154–64.

[16] *PR*, 363. For another move against the earl of Pembroke at this time, see E 368/5, m.13(2). For favours to Peter and Chester: *RLC*, 530b, 531.

shown. Indeed, it could have no long-term security since everything might be transformed once the king assumed control of his government. As early as March 1222 Bishop Peter may have suggested to the pope that the time had come for such a change. Hubert, given that he was already at the helm, could afford to be less hasty, yet ultimately he too must have planned to bring about the king's assumption of power. Until that happened it would be impossible to realize the final phase of the reassertion of royal authority, namely the resumption of the castles and sheriffdoms. Essentially, by 1222–23, the whole state of English politics rested on ice which was melting away as the king grew towards maturity. Hubert was content to let the ice melt slowly while he strengthened his control over the emerging king. It was Peter who had the nerve and incentive to shatter it.

Chapter 8

THE KING AND HIS CASTLES, 1223

i. *The papal letters of April 1223*

When Hubert returned to Westminster at the beginning of April 1223 he little knew that the next nine months would see a threatened invasion of Ireland by Hugh de Lacy, the death of the king of France and the conquest of south Wales by the earl of Pembroke. These events, and especially the last, controlled the timing and confirmed the political alliances which lay behind the king's assumption of regal powers at the end of 1223. That assumption made possible the recovery and redistribution of his castles and sheriffdoms. The programme set out in the papal letters of 1219, 1220 and 1221 was realized at long last. But, in contrast to the royal demesne in June 1222, the castles and sheriffdoms were resumed in circumstances which were highly partisan. The consequences remained with English politics for the next decade.

The starting point for events in England in 1223 lay in a series of papal letters of 13 April 1223, of which the chief was addressed to Hubert, Bishop Peter and William Brewer. The pope rejoiced to learn that what the king lacked in years, he made up for in prudence and discretion. Consequently, the three ministers were ordered to 'deliver to him the free and undisturbed disposition of his kingdom, and to resign to him, without any difficulty, the lands and castles which you hold as custodies, and to procure the resignation by others who hold his lands and castles in similar fashion'. Another letter was sent to Ralph de Neville in his capacity as keeper of the seal. Having explained about the order to the three ministers, Neville was enjoined 'now to use [the seal] at the pleasure [of the king], and in respect of it to be submissive to and obey only him, causing no letters henceforth to be sealed with the king's seal save at his will'. There was also a letter to the earls and barons of England. They too were informed of the letter to the three ministers and then told to be intendant henceforth on the king and to assist him against opposition, or else 'you can fear, not without cause, a sentence of excommunication'.[1]

Honorius had, of course, issued letters before ordering that the king's

---

[1] For the papal letters of 1223, see below note 4.

castles and possessions be surrendered. What was new about these was that they faced up to the block placed on such changes by the king's minority. Honorius did not declare Henry of age. What he did do, however, was to proclaim that the maturity of the king's understanding made up for his immaturity in years. He was thus deemed able to control the government of the kingdom. The castles were to be surrendered and the seal to be used at his will. The way was thus cleared for the whole structure of local and central government to be remodelled. On whose suggestion had Honorius acted?

'The representations which produced the papal letters of 1223', wrote Powicke, 'obviously came from quarters independent of the justiciar and his rivals, and later events confirm the impression that they came from Langton and his colleagues.'[2] Sir Richard Southern is even more specific: Langton and his colleagues 'sent messengers to Rome, who brought back a papal declaration dated April 1223 that the fifteen-year-old king was old enough to rule on his own'. Sir Richard suggests, indeed, that the messenger was none other than Robert Grosseteste, the famous theologian and later bishop of Lincoln.[3] These hypotheses are at odds with the actual course of events in 1223, since Langton and his colleagues intervened at a late stage of the crisis and, in the first instance, as mediators between Hubert and his rivals, not as executants of the papal letters. They also fly in the face of the actual terms of the letters and the one positive piece of evidence as to their origin.

The surviving letters of April 1223 mention no role for Langton and the bishops. The English prelates do not even appear in the somewhat tepid threat of excommunication at the end of the letter to the earls and barons. Instead, the key role was assigned to Peter, Hubert and William Brewer. It was they, not the bishops, who were mentioned in the letters to Neville and the earls and barons as the ones who were to give the king 'free disposition' of his kingdom. It was they who, having surrendered their own custodies, were to 'procure' a similar resignation from others.[4]

---

[2] Powicke, *Henry III*, 57.

[3] Southern, *Robert Grosseteste*, 80–1.

[4] The letters to the earls and barons, the three ministers and Ralph de Neville were copied (and supplied with incorrect dating clauses) in the Red Book of the Exchequer – E 164/2, f.171v. That to the earls and barons is printed from there in *F*, 190. An independent copy of the letter to Neville, with the correct dating clause – 13 April in the seventh year of Honorius's pontificate – is in *RL*, no. ccclviii. Extracts from the letter to the earls and barons were given in Hubert de Burgh's defence in 1239 to charges made against him (*Chron. Maj.*, vi, 69–70). This defence also gives extracts of a separate letter to the earl of Chester and says that one was addressed to Bishop Peter *sub eisdem verbis*. The former is in fact transcribed in the Red Book and is on the same lines as the other letters. Chester is informed of the instructions to the three ministers and then told to surrender the castles and lands in his custody. In November 1223 the pope refused to

The one direct piece of evidence about the origin of the April letters is contained in Hubert's reply to the king's charge, made in 1239, that he had sent messengers to Rome to get the king declared of age before he had reached his majority. The king was actually referring here to the events of 1227 but Hubert's answer dealt with 1223: 'he did not send messengers to Rome, but the bishop of Winchester sent to Rome W. de Sancto Albano for this affair, more to the harm of Hubert than to his benefit, in order that he and others should surrender their custodies, and so it happened at Northampton'.[5] This testimony cannot be dismissed.[6] In 1239 Hubert's defence would have seemed all the more impressive had he assigned responsibility for the letters to Langton. The only problem with the story is that William de Sancto Albino was sent to Gascony in October 1222 and was still there in April 1223.[7] He cannot, therefore, have been the envoy who obtained the April letters. This objection is not insuperable, however. William de Sancto Albino had made several visits to Rome on the king's behalf and with those in 1218 and 1220 Bishop Peter had been closely associated. William's last visit, prior to 1223, had been in March 1222, when Hubert himself had attested the relevant letters for the mission, which may officially have been connected with the affairs of Poitou.[8] It is not impossible,

withdraw letters in which Peter, Chester, Falkes and Hubert had been commanded to surrender their custodies: *RL*, 539. Probably these were simply the individual letters to Chester and Peter referred to above and ones on similar lines to Falkes and Hubert. Roger of Wendover (*Chron. Maj.*, 79) assigns an important role in 1223 to a papal letter which commanded the archbishops and bishops to proclaim that all who held custodies should surrender them immediately. They were also to coerce the recalcitrant with spiritual penalties. Wendover does not give the text of the letter, however, and his summary is clearly inaccurate, stating, for example, that Honorius had declared Henry 'of full age' when there is nothing else to suggest that this is what he did in 1223. Probably Wendover was merely inflating the letter which was almost certainly written to the archbishops and bishops in April 1223 in parallel with that to the earls and barons. The former would have ended with an injunction to coerce the recalcitrant with spiritual penalties but, like the others of the same date, probably left the key role in effecting the changes to the three ministers. Credit for sorting out the correct dates of the letters in the Red Book of the Exchequer belongs to Norgate, *Minority*, 286–90, 200–6. But, given the absence of their texts, she had no good grounds for supposing that the letter to the ecclesiastics summarized by Wendover and the letters which the pope refused to withdraw in November were on different lines and perhaps also different in date from the letters of April 1223 in the Red Book.

[5] *Chron. Maj.*, vi, 69. For events at Northampton, see below p. 325.

[6] Norgate leant towards the view that the initiative behind the April letters lay with Peter but believed that Langton prompted the other letters (see above note 4) written by the pope: *Minority*, 200–1, 205–6, 290.

[7] *RLC*, 518, 541.

[8] *PR*, 184, 237, 328; *RLC*, 384b, 422b. That William might indeed have been acting for Peter on his March 1222 mission was suggested to me by Mr Vincent. If so, the whole story cannot have come out till later. Otherwise it is unlikely that William would have been employed again by Hubert in 1222.

however, that on the side and in secret William acted for Bishop Peter and suggested to the pope that the king was ready to control affairs for himself. If so, his suggestion fell on deaf ears, for no letters were forthcoming. Ultimately, those which were conceded in April 1223 were secured and brought to England not by William de Sancto Albino, nor by Robert Grosseteste, but by Robert Passelewe.

In 1239 Hubert had good reasons for telling only half the story and ignoring the role of Passelewe, a personal enemy who was then high in the king's service. In the minority, however, Passelewe was a clerk of Falkes de Bréauté and very much part of Peter's circle. At the end of 1223 he was to go again to Rome on behalf of Peter, Chester, Falkes and other opponents of Hubert and Langton.[9] It is known that Passelewe was at the papal court early in 1223 from an order on the memoranda rolls of the exchequer. This instructed Thomas de Burgh, Hubert's brother, to deliver to a servant of Passelewe the lands which he had entered 'because he believed that Robert Passelewe was dead who is alive and attends to the affairs of the king in the Roman court'. Significantly, the next entry on the roll is a writ, dated 22 February, which was authorized by Peter.[10] Probably the order concerning Passelewe was issued when Peter was in charge of the exchequer after Hubert had left London. No wonder Hubert sent William de Cantilupe to watch what was going on there. Passelewe was back in England by 14 May, when, no doubt fulfilling a commission received from Guala, he was assigned 20 marks for the latter's annual fee.[11] The date of 14 May is significant. The papal letters were dated 14 April, exactly a month earlier. Since the journey from Rome to England took about a month, it looks as though Passelewe had left as soon as they were issued.

As Hubert said in 1239, Peter had sought the papal letters 'more to harm him than to benefit him'. Despite being removed from control of the king and accused of treason in 1221, Peter had held on to his position in the apparatus of government. He had been closely involved in dealings with Poitou and he and the earl of Chester had succeeded in raising once again the question of Caerleon. But nothing could alter the fact that Peter was very firmly Hubert's number two, called in to attest a writ in Hubert's favour or to mind the exchequer when Hubert was away. There may well have been recurrent friction between the two men. In March 1222, for example, when the court was at Winchester, Peter, acting alone, authorized a writ which gave bail to one of the

---

[9] *CRR*, xv, no.1058.

[10] E 368/5, m.13 (1)d.

[11] *RLC*, 546b. Passelewe had received Guala's pension on earlier occasions: *RLC*, 488, 497. A poem about Passelewe by his friend, Henry of Avranches, centres on his success in securing important papal letters and on his ungrateful reception when he returned home. It may refer to this mission: *Henry of Avranches*, 96, 91.

king's serjeants, a group with which he had been closely associated. This was cancelled almost immediately in favour of a writ, authorized by Hubert, which gave the serjeant bail only if the person he was accused of assaulting recovered.[12] Later, as has been seen, there was conflict over Engelard de Cigogné's tenure of Odiham.[13] That Bishop Peter deeply resented the situation is plain from Falkes's *querimonia*, which was probably the work of Robert Passelewe. This avers that when the king was freed from Peter's tutelage, the latter was unable to prevent him 'adhering to the counsels of the justiciar and his accomplices'.[14]

The king's emergence gave Peter every reason for acting as soon as possible. With Hubert's encouragement, Henry had begun, during his tour of Wales and the west in August 1222, to dispense gifts of wine, game and timber. In January 1223 he had confirmed Magna Carta. He was also beginning to display the personal enthusiasms which were to form so marked an element in his character. Since November 1221 he had become increasingly attached to two nuns (*puellae*), whom he had installed, in receipt of alms, at the convent of Kington in Wiltshire. In March 1223, soon after the king and Hubert had visited the priory, a writ, attested by Hubert, ordered thirty carts of firewood to be given to the nuns and expressed the king's astonishment that a previous order had not been carried out. At the same time William Brewer was told to repair their houses 'as was provided not long ago in our presence, and this omit on no account as you love us and since you know that it is expedient for our honour, and since (a note added perhaps by Hubert) you know we will cause the cost to be returned to you'.[15] The two nuns were still the recipients of the king's special favour in the 1230s.[16] A marked change had also come over the king's movements. The days when he lived for long periods apart from the government at Wallingford or Havering had ended. After November 1222 it is impossible to show that Henry and Hubert were ever separated.

The king's emergence was indeed closely linked to the development of his relationship with the justiciar. Just as Hubert and his allies had moved to sever Peter from the king in 1221 before they became too close, so it was vital now for Peter to act quickly in the face of Hubert's growing ascendancy, before Hubert indeed took the initiative and moved himself to change the status of the king. In that sense Peter was involved in a pre-emptive strike. His problem, of course, was that some of his principal allies, notably Falkes, Engelard and the earl of Chester,

---

[12] *RLC*, 490b.
[13] See above p. 293.
[14] *Walt. Cov.*, 260.
[15] *RLC*, 538b; for previous favours, see *RLC*, 479, 480b, 494b, 513b.
[16] *CR 1231-34*, 62, 115.

were themselves ensconced in the king's castles and sheriffdoms; Falkes had more to lose from the changes than anyone else. But Peter appreciated that the essential requirement was to have the controlling hand. For him, by far the most important papal letter was that to Ralph de Neville, who, henceforth, was to obey only the king and seal letters only at his will. Thus Hubert's grip was to be released at the very point where it had been strongest: his control over royal letters. If Peter could achieve that and become the man at the king's elbow, he could easily safeguard the interests of his own party in the resumption and redistribution of the castles and sheriffdoms.

ii. *The earl of Pembroke's conquest of south Wales*

Had the letters of 13 April been obtained without partisan intent, Peter, Hubert and William Brewer might have summoned a great council with the aim of resuming the castles and sheriffdoms in much the same way as the demesne had been resumed the year before. They would also have begun to negotiate the pay-offs and bargains which would have been the inevitable prelude to such a resumption. But the intent behind the letters was highly partisan. They provided Peter with the means of removing Hubert from power, provided he could implement them at the right time, a time, that is, when all the opposition to Hubert could be marshalled. But equally he now faced the possibility that Hubert would activate the letters at a moment of his own choosing. The government was at Westminster from late April to mid-June 1223. During this period concessions were made to Archbishop Langton, Bishop Peter, the earl of Chester and the count of Aumale. Hubert and Peter acted together to pardon Nicholas de Stuteville II a forest amercement. Peter also acted as a pledge, with William Brewer, for a loan to the earl of Salisbury.[1] The combatants circled round each other with the papal mandate lying on the floor like a gleaming knife. Who would reach out to grab it first?

Meanwhile, the government faced other problems. One was presented by Hugh de Lacy, the former lord of Ulster, whom John had disseized in 1210. Hugh had been in England at the end of 1222 seeking the restitution of his lands. He was offered his wife's *maritagium* and the lands given him by his brother Walter; Hugh's other lands and castles were to be committed for five years to Walter and the earls of Chester, Salisbury and Gloucester, with some hint that he might then receive seisin. Hugh had rejected these proposals and in early June 1223 the justiciar of Ireland was warned, in a letter authorized

---

[1] *RLC*, 545b, 547b, 548b; E 368/5, m.12(1)d. In May and early June Hubert presided at sessions of the bench: Meekings, 'Concords'.

by Hubert and the council, that he was 'plotting to invade Ireland in arms'.[2]

Events in Ireland, however, paled before those in Wales. As the papal letters made their way to England, the earl of Pembroke was destroying Llywelyn's dominance in south Wales and inflicting crushing retribution for the latter's invasion of Pembroke in 1220. This alone, as Powicke recognized, prevented the letters being given immediate effect.[3]

The political structure of south Wales, as Llywelyn had fashioned it during and after the war, had left the Marshal family in Pembroke isolated and surrounded. Llywelyn had given Maelgwyn ap Rhys Carmarthen in 1216 and Cardigan and Ceredigion below the Aeron after Rhys Ieuanc's death in 1222. He had also installed Maelgwyn in Cemais, St Clears, Laugharne and the Marshal lordships of Cilgerran and Emlyn. Further east, Llywelyn had allowed Rhys Gryg to retain Kidwelly, thus shutting out the earl of Pembroke's familiar, William Crassus, who had the custody of the de Londres heiress, and had installed John de Braose in Gower, to the exclusion of Pembroke's ally, Reginald de Braose.[4]

By the spring of 1223, the earl of Pembroke's preparations for bringing this hegemony to an end were complete.[5] Having spent the winter in Ireland gathering an army, he landed at St David's around 16 April 1223. With a *punctilio* worthy of his father, he waited until the truce with Llywelyn, renewed for a year back at Easter 1222, had expired and then struck. On Easter Monday, 24 April, he seized Cardigan and, on the following Wednesday, Carmarthen. He then headed south into Kidwelly. Llywelyn had been caught unprepared; perhaps he had dissipated his resources in the attacks on Kinnerley and Whittington earlier in the year. Certainly at no point in 1223 did he enter the field himself against Pembroke. Instead, the latter was met in Kidwelly by a force under Llywelyn's son, Gruffud. An inconclusive battle, which the Welsh accepted against the advice of Rhys Gryg, lasted all day. Gruffud was eventually forced to retire through lack of provisions, while Pembroke withdrew to the north to repair the castle at

---

[2]   *RLC*, 527b, 549b; *PR*, 374–5; Lydon, 'The expansion and consolidation of the colony', 158.

[3]   Powicke, *Henry III*, 58.

[4]   *Brut*, 99; Walker, 'Anglo-Welsh Wars', 119. See above pp. 75–7, 218.

[5]   The fullest account of Pembroke's campaign is in *Brut*, 99–100. See also *Ann. Camb.*, 75–6 (where the events of 1223 are placed incorrectly under 1221), and *Ann. Mon.*, iii, 82–3, where the events of 1220 and 1223 are intertwined. Pembroke gathered reinforcements from his lordship of Nether Went before landing at St David's, for he was at Chepstow on 22 March 1223: British Library MS Arundel 19, ff.1–7v (a reference I owe to Dr Crouch).

Carmarthen and start a new one in stone at Cilgerran. His concentration on Cilgerran was not surprising. King John had granted it to his
father in hereditary right. Situated, as Dr Walker has put it, 'in a very
strong position on the cliffs above the gorge of the Teifi', the castle was
only three miles up the river from Cardigan, but on the left of Pembrokeshire bank. It thus formed an obstacle to any Welsh invasion of north
Pembrokeshire, while facilitating the control of Emlyn to the east.[6]

The first phase of the campaign closed with Pembroke having
established his hold over Cardigan, Carmarthen, Cilgerran and
probably also Emlyn and Cemais. He had destroyed the position of
Maelgwyn ap Rhys and replaced Llywelyn's dominance in south
Wales with his own. The English government could only look on
open-mouthed but Hubert quickly grasped that his close relations with
Pembroke enabled him to share in the victory. On 10 May he signalled
the king's approval by authorizing a writ which gave Pembroke ten
deer from Windsor forest to stock his park at Caversham.[7] All question
of Caerleon was forgotten but Hubert and the council did move to
establish the king's rights over the lordships of Cardigan and Carmarthen. At the end of the month Robert de Vaux was sent to take
possession of these for the king.[8] Since Vaux had been in Pembroke's
army, and was a member of his *familia*, this move was designed to
safeguard the king's rights while leaving the reality of power in
Pembroke's hands.[9]

While summoning an army to Worcester, the government, with
Langton's help, also tried to arrange a meeting at which Pembroke and
Llywelyn might be reconciled.[10] This eventually took place at Ludlow,
probably between 8 and 10 July. However, no settlement was reached.
Llywelyn doubtless demanded the return of Cardigan and Carmarthen, which he held, under the terms of the treaty of Worcester, until
the king came of age; a demand the government was powerless to
concede had it wanted to. Thus the war continued. Langton, who
attended the meeting at Ludlow, excommunicated Llywelyn and
placed his lands under an interdict.[11] Meanwhile, Hubert, despite
opposition, presumably from Bishop Peter and the earl of Chester,
threw the government's full weight behind the earl of Pembroke. He
placed the earl, with his old friend and ally, the earl of Salisbury, in
command of an army which included 'a cavalry force of about 140
knights, the majority of them supplied by the contingents of six earls

[6] *Brut*, 313; Walker, 'Anglo-Welsh Wars', 159.
[7] *RLC*, 545.
[8] *PR*, 373–4.
[9] *RLC*, 569b; *PR*, 441; *Ormand Deeds*, 36, a reference I owe to Dr Crouch.
[10] *RLC*, 553; *PR*, 406; *Brut*, 100.
[11] *Brut*, 100; *PR*, 376; *RL*, no.cxci.

and the tenants in-chief of the south-western counties of England'.[12] In July or August Pembroke and Salisbury wrote jointly to Hubert thanking him fulsomely for his help and acknowledging that he had been 'greatly disturbed and had had a great dispute with certain people opposed to [support] being given us'.[13] The details of the campaign are obscure but Pembroke established his hold over Kidwelly. Then, exploiting the divisions between the native Welsh, he moved north in alliance with Cynan ap Hywel, whose father had been murdered by Maelgwyn ap Rhys in 1204, and expelled the latter from Ceredigion below the Aeron, putting Cynan in his place.[14]

iii. *The death of King Philip, July 1223*

In the middle of July, while the earls of Pembroke and Salisbury marshalled their forces for the campaign in south Wales, Hubert was contemplating a move on southern Powys, which Llywelyn held under the treaty of Worcester during the minority of Gwenwynwyn's heirs.[1] But all such thoughts were put into abeyance by the death, on 14 July, of the great scourge of the Angevin house, the conqueror of Normandy and Anjou and the victor of Bouvines: King Philip of France. The news probably reached Hubert at Gloucester on 20 July. He set off at once for London, despatching on the way a letter to the men of Normandy inviting them to return to King Henry's allegiance. On reaching London on 27 July it was decided to send Langton, with the bishops of London and Salisbury, to France to persuade the archbishop of Rheims to defer the coronation until Louis had surrendered Normandy in accordance with his promise at the end of the war.[2]

These vistas in Normandy encouraged the government to make more certain of the situation further south. The truce with Hugh de Lusignan was due to expire on 1 August. It had not gone smoothly. Savari de Mauléon had offended Hugh just as much as he had the towns. He had attempted to uphold the king's right to wardships by extracting the castles of Marans and Mauzé, late of Porteclie de Mauzé, from the hands of Hugh and Hugh's 'man', William Maingo. In the process he had taken William prisoner. Hugh warned the king that he would 'rather leave your service than suffer such injuries from [Savari] . . . without revenge'. The answer, he suggested, was the appointment of

---

[12] *App. Dig. Peer*, 3; *RLC*, 569; *PR*, 377, 406–7; Walker, 'Hubert de Burgh and Wales', 474.

[13] SC 1/1, no.121 (*CACW*, 3–4).

[14] *RLC*, 571b; *Ann. Camb.*, 76; Walker, 'Hubert de Burgh and Wales', 474, 476; Davies, *Wales*, 224–5.

[1] Walker, 'Hubert de Burgh and Wales', 475.

[2] *PR*, 406; *Ann. Mon.*, iii, 81.

Geoffrey de Neville as seneschal: 'with our aid . . . he will possess the land so peacefully that you will hear no complaints from anyone'.[3] In the event, the government did not dismiss Savari but early in August Geoffrey de Neville *was* sent out again to Poitou, a decision in which Hubert, Peter and the council were all involved. He, rather than Savari, was to act as custodian of Marans and Mauzé.[4] More important, the government began to retreat over the question of Joan's *maritagium* and conceded Saintes to Hugh until the king came of age.[5]

The government appreciated that a request to Louis and the friendship, or neutrality, of Hugh de Lusignan might not be quite all that was required for the recovery of Normandy. And so, at the beginning of August, ships and individuals with horses and arms were summoned to Portsmouth for 22 August and told to be ready to set out with the king in his service.[6] Richard de Umfraville in the north received his summons on 15 August and hastened south, though fearful that he would not make it in time. The archbishop of York equally hurried south with a contingent of knights.[7]

Against the background of a possible invasion of Normandy, Hubert and Peter may have formally agreed that the April letters should be withdrawn. At any rate, on 9 August William de Sancto Albino bade farewell to the two ministers and set out for the papal court. One of his tasks was to secure papal support against Louis.[8] But he had been appointed proctor not merely of the king but also of his *ministeriales*. Acting on their behalf he may well have secured the letter which Honorius wrote to the king in November, too late to influence the course of events. Honorius said that he had been asked by the king to quash the letters by which Peter, Hubert, Falkes and the earl of Chester had been ordered to surrender their royal castles and bailiwicks. The request had been put to him, Honorius continued, lest disturbances arose and since the ministers would surrender the custodies at a suitable time, for the moment there being no one to whom they could be more securely entrusted. Honorius declared that he was most reluctant to revoke his letters; hence, no doubt, the delay since William's arrival at the papal court in September. Instead, he merely forbad action on them without the king's consent.[9] The atmosphere which produced the representations to the pope may be reflected in Peter's appointment on

    [3] *PR*, 356, 370; *DD*, nos 120, 128, 79.
    [4] *PR*, 379–80; *RLC*, 557, 557b.
    [5] *PR*, 379. Hugh was also confirmed until the king came of age in possession of Cognac, Belmont and Merpins.
    [6] *RLC*, 570; SC 1/1, no. 205; *RLC*, 556b–7 for other measures.
    [7] SC 1/1, nos 205, 104.
    [8] *RLC*, 558b; *DD*, no. 121.
    [9] *RL*, 539.

24 August as custodian of the vacant bishopric of Coventry by a writ authorized by Hubert in the presence of Chester, William Brewer and the council.[10] By this time, however, the situation had changed again.

Hubert, Peter and the king hovered at Winchester from 13 to 19 August, as though unable to decide whether to proceed to Portsmouth. Then, on 20 August, the court returned to Westminster. The expedition had been called off.[11] There had been no spontaneous rising in Normandy. Langton and his colleagues, delayed by adverse winds in the Channel, had arrived after the coronation and had been received by Louis at Compiègne. He had treated their demands with contempt and threatened, if Henry made a hostile move, to launch a fresh invasion of England.[12] The government returned to reality.

iv. *Montgomery castle and the end of the Welsh war, September–October 1223*

With the invasion of France cancelled, the government could turn once more to Wales. Here, however, it was Llywelyn who took the initiative. Late in August he was still in diplomatic contact with the English government. Early in September he laid siege to Reginald de Braose's castle at Builth, at long last fulfilling apprehensions first expressed in 1219 and 1220. On 12 September the government summoned all tenants-in-chief, outside the Marcher counties whose forces were already involved in south Wales, to rendezvous in arms with the king at Gloucester.[1] The campaign was crowned with swift success: Builth was relieved between 21 and 23 September.[2] The army then moved north to Montgomery, where it encamped while a new castle was constructed.

The old castle at Montgomery commanded the Severn crossing but, for that reason, was down in the valley and thus easily surprised and attacked. According to Roger of Wendover, the leaders of the king's army surveyed the area carefully for a new site. As the great expert in castle warfare, Hubert doubtless had the deciding voice. He found a position which, in Wendover's words, 'seemed untakeable to everyone'.[3] From the great ridge of the Ceri Hills the high ground runs north, in the shape roughly of an arrow-head, until it reaches a final point high above the valley of the Severn. It was on this point that the new castle of

---

[10] *PR*, 382; for favours at this time to the earl and constable of Chester: *RLC*, 561.

[11] *RLC*, 571; SC 1/1, no. 104.

[12] *Ann. Mon.*, 81–2; *Chron. Maj.*, 77–8.

[1] *F*, 170; *Chron. Maj.*, iii, 64 (where misplaced in 1221).

[2] The date is suggested by the king's itinerary.

[3] *Chron. Maj.*, 64. Hubert's skill in these matters is amply confirmed by the remarkable site that he found for his castle at Hadleigh in Essex, started in 1230: *PR*, 417.

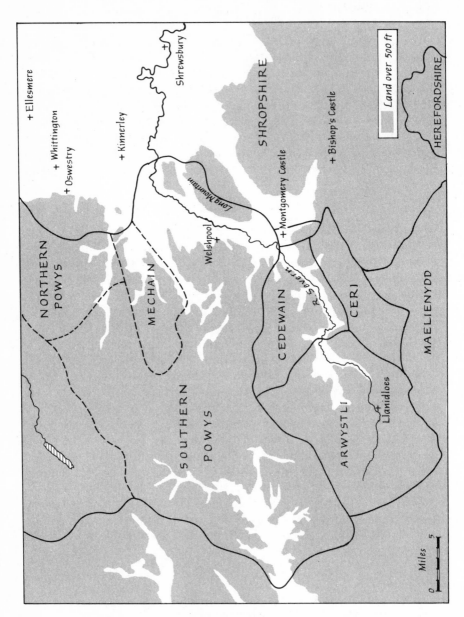

6. Montgomery and central Wales in the minority

Montgomery was built. Designed to occupy the whole of the promontory, it was almost impossible to attack and commanded the plain below and its strategic passes.

In general terms, as Wendover put it, the new castle was built 'for the security of the region on account of the frequent irruptions of the Welsh'.[4] There was an immediate background to this. During the civil war Llywelyn had seized both southern Powys and neighbouring Montgomery from the Welsh prince, Gwenwynwyn. Under the terms of the treaty of Worcester, he had been allowed to keep both during the minority of Gwenwynwyn's heir, which still had many years to run in 1223. By establishing royal power at Montgomery, therefore, Hubert deprived Llywelyn of one of his chief gains from the war. He also robbed Llywelyn of a strategic base from which he had probably launched his attacks on Kinnerley and Whittington. The large fertile plain commanded by the new castle is like a pocket amidst the mountains of the eastern Marches of central Wales. The mouth of that pocket towards England is almost stopped by the Long Mountain, but to the north-east there is a pass to Shrewsbury, while to the north the Severn valley runs through to Welshpool, by the thirteenth century the chief seat of the princes of southern Powys; from there the road continues to Oswestry and Chester. There are equally two holes in the bottom of the Montgomery pocket. One runs south-west, along the Severn valley into Cedewain and Arwystli, the principalities on the boundaries of southern Powys.[5] The other runs south to Bishop's Castle and thence into the plain of Herefordshire, from where the way is open to Builth, Carmarthen and Pembroke. The new castle at Montgomery, therefore, stopped up Llywelyn's invasion route from southern Powys into England and his path from Gwynedd to south-west Wales.[6]

The king and Hubert remained at Montgomery from 30 September to 11 October. A scutage of two marks on the fee was levied on those who did not join the army.[7] By 7 October Llywelyn and his principal allies, Maelgwyn ap Rhys and Rhys Gryg, had come in to make their submission. On that day Langton lifted Llywelyn's excommunication and the latter agreed to surrender Kinnerley and Whittington and, within a time limit set by Langton, to satisfy the king for the damage that he had done since he took the former.[8] The

---

4 *Chron. Maj.*, 64.

5 For Welshpool, see Davies, *Wales*, 230–1, 233, 235. There is a map of Powys on p. 232.

6 For further comment on the importance of eastern central Wales to Llywelyn, see Davies, *Wales*, 247.

7 Mitchell, *Taxation*, 143–7.

8 *PR*, 386, 411–12; *Ann. Mon.*, iii, 83. For much of what follows, see Walker, 'Hubert de Burgh and Wales', 475–6.

humiliating heart of the settlement, however, lay in the stipulation that Llywelyn and his followers were to recover only those lands which they had held 'in fee' when the war broke out.[9] Despite the treaty of Worcester, therefore, Llywelyn was to lose southern Powys and Montgomery, and Maelgwyn ap Rhys, as Llywelyn's deputy, Carmarthen and Cardigan. Maelgwyn was equally deprived of the Marcher lordships which he had been occupying since the war, in contravention of the treaty, namely Cemais, Cilgerran, Emlyn, St Clears, Laugharne and Llansteffan, while Rhys Gryg likewise was stripped of Kidwelly.

In fact, Llywelyn may have held on to southern Powys,[10] but for the rest the losses were real enough. The king retained Montgomery for himself,[11] while leaving southern Wales to the direction of the earl of Pembroke, who was soon to become bailiff of Cardigan and Carmarthen.[12] In August Pembroke had been told that he would not lose Kidwelly save 'at his will and pleasure', which meant he could decide if and when the de Londres heiress should be restored.[13] There was no question of returning Cemais to the fitz Martin heir while he remained in Falkes's custody.[14] Reginald de Braose, on the other hand, could now recover St Clears and perhaps also supplant his nephew John, Llywelyn's protégé, in control of Gower. Hubert authorized an order to the latter effect on 24 September. Meanwhile, until 1225, Pembroke maintained his ally, Cynan ap Hywel, in Ceredigion below the Aeron, in place of Maelgwyn ap Rhys, although the latter had held there 'in fee'.[15] The earl of Pembroke and Hubert de Burgh had reasserted the king's authority over Wales. It was time to do the same in England.

v. *Hubert's opportunity, October–November 1223*

After the completion of the Montgomery campaign, Hubert returned to Westminster in triumph. The army which he had led had raised

---

[9] *PR*, 481; *Ann. Mon.*, iii, 83.

[10] Davies, *Wales*, 235.

[11] *Ann. Mon.*, iii, 83.

[12] *PR*, 413–14.

[13] *RLC*, 571b. In July 1223, presumably with Pembroke's consent, the de Londres heiress was transferred from his familiar, William Crassus, to Reginald de Braose's younger brother, Walter: *PR*, 376.

[14] There seems no precise evidence as to when the fitz Martins recovered Cemais but see *ERF*, 120; *RLC*, ii, 140.

[15] *RLC*, 564; Walker, 'Hubert de Burgh and Wales', 476. Ultimately, however, John de Braose held on to Gower: *PR 1225–32*, 421–2; 'Neath Cartulary', 152–3. By 1228 Llansteffan had been recovered by its lord, William de Camville, and it is probable that Laugharne too was restored to its lord, William de Brian: Walker, 'Anglo-Welsh Wars', 193–4.

the siege of Builth, secured Montgomery for the king and brought Llywelyn to submission. That submission was equally a setback for the earl of Chester, who was both Llywelyn's ally and Hubert's enemy. All this had been achieved on the broad back of the earl of Pembroke. As a royal letter put it the following year, it was Pembroke who had 'boldly torn' the king's castles from the hands of Llywelyn, castles 'which could scarely have been freed without his power and industry'.[1] But Hubert could bask in Pembroke's glory. They had been allies since at least 1221, when Hubert had tried to arrange Pembroke's marriage to the king's sister, and their alliance had been confirmed in 1223 when Hubert, in the teeth of opposition, had given the government's full support to Pembroke's campaign.

One person above all must have been impressed by Hubert's success: the king. He had been in Hubert's company throughout the year. A suit of armour had been made for him, together with surcoats, banners and pennons. These were all in red cendal, adorned with the royal coat of arms, the leopards being of yellowish cendal adorned with gold leaf.[2] In August Richard de Umfraville had been careful to ask Hubert to make his excuses to the king for his late arrival at Portsmouth. In October Llywelyn had submitted in person to Henry at Montgomery.

Hubert, therefore, must have reflected that he would never be better placed to implement the papal letters of April 1223. He would be able to retain his position by the king and manipulate the resumption of the castles and sheriffdoms so as to destroy the power of his enemies and safeguard that of his own party. The earl of Pembroke, moreover, must have encouraged Hubert to take the initiative. Holding no royal castle or sheriffdom in England, he had nothing to lose from the resumption and much to gain, since it would slash the power of Falkes and the earl of Chester.

This does not mean that Hubert did not believe in the changes on grounds of public policy. In August he attested a royal letter which rebuked the justiciar of Ireland for usurping the liberties of the king. What made this 'the more offensive to your fame', the king told the justiciar, was that 'we have appointed you the protector in our place, in our kingdom of Ireland, to preserve our rights and to dispense justice to everyone else (ceteris), so that if anyone attempts [presumptions of this kind] you are bound, by the power committed to you, to punish them most severely'.[3] This letter surely reflected Hubert's view of his own office on the eve of the king's assumption of power. By bringing about the resumption of the king's castles and sheriffdoms he was doing his duty as justiciar in preserving the rights of the crown.

[1] DD, no. 140.
[2] RLC, 550b.
[3] RLC, 570–570b.

vi. *The collapse of Hubert's initiative, November 1223*

The stage was set for Hubert but he acted upon it with caution. The return to London, after the Montgomery campaign, brought about no immediate revolution. On 27 October Peter attested the writ giving Hubert his annual fee as castellan of Dover.[1] But Hubert was also sealing his alliance with the earl of Pembroke, to whom the custody of Cardigan and Carmarthen was formally committed on 7 November during the king's pleasure.[2]

It was in the first week of November that Hubert struck. According to Falkes's *querimonia*, 'the justiciar and his accomplices . . . procured that two barons should be called to the king's court, namely Walter de Lacy [sheriff of Hereford] and Ralph Musard [sheriff of Gloucester] . . . who, when they arrived, were not permitted to depart until they had assigned the castles, which they held as custodies, to the justiciar'.[3] These two 'victims' were carefully chosen. Walter de Lacy's brother, Hugh, was by now in open revolt in Ireland. Although Walter remained loyal, there were good reasons, quite apart from any general changes in the sheriffdoms, for removing him from office.[4] The selection of Musard, on the other hand, seems inexplicable, for he was a familiar of the earl of Pembroke, the last man whom Hubert wished to offend. The fact is, however, that, Musard's resignation was purely nominal. He was actually one of the few sheriffs who continued to hold office throughout 1223 and 1224. When Hubert and the king fled from London, a few days after Musard's 'resignation', it was precisely to Gloucester that they went for shelter.

The conclusion is inescapable: Musard and the earl of Pembroke were party to Hubert's plans. Musard, essentially, made a formal resignation of Gloucester *pour encourager les autres*, an encouragement which derived its force from the fact that his resignation, like that of Lacy, was demanded, and justified, on the grounds of the papal letters sent in April. The Dunstable annalist asserts that, after the king returned from Wales, 'the barons having been summoned to London, by order of the pope and with the assent of the barons it was provided, and the provision published, that the king should have his legitimate age as far as the free disposition of his castles, lands and wards were concerned'.[5] The implication was that where Lacy and

---

[1] *RLC*, 573.

[2] *RLC*, 574; *PR*, 413–14. On 26 October Pembroke's knight, Thomas Basset, was granted £20 to sustain him in the king's service: *RLC*, 567.

[3] *Walt. Cov.*, 261.

[4] This point, and the general interaction of English and Irish affairs in 1223–24, has been stressed to me in a letter by Dr R. F. Frame.

[5] *Ann. Mon.*, iii, 83.

Musard led, the others were to follow. Nonetheless, it was only an implication. Hubert, as far as the evidence goes, had yet to demand formally the resignation of everyone else. Equally, the papal letters giving the king control of the seal were not implemented, as Hubert's continued attestation of royal letters shows. Hubert, therefore, was attempting changes in the localities without, or at least before, loosening his grip at the centre. That had the advantage of enabling him to control the resumption and the disadvantage that he could not place the king's full authority behind it. Ultimately, things were to work better the other way round.

The facts of power, however, dictated this cautious approach. Hubert was in alliance with the earl of Pembroke, but the latter's strength was in Ireland and south Wales. He held no important English castle. The earl of Salisbury's two castles were Salisbury and Trowbridge, neither particularly powerful. Hubert's own strength lay in Kent and eastern England. By contrast, Falkes was entrenched across the midlands: castellan of four major castles, Oxford, Northampton, Bedford and Hertford, and sheriff of six counties. He held four more castles in south-west England. Meanwhile, Engelard de Cigogné held Windsor and Odiham, and Peter himself Winchester, Portchester, Southampton and Farnham. If it came to a fight, these men, in alliance with the earl of Chester, could mobilize formidable resources.

The relative paucity of the king's household forces made Hubert's position all the more dangerous. True, the financial recovery since the war had made possible an expansion of the military household. At the height of the Montgomery campaign there were at least thirty-seven knights *de familia regis*, as opposed to seven in 1218. Fifteen knights in 1223 were in receipt of annual fees, paid via writs of *liberate*, against four in 1219. Nonetheless, these forces remained smaller than those of John, or of Henry himself later in the 1220s: in 1228 Henry was paying fees to seventy household knights, while the total establishment around 1226 was 123.[6] Apart from the thirty-seven household knights, the king in 1223 also had a permanent establishment of fifty-eight serjeants, which was expanded to seventy-one during the Montgomery campaign.[7] But that still meant the total establishment of knights and serjeants was only 108 men, a force that Falkes could rival on his own for next year he put over eighty knights and serjeants into Bedford castle.[8] The army of Montgomery itself highlighted Hubert's danger. It was divided into constabularies, there being twenty-eight knights in the king's and twenty-four in Hubert's. But Peter, Falkes and Engelard

---

[6] Walker, 'Anglo-Welsh Wars', 70. C 72/2, m.20. See Critchley, 'Summonses to military service', 86.

[7] Walker, 'Anglo-Welsh Wars', 175–8.

[8] Norgate, *Minority*, 296–8.

also headed constabularies, each comprising between twenty and twenty-two knights. Falkes's own constabulary included Brian de Lisle with seven knights and ten knights of Falkes's own. Only the earl of Surrey, with fifteen knights, contributed a larger personal contingent.[9]

Hubert had one further difficulty: he had yet to reach an agreement with Archbishop Langton. Falkes's *querimonia*, as has been seen, blamed Hubert and his accomplices for the removal of Lacy and Musard. Only at a later stage in its narrative, as in that of the Dunstable annals, did Langton and the bishops become involved in the crisis. That a gap existed between Hubert and Langton is confirmed by a royal letter to Langton of 8 November which Hubert attested. It expressed the king's 'vehement astonishment' that Langton's officials were preventing rents from being collected from the vacant bishopric of Coventry, rents which the rolls of the exchequer showed that the king's predecessors had always received. Langton was told to prevent this happening, for, 'according to the certain hope which we have of your love, you should preserve us possessed and in enjoyment of those things which our ancestors . . . have rejoiced in through royal authority'. This letter would have been inconceivable had Hubert and Langton been working closely together. It went, moreover, beyond the immediate issue of the Coventry vacancy.[10] In effect Langton was reminded of the task in which Hubert was engaged and invited to help in securing for the king the 'enjoyment of those things which our ancestors . . . have rejoiced in through royal authority'.

Hubert indeed needed all the help that he could get. Essentially his move over Lacy and Musard had been to test the water before making more general changes. The water proved to be boiling. According to Falkes's *querimonia*, the earls of Chester and Gloucester and the count of Aumale, recognizing that if Hubert remained in power they would be at his mercy, decided to go to the king to expose the justiciar's malice. However, Hubert, so the *querimonia* continues, informed the king that there was a plot to seize and imprison him and the two fled to Gloucester.[11] Royal letters show that this flight from London took place on 9 November, the day after the appeal was sent to Langton. On the way to Gloucester the knight, Ralph fitz Nicholas, now back in the king's service after his spell as the steward of the earl of Derby, was put in Lacy's place as sheriff of Hereford.[12] Hubert and the king remained

---

[9] Walker, 'Anglo-Welsh Wars', 182–3, and appendix to chapter 3, i–vi, where the muster roll of the campaign (C 72/3, m.1) is analysed and transcribed.

[10] *RLC*, 629. The initial information on which this letter was based came from 'the custodians' of the bishopric, that is, from Bishop Peter and his officials, but there is no indication that Peter was responsible for the eventual letter sent to Langton.

[11] *Walt. Cov.*, 261.

[12] *PR*, 414–15.

at Gloucester from 15 to 22 November. On 16 November Hubert, the earl of Salisbury and William Brewer authorized a writ there.[13] So, at this climactic moment, Salisbury was at Hubert's side, just as he had been during the Christmas crisis of 1221. Behind Salisbury, of course, was the earl of Pembroke. Indeed, what had drawn Hubert to Gloucester were the resources, eighteen miles to the south-west, of the Marshal lordship of Nether Went and the security of its great castle of Chepstow.

William Brewer's presence at Gloucester was also significant. He had quarrelled with Bishop Peter over forest rights in Hampshire and perhaps, in November 1223, he was also reluctant to disturb his son's imminent election to the bishopric of Exeter.[14] Whatever the reason, two of the three ministers to whom the key papal letter of April 1223 had been addressed were now working together at the king's side.

Having gathered ample forces, Hubert and the king returned to London, going direct to the Tower, where they were on 27 November. As they approached, Chester, Aumale, Falkes, Brian de Lisle and their allies abandoned an attempt to seize the fortress and withdrew to Waltham. On 28 November Hubert took steps to protect Berkhampstead and Colchester castles 'from the attacks of [the king's] enemies'. His initiative had failed.[15]

vii. *Archbishop Langton's intervention, December 1223*

It was at this point, with the country on the brink of civil war, that Langton intervened. According to the Dunstable annals, being present in London with many of his suffragans, he sent messengers to those who had withdrawn to Waltham, bidding them come to the king to be reconciled and to give satisfaction for their excesses.[1] In Falkes's *querimonia* Langton and his colleagues likewise made their first appearance 'pretending to intervene to try and quiet the discord'.[2] On 3 December, presumably as a result of this mediation, a royal letter

[13] *RLC*, 575b.
[14] *PR*, 385, 415. See above p. 137.
[15] *Ann. Mon.*, iii, 83–4; *PR*, 416. It is not always clear who had custody of the Tower during the minority. In 1217 Louis surrendered it to Bishop Peter. Some time in 1217–18 the earl of Chester appears to have been custodian. Walter de Verdun was constable in 1218–19, perhaps as the regent's deputy. Pandulf was constable for a while, perhaps taking control on the regent's resignation. Stephen of Seagrave was constable from October 1221 till at least Easter 1223. When Hubert gained control is uncertain, although he seems to have been in charge by Christmas 1223: 'Southwark and Merton', 53; E 368/1, m.3; *Divers Accounts*, 46; *RLC*, 358, 525b, 472, 545; *Coggeshall*, 204.
[1] *Ann. Mon.*, iii, 83–4.
[2] *Walt. Cov.*, 261.

summoned and gave safe-conduct to the earls of Chester and Gloucester, the count of Aumale, John de Lacy, Robert de Vieuxpont, Falkes de Bréauté, Brian de Lisle and Engelard de Cigogné to attend a meeting the following morning at St John's Clerkenwell or the New Temple, 'where we will provide what is best by common counsel'.[3]

This is the fullest official list of the dissidents, whom Bishop Peter was soon to join, if he had not done so already. Probably Roger of Wendover was right to add the names of Peter de Maulay and the king's steward, William de Cantilupe. Both were certainly in the camp of the dissidents in 1224, Cantilupe by then having lost Kenilworth castle and the sheriffdom of Warwickshire–Leicestershire.[4] The forces and events which brought Bishop Peter, Chester, Falkes, Engelard and Maulay together and separated them in various degrees from Hubert have already been traced. Brian de Lisle had gone on crusade with the earl of Chester in 1218 and was in Falkes's *constabularia* in the army of Montgomery. Cantilupe too was probably connected with Chester.[5] All these men held extensive local office and had much to lose from the impending changes. Aumale had long been associated with Peter and since the end of the war had suffered a series of losses and humiliations.[6] The failure of his claim to the castle and honour of Tickhill perhaps rankled with Robert de Vieuxpont. John de Lacy was a major tenant of the earl of Chester and had married his niece. The presence of the earl of Gloucester may be explained by his conflict with his brother-in-law, the earl of Pembroke, over the castle of Dinas Powys in Glamorgan and by his thwarted claim to the Barton outside Bristol.[7]

The meeting planned for 4 December probably went ahead on that day or the next. Beforehand, there was at least an attempt at conciliation. On 4 December the king, by a writ authorized by Hubert in William Brewer's presence, allowed Peter to give the vacant church of Henley to whom he wished.[8] But the meeting swept all this away. Its explosive course is described in the annals of Dunstable, which were drawn up under the auspices of the prior, who may well have been present. When the dissidents came into the king's presence they 'declared unanimously that they had done and wished to do nothing against the king, but in every way it was necessary for Hubert de Burgh,

[3] *PR*, 481–2. Gloucester in the letter is obviously a mistake for London.

[4] *Chron. Maj.*, 83.

[5] *Ann. Mon.*, iii, 54, 60; C 72/3, m.1; C 60/27, m.4; *PR 1225–32*, 360; *CChR*, 115.

[6] Aumale may also have been influenced by moves in the Michaelmas term of 1223 to deprive him of part of the Egremont inheritance in Cumberland: *CRR*, xi, no.1223.

[7] The earl of Gloucester was the uncle of John de Braose and, like the earl of Chester, he had been a supporter of John against the latter's uncle, Reginald de Braose, Pembroke's ally: *BNB*, no.167.

[8] *PR*, 416. For a gift of fish to the earl of Pembroke on 4 December: *RLC*, 577.

called justiciar, to be removed from the administration as a dissipator of the king's treasure and an oppressor of the people. But the justiciar, then present, having heard these things with indignation, burst out in insulting words and, wishing to place the blame for everything on Peter, bishop of Winchester, he called him a traitor to the king and kingdom, and asserted that all the evils, which had happened in the times of King John and King Henry, had been perpetrated through his malice. The bishop, however, returning evil for evil, threatened that, if it cost him all he had, he would cause the justiciar to be removed from power, and, rising up from the middle of the assembly, with the accomplices named above [the earl of Chester, the court of Aumale, Falkes and Brian de Lisle], he left murmuring and complaining.'[9] It remained for Langton and the bishops to salvage what they could and on 6 December, according to Falkes's *querimonia*, they arranged a truce and a suspension of the matters in dispute until 20 January.[10]

viii. *The king receives control of his seal, 10 December 1223*

Langton had intervened to keep the peace between the two sides, much as he had in January 1221, but as soon as the truce was concluded on 6 December he decided to go much further. He joined with Hubert to give the king control over his seal. The decision was implemented at Westminster on 10 December. Down to that date royal letters had been attested by Hubert but on the tenth, in the presence of Langton, Hubert and the bishops of Bath and Salisbury, the king attested a letter himself.[1] This marked a new beginning. After 10 December 1223 all letters under the great seal were attested, in normal circumstances, by the king rather than by his justiciar.

Historians have sometimes implied that this change signalled the fact that the king, with certain restrictions, had been declared of age. But at the time the government never claimed this. It had merely implemented the papal letters of April 1223 which ordered Ralph de Neville to give the king control of his seal but did not declare him to be of age. Consequently the king continued to make concessions with his majority as their *terminus ad quem*. In fact, in one respect, the government went less far than the papal letters permitted. The latter had ordered the three ministers to give the king 'free disposition' of his kingdom but the king's freedom continued to be limited by the ban on permanent alienations until he came of age.[2]

---

[9] *Ann. Mon.*, iii, 84.

[10] *Walt. Cov.*, 261–2.

[1] *RLC*, 578. On 8 December a writ attested by Hubert in Langton's presence had been authorized by the king: *PR*, 417.

[2] See below, p. 389.

A great change had nonetheless taken place in the nature and authority of the government. Although for some time the king's influence is hard to gauge, the seal now followed his movements. He, not Hubert, took ultimate responsibility for the issuing of royal letters and for the decisions which they implemented. The change, however, had taken place at an ideal moment for Hubert. The last writ which Peter authorized was on 8 December.[3] After that his connection with central government was severed totally. He did not authorize another royal letter for nine years. His son or nephew, Peter des Rivaux, was soon to be removed as treasurer of the king's wardrobe.[4] There is no sign that Falkes or the earl of Chester remained at court. In November it had been too dangerous for Hubert to detonate the papal letter which gave the king control of the seal. Now he could do so in safety. With only his allies present, he had no difficulty in remaining at the king's side, exercising guidance over affairs. This was reflected in a new formula which was appended to a large number of letters in the chancery rolls as soon as the king took over their attestation: the letters were attested 'in the presence' of Hubert and the bishops of Bath and Salisbury.

This formula equally reflected the political alliance between Hubert, Langton and the bishops which had given the king control of his seal. The alliance was openly proclaimed in a royal letter sent to the pope on 19 December, itself attested by the king in the presence of Hubert and the bishops of Bath and Salisbury. The king thanked the pope for the April letters and rejoiced in the amelioration of his royal state due to the work of Langton and the bishops with Hubert 'assisting always by our side powerfully and publicly in all fidelity'.[5]

One point in the agreement between Hubert and Langton was that the ban on permanent alienations until the king came of age should remain in force.[6] This was a sensible move to reduce tension, in that it postponed the scramble for patronage which the relaxation of the ban would have brought. Its corollary was that Hubert and his allies could not, as yet, gain permanent reward for their faithful service. A second element in the agreement was the installation, at the very centre of

---

[3] *RLC*, 578. Peter's authorization (in company with the bishop of Durham) does not necessarily indicate that he was at court on 8 December.

[4] *Divers Accounts*, 50; Tout, *Chapters*, i, 191.

[5] *F*, 171.

[6] Hence no charter roll was opened until the restriction was lifted in January 1227. The Dunstable annalist (*Ann. Mon.*, iii, 83, see Norgate, *Minority*, 203, notes 2 and 3) implies that the restriction was introduced after the king's return from Montgomery as part of the provision that he should have his 'legitimate age' as far as the free disposition of his castles, lands and wards was concerned. But it is much more likely that it was inaugurated when the king gained control of his seal in December and the issue of what he could and could not do with it became a live one.

government, of the bishops of Bath and Salisbury: Jocelin of Wells and Richard le Poore. Both had served as justices on the great eyres of 1218–19 but neither had been active in central government since the war. Jocelin was a former chancery clerk of King John but had gone into exile on the latter's excommunication.[7] Richard, although from a curial family, had not risen through the royal administration in the same way. Rather, he was a celebrated scholar who had studied under Langton at Paris. As bishop of Salisbury (1217–26) he began the building of the new cathedral and promulgated a famous set of diocesan statutes. Indeed, his reform work at Salisbury 'was one of the formative influences in thirteenth-century church history'.[8]

Hubert's alliance with Langton, therefore, placed a new set of restrictions on his power. Previously he had worked with the king's council but the authorization note, 'by Hubert and the council', now virtually disappeared from the rolls. There was also a sharp decline in the number of letters for which Hubert took sole responsibility. Hubert had at his side two able bishops, neither of whom he knew particularly well, one of whom, Poore, was linked closely to Langton. The bishops rarely took sole responsibility for letters but clearly Hubert, quite apart from the necessity of working with the king, had more defined restrictions on his independence than when he worked with that nebulous and *ad hoc* body, the king's council.[9] Hubert's co-operation with the council had been an important factor in sustaining his power, demonstrating that he acted with consent. It is a measure of the authority conferred by Langton and the bishops that 'the council' could be replaced by the bishops of Bath and Salisbury.

In the broadest terms, what Langton was doing in 1223 was to support the king's recovery of his rights, just as he had supported the resumption of the demesne in June 1222, but in the process he had also become Hubert's partisan, whatever the restrictions he had placed upon him. Instead of postponing the matters in dispute until the expiry of the truce arranged on 6 December, Langton permitted the king to have his seal at a time when only the bishops and Hubert's supporters were at court. There may indeed have been no great assembly present at Westminster at all. The affair was hurried through almost in a corner. Thus no royal letter announced that the king would henceforth control the seal and no chronicler commented specifically on the fact.

The reason why Langton acted as he did in December 1223 was not due to some long-standing alliance with Hubert. It is true that Langton

    [7] Gibbs and Lang, *Bishops and Reform*, 11, 186.
    [8] Gibbs and Lang, *Bishops and Reform*, 25–7, 193. It was probably for spiritual reasons that John made Richard one of his executors.
    [9] The significance of the appearance of the bishops of Bath and Salisbury at Hubert's side has been discussed in an unpublished paper by Professor Cazel.

had been present again and again at key moments of Hubert's career: at Runnymede when he became justiciar; in the court adjudging him the Three Castles; at the councils in 1219 when he replaced the regent; and at his marriage in 1221. But around Christmas 1220 Hubert had headed the list of those urging the pope not to restore Simon Langton, the archbishop's brother, to England. In 1223 itself the alliance was not in place when Hubert launched his own initiative in November. Essentially, Langton sided with Hubert for public rather than for private reasons. His theological writings reveal him as a highly practical man.[10] Now he made a practical judgement about the situation in England. As he saw it, it was Hubert's opponents who were the disturbers of the peace. Thus when he first intervened, it was to summon the dissidents to court to give satisfaction for their excesses. These men had tried to seize the king before his flight to Gloucester; had attacked the Tower of London; and had skulked in arms at Waltham. By 9 December Langton knew, in addition, that they planned to meet for Christmas at Northampton 'in great array'. Against this background, he judged it vital to strengthen the government against the possibility of serious disturbances in the realm. The news about the Northampton assembly, indeed, may have been the immediate catalyst behind the move over the seal on 10 December. The first writ which the king attested dealt with preparations to forestall the hostile gathering by spending Christmas at Northampton himself.[11]

Other strands in the alliance are more speculative. Could Langton agree with Hubert, in a way he could not with Peter, or William Brewer, about the necessity of the Great Charter?[12] Was Langton's conduct influenced by his perception, as a native-born Englishman, that the trouble-makers were aliens, a perception that he could share with Hubert? Certainly, Langton's 'Englishness' was an important part of his make-up: 'from our tender years we have loved our kingdom with a tender, natural love' he declared in 1207. In 1220 one theme of his sermon preached at Becket's translation was the 'triumph of an Englishman'.[13] Of course, in 1223 the earls of Chester and Gloucester, John de Lacy, Brian de Lisle and Robert de Vieuxpont made up a strong native contingent amongst the dissidents. Conversely, Philip Mark, although from the Touraine and a kinsman of Engelard, remained aloof from the crisis and held on to both his sheriffdom and Nottingham castle until the end of 1224. Nonetheless, only one alien, Hugh de Vivonne, was named amongst the leading supporters of the

[10] Powicke, *Langton*, 94.

[11] *RLC*, 578.

[12] See below. p. 334.

[13] *Gervase*, lxxxi; Duggan, 'The cult of St Thomas Becket', 39; Powicke, *Langton*, 96–7.

government in December 1223, while the alien element amongst the dissidents was pronounced.[14] It included Peter himself, the count of Aumale, Falkes, his fellow Norman William de Cantilupe, Engelard and Peter de Maulay. It has been seen how Hubert was told in 1221 or 1222 that Falkes had threatened all native-born Englishmen with war. That was precisely the theme, according to Falkes's *querimonia*, of Langton's sermon to the people on the occasion of Falkes's absolution in 1224: 'here is the affliction of the natives to whom the people of England were so often given over as booty . . . take heed so that aliens are no longer permitted to act against you'.[15]

Langton and Hubert, therefore, had given the king control of his seal but they did not leave matters there. They moved on to implement the second thrust of the April letters. They would resume the king's castles and sheriffdoms, thus cutting the power of the dissidents and vindicating the rights of the king.

ix. *The king resumes his castles and sheriffdoms, 30 December 1223*

After the king received control of his seal on 10 December tension continued to mount. Both sides sent envoys to Rome, Langton, according to Falkes's *querimonia*, trying to prevent the departure of Robert Passelewe, emissary of the dissidents, lest he should seek the despatch of a legate.[1] Both sides planned to spend Christmas at Northampton, although eventually the schismatics, as the Dunstable annalist calls them, fixed on the earl of Chester's borough of Leicester instead.[2]

The king arrived at Northampton on 23 December. The Dunstable annalist observed that, what with Langton 'and so many bishops, earls, barons and armed knights, neither in the days of the [king's] father, nor afterwards, is such a feast known to have been been celebrated in England'.[3] Hubert and Langton had made sure of their chief supporters by 19 December, when their names were sent to the pope.[4] Not surprisingly, the list was headed by the earls of Salisbury and Pembroke; then came the earl of Surrey. But there was a large group of other magnates, many of them former rebels, namely Robert fitz Walter (who received a gift of game from the king on 29 December),[5]

---

[14] *F*, 171.
[15] *Walt. Cov.*, 268–9. For Langton's stance as an 'Englishman', see Powicke, *Langton*, 96–7.
[1] *Walt. Cov.*, 262–3; *F*, 171; *DD*, no. 136.
[2] *Ann. Mon.*, iii, 84.
[3] *Ann. Mon.*, iii, 84.
[4] *F*, 171.
[5] *RLC*, 579b.

Robert de Ros, William de Albini and the earls of Essex, Norfolk, Warwick and Hereford, the last appearing despite his continued exclusion from Trowbridge by the earl of Salisbury. Most surprising, perhaps, was the presence of the earl of Derby, given his close association with his brother-in-law, the earl of Chester, and his ejection from Bolsover and the Peak in 1222. Perhaps he had already been promised the custody of the the the castle and honour of Lancaster in succession to Chester. These magnates obviously commanded a formidable military force. Indeed, in the army of Montgomery, Robert fitz Walter, William de Albini and the earls of Derby and Surrey all headed constabularies of between fifteen and twenty-two knights. The earl of Surrey's fifteen knights, in a constabulary of twenty-two, were the largest contingent that an individual magnate brought to the army.[6]

The day after Christmas, Langton and his suffragans excommunicated all disturbers of the realm. Then the king, acting on the advice of Langton and Hubert, summoned the earl of Chester and his supporters to court. Chester's loyalty and restraint at this crucial moment were much praised by Powicke. Roger of Wendover was more cynical. Chester and his allies, he reported, decided to obey the summons, both through fear of excommunication and because they were aware, through their scouts, that their own forces were considerably smaller than the king's. Had they not been thus outnumbered, Wendover asserted, they would have taken up arms against the king 'on account of the justiciar'. As it was, faced with unpromising odds, Chester and the rest gave way and appeared at Northampton on 30 December. The papal letters which ordered the castles to be restored to the king were exhibited, thus hurdling the objection that he was not of age. Then the king, counselled by Hubert, demanded that Chester and his associates make restitution without delay. There was some hesitation. Should the order be obeyed without consulting the pope? But Langton intervened. He threatened the dissidents with excommunication but promised that in the surrenders everyone would be treated equally. In other words Hubert and his followers would also give up their castles.[7]

And so, at Langton's 'word and order', the earl of Chester came forward and surrendered his royal castles.[8] He was followed by the other schismatics. The chancery rolls show that on 30 December Chester resigned the castles of Shrewsbury, Bridgnorth and Lancaster together with their attendant sheriffdoms. Falkes gave up Hertford castle and the sheriffdoms and castles of Oxford and Northampton. Engelard surrendered the castles of Windsor and Odiham; Brian de Lisle the castles of Knaresborough, Bolsover and the Peak; and

[6] C 72/3, m.1; Walker, 'Anglo-Welsh Wars', 182–3, appendix to ch.3, i–vi.
[7] Powicke, *Henry III*, 50–1; *Chron. Maj.*, 82–3; *Walt. Cov.*, 262; *Ann. Mon.*, iii, 84.
[8] *Walt. Cov.*, 262.

William de Cantilupe the castle of Kenilworth and the sheriffdom of Warwickshire–Leicestershire.[9] Falkes may also have resigned his other sheriffdoms, for Bedfordshire–Buckinghamshire and Cambridgeshire–Huntingdonshire were transferred to new sheriffs in January 1224. In addition, on 7 January Bishop Peter was ordered to give up the castles of Winchester, Portchester and Southampton, and the sheriffdom of Hampshire.

On 30 December, however, as Langton had promised, it was not merely Chester and his followers who surrendered their custodies. Hubert, on his part, resigned the castles of Dover, Canterbury, Rochester, Norwich, Orford and Hereford; the earl of Salisbury resigned Salisbury; William Brewer, Devizes; and the household knights, John Russell and Ralph Gernun, the castles of Sherborne and Corfe, and the sheriffdoms of Somerset and Dorset.

According to Falkes's *querimonia*, Langton himself distributed the castles to their new keepers. Here too there was an attempt at conciliation. The custodies of the earl of Chester were given to the earl of Derby and Hugh Despencer, the latter being one of Chester's major tenants. Many of the castles and counties, moreover, were placed in the hands of ecclesiastics: namely the bishops of Bath, Salisbury, London, Lincoln and Hereford, and the archbishop of York. Langton himself took over Windsor and Odiham from Engelard. The intention was to show that the custodies had been placed in safe and also neutral hands, although whether the schmismatics saw it like that, in view of the alliance between Langton and Hubert, may be doubted.

Nonetheless, on 30 December the resumption and redistribution of the castles had some appearance of being as non-partisan as that of the demesne in June 1222. This appearance was quickly shown to be false. Both Ralph of Coggeshall and Falkes's *querimonia* pointed out that, while the custodies of Chester and his fellows were vacated bodily, those of their opponents were either retained or quickly recovered.[10] This was largely true. Admittedly, Brian de Lisle was still resisting the surrender of Knaresborough at the end of January but in the other cases Chester's party seem quickly to have surrendered physical possession. By contrast, Hubert's constable at Dover was merely told on 22 January to be obedient to a knight whom Langton was sending.[11] There is no evidence that Hubert actually vacated Norwich and Orford, and he certainly remained as sheriff of Kent and Norfolk–Suffolk. Meanwhile, Ralph fitz Nicholas, whom Hubert had put in at Hereford, remained as sheriff and castellan there, as did Ralph

---

[9] For this and what follows, see *PR*, 417–21.
[10] *Walt. Cov.*, 262; *Coggeshall*, 204.
[11] *PR*, 425.

Musard at Gloucester. William Brewer remained in place at Devizes and the earl of Salisbury at Salisbury. The latter also retained the sheriffdom of Wiltshire, as the earl of Surrey did that of Surrey.[12] Equally significant was the way in which Hubert and his supporters were quickly moved into the custodies vacated by Chester's party. On 7 February Langton vacated Windsor and Odiham in Hubert's favour. At one point it was intended to place the earl of Salisbury in all of the bishop of Winchester's custodies but instead he replaced the earl of Chester's successor, Hugh Despencer, as castellan of Shrewsbury and Bridgnorth, and sheriff of Shropshire and Staffordshire.[13]

The result, therefore, was that Hubert and his allies not merely retained their local power but greatly increased it at the expense of their enemies. Falkes's *querimonia*, not surprisingly, accused Langton of hypocrisy. This was to oversimplify. Langton certainly discriminated between the parties, taking physical control of Windsor and only nominal control of Dover,[14] but given the way that Chester and his allies had brought the country to the brink of civil war, this was inevitable. Had they then accepted the changes instead of challenging them at Rome and seeking the despatch of a legate, more might have been done to make a reality of the settlement. As it was, when tension persisted in the new year, that prospect slipped away and Langton accepted, after some hesitation, Hubert's installation at Windsor and Odiham,[15] followed, in March, by his return to Rochester.[16]

The changes in the sheriffdoms involved far more, however, than simply the removal of one party from office and its replacement by another. The new sheriffs were appointed on quite different financial terms from their predecessors: they were appointed as custodians answerable at the exchequer for all the revenue (the profits) which they collected above the county farms.[17] The same terms were imposed on

---

[12] *List of Sheriffs*, 86, 67, 59, 49, 152, 135; *PR*, 514, 554. Other sheriffs who remained in place were William Brewer junior (Northumberland), Philip Mark (Nottinghamshire–Derbyshire), Matthew fitz Herbert (Sussex), Walter de Beauchamp (Worcestershire): *List of Sheriffs*, 97, 102, 141, 157. In Yorkshire, Geoffrey de Neville (who was absent in Poitou for much of the crisis) was replaced as sheriff by his former deputy, Simon of Hale (who accounted from Michaelmas 1223), but Geoffrey retained control of Scarborough and Pickering: *List of Sheriffs*, 161; *RLC*, ii, 11.

[13] *PR*, 420, 421; *RLC*, ii, 5b; *List of Sheriffs*, 117; E 372/68, r. 14d, mm. 1,2.

[14] The physical possession of Windsor is proved by his account for the period 4 January – 6 February 1224: E 372/68, r. 14d, m.2.

[15] The hesitation may be indicated by the fact that an initial order on 12 January for the transferral of Windsor and Odiham to William de Rughedon and thence to Hubert was cancelled: *PR* 420. The castles were eventually transferred to Osbert Giffard (Hubert's deputy) on 6 February: *PR*, 421; E 372/68, r. 14d, m.2.

[16] *PR*, 430.

[17] Mills, 'Experiments in exchequer procedure', 167; Carpenter, 'Decline of the curial sheriff', 10.

the sheriffs who remained in office.[18] That the exchequer wished to move in this direction had been signalled at the end of 1220, when both the sheriffs of Berkshire and Northumberland had become custodians, but it was only with the wholesale removal of sheriffs at the end of 1223 that the policy could be given general application. Thus, at last, the government exploited the deletion of clause 25 of Magna Carta 1215, which had effectively banned the exaction of revenue above the county farms. In many ways the situation in December 1223 was unpropitious for the new policy. With the country wavering on the brink of civil war, it was essential to maintain, indeed to extend, the hold of great loyalists like the earl of Salisbury over the sheriffdoms. Such men, even in peaceful times, expected to draw off the revenue above the farm to sustain themselves in the king's service and to maintain the royal castles in their care. In the circumstances of 1223–24 it was necessary to allow them to do so. The new policy would have worked better had it been possible to replace the great curial sheriffs with county knights and minor professional administrators. Nonetheless, in the pipe roll of 1224 £407 were recorded as reaching the exchequer from profits and in the next roll the sum was £649.

That profits were demanded in such inclement weather is clear evidence that the government was not merely involved in party politics. It was determined to increase the king's cash revenues and assert tighter control over the sheriffs. Hubert himself was at the centre of the new policy. He made his own under-sheriffs in Kent and Norfolk–Suffolk answer for profits from Michaelmas 1223, before, that is, the general changes had taken place in the sheriffdoms, and they paid into the exchequer the largest sums, respectively £100 and £107, recorded in the pipe roll of 1224. Equally, Hubert, having taken control of Windsor and Odiham, accounted for the issues of their attendant manors, whereas Engelard de Cigogné had rendered no accounts at all.[19]

x. The resumption of the castles and sheriffdoms: perspectives and conclusions

The resumption of the castles and counties at the end of 1223 brought to a triumphal conclusion the programme which the papacy had first urged on the English government in 1219. Well might William de Sancto Albino, writing from Rome, congratulate 'your majesty who now fully and perfectly reigns' on having been delivered from those who 'were involved in the occupation of your patrimony'.[1]

This is not to say that in 1223 there was a clear-cut divide between

[18] The only sheriff, new or old, who did not acount as a custodian either from Michaelmas or Christmas 1223 was Simon of Hale in Yorkshire.

[19] E 372/68, r.9, m.2; r.11, m.1; r. 14d, mm. 1,2; E 372/70, r. 15, mm. 1, 2.

[1] *DD*, no. 136.

the advocates of centralized government, on the one hand, and of semi-independent local governorships on the other. On Hubert's side, after all, was the earl of Salisbury, who certainly believed in running his sheriffdoms with limited interference from the centre and who cherished a claim to hold Salisbury castle and Wiltshire in hereditary right. It was Falkes, in 1219, who had been employed to maintain the peace of the realm against Salisbury's attempted seizure of Lincoln castle. But although not clear-cut, a division between Hubert and his opponents about the proper structure of local government nonetheless existed. Hubert retained his royal castles until his fall, but it was in Wales, rather than in England, that he laboured to construct a permanent power base for his family. Once in control of the exchequer after 1219, he viewed matters increasingly from that vantage point. His aim was to build up a large cash revenue at the centre where he sat in control. He did not aspire to become a great multi-purpose regional governor, who drew on the revenues of his sheriffdoms to sustain his own 'great service'. Thus he accounted for profits from Kent and Norfolk–Suffolk from Michaelmas 1223 and in 1227 resigned both the sheriffdoms.

Precisely because they were not in control at the centre, the attitude of Peter's party was very different. Essentially, it remained rooted in the circumstances of the war and its immediate aftermath when regional governors had, of necessity, collected and spent the king's revenues as they thought fit. There was a feeling amongst the schismatics in 1223 that that was still the right way to do things. The alternative, after all, was to pay money in at the centre and see it dissipated by Hubert. In 1223, therefore, Hubert knew that he would never persuade members of Peter's party to account for revenue above their county farms. Their removal was a necessity both for the prosecution of the new financial policy and for tighter control over local officials in general. The revenue that Peter himself, as sheriff of Hampshire, paid into the exchequer was limited by the large allowances which he obtained for expenditure in the king's service. Some of these were legitimate enough. Others were clearly extracted as political bargains, notably that conceded in 1221 which set £266 of wartime expenditure against subsequent peacetime revenues. Peter also used his position to cover his encroachments on the royal forest, encroachments into which an inquiry was launched in 1224.[2] Engelard de Cigogné, meanwhile, avoided accounting for the manors associated with the castles of Windsor and Odiham. He was equally determined, as he made clear in insolent letters, to resist Hubert's efforts to subject him to the sheriff of Berkshire: 'You ought to write to me in the same form as you write to

[2] *Pipe Roll 1219*, 24–5; *Pipe Roll 1220*, 121–2; *Pipe Roll 1221*, 16–17; E 372/66, r.7, m.1; E 372/68, r.1, m.1; *RLC*, 655b; see above p. 144.

the sheriff. Therefore, if you wish the affairs of the king to proceed in this matter, you should send me the same summons as you send to the sheriff.'[3]

Falkes's record in respect of his county farms was particularly unimpressive, however much his hold over his sheriffdoms made possible the staging of forest eyres. Falkes had devoted extraordinary energy to exploiting the sources of revenue from which the county farms were obtained and had created many enemies as a result.[4] But the paradox of all this activity was that it brought no direct or quantifiable financial benefit to the king. Since 1221 Falkes, let alone accounting for profits, had often failed to clear the money which he owed for his county farms. Consequently, by the end of November 1223 he owed £258 worth of arrears under that heading, plus another £179 for the farms of various manors.[5] It looks as though, rather than pay this money into the exchequer, he had decided to keep it for himself to spend on what he deemed to be the king's good purposes. That was not exactly how the government saw it and Falkes was later accused, with some exaggeration, of converting to his own use 11,000 marks from his sheriffdoms which he ought to have paid into the exchequer.[6]

The reluctance of the schismatics to surrender their custodies in 1223 was partly, of course, because they were being asked to surrender them into Hubert's power. But, faced with that prospect, they also argued that the longevity and fidelity of their service justified their continuation in office. At Northampton, in the words of Falkes's *querimonia*, Chester and the rest surrendered 'all the castles which they had kept for the king faithfully and for a long time'. In Rome, early in 1224, Robert Passelewe demanded that the dispossessed be restored to their castles 'because they had been faithful to the king's father in the time of the war'.[7] Fundamentally, these men believed that there was no one to whom the king's castles could be more safely entrusted, as the pope was informed when urged to withdraw the letters of April 1223. But, of course, it was precisely the length of the tenure which made it dangerous to the crown, entrenching Falkes, Chester and their colleagues more deeply into local office and making their immediate control by the

---

[3] SC1/1, no. 83 (the affair in question concerned attachments for pleas of the forest); see also *RL*, no.cxxxix.

[4] See below pp. 333–4.

[5] E 372/68, r.1d, m.2. Falkes accounted (through deputies) for the sheriffdoms in which these debts arose in November 1223: E 368/6, mm.14, 14d, 20. For the year 1225–26 the profits for his sheriffdoms were over £200 gross: E 372/70, r.3, m.1; r.5d, m.1; r.12, mm.1, 2, 1d. It was only after Falkes's dismissal that the keepers of Woodstock began to account at the exchequer.

[6] *RL*, no.cclvii; see also *DD*, no. 203.

[7] *Walt. Cov.*, 262; *Ann. Mon.*, iii, 89.

exchequer and eventual removal by the king all the harder. This point was grasped by the Barnwell annalist when he said that the king in 1223 recalled 'to his demesne' many castles 'detained for a long time both by aliens and natives, for he held them suspect and feared they might do him great harm, if their power . . . was allowed to last any longer'.[8]

The irony of Peter's career, therefore, was that, while attached to the aggressive and absolutist forms of kingship practised by King John, he found himself supporting local governorships on a scale and of a type which John, in the circumstances of 1223, would not have tolerated for a moment. Whether the benefits to the crown, in terms of increased revenue and control over its local agents, would have been as great had Peter masterminded the changes is doubtful. If, in 1223, Peter's policy had been the counterpart of Hubert's, then Falkes, Chester, William de Cantilupe, Engelard, Brian de Lisle and Peter himself would merely have made nominal surrenders, while Hubert, the earls of Salisbury and Surrey, and Ralph Musard, amongst others, would really have resigned their castles and sheriffdoms.[9] But Peter would scarcely have vindicated the king's right to control local office as effectively as did Hubert, for the key issue in 1223 was not the king's ability to dismiss any custodian but his ability, or that of his government, to dismiss those who had been appointed by King John. The basic fact was that in Peter's party there were five such men, controlling eleven royal castles and eleven counties.[10] On Hubert's side there were only two, controlling four counties and five or six castles.[11] Even if there are added to these lists those on either side who were appointed by the young king during the war, the balance is much the same. On Peter's side, there were then six men, controlling twelve counties and thirteen

[8] *Walt. Cov.*, 253. The annalist went on to observe that the point was proved by subsequent events, meaning Falkes's rebellion.

[9] Peter may well have left in place Matthew fitz Herbert in Sussex and Walter de Beauchamp in Worcestershire, for neither seem to have been particular partisans of Hubert. Walter remained in office when Peter finally attained power in 1232.

[10] Counties: Oxfordshire, Northamptonshire, Bedfordshire–Buckinghamshire, Cambridgeshire–Huntingdonshire (Falkes); Lancashire, Shropshire, Staffordshire (the earl of Chester); Warwickshire–Leicestershire (William de Cantilupe): Castles: Oxford, Northampton, Cambridge, Hertford, (Falkes); Lancaster, Shrewsbury, Bridgnorth (Chester); Kenilworth (Cantilupe); Windsor, Odiham (Engelard); Knaresborough (Brian de Lisle). Falkes lost Cambridge and Hertford castles to Louis during the war but recovered them on its conclusion.

[11] Counties: Kent, Norfolk–Suffolk (Hubert); Gloucester (Ralph Musard); castles: Dover, Canterbury, Norwich, Orford (Hubert); Gloucester (Musard). I can find no evidence as to when Hubert acquired Rochester but it may have been under John. He recovered Norwich and Orford, having lost them to Louis during the war. He was also reappointed as sheriff of Norfolk–Suffolk in September 1217 during the king's pleasure: *PR*, 90; for his original appointment by John: *Pipe Roll 1215*, 10.

castles;[12] on Hubert's side, four men, controlling six counties and seven or eight castles.[13] The fact was that Peter's freedom of action was restricted because his allies, particularly thanks to Falkes's multitude of sheriffdoms, held the largest share of local office.[14] On the other hand, both Hubert's chief supporter, the earl of Pembroke, and the wider baronial and ecclesiastical constituency to which he appealed held no English custodies at all. Hubert, therefore, was far better placed to carry through radical changes.

On the part of schismatics there may, as Powicke believed, have been a degree of loyalty and restraint which prevented them plunging the kingdom into war. But essentially, as Roger of Wendover recognized, they submitted because they were compelled to. Their own forces at Leicester were simply outnumbered by the king's at Northampton. That was partly because the king could draw on the contingents brought by the church. It was also because large numbers of great magnates, most of them former rebels, rallied to his cause. Thus the victory in December 1223 followed the same pattern as that over Newark in 1218, Mitford in 1220, Bytham in 1221 and probably also over the resumption of the demesne in 1222. In December 1223 two former rebels, John de Lacy and the earl of Gloucester, stood with the earl of Chester. But against this, of the eighteen named supporters of the government in December 1223, fourteen were former rebels. Of these, the earls of Pembroke, Salisbury and Surrey had been on the edge of Louis's party, but the eighteen also included, as has been seen, Robert fitz Walter, Robert de Ros and the earls of Essex, Norfolk and Hereford.[15] An equally impressive array of former rebels supported the government in the following year when it came to the siege of Bedford castle.[16]

Past rebels were doubtless attracted to Hubert's side by the prospect of taking on old opponents from the war. Even more, the way some of Peter's party had run their local offices had made them many enemies. Engelard at Windsor had had bruising confrontations with the abbot of Reading and the bishops of Lincoln and Salisbury.[17] Falkes and his

[12] Counties: Hampshire. Castles: Winchester, and probably also Portchester (Peter).

[13] Counties: Wiltshire (the earl of Salisbury); Surrey (the earl of Surrey). Castles: Salisbury (Salisbury); Guildford (Surrey). In none of these cases does a record of appointment survive but both earls probably secured the custodies when they entered the king's allegiance in 1217.

[14] When Peter was in power between 1232 and 1234 his government did little to improve existing policies in the field of extracting revenue above the county farm: see Carpenter, 'Decline of the curial sheriff', 13–14.

[15] F, 171.

[16] See below p. 365.

[17] RL, no.cxxxviii; SC 1/1, nos 192, 193.

deputies, in the course of enforcing such shrieval rights as suit of court and sheriff's aid, had come into conflict with the earls of Pembroke, Salisbury, Essex and Gloucester, John Marshal, William de Beauchamp of Bedford, Thomas Basset of Headington, the bishop of Ely, the monastic houses of Dunstable, Thorney, Ramsey and West Dereham, the canons of St Paul's cathedral and the monks of Canterbury cathedral priory. With Falkes's dismissal a great sigh of relief must have gone up across the whole of central England.[18]

The wide support given to the government at the end of 1223, however, was also a tribute to its general conduct since the war and, in more recent years, to Hubert's own handling of affairs. The great councils of 1219 had preferred Hubert to Peter as the regent's successor because he seemed to promise a more moderate and acceptable form of government. Fundamentally, that hope had been realized. This was true in a variety of areas, none being more important than that of the Charters. There was a difference of attitude here between Hubert and Archbishop Langton. Langton's approach to the Charters was one of principle and derived from theories about the body politic. Hubert's was pragmatic and might change with circumstances. The imprecision of the Charters, especially over the question of deforestation, gave plenty of room for debate and manoeuvre, for advance and retreat. Occasionally, when it seemed necessary, Hubert blatantly transgressed the Charters – most notably when Constantine fitz Athulf was hung 'without judgement'. But if here, on a much smaller scale, he anticipated the conduct of Bishop Peter when the latter attained power between 1232 and 1234, he never pointed the moral by ridiculing the clause in the Great Charter which forbad such action.[19] Nor is there evidence throughout his long career, that he ever criticized the Charters in general, like William Brewer. Fundamentally, the justiciar, like the regent before him, treated the Charters with respect. He was a cautious politician and recognized that to do otherwise would both disturb the peace of the kingdom, as Langton warned William Brewer, and undermine his own position.

After the war the most important clause of all in the Great Charter for the barons – that which limited their relief to £100 – had been steadily observed. The clauses dealing with the administration of justice had also been fulfilled. Thus, as the Charter demanded, the use of the writ *praecipe* in such a way that 'a free man might lose his court' came to an end. If, as is not unlikely, the *praecipe* writ had been employed by the Angevin kings to remove cases from the feudal courts

[18] *CRR*, ix, 330–1; x, 147, 165–6; xiv, no.1188; E 159/3, m.8d; E 368/3, mm.1(2)d,2; *RL*, nos lxxxviii, cxcvi, cxcvii; *RLC*, 458, 458b, 499, 500; *Ann. Mon.*, iii, 54–5.
[19] See below p. 394.

of lords, this clause dealt with an important baronial grievance.[20] By 1219, in accordance with the Charter, the writ had been replaced by a new writ *praecipe in capite*, which 'was to give the lord an assured procedure so that he could normally recover his court'.[21] Significantly, the first known judgement founded on the new procedure took place at the bench while presided over by Hubert de Burgh and the earl of Oxford, the latter one of the twenty-five guarantors of Magna Carta in 1215 and the baron who had attested the writs which implemented the twenty-five's own judgements.[22]

The Charter was also upheld in the more general field of the dispensation of justice. The demand that the king make his civil justice more available was one of the most crucial features of the Charter. It showed that men appreciated the advantages that kingship could provide if properly directed. After the war the direction was much as desired. The clause commanding that common pleas be held in 'any certain place' was fulfilled both by setting up the bench at Westminster and by recommencing the eyres in the localities. The annalist of Waverley abbey described how the itinerant justices of 1218–19 'revived the laws and caused them to be observed in the pleas before them according to the Charter of King John'.[23] Likewise, the clause which stipulated that barons were to be amerced 'by their peers' was fulfilled on the eyres by reserving such amercements for the king's council.[24] The government also acted in the spirit of clause 18 of the 1215 Magna Carta which demanded that the king's judges should visit the counties, four times a year, to hear petty assizes, sitting with four knights of the county elected in the county court. In the Charter of 1217 this requirement was modified so that the judges were to come only once a year to hear the assizes 'with the knights of the counties', probably because it was thought more frequent visitations might both interfere with the general eyre and impose impossible burdens on the judiciary. But, in fact, it became increasingly the practice in the minority, perhaps at Hubert's suggestion, to deal with petty assizes by granting individual commissions to four judges to hear one or a few cases. On each commission some or all of these judges were county knights. In this way local society

[20] Miss Hurnard showed that there is little evidence in the plea rolls of John using the writ in this way: Hurnard, 'Magna Carta, clause 34', 157–79. However, Dr Brand points out to me that case records would not necessarily reveal when it had been used.

[21] Clanchy, 'Magna Carta, clause thirty-four', 543–4, 547; for the first known appearance, *CRR*, viii, 135–6, a reference I owe to Dr Brand.

[22] *CRR*, viii, 349; Meekings, 'Concords'; Clanchy, 'Magna Carta, clause thirty-four', 543. Another clause in the Charter that the government took steps to uphold was that which forbad sheriffs and others from holding pleas of the crown. For the new article of the eyre on this subject in 1221, see *Wiltshire Eyre*, 29.

[23] *Ann. Mon.*, ii, 291.

[24] See above p. 98.

exercised a large measure of control over the hearing of assizes, thus achieving in some part the aspirations which had been expressed in the 1215 Charter.[25]

The Charter had also been concerned about the quality of justice, laying down that the king was not to deny it or sell it to anyone. In this context, the salaries granted to senior justices in 1218 may well have been an attempt to prevent them accepting gifts and bribes, just as they were in the later reform programme of 1258.[26] They were also a significant step along the road to a professional judiciary. Of course, what men often wanted was less impartial justice than justice which they could control in their own interests. After the war former rebels were given some measure of reassurance here by the appointment of two of their number, first the earl of Arundel and then the earl of Oxford, as the senior justices of the bench. Equally, at a lower level, many former rebels became petty assize justices. Indeed, as memories of the war faded, the employment of former rebels became increasingly common. On the eyres of 1218–19 four such men served as judges; on those of 1226–29 as many as ten were appointed, including William of Lancaster, Roger Bertram, Maurice de Gant, John de Lacy and Thomas of Moulton, who was by now a justice of the bench.[27] That former rebels had confidence in the utility of the judicial process is clear from the large numbers who started legal actions after the war. Indeed, all but three of those named amongst the government's chief supporters in December 1223 had done so.

The minority witnessed, in fact, a rapid expansion in royal justice. A striking measure of this lies in the number of agreements, or concords, reached before the king's judges in settlement of cases, one of the most constructive aspects of the work of the courts. The number of agreements struck on the eyres of of 1218–19 was 1,037, as opposed to 737 when the same counties were visited in John's reign. When the counties were visited again between 1226 and 1229, the number of agreements was 1,704.[28] This expansion of justice was also reflected in the 1220s, in both the first registers of legal writs and the first drafts of *Bracton*, the great work on the laws and customs of England. Indeed,

---

[25] These commissions are found enrolled on the dorses of the patent rolls.

[26] *RLC*, 350, 365; Turner, *Judiciary*, 244–5; *DBM*, 108–9. A salary is found being paid to Stephen of Seagrave in 1220 (*RLC*, 411, 421, 444) but apart from that, if the judges were regularly paid after 1218, it was not through writs of *liberate* enrolled on the chancery rolls. This whole question will be discussed by Dr Brand in his forthcoming book on the origins of the English legal profession.

[27] Crook, *General Eyre*, 79–86; Meekings, 'Concords'.

[28] Crook, *General Eyre*, 71–6, 63–71, 79–86. I have not included the west-midland counties visited in 1220–21 in the comparison because the final concords for their last visitation in John's reign are lost.

the cases discussed in *Bracton* are drawn to a great extent from the minority of Henry III.[29]

After the war, therefore, the government did much to fulfil the spirit and letter of the Charter in the field of justice. This did not mean that the Charters were always observed by its local officials. Indeed, the Dunstable annalist explicitly asserted that they were not.[30] Late in the minority there were charges that sheriffs were holding local courts in defiance of Magna Carta. Likewise in 1219 and 1220 accusations were brought before Hubert and the council about the behaviour of forest officials. Hubert's response, however, had been sympathetic. He had ordered various clauses in the Forest Charter to be upheld and had enjoined the officials to behave 'in so friendly a fashion' that there were no more complaints.[31] Of course, it was the government itself which was accused of transgressing the Forest Charter by refusing significant deforestation but here it could plausibly argue that it was merely preventing the counties from taking far more than was their due. In 1223 itself the forest eyres had been resumed but on a very tentative basis. Brian de Lisle had visited Nottinghamshire, Derbyshire, Staffordshire, Hampshire and Somerset but there was probably little attempt to collect the debts arising before 1224–25 and even then the total issues were under £50.[32] In the early summer of 1223, moreover, collection of debts from the Yorkshire eyre of 1222 was respited by the exchequer until after Michaelmas, while Nicholas de Stuteville was pardoned (by Hubert and Peter) 30 marks of his 40 marks amercement for leading its boycott.[33]

Above all, the stance of Hubert's government in relation to the Charters was demonstrated by the events of January 1223. Hubert determined to push ahead with an inquiry into the king's rights in the counties but, in return, the king verbally confirmed the Charters. The recovery of his powers would take place within those fundamental limits.

Hubert's approach to the Charters was part and parcel of his general attitude to government and politics. When occasion demanded, he

---

[29] *Registers of Writs*, cxix–xxi; *Bracton*, iii, xiii–lii, for Professor Thorne's fundamental work on the date of *Bracton*.

[30] *Ann. Mon.*, iii, 93.

[31] See above pp. 164, 181–2.

[32] E 372/67, r. 1d, m. 2; r. 5d, m. 2; E 372/69, r. 14, m. 2; r. 7, m. 2.

[33] E 368/5, mm.12 (2)d, 12(1)d. The total sum reaching the exchequer in the pipe roll of 1223 from the eyres held in 1221–22 was only £167, the most significant amount – £89 7s 7d – coming from Northamptonshire: E 372/67, r.14d, m.2. For others pardoned forest amercements, including Richard de Percy and the earl of Derby: E 372/67, r.11d, m.2; E 372/69, r.4, m.2; r.9d, m.1; *RLC*, ii, 66b (where pleas of the crown is a slip for pleas of the forest); E 368/5, m.12(2).

could act with calculated harshness, as the Londoners discovered,[34] but his general way was cautious and moderate. Pandulf was seeing that essential characteristic from a different angle when he accused Hubert of 'travelling always over seas and mountains and seeking those things which are not to be had'.[35] Hubert *was* prepared to move slowly towards his objectives, with the patience of one used to long castle sieges. Thus the charges hurled at him by his enemies in 1223 did not strike deep chords outside their own circle. Hubert was accused of 'not ruling the kingdom with impartial laws' and of 'behaving towards the nobles far too imperiously in his acts and judgements'. Yet Hubert might fairly claim to have taken heed of the regent's reminder in 1218 that it was especially his task to maintain and favour justice.[36] He had presided on occasions at the bench, watched over difficult cases, heard petty assizes on journeys through the kingdom and rooted out malefactors by the use of approvers. He seems to have trodden cautiously in law suits, postponing controversial matters and trying to settle cases by compromises rather than by judgements. This was true, for example, of the suits between Falkes and the earl of Pembroke, between John and Reginald de Braose, and between Robert de Vieuxpont and the countess of Eu. The complaints of Falkes against Robert de Courtenay and of the earl of Pembroke and John Marshal against Falkes were shuffled off into law suits and inquiries. If Hubert squeezed the Three Castles from Reginald de Braose and Banstead from William de Mowbray, for both men there was a *quid pro quo*.[37]

The government, after the war, had struggled to implement the treaty of peace and restore former rebels to their lands, hence the long battles over Mitford and Bytham. Hubert had personally intervened in the cases of Roger de Montbegon and William de Marsh.[38] The government had also sought to appease former rebels in another way: in its handling of the debts which they owed the crown. King John had harried magnates to pay their debts with such ruthlessness that the rebellion of 1215, as Professor Holt has remarked, was a rebellion of the king's debtors.[39] After the war the Londoners payed a 2,000 mark fine for the lifting of the interdict imposed on the city, while Reginald of Cornhill, King John's renegade sheriff of Kent and an easy target, had to sell property in 1222 when forced to clear his huge debts to the

---

[34] For Peter de Maulay's allegations of threats made against him by Hubert later in the 1220s, see *CRR*, xv, no. 131; see also *CRR*, xvi, no. 1088.

[35] *F*, 162.

[36] *Chron. Maj.*, 79; *Coggeshall*, 203; *RLC*, 378.

[37] For Reginald, see above pp. 168, 216. Mowbray is discussed below.

[38] See above pp. 170, 179, 216.

[39] Holt, *Northerners*, 34.

crown.[40] But many of the greatest rebels, if sometimes burdened with ransoms, were treated with considerable laxity when it came to their ordinary debts to the crown. For some of those oppressed by King John, the minority of Henry III must have seemed like walking out into the sunlight after confinement in a debtors' prison.

Take the case of Gilbert de Gant. Between 1210 and 1214 he had reduced his Jewish debts in the king's hands by £436 13s 4d. When his debts were brought together and totalled in the pipe roll of 1219, they came to £810 7s 7d. They stood at exactly the same sum in the roll of 1223.[41] Gilbert may not have become earl of Lincoln but in 1219 he could afford to rebuild his castle at Folkingham in impressive style.[42] Gant was particularly fortunate because he had no ransom to pay. Another great northern baron and also one of the twenty-five guarantors of the Great Charter, William de Mowbray, had to clear his ransom by granting Banstead to Hubert de Burgh, yet there was some compensation in the treatment of his debts to the crown. King John had forced Mowbray to pay these off at £100 a year.[43] In the early minority, by contrast, William paid nothing in at the exchequer and his debts, when they were added up in 1221–22, came to £1,462 19s 10d, a sum which included the Poitevin scutage, the scutage of 1217, debts left over from John's reign and an ominous new item, £414 13s 4d worth of debts owed to the Jews. But no terms were fixed for the repayment of this potentially crushing sum. In the pipe roll of 1222 only £6 3s 6d reached the exchequer and in the roll of the next year, nothing at all.[44]

The government was also cautious in its approach to the controversial debts left over from the war and before. Little was done to collect the Poitevin scutage of 1214.[45] Likewise, it was not until the pipe roll of 1225 that William of Lancaster was saddled with his father's £8,000 fine for King John's grace, and he was then allowed to pay it off, with

[40] *Historiae Anglicanae*, 1878; *Pipe Roll 1221*, 202; E 372/66, r.5, m.1. Reginald, captured at Rochester in 1215, had also to pay a large ransom and was apparently still in prison in 1223: *Historiae Anglicanae*, 1878–9; *RLC*, 481b. For Reginald and Rochester castle where he was constable, see Rowlands, 'King John, Rochester castle and Stephen Langton', 270–7.

[41] *Pipe Roll 1211*, 61; *Pipe Roll 1212*, 109; *Pipe Roll 1214*, 150; *Pipe Roll 1219*, 122; E 372/67, r.8, m.1; see Holt, *Northerners*, 167, 173.

[42] *RL*, no. lii.

[43] *Pipe Roll 1209*, 130–1; *Pipe Roll 1210*, 152; *Pipe Roll 1211*, 52–3, 33; *Pipe Roll 1212*, 36; see Holt, *Northerners*, 172.

[44] E 372/66, r.10, m.1; E 372/67, r.11, m.1. The receipt roll for Easter 1223 shows £10 being received from Mowbray: E401/6, r.2d.

[45] *Pipe Roll 1219*, xxiii. Dr Harris's observation here about the non-payment of the scutage in the pipe roll of 1219 continued to be true down to 1224. However, the receipt roll of Michaelmas 1224 has sums received from the tenants of Robert fitz Walter, e.g. E401/7, r.3d.

his other debts, at £33 6s 8d a year, again some compensation for his heavy ransom.[46] The earl of Essex made no recorded payments down to 1225 towards what remained of the notorious 20,000 mark fine which his brother had made to marry the countess of Gloucester. In addition, he paid nothing towards his other debts, including the first scutage of the reign and his relief, both of which dated back to 1217.[47] When terms were set for the repayment of debts, even if the latter had arisen from offences committed in King Henry's reign, they could be quite reasonable. In 1221–22 the exchequer totted up the debts, hardly paid since the war, of another great Northerner and member of the twenty-five, Robert de Ros. They came to £398 6s 11d and included £333 6s 8d worth of amercements for convictions before the justices in eyre in 1219 and Hubert de Burgh a year later. In the pipe roll of 1222 Ros was credited with one payment of £55 6s 8d and was allowed to pay off the remainder of the debts at the rate of £33 6s 8d per annum. Next year he was sufficiently *persona grata* to be permitted to purchase a wardship which had been taken from him by the king in 1218.[48]

Another charge against Hubert in 1223 was that he was 'an oppressor of the people'.[49] But the conciliatory treatment which his government afforded to great magnates had its counterpart in its dealings with county society. Hubert had attempted to abolish scotale, had intervened to limit the number of shrieval and forest officials and had stressed that the counties and forests should be administered justly and without oppression.[50] He had also known when to draw back, postponing the forest eyres and withdrawing the January 1223 inquiry. Meanwhile, in the early summer of 1223, the collection of all *debita Judeorum*, the debts owed by Christians to the Jews which had come into the king's hands, was suspended until Michaelmas.[51] If this concession reflected the unpopularity of such exactions, the receipt rolls show that the money derived from the *debita* came from an accumulation of small sums and probably most debts were repaid on reasonable terms.

---

[46] E 372/69, r.6d, m.1. The fine of William's father, Gilbert fitz Reinfrey, was also for William's release (*RF*, 570–1), but, after Gilbert's second rebellion, William probably had to make a ransom agreement of his own. It was the burden of this ransom that Gilbert and William complained about in 1219–20. In 1223 William de Albini was allowed to pay off his 6,000 mark fine for the king's grace (see above p. 25 n.3), to which he had hitherto made no contributions, at 40 marks a year: E 372/67, r.8, m.2.

[47] E 372/69, r.8, mm.2, 2d.

[48] E 372/66, r.10, m.1; *ERF*, 17, 101.

[49] *Ann. Mon.*, iii, 84.

[50] See above pp. 164, 181–2, 191, 292.

[51] E 368/5, m.12(2)d. The immediate aim here (as in the remission of the Yorkshire forest amercements) was probably to create a favourable climate for the mobilization of the armies to fight in Wales.

Thus the £63 received from the Yorkshire *debita* in the Easter term of 1223 were contributed by seventy-one individuals, with the largest amount (from the abbot of Byland) being only £10 6s 8d.[52]

This moderation was not surprising because Hubert's government, like the regent's, was of necessity rooted in consent. Hence the delay in the earl of Pembroke's marriage to the king's sister when that consent was not forthcoming. Hubert had co-operated both with small groups of ministers and with frequently summoned great councils, and had attempted to demonstrate the fact by using the formula 'by the justiciar and the council' to authorize royal letters. Great councils had conceded the carucage tax, returned Bytham to William de Coleville, counselled the excommunication of the count of Aumale, acquitted Peter de Maulay of treason, advised the dismissal of the justiciar of Ireland, obtained the postponement of the forest eyres, supported the resumption of the royal demesne and secured the king's verbal confirmation of the Charters. Ultimately, it was a great council of the king's supporters, meeting in arms, which forced the surrender of the castles and sheriffdoms at the end of 1223.

Hubert de Burgh had stressed that there was an essential connection between the rights of the king and those of his subjects. Unless the king's rights were maintained he would be unwilling, indeed would be unable, to maintain the rights of everyone else. Between the interests of the king and his subjects, moreover, Hubert sometimes implied that there was a harmonious middle way. Thus he declared that both the king's rights would be better maintained and the counties oppressed less if the forests were run by a moderate number of officials.[53] In practice, of course, Hubert's approach was largely pragmatic, hence his readiness, when necessary, to retreat. Yet, precisely this pragmatism had enabled him to construct an acceptable or at least a sustainable relationship between the king and his subjects. In December 1223 itself there was one final and supreme guarantee of that, a guarantee which far outweighed the mixed blessing of William Brewer's support: Hubert was in alliance with Archbishop Langton. Langton had helped negotiate the Charter of 1215 and had demanded the confirmation of its successors in January 1223. Now he was at the centre of the king's government. There could be no more potent demonstration that its methods were to be utterly distinct from those of King John.

[52] E 401/6, r.5. See Stacey, *Politics*, 216. Numerous small payments are also found on the surviving Jewish receipt rolls from John's reign: E 401/1564. For the moderate levels of the taxation imposed on the Jews themselves in the early years of Henry III, explained perhaps by their impoverishment in the war, see Stacey, '1240–60: a watershed in Anglo-Jewish relations?', 136–7.

[53] See above pp. 160, 213, 164, 181–2.

On 30 December 1223 Langton got his reward. In the midst of the surrenders of the castles and sheriffdoms, or perhaps when the day's business was done, Hubert agreed to the return of his brother, Simon Langton, to England: Simon, the man who had been at the very heart of Louis's party, the man whom Hubert himself, with Chester, Falkes, Brian de Lisle, Engelard and William de Cantilupe, had stigmatized in 1220–21 as one who 'gloried in being the cause of John's death' and who 'thirsted after the blood of his son and all faithful men'. How times had changed.[54]

[54] *RLC*, 630b; *F*, 171.

Chapter 9

BEDFORD AND POITOU, 1224

i. *Confrontation or conciliation? The situation of the new government*

The events of December 1223 brought a huge change to English political life. The factional conflicts down to November 1223 had been essentially within the governing regime, the participants being both prominent at the centre and holders of local office. After December 1223 everything was different. Bishop Peter, the earl of Chester, Falkes, Engelard and the rest had lost their castles and sheriffdoms. Brian de Lisle was soon to be removed as the chief justice of the forests. These men were either excluded from or chose not to come to court. Thus Hubert and the bishops of Bath and Salisbury, and behind them Langton and their great lay supporters, were left to govern as they chose.

In domestic politics there was one major decision to take. Should the schismatics, now removed from office, be placated or punished? If the latter, the government had one lawful method, above all, which it could adopt. It could take possession of the few remaining royal manors, and the much larger number of escheats, which the schismatics held during the king's pleasure. Against Falkes himself, as will be seen, it could wield a range of other weapons. Already in January 1224 there were differences of opinion about which course to pursue. Some of the king's counsellors first opposed and then accepted an application to the pope for the removal of Falkes's protection as a crusader, the idea being that such a removal would make it easier to deprive him of the lands of the earldom of Devon.[1] In fact, between January and June 1224 the government oscillated between conciliation and confrontation. The conduct of the schismatics themselves, the pressures exerted by their enemies, Hugh de Lacy's invasion of Ireland and the situation in Poitou all influenced these changes of tack. Eventually the government stumbled into the great siege of Bedford castle and a life and death confrontation with Falkes de Bréauté.

The siege of Bedford was in a way a natural sequel to the course of English politics since 1216. It was the final and most formidable challenge to the king's authority from the great free-wheeling castellans who had won the war and gone on to dominate the peace. Falkes's ruin

[1] *DD*, no. 137.

seemed to bring to a victorious conclusion the government's struggle to assert its authority over such men. It was also a triumph for Falkes's long-standing private enemies. But the government's victory at home in 1224, although given added gloss by the defeat of Hugh de Lacy in Ireland, was overshadowed by the disaster in Poitou. While the king's army sat down from 20 June to 15 August around Bedford castle, King Louis overran Poitou with virtually no opposition. That too was a natural sequel to the crown's appalling weakness in the province since John's last visit in 1214. In 1224 the pope was persuaded that in crushing Falkes, rather than protecting Poitou, the government displayed a grievously distorted sense of proper priorities. In fact, until the last moment the choices never seemed as clear-cut as that.

ii. *Confrontation, February–March 1224*

In the early part of 1224 the government believed it could approach domestic problems free from imminent dangers in Poitou. Admittedly, the truce with the king of France was due to expire at Easter. Back in September 1223 the vicomte of Thouars had warned Hubert to provide either for its prolongation or for the defence of Poitou.[1] The government had no doubt which course to adopt. At Montgomery, that October, it despatched envoys to the king of France to seek the truce's prolongation. The atmosphere they found at the French court was disturbing. Philip de Albini was told that the towns and barons of Poitou would 'turn to the jurisdiction' of the king of France if the latter wished.[2] Perhaps the government should have taken more notice but, shortly afterwards, the threat to Poitou appeared to evaporate. In December 1223 the pope wrote to Louis, begging him to renew the truce with King Henry and intervene in the county of Toulouse where the heretics had expelled Amaury de Montfort. Next month Louis, asking that the truce with England be renewed for ten years rather than the customary four, agreed to go.[3] The English government was not altogether happy with this. The prolongation of the truce for ten years seemed to postpone for a shamefully long time the possibility of the king reclaiming his rights. Louis's installation in south-west France would place him in dangerous proximity to Gascony as well as extinguishing, for all practical purposes, the rights which kings of England claimed over the city of Toulouse.[4] Nonetheless, at least the immediate threat to Poitou and Gascony would be removed.

---

[1] *DD*, no. 123.
[2] *PR*, 412; *DD*, no. 127.
[3] Petit-Dutaillis, *Louis VIII*, 234–5.
[4] *DD*, no. 139 and also nos 136, 137.

Against this background, the government displayed considerable confidence in its dealings with Hugh de Lusignan. In August 1223, with a possible intervention in Normandy imminent, Geoffrey de Neville had been sent out with a new offer to Hugh. The negotiations, which began in October 1223, produced a 'form of peace' which Hugh sent to Hubert.[5] It was probably a watered down version of this which the king ratified in mid-January 1224, in the presence of Archbishop Langton, the bishops of Durham, London, Lincoln, Bath, Salisbury and Rochester, Hubert, the earls of Salisbury, Pembroke and Surrey, and William Brewer, a striking indication of the composition of the new regime and of the absence from court of Peter, the earl of Chester and Falkes. It was Hubert and the earls of Salisbury and Pembroke who swore on the king's behalf that he would observe the peace.[6]

The settlement, which was to last for four years, went further in some respects than what had been on offer back in August. In particular, compensation was given for the dower which Isabella had not received. She was to have the tin mines of Devon and the farm of Aylesbury in place of her Norman lands, and 100 marks a year at La Rochelle in place of Niort, despite the fact, so the king asserted, that Niort was not worth as much as that. She was also to receive 3,000 *livres tournois* (£800 sterling) over the next three years as compensation for all arrears of her dower. As for Joan's *maritagium*, however, the government was less forthcoming. In August 1223 Hugh had been offered Saintes until the king came of age, while nothing had been said about Oléron. This time, nothing was said about Saintes, but Hugh was conceded the 'land which he has in the isle of Oléron in the name of the county of Angoulême and in the name of the castle of Cognac', a formula which left open what exactly Hugh held in those names and avoided conceding him the island *tout court*.[7]

For the moment, it was the situation in Ireland rather than in Poitou which gave the government anxiety. The fears expressed in the spring of 1223 had been realized. Hugh de Lacy had invaded the country. He had gone, however, not to Ulster but to his brother Walter's province of Meath. There, in alliance with his half-brother, William de Lacy, he had 'pillaged and burnt the king's land, killing and holding his men to ransom'. In March 1224, therefore, under an agreement made before Langton, the bishops of London, Bath, Salisbury and Ely, Hubert and the earls of Pembroke and Salisbury, Walter de Lacy was sent to Ireland to make war on his brother.[8]

[5] *DD*, nos 124, 125, 123.

[6] *PR*, 422. Geoffrey de Neville returned to Poitou with the proffered settlement: *RLC*, 581.

[7] For the land of the count of Angoulême in Oléron, see *CPR 1232–47*, 156.

[8] *PR*, 483; *RL*, no. cxcv; Otway-Ruthven, *Medieval Ireland*, 91.

The central importance of the government's alliance with the earl of Pembroke was underscored by these disturbances in Ireland where Pembroke's cousin, John Marshal, had been in charge of Ulster since October 1223.[9] With Peter and the earl of Chester out of the way, therefore, steps were taken to confirm the alliance in the manner conceived by Pandulf and Hubert back in 1221. On 5 February Langton, Hubert and the bishops of Bath and Salisbury arranged for Eleanor, the king's youngest sister, to be handed over to Pembroke.[10] At long last their marriage was to proceed. The day after this decision Langton vacated the castles of Windsor and Odiham in Hubert's favour. Around the same time the earl of Salisbury took over the earl of Chester's former castles of Shrewsbury and Bridgnorth, and his sheriffdoms of Shropshire and Staffordshire.[11]

All this argues for rising tension between the government and the schismatics, as does the eventual agreement of the councillors to petition the pope about the future of the earldom of Devon. In the event, moreover, the government decided not to wait for papal permission. Towards the end of February the king, Hubert, the bishops of Bath and Salisbury, and William Brewer travelled to Marlborough. From there, on 29 February, Falkes was ordered to surrender all the lands of the earldom of Devon outside Devon, together with the castles of Christchurch and Carisbrooke, to William de Rughedon, the earl of Pembroke's deputy at court.[12] Falkes had been granted custody of the lands of the earldom, together with the heir, in 1218 until the king came of age, a concession that the government doubtless argued was nullified by the papal letters of April 1223. Falkes was not, however, attacked alone. On 29 February writs also went out ordering the seizure into the king's hands of William de Cantilupe's manors of Calne and Calstone, Peter de Maulay's manor of Upavon and Robert de Vieuxpont's manors of Titchfield and Milborne. Cantilupe, in all probability, was also deprived of Aston Cantlow in Warwickshire. The properties of William de Bréauté, Falkes's brother, at Kirtlington in Oxfordshire and elsewhere were also to be seized.[13] A few days later, on 9 March, the earl of Chester's familiar, Henry of Audley, was deprived of Edgmond, which he had held on to throughout the resumption of the royal demesne in 1222.[14]

[9] *PR*, 387.
[10] *PR*, 426.
[11] *PR*, 421; E 372/68, r. 14d, m. 2; *List of Sheriffs*, 117; *RLC*, ii, 5b.
[12] *PR*, 427.
[13] C 60/21, m.8. For Aston Cantlow, see *RLC*, 596.
[14] C 60/21, m.8. The writ mentions Newport rather than Edgmond but the two manors were linked together and it is certain that Audley was deprived of the latter: *CChR*, 55; *RLC*, 596.

Most of these properties had been 'lands of the Normans' which had come into John's hands after 1204, although Edgmond, Calne and Aston Cantlow were also ancient royal demesne. Since, as the writs noted, these properties were held *de ballio* of King John, they could be lawfully resumed. Nonetheless, the government was hitting at some of the most cherished possessions of these men. William de Cantilupe eventually acquired Calstone for life and Aston Cantlow, which became the chief home of his family, in hereditary right.[15] Audley likewise obtained Edgmond in perpetuity.[16] Peter de Maulay's determination to secure Upavon was still envenoming English politics in 1233.[17]

The government's offensive continued when it reached Bristol, where it met up with the earls of Salisbury and Pembroke. On 11 March a writ attested by the king, in the presence of Hubert and the two earls, conferred William de Bréauté's manor of Kirtlington on Pembroke's knight, Thomas Basset. Two days later a writ, attested in the presence this time of Hubert and the two bishops, told Falkes that he held Plympton castle merely *de ballio* of William Marshal when regent and ordered him to surrender it.[18] Not surprisingly, Falkes protested, pointing out that he had been given Plympton, as indeed he had, not *de ballio* but as part of his wife's dower. Langton shared with Hubert and the two bishops responsibility for the reply, sent from Reading on 21 March as the government returned to London. It explained that Plympton as *caput* of the earldom of Devon could not be held in dower and reiterated the demand for its surrender. On the same day a writ attested by the king in Langton's presence alone ordered Falkes to deliver up his stepson, the heir to the earldom of Devon.[19]

Clearly, responsibility for these measures was shared between Hubert, Langton, the two bishops and the earls of Pembroke and Salisbury. The earls may well have hoped to ruin Falkes, while Robert de Courtenay, who met the earl of Pembroke in February, must have urged his removal from Plympton.[20] But this was not simply a case of kicking men when they were down. Having been humiliated at Northampton, the schismatics did not pack up and go home. Instead, they waited eagerly for news from Rome, where Robert Passelewe was demanding the despatch of a legate who would recall them to court and restore their control over royal castles.[21] This was known to the

[15] *RLC*, 9, 14b; *CChR*, 66, 132; *VCH Warw.*, iii, 36.
[16] *CChR*, 55.
[17] Powicke, *Henry III*, 128, 132–3.
[18] *RLC*, 587b; *PR*, 429.
[19] *PR*, 430. See above pp. 78–9.
[20] *PR*, 426.
[21] *Ann. Mon.*, iii, 89–90; *DD*, no. 136, a letter which was written in mid to late rather than early January.

government by the end of February. Whether the schismatics waited in silence may also be doubted. The bishop of Winchester had munitioned his castle at Farnham. At Bedford Falkes was installing a garrison of over eighty knights and serjeants.²² The government's journey to Marlborough and Bristol in February and March may have been prompted by fears for the security of those castles. Both were given new constables when the king arrived. Work was also ordered on Marlborough castle and 1,000 crossbow bolts transferred there from Devizes.²³ It may be significant that the first three manors seized into the king's hands on 29 February were Calne, Calstone and Upavon, all within the immediate vicinity of Marlborough. Had there, perhaps, been gatherings and conjurations in the area?

Up to a point, therefore, the government was engaged in a pre-emptive strike. If it could remove Falkes from the possessions of the earldom of Devon he would have been reduced since December 1223 from eight major castles to only two: Bedford and Stogursey. He would no longer be the 'equal of an earl'. Equally, by removing the manors from William de Cantilupe, Peter de Maulay and the rest, the government taught them a lesson and hoped to bring them to heel. If these proceedings were harsh, they were also carefully measured. In stark contrast to the events of 1232–33, when Peter gained power, this was not a case of men being disseised unlawfully *per voluntatem regis* in contravention of the Great Charter. The argument that Plympton could not be included in the dower of Falkes's wife was a strong one. The other manors seized were all held during the king's pleasure. To that extent the door was left open for some future compromise. Indeed, that had already been apparent in the generous treatment of Engelard de Cigogné after he vacated Windsor.²⁴ There was a hint of compromise even with Falkes. He was told that Plympton could not be his wife's dower but was promised that, if she had less dower than was right, it would be made up to her 'according to the custom of the kingdom'. A compromise indeed was what the government soon attempted to achieve.²⁵

iii. *The settlement of April 1224*

Back at Westminster, after its journey to Marlborough and Bristol, the government faced again the problem of Hugh de Lusignan. Geoffrey de Neville had returned to England with Hugh's response to the treaty offered him in January. He had turned up his nose and demanded

²² HRO, Eccles II 159278, r. 4d; Norgate, *Minority*, 296–7; *Coggeshall*, 205.
²³ *PR*, 428, 429; *RLC*, 588b, 589.
²⁴ *RLC*, 581, 582, 585b.
²⁵ *PR*, 430.

more. The government, in royal letters of 27 March, decided to give it. The annual payment in place of Niort, already claimed as too high, was raised from 100 marks to 200 marks. Instead of the £800 for the arrears of Isabella's dower being paid over three years, it was to be paid all at once by 2 June. Above all, Hugh and Isabella, for the four-year duration of the treaty, could keep all the things of which they had been seized on 30 November 1223.[1] In other words, they could keep Joan's *maritagium* of Saintes, the Saintonge and the isle of Oléron. At last Hugh had got what he wanted: two *maritagia* for the price of one marriage. The reason for this capitulation may lie in the fact that the truce with the king of France was due to expire on 14 April, although, as will be seen, the belief was still that it would be renewed. But since, in any case, the government had no means of removing Joan's *maritagium* from Hugh, it made the best of a bad job.

The king attested the letter of 27 March, making these concessions to Hugh, in the presence of Langton, the bishops of London, Bath, Salisbury, Rochester and Ely, Hubert, the earls of Salisbury, Pembroke, Surrey, Essex and Norfolk, and Robert fitz Walter.[2] The government party, therefore, was much as it had been in December 1223 and January 1224. But its approach towards the opposition was softening[3] and, towards the end of April, a settlement was reached at a great council held at London. According to Falkes's *querimonia*, Langton had arranged for the barons to be summoned to the city. There 'with floods of tears he prayed [them] to come together in peace'. He was successful. According to a royal letter written two months later, at this London council there were 'brought together in peace the earl of Chester and all the other nobles who contended with the justiciar, and he with them, and the kiss of peace was given and received on both sides'.[4]

These ceremonies of reconciliation were accompanied by more material measures. At the end of April the manors which had been taken into the king's hands in late February and early March were restored, during the king's pleasure, to their previous holders. Calne, Calstone and Aston Cantlow went back to William de Cantilupe, Edgmond to Henry of Audley and Upavon to Peter de Maulay. At the same time, Robert de Vieuxpont was confirmed in his possession of Milborne and Titchfield, Brian de Lisle was repossessed of a number of properties and Engelard recovered Benson and Henley. Falkes and his family were included in the settlement. Falkes himself was restored to the manor of Moresk in Cornwall, despite its conferral a month

[1] *PR*, 431–2; *RLC*, 590, 594b.
[2] *PR*, 431–2.
[3] See *RLC*, 589, 589b, 590.
[4] *Walt. Cov.*, 263; *RL*, no. cxcix.

before on Walerand the German. William de Bréauté returned to Kirtlington despite the grant to Thomas Basset. Other restorations were made to Falkes's knights, Walter de Goderville and William Martel.[5]

There is no reason to challenge Falkes's view that Langton was at the heart of this settlement. Hubert and the two bishops were also closely involved, for the writs effecting the restorations were attested by the king in their presence. What had transformed the situation since the aggressive measures of February and March?

It is unlikely that the termination of the truce with the king of France on 14 April was a factor here, since the government remained confident of its eventual renewal. On the expiry of the truce, it had taken measures for the defence of the Channel Islands but had also permitted merchants in the power of the king of France to travel through King Henry's realms until 9 July.[6] On 28 April the bishops of Sens and Senlis were thanked for their message about the renewal of the truce and ambassadors were despatched, with powers to prolong it for four years, to a council to be held by Louis on 5 May.[7] Matters seemed to be proceeding equally satisfactorily with Hugh de Lusignan: £800 for the arrears of Isabella's dower and £133 for the annual payment for Niort (1,400 marks in all) were installed in the London Temple and, on 26 April, the master of the Paris Temple was authorized to hand over a like sum to Hugh's envoy as soon as he heard that Hugh and his barons had sworn to abide by the agreement. The same arrangement was made for the payment of the 500 mark fee of the vicomte of Thouars.[8]

Langton's enemies had no doubts about the reason for his intervention: he was desperate to prevent the despatch of a papal legate or envoy to England. By August 1224 the pope himself had come to believe this charge, which was repeated next year in Falkes's *querimonia*. There is certainly circumstantial evidence to support it. Robert Passelewe, when he arrived in Rome early in 1224, had justified his demand for a legate by pointing to the disturbed state of the country. Langton's envoys had countered by claiming that everything was peaceful. But Honorius was disturbed. He thought of sending an envoy to investigate the truth and, on 14 March, addressed a worried letter of advice to King Henry.[9] The king was to treat all parties alike and not to offend his vassals 'over the restitution of [his] revenues'. This letter probably reached England soon after the middle of April and it must

---

[5] *RLC*, 595b–6b. Early in May a concession was also made to Robert Passelewe: C 60/21, m.7.

[6] *PR*, 435.

[7] *PR*, 484; *F*, 174; *DD*, no. 141; Petit-Dutaillis, *Louis VIII*, 235.

[8] *PR*, 436; *RLC*, 594b, 601.

[9] *RL*, 540–1; *Walt. Cov.*, 263.

have been read to the king. It may well have influenced *him* in the direction of an amicable settlement. Certainly at this time leading *curiales* recognized that decisions could depend on their influence with Henry. In April 1224 itself William Brewer wrote to Ralph de Neville urging him to intervene vigorously with the king (*partes magnas interponatis versus regem*) so that his clerk might be presented to a particular benefice.[10] The pope's anxieties must equally have been made clear to Langton. After the settlement the latter hastened to send messengers to Rome, who announced that 'peace had been fully established in England', whereupon Honorius decided not to send his envoy after all.[11] That Langton, however, acted solely to keep a papal envoy out of England is incredible. He must also have wanted a settlement for its own sake. To help maintain the kingdom's peace and tranquillity was the duty of an archbishop and had been a theme in his career. He had intervened to secure peace after the Christmas crisis of 1221 and had warned William Brewer not to disturb it by challenging the Great Charter. He had intervened again to protect the peace in December 1223. Equally, the measures taken against the schismatics in February and March 1224, remaining as they did within the law, had always left open the possibility of reconciliation.

Of course, it took two to make a settlement. Chester and his followers had come to court. They had exchanged the kiss of peace with Hubert and recovered possession of some manors. They had not clamoured for Hubert's removal and their own reappointment as castellans and sheriffs. In short, they had recognized that the balance of power had tipped decisively against them and that they must salvage what they could. If they still hoped to transform the situation, they were prepared to wait and see what Passelewe could wring from the pope. In the meantime, while pressures mounted against Falkes, these men kept their heads down and did nothing to disturb the April settlement. Hence Engelard de Cigogné, Peter de Maulay, William de Cantilupe, Henry of Audley, Robert de Vieuxpont and Brian de Lisle all held on to the manors that they recovered in April 1224. For Falkes alone the April settlement did not stick.

iv. *The attack on Falkes, April 1224*

When Falkes looked back in his *querimonia* he considered the peace of April 1224 utterly hypocritical. Three days after its consummation, 'because of the open hatred with which the justiciar, the archbishop and certain of my enemies were persecuting me . . . by the procuration

[10] SC 1/6, no. 48; *PR*, 435.
[11] *RL*, 543–4; *Walt. Cov.*, 263.

of the justiciar and certain of my enemies, I was accused before the king of a capital crime, not, moreover, a recent crime but one allegedly committed eight years before'.[1] Some support is given to this complaint by a writ attested by the king on 26 April and addressed to the sheriff of Bedfordshire. It ordered him to summon Falkes from county court to county court to stand to right on a complaint of breach of the peace. The case was to proceed from the state in which it had been when adjourned by the king's order. If Falkes did not appear, he was to be outlawed according to the custom of the kingdom.[2] The penalty for conviction on a charge of breach of the peace could indeed be capital. Next year the annals of Dunstable had the following bleak entry: 'Roger de Cantilupe, a noble knight of Essex, was accused of breach of the king's peace. Having been convicted by a [judicial] duel he was at length hung and his sons were disinherited and outlawed.'[3] Falkes, therefore, was facing total ruin.

It is difficult to see how Falkes, by his immediate actions, can have provoked or deserved this treatment. True, he was still refusing to surrender Plympton castle but, if he was 'good' enough to be included in the April settlement, if indeed Moresk could be returned to him four days *after* the revival of the capital accusation, then he was surely 'good' enough to enjoy continued protection from the latter. There was, therefore, a conflict within the government as to how to deal with Falkes, just as there had been earlier in the year.

It is hard to believe that Langton himself revived a charge that might disturb the peace, which he had established, and provoke the pope into sending a legate after all. Falkes, indeed, does not include Langton as one of the immediate 'procurers'. He also says that the charge was brought before the king himself and indeed the writ to the sheriff of Bedfordshire was not merely attested by the king but also authorized by him. It is, in fact, only the second writ, since taking over his seal, for which the king took responsibility as authorizor. It was also not enrolled on the close roll until the following year.[4] These singular facts suggest that there was something highly unusual about the circumstances in which the charge against Falkes was revived. Was it a case of a small group of men persuading the king to take a personal initiative, thus bypassing Langton and other members of the government?

Falkes claimed that the charge was laid against him 'by the procuration of the justiciar and certain of my enemies' and it can scarcely have gone forward without Hubert's compliance. Back in 1219

[1] *Walt. Cov.*, 263–4.
[2] *RLC*, ii, 72b–3; for the date of this writ, see Norgate, *Minority*, 230, n. 2; for the custom of the kingdom in respect of outlawry, see *Bracton*, ii, 354.
[3] *Ann. Mon.*, iii, 95.
[4] *Walt. Cov.*, 263–4; *RLC*, ii, 72b–3; Norgate, *Minority*, 230 n. 2.

and 1220 Falkes had regarded Hubert as a close friend.[5] They had co-operated together as late as August 1222 in suppressing the London riots; but clearly Falkes could never forgive his ejection from his castles and sheriffdoms. He may well have said and done much since then to convince Hubert of his undying enmity.

Hubert, however, must have come under intense pressure to allow the charge to proceed from Falkes's 'enemies'. Later Falkes demanded that three of these be excluded from any court passing judgement on him.[6] It is easy to suggest who they may have been, namely William de Beauchamp of Bedford, Hugh de Neville and the earl of Pembroke. All had been deprived of property by Falkes. All were to recover that property as a result of his fall.

William de Beauchamp, of course, was being excluded from Bedford castle. He had constantly sought its return under the terms of the peace of 1217 and had got nowhere. In fact, whether Falkes or William had the better right to Bedford castle was a complex question, best settled by a law case.[7] Perhaps, in the changed atmosphere after December 1223, William would have brought one. But the capital charge against Falkes provided a marvellous short cut. If Falkes was convicted and hung, or if he failed to answer the charge and was outlawed, his property would come into the king's hands and William could expect to be restored to his castle. It is possible that William may have had something to do with moving the charge in the first place. It presumably arose from some incident in Bedfordshire in or soon after the civil war. While Falkes ruled Bedfordshire as sheriff, an appeal could scarcely have been brought against him in the county court. Almost certainly, the case began, and Falkes was summoned for the first time, at the first Bedfordshire county court after his dismissal, which met in February 1224.[8] That fits well with the fact, as will be seen, that Falkes was due to be summoned for the last time and, if he failed to appear, outlawed, five county courts later in June 1224. (The customary procedure was that the acccused had to be summoned at five county courts before outlawry was pronounced.)[9] The new sheriff who presided over the county court during this period was Walter of Pattishall, a 'man and knight' of William de Beauchamp.[10]

Hugh de Neville and Falkes had married half-sisters, the daughters

---

[5] This is apparent from the very openness of Falkes's letters to Hubert, notably *RL*, nos v, cxlix.

[6] *Walt. Cov.*, 266.

[7] *Chron. Maj.*, vi, 68; see above p. 87.

[8] Although Falkes may have resigned the sheriffdom at Northampton on 30 December, a new sheriff was not appointed until 18 January, which was probably later than that month's session of the county court: *PR*, 421; *RLC*, ii, 73.

[9] *RLC*, ii, 73; *Bracton*, ii, 354.

[10] *PR*, 421; *RL*, no. ccvi.

of Alice Curcy, by, respectively, her first marriage to Henry of Cornhill and her second to Warin fitz Gerald. As a result they should have shared the Curcy inheritance between them, with Stogursey castle itself going to Hugh as the husband of the senior sister. Falkes, however, had persuaded Warin and Alice, in return for a payment of 2,000 marks, to grant him in hereditary right the manor and hence also the castle of Stogursey, thus depriving Hugh's wife of what would otherwise have been her inheritance. In 1220 Hugh had brought an unsuccessful action at the bench to recover his wife's share of Stogursey.[11] An assured route to the same end would be provided by Falkes's execution or outlawry. Since Falkes and his wife held Stogursey from Hugh and his wife, after the king's year and a day, Stogursey should come into their hands as a matter of course. Despite his rebellion in the war, Hugh had connections at court through his near kinsman, Ralph de Neville.[12] His own position was fully restored precisely in April 1224. The previous January, on Brian de Lisle's removal from the chief justice-ship, Hugh had received custody of the forest on a temporary basis. On 29 April he was formally appointed chief justice of the forest during the king's pleasure.[13]

Hugh de Neville's influence, however, paled before that of Falkes's most powerful and deadly enemy: the earl of Pembroke. Pembroke had accused Falkes of forging his charters 'wickedly (*nequiter*) to disinherit him'. He had begged Hubert to punish 'the excesses of this capricious and evil man' (*tam inconstantis et mendacis viri excessus*). The hostility between the two men had derived, in part, from Falkes's activities as sheriff in counties where Pembroke had extensive lands. At least Falkes's dismissal had removed this area of friction, but another running sore remained in the way Falkes had extracted from the earl the manors of Luton, Brabourne, Kemsing and Sutton. Pembroke had ultimately conceded these to Falkes in hereditary right and could recover them only through Falkes's forfeiture.[14] In April 1224 Pembroke wielded huge influence. On 23 April he had married the king's sister.[15] He was also coming to the government's rescue in Ireland. There, Hugh de Lacy was carrying all before him. The justiciar of Ireland, the archbishop of Dublin, spent £500 from the proceeds of the Easter exchequer trying vainly to combat him.[16] In this desperate

---

[11] *CRR*, ix, 347–8; *Rutland MSS*, 55–6. There was a clause, however, allowing for repurchase.

[12] *RL*, no. lvi.

[13] *PR*, 423, 436–7.

[14] There was also tension between Falkes and Pembroke over the future of Cemais: see above pp. 293–4.

[15] *Gervase*, 113.

[16] SC 1/60, no. 120; Otway-Ruthven, *Medieval Ireland*, 91.

situation the government turned to Pembroke and on 2 May he was appointed justiciar of Ireland in the archbishop's place.[17] The great earl would conquer Hugh de Lacy just as he had conquered Llywelyn. The issues, indeed, were interlinked. Hugh was an ally of the Welsh prince, as also of the earl of Chester. Indeed, in 1222, styling himself earl of Ulster, he attested the marriage agreement between Llywelyn's daughter and Chester's nephew.[18] Pembroke had, therefore, strong personal reasons for going to Ireland. But he extracted a *quid pro quo*. He could not prevent Falkes's inclusion in the April settlement; indeed his knight, Thomas Basset, was turned out of Kirtlington in favour of William de Bréauté. But, in another way, through the capital charge, the attack on Falkes was to continue.

v. *The defection of Hugh de Lusignan, May–June 1224*

After the conclusion of the London council, the seal was left at Westminster, where royal letters were attested by the bishop of Salisbury, while the king and Hubert set out for Shrewsbury for a meeting with Llywelyn. They got as far as Oxford on 9 May when they were recalled to London by a letter from Archbishop Langton.[1] Almost certainly he warned them of an event which was to falsify the government's calculations and destroy much of what remained of the Angevin empire. King Louis had decided not to renew the truce after all. His decision, formally announced on 5 May, was the consequence of the reconciliation between the count of Toulouse and the pope. In the new year William de Sancto Albino had reported to King Henry that the count's envoy was at the papal court seeking his master's absolution. The pope, wishing to clear the decks for a crusade, was sympathetic and, early in April, he asked Louis to make peace with the count. Louis, therefore, found himself dressed up but his party cancelled. Fortunately, there was somewhere else to go. He would take his army not to Toulouse but to Poitou.[2]

This possibility had not occurred to the English government when it had urged the pope to reach a settlement with the count of Toulouse. It hoped to square the circle: to have Louis barred from Toulouse *and* the truce renewed for four years. Once the facts were known, it busied itself fitting out a force to be sent to La Rochelle. This was to be commanded by Geoffrey de Neville and included at least fifteen household knights.

---

[17] *PR*, 437–8.

[18] British Library Cotton Charter, xxiv, no. 17. Hugh's half-brother and ally, William de Lacy, had married a daughter of Llywelyn: Lydon, 'The expansion and consolidation of the colony', 158–9.

[1] *RLC*, 631b.

[2] Petit-Dutaillis, *Louis VIII*, 235; *DD*, no. 136; *Recueil*, xviii, 305; xix, 750.

In contrast to former years, money was available and, on 26 May, 2,000 marks were provided for the expedition. At the same time, dispensing with the banking facilities of the Templars, the government decided to send direct to Hugh de Lusignan the 1,400 marks which were owed him, together with another 200 marks as a loan.[3]

Preparations for Neville's expedition, however, did nothing to diminish the attack on Falkes at home. Indeed the two, in the late May of 1224, ran on side by side. Falkes himself had recognized the unlocking of the capital charge for what it was: an attempt to ruin him. When he last saw his constable of Stogursey, Henry de Vernay, he told him not to surrender the castle 'unless you see my person or the person of the king'.[4] Yet Falkes's tenure of Stogursey was only likely to be challenged if his estates were subject to forfeiture. Falkes's reaction to this pressure was far from submissive. He continued to defy the king's order to surrender Plympton castle and had it 'very strongly fortified with serjeants, arms and other munitions', as the sheriff of Devon reported later in the year.[5] He also built up a huge garrison at Bedford castle, a garrison commanded by William de Bréauté.

Against this background Falkes's enemies raised the bidding. On 19 May a writ returned Kirtlington to Pembroke's knight, Thomas Basset, 'notwithstanding [the] order to give seisin of it to William de Bréauté'. Then, on 25 May, Moresk was transferred once more from Falkes to Walerand the German. For Falkes and his *familia*, therefore, the April settlement had been overturned. This change of policy was explained, in part, by Falkes's continued refusal to surrender Plympton: another writ on 25 May instructed him to resign the castle 'without delay'. Responsibility for these measures was publicly taken by Hubert and the bishops of Bath and Salisbury, the relevant writs being attested, by the king, in their presence, just like the writs which had included Falkes and his *familia* in the settlement in the first place.[6] There must also have been pressure from the earls of Pembroke and Salisbury, who were both at court at this time, Pembroke making the final arrangements before his departure for Ireland.[7] It was probably Pembroke's influence which ensured that the capital charge against Falkes also rumbled on, despite opposition within the government. By the third week in May, Falkes had been summoned at four county courts. At the next, if he did not appear, he would be outlawed. The sheriff of Bedford informed the king, evidently in reply to an inquiry,

3 *RLC*, 599, 600, 601, 602b; *PR*, 441–2.
4 *PR*, 490.
5 *RL*, no. cciii.
6 *RLC*, 599, 599b, 601; *PR*, 440.
7 *RLC*, 600, 603b. It was at this time that a huge writ of allowance was made out in favour of the regent's executors: *RLC*, 601–3; *Divers Accounts*, 32–7.

that this county court would be held on 17 June. On 28 May he was told to summon Falkes at the meeting but to adjourn his outlawry until another order. Two days later this restriction was lifted. If Falkes did not appear, the sheriff was 'to cause him to be outlawed without delay according to the custom of the kingdom'.[8]

Around the same time a new method of attacking Falkes was developed, one which, while it did not threaten his castles or his life, would inflict on him humiliation and expense. On 23 May judges were commissioned to hear all assizes of novel disseisin from Bedfordshire and Buckinghamshire at Dunstable on 10 June, while assizes from Northamptonshire and Rutland were to come before the king himself at Northampton on 16 June, the day before, twenty miles away, Falkes's outlawry was due to be pronounced in the Bedfordshire county court.[9] These judicial commissions were aimed at Falkes, the hearing of assizes being confined to counties where he had been sheriff and possessed extensive private interests. Essentially, the government was calling in against him the people whom he had injured during the years of his power. As it explained in a letter written to the pope in June 1224, the judges were commissioned 'to hear and correct complaints of many people of rapine and plunder of their lands and goods which many brought to our ears'.[10] Dunstable itself was chosen as the seat of the judges because it adjoined Falkes's manor at Luton, where he had allegedly disseized many small freemen, as well as damaging property of the abbot of St Albans.[11] One at least of the judges was carefully chosen. This was Henry of Braybrooke. He had defended Mountsorrel against the Henricians in 1217 and escaped by the skin of his teeth after the battle of Lincoln. Henry was another 'man and knight' of William de Beauchamp. He was also, as Falkes dolefully recorded in his *querimonia*, a personal enemy of William de Bréauté.[12]

Instead, therefore, of hastening forward an expedition to follow Geoffrey de Neville, the government intended on 16 June to be in Northampton to hear petty assizes against Falkes de Bréauté. Was it not behaving with extraordinary irresponsibility? That certainly was the view taken later by the pope and, indeed, when he looked back in 1239, by the king himself.[13] The truth is, however, that Hubert imagined that he could do everything at once: bring Falkes to

[8] *RLC*, ii, 73.
[9] *RLC*, 631–631b.
[10] *RL*, no. cxcix.
[11] *CRR*, xi, nos 1916–34; *Chron. Maj.*, 88, 120. Falkes's response to the abbey's complaint, according to Matthew Paris's story, was to say that he only wished he had waited till autumn so that its barns would have been full of corn when flooded by his operations in making a new fish-pond!
[12] *Chron. Maj.*, 15; *Ann. Mon.*, iii, 49; *RL*, no. ccvi; *Walt. Cov.*, 264.
[13] *RL*, 543–4; *Chron. Maj.*, vi, 67.

submission, if not to ruin, subdue Hugh de Lacy in Ireland *and* protect Poitou. This was not quite so improbable as it sounds. Despite the intensity of the pressure which was being placed upon him, there was no expectation that Falkes was going to launch a rebellion. Pembroke would never have gone off to Ireland in June had *that* been in the offing.

Up to a point, moreover, the government still imagined that the situation in Poitou left it free for domestic politics. When the king and Hubert first heard of Louis's decision not to renew the truce, they still thought that they could be back at Shrewsbury on 28 July.[14] Louis, perhaps by design, gave no indication that hostilities were imminent. Indeed, on 14 June the government still believed that merchants could pass safely through the realms of both kings until 9 July.[15] In any case, the safety of Poitou seemed assured by the settlement with Hugh de Lusignan. Any French invasion was likely to be halted by Hugh's castles at Frontenay, Chizé, Melle, Lusignan and Civray.[16] On 21 May one of Hugh's clerks was granted an annual fee of 10 marks and next day Hugh's attorney was given seisin of his master's lands in England.[17] Evidently the government thought that Hugh and his barons had now sworn to the agreement offered back in March.

It was not until 2 June, when the measures against Falkes had been taken, that the government knew the awful truth.[18] At Bourges, some time during May, King Louis and Hugh de Lusignan had come to terms. Louis had made Hugh an offer which he could not refuse, one far better than he could ever extract from the English government: instead of remaining unchallenged in Saintes and Oléron, Joan's *maritagium*, merely for four years, he was to hold them in perpetuity. In place of his wife's dower in England, which, of course, he would lose, he was to receive 2,000 *livres parisis* a year until assigned land of equivalent value in conquered Poitou; in place of Saumur, which had also been part of the dower, he was promised Langeais. But the greatest prize, one no English government could concede, was Bordeaux itself. If it was conquered, Hugh was to hold it instead of the other compensations offered for the dower.[19]

The English government reacted immediately to this disastrous news. As the king explained to the pope later in the month, the archbishops, bishops 'and all the magnates of all our kingdom' were summoned to Northampton for 16 June 'to give us there counsel and aid for the defence of our land of Poitou, which the king of France

---

[14] *RLC*, 631b.
[15] *RLC*, 603–603b; *PR*, 443–4.
[16] Petit-Dutaillis, *Louis VIII*, 238.
[17] *PR*, 439–40.
[18] On this day Hugh was described as 'the king's enemy': *RLC*, 603.
[19] Petit-Dutaillis, *Louis VIII*, 236–7.

prepared to invade'.[20] Falkes, in his *querimonia*, alleged that this explanation for the gathering at Northampton was totally disingenuous. The king, he declared, summoned an army to Northampton, 'falsely giving as a reason that it was needed to give help to Poitou'. Its real purpose was to crush Falkes himself. Hence the army was summoned not to Portsmouth but to Northampton, which was 'five days distance from the sea'.[21] This argument has convinced later historians but it is specious. The king's original decision, on 23 May, to be in Northampton on 16 June to hear petty assizes was certainly part of a package of measures against Falkes. He may have intended to be there in some force in case of trouble. But he had as yet made no general summons of lay and ecclesiastical magnates to the town. The royal letter to the pope, quoted above, states specifically that it was '*after* Pentecost', after, that is, 2 June, that the king issued the general summons.[22] In other words, it was issued only when the king knew of Hugh de Lusignan's defection. This strongly supports his statement that the purpose of the gathering at Northampton was to bring succour to Poitou.

But why summon an army to Northampton rather than to Portsmouth? The answer is that no *army* was summoned. Convoked at Northampton was a council to give advice about Poitou, not a military force to proceed immediately to its rescue. This was how the chroniclers understood it. Roger of Wendover described the Northampton assembly as a *colloquium* where the king wished to take counsel with his magnates about his lands overseas which were being occupied by the king of France. The Dunstable annals likewise stated that the king and magnates discussed at Northampton how to assist Poitou. When, therefore, the king eventually moved against Falkes, it was, as he told the pope, 'with our army which we soon (*in proximo*) hope to have in battle array (*in bello*), God willing', not with an army already assembled.[23]

There was nothing surprising about this. Once the king of France and Hugh de Lusignan were in alliance, measures for Poitou's defence needed to be taken on an altogether different scale than before. The government may have intended to despatch reinforcements soon after the council[24] but essentially the situation called for a major expedition, carefully planned and plentifully funded. When the king explained that the magnates were summoned to Northampton to give 'counsel and aid' for the defence of Poitou, the aid envisaged was probably financial,

[20] *RL*, no. cxcix; *Chron. Maj.*, 84.
[21] *Walt. Cov.*, 264, 269.
[22] *RL*, no. cxcix.
[23] *Ann. Mon.*, iii, 86; *Chron. Maj.*, 84; *RL*, no. cxcix; compare Norgate, *Minority*, 223.
[24] For the dispersal of ships once the siege had begun: *RLC*, 607.

the government intending to seek a tax on movable property, like the one which was conceded for the defence of Gascony seven months later. Given that this was the purpose of the assembly, Northampton, easy of access in the centre of the kingdom, was an ideal place for it.

The council at Northampton, however, opened not with discussions about Poitou but with Langton and the other bishops formally urging the king to restore Peter, Chester and their allies to his counsels. They were acting in accordance with letters which the pope had addressed to them, perhaps when he decided not to send an envoy to investigate the situation in England.[25] Under this pressure from the pope, and faced with catastrophe in Poitou, it seems highly probable that another attempt was begun to construct a general settlement. Hence the government backtracked once more over Falkes. He was due to be summoned at the Bedford county court on 17 June and outlawed if he did not appear. Powicke boldly stated that the outlawry was pronounced but there is no evidence of this.[26] Not one of the numerous royal letters dealing with Falkes after 17 June 1224 calls him an outlaw. Rather, he is simply the king's 'manifest' or 'public' enemy.[27] Of course, 17 June in Bedford, as will be seen, was a day of turmoil. It is possible that the county court was prevented from meeting. But both Falkes and the king assumed that Falkes's place on 17 June was at the council at Northampton, not the county court at Bedford. Falkes, in his *querimonia*, indicates that on 17 June he was actually 'at Northampton, where I had gathered with other barons of the land to do the king's service'. The royal letter to the pope, written later in the month, says that Falkes was summoned to 'the council of magnates of all the realm who were with us' at Northampton.[28] Evidently there had been yet another change of mind about the process of the capital charge. Another writ had been issued to the sheriff of Bedford telling him to adjourn it. For Falkes, however, it was to prove a false dawn.

vi. *The siege of Bedford, 20 June–15 August 1224*

If the government had stopped one train running towards Falkes, it had let another proceed on its way. The justices had been sitting at Dunstable since 10 June hearing petty assizes. Falkes himself had been convicted of sixteen disseisins and been condemned to pay substantial damages.[1] William de Bréauté was in similar difficulties. That the

---

[25] *RL*, no. cxcix.

[26] Powicke, *Henry III*, 63.

[27] For example, *PR*, 450, 462. Llywelyn's protestation (*RL*, no. cci) does not prove that Falkes had been outlawed.

[28] *Walt. Cov.*, 264; *RL*, no. cxcix.

[1] *RL*, no. cxcix; Norgate, *Minority*, 292–3.

justice, Henry of Braybrooke, a personal enemy of William, acted 'dishonestly' towards the Bréautés was stated by Ralph of Coggeshall as well as by the *querimonia*.[2] His conduct provided the final provocation. On 17 June, as he made his way towards the council at Northampton, Henry was seized by William de Bréauté. Falkes always denied instigating his brother's action, which may be true. Certainly there could be no worse time to start a rebellion than with a great council in session at Northampton and with Falkes's allies, as events were to show, unwilling to assist him. The assizes at Dunstable, moreover, while embarrassing and expensive, did not strike at the heart of Falkes's power, which was why the government had allowed them to proceed. On 17 June Falkes knew that the capital charge, the direst threat to his position, had been suspended. He also hoped, as a remark in the *querimonia* shows, that an expedition to Poitou would transform the situation in England, with those going in the army being replaced as castellans of royal castles. Fear of that happening, Falkes alleged, was a reason why Langton wished to delay the expedition.[3]

If, however, Falkes did not incite William's action, he immediately endorsed it and thus chose the path of revolt. The first response of the government, the day after the outrage, was to send envoys, who ordered Falkes both to release Braybrooke and produce his seizors to suffer judgement in the king's court. Falkes claimed that he was powerless to do this. On hearing at Northampton of Braybrooke's seizure, he had, he said, gone at once to Bedford to secure his release, only to find that William de Bréauté had vanished with his captive. The king's envoys also summoned Falkes himself to Northampton to answer, *inter alia*, the charge of breach of the peace. This order Falkes refused to obey. Instead, he sent messengers to explain to the king, through the good offices of Bishop Peter and the earl of Chester, that he intended to continue the search for William and Henry of Braybrooke.[4]

Falkes's story that he could not find his brother is incredible. The king's forces had no difficulty finding him when they arrived outside Bedford castle on 20 June. In Hubert's later recollection, William then declared that 'he would not give up Henry [of Braybrooke] without Falkes his brother, and his brother certainly avouched what he had done'.[5] That was the truth of the matter. Falkes must have told William to surrender neither Braybrooke nor the castle. The long siege is inexplicable on any other basis. Instead of taking his chances at

---

[2] *Coggeshall*, 206; *Walt. Cov.*, 264.

[3] *Walt. Cov.*, 269. There is no indication in either Falkes's *querimonia* or the government records that Falkes had been ordered to give up Bedford castle itself; compare *Coggeshall*, 205–6.

[4] *RL*, no. cxcix; *Walt. Cov.*, 264–5.

[5] *Chron. Maj.*, vi, 68.

Northampton, Falkes staked everything on Bedford holding out until the pope intervened and his friends in England rallied to his support. He hoped, in effect, that the siege would lead to the government's overthrow or defeat in what might well become a general civil war.

The government received Falkes's replies at Northampton on Wednesday, 19 June. That evening it directed forces on Bedford. Next morning the castle was surrounded. Even Falkes admitted that William de Bréauté now declared that 'there was no law or custom' by which the castle should be surrendered. William produced the papal letters which protected Falkes and his possessions as a crusader and demanded that nothing be done until the pope had sent a *nuncius* or legate to investigate the situation. Langton and his fellow bishops thereupon excommunicated the castle garrison and Falkes himself, who by this time had fled, and the siege began.[6]

Falkes later alleged that the decision to besiege Bedford was taken with indecent haste and by only a proportion of those assembled at Northampton[7] but it must, in fact, have commanded a wide measure of consent. Otherwise the government could never have acted so quickly and decisively. The royal letter to the pope described the decision to besiege the castle as made 'by the counsel of our court'. Hubert later put it another way. The castle was besieged 'by the common counsel of the kingdom' and 'by the counsel of the archbishop, bishops and magnates of the land'. This was important for Langton, whose backing was clearly of key importance. In his university days he had argued that subjects were bound to support the king, even if he attacked a castle unjustly, provided that there had been a formal judgement in the matter. In effect, such a judgement was precisely what the council at Northampton had given.[8]

Nonetheless, in besieging Bedford rather than succouring Poitou, did not the government show a twisted sense of priorities? As the pope put it in a letter to Langton: 'perhaps you may say that justice demanded that arms were moved against [Falkes]. But certainly expediency (*utilitas*) demanded the contrary, which should rather have been consulted in the present case. For where is your abundant wisdom if you counsel the king to begin war with his own subjects when he sees external enemies making war on him?'[9] The government was well aware of the choice. As it told the pope in the letter written soon after 20 June, the king had gone to Bedford leaving aside urgent affairs in Ireland and Poitou.[10] But it is difficult to see what else could have been

---

[6] *Walt. Cov.*, 265.
[7] *Walt. Cov.*, 265.
[8] *RL*, no. cxcix; *Chron. Maj.*, vi, 67–8; Powicke, *Langton*, 95.
[9] *RL*, 543–4.
[10] *RL*, no. cxcix.

done. Having given both Falkes and William de Bréauté' a chance to submit, the government could not simply ignore the affront to the king's dignity caused by the seizure of a royal justice and leave Bedford to the mercies of its recalcitrant castellan. 'We realized', the king told the pope, 'that it was vain to attend to affairs outside our kingdom of England, when everyone [around Bedford] was hurrying to churches and cemeteries as though in time of war, and worse would have happened if we had not gone there.' Equally, to have simply sat down and negotiated with Falkes would have signalled to his allies and everyone else that one could rebel with impunity. 'If Falkes had escaped unpunished, and the castle had not been taken', Hubert later observed, 'the kingdom would have been more disturbed than it was.'[11]

Falkes in 1224 placed his trust in Bedford castle, the pope and his allies in England. At the castle, he had built well. Demolishing the churches of St Paul and St Cuthbert to clear the space, he had added to the old tower and small bailey a barbican, a large outer bailey and a new keep, both the last two protected with moats dressed with stone.[12] Forbidding the despatch of further messengers demanding their surrender, William de Bréauté and the garrison defended this formidable structure, in the words of Ralph of Coggeshall, 'with foolish bravery and stubborn probity'.[13]

Thus the siege of Bedford lasted for a full eight weeks. But that was not long enough to allow for papal intervention. Honorius was persuaded to write to England deploring the government's priorities and commanding it to cease Falkes's persecution but these letters were dated around 17 August, three days after the fall of Bedford castle.[14] Long before, Falkes's allies in England seem to have given up hope of effective papal intervention. As early as 29 June, at the instance of Langton and Chester, Robert Passelewe was given licence to return to England.[15] If this was a concession to Chester, it equally suggested that he was no longer challenging the regime at the papal court. The fact was that Falkes's hope for support from his friends in England had proved illusory. As the royal army closed around Bedford, Falkes had fled to the lands of the earl of Chester. But Chester, Bishop Peter, the count of Aumale, William de Cantilupe, Brian de Lisle and Peter de

[11] *DD*, no. 149; *Chron. Maj.*, vi, 67.

[12] *Coggeshall*, 205; *Ann. Mon.*, iii, 87–8; *RLC*, 632, 632b. Remains of the stone linings to the moats or ditches, together with some of the missiles thrown by the siege engines, have been discovered during excavations at Bedford castle: Baker, Baker, Hassall, Simco, *Excavations in Bedford 1967–1977*, 13–17, 31–5, 53.

[13] *Coggeshall*, 206; *Chron. Maj.*, 86.

[14] *RL*, 543–5.

[15] *PR*, 447–8.

Maulay all answered the summons to the army of Bedford. Admittedly they showed themselves less than enthusiastic about proceedings once they got there. Bishop Peter and Chester ultimately went home, finding themselves 'excluded from the most secret royal counsels'.[16] But the government did what it could to appease Falkes's potential allies. Chester was sufficiently included in the king's counsels to be one of the magnates, on 10 July, in whose presence the king made a grant to the citizens of Bordeaux.[17] During the siege, concessions were made to William de Cantilupe, Peter de Maulay, Engelard and Bishop Peter.[18] The bishop sent munitions to the parallel siege of Stogursey castle and was involved around the same time in despatching the king's money to Poitou.[19]

Chester's attitude was summed up in a letter, at turns disputatious and dutiful, which he wrote to the king after his return to Chester early in August. He already knew perfectly well, he said, what the king told him about the siege of Bedford. What he did not know, indeed did not believe, was that Falkes was attempting to harm the king. Rather, he had behaved patiently and peacefully, wishing above everything to recover the king's grace. Chester, however, still agreed to do all he could to maintain the security of his parts: 'I have always wished, constantly and faithfully, to serve and assist you and your ancestors.'[20]

Such professions of loyalty had recurred frequently in Chester's career. They were encouraged on this occasion, as on others, by sober calculation. However much he and his allies sympathized with Falkes, they knew that to rebel on his behalf would be merely to share his ruin. In the first place, the king was reasonably supplied with money. True, in July, 'for his great necessity' he took two loans of £200 but one of these was repaid almost immediately.[21] During the same month, despite the drain of the siege, the king made arrangements to despatch £500 to Poitou.[22] In fact, the accounts of the king's wardrobe show that its keepers received a total of £9,064 16s $\frac{1}{2}$d between 4 January and 28 October 1224, a sum not equalled in either of the next two regnal years. It was possible, therefore to spend £1,311 18s 2d on expenses during the siege, much of it going on the wages of knights, serjeants and engineers.[23] An important contribution to these financial resources was made by a tax imposed by Langton and the bishops of 6s 8d on the

[16] Ann. Mon., iii, 87.
[17] PR, 449–50.
[18] RLC, 606b, 608, 611b; C 60/21, m.5.
[19] HRO, Eccles II 159278, r.11; RLC, 612b.
[20] RL, no. cciv.
[21] PR, 453–4, 455–6.
[22] RLC, 612b.
[23] Divers Accounts, 50–2.

demesne ploughs of ecclesiastics and 2s on the ploughs of their tenants. From this the keepers of the wardrobe, by 28 October, had received £2,377 6s. The rate of 6s 8d on the plough compared with the 2s imposed by the carucage of 1220 and the £2,377 raised was only £294 less than the sum accounted for by the receivers of the 1220 tax.[24] There could be no more striking testimony to the strength of the alliance in 1224 between church and state.

Chester must also have recognized that the great majority of the magnates had rallied to the government's support. High in the king's counsels at Bedford were the earls of Salisbury and Surrey, as one would expect, but so too were the earls of Derby and Gloucester, the latter now clearly wrested from the ranks of the schismatics.[25] The king's declaration that the clerical carucage should not create a precedent was made in the presence of Hubert, the earls of Salisbury, Surrey, Gloucester, Essex, Norfolk, Hereford and Warwick, and John de Lacy, Peter fitz Herbert, Thomas of Moulton, John fitz Robert, Richard de Muntfichet and the Northerners, William of Lancaster, Robert de Ros, Richard de Percy and William de Ros. Apart from Hubert, every one of these men had been a rebel in the civil war.[26] Likewise, during the siege, another group of Northerners, including Roger Bertram, Richard de Umfraville and Nicholas de Stuteville II, were conceded the scutage of Montgomery owed on their fees in return for their 'faithful service'.[27]

Thus the knot slowly tightened around Bedford castle. Mangonels were established on its four sides and two towers were built whose projectiles forced the garrison to go everywhere in armour. Anxious to do his part, the judge Martin of Pattishall, observing that 'in the siege of castles, doctors are necessary and especially those knowing how to cure wounds', sent on to the army a Master Thomas, 'whom I know is skilled in such science'.[28] There were four main assaults. First the barbican was taken; second the outer bailey, where 'our men', the annals of Dunstable reported, plundered horses, shields, crossbows, cows, bacon and live pigs. Then the miners, operating under the protection of a large 'cat', mined the wall of the inner bailey by the old tower. That left only the heart of the castle, Falkes's new keep. This too was mined. The props holding up the tunnels were fired on 14 August around vespers. Smoke filled the rooms and a great crack appeared in

[24] PR, 464–5; Divers Accounts, 51; Mitchell, Taxation, 153–9.
[25] PR, 450, 458, 465; for concessions to the earls of Salisbury, Gloucester and Norfolk, RLC, 609b, 610, 611, 611b.
[26] PR, 465. The muster for the army meant that the scutage for the siege was only levied on between 600 and 700 out of 5,000 fees: Mitchell Taxation, 152, 151 n.6.
[27] RLC, 609b.
[28] SC 1/6, no. 75 (a letter to Ralph de Neville).

the masonry. The garrison sent out Falkes's wife, her women and Henry of Braybrooke, hauled up the king's standard on the summit of the tower and spent a last miserable night there effectively in captivity.[29]

Next morning William de Bréauté and his men came out of the castle, received absolution from Langton and the bishops, and flung themselves at the king's feet, begging tearfully for mercy.[30] When Henry, according to the story in the *querimonia*, asked innocently what he should do, Langton, 'not as pastor of the country but as a tyrant', referred him grimly to the justiciar.[31] Other accounts imply that the king's anger, and his oath to hang all the garrison if it was taken by force, was a factor in the decision which was now taken.[32] In any case, 'by order of the king and the justiciar', as the Dunstable annalist put it, the whole garrison, consisting of William de Bréauté and upwards of eighty knights and serjeants, was hanged.[33]

There may have been disagreements about the executions at the end of the siege but, if there is any truth in the narrative in the *querimonia*, it is that Langton and Hubert were at one about them. They thus carried through a brutal but necessary vindication of the king's authority. Perhaps the nearest parallel to the siege of Bedford was that of Exeter castle in 1136 which continued for over three months. Then, King Stephen had spared the garrison but since neither it, nor its lord, Baldwin de Redvers, had ever sworn fealty to him, there were grounds for clemency.[34] The Bedford garrison had no such excuse. If William de Bréauté claimed, as Roger of Wendover says, that he did not owe fealty to the king, he was hardly telling the truth. Indeed, immediately after the war he had been bound to the king by a special oath as one of his household knights.[35] The essential reason for the executions, however, lay not in considerations of right and custom but in practical politics. Stephen's failure to execute the Exeter garrison was arguably one of his greatest mistakes, advertising to everyone that there were no penalties for defying the king.[36] The minority government had followed the same lenient path after the sieges of Newark, Rockingham and Bytham. These bad examples were very much in men's minds in 1224. When

---

[29] *Ann. Mon.*, iii, 87–8.

[30] *Hist. Angl.*, ii, 264.

[31] *Walt. Cov.*, 267–8.

[32] *Chron. Maj.*, 86; *Walt. Cov.*, 254.

[33] *Ann. Mon.*, iii, 88. Norgate, *Minority*, 296–8, brings together the evidence for the numbers actually hung. Three men were cut down from the gallows and spared.

[34] *Gesta Stephani*, 28; Davis, *King Stephen*, 24.

[35] *Chron. Maj.*, 85; *RLC*, 362. For the oath taken by members of the king's household, see *CRR*, vii, 170.

[36] Davis, *King Stephen*, 24–6.

Langton referred the king to Hubert's counsel, the bishop of Bath gave a broad hint as to its likely tenor: 'if those captured at Bytham had been hung, those now taken would not have held the castle against the royal will'.[37] The siege of Bytham, like those of Newark and Rockingham, had only lasted a few days. That of Bedford had continued for eight weeks. Capital punishment for the offenders seemed an absolute necessity.

Before the fall of Bedford castle, Falkes had already yielded to the entreaties of the earl of Chester and the bishop of Coventry to wait for better times and had indicated his willingness to submit. He finally placed himself in the king's mercy at Elstow or Kempston, just south of Bedford, on 19 August and was sent to London, where Langton absolved him in a humiliating ceremony on, or shortly before, 25 August.[38] In the picture later relayed to Matthew Paris by the bishops of Coventry and London, Falkes was a broken man. He fell down in a trance when he heard of his brother's execution and lamented, when he saw the bodies, that he had caused the deaths of so many noble men. Recalling his oppression of the abbey, he acknowledged that St Alban was indeed revenged. He was little consoled when the bishop of London produced a quotation from Ovid to sum up his situation.[39]

Falkes resigned all his possessions to the crown, including £698 stored in the London Temple, and Plympton and Stogursey castles, which had held out till after the fall of Bedford.[40] Resignation, as opposed to forfeiture, sidestepped the protection which Falkes enjoyed as a crusader and gave the king total control over the property. Nonetheless, Falkes's enemies now reaped their reward. On 20 August orders were given for the remains of Bedford castle to be restored to William de Beauchamp; this, so Hubert later averred, being done 'by the counsel of the magnates of England' in fulfilment of the peace treaty of 1217.[41] Seven days later, in return for a fine of 100 marks, Hugh de Neville was conceded Stogursey castle as his wife's inheritance.[42] Next year the earl of Pembroke obtained seisin, during the king's pleasure, of Luton, Sutton, Brabourne and Kemsing. In 1229 the king conceded them to him in hereditary right.[43]

Falkes publicly abjured the realm in October. For a while he became

[37] *Walt. Cov.*, 268.

[38] *Walt. Cov.*, 266–9; 254; *F*, 175. The date of the submission is suggested by the king's presence at Kempston, just by Elstow, on 19 August: *RLC*, 617.

[39] *Hist. Angl.*, ii, 265–6; *Chron. Maj.*, 87. After his surrender, Falkes was placed in the bishop of London's custody.

[40] *F*, 175; *Walt. Cov.*, 269.

[41] *RLC*, 632; *Chron. Maj.*, vi, 68. The castle was partly dismantled before being given to William.

[42] C 60/21, m.3.

[43] *RLC*, ii, 27; *Ann. Mon.*, iii, 92; *CChR*, 102.

a prisoner of the king of France, which at least disproved the accusation that his rebellion was timed to give the latter a clear run in Poitou. Then, in the company of Robert Passelewe, arrangements for whose return to England had fallen through, he made his way to the papal court. It was Passelewe, almost certainly, who drew up his *querimonia* to the pope but although papal pressure was exerted on his behalf, it proved insufficent to effect his restoration.[44] Still, all Falkes needed was time. On Hubert's fall and Richard earl of Pembroke's rebellion in 1232–33, he would doubtless have returned to recover his lands and his wife from a grateful and penitent king. For Falkes, however, there was to be no happy ending, no dignified last days surrounded by family and friends at Bedford, Luton or Stogursey. Nor, like other exiles, did he enjoy or endure 'long years of indolence and insignificance – sinking away into forgetfulness through the monotony of Roman afternoons'. At Santo Ciriaco in Rome, in 1226, in the words of Matthew Paris, 'he lay down to sleep after supper, and was found dead, black and fetid, having died intestate and without viaticum, and . . . was quickly buried in an ignoble fashion'. Paris drew a picture of the devil pushing the poisoned fish, the cause of death, into Falkes's mouth.[45]

It was 'for love of the king', Falkes cried out to the bishop of London, after his fall, that he had made so many enemies.[46] There was something in that, for he had certainly displayed an extraordinary energy and determination in upholding the rights of the king, as he saw them, in his sheriffdoms, although, equally, it was often Falkes, rather than the king, who reaped the benefit. He had shown the same force and ruthlessness in administering his private affairs. Falkes had always been more than the brutal, disobedient soldier of his enemies' caricature. His letters to Hubert have a sinuous cleverness quite foreign to the blunt epistles of, say, Engelard de Cigogné. If he used his huge wealth to rebuild castles and maintain soldiers, he also gathered a talented body of men to run his sheriffdoms and estates. If he threatened native-born men with war, he also named his son after St Thomas of Canterbury. When the men of Essendon and Bayford complained of his oppressions, he called them before him to hear their complaints. He apologized to the monks of Wardon and St Albans (not in the latter case to much effect) for past injuries and accepted discipline at their hands. While he disseized the men of Luton of their properties, he also brought law cases against them at the bench.[47] In the years after the war it was

---

[44] *PR*, 478–9; *Chron. Maj.*, 94, 97 (where the events narrated belong to October 1223); *Ann. Mon.*, iii, 89; *Walt. Cov.*, 270; *Coggeshall*, 208; *RL*, 547.

[45] *Chron. Maj.*, 119–21; *Ann. Mon.*, iii, 89; *DD*, no. 203.

[46] *Hist. Angl.*, ii, 266.

[47] See above pp. 333–4; *Chron. Maj.*, 12–13; *Ann. Mon.*, iii, 52–3: *RL*, no. lxxxviii; *CRR*, x, 81–2. Falkes's son became an Oxfordshire county knight: *VCH Oxon.*, vi, 197.

difficult to know whom to fear most: Falkes's castellans or his lawyers. He had always more than one method of attack. Like Dr Johnson in conversation, if his pistol misfired, he knocked you down with its butt.

Part of Falkes's tragedy was that, once stripped of office, he could not sit back, like Peter de Maulay, on a secure inheritance which he could pass on to his heirs. Falkes's tenure of Plympton was easily challenged on the grounds that it could not be his wife's dower. His tenure of the other lands of the earldom of Devon was conceded to him only until the king came of age and, arguably, could be revoked under the papal letters of April 1223. The fact was that Falkes's marriage looked far better than it was. Since Margaret had a son by her previous husband, there was virtually nothing which would descend to her son by Falkes. The castles and manors that Falkes claimed to hold in hereditary right – Bedford, Stogursey, Luton – he had acquired in other ways, thereby making implacable enemies.

What Falkes may have said or done, in the early months of 1224, to justify the attack which was made on him cannot be known. What is certain is that, however great the provocation, his only course, as the earl of Chester recognized, was to wait for better times. As it was, his brother's action, and his own failure to disavow it, played into the hands of his enemies at the very moment when the crisis in Poitou meant that salvation was at hand. Falkes's conduct in June 1224 summed up all the public grounds which his enemies alleged for objecting to him. Here, as both Ralph of Coggeshall and the Barnwell chronicler put it, was a man who, having risen from nothing to great power, disdained to have a peer,[48] a man who freely proclaimed his refusal to obey thirty pairs of royal letters and threatened all native-born Englishmen with war. Now, rather than bow down to judgements passed against him, he had seized a royal justice, refused to surrender him or the castle in which he was held captive and brought England to a state of war. Roger of Wendover, indeed, confused Falkes's outburst in 1221–22 with the events of June 1224, stating that at Dunstable he fell 'into the mercy of the king for more than thirty pairs of letters'.[49] Falkes, thus represented, seemed the over-mighty subject *par excellence*, the 'more than king in England' (*plusquam rex in Anglia*), of his description in the Tewkesbury annals.[50] As a royal letter written to the pope put it, in seizing Braybrooke, Falkes 'exercised the venom which for a long time he had conceived, being indignant . . . that he was compelled to be under a master, when he burned with a desire to have dominion'.[51] In this perspective, the siege of Bedford castle was more

[48] *Coggeshall*, 81–2; *Walt. Cov.*, 253.
[49] *Chron. Maj.*, 84; Norgate, *Minority*, 292–3.
[50] *Ann. Mon.*, i, 64.
[51] *RL*, no. cxcix.

than a private vendetta against Falkes. It concluded the triumph of central government over the centrifugal forces which had threatened to pull Angevin kingship apart.

vii. *The loss of Poitou*

While the king besieged Bedford, the earl of Pembroke carried all before him in Ulster. He had landed at Waterford on 19 June. Part of his force defeated Hugh de Lacy's half-brother, William; another drove Hugh himself off from a siege of Carrickfergus. Pembroke, assisted by Geoffrey de Marsh, concentrated on the siege of Trim, much encouraged by the news from England. Soon after 4 August he wrote to congratulate the king on the course of events.[1] A week later Trim finally surrendered. Next year Hugh de Lacy gave himself up and was sent to England.[2]

Success in Ireland, however, was far outweighed by disaster in Poitou. On 24 June, four days after the ring closed around Bedford, Louis gathered his army at Tours.[3] He then proceeded to Montreuil-Bellay and secured a truce with the vicomte of Thouars, the latter becoming Louis's man for a year and obtaining pensions for his closest followers.[4] With his rear thus secured, Louis advanced on the smaller Poitevin towns. Niort surrendered on 5 July, after a siege of two days, the garrison under Savari de Mauléon securing passage to La Rochelle. St Jean d'Angély gave up next without a struggle. Louis was now ready to take on La Rochelle itself.

La Rochelle was 'the key' to Poitou, as Matthew Paris put it later. It was 'the port . . . where kings of England and knights for the defence of these regions were accustomed to disembark'. It was also, as the citizens had reminded Hubert in 1219, the one place which King Philip had failed to conquer in 1204, with the result that ultimately he had lost most of the rest of the county. The conclusion was obvious: 'if [the king of France] can in any way subdue the vill of la Rochelle, thenceforth he will easily possess the rest of the land of Poitou'.[5] Louis began the siege on 15 July and the first news that reached England was of Savari's vigorous defence aided by the contingent sent from England under Geoffrey de Neville.[6] There is some obscurity over what happened

[1] SC 1/4, no. 71 (*CDI*, no. 1202).
[2] *RL.*, no. cci (*bis*) and pp. 500–3; Otway-Ruthven, *Medieval Ireland*, 91–2; Lydon, 'The expansion and consolidation of the colony', 159–61.
[3] The progress of Louis's campaign is described by the Chronicle of St Martin of Tours, *Recueil*, xviii, 305.
[4] Petit-Dutaillis, *Louis VIII*, 240–1.
[5] *Hist. Angl.*, ii, 262; *Chron. Maj.*, iii, 84; *DD*, no. 52.
[6] *Ann. Mon.*, iii, 86.

next. On 3 August, according to the chronicle of St Martin of Tours, the town was surrendered to Louis, and it is certain that French troops were allowed into La Rochelle on, or very soon after, that date. On the other hand, it was not until 13 August that the burgesses swore fealty to Louis, a prior agreement that he should come to La Rochelle on 24 December to receive their fealty being then set aside. Ralph of Coggeshall adds the point that the citizens surrendered their town 'conditionally'. Perhaps there had been an initial agreement to enter the faith of the king of France if no help arrived from England by Christmas. On 13 August, having already let French troops into the town, this was set aside and the burgesses decided to enter Louis's faith at once.[7]

The English garrison had no part in this surrender and was allowed to go free with its arms. Indeed, Savari and the citizens were stigmatized by the English for treachery,[8] although the former seems to have resisted the final surrender to Louis on 13 August. Certainly, he tried to come to England to explain matters to the king and did not enter the service of the king of France until Christmas as originally agreed.[9] Essentially, it was the citizens themselves who decided to give up the fight.

There was one immediate reason for this collapse of resistance. As Ralph of Coggeshall explained, the citizens surrendered La Rochelle 'since they despaired of help from King Henry, who was meanwhile besieging the castle of Bedford'.[10] The story quickly reached St Martin of Tours that, instead of money, Savari received only barrels full of stones, a charge which Henry III himself revived against Hubert as late as 1239.[11] What is true is that the troops and money which arrived under Geoffrey de Neville in early June were the last. The sum of 500 marks destined for the burgesses on 13 June was recalled, presumably now needed for the siege of Bedford. Instead, on 25 June Neville was simply ordered to give Savari 500 marks, apparently from the 2,000 marks which he had taken out with him. In addition, Savari was sent a letter empowering him to seek a loan of 1,000 marks.[12] Well might he have cried out that he was being sent no more than stones. The £500 destined for Poitou on 18 July probably arrived too late to affect the issue.[13]

[7] *Recueil*, xviii, 305; *DD*, no. 145; *Layettes*, ii, no. 1661; *Coggeshall*, 208; Petit-Dutaillis, *Louis VIII*, 245–6.

[8] *Ann. Mon.*, iii, 91; *Chron. Maj.*, vi, 67; *DD*, no. 145.

[9] *Recueil*, xviii, 307; *PR*, 477.

[10] *Coggeshall*, 208.

[11] *Recueil*, xviii, 305; *Chron. Maj.*, vi, 66.

[12] *RLC*, 601, 604b; *PR*, 447.

[13] *RLC*, 612b.

The siege of Bedford, therefore, was certainly an immediate factor in the loss of La Rochelle. At the very least the £1,311 spent there, amongst other things on the wages of knights and serjeants, could have gone out to Savari, as could the knights and serjeants themselves.[14] Even more devastating was simply the news of the siege. To those in La Rochelle it must have seemed that the English government had taken leave of its senses.

The irony of the events of 1224 was that Poitou was lost at the very moment when the English government, in terms of financial resources, was better equipped to defend it than at any time since the war. That still did not make the contest very equal in terms of resources. The ordinary annual revenue of the king of France has been estimated, on the basis of the budget of November 1221, at around 200,000 *livres parisis* or nearly £65,000 sterling. By contrast, around 1224, the ordinary annual revenue of the king of England was probably not much more than £15,000. Louis VIII could also utilize the huge treasure built up by his father, who probably spent only two thirds of his income every year. It was with easy confidence that Louis ridiculed Henry III, at the end of 1224, as 'a boy and a pauper'.[15]

It was not, however, merely lack of material support which brought the loss of Poitou. The citizens of La Rochelle, like those of the other towns, had simply lost the will to fight for the Angevin cause. Could one blame them, given the utter failure of the English government to protect them from the depredations of the great Poitevin magnates? When faced by the attacks of Hugh de Lusignan and his allies in 1220, Niort had already warned King Henry to take care 'lest it becomes necessary for us and your *fideles* to leave your land on account of such great grievances'.[16] Throughout the autumn of 1223 La Rochelle had been embroiled in a conflict with Hugh de Thouars, son of the vicomte. Hugh had declared that neither for the king of England nor the burgesses would he cease to construct a castle which threatened the town. When the citizens sallied forth and destroyed it themselves, Hugh threatened to lay waste their vines and wine presses, and compelled them to promise him 700 marks. Meanwhile, the burgesses had, in effect, been forced to lend Savari £3,027.[17] A letter to the king in November 1223 concluded with the observation that 'the suburbs of La Rochelle have become enfeebled, and a great multitude of your men of La Rochelle have fallen from wealth into great poverty, on account of the dangers from wars in times past,

---

[14] *Divers Accounts*, 52; see the king's later comment, *Chron. Maj.*, vi, 67.
[15] Baldwin, *Philip Augustus*, 239–48, 351–4; *Ann. Mon.*, iii, 92.
[16] *DD*, no. 90.
[17] *DD*, nos 126, 131.

and on account of the exertions that they still have to sustain daily'.[18]

What the men of La Rochelle wanted at this time, in recompense for their losses, was to hold the provostship of the city themselves and receive its farm to wall in the suburbs so that when the truce expired 'they may be better defended from your enemies'.[19] This request, however, the English government did not meet, perhaps because it was so certain that the truce would be renewed. Instead, it had accepted Savari's suggestion that the provostship should be entrusted to Bartholomew de Puy, an appointment it was still trying to effect in January 1224 after Savari himself had changed his mind about it.[20] Against this background the defection of La Rochelle and the other Poitevin towns, when attacked by Louis, was understandable.

The English government had one last card to play, that of enlisting papal intervention. Envoys were despatched to the papal court on 26 May. They arrived to find only two cardinals in Rome, both of whom were pro-French, and the pope unwilling to act until he had taken further advice. In the end, on 3 August, Honorius wrote to Louis expressing regret that he had not renewed the truce and surprise that, forgetful of the needs of the Holy Land, he had actually resorted to war. He then rather feebly 'asked and begged' him to cease attacking the lands of the king of England.[21] Louis's reply was altogether more robust. Having pointed out that King John had been justly sentenced to forfeiture, he complained that England was a papal fief, yet its resources were being used to oppose him in Poitou. If this was occurring with the pope's consent he was 'asked and required' (not 'asked and begged') to put a stop to it. In December, when Louis's own envoys reached Rome, they threatened a fresh invasion of England if the pope did anything against their master's interests and they put it about that English magnates were still prepared to hand the kingdom over to him.[22]

When the vicomte of Thouars became Louis's man for a year in June 1224, he added a rider permitting the king of England to disembarrass him of the agreement.[23] The immediate chance of Henry doing this, or of recovering Poitou, was remote. Louis established garrisons in the towns, confirmed their old privileges and granted new.[24] He

[18] *DD*, no. 127. There was also hostility within La Rochelle between the burgesses and the Templars who had 'converted nearly a third part of the town to their demesne': *DD*, no. 113.

[19] *DD*, nos 126, 127.

[20] *PR*, 366, 380; *RLC*, 525b, 582.

[21] *DD*, no. 144; *RL*, 541–3; *Recueil*, xix, 759.

[22] *Recueuil*, xix, 760; *DD*, no. 153; *Ann. Mon.*, iii, 92.

[23] Petit-Dutaillis, *Louis VIII*, 240–1.

[24] Petit-Dutaillis, *Louis VIII*, 253–5.

demonstrated that they would enjoy far more security and prosperity under his lordship than under that of the king of England.

If Poitou was lost, however, there were indications that Gascony might be saved. Once La Rochelle had been secured, Louis had gone to Poitiers, leaving Hugh de Lusignan and the new seneschal of Poitou, Geoffrey de Builli, to invade Gascony.[25] Towards the end of September the men of Bordeaux wrote to the king of England with what seemed a catalogue of disaster. The towns of Blaye, Bourg, St Émilion, La Réole, St Macaire, Langon and Bazas had all surrendered 'without suffering any harm or coercion'. Nothing remained to the king save Dax, Bayonne and Bordeaux.[26] In fact, however, this conquest was superficial. Hugh de Vivonne, who had come on to Gascony after the fall of La Rochelle, reported the crucial fact that no garrisons had been placed in any of the towns which had submitted. Although many of the barons of the province had gone over, 'I count it for nothing and think that you will recover all that they [Hugh and Geoffrey] have acquired in these parts if you send speedy aid and succour'.[27] Above all, however, the two dominant towns of Gascony, Bordeaux and Bayonne, were determined to adhere to the king of England. Bordeaux spurned Hugh's attempt to secure a truce until the following Easter and maintained a force of 200 knights and 500 serjeants against him. As a result Hugh dared approach no closer than four leagues to Bordeaux. He then retired from Gascony 'in confusion'.[28]

That Bordeaux, and consequently Gascony, was much harder to conquer than La Rochelle and Poitou was understandable. In terms of history and dialect the two provinces were distinct.[29] Louis himself had little interest in helping Hugh to Bordeaux and in September he returned to Paris.[30] The towns of Gascony had not suffered from the depredations of great local magnates in the same way as those of Poitou, partly because there were not the same concentrations of power in the hands of a few great noble families.[31] In 1224 itself the king's government moved to confirm Bordeaux's allegiance. In July it was allowed to form a commune and choose its own mayor. In August it was conceded the customs on its wines for four years to assist work on the walls. In November 550 marks were sent out to complete the 2,000 marks given to fortify the town and sustain it in the king's service.[32]

---

[25] Petit-Dutaillis, *Louis VIII*, 250.
[26] *DD*, no. 147.
[27] *DD*, no. 148.
[28] *DD*, no. 147. For the equally robust attitude of Bayonne, *DD*, no. 145.
[29] See Stacey, *Politics*, 162, for a useful survey.
[30] Petit-Dutaillis, *Louis VIII*, 251.
[31] Stacey, *Politics*, 162.
[32] *PR*, 449–50, 458, 497. For concessions to Bayonne, *PR*, 467.

If, however, the king was to maintain and recover his position in Gascony, the problem was much the same as it had been before in Poitou. It was vitally necessary to send out troops and money from England on an altogether different scale from that attempted hitherto. 'If it pleases you to send us help in both men and money, you will recover your lands', concluded the mayor and commune of Bordeaux.[33] Other advice was even more specific. The king should despatch Richard, his younger brother, together with money and a great man to oversee its expenditure. It was exactly this advice which the government followed in 1225.[34]

[33] *DD*, no. 147.
[34] *DD*, no. 146.

Chapter 10

GASCONY, TAXATION AND MAGNA CARTA, 1225

In 1225 Gascony was recovered by an expedition sent from England and plentifully supplied with money; it was to be retained for the next 225 years. The financial resources which made this victory possible in 1225 came from taxation in the form of a fifteenth on movable property, taxation which raised some £40,000. The contrast between that sum and the few thousand pounds of the scutage of 1217 and the carucage of 1220 was ample testimony to the renewed authority and power of the king's government in England. The quid pro quo for the tax, however, was the reissue of Magna Carta and the Charter of the Forest. Thus the events of 1225 showed where English kingship stood after the traumas of the war and the early minority. It held Gascony but not Poitou. It dispensed justice throughout the kingdom and controlled its manors, castles and sheriffdoms as it wished. Its revenues had substantially increased since the period immediately after the war. But kingship had also accepted the limits imposed by the Charters. The events of 1225, indeed, marked a decisive stage in the implantation of the Charters into English political life.

i. *Gascony, 1225*

The decision to send Richard, the king's brother, to Gascony was taken at a great council held in London in February 1225. Richard, who was sixteen, was knighted and granted the county of Cornwall during the king's pleasure. The great man who was to accompany him and, in effect, control the expedition was the earl of Salisbury.[1] Salisbury thus acted in accord with his constant protestations of loyalty and fidelity to the king. He was supported materially by being granted the wardship of the lands of the earl of Norfolk, who died in February 1225.[2] In November 1224 Salisbury had already received a writ of allowance covering many of his debts to the king; for example, £1,009 15s of the £1,340 that he owed for the peacetime farms of Lincolnshire down to

---

[1] Denholm-Young, *Richard of Cornwall*, 4; *Chron. Maj.*, 92–3; *PR*, 507.
[2] *PR*, 508.

1221 were allowed against his wartime expenditures on Lincoln castle, for which no doubt he had enjoyed wartime resources.[3] If this, therefore, was simply a means of writing off the debt it was worth doing. In 1225 the earls of Salisbury and Pembroke, Hubert's two greatest allies in the period since 1220, were both hard at work for the king, the former his representative in Gascony, the latter in Ireland.

Richard was received at Bordeaux with enthusiasm and immediately used his money to hire soldiers. The towns which had entered the faith of the king of France returned to that of the king of England. On 2 May, having received the allegiance of the citizens of Bazas, Richard proclaimed, in a letter home to his brother, that he 'already had all Gascony free and cleared of your enemies, save La Réole, and all the magnates of Gascony are in your faith, save Elyas Ridel [of Bergerac]'.[4] The exceptions were important. Elyas, as Geoffrey de Neville had explained to the king in 1219, 'holds the March of your land towards the Agenais and Périgeux against your enemies'. In 1225 it was the count of Périgueux whom Hugh de Lusignan had left behind in Gascony to look after his interests.[5] La Réole, too, held a key strategic position on the Garonne and was frequently in conflict with Bordeaux over the free passage of its merchandise down the river. Consequently there was a strong Francophile party in the town which had wanted to hand it over to Louis in 1219. In 1224 Louis had showered La Réole with privileges; pronounced the renewed banishment of the Piis family, the great supporters of the king of England; and finally succeeded in installing his own garrison.[6]

Richard's campaign against La Réole and Elyas Ridel was held up, at first, because his money had run out. Late in July, Henry de Trubleville wrote home to Hubert describing the utter poverty of the army and the impossibility of getting substantial loans. He begged the latter to act up to his promises, made when they were all in England, and send money at once.[7] This was the point at which the campaign might have run into the ground. Instead, the tap, fed by the fifteenth, was about to be turned on. On 6 August a fleet left England with 6,000 marks of silver, together with jewels and cloths, and arrived in Gascony ten days later. Another 3,000 marks were sent out on 18 August.[8] Ultimately, between 15 June 1225 and the end of August 1226, 40,800 marks were despatched to support the expedition. Another 6,124 marks were given to knights and serjeants going out to join Richard. In all,

[3] RLC, ii, 4b–5; Divers Accounts, 44.
[4] DD, no. 166; Chron. Maj., 92–3; Ann. Mon, iii, 94.
[5] DD, nos 38, 147.
[6] DD, no. 48; Petit-Dutaillis, Louis VIII, 254–5.
[7] DD, no. 176.
[8] DD, nos 180, 181; RLC, 59.

the accounts for the fifteenth show that some 52,341 marks were spent on purposes related to the defence of Gascony.[9]

With these funds at his disposal, Richard ultimately succeeded, as Roger of Wendover put it, in 'subjugating all Gascony'.[10] As he tightened his grip around La Réole, Louis sent Hugh de Lusignan and a force of stipendary knights to the rescue. Richard, however, left the siege, caught Hugh in an ambush and prevented him from crossing the Dordogne. Hugh went instead to secure Bergerac, but after his withdrawal Elyas Ridel entered Richard's service. La Réole itself surrendered on 13 November.[11]

By this time the earl of Salisbury had been forced by illness to return to England. No real attempt was made to push the campaign further north into Poitou, which Louis held in force and would personally have defended. The recovery of Gascony, however, proved to be permanent. Hugh de Lusignan lacked the power to conquer it on his own, while Louis's interest in the area was limited. In any case, the latter became involved again in Toulouse and died in 1226, whereafter there was the long minority of his son, Louis IX. The Gascons themselves soon appreciated the value of the English connection. With the defection of Poitou, their wine would monopolize the English market. Already in July 1225 the king had sent a great ship to Gascony for 200 casks of wine.[12] Next month the first of the annual wine fleets was assembled by the barons of the Cinque Ports to bring the year's harvest home to England.[13] Since Gascon towns and nobles alike were engaged in viticulture, they both had an interest in maintaining the English connection. Bordeaux, in particular, benefited from it, since the great bulk of the wine was shipped from there to England. As the wine trade increased, moreover, so did the value of the customs imposed at Bordeaux on the exports. These were to become the most valuable single item in the king's revenue in Gascony, amounting in 1306–7 (the first year for which accounts survive) to £6,267.[14] Gradually, therefore, the king of England enjoyed in Gascony something which in Henry's early minority had been completely wanting in Poitou: a substantial annual revenue. Gascony had both the will and also ultimately the resources to contribute to its own defence.

[9] *Divers Accounts*, 54–63.

[10] *Chron. Maj.*, 93.

[11] *Recueil*, xviii, 308, 310; *Chron. Maj.*, 93.

[12] *PR*, 540.

[13] *PR*, 546.

[14] Trabut-Cussac, 'Les coutumes ou droits de douane perçus à Bordeaux', 135–50. For the wine trade, see Renouard, *Histoire de Bordeaux*, iii, 53–68, 233–66.

ii. *The fifteenth on movables and the recovery of government*

In succouring Gascony, the government commanded financial re-sources undreamt of since John's reign. There was nothing, in principle, surprising about the yield of the tax granted in 1225. The great council which conceded it knew that, if properly paid, it would raise money on a wholly different scale from the scutage of 1217 and the carucage of 1220. The last tax on movables, the thirteenth of 1207, had brought in over £60,000. Its memory had lain behind the clauses in the Charter of 1215 which regulated in detail how consent was to be obtained for future taxation.

The great council conceded such a tax in 1225 because it secured in return a renewed grant on the Charters. But it also seems likely that it made conditions about how the money should be collected and spent, conditions which anticipated the efforts of parliaments in the fourteenth century to exercise control over the taxation which they had voted. In 1225 the bishops of Bath and Salisbury were placed in charge of special exchequers, respectively at London and Salisbury, where the tax was received and accounted for. They were equally in charge of the disbursement of the money and were clearly enjoined to spend it exclusively on the purpose for which it had been conceded. Thus when the king and justiciar received money from the fund for other uses they were expected to repay it.[1]

The purpose of the taxation itself helps to explain why it was granted. This was not simply to recover Poitou and defend Gascony, areas where no English baron had significant interests. When Hubert put forward the king's case, he was able to argue that, quite apart from the situation overseas, money was needed to defend England from a French invasion. Thus, as a royal letter put it later, the tax was for 'the tranquillity and protection of the kingdom, and the common defence and utility of all'.[2] What had become widely known, early in 1225, were Louis's threats to mount another invasion, his claims that English magnates were prepared to hand the country over to him, and his letters to French and English ports trying to rally support. Thus King Henry paid a visit to the Cinque Ports in January 1225 to concert measures of defence and told them to advise him at the great council in February as to what should be done 'for the conservation of the kingdom'.[3] As it turned out, Louis was merely sabre rattling but Hubert, as a result, was able to link the king's cause in Poitou and Gascony with the general defence of the kingdom.

[1] *Divers Accounts*, 54–63; Mitchell, *Taxation*, 167–8; Cazel, 'The fifteenth of 1225', 67–81.

[2] *Chron. Maj.*, 91; *PR*, 572; see *Ann. Mon.*, iii, 93, where the aid is described as being 'for the defence of the kingdom'.

[3] *DD*, no. 153; *Ann. Mon.*, iii, 92–3; *PR*, 503.

The government which secured the tax in 1225 also appeared soundly based politically. The danger from the schismatics of 1223–24 had receded with the crushing of Falkes's rebellion. Indeed, Engelard de Cigogné, and several of Falkes's former knights, all went with Richard to Gascony, while Bishop Peter lent 1,000 marks towards the initial costs of the expedition.[4] According to Roger of Wendover, having heard Hubert present the king's case, Archbishop Langton and the bishops and the barons deliberated upon it. The result, however, was that the church lent its full support to the tax. Langton bound everyone to pay it under pain of excommunication[5] and the bishops of Bath and Salisbury were at the centre of its collection. Although, moreover, the church was allowed to assess and collect the tax on its own properties, it was still subject to it, in contrast to the carucage of 1220.

The authority of the government in the localities was apparent in the way the tax was assessed and collected. Like the carucage of 1220, although in a different form, this was the responsibility of local knights. Under the supervision of panels of these in each hundred, stewards were to swear to the value of the movables of earls, barons and knights. Everyone else was to swear to the value of their own movables, disputes being settled by juries.[6] The returns of the assessors and collectors were extraordinarily detailed, listing not merely the tax owed by each individual but also the property upon which the assessment was based. The return for the wapentake of Aswardhurn in Lincolnshire, one of the few to survive, runs to forty printed pages.[7] According to Professor Cazel, who has edited the surviving returns, 'the valuations appear to have been made with care and may be judged reasonably accurate'. Indeed, the returns 'suggest a quite remarkable degree of proficiency on the part of the assessors'.[8]

The results were correspondingly impressive, especially when compared to the carucage of 1220. In 1220, as has been seen, there were considerable difficulties imposing the tax in the former rebel-held counties of eastern England. In 1225, on the other hand, Lincolnshire, Yorkshire, Norfolk and Suffolk made the largest contributions of all, Lincolnshire paying £2,925 as opposed to £40 five years before. In all, when the accounts of the two bishops were audited in 1227, they

---

[4] *Divers Accounts*, 52. The knights were Walter de Goderville, Henry de Frankesney and Hugh Grandin: *PR*, 573–4.

[5] *Chron. Maj.*, 91; *Walt. Cov.*, 257. However, it is possible that Langton may have been disappointed in not securing the concession of ecclesiastical liberties over and above Magna Carta in return for the tax: see *Councils and Synods*, ii, part 1, 162.

[6] *PR*, 560–1.

[7] *Rolls of the Fifteenth*, 4–45.

[8] *Rolls of the Fifteenth*, x.

revealed receipts of £37,933, the total yield, including money paid elsewhere, being some £39,190 19s 8d or roughly 60,000 marks.[9]

The success of the tax of 1225 was a measure of both the political and administrative strength of the government in England. Equally significant, however, was the size of the king's ordinary revenue between 1224 and 1226, for this reveals just how much his power had increased since the catastrophic days of the early minority.[10] The sheriffs at the *Adventi* of Michaelmas 1224 and Easter 1225 brought to the exchequer respectively £1,815 and £995, as against £334 and £52 at the *Adventi* of Michaelmas 1219 and Easter 1220. The total receipts for the Michaelmas term of 1224, as recorded on the sole Michaelmas receipt roll of this period, were £9,095 from the counties and another £508 from Jewish debts, a total of £9,603. The proceeds of the Easter term of 1226, as found on the last receipt roll to survive from the early part of the reign, were £5,837, compared with £1,733 six years before.[11] The cash revenue in the pipe roll of 1224, adjusted for doubled and missing accounts, amounts to £12,980, while that in the roll for 1225 is £14,280. This compares with a cash revenue of £5,350, again on the adjusted figures, from the roll of 1220. Authorized expenditure in the rolls of 1224 and 1225, to take the adjusted figures, was respectively £2,410 and £2,220, making grand totals for the rolls of £15,390 and £16,500, as compared with £7,390 for the roll of 1220. The king's ordinary revenue, therefore, was more than double the level which it had been early in the minority and, in cash terms, approached three times as much. That is the best measure of the achievement of King Henry's government since the war.

The level of income in the roll of 1225 at around £16,500 was still less than half that reached in the roll of 1203 and indeed was between £11,000 and £15,000 less than in the rolls of the 1240s as analysed by Dr Stacey.[12] But the disastrous situation of the early minority had been

---

[9] *Divers Accounts*, 56, 60, 16, 54–63; Cazel, 'The fifteenth of 1225', 70–1. The tax base indicated by the proceeds of the 1225 tax was £600,000 and thus not very different from the £660,000 and £675,000 for the taxes on movables in 1232 and 1237: *Rolls of the Fifteenth*, x. The base for the tax of 1207 was some £780,000 but this was a levy on rents as well as movable property: *RLP*, 72.

[10] For the figures which follow, see Appendix, pp. 413–15.

[11] The roll of 1226 also recorded £371 received from Jewish debts (from Jews and Christians) and another £450 from a tallage on the Jews.

[12] Holt, 'The loss of Normandy and royal finances', 97; Stacey, *Politics*, 210. John's income was probably considerably larger after 1204. According to Dr Stacey's tables, between 1241 and 1245 the king's pipe roll income, leaving aside the exceptional roll of 1242, varied between £27,205 and £31,219. The king's total income, of course, was considerably larger because the pipe rolls, as in the minority, did not include the revenues accounted for at the Jewish exchequer or received from Ireland; see the tables in Stacey, *Politics*, 208, for total revenue between 1241 and 1245.

remedied and a firm basis laid for further recovery. In the later 1220s that recovery was aided in two ways.[13] The first was through the beginnings of an income from ecclesiastical vacancies. The speed with which these had been filled in the minority had deprived the crown of a considerable income. After 1225, however, this situation was modified by the disputed election at Durham, which produced a two-year vacancy between 1226 and 1228 and a welcome £5,861 for the crown.[14] The second cash injection was provided by the revival of the general eyres. With the last of these having taken place in 1221, there had been a decline in the revenue from justice, which makes the rising income in the rolls after 1221 all the more remarkable. By the roll of 1225 judicial issues were worth no more than £357.[15] The restarting of the eyres in 1226 soon altered this picture. In the rolls of 1227 to 1229 they generated a cash revenue of over £7,000, as against £2,680 produced by the first eyres of the reign in the rolls of 1219 to 1221.[16] That again is a measure of the government's advance since the early years of the minority.

Increased revenue, of course, meant increased power and in terms of projecting power nothing was more important than the size of the king's military household. It was precisely here that a significant portion of the additional revenue was spent. In 1219 annual fees had been paid to only four household knights; in 1223 they were paid to fifteen; in 1228 they were paid to seventy. In all, the number of household knights rose from seven in 1218 to 123 around eight years later.[17] There could be no more clear demonstration of the growth in royal power.

iii. *Magna Carta and the Charter of the Forest, 1225*

The government had made long advances in restoring its finances and authority but it had done so within acknowledged limits. What, above all, secured consent to the fifteenth on movables was the fresh grant in February 1225 of Magna Carta and the Charter of the Forest. The events of 1225 were a landmark in the establishment of the Charters. This was

[13] Later there is no doubt that the reforms of 1236 markedly increased the king's income: Stacey, *Politics*, ch. 2.

[14] Howell, *Regalian Right*, 234–5. In the pipe rolls of 1241 to 1244 vacancies produced between £4,635 and £7,196 a year: Stacey, *Politics*, 210.

[15] Between 1241 and 1245 judicial issues varied between £2,128 and £6,083: Stacey, *Politics*, 210.

[16] £6,953, according to my calculations, was the sum received in these rolls from the amercements of the eyre recorded 'in block' on the pipe rolls and from the 'common fines' imposed on some counties.

[17] Walker, 'Anglo-Welsh Wars', 70; C 72/2, m.20 and mm. 13, 15d, for other lists of household knights; *RLC*, 345b. The numbers of the late 1220s are partly explained by the exigencies of the conflict with France.

true, in the first place, in the purely textual sense, because in 1225 the Charters received their final form. Henry III in 1237 and 1253, and Edward I in 1297, rather than issuing new Charters, merely confirmed those of 1225. It is clauses from the Magna Carta of 1225, in Edward I's 1297 confirmation, which are still on the Statute Book today.[1]

In nearly all respects the Charters of 1225 were the same as those of 1217 but a new preamble stated that the king had granted them of his own 'spontaneous and free will' rather than, as in 1217, on the advice of his bishops, earls and barons.[2] This formula stepped around the problem that the king was still barred, until he came of age, from making grants in perpetuity,[3] but it could be justified by Henry's partial assumption of regal powers at the end of 1223. It also gained credibility from the new Charters being part of a mutual bargain between the king and his realm. This was because they had been paid for.[4] As the Charters themselves stated, in return for the concession of the liberties, everyone in the kingdom had granted the king a fifteenth of their movable property.[5] William Brewer's objection in 1223, therefore, no longer applied. In 1225 there was no element of coercion. The king had indeed granted the charters of his 'spontaneous and free will'.

The government itself was keen to maintain the connection between the tax and the Charters since it was the best way of getting it paid. Thus the orders for the tax's assessment and collection were sent to the sheriffs at exactly the same time (15, 16 February) as the orders to proclaim and observe the Charters and to carry through the new perambulations of the forest. The next month the sheriffs were to inform crusaders that, unless they paid the tax to the king, they and their heirs could not share in the liberties which the king had conceded in return for it.[6] Thus the Charters of 1225 were always remembered as part of a mutual bargain between the king and his subjects. This was why the king had a peculiar obligation to observe them.[7]

That the Charters of 1225 were well remembered was also because the government took good care to publicize them. The sheriffs were ordered to publicly proclaim the Charters both in February and again,

---

[1] *Halsbury's Statutes*, x, 14–17.

[2] Holt, *Magna Carta*, 350. The text, with that of the Charter of the Forest, is printed on pp. 350–62. For discussion, *ibid.*, 282.

[3] See *RLC*, ii, 75b.

[4] Maddicott, 'Magna Carta and the local community', 38.

[5] Holt, *Magna Carta*, 357. For the element of bargain in respect of the earlier versions, see below p. 403.

[6] *PR*, 560–7, 572–3. Although the enrolled orders to proclaim and uphold the Charter or Charters were only addressed to the sheriffs of Yorkshire, Northumberland, Lincolnshire and Cambridgeshire (*RLC*, ii, 70), it seems fairly certain that broadly similar letters were sent to the other sheriffs.

[7] *DBM*, 81.

with the first payment of the tax coming due, in May.[8] To this end, copies of the Charters, as both Roger of Wendover and the Barnwell annalist noted, were sent to all the counties.[9] Wiltshire's was deposited by the knights of the county in Lacock abbey and is now in the British Library.[10] Knights and magnates, indeed, were soon involved in struggles to uphold and exploit the Charters' provisions.[11] As early as July 1225 the government was concerned about attempts, under the pretext of the Great Charter, to withdraw suits from the local courts and exclude the sheriffs from wapentakes and ridings in Yorkshire and Cumberland. The sheriffs were told not to allow these usurpations to be defended by reference to the bad example of the county of Lincoln.[12] What was going on in Lincolnshire was revealed in a case of 1226 where two knights of the county upbraided the sheriff for attempting to hear pleas 'contrary to the liberty which they ought to have by the lord king's Charter'. The dispute here turned on the clause introduced into the Charter in 1217, which regulated the intervals between the meetings of the county court and restricted the tourn of the sheriff to two sessions a year. The upshot of this dispute in 1226 was the summons of elected knights from eight counties, including Lincoln-shire, to present 'on behalf of all the county' complaints against the sheriffs over certain articles in Magna Carta. Next year, virtually all the counties were ordered to elect knights to come before the king to present similar complaints.[13]

By this time the Charter had sunk deep roots into county society. That was not simply, of course, the work of the Charter of 1225. The previous versions had also been publicized, cherished and exploited. The extent of the deforestation promised by the Charter of the Forest, in particular, had been in dispute between the government and the counties since 1218. If any additional stimulus was needed to make the counties feel strongly about the issue, it was provided by the order in October 1224, authorized by 'all the council', instructing the new chief justice of the forest, Hugh de Neville, to keep the boundaries of the forest the same as they had been in John's time before the war.[14] Next year, above everything else, the counties were determined to seize their opportunity and force the government, at long last, to give way to their interpretation of the clauses on deforestation in the Forest Charter.

[8] *RLC*, ii, 70, 73b.

[9] *Chron. Maj.*, 91–2; *Walt. Cov.*, 256.

[10] Poole, 'Publication of the Charters', 451–2.

[11] See Maddicott, 'Magna Carta and the local community', 30–6, and Holt, *Magna Carta*, 279–81, where the incidents mentioned below are discussed.

[12] *RLC*, ii, 48b–9, 79b. The clause on the holding of courts was 42 in the 1217 Charter and 35 in the Charter of 1225.

[13] *CRR*, xii, no. 2142; *RLC*, ii, 153–153b; 212b–13.

[14] *PR*, 491.

In this they succeeded. The results of the perambulations ordered in February 1225 were to be sent to the king by 27 April so that he could decide, having taken counsel, what was to be done about them. Meanwhile, things were to remain as they were.[15] This, of course, was exactly the line the government had taken between 1218 and 1220. The new perambulations, when they came in, proved just as demanding as the old. Those in Nottinghamshire, Leicestershire, Huntingdonshire and Rutland left the king virtually no forest in the counties outside his demesne.[16] In Yorkshire large parts of Galtres and the forest between the Ouse and the Derwent were to be deforested.[17] The government, however, now gave way. On 8 May the sheriffs were ordered to proclaim and observe the perambulations so far made and to do the same with the others once they were completed. When Hugh de Neville protested that the perambulators of Dorset intended to deforest a large part of the county to the king's 'damage and injury', he was told to warn them not to do this, 'but if they nonetheless persist', the king observed, 'it is necessary for us to put up with it at present until at an opportune time we are able to emend it'; a statement which sums up much of Hubert's approach to government.[18] Thus, Roger of Wendover gives a graphic picture of how men throughout the forest counties hastened to exploit the new perambulations, selling their woods, making assarts, hunting beasts and creating new arable land.[19]

Having held the line on the forest after the war when it was weak, the government thus retreated when it was much stronger. It did so essentially as the quid pro quo for the payment of the tax on movables. Thus, if it accepted the encroachments on the forest in Dorset, at least it received £394 from the fifteenth in the county.[20] The intention of putting matters right at an opportune time was also more than a pious hope and as soon as the king assumed full power in 1227 the perambulators in many counties were forced to admit their errors.[21]

In 1225 itself, however, the king, according to the Barnwell chronicler, conceded the Charters willingly and happily, *benigne et hilariter*.[22] Indeed, one of the most striking and significant features of 1225 was the way the government learnt to live with the Great Charter,

---

[15] *PR*, 567–8; *RLC*, ii, 70.

[16] *RLC*, ii, 169b–70. The perambulation of Nottinghamshire in 1225 was much the same as in 1218 save that it made some acknowledgement of the forest which belonged to the royal demesne: Crook, 'The forest boundaries in Nottinghamshire', 38.

[17] C 47/11/1, no. 21; see the map below, p. 391. Deforestation was also demanded in Farndale: *CR 1227–31*, 225.

[18] *RLC*, ii, 73b. The perambulation itself is found in 'Cerne Cartulary', 195–7.

[19] *Chron. Maj.*, 94–5.

[20] *Divers Accounts*, 60.

[21] See below p. 392.

[22] *Walt. Cov.*, 257.

accepting the limitations which it imposed on kingship and working out how it could turn them to its advantage. In this it set a precedent for the rest of Henry's reign.

In 1225 the king was clear that he was subject to the law and custom of the kingdom. When, that October, the papal envoy, Master Otto, arrived to plead Falkes's cause, the king replied, according to Roger of Wendover, that Falkes had been exiled by the 'judgement of his court'. 'Although', the king continued, 'the care of the kingdom is seen to belong especially to [us, we] ought to observe the laws and good customs of the kingdom.'[23] Amongst these laws, of course, the Charters were now an acknowledged part. King Henry was equally clear that he ought not to deprive men of property unlawfully, thus breaching one of the most coveted clauses of the Great Charter. In February 1225 the tin mines of Cornwall had been given to Richard, the king's brother, despite an agreement under which they were held by John fitz Richard and Stephen de Croy. When John and Stephen protested, they recovered the mines, 'since', as a royal letter put it, 'it is neither fitting nor right for the king to infringe . . . the agreement made with them by his letters patent'. Likewise, in respect of the knights of Cornwall's privilege of choosing their own sheriff, the king declared that 'we neither wish nor is it right for us to infringe what our father conceded to them by his charter and we afterwards approved.'[24]

The king, therefore, was subject to the law. It was neither 'fitting nor right' for him to act unjustly. His *duty*, moreover, was to dispense justice to everyone. This was stressed in a letter of June 1225 to the bishop of Durham, a letter with whose issue Hubert was closely associated. 'We who are bound by our office as ruler (*ex officio regiminis nostri*)', the king told the bishop, 'to give justice to all and each in our kingdom, cannot omit to give full justice to the prior and convent [of Durham], according to the custom of the kingdom.' Hubert was equally clear that it was the king's duty to see that everyone enjoyed the benefits of the Charters. Nine days later the king was writing again to the bishop of Durham, a letter he attested in Hubert's presence: 'since to all in our kingdom, as you well know, we have conceded certain liberties in our Great Charter of liberties, we cannot rightfully allow the prior and monks of Durham to be prevented from using and enjoying the liberties in our foresaid Charter in the same way as others in our kingdom'.[25]

What the king was doing in these cases was to make a virtue of the limitations on his power imposed in the Great Charter. His obligation to observe the law meant that he could not restore Falkes; his duty to

[23] *Chron. Maj.*, 97–8.
[24] C 60/23, mm. 6,5 (*quia non decet dominum Regem sicut nec debet de iure conventionem eis factam per literas suas patentes . . . infringere*); *RLC*, ii, 25.
[25] *RLC*, ii, 73.

dispense justice and enforce the Charter meant he could protect the prior and monks of Durham when they were attempting to override the claims of the bishop and present one of Hubert's clerks to the valuable church of Heighington.[26] Here, as elsewhere in Hubert's career, principle and self-interest were conveniently intertwined.

There were other ways, too, in which the government strove to profit from the Great Charter. One was by developing the concept of reciprocity, which had been a feature of writs attested by Hubert in the early minority.[27] On 8 May 1225 the sheriffs were not only to proclaim the Charters, they were also to declare that, as the king wished the liberties which he had conceded in them to be observed, so 'all and everybody should preserve all our rights and all our liberties unharmed'.[28] The same point was repeated in June when the government learnt that, in the lands of the earls of Chester and Surrey, the Charter was being exploited so as to damage the liberties of the king and threaten his peace. The earls were informed that this must stop: 'since to you and the other . . . men of our kingdom we have conceded liberties which we wish and have ordered to be preserved, so no less do we wish our liberties and peace, as is fitting and just, to be inviolably observed'.[29] Later, in July, when the king became anxious about encroachments on his rights in Yorkshire and Cumberland, this was given a slightly different twist. A writ, attested by the king in the presence of Hubert and the bishops of Bath and Salisbury, pointed out that since the Charter had reserved to everyone all the liberties which they enjoyed before, so the king should enjoy the liberties possessed before by his ancestors, provided they had not been specifically given away in the Great Charter.[30] The use of such reciprocal sentiments to defend the king's liberties became a common feature of writs for the rest of Henry's reign.[31]

Another tack which appears in 1225, and to which the king equally reverted throughout his reign, was to pick up the clause in the Charters which stipulated that everyone should observe towards their own men the liberties which they themselves had received from the king. This was to exploit an issue – that of the relations between magnates and their subjects – which was to grow in importance throughout Henry's reign and become a cardinal feature of the period of revolution and reform in 1258–59. By insisting that this clause in the Charters be obeyed, the king could hope to win the favour of sections of society

[26] *RLC*, ii, 73.
[27] See above pp. 160, 213.
[28] *RLC*, ii, 73b.
[29] *RLC*, ii, 78.
[30] *RLC*, ii, 79b.
[31] *CR 1242–7*, 242, for the most famous example.

below the magnates. Thus, at the end of June 1225, following a complaint from the knights and men of Westmorland and elsewhere, William of Lancaster, John de Lacy, Robert de Vieuxpont and the earl of Surrey, amongst others, were ordered to deforest areas which had been afforested by their ancestors since the beginning of Henry II's reign.[32] As a result, John de Lacy was soon writing to Hubert to explain that he was detained in the area of Bowland, warding off an attempt by the men there to deprive him of the whole forest, although his ancestors had possessed it before the time of Henry II. Lacy, therefore, was trying to prevent, in Bowland, exactly the same type of illegitimate deforestations as was the king in the counties of England.[33]

When he put the king's case for the tax of 1225 Hubert knew that the quid pro quo would be a new grant of the Charters. Thenceforth they would be a permanent feature of English political life. What Hubert equally saw was the way that the king could live with this situation and exploit it. For the future of Plantagenet kingship, that service was on a par with his defence of Dover and his resumption of the king's demesnes, sheriffdoms and castles.

The concession of the Charters in 1225 thus laid tracks for the future but also sealed up the divisions of the past. On the great day at Westminster, 11 February 1225, when the documents were issued, they were witnessed by those who had stood on either side of the great divide in 1215–16. Angevin loyalists like Hubert, Bishop Peter, Robert de Vieuxpont, William Brewer, John of Monmouth, Hugh de Mortimer, Brian de Lisle, Geoffrey de Neville, Peter de Maulay and the earls of Chester and Derby stood side by side with Archbishop Langton and eight of the twenty-five barons of the 1215 Charter's security clause, namely Robert fitz Walter, Robert de Ros, Richard de Muntfichet, John de Lacy, William de Albini, the earls of Gloucester and Norfolk, and the count of Aumale. The process of settlement after the war was indeed complete.

---

[32] *PR*, 575–6. The way this concept was exploited later in Henry's reign is discussed in Maddicott, 'Magna Carta and the local community', 52–3. Another later feature of Henry's kingship (see *ibid.*, 54) to appear in 1225 is his concern to prevent his government bearing too heavily on the poor: *PR*, 572–3.

[33] SC 1/1, no. 108.

Chapter 11

THE END OF THE MINORITY

When John de Lacy wrote to Hubert in 1225 about his problems regarding Bowland forest, he did not ask him to deal with the matter himself but 'to intervene on my behalf with the king'.[1] The request reflected the fact that, since the end of 1223, the king had been directly involved in day-to-day government. By 1226 his influence was very clear, most notably in his desire to emulate his brother Richard and lead an expedition to recover Poitou. The minority was never formally brought to an end. In January 1227 the king announced that 'by the common council of Stephen archbishop of Canterbury and our bishops, abbots, earls, barons and other magnates and *fideles*' he would henceforth issue charters under his seal.[2] Thus the restriction imposed on his kingship in December 1223 was lifted. The immediate reason for this move was to increase the king's authority as opportunities opened up following the death of Louis VIII.[3] The move was not, however, accompanied by a declaration that the king had reached his majority. No letter was obtained from the pope to that effect, whatever Henry later believed. Nor had January 1227 any significance in terms of the king's age: he was still a year and eight months short of his twenty-first birthday on 1 October 1228. As has been seen, the feeling continued that in fact Henry remained a minor until that point.[4] Nonetheless, from January 1227 onwards he was in full possession of regal powers.

The lifting of the restrictions on the concession of charters meant a huge change in the nature of politics. The king could at last dispense patronage on a permanent basis. For Hubert above all this was important. He was an old man in a hurry, eager to cash in before it was too late on long years of faithful service. The king made him earl of Kent and gave him in hereditary right the honours of Haughley and Rayleigh. More remarkably, he was also conceded in hereditary right the castles and honours of Montgomery, Cardigan and Carmarthen. With his tenure of the Three Castles also confirmed, Hubert had

---

[1] SC 1/1, no. 108.

[2] *RLC*, ii, 207.

[3] There was also the more immediate purpose of making money by charging for the confirmation that the king could now issue: *RLC*, ii, 207.

[4] *Chron. Maj.*, vi, 69; see above pp. 123–4.

created a formidable power-base in the Welsh Marches.[5] Equally impressive was his success in Ireland, where he established his nephew, Richard, in Connaught. Here too he had bided his time, having, throughout the early minority, postponed decisions on Richard's claims so as not to offend Cathal Crovderg, the king of Connaught (who died in 1224).[6] In all this, Hubert's star increasingly shone alone beside the king. Langton ceased to be involved in active politics in 1227 and died the following year.[7] The year 1228 also saw the withdrawal from court of Richard le Poure, bishop of Salisbury, on his elevation to the bishopric of Durham. Meanwhile, the earl of Salisbury had died in 1226 after his return from Gascony.

Hubert's success depended on his relationship with the king. Henry was not an easy man to serve. He was impulsive, enthusiastic and ignorant of political realities. In matters large and small Hubert struggled to keep him off the rocks. In 1226, for example, the king, in trying to persuade the monks of Durham to elect Hubert's chaplain as bishop, threatened to pull down Durham castle. Hubert had to point out that nothing would please the monks more, the castle being the property of the bishop.[8] Above all Hubert had to cope with the young king's passionate desire to lead an expedition which would recover the Angevin empire, a project to which Hubert, fully aware of the pitfalls, was less than committed. Yet the justiciar had many strengths to put in the balance. His prestige was immense; his men were carefully placed throughout the royal administration. The king had objectives without expertise and ambition without energy. He needed someone to advise him about means to ends. He also liked an easy life. In that sense the cautious approach of the aging justiciar suited him well enough.

Hubert's relations with the great magnates were inevitably prejudiced by the sudden flowering of his material ambitions. As late as 1228 he was able to secure general consent to his becoming justiciar for life.[9] But there was little support next year when he was conceded Cardigan and Carmarthen in hereditary right.[10] As early as 1226 the installation of Richard de Burgh in Connaught had broken up his alliance with the earl of Pembroke. Nonetheless, it was not, in the end, the great magnates who brought Hubert down, however much they resented his accumulation of wealth and power. Hubert continued to

[5] CChR, 12–13, 81, 83, 100.

[6] RLC, 401, 584–584b, 604b; RL, no. cxcviii; Otway-Ruthven, Medieval Ireland, 69, 72, 76, 92–4; Lydon, 'The expansion and consolidation of the colony', 162–3.

[7] Cazel, 'The last years of Stephen Langton', 673–97.

[8] Durham Cathedral MSS, Misc. 5520, transcribed in Evers, 'Disputes about Episcopal Elections', 107.

[9] CChR, 74; Ellis, Hubert de Burgh, between pp. 120 and 121.

[10] No earl attested the relevant charter: C 53/21, m.3.

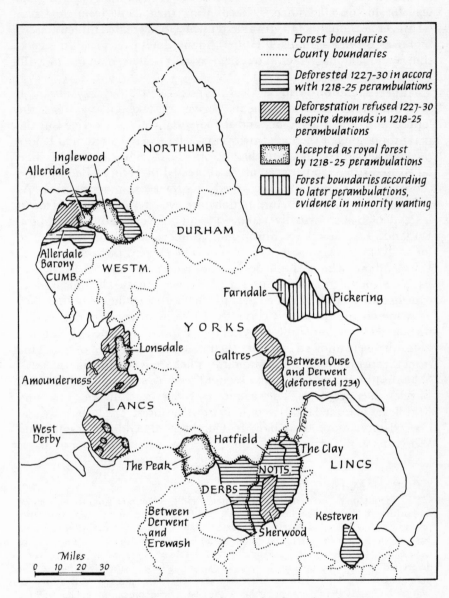

7. Northern royal forests in the minority

filter their requests for justice and favour through the king, clearing the way for his own advance by facilitating their own. John de Lacy, whatever he thought of the royal letter which had created difficulties for him over Bowland, thanked Hubert 'many times over for all the good things and honours which [you] have always conferred on me and still will, if it pleases you'.[11]

Hubert's relations with the localities also soured after 1227, although here too there remained elements of give and take. In 1227 itself the 'opportune time' had come, and the knights who had carried out the perambulations of the forest two years before were summoned before the king and forced to admit their errors, the chief being that they had failed to distinguish between areas afforested by Henry II *de novo* and those which he had merely recovered after their loss under Stephen. As a result, the whole of Huntingdonshire was restored to the forest instead of being virtually removed from it. Yorkshire, Lancashire, Rutland, Leicestershire, Shropshire, Staffordshire and Surrey also found themselves back to square one. The exigent perambulation in Dorset about which Hugh de Neville had complained in 1225 was likewise modified. Henry and Hubert were naturally accused of overthrowing the Forest Charter, to which they could reply that they were merely interpreting it correctly. Certainly, they were engaged in no blanket rejection of the 1225 perambulations. The men of Nottinghamshire were allowed to realize their chief ambition, that of removing from the forest both The Clay and the other areas outside Sherwood.[12] 'The disafforestments actually secured were considerable', Margaret Bazeley has written. 'The counties of Sussex, Lincoln . . . and Middlesex obtained total exemption from the forest. In Derbyshire and Oxfordshire, more than half; in Cumberland, Gloucestershire and Worcestershire, more than a third; in Nottinghamshire, perhaps as

---

[11] SC 1/1, no. 108.

[12] The map on p. 391 is derived from that in Holt, *Northerners*, from the secondary authorities cited there in note 1 to p. 195, and from the perambulations and other primary evidence listed in Bazeley, 'The extent of the forest', 167–70. Northumberland has not been included since no perambulations survive from the minority. For Lancashire, see below note 13. Much of West Derby may in practice have become deforested since there is little later evidence for it being within the forest. The perambulations of Galtres forest (C 47/11/1, nos 10, 21) are ambiguous and it may be that the boundary should extend further to the east. The modifications in Cumberland are based on later evidence; that they took place between 1227 and 1230 is my speculation: Parker, 'Inglewood forest', 35–61, and the map in Bazeley. With the exception of a few counties (see notably Fisher, *The Forest of Essex*), it is not possible to draw for the southern forests the same kind of detailed map as it is for the northern. The evidence exists but it has not been analysed in the same way by local historians. However, map 2, p. xxii, which largely reproduces that in Bazeley, gives an impression of the extent of the forest after the modification of the perambulations of the minority.

much as two-thirds, and in Berkshire four-fifths of the forest area was surrendered by the Crown . . . In Northamptonshire, Hampshire and Wiltshire districts more or less considerable were exempted.' Although the men of Essex obtained much less than they wanted, they did secure the deforestation of Tendring hundred.[13]

In effect, what the government sought in and after 1227 was the type of compromise with the counties envisaged in the early minority. Thus, just as in 1219–20, while refusing to give way over deforestation, Hubert had ordered other clauses in the Forest Charter to be respected, so in 1229 Henry III, declaring that he had sworn to the Forest Charter and wished to see the liberties in it preserved unharmed, specifically ordered the upholding of the clause which exempted those outside the forests' bounds from answering the common summons to appear before the justices of the forest.[14] In seeking such a compromise, the government was not entirely unsuccessful. Although grievances over the modification of the 1225 perambulations long rankled, the administration of the forest under Henry III was nowhere near so unpopular as it had been under King John.

Ultimately it was Bishop Peter and the party of 1223–24 which proved fatal to Hubert. Peter might continue to assist the government in its dealings with Poitou and Gascony but he was never reconciled to Hubert's regime. At long last, in 1232, having returned in glory from a crusade, he persuaded the king to remove the justiciar from office, thus fulfilling his threat made nine years before.[15] The surviving schismatics of 1223–24, Peter de Maulay, Engelard de Cigogné, Robert Passelewe, and Falkes's chief servant, Ralph de Bray, all returned to court or to local office. Brian de Lisle too was an important prop of the bishop's regime. If only Falkes himself had lived to see the day. Had Peter behaved wisely, he could have ended his days as the king's chief minister. Instead, he induced the king to restore Peter de Maulay to the manor of Upavon, thus disseising Gilbert Basset unjustly and without judgement, in flagrant contravention of the Great Charter. This was

[13] Bazeley, 'The extent of the forest', 149–52; Crook, 'The forest boundaries in Nottinghamshire', 38–40; *Chron. Maj.*, 122; see also Maddicott, 'Magna Carta and the local community', 36–40. Many of the deforestations referred to by Bazeley were accepted by the king at various dates between 1227 and 1230. For Cumberland, see above note 12. In 1234 most of the forest between the Ouse and Derwent in Yorkshire was deforested, as, in 1235, was nearly all the forest of Leicestershire. Such individual concessions were usually paid for. W. H. Farrer ('Forestry', 438) believed that extensive deforestation was authorized in Lancashire in 1228 but the perambulation on which he relied was probably the rejected one of 1225: see Bazeley, 'The extent of the forest', 168.

[14] *CR 1227–31*, 174–5; but for the later breach of the clause, see Crook, 'The forest boundaries in Nottinghamshire', 40.

[15] I have discussed Hubert's fall in 'The fall of Hubert de Burgh', 1–17.

dangerously provocative since Gilbert Basset, like his elder brother Thomas before him, was a familiar of the earl of Pembroke. Other disseisins *per voluntatem regis* followed. These Peter justified in the light of 'the plenitude of royal power'. Equally, he ridiculed the fundamental clause in the Great Charter which forbad such conduct: there were no 'peers' in England, he declared.[16] All this provoked a rebellion led by Richard Marshal earl of Pembroke, the brother of William, who had died in 1231. In a revival of the old alliance Richard rescued Hubert from imprisonment at Devizes castle. By the summer of 1234 Richard's revolt and Edmund archbishop of Canterbury's intervention forced the king to dismiss Bishop Peter. His regime had lasted less than two years. What a contrast to Hubert's thirteen patient years of power!

The politics of the early minority, therefore, created a legacy of political instability which remained until 1234. Only then, with the final retirement of Hubert and Peter, was Henry free from the rivalries which had developed in the period after the war. Only then could he rule without one of King John's former justiciars at his elbow. One legacy of Bishop Peter's regime, however, exacerbated Henry's later difficulties, for the bishop's conduct encouraged the distinctively English view of recent history which had been developing since the war and thus helped to accelerate the growth of English national feeling. Already, in the early minority, the Barnwell chronicle could ascribe John's problems to his placing more trust in aliens than in his own people. Likewise, Ralph of Coggeshall believed that in the sea fight off Sandwich 'the Lord struck the heads of his enemies coming to destroy the English race'. A poet expressed similar sentiments about the battle of Lincoln.[17] The politics of the minority, when aliens appeared repeatedly as the fountain-heads of trouble, reinforced this view of events. The final seal was put on it by the return in 1232 of Bishop Peter and 'the Poitevins'. Against this background Hubert's role as the loyal Englishman stood out all the more. He was the man who had 'rescued England from the devastation of aliens, and restored England to England', as a smith who refused to fetter him in 1232 exclaimed, according to Matthew Paris's story.[18] King Henry himself was the most English of kings since the Norman conquest but he also gave large amounts of patronage to foreigners, notably the Savoyard relations of his wife and his own Lusignan half-brothers. 'He loved aliens above all Englishmen, and enriched them with innumerable gifts and possessions',

[16] *BNB*, no. 857; CRR, xv, nos 131, 1026, 1047, 1308, 1426–7, 1475, 1895; *CR 1231–34*, 401; *CChR*, 114; *RL*, no. ccclxxxix; *Chron. Maj.*, 252.
[17] *Walt. Cov.*, 232; *Coggeshall*, 185; *Political Songs*, 19–20. See the discussion in Clanchy, *England and its Rulers*, 241–4.
[18] *Chron. Maj.*, 227.

noted the Osney abbey chronicler dolefully.[19] Feelings of xenophobia
were to play a important part in the period of reform and rebellion
between 1258 and 1265.

Bishop Peter died in 1238, Hubert de Burgh 'in melancholy
retirement' five years later.[20] Melancholy because his hopes of creating
a great English comital house had fallen to the ground. He had been
forced to resign to the king the great gains of his career: Haughley and
Rayleigh, the Three Castles, Montgomery, and Cardigan and Carmarthen. His only child by his marriage to Margaret, King Alexander's
sister, known universally by her affectionate diminutive Meggotta, had
died in 1237. Hubert's son by his first marriage, John de Burgh, would
be a great magnate but he had no castle and could inherit no earldom,
that of Kent being entailed on Hubert's issue by Margaret. In another
way, however, Hubert had emerged victorious, for time increasingly
invested his period as justiciar with a golden glow. Hubert was, in fact,
the last effective justiciar, since the office was allowed to lapse two years
after his dismissal. Ten years later the abortive Paper Constitution of
1244 demanded its revival. The demand was reiterated at successive
parliaments in the 1240s and 1250s until it was finally realized in the
great revolution of 1258.

[19] *Ann. Mon.*, iv, 254. See Ridgeway, 'Henry III and the "Aliens" ' and 'Foreign
favourites and Henry III's problems of patronage'.
[20] Powicke, *The Thirteenth Century*, 61.

Chapter 12

THE MINORITY AND ITS AFTERMATH

By the time that King Henry began to influence the course of events in 1226, the great issues raised by the minority had been settled. England was to be ruled by the Plantagenet, not the Capetian house with all the incalculable consequences that might have brought. Equally, after a period of almost total collapse, much of the power and authority of kingship had been restored. The dangers of anarchy and civil war had been averted. England was not to be broken up into semi-independent principalities under great sheriffs and castellans, on the one hand, and areas where the king's local agents were overrun by magnates and communities on the other. The king's ordinary revenue, as recorded in the pipe rolls, had more than doubled from £7,390 in the roll of 1220 to £16,500 five years later. The rise in the cash income had been even more spectacular: from £5,350 in 1220 to £14,280 in 1225.[1] If, however, the king had recovered power, he had publicly accepted the limits imposed by Magna Carta and the Charter of the Forest. The minority of Henry III had thus refashioned the nature of England's polity. It had also accelerated the growth of English national feeling and ensured that kings of England would retain possessions on the continent, possessions whose preservation and expansion would be a major preoccupation for the rest of the middle ages.

Purely military factors had gone a long way towards explaining the Angevin victory in the war. King John's death, the succession of his innocent son and the proclamation of the new Charter did little to thin the ranks of Louis's supporters. Concepts of loyalty made desertion difficult but the essential factors keeping apart the two camps, much as in Stephen's reign, were hard material rivalries over castles, lands and rights. The politics of the war thus pointed to those of the minority, where so much depended on the struggle to recover or retain material possessions. In the war the deadlock was broken at Lincoln, second only to Hastings as the most decisive battle in English medieval history. The regent's decision to commit the fortunes of the Angevin house to the hazard of one great fight was the finest moment of his career.

[1] In all cases these are the adjusted figures from the respective pipe rolls: see Appendix, p. 413.

It was based on cool calculation, not flashy chivalry. With Louis's forces divided, the moment had come. Two other great men of the minority played a central part in this victory. Peter bishop of Winchester's discovery of the blocked gate at Lincoln provided the means of entry to the town, while Hubert de Burgh's defence of Dover had ensured the division of Louis's army.

After the war, rebuilding the king's government and implementing the peace settlement were hugely difficult tasks. With the king a minor, the authority of those who governed in his name was limited and largely dependent on the backing of great councils. In the localities magnates and local communities were determined to profit from the weakness of royal authority and exploit the concessions in Magna Carta and the Charter of the Forest. Even more serious were the problems presented to the government by its own local agents, who disobeyed its orders and drew off for themselves the revenues from the county farms and royal demesne.

The extraordinary difficulty of dismissing such men while the king was under age is plain from the way they usually had to be either bought out or forced out, sometimes both. Robert de Vieuxpont's price for vacating Tickhill in 1218 was the concession of the county farm of Cumberland; that of the earl of Pembroke for vacating Marlborough, his marriage to the king's sister. Likewise, the resumption of the demesne went through in 1222 after a multitude of bargains and concessions. The threat of force was equally apparent in securing government victories. It underpinned the removal of Philip of Old-coates from Mitford, the ejection of Henry fitz Count from Cornwall and the surrender of the castles and sheriffdoms at the end of 1223. Indeed, in December 1223 the government won the day because its army at Northampton outnumbered the dissidents' forces at Leicester. On occasions threats spilled over into the actual use of force; Newark was besieged in 1218, Rockingham in 1220, Bytham in 1221 and Bedford in 1224.

In all this, the immediate danger was that, faced with insubordinate castellans, private wars and mutinous local communities, the authority of the government would simply collapse. At times, indeed, anarchy seemed very close. Alternatively there might be full-scale civil war. Such a war was rumoured to be imminent during the Christmas crisis of 1221, nearly broke out at Christmas 1223 and was begun by Falkes, if not continued by others, in 1224.

For the state to hold together and royal power to recover, in this situation, required two things: a clear programme of action at the centre and the ability to mobilize support for its execution. In providing that programme and in urging its prosecution, the role of Pandulf and the papacy was pre-eminent. Indeed, the papacy never played a more important and constructive role in English history than during the minority of Henry III. In April 1219 the pope, as the young king's overlord and guardian, unfolded for the first time the programme of resumption. It was repeated more urgently in further letters in 1220 and again in 1221. The pope also sanctioned the king's second coronation, in May 1220, where special significance probably attached to the royal oath to maintain and recover the rights of the crown. These moves almost certainly took place at Pandulf's instigation. The programme of resumption was not achieved during his legation but it had been put on the political agenda in so forceful a fashion as to be irremovable. It was not, moreover, merely a case of Pandulf unveiling a programme and leaving its implementation to others. He was perfectly prepared to muddy his hands in politics. He was at the centre of Oldcoates's removal from Mitford, fitz Count's from Cornwall and Pembroke's from Marlborough. Pandulf's last recorded advice on English affairs (in a letter of 1225) summed up his attitude: referring to the dissidents of 1223–24, he told Hubert to ensure above all that 'the pride of the traitors does not ascend further than is expedient'.[2]

The programme enunciated in April 1219 fitted in with existing principles in England, if not with existing practice. Already at his first coronation the king had sworn to maintain and recover royal rights. If, in reality, the regent had presided over a rapid passage of manorial and county farms out of the king's control, he at least acknowledged the principle that the king should be kept in seisin of all that King John had held at the beginning of the war. He had attempted a resumption of the royal demesne, if with little success. He had refused to sanction the deforestations demanded by the counties. By and large he did maintain, as a bottom line, that the king could make no permanent alienations until he came of age. Already in January 1218 the exchequer was critical of the practice of the great local governors. The latter, it implied, should pay their revenues into the exchequer and then receive them back to fund local expenditures as and when necessary. Clearly this system would give the exchequer both greater reserves of cash and greater control over how it was spent than where the local governors simply absorbed the king's revenues themselves.

Familiar as they were with these ideas, Hubert and Bishop Peter were ready to work with Pandulf towards the restoration of royal authority. Peter had been closely associated with King John's assertive kingship and must have shared the legate's objectives. The duty of Hubert as justiciar, as numerous letters written to him stressed, was precisely to maintain the rights of the crown. His zeal in doing so was increased by his own control at the centre. The greater the revenue

---

[2] *DD*, no. 177.

received there, the greater his own power. Both ministers, therefore, were involved in the struggles over Mitford, Rockingham and Fotheringhay. Then, while Peter was abroad in 1221, Hubert gained control of Corfe castle and, working hand in hand with Pandulf, persuaded the earl of Pembroke to surrender Marlborough. Pandulf's departure brought no slackening of pace, for Hubert took the lead himself. He was almost certainly behind the abortive attempt to resume the demesne in September 1221; by the same token, his was probably the immediate initiative behind the successful resumption of June 1222. By this time, however, English politics were rent by faction. Hubert had strengthened his control at the centre at Peter's expense, had accused him of treason and discontinued his guardianship of the king. It was in the hope of unhorsing his rival that Peter secured the papal letters of April 1223 which gave the king control of his seal and commanded the surrender of the castles and sheriffdoms. How effectively Peter would have executed such a resumption is open to question. He was hampered, to a degree that Hubert was not, by supporters entrenched in local office. As it was, in November 1223 Hubert used the letters himself and began the process of resuming the king's castles and sheriffdoms, a task he completed in alliance with Langton and the bishops. At the same time more stringent financial terms were imposed on all the sheriffs, both those who were new appointments and those, like Hubert himself, who remained in office. The justiciar was thus engaged in more than party warfare. He was positively concerned to vindicate the rights and increase the revenues of the crown.

After 1219, therefore, there *was* a clear programme for the recovery of royal power. It was a programme laid out by the papacy and prosecuted by those in control of central government. It was not enough, however, merely to have clear objectives. The government had also to enlist support for their implementation. For Hubert two alliances were of paramount importance, the first with the earls of Salisbury and Pembroke, the second with Archbishop Langton and the bishops. It was Salisbury who stood by Hubert's side during the Christmas crisis of 1221 and who accepted, and thus did much to further, the act of resumption in 1222, despite suffering considerable losses. It was Pembroke's triumph over Llywelyn which gave Hubert the strength to take the initiative over the castles and sheriffdoms in November 1223. In their letters, Pembroke and Salisbury frequently protested their readiness to obey the orders and further the interests of the king. But Pembroke equally threatened to withdraw from the king's court if he failed to get his way or, as he preferred to put it, if Hubert denied him justice. The fact is that material concerns help explain the two earls' support for the government, concerns which Hubert safeguarded and exploited with skill. If Pembroke gave a good example to others by vacating Marlborough, he did so because of his promised marriage to the king's sister. If Salisbury lost much under the 1222 act, there was much also that he retained, notably, in partnership with Hubert and Pembroke, the lands of the count of Perche. In 1223 Pembroke had nothing to lose from the resumption of the castles and sheriffdoms, while Salisbury was exempted from it. Both could expect it to undermine the power of their enemies.

Hubert's co-operation with Langton after 1221 was even more vital. From the start of the minority ecclesiastics had worked within the government: bishops were active both at the exchequer and as justices in eyre. But it was not till Pandulf's departure in 1221 that Langton came right to the fore. His role, thereafter, as it had been in 1215, was very much that of a mediator and a peacemaker. He intervened to keep the peace in 1222, 1223 and 1224, not always with success. He was not the immediate force behind the prosecution of the programme of resumption but equally it was a programme which he could understand and support. It was, therefore, Langton's backing and those of his allies on the episcopal bench which saw through the measures over the demesne in 1222 and the castles and sheriffdoms in the following year. At the end of 1223, indeed, Langton, with the bishops of Bath and Salisbury, effectively joined with Hubert to form a new government.

The recovery of royal authority, however, also depended on the ability of central government to win support from laymen who were outside the circle of the regime, hence the repeated oaths designed to rally barons and knights to its cause. Those whose assistance was enrolled in this way inevitably included many former rebels. Indeed, it was former rebels who formed large parts of the armies on which the victories of the government depended at Newark in 1218, in the operations against the count of Aumale in 1221, at Northampton in 1223 and at Bedford in 1224. Equally, it was pressure from former rebels which extracted Philip of Oldcoates from Mitford and, in all probability, helped push through the resumption of the demesne in 1222.

Essentially, the government was able to secure this support because it tackled effectively the second great problem after the war, namely that of enforcing the peace settlement. Of course, it was helped here by the way the private business of individuals soon cut across wartime divisions, but with many former rebels embittered by large ransoms and frustrated ambitions, failure to implement the peace treaty might have led to a fresh outbreak of war. By and large the government did not fail. The centrepiece of the treaty was the restoration of former rebels to the lands which they had held at the beginning of the war. The process got successfully under way in 1217–18 and when it was obstructed, the regent demonstrated to former rebels that he was on their side. The same line was followed by his successors, who ultimately effected the restoration of Roger de Montbegon to his Nottinghamshire lands, Roger Bertram to Mitford, Hugh de Neville, Walter of Preston and Henry of Braybrooke to the Rockingham forest and surrounding manors, Reginald de Braose to Totnes, William de Coleville to Bytham and indeed William de Beauchamp to Bedford.

The peace treaty also implied that the government would confirm, indeed would improve, the version of Magna Carta which it had conceded in November 1216 and here again it was true to its word. From 1218 there was a wavering tussle with the counties over the Charter of the Forest but in many areas the kingdom could see clearly that the Great Charter was being upheld. It was equally clear that the style of government was moderate and malleable. Up to a point the magnates had the control of that in their own hands since so many important decisions were the prerogative of great councils. Great councils in 1219 had preferred Hubert to Bishop Peter as the regent's successor, in the belief that he would prove pliant and reasonable, which indeed he did. He treated former rebels with care and knew when to draw back in his dealings with the counties. 'If they nonetheless persist, it is necessary for us to put up with it at present until at an opportune time we are able to amend it' – the advice given to Hugh de Neville about the men of Dorset's perambulation of their forest – was typical of Hubert's pragmatic method.[3]

As justiciar, Hubert's duty, like the king's, was to dispense justice as well as maintain the rights of the crown. The tasks were related. If justice was dispensed and peace maintained, men would more readily accept that the king's rights too must be safeguarded. Unless they were, the king would be unable to preserve peace and protect the rights of everyone else. A recognition of this truth had informed Langton's approach after the war. It had, likewise, underlain the crucial early decision that the king could not make permanent alienations until he came of age. If the king's rights were not protected in a minority then there would be no protection for the rights of other minors. This reciprocity of interest was a theme of writs for which Hubert was responsible. Its general acceptance depended on whether the benefits of kingship seemed to outweigh its burdens. After the war, those benefits had been provided above all by the expansion of the system of justice, the one area where Magna Carta had demanded a positive and increasing role for kingship. It was no accident that the minority saw the origins both of *Bracton* and of a salaried professional judiciary. Royal justice had been made available by the re-establishment of the bench, the revival of the eyres and the growing number of individual

---

[3] *RLC*, ii, 73b.

commissions to hear petty assizes. The Waverley abbey annalist welcomed the first eyre of the reign, declaring that its judges caused the laws to be observed in accordance with the Great Charter. The Dunstable annalist likewise regarded the visitation of the judges in 1225 to hear petty assizes and deliver gaols as an impressive and constructive attempt to curb rising crime.[4] Thus kingship was seen to fulfil its most basic and essential task, that of maintaining peace and dispensing justice. Of course, the king could perfectly well have done this, yet caused offence by aggressively prosecuting his local rights, as the inquiry of January 1223 seemed to threaten. If Hubert liked to suggest that a mutually beneficial balance could be struck between the rights of the king and those of his subjects, he was also continually adjusting that balance one way or the other according to circumstances. Through such a process of give and take, however, a middle way was often found in the minority between the claims of the king and his people. The Charters were publicly accepted; ministers were governing in co-operation with great councils; justice was being dispensed; the government as a whole was very different from King John's. In these conditions a wide body of opinion was prepared to support the recovery of royal power.

There was, however, nothing permanent about the *modus vivendi* reached in the minority and by 1244 schemes of political reform more radical than the Charters were being propounded. This was not because the Charters themselves had been overthrown. Indeed, the minority had made them irreversible, but it had also revealed problems over their interpretation and enforcement. In respect of the forest Hubert himself intended to modify the verdicts of 1225 at an 'opportune' moment and did so two years later, as has been seen. In part, therefore, the conflicts later in Henry's reign were foreshadowed in the minority. Yet they were also the result of his dispensing with great officers of state like the justiciar and refusing to allow appointments and policies to be determined by great councils. Precisely for that reason it was the minority which seemed to provide the solution to the problems posed by Henry's personal rule. Essentially, from 1244 onwards, the king's critics demanded a return to its constitutional structure. The minority of Henry III, therefore, had a dual constitutional significance. It planted the Charters into English political life and it also engendered the belief that great councils, or as they were soon to be called, parliaments, should have a large say in deciding the personnel and policies of the king's government. It thus secured the acceptance of one political programme and laid the foundations for another.

The Charters had become firmly established during the minority,

---

[4] *Ann. Mon.*, iii, 95.

however much their enforcement and interpretation might be matters of controversy and debate. The king had conceded versions of the Great Charter in 1216 and 1217, in 1217 with an altogether new document: the Charter of the Forest. In 1223 he proffered a verbal confirmation of the Charters. And then, in 1225, he granted them again in what was to be their final form. All this had taken place with considerable publicity. In 1217 the sheriffs were instructed to read and proclaim Magna Carta in the county courts. Likewise, in 1218, the Charters were sent to all the sheriffs, who were ordered to 'read them publicly in full county court, having called together the barons, knights and all the free tenants of the county'. In 1225 the Charters were sent to the counties and twice ordered to be proclaimed. Meanwhile, between 1218 and 1220 and again in 1225 and 1227, the struggles over its implementation gave huge publicity to the Charter of the Forest.

The Charters were given the more stability by appearing from the first as part of a mutual bargain between the king and his subjects. The unstated quid pro quo for the Charters of 1217 was the grant of taxation in the form of a scutage. That quid pro quo was made clearer next year when measures to collect the scutage were linked to the proclamation of the Charters. Moreover, the barons, knights and free tenants of the counties were to swear fealty to the king at the same time as they swore to observe the Charters. It would be hard to think of a more public and potent demonstration that kingship and the Charters would henceforth go hand in hand. Then, in 1223 the verbal confirmation proffered by the king was, in effect, the price for the inquiry into his local rights. Finally, in 1225 the Charters were explicitly granted in return for the great tax on movables.

If the king conceded the Charters, individuals and communities digested and exploited them. The county court of Lincolnshire, the abbot of St Augustine's, Bristol, and Richard de Umfraville all appealed to the clause in the Charter which forbad disseisin save by judgement of peers or by the law of the land. In Yorkshire, the stewards of the magnates took their stand on the 1215 Charter when they refused to agree to the carucage of 1220 since their lords had not been consulted about it. The counties likewise struggled to enforce their own interpretation of the deforestations promised by the Charter of the Forest. The men of Huntingdonshire, Nottinghamshire, Somerset, Dorset and Cumberland all made individual proffers for perambulations to establish the new bounds in accordance with its terms. The men of Huntingdonshire drew up a great remonstrance in 1220 at the failure to implement the results. The knights and magnates of Yorkshire, led by Nicholas de Stuteville II and his steward, Walter of Sowerby, boycotted the forest eyre of 1222 and appealed to the pope, almost certainly against the breach in the Charter which it constituted. In

1225 the counties at last enforced the deforestations that they thought the Charter permitted. In the same year, in Yorkshire and Cumberland, Magna Carta was used as a pretext for the withdrawal of suits from the county courts and the exclusion of the sheriffs from wapentakes and ridings. Next year, Lincolnshire knights rebuked the sheriff for attempting to hear pleas 'contrary to the liberty which they ought to have by the lord king's Charter'[5] while in 1227 nearly all the counties were instructed to elect knights to come before the king to present complaints about breaches of the Great Charter by the sheriffs.

The king's concession of the Charters in 1225 could not be taken as his last word on the subject, for he was still under age and barred, in all other respects, from making permanent alienations. Hence the importance of Henry's confirmation of the 1225 Charters in 1237 'notwithstanding' that he had granted them while a minor.[6] Yet, in truth, the Charters had taken such a hold in the minority that they could never be set at nought by a style of kingship totally contrary to their spirit, much less completely overthrown. The reaction to the bishop of Winchester's regime between 1232 and 1234 was clear proof of that.[7]

Henry III and his successors might evade, twist and break some of the provisions in the Charters but nothing could alter the fact that a fundamental principle had been asserted by the kingdom and accepted by the king: monarchy was subject to the law. At the very least the Charters thus set a standard by which the activities of kings might be judged, making absolutism more difficult and protest more legitimate. Henry himself took an exalted view of the royal position, yet he accepted his subjection to the law and much of his kingship after 1234 was congruent with the Charters. In that sense, the responses worked out in 1225 created the pattern for his later rule. He confirmed the Charters in 1237 and again in 1253 'with cheerful face and spontaneous will'.[8] He frequently attempted to turn them to his advantage in the manner of the various writs of 1225. He would observe the Charters, he said, but so likewise must his magnates in their dealings with their own men. He would preserve the liberties of his people but that meant that his own liberties must be preserved. In the style of his personal rule Henry remained a product of the minority. He attempted, if with less skill, to conciliate the great magnates much as had Hubert de Burgh. He did not challenge their liberties or force them to pay their debts. 'I prefer to be considered a stupid king rather than a cruel and tyrannical

---

5   *CRR*, xii, no. 2142.
6   Holt, *Magna Carta*, 357, 282–3.
7   See above pp. 393–4.
8   *Chron. Maj.*, 382; v, 377.

one' Roger of Wendover reported him as saying.[9] Henry was deeply influenced by the war of 1215–17, when he nearly lost his throne, and by Bishop Peter's aggressive regime between 1232 and 1234, which led to a revival of discord. He heeded the Marshal's death-bed advice. Just as his personal life – his piety, his chastity – was in stark contrast to his father's, so, in politics, he wanted no return to the ways of his 'criminal ancestor'.[10] Thus, whatever the anxieties left behind by the events of 1232 to 1234, there was no suggestion in 1258 that Henry had proceeded against men *per voluntatem*, thus transgressing the fundamental clause in the Charter. There was no equivalent to the magnates of 1215, who believed that they had been disseised unjustly by the king. No machinery was set up, as it had been in 1215, to deal with such grievances, nor were they ventilated in the courts as they had been after Bishop Peter's fall in 1234.[11]

What then went wrong? Why was Henry plagued from 1244 and overtaken in 1258 by schemes of political reform more radical than the Charters; schemes which both took control of central government out of his hands and regulated in detail the running of local government? The problem was that while Henry formally accepted the Charters, in important areas they were too silent, too ambiguous or, where perfectly specific and transgressed by Henry and his agents, too unenforceable. In the first place the Charters said nothing about how patronage should be distributed, the king's councillors appointed and policy decided: key issues during Henry's personal rule.[12] Equally, in the local sphere the Charters said nothing about the type of person who should be sheriff and the financial terms on which they should hold office: both major concerns after 1241. On other local matters – notably the forest and the holding of county and hundred courts – the clauses in the Charters were vague and open to differing interpretations. And, finally,

---

[9] *Chron. Maj.*, 233.

[10] For more detailed discussion: Carpenter, 'The personal rule of King Henry III', 39–70, and the different perspective in Clanchy, 'Did Henry III have a policy?', 203–16, and the same author's *England and its Rulers*, 222–30.

[11] The clause in the Charter forbidding action against freemen save 'by lawful judgement of their peers or by the law of the land' was open to interpretation and manipulation: see Powicke, 'Per judicium parium vel per legem terrae', 96–121; Holt, *Magna Carta*, 226–9. Perhaps Henry came nearest to transgressing its spirit, during his personal rule, in the pressure put on Hubert de Burgh in 1239 to resign Hadleigh and the Three Castles: *Chron. Maj.*, 619–20; *CChR*, 248. For Edward I's practices, see McFarlane, 'Had Edward I a "policy" towards the earls?', 145–59. For a more general discussion of the effects of Magna Carta on royal lordship under Henry III, see Waugh, *The Lordship of England*, 83–91.

[12] For Henry III's foreign relatives and the patronage given to them, see Ridgeway, 'King Henry III and the "Aliens"' and his 'Foreign favourites and Henry III's problems of patronage'.

where the king did transgress the Charters, notably in his occasional denial of justice, or where the Charters were breached by his local agents in their administration of wardships and ecclesiastical vacancies, and in their imposition of amercements at the sheriff's tourn, there was no constitutional remedy.[13]

Some of these problems were already clear in the minority. The ambiguity of the clauses on the forest had given rise to prolonged conflict. Indeed, the grievance over the revision of the 1225 perambulations was aired, although not redressed, in 1258. Another important clause open to varying interpretations was the one introduced into the 1217 Charter which regulated the holding of the county and hundred courts. There was a dispute over the meaning of this in Lincolnshire in 1226 and it remained a point of controversy throughout Henry's personal rule.

Difficulties with Magna Carta also resulted from the watering down of the original of 1215 in the versions of the minority. If the Charter said nothing about the financial terms on which sheriffs should be appointed, this was because of the removal from Henry's versions of clause 25 of 1215, which stipulated that the counties should be held at the 'ancient farm without any increment'. The government had exploited this omission at the end of 1223 when it made the sheriffs answer for revenue above the county farms and ultimately, in the 1240s and 1250s, increments of very large size were imposed. At the same time the sheriffs were frequently the more ruthless for being 'strangers' in their shires.[14] The counties would have preferred local gentlemen as sheriffs but this was a subject on which the Charter had always been silent.

The most important change to the 1215 Charter, however, was the omission of the security clause: the twenty-five barons who were to force the king to emend breaches of the Charter. The emphasis in 1225, 1237 and 1253 on the excommunication of those who transgressed the Charters reflected the lack of such a guarantee but provided no real substitute for it. The problem was not simply one of the king's good faith. Those accused of breaking the Charters were often local officials over whom the king had limited control. What was needed was an administrative procedure to bring these men to justice. But that was not provided until the *Articuli super Cartas* of 1300, when three knights

[13] *DBM*, 269, 109, 127. For the inadequacy of the Charters in the local sphere under Henry III, see Maddicott, 'Magna Carta and the local community', 25–65. For Henry III's denial of justice in the course of conciliating friends at court, see Carpenter, 'The personal rule of King Henry III', 44–9.

[14] Carpenter, 'The decline of the curial sheriff', 21–32; Maddicott, 'Magna Carta and the local community', 43–8.

were to be elected in each county to hear complaints about breaches of the Charters.

Problems arising from the omissions, ambiguity and unenforceability of the Charters were, therefore, already apparent in the minority. They particularly bore on the king's relations with local society, a society whose powers had been abundantly shown in the struggle over the forest. Thus the politics of the minority foreshadowed those of 1258–59 when pressure from the localities brought about an extensive reform of local government.

In another area, however, the conflicts of Henry's personal rule were related to his overturning of the minority system. In the minority Magna Carta's failure to lay down how the king's ministers were to be chosen, patronage distributed and policy decided had not mattered. The system of government had been open and controllable. At the centre were great ministers with defined duties and responsibilities, who frequently deferred to, indeed had been appointed by, great councils. 'You are justiciar of England, held to dispense justice to everyone,' Falkes de Bréauté reminded Hubert de Burgh in 1219.[15] Hubert needed little reminding, for he dealt carefully and responsibly with the mass of petitions for justice and favour which poured in to him. Ralph de Neville, as keeper of the seal and later chancellor, dealt with the same type of business. His position was particularly important, for he frequently decided whether or not to grant the *ad hoc* judicial writs which many petitioners sought to cope with particular problems.

During the minority these and other ministers had been appointed by great councils and were, in effect, responsible to them. It was a great council of the young king's supporters which had made the Marshal regent in 1216; indeed, William purposely waited until the arrival of the earl of Chester so that consent should be as full as possible. Later, in 1219 on the regent's resignation, Pandulf was made 'first counsellor and chief of all the kingdom by the common consent and provision of all the kingdom'. Likewise, it was great councils in 1219 which gave Hubert control of government. As he put it later, he remained justiciar 'by the counsel of [the legate], the archbishop of Canterbury and the bishops and magnates of the land'.[16] Even in 1228, when the king made Hubert justiciar for life, he acted 'by the counsel of our magnates . . . at our petition', the relevant charter being attested by the earls of Chester, Pembroke, Gloucester and Surrey.[17] Great councils in the minority were equally involved with a series of lesser appointments: in 1218

[15] *RL*, no. 5.
[16] *Chron. Maj.*, vi, 64–5.
[17] Ellis, *Hubert de Burgh*, between pp. 120 and 121.

those of the justices of the Jews and the seneschal of Poitou; in 1222 that of the justiciar of Ireland.

Men were reminded of these appointments by great councils long after the minority was over through the career of Ralph de Neville, bishop of Chichester. Neville was in day-to-day charge of the king's seal from 1218 down to 1238. He was formally chancellor from 1226 until his death in 1244, the very year of the Paper Constitution. Neville's initial appointment as keeper had been at the great council of November 1218, which inaugurated the king's seal. Later, in 1236, he refused to surrender the seal to the king precisely because, having been appointed by one great council, he could only be dismissed by another. There could have been no clearer demonstration that those appointed by great councils felt a continuing responsibility to them. Equally, since Neville on several occasions resisted irresponsible acts of the king and generally discharged his office in an even-handed manner, his whole career broadcast the value of great officials appointed in this way.[18]

In addition to appointments, great councils in the minority were also involved with many other decisions. Philip of Oldcoates thought it pointless to come south until one was assembled;[19] only such a body had the authority to deal with his affairs. Naturally, it was great councils which granted the scutage of 1217, the carucage of 1220 and the fifteenth of 1225, in the last year probably laying down conditions about how the money was to be spent. They were also involved in the concession of patronage, for example, to Philip of Oldcoates; in the decision of law cases like those between the earl of Chester and Maurice de Gant; in the permitting of excommunications, notably the count of Aumale's; and in the sanctioning of marriages like that of Hubert de Burgh. Indeed, the marriage of the earl of Pembroke to the king's sister was made conditional on the consent of 'the magnates of the kingdom'. Great assemblies also counselled the return of Newark to the bishop of Lincoln; the appointment of knights to assist in collecting the eyre amercements; the postponement of the forest eyres; the resumption of the royal demesne; the laying siege to Bedford castle; the restoration of the castle to William de Beauchamp; and, in January 1227, the lifting of the final restrictions on the king's powers. Of course, the Norman and Angevin kings had always received counsel and support from great assemblies. But in the minority, there was both new practice and new theory; practice because the great councils wielded greater power and responsibility than before; theory because the extent of that power and responsibility was publicly enunciated. In 1215 Magna Carta had

---

[18] *Chron. Maj.*, 364, 74. I have discussed the importance of Neville's career in 'Chancellor Ralph de Neville', 69–80.

[19] *RL*, no. xxi. See above p. 130.

stipulated that extraordinary scutages and aids must be imposed by 'common counsel'. In the minority this principle of assent was extended to a range of other decisions. By far the most important political statement in the period came from the earl of Salisbury and Robert de Vieuxpont when they objected to the order for the dismantling of Richard de Umfraville's castle at Harbottle. Such an order, Salisbury declared, 'is not held to be done rightfully without our assent and counsel who are and are held to be of the chief council of the king with other chief men'. What Salisbury meant here by the 'chief council' was made plain in the parallel letter from Robert de Vieuxpont: the order complained of had been made 'without the common counsel and assent of the magnates of England who are held to be and are of the chief council of the king'.[20]

During Henry's personal rule much of this came to an end. True, the king continued to take advice from councils, which, as in the minority, were both small gatherings of ministers and large assemblies of ministers and magnates. Indeed, in 1236 the small council was given a formal structure with the inauguration of a councillor's oath, and its composition soon became a major issue of politics.[21] After 1234, however, the office of justiciar was allowed to lapse, partly because Henry wanted more independence, partly because the office seemed redundant now that the king spent all his time in England. Then, in 1238, the great seal was taken from Ralph de Neville and given to *curiales* with far less stature and independence. With Neville's death early in 1244 the title of chancellor was frequently left in abeyance.[22] While Henry continued to summon great councils, he was determined to decide questions of appointments, patronage and policy himself, in the fashion of his predecessors. As he said, any great baron decided upon his own officials, why should the king be of lesser liberty?[23]

Had Henry's decisions and policies been carefully judged these changes would have mattered less. As it was, Henry was regarded as *simplex* and much that he did was highly controversial. The Poitevin expedition of 1242 and the Sicilian scheme of 1254, both conceived without general consent, provoked widespread opposition amongst the magnates; so did the marriage of Simon de Montfort to the king's sister (carried through in private) and the later patronage given to the king's Lusignan half-brothers. The fact that magnates were treated in a conciliatory fashion by the king, and were often at court,

[20] SC 1/2, nos 10, 17; see above p. 209.

[21] Stacey, *Politics*, 96.

[22] *DBM*, 252–3; Carpenter, 'Chancellor Ralph de Neville', 69–80. The immediate reason for the removal of the seal from Neville in 1238 was his refusal to withdraw his candidature for the bishopric of Winchester.

[23] *Chron. Maj.*, v, 20; *The Song of Lewes*, 16–17; see Prestwich, *Edward I*, 563.

did not mean that they were consulted about all decisions or agreed with them when they were.

For those outside the circle of the court the changes had other consequences. The long years of peace after 1217 saw the king's government steadily expand in scope. It benefited, or oppressed, increasing numbers of people, as the rapidly expanding rolls of the bench, the eyres and the exchequer show.[24] Yet at the very time when the affairs of more and more people were touched by the king's government, so defined and navigable channels of communication with the centre of that government were closing down. After 1234 there was no longer a justiciar at the centre specifically charged with dispensing justice to everyone. After 1238 there was no longer a keeper of the seal with an independent status which enabled him to decide judiciously what writs should be granted. Instead, the king's seal moved rapidly from one hand to another and was sometimes the responsibility of more than one person at the same time. All this made the apparatus of government harder for those on the outside to penetrate and easier for those on the inside to manipulate and corrupt. Hence the rising volume of complaints down to 1258 about the concession of writs 'against justice'.[25]

The solution to all this, first propounded in 1244, was essentially a return to the system of the minority. Under the abortive Paper Constitution, the offices of justiciar and chancellor were to be restored and their holders to be appointed 'by all', just as they had been in the minority. Four members of the king's council were to be appointed in the same way and, the Constitution continued, 'since they have been chosen by the assent of all, so they cannot be removed without common assent'. This principle, which was also to apply to the justiciar and chancellor, was precisely that which Ralph de Neville had claimed applied to his own keepership of the seal as a result of his appointment by the great council of 1218. The Constitution, however, did not stop with the four councillors and the justiciar and chancellor. Just as in 1218 the justices of the Jews had been appointed by 'common counsel', so it laid down that at least one justice of the Jews, two barons of the exchequer and two justices of the bench were to be chosen in that way. The Constitution also said something of the roles to be played by the new ministers. Two of the four elected councillors were to remain permanently at court 'so that they can hear the complaints of everyone and can speedily help those suffering injury', much the role that had been played by Hubert de Burgh as justiciar. Equally, the chancellor,

[24] For another measure of the expansion of royal government, namely the increasing amount of wax required for the sealing of writs, see Clanchy, *From Memory to Written Record*, 45–6, 58–9.

[25] Carpenter, 'Chancellor Ralph de Neville', 77–9.

by implication, was to resist the issue of irregular writs, much as Neville had done in his long career. The elected councillors were also to oversee the spending of the king's treasure and the taxation which was to be granted in return for the new Constitution, a stipulation which had its origins in the control exercised by the bishops of Bath and Salisbury over the tax conceded in 1225.[26]

This new structure of government had several advantages. For the great magnates it promised control over the king's distribution of patronage, disbursement of revenue and direction of policy. For lesser men, the reforms prised open the institutions of central government and provided clear pathways for the redress of grievances. The measures also solved the problem of the unenforceability of the Charters; indeed, the demand for elected officials was justified by the allegation that the Charters had been infringed. Clearly officials, appointed by great councils, would ensure that the king 'executed what he promised'.[27]

In 1244 the Paper Constitution remained a mere proposal and may not even have been put to the king. But thereafter the demand that Henry should appoint a justiciar, chancellor and treasurer by common counsel was reiterated at parliament after parliament (as great councils were increasingly called) until he finally bowed to reform in 1258. The programme of 1244 was no longer the complete answer. The way that Henry had run local government since 1241 – the high increments, the sheriffs 'strangers' in their shires – was remedied by making the sheriffs 'vavasours' of their counties and giving them a salary. The increasingly burdensome jurisdiction of private courts and the oppressions of private officials – a by-product of Henry's appeasement of his magnates – also called forth special remedies. But, as far as central government was concerned, the reforms of 1258 were variations of those pro-pounded in 1244. The office of justiciar was at last revived and a council of fifteen imposed on the king. A proclamation of October 1258 declared that this council had been elected by the king and the 'community of the realm', and certainly the magnates exercised a decisive influence over its composition. The council in its turn was to choose the justiciar, chancellor and treasurer. In practice, therefore, as the king later complained, these officials were appointed 'by the councillors whom the barons placed in the king's council'.[28] The council was to co-operate closely with parliament, which was to meet

[26] *Chron. Maj.*, iv, 366–8. For the date: Cheney, 'The "Paper Constitution" preserved by Matthew Paris', which disposes of the argument that it belongs to 1238, for which see Denholm-Young, 'The "Paper Constitution" attributed to 1244', 401–23.

[27] Holt, *Magna Carta*, 285.

[28] *DBM*, 116–17, 252–3.

thrice annually to 'review the state of the realm and to deal with the common business of the realm and of the king together'.[29] Thus, although parliament did not appoint the king's ministers and councillors directly, the whole spirit of the programme was that they were responsible both to it and to the wider community of the realm.

The measures of 1258 foreshadowed the Ordinances of 1311. Indeed, the Ordinances followed the Paper Constitution of 1244 even more exactly, demanding that the king's chief ministers and officials be appointed directly by the magnates in parliament. Such schemes marked the high watermark of medieval constitutional reform. Their origins lay in the minority of Henry III. The minority made Magna Carta a fundamental feature of English political life. It also saw the genesis of the constitutional programme over which king and country were still fighting in the seventeenth century.

[29] To save the expense of large numbers of people having to attend the three annual parliaments, the barons were to choose twelve of their number to appear and represent 'the whole community of the land in the common business': *DBM*, 110–11, 104–5. However, parliaments between 1258 and 1260 were certainly not confined to meetings of the fifteen and the twelve.

Appendix

FINANCIAL TABLES

1. *Pipe roll figures*

No two people, working independently, are likely to produce the same figures when adding up the pipe rolls of the thirteenth century. Apart from the first roll of Henry III's reign, the sums involved are so numerous that mistakes are inevitable. An attempt to throw light on current revenue and expenditure from the rolls of the minority also encounters special problems which no two people will tackle in exactly the same way.[1] In the tables below all revenue and expenditure which clearly dates to the period during and before the war has been excluded from consideration. The adjusted totals have been arrived at partly by attempting to redistribute to what seems the appropriate roll revenue and expenditure which appears in later or nominally earlier pipe rolls and in an allied roll of foreign accounts. This is explained in more detail in the footnotes. In addition, doubled and missing accounts have been compensated for as follows. Where the accounts of a county in a particular roll are for two years, not one, the receipts and expenditure are divided equally between that roll and its predecessor. Cash revenue, unless indicated, is always revenue paid into the exchequer. The question of the chronology of the revenue audited in a pipe roll is discussed above, pp. 109–12. When all the problems and qualifications have been taken into account, two important conclusions can still be drawn from the figures presented below, which are all given to the nearest £10. First, Henry III's income, as recorded in the pipe rolls, was far smaller than that recorded in the rolls of John's time and of Henry himself later in his reign. Second, after 1220 the pipe roll revenue steadily increased.[2]

| | CASH TOTALS | | EXPENDITURE TOTALS | | GRAND TOTALS | |
	Actual	Adjusted	Actual	Adjusted	Actual	Adjusted
1218	£2,800	£9,030[3]	£1,830	£7,320[3]	£12,540[3]	£16,350[3]
1219	£5,880		£2,030			
1220	£4,560	£5,350[4]	£4,000	£2,040[4]	£8,560	£7,390
1221	£7,600	£8,280	£1,780[5]	£1,940	£9,380	£10,220
1222[6]	£11,690	£10,340	£1,820	£2,200	£13,510	£12,540
1223[7]	£11,650	£12,180	£2,250	£1,800	£13,900	£13,980
1224[8]	£12,530	£12,980	£2,610	£2,410	£15,140	£15,390
1225[9]	£14,130	£14,280	£2,200	£2,220	£16,330	£16,500

[1] See above pp. 109–12.
[2] One should stress that the pipe rolls do not include all the king's income, since they omit the revenue received from Ireland, the revenue from much extraordinary taxation (notably in this

period the carucage of 1220 and the fifteenth of 1225) and the revenue accounted for at the separate exchequer of the Jews.

[3] The two rolls for 1218 and 1219 overlap to such an extent that it is pointless to try to separate their adjusted figures. The adjusted cash total includes revenue from *Divers Accounts*, 46, and *Pipe Roll 1215*, 14–15. The adjusted total for expenditure includes £3,460, of which the great bulk comes from later pipe rolls and some smaller sums from *Divers Accounts*, 46, 32–7, and *Pipe Roll 1215*, 20–2.

[4] The rise in the adjusted cash total is chiefly because of compensation for the absence of Yorkshire and Somerset-Dorset, the accounts for which appear in the next roll. The sharp decline between the actual and adjusted figure for expenditure is largely explained by the redistribution to the rolls of 1218 and 1219 of various allowances for expenditure, for example some of those to Hubert de Burgh in *Pipe Roll 1220*, 58–9.

[5] These figures exclude the sums involved in the writing off of Peter de Maulay's debts: *Pipe Roll 1221*, 93–5. They have been partly included in the adjusted expenditure for 1218–19.

[6] E 372/66. The drop in the adjusted cash total is chiefly because Essex-Hertfordshire is accounted for in this roll for two years and Cornwall for the period from Christmas 1220. The redistribution of the sums involved helps explain why the adjusted totals in the rolls of 1220 and 1221 are larger than the actual ones.

[7] E 372/67. The drop in the adjusted total for expenditure is partly because the Barton of Bristol is accounted for in this roll for the whole period since January 1221.

[8] E 372/68. Hampshire is accounted for in this roll for two years. The adjusted figures include sums from *Divers Accounts*, 1–11, 37–42, 43, 47–50. The cash total here includes sums paid into the king's wardrobe and chamber.

[9] E 372/69. The adjusted figures include sums from *Divers Accounts*, 1–11, 27–32, 47–50. Again the cash total includes sums paid into the wardrobe and chamber.

2. *Surviving receipt roll figures*

The Easter and Michaelmas receipt rolls provide a far more accurate guide to the king's revenue than do the pipe rolls but their survival from the minority is intermittent and only one roll, that for Easter 1220, provides a total for the receipts which it records. In the other rolls I have calculated the amounts myself by adding up the totals given at the end of each county and town section. (The sums received are arranged under counties and, in the case of Jewish debts, under counties and towns.) Unfortunately, in some cases totals are not given, while in others the precise number of payments that they cover and their relationship to earlier running totals is unclear. I have used the totals where they appear tolerably accurate but have sometimes made my own calculations. In several rolls a few figures are lost but the amounts involved are not large. My totals are given to the nearest whole pound. The portion of the receipt roll dealing with Jewish affairs usually records both money received from Jews and money received from Christians owing debts to the Jews.

	Counties	Jewish debts	Jewish tallage	Ireland
Easter 1220[1]	£1,733 12s 8½d	£186 19s ½d		
Easter 1221[2]	£2,332	£304	£654 3s 5½d[3]	£1,693
Easter 1222[4]	£3,440			
Easter 1223[5]	£4,275	£254	£1,690 1s 5½d	
Mich. 1224[6]	£9,095	£508		
Easter 1226[7]	£5,837	£371	£450	

[1] E 401/3B.

[2] E 401/4. The section dealing with the receipts of the Jewish tallage is printed in 'A Jewish Aid to Marry', 92–111.

³ Easter and Michaelmas terms 1221.
⁴ E 401/5.
⁵ E 401/6. The sum given in the roll for the tallage is £1,676 8s 3¹/₂d, to which two further sums totalling £13 13s 2d are appended.
⁶ E 401/7. I have calculated the sums for Lincolnshire and Essex-Hertfordshire myself since the final totals given for them in the roll seem considerably too small.
⁷ E 401/9. Save for r. 1d where it is lost, I have added the total for each *rotulus* given at its foot.

3. *Adventus Vicecomitum figures*

Only a small proportion of the revenue recorded on the receipts rolls came in on the first day of the Easter and Michaelmas terms at the *Adventus Vicecomitum*. Nonetheless, the rising amounts of money presented at the *Adventus* are a useful reflection of the recovery of the king's income in the minority. I have calculated all these totals myself by adding up the sums brought by the sheriffs and by those responsible for the farms of boroughs. In the final total I have omitted the shillings and pence.

Michaelmas 1217[1]	£32	Michaelmas 1221[9]	£582
Hilary 1218[2]	nothing received	Easter 1222[10]	£558
Easter 1218	missing if held	Michaelmas 1222	missing
Michaelmas 1218[3]	£216	Easter 1223	missing
Easter 1219[4]	£65	Michaelmas 1223[11]	£997
Michaelmas 1219[5]	£334	Easter 1224[12]	£370
Easter 1220[6]	£52	Michaelmas 1224[13]	£1,815
Michaelmas 1220[7]	£301	Easter 1225[14]	£995
Easter 1221[8]	£145		

¹ E 368/1, m.4.
² E 159/1, m.4; E 368/1, m.6.
³ E 159/2, m.15. This roll is partly illegible and a few of the sums have been lost. I have followed the suggestion in the typescript of the roll at the PRO that Walter de Verdun brought £15.
⁴ E 159/2, m.1. I have followed the PRO typescript's suggestion that Philip Mark brought 5 marks.
⁵ E 368/2, m.8. Three keepers of boroughs said that they had brought their farm but the amount was not specified.
⁶ E 159/3, m.6.
⁷ E 159/4, m.1. Three keepers of boroughs said that they had brought their farm but the amount was not specified.
⁸ E 159/4, m.11.
⁹ E 159/5, m.7. I have followed the PRO typescript's suggestion that Ralph Musard brought 20 marks.
¹⁰ E 159/5, m.4. I have assumed that William de Cantilupe brought £140 not 140 marks.
¹¹ E 159/6, m.1.
¹² E 368/6, m.6. Two sheriffs were stated to have brought all their farm, the amount being unspecified.
¹³ E 159/7, mm.15, 15d.
¹⁴ E 159/7, m.18.

4. *Cash revenues from the county farm in the pipe rolls*

These figures include sums accounted for as increments and profits. The adjusted totals are achieved as follows: where the accounts of a county are for two years, not one, the sum received from the farm is divided equally between the pipe roll in which the account is found and its predecessor. Unless specified, all sums were paid into the exchequer. I have omitted the shillings and pence from all the totals.

	Actual totals	Adjusted totals
1218	£58	
1219	£65	
1220	£133	£133
1221	£346	£563
1222	£1,657	£1,473
1223	£1,453	£1,450
1224	£1,823[1]	£2,009
1225	£2,167[2]	£1,940

[1] This sum includes £80 paid into the chamber at Bedford.
[2] This sum includes £38 paid into the wardrobe.

5. *Cash revenues from the demesne in the pipe rolls*

These figures do not include demesne within the county farm. All revenue was paid into the exchequer. The adjusted sums are arrived at in the same way as for the county farms as explained in section 4 above. The shillings and pence are omitted from all the totals.

	Actual totals	Adjusted totals
1218	£371	
1219	£2,048	
1220	£1,365	£1,805
1221	£2,616	£2,370
1222	£2,816	£2,694
1223	£3,500	£3,668
1224	£3,642	£3,501
1225	£4,421	£4,309

6. *Sums ordered to be dispensed by the exchequer by writs of* liberate

The amounts given here run from Michaelmas to Michaelmas. Although some writs of *liberate* in this period were not honoured by the exchequer,[1] the rising sums ordered to be dispensed reflect the government's sense of its growing resources and broadly match up with the rise in income recorded in the pipe rolls, although that income does not, of course, run neatly from Michaelmas to Michaelmas. The totals are given to the nearest £5.

1217–18	£3,580[2]
1218–19	£2,775
1219–20	£5,295
1220–21	£10,785[3]
1221–22	£9,835
1222–23	£11,480

[1] However, my impression, judging from the writs of *liberate* enrolled on the receipt rolls from 1220 onwards, is that the great majority of writs did result in payments.

[2] I have made some adjustment to the figures in this year so as not to count twice the sums involved when writs ordered the repayment of loans and the dispensation of the money received from them. There are probably other occasions when it is not possible to detect this happening, however.

[3] This sum is explained by the additional revenue received from the carucage of 1220 and the aid paid by the church.

GENEALOGICAL TABLES

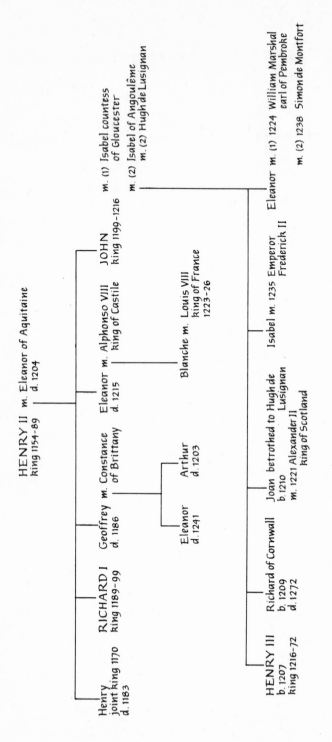

HENRY II m. Eleanor of Aquitaine
king 1154-89   d. 1204

Henry   RICHARD I   Geoffrey m. Constance   Eleanor m. Alphonso VIII   JOHN   m. (1) Isabel countess
joint king 1170   king 1189-99   d. 1186   of Brittany   d. 1215   king of Castile   king 1199-1216   of Gloucester
d. 1183   m. (2) Isabel of Angoulême
                                                                                                                        m. (2) Hugh de Lusignan

                                       Arthur   Blanche m. Louis VIII
                                       d. 1203   king of France
                                                                           1223-26
                         Eleanor
                         d. 1241

Richard of Cornwall   Joan betrothed to Hugh de   Isabel m. 1235 Emperor   Eleanor m. (1) 1224 William Marshal
b. 1209   b. 1210   Lusignan   Frederick II   earl of Pembroke
d. 1272   m. 1221 Alexander II
                               king of Scotland   m. (2) 1238 Simon de Montfort

HENRY III
b. 1207
king 1216-72

1. The Angevin royal family

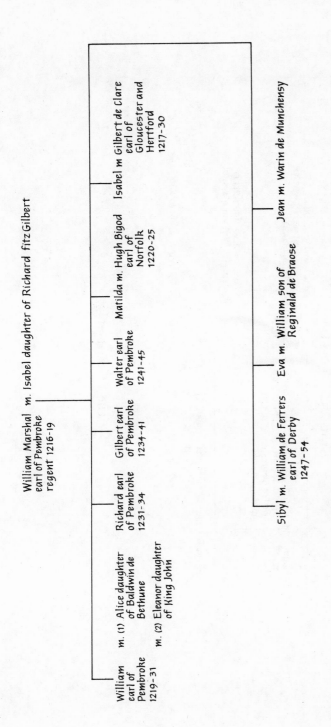

William Marshal m. Isabel daughter of Richard fitz Gilbert
earl of Pembroke
regent 1216-19

William   Richard earl   Gilbert earl   Walter earl   Matilda m. Hugh Bigod   Isabel m Gilbert de Clare
earl of   of Pembroke   of Pembroke   of Pembroke   earl of   earl of
Pembroke   1231-34   1234-41   1241-45   Norfolk   Gloucester and
1219-31   1220-25   Hertford
                                                                                                                         1217-30
m. (1) Alice daughter
of Baldwin de
Bethune

m. (2) Eleanor daughter
of King John

Sibyl m. William de Ferrers   Eva m. William son of   Jean m. Warin de Munchensy
         earl of Derby   Reginald de Braose
         1247-54

2. The Marshal family

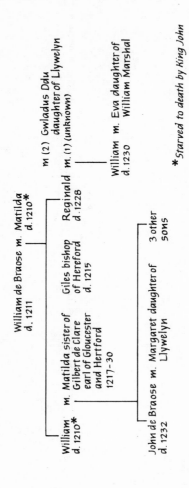

William de Braose m. Matilda
d. 1211   d. 1210*

William   m. Matilda sister of   Giles bishop   Reginald   m. (2) Gwladus Ddu
d. 1210*   Gilbert de Clare   of Hereford   d. 1228   daughter of Llywelyn
          earl of Gloucester   d. 1215   m. (1) (unknown)
          and Hertford
          1217-30

John de Braose m. Margaret daughter of   3 other   William   m.   Eva daughter of
d. 1232   Llywelyn   sons   d. 1230   William Marshal

* Starved to death by King John

3. The Braose family

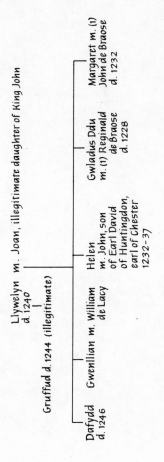

4. Llywelyn, prince of North Wales and his children

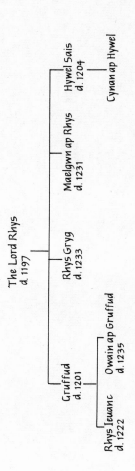

5. Sons and grandsons of Lord Rhys of Deheubarth

BIBLIOGRAPHY

The following bibliography is intended to provide details of works cited by short title in the footnotes and to give recognition to secondary works which have assisted in the preparation of this book. It is divided betwen primary and secondary sources, although the scholarly introductions to many of the former and the occasional publication of primary documents in the latter make the distinction to some extent an artificial one. Unless stated, the place of publication is London.

1. UNPRINTED PRIMARY SOURCES

Classes of unprinted or only partly printed sources
in the Public Record Office, Chancery Lane, London

C 47	chancery miscellanea
C 53	charter rolls
C 54	close rolls
C 60	fine rolls
C 72	scutage and muster rolls
CP 25(1)	feet of fines
E 32	forest proceedings
E 101	exchequer, king's remembrancer, accounts various
E 159	memoranda rolls, king's remembrancer
E 368	memoranda rolls, lord treasurer's remembrancer
E 372	pipe rolls
E 401	receipt rolls (some of these also record issues authorized by writs of *liberate*)
E 403	issue rolls
SC 1	ancient correspondence
SC 8	ancient petitions

Other important unprinted sources

HRO	Hampshire Record Office, Eccles II 159274–9. These are the bishop of Winchester's pipe rolls from between 1217–18 and 1224–25.
VL	Vatican Library, Rome. The papal registers of Pope Honorius preserved there have been consulted in the microfilm copies kept at the Institute of Historical Research, London.

2. PRINTED PRIMARY SOURCES

'A Jewish Aid to marry'   H.M. Chew, 'A Jewish Aid to marry, A.D. 1221', *Transactions of the Jewish Historical Society*, xi (1924–27), 92–111.

Accounts of Bristol Castle   Accounts of the Constables of Bristol Castle in the Thirteenth and early Fourteenth Centuries, ed. M. Sharp (Bristol Rec. Soc., xxxv, 1982).

Acta Stephani Langton   Acta Stephani Langton, ed. K. Major (Canterbury and York Soc., l, 1950).

Acts of the Parliament of Scotland   The Acts of the Parliament of Scotland, i (1844).

'An unpublished document on the great interdict'   G. Lacombe, 'An unpublished document on the great interdict (1207–1213)', *Catholic Historical Review*, xv, new ser., ix (1929–30), 408–20.

Anglo-Scottish Relations   Anglo-Scottish Relations 1174–1328: Some Selected Documents, ed. E.L.G. Stones (Oxford, 1965).

Ann. Camb.   Annales Cambriae, ed. J. Williams ab Ithel (Rolls ser., 1860).

Ann. Cest.   Annales Cestrienses or Chronicle of the Abbey of S. Werburg at Chester, ed. R.C. Christie (Lancashire and Cheshire Rec. Soc., xiv, 1886).

Ann. Eccles.   Annales Ecclesiastici, xx *(1198–1228)*, ed. A. Theiner (Bar-le-Duc, 1870).

Ann. Mon.   Annales Monastici, ed. H.R. Luard, 5 vols (Rolls ser., 1864–9). Vol. i: the annals of Tewkesbury abbey; vol. ii: the annals of Winchester cathedral priory (pp. 1–125) and Waverley abbey (pp. 133–411); vol. iii: the annals of Dunstable priory; vol. iv: the annals of Osney abbey and of Thomas Wykes (pp. 3–352) and of Worcester cathedral priory (pp. 355–564).

App. Dig. Peer   Appendix No.1 to Report on the Dignity of a Peer of the Realm, part I printed in *Reports from the Lords Committees touching the Dignity of a Peer of the Realm*, iii, (1829).

BF   Liber Feodorum. The Book of Fees commonly called Testa de Nevill, 3 vols (1920–31).

BNB   Bracton's Note Book, ed. F.W. Maitland, 3 vols (London, 1887).

Beauchamp Cartulary   The Beauchamp Cartulary Charters 1100–1268, ed. E. Mason (Pipe Roll Soc., new ser., xliii, 1971–73).

Beds. Fines   A Calendar of the Feet of Fines for Bedfordshire of the Reigns of Richard I, John and Henry III, ed. H.G. Fowler (Bedfordshire Historical Rec. Soc., vi, 1919).

Bernewelle   Liber Memorandum de Ecclesie de Bernewelle, ed. J.W. Clark (Cambridge, 1907).

Bracton   Bracton de Legibus et Consuetudinibus Angliae, ed. G.E. Woodbine, translated with revisions and notes by S.E. Thorne, 4 vols (Cambridge, Mass., 1968–77).

Brut   Brut Y Tywysogyon or The Chronicle of the Princes Peniarth MS. 20 Version, ed. T. Jones (Cardiff, 1952). For the original Welsh text of which this is a translation, see *Brut Y Tywysogyon, Peniarth MS. 20*, ed. T. Jones (Cardiff, 1941).

CACW *Calendar of Ancient Correspondence concerning Wales*, ed. J.G. Edwards (Cardiff, 1935).

CChR *Calendar of the Charter Rolls Henry III 1226–1257* (1903).

CDI *Calendar of Documents relating to Ireland 1175–1251*, ed. H.S. Sweetman (1875).

CPR 1232–47 *Calendar of the Patent Rolls Henry III 1232–1247* (1906).

CPReg *Calendar of entries in the Papal Registers relating to Great Britain and Ireland 1198–1304*, ed. W.H. Bliss (1893).

CR *Close Rolls of the Reign of Henry III*, 14 vols (1902–38). The volume cited is indicated by years.

CRR *Curia Regis Rolls of the reigns of Richard I, John and Henry III preserved in the Public Record Office*, 16 vols (1922–79).

'Cerne Cartulary' 'The Cartulary of Cerne Abbey', *Proceedings of the Dorset Natural History and Antiquarian Field Club*, xxix (1908), 195–204.

Chartulary of St. Werburg Chester *The Chartulary or Register of the Abbey of St. Werburgh Chester*, 2 parts, ed. J. Tait (Chetham Soc., new ser., lxxix, lxxxii 1920, 1923).

Chron. Maj. *Matthaei Parisiensis, Monachi Sanctii Albani, Chronica Majora*, ed. H.R. Luard, 7 vols (Rolls ser., 1884–9). Down to 1235 this is Roger of Wendover's chronicle with additions by Matthew Paris. All references are to vol. iii unless indicated.

Chron. Petroburgense *Chronicon Petroburgense*, ed. T. Stapleton (Camden Soc., 1849).

Coggeshall *Radulphi de Coggeshall Chronicon Anglicanum*, ed. J. Stevenson (Rolls ser., 1875).

Coucher Book of Furness *The Coucher Book of Furness Abbey*, vol. i in 3 parts, ed. J.C. Atkinson (Chetham Soc., 1886–87), vol. ii in 3 parts, ed. J. Brownhill (Chetham Soc., 1915–19).

Councils and Synods *Councils and Synods with other documents relating to the English Church*, ii, part i, *1205–1265*, ed. F.M. Powicke, C.R. Cheney (Oxford, 1964).

DBM *Documents of the Baronial Movement of Reform and Rebellion 1258–1267*, ed. R.F. Treharne and I.J. Sanders (Oxford, 1973).

DD *Diplomatic Documents preserved in the Public Record Office 1101–1272*, ed. P. Chaplais (1964).

Dialogus de Scaccario *De Necessariis Observantiis Scaccarii Dialogus qui vulgo dicitur Dialogus de Scaccario*, ed. C. Johnson (1950).

Die Gesetze *Die Gesetze der Angelsachsen*, i, ed. F. Liebermann (Halle, 1903).

Digest of Justinian *The Digest of Justinian*, vols i–ii, ed. T. Mommsen, P. Krueger, A. Watson (Philadelphia, Pennsylvania, 1985).

Divers Accounts *Roll of Divers Accounts for the early years of the Reign of Henry III . . .*, ed. F.A. Cazel Jr (Pipe Roll Soc., new ser., xliv, 1974–5).

Documents of English History *Documents illustrative of English History in the Thirteenth and Fourteenth Centuries*, ed. H. Cole (Record Commission, 1844).

EHD *English Historical Documents 1189–1327*, ed. H. Rothwell (1975).

ERF   *Excerpta e Rotulis Finium in Turri Londinensi Asservatis . . . A.D. 1216–72*, ed. C. Roberts, 2 vols (Record Commission, 1835–6). All references are to vol. i unless indicated.

EYC   *Early Yorkshire Charters*, vols i–iii, ed. W. Farrer (Edinburgh, 1914–16), vols iv–x, ed. C.T. Clay (Yorkshire Archaeological Soc., Record ser., extra ser., 1935–55).

Election of Abbot Hugh   *The Chronicle of the Election of Hugh, Abbot of Bury St Edmunds and later Bishop of Ely*, ed. R.M. Thomson (Oxford, 1974).

F   *Foedera, Conventiones, Litterae et cujuscunque generis Acta Publica*, ed. T. Rymer, new edn, vol. i, pt. I, ed. A. Clark and F. Holbrooke (Record Commission, 1816).

Flores Hist.   *Flores Historiarum*, ed. H.R. Luard, 3 vols (Rolls ser., 1890).

Fouke le Fitz Waryn   *Fouke le Fitz Waryn*, ed. E.J. Hathaway, P.T. Ricketts, C.A. Robson and A.D. Wilshere, Anglo-Norman Text Soc. (Oxford, 1975).

Gervase   *The Historical Works of Gervase of Canterbury*, ed. W. Stubbs, 2 vols (Rolls ser., 1879–80). All references are to vol. ii.

Gesta Abbatum   *Gesta Abbatum Monasterii Sancti Albani*, ed. H.T. Riley, 3 vols (Rolls ser., 1867–9).

Gesta Stephani   *Gesta Stephani*, ed. K.R. Potter (1955).

Giraldi Cambrensis Opera   *Giraldi Cambrensis Opera*, ed. J.S. Brewer, J.F. Dimock and G.F. Warner, 8 vols (Rolls ser., 1861–91).

Glanvill   *Tractatus de legibus et consuetudinibus regni Anglie qui Glanvilla vocatur*, ed. G.D.G. Hall (1965).

Gloucester Pleas   *Pleas of the Crown of the County of Gloucester 1221*, ed. F.W. Maitland (1884).

Gloucs. Warw. Eyre   *Rolls of the Justices in Eyre for Gloucestershire, Warwickshire and [sic] Staffordshire 1221, 1222*, ed. D.M. Stenton (Selden Soc., lix, 1940).

Guisborough   *The Chronicle of Walter of Guisborough previously edited as the chronicle of Walter of Hemingford or Hemingburgh*, ed. H. Rothwell (Camden Soc., lxxxix, 1957).

HRO   Hampshire Record Office. See 'Unprinted Sources' above.

Halsbury's Statutes   *Halsbury's Statutes of England and Wales*, 4th edn, vol. x, *Constitutional Law* (1985).

Henry of Avranches   *The Shorter Latin Poems of Master Henry of Avranches relating to England*, ed. J.C. Russell and J.P. Heironimus (Cambridge, Mass., 1935).

Hist. Angl.   *Matthaei Parisiensis Historia Anglorum*, ed. F. Madden, 3 vols (Rolls ser., 1866–69).

Historiae Anglicanae   *Historiae Anglicanae Scriptores X*, ed. R. Twysden (1652). The chronicle of William Thorne printed on pp.1753–2206 relates the affairs of St Augustine's abbey, Canterbury.

Honorii III Opera   *Honorii III Opera Omnia*, ed. C. Horoy, *Medii Aevi Bibliotheca Patristica ab anno 1217 ad Concilii Tridentini tempora i–ii* (Paris, 1879–80).

Institutes of Justinian   *The Institutes of Justinian*, ed. J.A.C. Thomas (Amsterdam, 1975).

Lanercost   *Chronicon de Lanercost 1201–1346,* ed. J. Stevenson (Maitland Club, 1839).

Layettes   *Layettes du Trésor des Chartres,* ed. A. Teulet, H-F. Delaborde and E. Berger, 5 vols (Paris 1863–1909).

'Letters to Ralph de Nevill'   W.H. Blaauw, 'Letters to Ralph de Nevill, bishop of Chichester (1222–24), and chancellor to King Henry III', *Sussex Archaeological Collections,* iii (1850), 35–76.

Liber de Antiquis Legibus   *De Antiquis Legibus Liber. Cronica Maiorum et Vicecomitum Londoniarum,* ed. T. Stapleton (Camden Soc., 1846).

Lincs. Worcs. Eyre   *Rolls of the Justices in Eyre for Lincolnshire, 1218–19 and Worcestershire, 1221,* ed. D.M. Stenton (Selden Soc., liii, 1934).

List of Sheriffs   *List of Sheriffs for England and Wales* (Public Record Office, Lists and Indexes IX, 1898).

Maréchal   *L'Histoire de Guillaume le Maréchal,* ed. P. Meyer, 3 vols (Société de l'histoire de France, 1891–1901).

Melrose   *The Chronicle of Melrose,* ed. A.O. and M.O. Anderson (1936).

Melsa   *Chronica de Monasterii de Melsa,* ed. E.A. Bond, 3 vols (Rolls ser., 1866–68).

Memoranda Roll 1208   *The Memoranda Roll for the tenth year of King John (1207–8)* . . ., ed. R.A. Brown (Pipe Roll Soc., new ser., xxxi, 1955).

'Neath Cartulary'   F.R. Lewis, 'A history of the lordship of Gower from the missing cartulary of Neath abbey', *Bulletin of Celtic Studies,* ix, part 2 (May 1938), 149–54.

Nicholai Triveti Annales   *Nicholai Triveti Annales,* ed. T. Hog (1845).

Normandie   *Histoire des Ducs de Normandie et des Rois d'Angleterre,* ed. F. Michel (Société de l'histoire de France, 1840).

Ormond Deeds   *Calendar of Ormond Deeds 1172–1300,* i, ed. E. Curtis (Dublin, 1952).

PR   *Patent Rolls of the Reign of Henry III* . . . *1216–1225* (1901).

PR 1225–32   *Patent Rolls of the Reign of Henry III* . . . *1225–1232* (1903).

Peerage   *The Complete Peerage,* ed. G.E. Cokayne, revised by V. Gibbs, H.E. Doubleday and Lord Howard de Walden, 12 vols in 13 (London, 1910–57).

Pipe Rolls   Citations to pipe rolls are to the volumes published by the Pipe Roll Society. The following volumes have been used extensively.

Pipe Roll 1214   *The Great Roll of the Pipe for the sixteenth year of the reign of King John Michaelmas 1214,* ed. P.M. Barnes (Pipe Roll Soc., new ser., xxxv, 1962).

Pipe Roll 1215   *Pipe Roll 17 John and Praestita Roll 14–18 John,* ed. respectively by R.A. Brown and J.C. Holt (Pipe Roll Soc., new ser., xxxvii, 1961).

Pipe Roll 1218   *The Great Roll of the Pipe for the second year of the reign of King Henry III Michaelmas 1218,* ed. P. Ebden (Pipe Roll Soc., new ser., xxxix, 1964).

Pipe Roll 1219   *The Great Roll of the Pipe for the third year of the reign of King Henry III Michaelmas 1219,* ed. B.E. Harris (Pipe Roll Soc., new ser., xlii, 1969–70).

Pipe Roll 1220 The Great Roll of the Pipe for the fourth year of the reign of King Henry III Michaelmas 1220, ed. B.E. Harris (Pipe Roll Soc., new ser., xlvii, 1981–83).

Pipe Roll 1221 The Great Roll of the Pipe for the fifth year of the reign of King Henry III Michaelmas 1221, ed. D. Crook (Pipe Roll Soc., new ser., xlviii, 1984–86). I have been unable to provide page references to Dr Crook's introduction since these were not available at the time of going to press.

Pipe Roll 1230 The Great Roll of the Pipe for the fourteenth year of the reign of King Henry III Michaelmas 1230 (Pipe Roll Soc., new ser., iv, 1927).

Pipe Rolls Cumberland The Pipe Rolls of Cumberland and Westmorland, ed. F.H.M. Parker (Cumberland and Westmorland Antiquarian and Archaeological Soc., extra ser., xii, 1905).

Pleas of the Forest Select Pleas of the Forest, ed. G.J. Turner (Selden Soc., xiii, 1899).

Political Songs The Political Songs of England, ed. T. Wright (Camden Soc., 1839).

RBE The Red Book of the Exchequer, ed. H. Hall, 3 vols (Rolls ser., 1896).

RCh Rotuli Chartarum in Turri Londinensi asservati, ed. T. Duffus Hardy (Record Commission, 1837).

RF Rotuli de Oblatis et Finibus in Turri Londinensi asservati, ed. T. Duffus Hardy (Record Commission, 1835).

RH Rotuli Hundredorum in Turr' Lond', 2 vols (Record Commission, 1812, 1818).

RL Royal and other Historical Letters illustrative of the Reign of Henry III, ed. W.W. Shirley, 2 vols (Rolls ser., 1862, 1866). All references are to vol. i.

RLC Rotuli Litterarum Clausarum in Turri Londinensi asservati, ed. T. Duffus Hardy, 2 vols (Record Commission, 1833–4). Unless indicated, all citations are to vol. i.

RLP Rotuli Litterarum Patentium in Turri Londinensi asservati, ed. T. Duffus Hardy (Record Commission, 1835).

Recueil Recueil des Historiens des Gaules et de la France, 24 vols (Paris, 1734–1904).

Regesta Regesta Regum Anglo-Normannorum, iii, *1135–54*, ed. H.A. Cronne and R.H.C. Davis (Oxford, 1968).

Regesta Pontificum Regesta Pontificum Romanorum 1198–1304, ed. A. Potthast, 2 vols (repd Graz, 1957).

Registers of Writs Early Registers of Writs, ed. E. de Haas and G.D.G. Hall (Selden. Soc., lxxxvii, 1970).

Rolls of the Fifteenth Rolls of the Fifteenth . . . and Rolls of the Fortieth, ed. F.A. Cazel Jr and A.P. Cazel (Pipe Roll Soc., new ser., xlv, 1976–1977).

Rot. Lib. Rotuli de Liberate ac de Misis et Praestitis, ed. T. Duffus Hardy (Record Commission, 1844).

Rot. Norm. Rotuli Normanniae in Turri Londinensi asservati, ed. T. Duffus Hardy (Record Commission, 1835).

Rutland MSS *The Manuscripts of the Duke of Rutland at Belvoir Castle*, iv, Historical Manuscripts Commission (1905).

Sandford Cartulary *The Sandford Cartulary*, ed. A.M. Leys (Oxford Rec. Soc., xix, xxii, 1938, 1941).

Select Charters *Select Charters, and other Illustrations of English Constitutional History, from the earliest times to the reign of Edward I*, ed. W. Stubbs, 9th edn, revised by H.W.C. Davis (Oxford, 1921).

Sherwood Forest Book *The Sherwood Forest Book*, ed. H.E. Boulton (Thoroton Soc., record ser., xxiii, 1965).

The Song of Lewes *The Song of Lewes*, ed. C.L. Kingsford (Oxford, 1890)

'Southwark and Merton' M. Tyson, 'The annals of Southwark and Merton', *Sussex Archaeological Collections*, xxxvi (1925), 24–57.

VL Vatican Library. See 'Unprinted Sources' above.

Walt. Cov. *Memoriale fratris Walteri de Coventria*, ed. W. Stubbs, 2 vols (Rolls ser., 1872–3). All references are to vol. ii which contains the so called Barnwell chronicle. The MS was in the possession of Barnwell priory, although the author may not have come from there: see Gransden, *Historical Writing*, 339–41.

Wiltshire Eyre *Crown Pleas of the Wiltshire Eyre, 1249*, ed. C.A.F. Meekings (Wiltshire Archaeological and Natural History Soc., Records Branch, xvi, 1960).

Winchester Chartulary *Chartulary of Winchester Cathedral*, ed. A.W. Goodman (Winchester, 1927).

Winchester Pipe Roll 1208–9 *The Pipe Roll of the Bishopric of Winchester 1208–9*, ed. H. Hall (1903).

Winchester Pipe Roll 1210–11 *The Pipe Roll of the Bishopric of Winchester 1210–11*, ed. N.R. Holt (Manchester, 1964).

Worcester Cartulary *The Cartulary of Worcester Cathedral Priory*, ed. R.R. Darlington (Pipe Roll Soc., new ser., xxxviii, 1962–3).

Yorks. Eyre *Rolls of the Justices in Eyre for Yorkshire, 1218–19*, ed. D.M. Stenton (Selden Soc., lvi, 1937).

Yorks. Fines *Feet of Fines for the County of York 1218–1231*, ed. J. Parker (Yorkshire Archaeological Soc., record ser., 1921).

3. SECONDARY SOURCES

The following abbreviations are employed:

BIHR	*Bulletin of the Institute of Historical Research*
EHR	*English Historical Review*
TRHS	*Transactions of the Royal Historical Society*
Thirteenth Century England I	*Thirteenth Century England I: Proceedings of the Newcastle upon Tyne Conference 1985*, ed. P.R. Coss and S.D. Lloyd (Woodbridge, 1986).
Thirteenth Century England II	*Thirteenth Century England II: Proceedings of the Newcastle upon Tyne Conference 1987*, ed. P.R. Coss and S.D. Lloyd (Woodbridge, 1988).

ABULAFIA, D., *Frederick II: a Medieval Emperor* (1988).

ALEXANDER, J.W., *Ranulph of Chester: a Relic of the Conquest* (Athens, Georgia, 1983).

ALTSCHUL, M., *A Baronial Family in Medieval England: The Clares 1217–1314* (Baltimore, 1965).

BAKER, D., BAKER, E., HASSAL, E. and SIMCO, A., *Excavations in Bedford 1967–1977* (Bedfordshire Archaeological Journal, xiii, 1979).

BALDWIN, J.F., 'The beginnings of the king's council', *TRHS*, new ser., xix (1905), 27–59.

——, *The King's Council in England during the Middle Ages* (Oxford, 1913).

BALDWIN, J.W., *The Government of Philip Augustus: Foundations of French Royal Power in the Middle Ages* (Berkeley, 1986).

BALLENTYNE, A.W.G., ' "Gerardus de Atyes et tota sequela sua": a study into the establishment in 13th-century England of a "notorious body of foreigners", unpublished University of Cambridge M.Litt. thesis (1979).

BARTLETT, R., *Gerald of Wales 1146–1223* (Oxford, 1982).

——, *Trial by Fire and Water: the Medieval Judicial Ordeal* (Oxford, 1986).

BAZELEY, M.L., 'The forest of Dean and its relations with the crown during the twelfth and thirteenth centuries', *Transactions of the Bristol and Gloucester Archaeological Society*, xxiii (1910), 153–282.

——, 'The extent of the English forest in the thirteenth century', *TRHS*, 4th ser., iv (1921), 140–72.

BERGER, A., *Encyclopedic Dictionary of Roman Law* (Transactions of the American Philosophical Soc., xliii, part 3, 1953).

BISSON, T.N., *The Medieval Crown of Aragon: A Short History* (Oxford, 1986).

BOLTON, J.L., *The Medieval English Economy 1150–1300*, 2nd edn (1985).

BROOKS, F.W. and OAKLEY, F., 'The campaign and battle of Lincoln, 1217', *Associated Architectural Societies' Reports and Papers*, xxxvi, pt 2 (1922), 295–312.

BROWN, R.A., COLVIN, H.M. and TAYLOR, A.J., *The History of The King's Works: The Middle Ages*, 2 vols, general editor H.M. Colvin (1963).

BUCKLAND, W.W., *A Text-book of Roman Law from Augustus to Justinian*, 3rd edn, revised by P. Stein (Cambridge, 1963).

CANNON, H.L., 'The battle of Sandwich and Eustace the Monk', *EHR*, xxvii (1912), 649–70.

CARPENTER, D.A., 'Sheriffs of Oxfordshire and their subordinates 1194–1236', unpublished University of Oxford Ph.D. thesis (1974).

——, 'The decline of the curial sheriff in England, 1194–1258', *EHR*, xci (1976), 1–32.

——, 'The fall of Hubert de Burgh', *Journal of British Studies*, xix (1980), 1–17.

——, 'King, magnates and society: the personal rule of King Henry III, 1234–1258', *Speculum*, lx (1985), 39–70.

——, 'Chancellor Ralph de Neville and plans of political reform, 1215–1258', *Thirteenth Century England II*, 69–80.

CATE, J.L., 'The church and market reform in England during the reign of Henry III', *Essays in Honor of J.W. Thompson*, ed. J.L. Cate and E.N. Anderson (Chicago, 1938), 27–65.

CAZEL, F.A., 'The fifteenth of 1225', *BIHR*, xxxiv (1961), 67–81.

——, 'The last years of Stephen Langton', *EHR*, lxxix (1964), 673–97.

——, 'Religious motivation in the biography of Hubert de Burgh', *Religious Motivation: Biographical and Sociological Problems for the Church Historian*, ed. D. Baker, *Studies in Church History* xv (Oxford, 1978), 109–19.

——, 'The legates Guala and Pandulph', *Thirteenth Century England II*, 15–21.

CHAPLAIS, P., 'Le traité de Paris de 1259 et l'inféodation de la Gascogne allodiale', *Le Moyen Age* (1955), 121–37, reprinted in the same author's *Essays in Medieval Diplomacy and Administration* (1981).

CHAYTOR. H.J., *Savaric de Mauléon Baron and Troubadour* (Cambridge, 1939).

CHENEY, C.R., 'The "Paper Constitution" preserved by Matthew Paris', *EHR*, lxv (1950), 213–21.

CHENEY, M., 'Inalienability in mid-twelfth-century England: enforcement and consequences', *Monumenta Iuris Canonici*, series C: Subsidia, vii (1985), 467–78.

——, 'The litigation between John Marshal and Archbishop Thomas Becket in 1164: a pointer to the origin of novel disseisin?', *Law and Social Change in British History*, ed. J.A. Guy and H.G. Beal (1984), 9–26.

CLANCHY, M.T., 'Magna Carta, clause thirty-four', *EHR*, lxxix (1964), 542–7.

——, 'Did Henry III have a policy?', *History*, liii (1968), 203–16.

——, *From Memory to Written Record: England 1066–1307* (1979).

——, *England and its Rulers 1066–1272: Foreign Lordship and National Identity* (Glasgow, 1983).

——, 'Magna Carta and the Common Pleas', *Studies in Medieval History presented to R.H.C. Davis*, ed. H. Mayr-Harting and R.I. Moore (1985), 219–32.

COSS, P.R., 'Knighthood and the early thirteenth-century county court', *Thirteenth Century England II*, 45–58.

CRITCHLEY, J.S., 'Summonses to military service early in the reign of Henry III', *EHR*, lxxxvi (1971), 79–95.

CRONNE, H.A., *The Reign of Stephen 1135–54: Anarchy in England* (1970).

CROOK, D., 'The Great Roll of the Pipe for the 5th year of the reign of Henry III, Michaelmas 1221', unpublished University of Reading Ph.D. thesis (1973).

——, 'The struggle over forest boundaries in Nottinghamshire, 1218–1227', *Transactions of the Thoroton Society of Nottinghamshire* (1979), 35–45.

——, *Records of the General Eyre* (1982).

——, 'The later eyres', *EHR*, xcvii (1982), 241–68.

CROUCH, D., 'Strategies of lordship in Angevin England and the career of William Marshal', *The Ideals and Practice of Medieval Knighthood II*, ed. C. Harper-Bill and R. Harvey (Woodbridge, 1988).

DAVIES, R.R., *Conquest, Coexistence, and Change. Wales 1063–1415* (Oxford, 1987).

DAVIS, R.H.C., 'What happened in Stephen's reign, 1135–54', *History*, xlix (1964), 1–12.

——, *King Stephen 1135–1154* (1967).

DENHOLM-YOUNG, N., 'The "Paper Constitution" attributed to 1244', *EHR*, lviii (1943), 403–23, reprinted in *Collected Papers of N. Denholm-Young* (Cardiff, 1969).

——, 'A letter from the council to Pope Honorius III, 1220–1221', *EHR*, lx (1945), 88–96.

——, *Richard of Cornwall* (Oxford, 1947).

DIBBEN, L.B., 'Chancellor and keeper of the seal under Henry III', *EHR*, xxvii (1912), 39–51.

DUBY, G., *Guillaume le Maréchal ou le Meilleur Chevalier du Monde* (Paris, 1984).

DUGGAN, A.J., 'The cult of St Thomas Becket in the thirteenth century', *St Thomas Cantilupe Bishop of Hereford: Essays in his Honour*, ed. M. Jancey (Hereford, 1982), 21–44.

DUNCAN, A.A.M., *Scotland: The Making of the Kingdom* (Edinburgh, 1975).

EALES R., 'Henry III and the end of the Norman earldom of Chester', *Thirteenth Century England I*, 100–12.

——, 'Castles and politics in England, 1215–1224', *Thirteenth Century England II*, 23–43.

ELLIS, C., *Hubert de Burgh: A Study in Constancy* (1952).

ENGLISH, B., *The Lords of Holderness 1086–1260* (Oxford, 1979).

EVERS, W.K., 'Disputes about episcopal elections in the reign of Henry III, with special reference to some unpublished Durham documents', unpublished University of Oxford B.Litt. thesis (1936).

FARRER, W., 'Forestry', in *The Victoria History of The County of Lancaster*, ii, ed. W. Farrer and J. Brownbill (1908), 437–66.

FISHER, W.R., *The Forest of Essex: its History, Laws, Administration and Ancient Customs and the Wild Deer which lived in it* (1887).

FLANAGAN, M., 'Strongbow, Henry II and Anglo-Norman intervention in Ireland', *War and Government in the Middle Ages: Essays in honour of J.O. Prestwich*, ed. J. Gillingham and J.C. Holt (Woodbridge, 1984), 62–77.

FOSTER, J.E., 'The connection of the church of Chesterton with the abbey of Vercelli', *Proceedings of the Cambridge Antiquarian Soc.*, new ser., vii (1908–9), 185–211.

FOWLER, G.H., 'Munitions in 1224', *Bedfordshire Historical Record Soc.*, v (1920), 117–32.

GIBBS, M. and LANG, J., *Bishops and Reform 1215–1272 with special reference to the Lateran Council of 1215* (Oxford, 1934).

GILLINGHAM, J., *Richard the Lionheart* (1978).

——, 'Richard I and Berengaria of Navarre', *BIHR*, liii (1980), 157–73.

——, *The Angevin Empire* (1984).

——, 'War and Chivalry in the *History of William Marshal*', *Thirteenth Century England II*, 1–13.

GOLOB. P.E., 'The Ferrers earls of Derby. A study of the honour of Tutbury 1066–1279', unpublished University of Cambridge D.Phil. thesis (1984).

GRANSDEN, A., *Historical Writing in England c.550 to c.1307* (1974).

GREEN, J.A., ' "Praeclarum et Magnificum Antiquitatis Monumentum": the earliest surviving Pipe Roll', *BIHR*, lv (1982), 1–16.

HAJDU, R., 'Castles, castellans and the structure of politics in Poitou, 1152–1271', *Journal of Medieval History*, iv (1978), 27–53.

HAJDU, R., 'Family and feudal ties in Poitou, 1100–1300', *Journal of Interdisciplinary History*, viii (1977), 117–39.

HALLAM, E.M., *Domesday Book Through Nine Centuries* (1986).

HARCOURT, L.W. VERNON, 'The amercement of barons by their peers', *EHR*, xxii (1907), 732–40.

HARRIS, B.E., 'King John and the sheriffs' farms', *EHR*, lxxix (1964), 532–42.

——, 'Ranulph III, Earl of Chester', *Journal of the Chester Archaeological Soc.*, lviii (1975), 99–114.

HARRISS, G.L., *King, Parliament, and Public Finance in Medieval England to 1369* (Oxford, 1975).

HILL, J.W.F., *Medieval Lincoln* (Cambridge, 1948).

HOLT, J.C., 'Philip Mark and the shrievality of Nottinghamshire and Derbyshire in the early thirteenth century', *Transactions of the Thoroton Society of Nottinghamshire*, lxvi (1952), 8–24.

——, 'King John's disaster in the Wash', *Nottingham Medieval Studies*, v (1961), 75–86, reprinted in the same author's *Magna Carta and Medieval Government*.

——, *The Northerners. A Study in the Reign of King John* (Oxford, 1961).

——, *King John* (1963), reprinted in *Magna Carta and Medieval Government*.

——, *Magna Carta* (Cambridge, 1965).

——, 'A Vernacular-French text of Magna Carta', *EHR*, lxxxix (1974), 346–64, reprinted in *Magna Carta and Medieval Government*.

——, 'The end of the Anglo-Norman realm', *Proceedings of the British Academy*, lxi (1975), 3–45, reprinted in *Magna Carta and Medieval Government*.

——, 'The prehistory of parliament', *The English Parliament in the Middle Ages*, ed. R.G. Davies and J.H. Denton (Manchester, 1981), 1–28.

——, 'The loss of Normandy and royal finance', *War and Government in The Middle Ages: Essays in Honour of J.O. Prestwich*, ed. J. Gillingham and J.C. Holt (Woodbridge, 1984), 92–105.

——, 'Feudal society and the family in early medieval England: iii. Patronage and politics', *TRHS*, 5th ser., xxxiv (1984), 1–25.

——, 'Feudal society and the family in early medieval England: iv. The heiress and the alien', *TRHS*, 5th ser., xxxv (1985), 1–28.

——, *Magna Carta and Medieval Government* (1985).

HOWELL, M., *Regalian Right in Medieval England* (London, 1962).

HOYT, R.S., *The Royal Demesne in English Constitutional History: 1066–1272* (Ithaca, New York, 1950).

HURNARD, N.D., 'Magna Carta, clause 34', *Studies in Medieval History presented to F.M. Powicke*, ed. R.W. Hunt, W.A. Pantin, R.W. Southern (Oxford, 1948), 157–79.

JENKINSON, A.V., 'The Jewels lost in the Wash', *History*, viii (1923), 161–8.

JENKINSON, H., 'The records of exchequer receipts from the English Jewry', *Transactions of the Jewish Historical Society* (1915–17), 19–54.

JOHNSTON, S.H.F., 'The lands of Hubert de Burgh', *EHR*, l (1935), 418–32.

KANTOROWICZ, E., *Laudes Regiae: A Study in Liturgical Acclamations and Medieval Ruler Worship* (Berkeley, 1946).

——, 'Inalienability. A note on canonical practice and the English coronation oath in the thirteenth century', *Speculum*, xxix (1954), 488–502.

KANTOROWICZ, E., *The King's Two Bodies: A Study in Medieval Political Theology* (Princeton, 1957).

KING, E., 'King Stephen and the Anglo-Norman aristocracy', *History*, lix (1974), 180–194.

——, 'Mountsorrel and its region in King Stephen's reign', *Huntingdon Library Quarterly*, xliv (1980), 1–10.

KNIGHT, G.A., 'The Great Roll of the Pipe for the sixth year of the reign of Henry III', unpublished University of Liverpool Ph.D. thesis (1980).

LABARGE, M.W., *Gascony: England's First Colony 1204–1453* (1980).

LAWLOR, H.J., 'An unnoticed Charter of Henry III, 1217', *EHR*, xxii (1907), 515–18.

LAWRENCE, C.H., ed., *The English Church and the Papacy in the Middle Ages* (1965).

LEMOSSE, M., 'L'incapacité juridique comme protection de l'enfant en droit romain', *Recueils de la Société Jean Bodin pour l'Histoire Comparative des Institutions*, xxxv (Brussels, 1975).

LIDDELL, W.H., 'Some royal forests north of Trent 1066–1307', unpublished University of Nottingham M.A. thesis (1961).

——, 'The private forests of S.W. Cumberland', *Transactions of the Cumberland & Westmorland Antiquarian & Archaeological Society*, new ser., lxvi (1966), 106–29.

——, 'The bounds of the Forest of Essex', *An Essex Tribute: Essays presented to F.G. Emmison*, ed. K. Neale (Leopard's Head press, 1987), 110–13.

LLOYD, J.E., *A History of Wales from the Earliest Times to the Edwardian Conquest*, 2 vols (1911). All references are to vol. ii.

LLOYD, S.D., ' "Political Crusades" in England c.1215–17 and c.1263–5', *Crusade and Settlement: Papers Read at the First Conference of the Society for the Study of the Crusades and the Latin East and Presented to R.C. Smail*, ed. P.W. Edbury (Cardiff, 1985), 113–20.

——, *English Society and The Crusade 1216–1307* (Oxford, 1988).

LODGE, E.C., *Gascony under English Rule* (1926).

LUNT, W.E., *Financial Relations of the Papacy with England to 1327* (Cambridge, Mass., 1939).

LYDON, J.F., 'The expansion and consolidation of the colony, 1215–54', *A New History of Ireland*, ed. A. Cosgrove, ii, *Medieval Ireland 1169–1534* (Oxford, 1987), 156–78.

MADDICOTT, J.R., 'Magna Carta and the local community 1215–1259', *Past and Present*, cii (1984), 25–65.

MADOX, T., *The History and Antiquities of the Exchequer of the Kings of England . . .* 2 vols, 2nd edn (1769).

MAJOR, K., *The D'Oyrys of South Lincolnshire, Norfolk and Holderness 1130–1275* (Lincoln, 1984).

MARTIN, F.X., 'John, lord of Ireland, 1185–1216', *A New History of Ireland*, ed. A. Cosgrove, ii, *Medieval Ireland 1169–1534* (Oxford, 1987), 127–55.

MASON, E., 'St Wulfstan's staff: a legend and its uses', *Medium Aevum*, liii (1984), 157–79.

McFARLANE, K.B., 'Had Edward I a "policy" towards the earls?', *History*, l (1965), 145–59, reprinted in his *The Nobility of Later Medieval England* (Oxford, 1973).

MEEKINGS, C.A.F., 'Final Concords'. These are lists compiled by Meekings of the justices of the bench before whom final concords were made from Easter 1218 until the end of Henry III's reign. They are kept at the Public Record Office.

——, 'Justices of the Jews, 1216–68: a provisional list', *BIHR*, xxvii (1955), 173–88, reprinted in Meekings's collected articles, *Studies in 13th–Century Justice and Administration* (1981).

MEISEL, J., *Barons of the Welsh Frontier: The Corbet, Pantulf, and fitz Warin Families, 1066–1272* (Lincoln, Nebraska, 1980).

METZ, R., 'L'enfant dans le droit canonique medieval: orientations de recherche', *Recueils de la Société Jean Bodin pour l'Histoire Comparative des Institutions*, xxvi (Brussels, 1976), 9–96.

MILLS, M., 'Experiments in exchequer procedure, 1200–1232', *TRHS*, 4th ser., viii (1925), 151–70.

——, Review of J.H. Ramsay, *A History of the Revenues of the Kings of England*, *EHR*, xli (1926), 429–31.

MILSOM, S.F.C., *The Legal Framework of English Feudalism* (Cambridge, 1976).

MITCHELL, S.K., *Studies in Taxation under John and Henry III* (New Haven, 1914).

——, *Taxation in Medieval England* (New Haven, 1951).

MORRIS, W.A., *The Medieval English Sheriff to 1300* (Manchester, 1927).

NORGATE, K., *John Lackland* (1902).

——, *The Minority of Henry the Third* (1912).

ORME, N., *From Childhood to Chivalry: the education of the English kings and aristocracy 1066–1530* (1984).

OTWAY-RUTHVEN, A.J., *A History of Medieval Ireland* (1968).

PAINTER, S., *William Marshal: Knight-Errant, Baron, and Regent of England* (Baltimore, 1933).

——, *The Scourge of the Clergy: Peter of Dreux, Duke of Brittany* (Baltimore, 1937).

——, *Studies in the History of the English Feudal Barony* (Baltimore, 1943).

——, *The Reign of John* (Baltimore, 1949).

——, 'The house of Quency, 1135–1264', *Feudalism and Liberty: Articles and Addresses of Sidney Painter*, ed. F.A. Cazel Jr (Baltimore, 1961).

PARKER, F.H.M., 'Inglewood Forest', *Transactions of the Cumberland & Westmorland Antiquarian & Archaeological Soc.*, new ser., v (1905), 35–61.

PETIT-DUTAILLIS, C., *Étude sur la Vie et le Règne de Louis VIII 1187–1226* (Paris, 1894).

PHILADELFO LIBICO, *Gualae Bicherii Presbyteri Cardinalis S. Martini in Montibus Vita et Gesta* (Milan, 1767).

POLLOCK, F. and MAITLAND, F.W., *The History of English Law*, 2nd edn (Cambridge, 1898).

POOLE, R.L., 'The publication of Great Charters by the English Kings', *EHR*, xxviii (1913), 444–53.

POWICKE, F.M., 'The chancery during the minority of Henry III', *EHR*, xxiii (1908), 220–35.

——, *The Loss of Normandy, 1189–1204. Studies in the history of the Angevin Empire*, 2nd edn (Manchester, 1961).

——, 'Per iudicium parium vel per legem terrae', *Magna Carta Commemoration Essays*, ed. H.E. Malden (1917), 96–121.

POWICKE, F.M., *Stephen Langton* (Oxford, 1928).

——, *King Henry III and The Lord Edward. The Community of the Realm in the Thirteenth Century*, 2 vols (Oxford, 1947).

——, *The Thirteenth Century 1215–1307* (Oxford, 1953).

—— and FRYDE, E.B., *Handbook of British Chronology* (2nd edn, London, 1961).

PRESTWICH, J.O., 'The military household of the Norman kings', *EHR*, xcvi (1981), 1–35.

——, 'The treason of Geoffrey de Mandeville', *EHR*, ciii (1988), 283–312.

PRESTWICH, M., *Edward I* (1988).

PRYNNE, W., *The Third Tome of an Exact Chronological Vindication . . . of the Supreme Ecclesiastical Jurisdiction of our . . . English Kings* (1668).

RAMSAY, J.H., *The Dawn of The Constitution or the Reigns of Henry III and Edward I* (Oxford, 1908).

——, *A History of the Revenues of the Kings of England 1066–1399*, 2 vols, (Oxford, 1925).

RENOUARD, Y., ed., *Histoire de Bordeaux*, iii, *Bordeaux sous les Rois d'Angleterre* (Bordeaux, 1965).

REYNOLDS, S., *Kingdoms and Communities in Western Europe 900–1300* (Oxford, 1984).

RICHARDSON, H.G., 'The exchequer year', *TRHS*, 4th ser., viii (1925), 171–90.

——, 'Letters of the Legate Guala', *EHR*, xlviii (1933), 250–9.

——, 'William of Ely, the king's treasurer', *TRHS*, 4th ser., xv (1932), 45–90.

——, *The English Jewry under the Angevin Kings* (1960).

——, 'The coronation in medieval England', *Traditio*, xvi (1960), 111–202.

RIDGEWAY, H.W., 'King Henry III and the "Aliens", 1236–1272', *Thirteenth Century England II*, 81–92.

——, 'Foreign favourites and Henry III's problems of patronage, 1247–58', *EHR*, cix (1989), 590–610.

RIESENBERG, P.N., *The Inalienability of sovereignty in Medieval Political Thought* (New York, 1956).

ROWLANDS, I.W., 'King John, Stephen Langton and Rochester castle, 1213–15', *Studies in Medieval History presented to R. Allen Brown*, ed. C. Harper-Bill, C.J. Holdsworth and J.L. Nelson (Woodbridge, 1989), 267–80.

RUSSELL, J.C., 'Master Henry of Avranches as an international poet', *Speculum*, iii (1928), 34–63.

SANDERS, I.J., *Feudal Military Service in England* (Oxford, 1956).

——, *English Baronies: A Study of their Origin and Descent 1086–1327* (Oxford, 1960).

SAYERS, J.E., *Papal Government and England during the Pontificate of Honorius III (1216–1227)* (Cambridge, 1984).

SMITH, J. BEVERLEY, 'The treaty of Lambeth, 1217', *EHR*, xciv (1979), 562–79.

SOUTHERN, R.W., *Robert Grosseteste: The Growth of an English Mind in Medieval Europe* (Oxford, 1986).

STACEY, R.C., 'Royal taxation and the social structure of medieval Anglo-Jewry: the tallages of 1239–42', *Hebrew Union College Annual*, lvi (1985), 175–249.

——, *Politics, Policy and Finance under Henry III 1216–1245* (Oxford, 1987).

STACEY, R.C., '1240–60: a watershed in Anglo-Jewish relations?', *Historical Research*, lxi (1988), 135–50.

STENTON, D.M., *English Justice Between the Norman Conquest and the Great Charter* (1963).

STENTON, F.M., *The First Century of English Feudalism 1066–1166*, 2nd edn (Oxford, 1961).

STEVENSON, W.B., 'England and Normandy, 1204–1259', unpublished University of Leeds Ph.D. thesis (1974).

STONES, J. and L., 'Bishop Ralph Neville, Chancellor to King Henry III and his correspondence: a reappraisal', *Archives*, xvi (1984), 227–57.

STRINGER, K.J., *Earl David of Huntingdon 1152–1219: A Study in Anglo-Scottish History* (Edinburgh, 1985).

——, 'The early lords of Lauderdale, Dryburgh abbey and St Andrew's priory at Northampton', *Essays on the Nobility of Medieval Scotland*, ed. K.J. Stringer (Edinburgh, 1985), 44–71.

SUMMERSON, H.R.T., 'The structure of law enforcement in thirteenth-century England', *American Journal of Legal History*, xxiii (1979), 314–27.

TITOW, J.Z., 'Land and population on the Bishop of Winchester's Estates 1209–1350', unpublished University of Cambridge Ph.D. thesis (1962).

TOMKINSON, A., 'The carucage of 1220 in an Oxfordshire hundred', *BIHR*, xli (1968), 212–16.

TOUT, T.F., 'The Fair of Lincoln and the "Histoire de Guillaume le Maréchal"', *EHR*, xviii (1903), 240–65.

——, *Chapters in the Administrative History of Medieval England: the Wardrobe, the Chamber and the Small Seals*, 6 vols (Manchester, 1920–33).

TRABUT-CUSSAC, J.P., 'Les coutumes ou droits de douane perçus à Bordeaux sur les vins et les marchandises par l'administration anglaise de 1252 à 1307', *Annals du Midi*, lxii (1950), 135–50.

TURNER, G.J., 'The minority of Henry III (part I)', *TRHS*, new ser., xviii (1904), 245–95.

——, 'The minority of Henry III (part II), *TRHS*, 3rd ser., i (1907), 205–62.

TURNER, R.V., *The King and his Courts: The Role of John and Henry III in the Administration of Justice, 1199–1240* (Ithaca, New York, 1968).

——, 'The royal courts treat disseizin by the king: John and Henry III, 1199–1240', *American Journal of Legal History*, xii (1968), 1–17.

——, 'William de Forz, count of Aumale: an early thirteenth-century baron', *Proceedings of the American Philosophical Society*, cxv (1971), 221–49.

——, *The English Judiciary in the Age of Glanvill and Bracton, c.1176–1239* (Cambridge, 1985).

——, *Men Raised from the Dust: Administrative Service and Upward Mobility in Angevin England* (Philadelphia, 1988).

TYERMAN, C.J., *England and The Crusades 1095–1588* (Chicago, 1988).

VAN CLEVE, T.C., *The Emperor Frederick II of Hohenstaufen* (Oxford, 1972).

VAUGHAN, R., *Matthew Paris* (Cambridge, 1958).

VCH, Victoria County History.

WALKER, R.F., 'The Anglo-Welsh Wars, 1217–1267; with special reference to English military developments', unpublished University of Oxford Ph.D. thesis (1953).

WALKER, R.F., 'Hubert de Burgh and Wales, 1218–1232', *EHR*, lxxxvii (1972), 465–94.

WARREN, W.L., *King John* (1961).

——, *Henry II* (1973).

——, *The Governance of Norman and Angevin England 1086–1272* (1987).

WAUGH, S.L., 'From tenure to contract: lordship and clientage in thirteenth-century England', *EHR*, ci (1986), 811–39.

——, *The Lordship of England: Royal Wardships and Marriages in English Society and Politics 1217–1327* (Princeton, New Jersey, 1988).

WEST, F.J., *The Justiciarship in England 1066–1232* (Cambridge, 1966).

WEISS, M., 'The castellan: the early career of Hubert de Burgh', *Viator*, v (1974), 235–52.

WHITWELL, R.J., 'The revenue and expenditure of England under Henry III', *EHR*, xviii (1903), 710–11.

WILLIAMS, G.A., *Medieval London from Commune to Capital* (1963).

WOLFFE, B.P., *The Royal Demesne in English History: The Crown Estate in the Governance of the Realm from the Conquest to 1509* (1971).

YOUNG, C.R., *The Royal Forests of Medieval England* (Pennsylvania, 1979).

INDEX

Abbreviations: abp (archbishop), Alexander II (Alexander II, king of Scotland), bp (bishop), Bp Peter (Peter des Roches, bishop of Winchester), c. (count), d. (died), dau. (daughter), e. (earl), e. of Pembroke (William Marshal e. of Pembroke 1219–31), Engelard (Engelard de Cigogné), Falkes (Falkes de Bréauté), Hubert (Hubert de Burgh), John (King John), jun. (junior), King Philip (Philip Augustus, king of France), Louis (Louis, son of Philip Augustus, king of France 1223–6), regent, the (William Marshal, e. of Pembroke 1199–1219, regent 1216–19), s. (son).

Abergavenny (Monmouth), 246 n.15
Acaster, Roger of, 241
Agenais, the, 154, 377
Alan, John fitz, 56, 74
Alan, Ruald fitz, 33, 122
Albermarle, Robert de, 81
Albini, Philip de, 27–8, 68, 171, 216, 228–9, 234, 253, 288 n.48, 294, 298, 344; as *dux milicie Christi*, 28; as king's tutor, 243, 258
Albini, Philip de, jun., 253, 255
Albini, William de, lord of Belvoir, 101 n.44; his fine for the king's grace, 25 n.3, 340 n.46; his pledges 1220, 205; boycotts Yorkshire forest eyre 1222, 277; his knights in army of Montgomery, 326; supports government 1223, 326; one of twenty-five of 1215 attesting 1225 Charter, 388
Aldbourne (Wilts), 92
Alexander II, king of Scotland, 19, 33, 35, 57, 60, 68, 165, 188, 194, 199, 211, 219–21, 225, 231, 245, 250; and peace of Kingston/Lambeth, 69; and Anglo-Scottish treaties of 1209/1212, 152; settlement with king of England 1220, 196, 246 n.12; marriage to Joan, sister of Henry III, 253; his sister's marriage to Hubert, 245–6
Alexander III, pope (1159–81), on the Roman law on minors, 18, 142
Alnwick (Northumb), castle of, 71

Alveston (Gloucs), forest of, 151
Andover (Hants), 288 n.48
Angoulême, 153, 155, 193, 221, 345
Anjou, 7, 9, 153, 177, 179; seneschal of king of France in, 173
Apethorpe (Northants), 119, 283 n.18, 284, 286 n.35
Aragon, kingdom of, 143 n.43
Arras, castellan of, 36
Arthur, of Brittany, nephew of John, 7, 138, 251
Articuli super Cartas of 1300, 406–7
Arundel, William de Albini, e. of (1193–1221), 31, 42, 83, 336; and peace negotiations, 47; as justice of bench, 101, 103, 180; on crusade, 103; and 1220 carucage, 225
Arwystli, cantref of, 313
Aston Cantlow (Warw), 346–7, 349
Attestation and authorization of royal letters, its meaning, *see* text to plate 12
Aswardhurn (Lincs), wapentake of, 380
Athée, John de, 282, 283 n.18, 284
Athulf, Constantine fitz, 290–1, 334
Audley, Henry of, familiar of e. of Chester, escapes resumption of demesne 1222, 288; attack on 1224, 346–7, 349, 351
Aumale, William de Fors, c. of, references to in sequence, 6, 22, 35, 46–8, 51–2, 57, 59, 72–3, 80, 84–7, 99, 102–3, 109, 140, 145, 147–8, 158, 159 n.10, 166–7, 178, 184, 186–7, 189, 197–201, 211,

Aumale, William *contd:*
222, 227–37, 240, 246, 256, 261–2,
281–5, 287–9, 306, 318–21, 325, 341,
363, 388, 408; early career, 57; and
peace of Kingston/Lambeth, 47–8, 47
n.23, 51; and eyre of 1218–19, 99,
102–3, 166; surrender of Rockingham,
198–9; revolt, siege of Bytham, 227–34;
his pledges 1221, 233–4, 261; and resumption of demesne 1222, 283 n.18,
284–5, 287, 288 n.48; dissident in 1223,
318–21, 325; at siege of Bedford,
363–4; one of twenty-five of 1215 attesting 1225 Charter, 388; and case against
Gilbert de Gant, 99, 102–3, 159 n.10,
165–6; and Bytham, 57, 72–3, 84–7,
109, 145, 147, 166–7, 184, 186–7, 189,
211, 227–34, 236, 262, 289; and
Driffield, 230–1, 246, 282, 283 n.18,
284–5, 287, 288 n.48; excommunications of, 166–7, 229, 231, 233, 341, 408;
his grievances, 87, 232, 234; and Rockingham, 35, 72–3, 84–5, 109, 145,
147–8, 158, 166–7, 184, 187, 189, 198–
199, 211, 231, 256, 262; rejected as
seneschal of Poitou, 178, 230; ally of Bp
Peter, 140, 166, 199, 262; and Pandulf,
166–7, 233; and e. of Salisbury, 178
Avenel wardship, 78
Avranches, Henry of, 139, 241, 304 n.11
Awre (Gloucs), 89, 119, 281, 283 n.18
Aylesbury (Bucks), 345

Balliol, Hugh de, 20, 58, 80; and Mere,
88, 121, 147, 162, 176
Bamburgh (Northumb), 68, 72, 119, 221,
226, 226 n.25, 283 n.21; castle of, 20, 86,
226
Banaster, Turstin, 152
Banstead (Surrey), 141, 338–9
Bardolf, Doun, 141
Bardsey (Yorks), 96, 119, 226 n.25
Bareville, Robert de, 283 n.18
Barnstaple (Devon), castle and honour
of, 35, 85, 87, 87 n.12, 141, 179
Barnwell priory (Cambs), canons of, 60,
124; chronicle of, 17, 21, 37, 45, 50, 56,
59–60, 79, 196, 231, 270–1, 384–5; on
activities of Guala, 28; on king's second
coronation, 191; on siege of Rockingham, 198; on c. of Aumale's rebellion,
231–2; on threat to royal power 1223,
332; on Falkes, 369; on John's prefer-
ence for aliens, 394

Barre, Gerard de la, 283 n.18, 284, 288
n.48
Barres, William de, 44
Basingstoke (Hants), 283 n.20
Basset, Alan of High Wycombe (d.1231/
2), 16, 40
Basset, Gilbert (d.1241), s. of Alan, 282
n.15; disseized *per voluntatem regis*, 1233,
393–4
Basset, Thomas of Headington (d.1220),
brother of Alan, 11, 40; and Falkes, 334
Basset, Thomas (d.1230), s. of Alan,
knight of earls of Pembroke, 270–1,
282, 283 n.18, 284, 316 n.2, 347, 350,
355–6, 394
Basset, William, 160
Bath, Hugh of, 117
Bath, Jocelin of Wells, bishop of
(1206–42), 121, 327; early career, 323;
as justice in eyre 1218–19, 100 n.33; at
centre of government 1223–4, 322–3,
343, 345–7, 349, 356, 400; and collection of fifteenth of 1225, 379–80, 411;
and date of king's coming of age, 124;
says Bytham garrison should have
hung, 233, 367; and Magna Carta, 387
Bayford, see Essendon
Bayonne, loyalty of in 1224, 374, 374 n.28
Bazas (Gironde), 374, 377
Beauchamp, Walter de; and hereditary
claim to sheriffdom of Worcester 125,
125 n.69; retains 1223, 328 n.12, 332
n.9
Beauchamp, William de, 101; kept out of
Bedford castle by Falkes, 85, 87, 205
n.12; recovers, 367, 401; and attack on
Falkes, 1224, 353, 357; and Falkes as
sheriff, 334
Beaulieu (Hants), abbey of, 226 n.25
Beaumont, Adam de, 29
Becket, Thomas, abp of Canterbury, 368;
translation of 1220, 193, 198, 200
Bedford, 29, 273, 360; castle of, 20, 32,
317, 348, 356; siege of, 86, 232 n.36,
233, 333, 343, 361–70, 397, 400, 408;
leads to loss of Poitou, 362, 371–2; rival
claims of Falkes and William de
Beauchamp to castle, 87, 205 n.12, 353;
returned to William, 367, 401
Bedfordshire, 243, 352–3, 357
Bedfordshire-Buckinghamshire, sheriffdom of, 51, 117, 327, 332 n.10; 1220
carucage in, 224
Beeston (Norfolk), 140 n.28

Bek, Henry, 101–2

Belmont (Angoulême), 310 n.5

Bench, judicial, 121, 147, 164–6, 175–6, 179, 182, 185, 188; suspension by John, 8, 64; revival after war, 64–5, 70, 96, 108, 335, 401–2; see also Burgh, Hubert de

Benson (Oxon), 96, 119, 281, 285, 293, 349

Bere (Hants), forestership of, 137 n.13

Bere Regis (Dorset), 282 n.17, 283 n.19, 284

Bergerac (Dordogne), 154, 378

Berkeley (Gloucs), castle of, 194–5, 203–4, 212–13

Berkeley, Robert of, 194, 203–4

Berkeley, Thomas of, 194, 203–4, 255

Berkhampstead (Herts), castle of, 25, 27, 221, 319

Berkshire, 27, 29, 225; demands for deforestation in, 181, 252; deforestation after 1227, 392–3; sheriffdom of, 185, 226–7 (exaction of revenue above county farm), 329

Bertram, Roger, 56, 69, 210–11, 234; 'faithful service' 1224, 365; as justice in eyre, 336; struggle to recover Mitford, 57–8, 83–5, 130, 147, 168, 174–6, 196–197, 203–8 (recovers), 214, 234–5, 401; and Hubert, 174, 197, 204; and Richard de Umfraville, 58, 58 n.13, 88, 88 n.18; and Robert de Vieuxpont, 88, 88 n.18; and Pandulf, 205; and e. of Salisbury, 88, 205

Beverley (Yorks), 26

Bicknor [English] (Gloucs), castle of, 78, 78 n.3, 109

Bigod, Ralph, 46

Bigstrup, Matthew of, 117

Bingley (Yorks), 82, 129

Bishop's Castle (Shrops), 313

Blancmuster, Reginald de, 287

Blaye (Gironde), 374

Bloxham (Oxon), 119, 283–4, 283 n.19

Blyth (Notts), tournament at, 50

Bolebec, Hugh de, 197, 204, 208

Bolsover (Derbs), 119, 119 n.40, 269, 283 n.18, 284–5, 326; castle of, 17, 18 n.22, 41, 124

Bordeaux, 155, 168, 202, 217, 295, 358, 364, 377–8; customs of, 156, 156 n.15, 168; loyalty 1224, 374–5

Bordeaux, Guillaume Amanieu, abp of, 80

Boroughbridge (Yorks), 33, 59 n.19, 118; see also Knaresborough

Bosham (Sussex), 91

Bouvines, battle of, 9, 30, 36

Bourg (Gironde), 374

Bourges (Cher), 358

Bowland, forest of (Lancs), 388–9, 392

Boxley (Kent), William abbot of, 294, 297

Brabourne (Kent), 165, 203, 354, 367

Bracton (Bracton De Legibus et Consuetudinibus Angliae), 246, 286; a product of minority, 336–7, 401

Bramber (Sussex), castle, honour, of, 91, 97 n.7, 168, 246, 246 n.15

Brand, P.A., 335 ns.20, 21, 336 n.26

Braose, Giles de, bishop of Hereford (1200–15), 6

Braose, John de (d.1232), s. of William (d.1210), 247 n.16; release from prison, 83; and Reginald de Braose (his uncle), 141, 152, 168, 218, 246–7, 246 n.15, 260 n.26, 307, 314, 314 n.15, 338; supported by e. of Chester, 320 n.7; supported by e. of Gloucester, 320 n.7; installation in Gower, 218–19, 307, 314, 314 n.15; protégé of Llywelyn, 218, 307; marriage to his dau., 218

Braose, Matilda de, wife of William (d.1211), murdered by John, 6–7

Braose, Reginald de (d.1228), younger s. of William (d.1211), 20, 26, 42, 180, 200, 205–6; struggle to recover Barnstaple, 35, 85, 87, 87 n.12, 141, 179; and Hubert, 138–9, 141–2, 168, 246–7, 338; conflict with John de Braose (his nephew), 141–2, 152, 168, 218, 246–7, 246 n.15, 260 n.26, 307, 338; and Llywelyn, 42–3, 91, 168, 217–18, 253, 279, 307, 311; ally of Marshal earls of Pembroke, 91, 218, 260 n.26, 314, 320 n.7; struggle to recover Totnes, 35, 85, 87 n.12, 141, 179, 216, 235, 401; unfulfilled promises to on return to king's faith, 35, 179

Braose, Walter de, 314 n.13

Braose, William de (d.1211), 6, 87, 138

Braose, William de (d.1210), eldest s. of William (d.1211), murdered by John, 7, 83

Braose, William de (d.1230), s. and heir of Reginald (d.1228), 215, 246, 246 n.15; marriage to Eva dau. of regent, 91, 91 n.7.

Braunton (Devon), 288 n.48

Bray, *see* Cookham

Bray, Ralph de, 117, 393

Braybrooke, Henry of, 72, 199, 235, 269, 401; justice at Dunstable 1224, 357, 361; seized 361, 366, 369

Bréauté, Falkes de, 14 n.6, 20, 29, 36, 51, 59 n.16, 73 n.12, 79 n.5, 96, 99, 206, 215, 222, 232–4, 270, 275, 282, 285, 295, 304–5, 315, 332 n.10, 342; early career, 20–1, 117; his castles in the war, 20; at battle of Lincoln, 39; garrisons Lincoln castle against e. of Salisbury 1219–20, 159, 175, 184, 271; and Christmas crisis of 1221, 271–3; and resumption of 1222, 282–3, 283 n.18; and London riots 1222, 291; and papal letters April 1223, 302 n.4, 310; dissident in 1223, 317–22, 325; surrenders custodies, 326–7; disappears from court, 322, 343, 345; and earldom of Devon, Plympton castle 1224, 343, 346–8, 356, 369; and settlement April 1224, 349–52, 356; fortifies Bedford and Plympton, 348, 356; capital charge against, 351–6, 360–1; petty assizes at Dunstable, 357, 360; on purpose of council at Northampton, 359–60; false dawn, 360–1; and seizure of Henry of Braybrooke, 361, 369; and siege of Bedford, 343–4, 361–7; pope intercedes for, 363, 368, 386; submission, exile, death, 367–8; assessment of, 368–70; and Bedford castle, 85, 87, 205 n.12, 353, 363 (works at); and Cemais, 293–4, 314; disseisins by, 100, 273, 357, 360, 368; his officials, 117; outburst against *naturales*, 272–3; *plusquam rex in Anglia*, 100, 100 n.39, 122, 369–70; scourge of English, 325; and Normandy, 262, 262 n.36; and sheriffdoms, 51, 101, 116–17, 122, 122 n.56, 148–9, 224 (1220 carucage), 277 (forest eyres), 281, 326–7 (surrenders), 331, 331 n.5, 333–4 (exactions within); his castles, 20, 117, 199, 326–7 (surrenders) 348; and St Albans abbey, 26, 357, 367; his jest about, 357 n.11; and Henry of Braybrooke, 269, 357; and e. of Chester, 271–2, 361, 363–4, 367; and earldom of Devon, conflict with Robert de Courtenay over, 78–9, 84, 184–5, 269, 274, 281, 338, 347; and Hubert, 140, 149, 175, 182, 184–5, 228, 247, 273, 291, 352–3, 362–3; and Abp Langton,

325, 347, 361, 367; quarrel with Hugh de Neville, 353–4, 367; quarrels with e. of Pembroke, 149, 164–5, 165 n.16, 175–6, 203, 243–4, 247, 249, 293–4, 315, 338, 347, 354–5, 367; and Bp Peter, 140, 250, 260–2, 270, 361, 393; his wife, 78–9, 353–4, 366, 368–9; *see also* Dissidents of 1223–4

Bréauté, William de, attack on 1224, 346–7, 350, 355–6; seizes Henry of Braybrooke, 360–1; defends Bedford, execution, 361–3, 366

Brewer, William, 14 n.6, 96, 117, 137, 137 n.13, 171–2, 205–6, 215, 229, 238, 248, 267–8, 270, 275, 281, 285, 290, 295, 305, 311, 351; and triumvirate 1219–20, 133–4; and papal letters of April 1223, 301–2, 306; supports Hubert 1223–4, 319–20, 345–6; retains custodies, 327–8; as baron of exchequer, 65, 65 n.9, 133, 170, 248; and Hubert, 170–1, 171 n.11, 172, 319; attacks Magna Carta, 22–3, 296, 334, 383; witnesses 1225 Charter, 388; and Bp Peter, 137, 170, 319; on Pandulf, 174

Brewer, William jun., 78, 184, 224 n.15, 328 n.12

Brian family, of Laugharne, 76

Brian, William de, 314 n.15

Bricheville, William de, 158

Bridgnorth (Shrops), castle of, 326, 328, 332 n.10, 346

Brigstock (Northants), 72, 119, 199, 282

Bristol, 21, 25, 26, 67, 118, 122–3, 229, 235, 251, 255, 347–8; the Barton outside, 83, 83 n.10, 84, 104–5, 109, 118, 147, 147 n.6, 229, 320; castle of, 118, 122–3 *and see* Gloucester, e. of

Bristol, abbot of St Augustine's, 237 n.6; and Magna Carta, 137, 237, 403

Brittany *see* Arthur, Eleanor

Brittany, Peter de Dreux, duke of, 30, 42; and Richmond, 33, 33 n.12, 82

Brackley (Northants), 166

Brochard, Gerard, master of Templars in Aquitaine, 168, 202

Brokehampton in Kineton (Warw), 282 n.15

Bromsgrove (Worcs), 119, 288 n.48

Brus, Peter de, 6, 197, 234

Buckingham, castle of, 20

Buckinghamshire, sheriffdom of, *see* Bedfordshire

Buckinghamshire, demands for deforestation in, 180–1

Buckland, Geoffrey of, 65 n.9

Builli, Geoffrey de, seneschal of Poitou, 1224, 374

Builth (Radnor), castle of, 168, 311, 313, 315

Bulwell (Notts), 284

Burgh, Hubert de, justiciar 1215–32, 22, 46, 59, 68, 95, 103, 108, 200, 206, 229, 248, 319 n.15; and John, 21 n.14, 33, 136, 138–41, 332 n.11; loyalty to Angevin cause, 32–3, 122; defence of Dover, 12, 20–1, 21 n.14, 136, 138, 397; works on after war, 53 n.16, 116, 116 n.31, 118, 265, 265 n.11; in sea fight off Sandwich, 43, 43 n.37, 136, 138; and regent, tensions with, 21–2, 27, 53, 65–6, 70, 103–4; petty assize eyre 1218, 53, 97, 99; and creation of triumvirate, 128; takes over attestation of royal letters from Bp Peter, 129, 131, 134–5, 146, 148; and Pandulf 1219–20, 130–1 (initial dispute with), 134, 146, 148–53, 155, 160–2, 166–8, 171–6, 185, 187, 195, 213–14, 229, 239; Pandulf's criticism of him, 214, 217; and Bp Peter 1219, 104, 129–32, 132, 138–9; early co-operation 1219–20, 143–72, 176; May 1220–1221, 198–9, 213–14, 217, 220, 229; increasing tensions with 1220–21, 170, 172, 172 n.14, 182–3, 225–6, 238–43; orders Forest Charter to be upheld, 164; alone with seal 1219, 1220, 160, 169–74; intervenes for Roger de Montbegon 1220, 170, 179, 182, 216, 338; increasing use of note of authorization 'by the justiciar and the council', 182–4; achievement in first year, 182; and Henry fitz Count 1219–20, 161–2, 213–15; and Philip of Oldcoates 1219–20, 57, 130, 104–5, 162, 174–5, 182, 197, 204, 214, 216–17; and Harbottle castle 1220, 202, 208; and carucage, 207; and Roger Bertram, 174, 204–5, 208; and c. of Aumale 1219–21, 147, 158–9, 198–9, 246; co-operation with Pandulf 1221, 243–4; marriage to Margaret of Scotland, 245–6, 245 n.11, 256; alliance with e. of Pembroke, 243–9; accuses Bp Peter and Peter de Maulay of treason, 249–52; removal of Bp Peter as king's guardian, 257–9; his government's aims, situation, July
1221, 263, 265–6; and control of royal letters 1221–3, 280–1, 293, 306; and Abp Langton down to 1221, 136, 139, 157–8, 228, 245 n.11; relationship with him 1221–3, 262–5, 279, 289; relations with Bp Peter, friction, co-operation 1221–3, 259–60, 263, 267, 275, 280–1, 293, 295, 298–300, 304–6; and Christmas crisis of 1221, 270–4; and bringing counties under exchequer control 1221–2, 274–6; and resumption of the demesne, 239, 265; failure 1221, 269–70, 279; success 1222, 278–90, 292–3, 296, 298; situation after resumption, 289–90; increasing hold over king 1222–3, 276, 289–90 and 300 (question of his assuming power), 295, 305, 315; and resumption of castles and sheriffdoms 1221–3, 239, 247–9, 251, 265, 289, 300, 315, 399; and London riots, execution of Constantine fitz Athulf, 290–1; and inquiry, confirmation of Magna Carta, Jan. 1223, 296–8; achievement 1221–3, 299; and papal letters of April 1223, 301–6; supports e. of Pembroke in south Wales, 308–9; alliance with 1223–4, 315–17, 319, 325, 345–6; alliance with e. of Salisbury 1223–4, 319, 325, 345–6; reaction to King Philip's death, 309–11; and withdrawal of April letters, 310–11; and Montgomery campaign, 311, 311 n.3, 314–15; his situation Nov. 1223, 317–18; no alliance with Abp Langton, 318; attempt to resume the king's castles, 314–19; appeal to Abp Langton, 318; accusations against Bp Peter, 321; his alliance with Abp Langton, 1223–4, 322–5 and ff; its importance, 341, 399–400; works with bps of Bath and Salisbury 1223–4, 321–3, 343–9, 356; with Abp Langton gives king control of seal, 321–3; and resumes castles and sheriffdoms Dec. 1223, 325–8; exaction of revenue above county farms, 328–9, 399; retains his custodies, 327–8; crisis of 1223, support from former rebels, 333; charges against him, 338–41; attack on Falkes 1224, 347, 351–3, 356; and siege of Bedford, 362–6; and the Charters of 1225, 386–8; sees how to work within, 386–8; benefits to be available to everyone, 386–7; gives way over forest, 385;

Burgh, Hubert de *contd:*

and king's duty to dispence justice 386–7; last advice from Pandulf, 398; his rewards after Jan. 1227, 389–90; establishes his nephew in Connaught, 390; modification of forest boundaries 1227, 392–3; later relations with magnates, 390, 392; relations with king, 390, 404; brought down by Bp Peter 1232, 393; rescued by Richard e. of Pembroke, 394; loses gains of his career, death, 395; influence of his time as justiciar, 395, 410–11; early career, material position, outlook, 135–6, 138, 140–1; first marriage to Beatrice of Wormegay, 140–1; second to countess of Gloucester, 43 n.36, 141; third to Margaret of Scotland, 231–2, 232 n.22, 245 n.11, 245–6, 256, 268, 395, 408; and lands of count of Perche, 244, 287; duties as justiciar, 78, 135, 144, 149, 157, 169, 315, 339, 398–9; defence of crown's rights, 143–5, 157, 160, 162, 170, 182, 213, 290, 315, 387, 398–9, 401; *see also* above for resumption of demesne, castles and sheriffdoms, and exaction of revenue above county farms; and exchequer, 53 and 65 (absence from during regency), 65 n.9, 132, 135, 144, 162–3 (reform at), 170–1, 225–6 (reform at), 225 n.21, 244, 248, 254, 265, 276, 280, 292; prefers cash at exchequer to it being absorbed locally, 265–6, 328–31, 398–9; and dispensation of justice, 144–5, 290, 292, 315, 335, 338, 398, 401–2; and bench, virtual absence from during regency, 53, 65, 70; presence thereafter and handling of individual law-suits, 132, 132 n.14, 135, 147–8, 148 n.12, 157–8, 164 n.14, 164–6, 168, 180, 185, 187–8, 273, 275, 280–1, 306 n.1, 335, 338; and use of approvers, 213, 213 n.6, 338; hears petty assizes, 53, 195, 338; individual commissions to hear, 335, 401–2; as sheriff of Kent, Norfolk-Suffolk, 116, 118, 122, 144, 162, 265, 329–30; and the council, 162, 164, 169–170, 178, 180 n.4, 182–4 (note of authorization by the justiciar and the council, its development), 323 (its disappearance), 194, 197, 202, 208–9, 211, 215–16, 221, 226 n.25, 236, 240, 253, 267, 274–5, 280–1, 293, 298, 307–

308, 310, 323, 341; acceptability of his government, 135–6, 140–2, 279, 288–9, 295–7, 299, 334–42, 401–2; breaches Magna Carta, 291, 334; government congruent with, 139–40, 211, 266, 291, 296–7, 334–7, 386–8; and royal forest, Charter of the Forest, 129, 145, 150, 159, 163–4 (orders Charter to be upheld), 169, 182, 337, 385, 392–3 (accused of overturning); and process of settlement after war, 53, 179–82, 186, 334–41, 401; handling of debts of former rebels, 338–40; dealings with individual rebels; Reginald de Braose (and Three Castles), 138–9, 141–2, 149 n.19, 168, 212, 216, 246–7, 246 n.15; 247 n.16, 290; Matilda de Cauz, 216; John de Lacy, 388, 392; William de Marsh, 216, 338; Roger de Montbegon, 170, 179, 182, 216, 338; William de Mowbray, 141, 141 n.34, 338–9; Robert de Ros, 195, 340; and reciprocity, middle way between rights of king and subjects, 160, 164, 181–2, 213, 292, 295, 341, 387, 401–2; readiness to conciliate, draw back, 163–4, 181–2, 207, 211, 252, 266, 279, 298, 337, 340–1, 385; harshness, 291, 339; as an Englishman, 135, 273, 324–5, 394; and Arthur of Brittany, 138; and Ralph of Coggeshall, 138; and Falkes (down to 1223), 140, 149, 165, 175, 182, 184–5, 228, 247, 250, 260–1, 273, 291, 317–19; and e. of Chester, 141, 212, 228, 234, 239, 260–1, 270–3, 317–19, 349, 351; and Engelard, 225, 228, 249–51, 260–1, 293, 330; and Simon Langton, 228, 342; and Llywelyn, 168, 212–13; and e. of Pembroke, 149, 157–8, 165, 174, 182, 185, 204, 212, 219–20, 239, 243–9 (alliance with), 250, 260–1, 271–4, 287 (and act of resumption 1222), 290, 299, 308–9, 315–17, 319, 325, 345–6, 390, 399–400 (importance of their alliance); and Matthew Paris, 43 n.37, 138; and e. of Salisbury, 159, 163, 194–5 (their alliance), 204, 238, 244, 246, 250, 260–1, 271–4 (and Christmas crisis 1221), 287 and 288 n.48 (and act of resumption 1222), 299, 319, 325, 345–6, 399–400 (importance of their alliance); and e. of Surrey, 140, 161, 161 n.17, 164, 246, 325; and Robert de Vieuxpont, 157–8, 160, 169,

Burgh, Hubert, de, *contd:*
182, 187–8, 275, 320; *see also* Triumvirate

Burgh, John de, s. of Hubert by first marriage, 395

Burgh, Margaret de (Meggotta), dau. of Hubert by Margaret of Scotland, 395

Burgh, Richard de, Hubert's nephew, established in Connaught, 390

Burgh, Thomas de, Hubert's brother, 304

Burgh, William de, Hubert's brother, in Ireland, 140

Burgh next Aylsham (Norfolk), 135, 140 n.28, 160

Burton, in Fordington (Dorset), 282 n.15

Burton, Hamo of, 282 n.15

Bury St Edmunds (Suffolk), monks of, 55

Byland (Yorks), abbot, of, 341

Bytham, Castle Bytham (Lincs), 57, 59, 72–3, 84–7, 102, 145, 165–7, 187, 211, 236, 262, 289, 338, 341, 401; siege of, 86, 227–34, 239, 248, 366–7, 397; *see* Coleville, William de; Aumale, c. of

Caerleon, lordship, castle of, 70, 77, 192, 218–19, 294, 307–8, 314

Caerleon, Morgan of, 70, 77, 192, 294

Caistor (Lincs), 283 n.18

Calais, 21, 43

Calne (Wilts), 283, 283 n.18, 346–9

Calstone Wellington (Wilts), 346–9

Cambridge, 25; castle of, 20, 332 n.10

Cambridgeshire-Huntingdonshire, sheriffdom of, 51, 117, 327, 332 n.10

Camville family of, of Llansteffan, 76–77

Camville, Richard de, 66; Idonea dau. of, 66

Camville, William de, of Llansteffan, 314 n.15

Canterbury, 200, 203, 256; castle of, 327, 332 n.11; cathedral of, 193, 198

Canterbury, Edmund Rich, abp of (1234–40), 394

Canterbury, Stephen Langton, abp of (1207–28), 64–5, 95, 98, 200, 209, 306, 308; and king's first coronation, 20, 20 n.6; return to England 1218, 65 n.4, 94, 101; political activities 1219–20, 158, 168, 191, 205, 263; and king's second coronation, 162, 187–8; in Rome 1220–1, 228, 254; in politics 1221–4, 265; supports programme of resumption,

264–6; restores peace after crisis Christmas 1221, 271, 273, 280; supports resumption of royal demesne 1222, 281, 287, 289; obtains confirmation of Magna Carta Jan. 1223, 296–7; and papal letters April 1223, 302–4, 302 n.4; mission to France 1223, 309–11; excommunicates Llywelyn, 308, 313; intervenes during crisis over castles, 319–21; his alliance with Hubert, 322–5; gives king control of seal and redistributes castles and sheriffdoms, 321–8; demands return of Simon Langton, 342; role at centre 1224, 343–9, 355; and attack on Falkes, 347–8, 351–2, 361; attempts settlement April 1224, 349–52; and fear of papal legate, 325, 350–1; attempts settlement June 1224, 360; supports siege of Bedford, 362–7; and fifteenth of 1225, 380; witnesses 1225 Charter, 388; and king beginning to grant charters, 389; death, 390; an Englishman, 324–5; political approach: support for Magna Carta and the rights of the crown, 101, 137–8, 263–6, 334, 348, 362, 380 n.5, 401; strives for peace of realm, 271, 319, 321, 324, 349, 351–2, 360; a practical man, 264; and Hubert, 136, 139, 157–8, 228, 245 n.11, 263–5, 268, 299, 318, 322–5, 342–3; importance of their alliance, 399–400; and Pandulf, 133, 254; and Bp Peter, 136–8, 258

Canterbury, cathedral priory of (Christ Church), and Falkes's exactions, 334

Canterbury, St Augustine's abbey, monks of, 238, 256

Cantilupe, William de (d.1239), 228, 270, 283, 283 n.18, 298 n.9, 304, 342; dissident in 1223, 320, 325, 332, 332 n.10; surrenders custodies, 327; attack on 1224, 346–9, 351; at siege of Bedford, 363–4; baron of exchequer, 65 n.9, 298; king's steward, 172, 241, 242 n.14; sheriff of Warwickshire-Leicestershire, 120 n.46, 163, 327 (surrenders)

Cantilupe, William de jun. (d.1251), 290

Cantref Bychan, 77 n.7

Cantref Mawr, 77 n.7

Cardigan, lordship of, 76, 77 n.7, 218, 219 n.6, 253, 307–8, 314, 316, 389–90, 395

Carisbrooke, castle of (isle of Wight), 346

Carlisle, castle of, 69, 157, 160, 169, 275

Carlisle, bishop of, *see* Mauclerc

Carlton, Carlton and Darlton (Carlton-on-Trent and Darlton [Notts], manors with joint farm), 68, 282, 283, 283 n.18

Carlton in Lindrick (Notts), 284, 288 n.48

Carmarthen, lordship, castle of, 76, 77 n.7, 218–19, 307–8, 313–14, 316, 389–90, 395

Carrickfergus (Antrim), 370

Castle Cary (Som), 213

Castles, adulterine, 50, 74, 142

Catthorpe (Leics), 85

Cauz, Matilda de, 59, 59 n.20, 216

Caversham (Berks), 70, 91, 105–6, 108, 308

Cazel, F. A. Jr., 270 n.2, 380

Cedewain, commotte of, 313

Cemais, lordship of, 76, 77 n.7, 219, 293–4, 294 n.8, 307–8, 314, 314 n.14, 354 n.14

Ceredigion, 77 n.7, 307, 309, 314

Ceri Hills, 311

Chaceporc, Hugh, 171

Chalons, William bishop of, c. of Perche, 92

Channel Islands, 253, 350

Charter of the Forest, *see* Forest, Charter of

Charter Rolls of first and second years of reign, their possible destruction, 95, 322 n.6

Chauntemerle, Robert de, 282 n.15

Chavencurt, Nicholas de, 102

Cheltenham (Gloucs), 89, 119, 281, 283 n.18; 284, 298

Chepstow, castle, lordship of, 14, 43, 77, 212–13, 307 n.5, 319

Chertsey (Surrey), 27, 41

Cheshire, Charter of Liberties of, 23

Cheshire, position of Ranulf earl of Chester in, 122

Chester, 212, 313, 364

Chester, Ranulf e. of, 9, 14 n.6, 22, 28 n.7, 42, 48, 51, 64, 83, 117, 185, 229, 248, 254, 266–7, 270, 274, 285, 288, 291, 299, 304–6, 315, 319 n.15, 332 n.10, 342, 360; loyalty to Angevins, 31, 33; alternative to William Marshal as regent, 16–17, 36, 135; causes difficulties for regent, 26–7, 36, 77; and Mountsorrel and e. of Winchester, 34–6, 40, 103; at battle of Lincoln, 37, 39 n.11, 40; becomes e. of Lincoln, 34, 40, 95; claim to Lincoln castle, 125, 271, 271 n.6; and peace of Kingston/Lambeth, 47–8, 82, 122; on crusade, 84, 103; returns, 212; does not pay 1220 carucage, 225; and c. of Aumale's revolt, 229, 231–3; and e. of Pembroke's marriage, 245, 271–2; and 1221 Christmas crisis, 270–4; and papal letters April 1223, 302 n.4, 310–11; dissident in 1223, 317–25, 331–2; surrenders custodies, 326–7; disappears from court, 322, 343, 345–6; submission 1224, 349, 351; at siege of Bedford, 361–5; protestation of loyalty, 364; advises Falkes to submit, 367, 369; witnesses 1225 Charter, 388; and exploitation of 1225 Charter, 387; position in Cheshire, 122; attitude to Magna Carta, 23; oath to keep custodies safe till king of age, 123; gains earldom of Lincoln, 40, 95; other patronage received by, 228, 231–2, 253; and honour of Richmond, 33, 33 n.12, 82; and Richmondshire, 122; and sheriffdoms of Lancs, Shrops and Staffs, 80–1, 119–20, 120 n.47, 122, 125, 225, 239, 253, 255, 274, 326–7 (surrenders); supports John de Braose, 260 n.26; ransom dispute with Maurice de Gant, 48, 82, 129, 408; and Hubert, 141, 212, 228, 234, 260–1, 280–1, 315, 349, 351; and Falkes, 271–2, 361, 364, 367, 369; ally of Hugh de Lacy, 22, 271, 306, 355; ally of Llywelyn, 81, 212, 260–1, 293–4, 298, 315; and Bp Peter, 260, 271; *see also* Dissidents of 1223–4

Chesterfield (Derbs), 119

Chesterton (Cambs), 60, 119, 124, 266, 283 n. 20; advowson of, 68, 95

Chewton Mendip (Som), 119, 288 n.48

Chichester, bishop of, *see* Salisbury, bishop of; and Neville, Ralph de

Chinon (Indre-et-Loire), 57, 136, 138, 201

Chizé (Deux-Sèvres), 358

Christchurch (Hants), castle of, 346

Church and state, relations between, 53, 86, 143, 365

Church, Stephen, 52 n.4

Cigogné, Engelard de, 10, 24, 232, 270, 281, 342, 368; during war, 20; accused of treason 1221, 249–51; mission to Poitou, 267; evades resumption of demesne 1222, 281–2, 285, 288, 293, 329; dissident in 1223, 317–18, 320, 325, 332; surrenders custodies, 326–7; submission 1224, 348, 351; and siege of

Cigogné, Engelard de, *contd:*
Bedford, 364; on 1225 Gascon expedition, 380; returns to office with Bp Peter 1232, 393; demand for patronage, 96; and Hubert, 225, 228, 293, 330–1; close associate of Bp Peter, 139, 251, 260–2, 293; custodian of Windsor and Odiham, 20, 250, 305, 326–7, 329–30, 333; *see also* Dissidents of 1223–4
Cilgerran, castle, lordship of, 76, 77 n.7, 218–19, 307–8, 314
Cinque Ports, 21, 27, 160, 237, 261, 378–9
Cirencester (Gloucs), 129
Civray (Deux-Sèvres), 358
Clanchy, M. T., 64 n.1, 96 n.18, 136 n.9, 259
Clare, Gilbert de, *see* Gloucester, e. of
Clare, Richard de, *see* Hertford, e. of
Clarté Dieu (north of Tours), Bp Peter's executors found religious house at, 139
The Clay (Notts), its deforestation, 90, 392
Clayworth (Notts), 170
Clifford, Walter of jun., 283 n.18, 284, 288 n.48, 290
Cockermouth (Cumb), 233
Cockfield, Robert of, 85 n.6
Coggeshall, Ralph of, chronicler, 28, 249, 270, 327, 361, 363, 371, 394; on Falkes, 369; on Hubert, 138; on Bp Peter's appointment as justiciar, 140
Cognac (Deux-Sèvres), 310 n.5, 345
Colchester (Essex), castle of, 25, 319
Coleville, William de, 102, 211; struggle to recover Bytham castle, 57, 72, 84–7, 147, 166–7, 184, 186, 227, 231, 234–5, 341, 400–1
Collingham (Yorks), 96, 119, 226 n.25
Colomb, Rostand de, 202
Combe, church of, 175
Compiègne (Oise), 311
Connaught, 390
Connaught, Cathal Crovderg O'Connor, king of (d.1224), 390
Cookham (Berks), 105
Cookham and Bray (Berks), (manors with joint farm), 119, 281, 293
Corbridge (Northumb), 68, 72, 119, 226, 283 n.20
Corby (Northants), 72, 119, 199, 269, 283 n.20
Corfe (Dorset), castle of, 20, 26, 46, 239, 249–52 (its surrender by Peter de

Maulay), 256, 260, 262, 275, 290, 327, 399
Cornhill, Henry of, 354
Cornhill, Reginald of, 338–9, 339 n.40
Cornwall, 121, 125, 145, 184, 187, 212–15, 397–8; demand for local man as sheriff, 211–12, 386; granted to Richard, the king's brother, 376; sheriffdom of, revenues outside exchequer control, 120, 185, 189, 215 (recovery of), 223, 235, 255, 274, 276, 292, 292 n.1; tin mines of, 120, 201, 212, 215, 224–5, 386; *see also* fitz Count, Henry
Cornwall, Reginald earl of (1141–75), 125, 212
Coronation, king's first at Gloucester 1216, 13–14, 19–20, 162; second at Westminster 1220, 162, 187–8; a turning point, 187–91, 196, 236–7; king's coronation oath, 188–9; oath of barons, 189
Costentin, Thomas de, 102, 255, 255 n.13
Count, Henry fitz (d.1222), 35, 66, 85, 87 n.12, 179, 224, 235; pretensions as sheriff of Cornwall, 120–2, 125, 145, 161, 184–5, 187, 201; expulsion from 1220, 211–15, 255, 274, 397–8
Councils, Great: role in minority, 3–4, 54–5, 61, 96, 183–4, 187, 236, 246, 270, 279, 341, 401–2, 407–9; and appointments, 17, 82–3, 94–5, 106–7, 128, 134–5, 253–4; ideas about, 4, 54, 94–5, 130, 207–11, 209 ns. 7 & 8, 236
individual councils: *1216,* at Gloucester, 14, 17; at Bristol, 19, 21–5; *1217,* at Oxford, 43; at Westminster, 56–8, 60, 66–8; *1218,* in West Country, 71, 73–4; at Worcester, 74, 77, 84; at Westminster (May), 81–3; Westminster (Nov.), 94–6, 101; *1219,* at Rochester, 104; at Reading, 106–7, 128; at Oxford, 128–130, 137; at Gloucester, 131, 131 n.12, 137, 146–8, 160; *1220,* at Westminster, 177; at London, 200; at Oxford 203–7, 231, 236 (Christmas court), 231, 236; *1221,* at Shrewsbury, 253; at London (July), 256; at London (Oct/Nov.), 268, 270; *1222,* at Westminster (and resumption of demesne), 281, 288–9; *1223,* at

Westminster 296–7 (and confirmation of Magna Carta);
at Northampton (Christmas
court), 325; *1224*, at London (?
March), 349; London (April),
349, 355; at Northampton,
358–60, 362 (and siege of Bedford); *1225*, at Westminster,
379, 388 (grant of taxation, concession of the Charters) *1227*
(Jan), 389 (allows king to issue
charters)
small councils, 54, 96, 183–4, 267,
275; and formal structure in 1236,
409; 'the council' (of indetermin-
ate size), 70, 73, 77, 81, 94,
119–20, 129, 147, 149, 160, 162,
183–4, 187, 191, 206, 208, 220 (*and
see* Hubert de Burgh)
Counties, revenues from, *see* Finance
Courtenay, Robert de, butler of Louis,
44
Courtenay, Robert de (of Devon), 282; as
sheriff of Devon, 66, 71, 79–81 (failure
of attempt to remove 1218), 121, 157,
281 (removal); conflict with Falkes,
78–9; 184–5, 269, 338, 347; and
Hubert, 157, 246; his wife, 79
Coventry, William of Cornhill, bishop of
(1215–23), baron of exchequer, 53, 65
n.9, 131, 282 n.17
Coventry, Alexander of Stavensby,
bishop of (1224–38), 367
Coventry, bishopric of, during vacancy,
311, 318
Cowley (Oxon), 46
Crassus, William, 217–18, 307, 314 n.13
Crook, David, 226, 230, 275
Crouch, David, 11 n.11, 30 n.15, 92 n.12,
122 n.53, 294 n.11, 307 n.5, 308 n.9
Crowcombe, Godfrey of, 270, 282, 283
n.18, 284
Croy, Stephen de, 386
Cumberland, exploitation of 1225 Charter in, 384, 387, 404; proffer for deforestation, 150, 403; deforestation after
1227, 392, 392 n.12; sheriffdom of,
outside exchequer control, 89, 119–21,
185, 188–9, 263, 274–6 (recovery
1222), 292, 397; complaints about
number of shrieval officials, 115, 150;
and number of forest officials, 292
Curcy, Alice de, 354
Cynan ap Hywel, 309, 314

Dafydd, s. of Llywelyn, 192
Damietta, 170; archbishopric of, 170
Darley (Derbs), abbey of, 151; canons of,
124
Darlton (Notts), *see* Carlton (Notts)
Davis, R. H. C., 33
Deeping (Lincs), 229
Deheubarth, Lord Rhys of (d.1197), 43,
76, 77 n.7
Demesne, Royal, *see* Resumption
Dent de Fer, Robert, 279–80
Derby, 68, 119, 282, 283 n.18, 284–5
Derby, William de Ferrers, earl of (1190–
1247), 9, 14 n.6, 22, 36, 47, 47 n.23, 83,
234, 318; on crusade, 84; and act of
resumption, 1221, 269–70; and resumption 1222, 283–5; supports government 1223–4, 326–7, 365; witnesses
1225 Charter, 388; struggle to secure
the Peverel inheritance (Bolsover and
the Peak), 17–19, 26, 26 n.14, 41, 124,
126, 269, 284–5 (deprived of), 326
Derbyshire, 59, 59 n.20, 151, 181; protest
to Pandulf over forest 1219, 151, 159;
forest eyre postponed 1221, 236, 252,
276; postponed 1222, 277 n.6; takes
place 1223, 337; deforestation after
1227, 391–2, 403; and number of
shrieval officials, 181; sheriffdom of, *see*
Nottinghamshire-Derbyshire
Dereham, Elias of, 19, 42
Despencer, Hugh, 327–8
Devizes (Wilts), 119, 216, 290; castle of,
26, 327–8, 348, 394; surrender to Pandulf, 253, 255; forest of, 121
Devon, lands of earldom, 78–9, 269, 343,
346
Devonshire, 31; general eyre in, 146;
private wars in, 66, 71, 184; desire for
local man as sheriff, 81; sheriffdom of,
66, 71, 79–80, 121–2, 281; tin mines,
200, 345
Dialogus de Scaccario, 110
Dinas Powys (Glamorgan), 290, 320
Dissidents of 1223–4, attempt to seize
Tower, 319; armed gathering at Leicester, 325; submit as outnumbered, 326;
intervention at Rome, 325, 347–8, 350–
1; military preparations 1224, 347–8;
submission, 351; reluctance over
paying revenue into exchequer,
329–31; their case for retaining office,
331–2; dangers posed by to royal power, 331–3; *see* Chester, Ranulf e. of;

Dissidents *contd:*
  Cigogné, Engelard de; Bréauté, Falkes de; Winchester, Peter des Roches, bishop of
Dore, abbot of, and the king coming of age, 124
Dorchester (Dorset), 213
Dordogne, river, 378
Dorking (Surrey), 27
Dorset, demands for deforestation in, 129, 403; deforestation in 1225, 385, 385 n.18, 401; modified 1227, 392; fifteenth of 1225 in, 385; sheriffdom of, *see* Somerset
Dover, 12, 22, 167; siege of 1216–17, Hubert's defence of, 20–1, 27, 32–3, 36, 41, 136, 138, 388, 397; works, costs after war, 53 n.16, 77 n.10, 116, 116 n.31, 259, 265, 280–1, 293, 316; Hubert retains 1223–4, 327–8
Downton (Hants), 71
Dreux, Robert count of, brother of Peter duke of Brittany, 30, 92, 244–5
Driffield (Yorks), 119, 230–1, 246, 282, 283 n.18, 284, 287, 288 n.48, 292
Droitwich (Worcs), 119, 288 n.48
Drumare, Luke de, 284 n.24
Dublin, Henry of London, archbishop of (1213–28), 19 n.5, 161, 170, 206; as justiciar of Ireland, 253, 315, 354–5
Dunstable (Beds), 187, 334, 357, 360–1, 369
Dunstable priory, and Falkes as sheriff, 334; annals of, 28, 33, 33 n.14, 39, 44, 230 n.12, 247, 250, 298, 316, 318–19, 320–1, 325, 359, 366; on obedience to 'reasonable' orders of king, 54, 99, 127; on king's second coronation, 188–9; asserts that Magna Carta broken, 337
Dunstanville, Walter de, 56
Durham, 148, 390
Durham, Richard de Marsh, bp of (1217–26), chancellor of the king (1214–26), 60 n.2, 85 n.6, 94 n.10, 98, 102, 129, 129 n.6, 145–6, 148, 148 n.11, 188, 197, 205, 208, 221, 240 n.3, 275, 345, 386; conflict with Philip of Oldcoates 148, 148 n.11
Durham, bishopric of, revenues from vacancy 1226–8, 382
Durham, prior and monks of, 386–7, 390
Dymock (Gloucs), 119

Earley, John of, 15–16, 19, 26 n.9, 32, 68, 78, 107

Easingwold (Yorks), 186 n.11
Edenham (Lincs), 102, 165, 229
Edgmond (Shrops), 119, 288, 288 n.49, 346 n.14, 347, 349
Edwinstowe (Notts), 68, 119, 282, 283, 283 n.18, 284–5
Eleanor of Brittany, 249, 251
Eleanor, sister of Henry III; marriage to e. of Pembroke, 244, 341, 354; marriage to Simon de Montfort, 409
Ellesmere (Shrops), 294
Elstow (Beds), 367
Ely, John of Fountains, bishop of (1220–5), 143, 345, 349; and Falkes as sheriff, 334
Emlyn, lordship of, 76–7, 77 n.7, 218–19, 307–8, 314
English national feeling, development of, 4, 29, 261–2, 273, 324–5, 394–5; aliens against natives in crisis of 1223, 324–5
Erdington, Thomas of (d.1218), 65 n.9
Essendon and Bayford (Herts), manors with joint farm, 119, 283 n.18, men of, 368
Essex, carucage in 1220, 224; demands for deforestation in, 252; forest eyre in 1221, 236, 252, 276–7; deforestation of Tendring hundred after 1227, 393
Essex, Geoffrey de Mandeville, e. of and e. of Gloucester (1213/14–16), 6, 136, 264
Essex, William de Mandeville, e. of (1216–27), 58, 63, 83, 93, 101, 108, 205, 232; and Falkes, 334; supports government 1223–4, 326, 333, 349; at siege of Bedford 1224, 365; lenient treatment of his debts, 340
Essex-Hertfordshire, sheriffdom of, 117, 180, 191, 226; resistance to shrieval authority in, 115–16; ex-rebel appointed as sheriff, 179–80
Étampes (Seine-et-Oise), 221
Eu, Alice, countess of, 89, 156, 160–1, 187–8, 261, 275
Eu, county of, 173
Evesham, battle of, 47
Exchange, Royal, 73, 77, 77 n.10, 200, 224
Exchequer, 8, 135, 268; exchequer procedure and revenue in the pipe rolls, 109–12, 413–14; collapse during war, 51; restart afterwards and early difficulties, 64–6, 70, 73, 80, 93, 108, 118; reforms at, 163, 226; insists revenue must be paid to it not expended locally, 70, 118, 398

Exeter, 71–2, 74, 193, 214–16; bishopric of, 319, 366; castle of, 66

Exeter, Simon of Apulia, bishop of (1214–23), 211, 215

Falaise (Normandy), 138

Falkes's *querimonia* (the *querimonia* to the pope of Falkes in 1225), 249, 257, 259–60, 316, 318–19, 321, 325, 327, 331, 349, 351, 359, 361, 366, 378

Farndale (Yorks), forest of, 278, n.9, 385 n.17

Farnham (Surrey), castle of, 28, 31, 317, 348

Faukenburg, Eustace de, bishop of London (1221–8), 143, 275, 309, 327, 345, 349; and Falkes, 367–8, 367 n.39; as treasurer of exchequer, 65, 65 n.9, 105, 131, 248

Fawsley (Northants), 282 n.15

Feckenham (Worcs), 119, 288

Fidelity and fame, concepts of, 31–2

Finance, royal, poverty at beginning of reign, 26; at end of war, 51, 70, 93–4; in first years of peace, 112–20 (causes), 177–8; causes analysed by pope 1220, 189–90; payment of Louis's indemnity, 45, 67, 93; damage in war, 115; resistance to shrieval authority, 80, 115–16; revenue in pipe roll 1130, 126; revenue in pipe rolls 1155–7, 126; revenue in pipe roll 1203, 113; *Adventus* Easter 1208, 115; of Nov. 1217, 66; of Jan. 1218, 70; of Mich. 1218, 93; revenue in pipe rolls 1218, 1219, 93, 112–14; *Adventus*, Easter 1219, 114; at Mich. 1219, 163; at Easter 1220, 186; receipts Easter 1220, 186, 188, 202, 223; *Adventus* Mich. 1220, 222–3; writs of *liberate* 1220–1, 223, *Adventus* Easter 1221, 248; receipts Easter 1221, 248; revenue in pipe roll 1221, 255; writs of *liberate*, 1221–2, 255; *Adventus*, receipts Easter 1222, 276; revenue in pipe roll 1222, 292–3; receipts Easter 1223, 299; revenue in pipe roll 1223, 299; writs of *liberate* 1222–3, 299; financial situation during siege of Bedford, 364–5; resources 1224 compared with king of France's, 372; *Adventus* Mich. 1224, 381; receipts Mich. 1224, 381; revenue in pipe roll 1224, 381; *Adventus*, Easter 1225, 381; revenue in pipe roll 1225, 381; receipts Easter 1226, 381; re-

venues in pipe rolls of 1240s, 381, 381 n.12; general rise in king's revenue 396; county farms, revenue from, 114–16, 185, 274–6, 292–3; revenue from ecclesiastical vacancies, 382; revenue from general eyres, 99, 255, 382, 382 n.16; royal demesne, proceeds of resumption, 283; Financial Tables, 413–17; *see also* Exchequer, Jews, Ireland, Resumption, Taxation

Finedon (Northants), 88, 119, 281, 283 n.18, 284, 286 n.35

Foliot, Henry, 220

Foliot, Richard of Warpsgrove, 101

Folkingham (Lincs), castle of, 339

Ford, Roger of, 274

Forest, Charter of, 60 n.2, 61, 95, 108, 191, 262, 396–7, 401; analysis of, 62–3; clauses on deforestation, 89–90, 278; proclamation of Feb. 1218, 73–4; orders for its observation, April 1218, 81, 89; perambulations ordered under its terms July 1218, 91, 168; Dec., 1219, 168–9, 180–1; individual clauses to be upheld, 1219, 164; Huntingdonshire complaints about failure to implement perambulations, 180–1; appeal of Yorkshire to Charter, 277–9; Charter of 1225, 376; deforestation under its terms, 384–5; these modified 1227, accusations of breach of Charter, 392–3; clause in Charter to be observed 1229, 393; *see also* Forest, Royal

Forest, Royal, its nature and extent, 61–2, and Maps on pp. xxii and 391; chief justices *see*, Marshal, John; Lisle, Brian de; Neville, Hugh de; assarts inquiry 1219, 150–1, 159, 163–4; demands for deforestation, process of, 62–3, 89–91, 129, 145, 150, 168–9, 180–1, 277–9, 337, 406, deforestations of 1225, 384–5; modifications in and after 1227, 385, 392–3, *and see particularly under* Buckinghamshire, Cumberland, Dorset, Derbyshire, Huntingdonshire, Nottinghamshire, Oxfordshire, Somerset, Yorkshire; forest eyres 1221, 236, 252, 263, 276–7; 1222, resistance in Yorkshire, 276–9; postponed for year June 1222, 279, 295–6; eyres 1223, 296, 298, 337; officials to behave 'amicably', 164, 181–2, 191, 340

Fors (Deux-Sèvres), 178 n.8

Fossard barony, 256

Fotheringhay (Northants), 158; castle of, struggle to prize it from e. of Pembroke, 145, 148–9, 158, 187, 189, 196, 199, 200, 211, 219–20 (its surrender), 235, 239, 399; in revolt of c. of Aumale, 230, 230 n.12, 231–2, 232 n.22, 233

Fountains, abbey of (Yorks), 233

Frame, R. F., 316 n.4

France, marshal of, 37

Frankesney, Henry de, knight of Falkes, 192, 380 n.4

Frederick II, emperor of the Romans, 123

Frigido Monte, Merlet de, 154 n.3

Frontenay-Rohan-Rohan (Deux-Sèvres), castle of, 358

Furnivall, Gerard de, 18 n.22

Galtres (Yorks), forest of, 278, 392 n.12; deforestation in 1225, 385; reversed after 1227, 392

Gant, Gilbert de, 6, 40, 46–7, 56, 59, 87; and earldom of Lincoln, 34, 46; loyalty to Louis, 34–5; his case against c. of Aumale, 102–3, 159 n.10, 165–6; his debts in minority, 339

Gant, Maurice de, 101–2; and ransom dispute with e. of Chester, 48, 82, 129, 408; as justice in eyre, 336

Garonne, river, 377

Gascony, 1–2, 4, 7, 45, 153, 153 n.1, 177, 193, 200, 202, 221, 229, 226, 291, 295, 303, 344, 360, 374–80, 390, 393; retention of in 1224–5, 374–6, 379; resources of fifteenth devoted to, 377–8; revenues of, 378

Gaugi, Robert de, 20, 36, 51, 108, 198, 232; and Newark, 43 n.36, 58, 84–6, 227, 262, 289

Geddington (Northants), 119, 253, 283 n.20; forest of, 73 n.12

General eyre, revival of in 1218–19, 96–103, 108; difficulties of, 99; success of, 99–103; final concords before, 100, 336; dispenses justice in accordance with Great Charter, 100, 103, 335; letter of protest from judges in Lincoln-shire, 99–100, 102–3; oath before judges, 98; in West Midlands 1221–2, 255; eyres of 1226–9, 382; money from eyres, 99, 255, 382; additions to articles of eyre in 1218, 97–8, 121; in 1221, 121, 122 n.53

Gentry, *see* Local society

Gerald, Henry fitz, 107

Gerald, Warin fitz, 25 n.3, 355

German, Walerand the, 350, 356

Germany, 257, 257 n.6

Gernun, Ralph, retains custodies 1223, 327–8

Giffard, Osbert, 328, n.15

Gilbert, John fitz (father of the regent), 29–30

Gilling (Yorks), 278, 279 n.13

Gillingham, John, 177 n.2

Gilsland (Cumb), 60

Girros, Robert de, 102, 255, 255 n.3

Gisnes, Baldwin de, 283 n.18, 289

Glamorgan, 21; lordship of, 49

Glanvill (Tractatus de legibus et consuetudini- bus Anglie qui Glanvilla vocatur), 18

Gloucester, 13–14, 26–7, 69, 131, 243, 251, 290, 298, 309, 311, 318–19, 324; castle of, 125, 316, 328, 322 n.11; king's first coronation at, 13, 20, 162

Gloucester, countess of, 43 n.36, 136, 141

Gloucester, Gilbert de Clare, e. of (1217– 30), also e. of Hertford, 56, 63, 83, 83 n.12, 93, 101, 108, 131 n.12, 233, 270, 281, 306; marriage to regent's daugh-ter, 49, 49 n.34, 63, 91; and Falkes's exactions, 334; amongst dissidents 1223–4, 318, 320, 320 n.7, 324, 332–3; returns to side of government 1224, 365, 365 n.25; at siege of Bedford 1224, 365; one of twenty five of 1215 (when Gilbert de Clare) attesting 1225 Char-ter, 388; accepts Hubert becoming jus-ticiar for life, 407; and the Barton outside Bristol, 83–4, 104–5, 147, 147 n.6, 320; and 1220 carucage, 225; dis-pute with e. of Pembroke, 290, 320

Gloucestershire, forest in, 151; deforesta-tion after 1227, 392; general eyre in 1221, 255; sheriffdom of, 220, 316, 328, 328 n.11

Goderville, Walter de, 350, 380 n.4

Godmanchester (Hunts), 119, 222, 222 n.2

Goodrich (Heref), castle of, 20, 43

Government, structure of Angevin, 7–9

Gower, lordship of, 43, 77, 77 n.7, 217–19, 246, 246 n.15, 307, 314, 314 n.15

Great Bedwyn (Wilts), 30 n.15

Great Councils, *see* Councils, Great

Grelley, Robert, 40

Gretton (Northants), 72, 119, 199, 283 n.20

Grimsby (Lincs), 60, 119, 253, 283 n.20

Grosmont (Monmouth), 138, *see* Three Castles

Grosseteste, Robert, 302, 304

Gruffud, illegitimate son of Llywelyn, 172, 307

Guala Bicchieri, papal legate, 14 n.6, 17, 20 n.6, 31, 36, 40, 60 n.2, 71, 73–4, 76, 84, 86, 95–6, 104 n.2, 133, 146, 190, 278, 285, 304; powers, 13, 52–3, 133 n.17; and Magna Carta 1216, 22–3; turns the war into a crusade, 28; and peace negotiations, 42, 44–5, 48; secures grant for Vercelli, 68, 95, 142; resignation, 93, 95 n.12, 103

Gualer, William, 168

Guestling, John of, 64, 101, 101 n.44

Guildford (Surrey), 94, 258, 333; castle of, 333 n.13

Gwent, 246 n.15

Gwenwynwyn ab Owain Cyfeiliog (d.1216), 76, 309, 313

Gwynedd, 192, 313

Hadleigh (Essex), castle of, 311 n.3, 405 n.11

Hailsham, Lord, 2 n.4

Hajdu, R., 156

Hale, Simon of Great, 80, 163, 328 n.12, 329 n.18

Hallikeld (Yorks), 278, 279 n.13

Hampshire, sheriffdom of, 116, 259, 327, 333 n.1; revenues under Bp Peter as sheriff, 256, 330; deforestation after 1227, 393; royal forest in, 144, 150–1, 170; forest eyre in 1223, 337

Hamstead Marshall (Berks), 30 n.15, 70, 91

Hang (Yorks), 278, 279 n.13

Harang, Ralph, 64

Harbottle (Northumb), castle of, 202, 207–11, 214, 236, 409

Harris, B. E., 11 n.9, 121 n.52, 339 n.45

Hartshill, William of, 271

Hastings (Sussex), 396

Haughley (Suffolk), honour of, 33, 141, 244, 389, 395

Hauvill, Geoffrey de, 173

Hauvill, Gilbert de, 173

Hauvill, Henry de, 282

Hauvill, Walter de, 173

Haverford (Pembroke), 218, castle of, 43, 218

Havering (Essex), 94, 241, 258–9, 284, 305

Hay, barony of in Lincolnshire, 66, 66 n.13

Headington (Oxon), 11, 286, n.40

Heighington (Durham), church of, 387

Hedingham, Castle (Essex), castle of, 25

Henley (Oxon), 96, 281, 285, 320, 349

Henry II, king of England, 6, 11–12, 30, 51; afforestations of, 62–3, 89–90, 169, 180–1, 278; legal measures of, 8, 10–11, 125; situation and actions at start of reign, 67, 85, 109, 126

Henry III, king of England, 26, 44, 159, 162, 243, 251, 284–6, 379; accession, 1, 13; coronation 1216, 13, 19–20; takes cross 1216, 13; his own seal, 94; derided as boy, 160–1; coronation 1220, 162, 188; pattern of life 1218–22, 94, 258; changed pattern 1223, 305; progress of education, 241–2; age of his majority, fourteen as against twenty-one, 123–4, 241–3; significance of fourteenth birthday, end of Bp Peter's guardianship, 240–1, 243, 257–8, 268–9; verbal confirmation of Charters 1223, 295–7; papal letters of April 1223 giving him control of his seal, 301–2; emergence 1223, 315; his new powers Dec. 1223 (but not declared of age), 321–3; role of 1224, 351–2; ridiculed by Louis VIII as boy and pauper, 372; works within and exploits Charters, 385–8; and Durham election 1226, 390; begins to grant charters Jan. 1227, 389; and forest/Charter of the Forest, 392–3; his personal rule, 404–12; congruent with Charters, 404–5; distinct from that of John, 405; household (Christmas 1217), 69, 227; household knights, increasing numbers, 227 n.1, 242, 317, 382; rising costs of household, 242, 299; and Hubert, 257, 290, 305, 315, 390, 404; and English national feeling, 394–5; and Bp Peter, 17, 78 n.1, 160, 169–70, 172, 238, 240, 259, 405; *see also* Coronation, Minority

Henry, Meiler fitz, 32 n.9

Herbert, Matthew fitz, 66, 332 n.9; remains in office as sheriff of Sussex 1223, 328 n.12

Herbert, Peter fitz, 101; at siege of Bedford 1224, 365

Hereford, 67, 148–9, 153, 168, 327; gaol delivery at, 213 n.6

Hereford, Bohun earls of, 125

Hereford, Henry de Bohun, e. of (1200–20), 6, 40, 46, 59, 101; and Trowbridge, 195; loyalty to Louis, 30, 35

Hereford, Hugh Foliot, bishop of (1219–34), 148, 168, 245 n.9, 327

Hereford, Humphrey de Bohun, e. of (1220–75), 195; supports government 1223, 326, 333; at siege of Bedford 1224, 365

Herefordshire, sheriffdom of, 125, 313, 316

Hershey, Andrew, 48 n.31

Hertford, 119, 259, 282; castle of, 20, 25, 33–4, 45, 282, 317, 326, 332 n.10

Hertford, e. of, *see* Gloucester, e. of

Hertford, Richard de Clare, e. of (1173–1217), 6–7, 40

Hertfordshire, sheriffdom of, *see* Essex

Heybridge, Gervase of, 19

High Wycombe (Bucks), 286 n.40

Hingham (Norfolk), 220 n.7, 288 n.48

Hintlesham (Suffolk), 220 n.17, 288 n.48

Histoire des Ducs de Normandie, 20, 47, 117

Hodenet, Baldwin de, 298

Holderness (Yorks), 57

Holt, J. C., 46, 297 n.5, 338

Honorius III, pope (1216–27), 12, 25, 28, 32, 36, 93–4, 132, 245, 258, 355; for his letters calling for act of resumption, *see* Resumption; vital role in providing this programme, 397–8; and protection of king's rights, 142–3, 189; sanctions king's second coronation, 187, 189; letters of April 1223, 301–6, 310, 321, 346; and Louis VIII 1224, 344, 373; urges moderation 1224, 350–1; intercedes for Falkes, 363, 368, 386; and Hugh de Lusignan, 217, 221, 280, 291, 294; and Pandulf, 133, 189–90

Hornington, in Bolton Percy (Yorks), 102

Horwell, *see* Ombersley

Hugh, John fitz, 32, 46

Hulcote, John of, 117

Hungary, abp from, 200

Hungary, king of, his coronation oath, 143, 189

Huntingdon, 67, 253

Huntingdon, David earl of (1185–1219), 6, 69, 73; control of his lands, 148–9, 157–8, 212, 228, 231–2, 253

Huntingdon, John le Scot, earl of (1227–37), earl of Chester (1232–7), marries daughter of Llywelyn, 260

Huntingdonshire, demands for deforestation in, 89–91, 91 n.6, 150–1, 168–9, 180–1, 403; deforestation in 1225, 385; reversed 1227, 392; forest eyre in 1212; 277; in 1221–2, 236, 276–7; forest remonstrance 1220, 180–1, 277, 403; sheriffdom of, *see* Cambridgeshire

Ilchester (Som), 214

Inalienability, *see* Resumption

Innocent III, pope (1198–1216), 12, 278

Ireland, 1, 4; Angevin bastion during war, 15, 15 n.11, 19–20, 26; revenue from, 93 n.3, 109, 113, 205, 248, 253, 253 n.10, 414; *see* Marsh, Geoffrey de; Lacy, Hugh de

Isabella of Angoulême, queen of England, 44, 47, 117, 155, 267, 280; returns to Angoulême, 153; complaints of, 155, 167, 200; marries Hugh de Lusignan, 193; her dower, 193, 200, 221, 267, 280, 345, 349, 358

Isabella, sister of Alexander II king of Scotland, 196

Isabella, sister of Henry III, 196

Jedburgh (Scotland), 69

Jerusalem, king of, 281

Jews, 53 n.10; and the crown, 82–3; *debita Judeorum*, 121, 186, 340–1, 381, 414; exchequer of, 82–3, 83 n.8, 109, 110 n.4; tallages on 248, 299, 414; the *tabula*, 83

Joan, sister of Henry III; and Hugh de Lusignan, 155, 193, 196, 200, 221; married to Alexander II, 245, 253; *and see* Lusignan, Hugh de

John, king of England, 1, 5, 12, 14–16, 21–2, 25–6, 28 n.7, 29–30, 32, 35, 47–8, 57, 66, 76, 80, 86–7, 89–90, 95, 105, 123, 133, 170–1, 180, 185, 193, 228, 332, 344, 393; aspects of his government, 5–9, 30, 33, 59–60, 62–3, 136–7, 145, 195, 212, 237, 256, 264, 286; treatment of debts, 338–9; and claims to hereditary local office, 124 n.67, 125; his military household, 52, 317; and loss of Angevin empire, 7, 9, 153, 373; and Anglo-Scottish treaties of 1209, 1212, 196; concedes kingdom to papacy, 13; grants of demesne during war, 117–18, 125, 230, 285, 288, 288 n.48; his executors, 14, 14 n.6; and Hubert, 21 n.14, 136, 138–41; and Hugh de Lusignan, 178–9; and regent,

John, king of England *contd:*
14–15, 77, 106; and e. of Winchester,
34, 34 n.19; minority government distinct from his, 341; Henry III's government also, 405
Judges, salaried, 65, 108, 336, 336 n.26,
401; former rebels employed as, 64–5,
101, 101 n.44, 180, 336
Justice, king's dispensation of, demand
for, 10–11, 96, 100, 108; development
during minority, 336–7, 401–2; regulations in Magna Carta, 9–10, 96–7; writ
pone, 100; *see also* Burgh, Hubert de;
Bench, the judicial; Judges; General
eyre
Justiciarship, office of, 21–2; demands for
its revival, 395; for duties *see* Burgh,
Hubert de

Kempston (Beds), 367
Kemsing (Kent), 165, 203, 354, 367
Kenilworth (Warw), castle of, 320, 327,
332 n.10
Kensham, William of (Willikin of the
Weald), 27, 29
Kent, 53, 59, 317; earldom of, 246, 388,
395; sheriffdom of, 53, 116, 118, 265,
327, 329, 330, 332 n.11
Kidwelly, lordship of, 77, 77 n.7, 217–19,
307, 309, 314
Kimbolton (Hunts), castle of, 58, 229,
232
King's Cliffe (Northants), 72, 119, 199,
283 n.20; forest of, 73 n.12
Kingston/Lambeth, peace of, 44–8, 74,
77, 216; and Alexander II, 69; and
Llywelyn, 69, 76; and Magna Carta,
45, 57, 296; and ransoms, 46, 81–2, 82
n.4; on return of seisin, 45, 50, 56–9,
122; breaches of alleged, 82 n.4, 216; *see*
Rebels under ransoms, process of set-
tlement
Kingston upon Thames (Surrey), 44, 282,
283 n.18, 284
Kington (Heref.), 168
Kington St Michael (Wilts), prioress of,
290
Kinnerley (Shrops), castle of, 298, 307
Kirby Moorside (Yorks), 46
Kirtlington (Oxon), 346–7, 350, 355–6
Knaresborough (Yorks), 40–1, 59 n.19,
119, 270; castle of, 20, 26, 33–4, 35, 270,
326–7, 332 n.10
Knepp (Sussex), honour of, 91

Knighton (Maelienydd), 192 n.4
Knights, *see* Local society; Henry III (for
household knights)
Kyme, Simon of, 46

Lacock (Wilts), abbey of, 384
Lacy, Hugh de, earl of Ulster (1205–44),
deprived of Ulster by John, 22, 271,
306; invasion of Ireland, 301, 306–7,
316–17, 343–5, 354–5, 358; submission, 370; ally of e. of Chester, 355
Lacy, John de, constable of Chester, earl
of Lincoln (1232–40), 6, 60, 63, 80,
233–4, 311 n.10; in civil war, 34, 42; on
crusade with e. of Chester, 84, 103;
marriage, 103; dissident in 1223, 320,
324, 333; justice in eyre, 336; at siege of
Bedford, 365; one of twenty-five of 1215
attesting 1225 Charter, 388; and
Hubert, 388, 392; private forest of
Bowland, 388–9, 392
Lacy, Walter de (brother of Hugh), 14
n.6, 15 n.11, 149, 149 n.19, 162–3, 206,
282, 282 n.17; dismissal from sheriffdom of Hereford 1223, 316, 318; and
revolt of Hugh de Lacy, 316, 345
Lacy, William de (half-brother of Hugh),
345, 355 n.18, 370
Laigle, Gilbert de, 234
La Marche, county of, 155
Lancashire, 51; sheriffdom of, 326, 332
n.10; its revenues outside exchequer
control, 80–1, 119–22, 185, 189, 239,
253, 255, 274, 276; and the carucage of
1220, 225; reversal of 1225 deforestation 1227, 392, 392 n.12, 393 n.13
Lancaster, castle of, 326, 332 n.10
Lancaster, William of, 26, 234; his debts,
poverty and ransom, 197, 197 n.14,
339–40, 340 n.46; justice in eyre, 336;
at siege of Bradford, 365; private forests
of, 388
Langeais (Indre-et-Loire), 358
Langon (Gironde), 374
Langton, Simon, 19, 42, 45, 233, 324;
protest over his return to England, 228;
Abp Langton secures permission for,
342
Lanvallei, William de (d.1215), 6
La Réole (Gironde), 153–4, 154 n.3, 156;
surrender to Richard of Cornwall 1225,
377–8
La Rochelle (Charente-Maritime),
155–6; mayor and burgesses of, 173;

La Rochelle—*contd*
  unconquered 1204, 153, 173, 370; 'key' to Poitou, 370; surrenders 1224, 371–3
La Rugge, part of Windsor forest, 290
Lateran Council, Fourth, 82, 153; and judicial ordeal, 99
Laugharne, lordship of, 76, 77 n.7, 219, 307, 314, 314 n.15
Launceston (Cornwall), castle of, 215
Laughton en le Morthen (Yorks), 160
Laxton, Robert of, 233
Leeds (Yorks), 82, 129
Leicester, 91, 195, 198–9, 228, 325, 397
Leicester, Montfort half of honour of, 228, 228 n.2
Leicestershire, deforestation 1225, 385; reversed 1227, 392; deforestation 1235, 393 n.13
Leinster, 14, 32 n.9
Lichfield (Staffs), precentor and treasurer of, 133
Liddell (Cumb), 46
Limoges, Guy vicomte of and his brother, 212, 215, 215 n.16
Lincoln, 195, 268; battle of, 21, 31, 36–40, 48–9, 82, 136, 357, 394, 396–7; castle of, 20, 26, 36–9, 66–7, 157, 159–60, 175–6, 186, 260, 271, 271 n.6, 330, 337; cathedral, 36, 39; earldom of, 34, 40, 46
Lincoln, Hugh of Wells, bishop of (1209–35), 58, 84–6, 232, 237, 333, 345
Lincolnshire, 56, 59, 254, 298, 380, 383 n.6; and carucage 1220, 244; fifteenth 1225, 380; disturbances, private wars in, 145, 159; 184; deforestation 1230, 391–2; eyre in 1218–19, 99–100, 102–3, 147, 255; protest of county before judges, appeal to Magna Carta, 102–3, 137, 403; exploitation of 1225 Charter in, 384, 404, 406; knights of, at siege of Bytham, 234; e. of Salisbury as sheriff, 40, 55, 66–7, 119–20, 271, 274, 376–7; revenues outside exchequer control, 146, 185, 189, 194, 263, 274–6, 292, 376–7
Lisle, Brian de, 20, 36, 160, 228, 234, 281, 332 n.10, 342; and the Peak, 18, 26, 41, 285, 326–7; evades 1221 resumption, 270; as forest chief justice, 236, 236 n.3; eyres 1221–2, 252, 277; protest in Yorkshire, 277–9; eyres 1223, 337; dissident in 1223, 318–21, 324, 332; surrenders custodies, 326–7; removed as forest chief justice, 343, 354; submission 1224, 349, 351; at siege of Bedford,

363–4; witnesses 1225 Charter, 388; prop of Bp Peter's regime 1232–4, 393; and Knaresborough, 35, 40, 270, 326–7
Llansteffan, lordship of, 77, 77 n.7, 219, 314 n.15
Lloyd, S.D., 28 n.7
Llywelyn, prince of North Wales, 19–20, 26, 109, 151–2, 166, 168, 170–1, 174, 202–3, 241, 279, 355; invasion of south Wales 1217, 42–3, 69, 76–7, 218; and peace of Kingston/Lambeth, 69; invasion of south Wales 1220, 187, 211–13, 217–20; seizes Whittington 1223, 298, 307, 313; defeat of, 311–15; ambitions, outlook, 74, 76, 171, 192, 218–19; ally of e. of Chester, 81, 212, 260–1, 298; and Hugh de Lacy, 355; controls Maelienydd, 77 n.7, 192, 192 n.4; conflicts with Marshal earls of Pembroke, 43, 192, 217–20, 253, 260; and with Reginald de Braose, 42–3, 212–13, 217–18, 253, 307, 311; supports John de Braose, 218, 307; and Rhys Gryg, 43, 217–19, 218 n.2, 307; and southern Powys and Montgomery, 69, 76, 313–14; dominance in south Wales, 76–7, 218–19, 307; destroyed in 1223, 307–9; and treaty of Worcester, 76–7, 142, 192, 217–19, 293, 308, 314
Local society, structure of (knights, gentry, magnates), 11–12; ambition to control local government, for local officials to be local men, 11, 81, 179–80, 211–2, 274–5, 335–6; struggles over Forest, *see* Forest; struggles to exploit Magna Carta, 102–3, 210–11, 384, 403–4, 407; to limit number of local officials, 115, 150, 164, 181–2, 235 n.1, 292, 340; government's relationship with, 146, 206–7, 235–6; *see also under* individual counties
London, 41, 47, 56, 78, 131, 134, 158, 167, 173–6, 187, 192, 200–1, 210, 220, 223, 228–9, 245 n.11, 271, 279, 280, 285, 292, 297 n.5, 304, 309, 316, 318–19, 347, 349, 353, 355, 367, 378; and Louis, 19, 44, 290; blockade during war, 44, 47; fine for lifting interdict, 113, 113 n.16, 114 n.19, 291, 291 n.5, 338; riots in 1222, 290–1; St John's, Clerkenwell, 320; New Temple, 130, 161, 206, 320, 350, 367; Temple Church, 108; Tower of, 42, 105, 178, 291, 319, 319 n.15 (custody during minority), 324

London, bishop of, *see* Faukenburg, Eustace de

London, William de Sainte-Mère-Église, bishop of (1199–1221), 188; baron of exchequer, 53, 65 n.9

de Londres, family, heiress, 77, 217, 307, 314 n.13

Long Crendon (Bucks), 91

Longueville (Seine-Inférieure), 14–15

Louis, eldest son of King Philip Augustus, 51, 67, 138, 290; in England, 1, 12, 15, 19–49; character, 32; claim to throne, 12–13; appreciates military difficulties, 21; desertions while in France, 27–31; loyalty to his followers, 32, 42, 44, 47; and patronage, 29, 30, 33–4, 122; cement of his party, 32–5; splits his army, 36; peace negotiations, 41–2, 44, 47; and peace of Kingston/Lambeth, 44–5, 49; payment to, *see* Finance; promise over Normandy, 45, 309; threat to Poitou and Gascony 1219, 153, 167; as Louis VIII, king of France (1223–6): coronation, 309, 311; negotiations for renewal of truce 1224, 344, 349–50, 355, 358; agreement with Hugh de Lusignan, 358; conquers Poitou, 177, 344, 355, 370–4; resources 1224 compared with king of England's, 372; ridicules Henry III, 372; defies pope, 373; limited interest in Gascony, 374, 378; and La Réole, 153–4, 377–8; threatens fresh invasion of England, 344, 373, 379; death, 378, 388

Louis IX, king of France (1226–70), 378

Lucy, Geoffrey de, 158

Lucy, Richard de, widow of, 78

Ludgershall (Wilts), castle of, 247, 247 n.18

Ludlow (Shrops), 308

Lugwardine (Heref), 282 n.17

Lusignan (Vienne), 155; castle of, 358

Lusignan, family of, 156

Lusignan, Hugh de, lord of Lusignan, count of La Marche (1219–48), references to in sequence: 109, 154–6, 161, 167, 173, 178–9, 193–4, 196, 199–201, 211, 217, 221, 267–8, 279–80, 291–2, 294–5, 298, 309–10, 345, 348–9, 350, 356, 358–9, 372, 374, 378; position in Poitou, 155; aims, demands, 179, 193–4, 199–201, 267; and Joan, Henry III's sister, 155, 178–9, 193, 196, 200, 211, 221; retains her *maritagium*, 200,

217, 221, 267, 291, 294, 310, 345, 349, 358; marriage to Queen Isabella, 193, 200; for her dower *see* Isabella; negotiations for settlement 1224, 345, 348–50, 356, 358; defection to Louis, 358–9; invasion of Gascony, 374, 378; and Savari de Mauléon, 309–10

Lusignan, Ralph de, count of Eu (d.1219), 89, 155, 160

Lusignans, the half-brothers of king, 394, 409

Luton (Beds), 165, 203, 354, 357, 367–9; men of and Falkes, 368

Madoc ap Gruffyd, 298

Maelgwn ap Rhys, 77 n. 7, 218–19, 294 n. 8, 307–9, 313–14

Maelienydd, lordship of, 77 n.7, 192

Magna Carta, 50, 53–4, 95, 108, 137–40, 262, 396–7, 401; first appearance of name, 2; breaches of, 102–3, 166, 291, 334, 337, 393–4, 405–6, 405 n.11, 406 n.13; defects of, 3, 61, 405–6; disputes over interpretation, 384, 405–6; clauses still on Statute Book, 2, 2 n.4, 383; clauses obeyed, 63, 98, 100, 103, 191, 197, 210–11, 334–7, 348, 385–8, 404–5; takes root in minority, struggles of local society to exploit, 2, 102–3, 210–11, 383–4, 402–4, 407; as part of bargain between king and subjects, 383, 403; publicity, 383–4, 403

Magna Carta 1215: 12, 23–4, 30, 47; analysis of, 9–11, 62; individual clauses: *1* (liberties of church), 23; *2* (relief), 63, 191, 197, 204, 334; *4, 3–5* (wardships), 23 n.11, 24, 406; *7* (widow's dower), 24; *12 & 14* (scutages and aids), 24, 54–5, 61, 210–11, 278, 379, 408–9; *17* (common pleas), 64, 96, 335; *18* (petty assizes), 10–11, 97, 335; *21* (amercement by peers), 98, 335; *24* (pleas of crown), 121 n.52, 335 n.22; *25* (revenue above county farm), 24, 114, 226, 286, 329, 406; *34 (praecipe)*, 334–5, 335 n.20; *39* (judgement by peers, [clause *29* 1225]), 2, 103, 137–9, 166, 209, 237, 264, 334, 348, 386, 393–4, 403, 405, 405 n.11; *40* (denial of justice), 336, 406; *48* (inquiry into local government), 24, 61, 63 n.8;

Magna Carta—*contd*

> *60* (everyone to observe Charter), 61, 387–8 (exploited by king 1225); *61* (security clause), 3, 63, 180, 195, 388, 406
>
> Magna Carta 1216: 123; issue of and significance, 22–4; on ecclesiastical vacancies, 23 n.11, 143, 406; proclamation of 1217, 42, 403; and peace negotiations 1217, 41, 45, 45 n.7
>
> Magna Carta 1217: issue of, 60–2; its date, 60 n.2 and plate 8; proclamation 1218, 73–4, 403; oath to observe, 73, 403; new clauses: *14 & 15* (the bench), 64; *20* (riverbanks), 61; *39* (alienations), 61; *42* (counties and hundreds, [clause 35 1225]), 61, 63, 63 n.8, 384, 405–6; *43* (alienations to religious houses), 61; *46* (saving previous liberties), 61, 387 (exploited by king 1225); *47* (adulterine castles), 74
>
> Confirmation by king Jan, 1223, 266, 296–7, 297 n.5 (for discussion of date), 337, 403
>
> Magna Carta 1225, its concession and exploitation, 376, 382–5; its witnesses, 388; final form, 383; king works within, 385–8; acknowledges he is subject to law, 386–7, 386 n.24; duty to dispense justice, 386–7; king's liberties, liberties of others, 387; everyone must observe Charter to own men, 387–8; confirmations 1237 and 1253, 383, 404; and 1297, 2, 383; *see also* Twenty-five

Maidenhead (Berks), 105

Maingo, William, 309

Malmesbury (Wilts), 175, 290; abbot of, 213, 237

Mansfield (Notts), 119, 283 n.18, 284

Mantell, Robert, 179–80, 191

Marans (Charente-Maritime), castle of, 309–10

Marden (Heref), 282 ns.15, 17

Margaret, sister of Alexander II, 196; wife of Hubert, 231–2, 232 n.22, 268, 395, 408

Mark, Philip, 10, 20, 24, 26, 36, 51, 68, 84, 176; grants to 1217, 68; at siege of Bytham, 232–3; and fall of Peter de

Maulay 1221, 250, 260; and resumption of demesne 1222, 281–3, 283 n.18, 284–5; retains office in 1223, 324, 328 n.12; as sheriff of Nottinghamshire-Derbyshire, 117, 181, 199, 328 n.12; resists return of seisin to Roger de Montbegon, 58–9, 170, 179, 234, 269; controls forest, resists return to

Matilda de Cauz, 59, 59 n.20, 151, 181, 216

Markets and fairs, licences for only valid until king comes of age, 227

Marlborough (Wilts), 70, 91, 119, 124, 283 n.21, 284, 296; castle of, 28, 348; and the e. of Pembroke, 29–30, 30 n.15, 185, 189, 239, 244, 247, 247 n.18, 249, 251–2, 255, 316, 397–400

Marsh, Geoffrey de, justiciar of Ireland (1215–21), struggle to control, 73, 142, 161, 203, 205–6, 211, 239, 253–4 (dismissal), 256, 266, 270, 341

Marsh, Richard de, *see* Durham, bishop of

Marsh, William de, lord of Lundy island, 216, 234

Marshal, John, nephew of regent, 19, 46, 220, 220 n.7, 288, 288 n.48; advises William Marshal to accept regency, 16; as forest chief justice, 68, 81, 90 n.1, 91, 150, 169, 236 n.3; and Falkes, 272–3, 334, 338; in charge of Ulster 1223–4, 346

Martel, Alan, 207

Martel, William, 350

Marshal, William father and son, *see* Pembroke, earls of

Martin fitz, family, wardship of heir, 76, 293–4, 314

Mauclerc, Walter, bishop of Carlisle (1223–46), 240 n.3, 275

Mauduit, William, 6, 34–5, 46, 73 n.12

Maulay, Peter de, 20, 26, 46, 71 n.5, 232, 241, 274, 369; private war with e. of Salisbury over Sherborne and Somerset 1217–18, 31, 35, 66, 71, 121, 250; accused of treason 1221, 239, 249–52, 256, 341; removed from Corfe, 239, 249–52, 256, 262; debts pardoned, 256, 275; dissident in 1223, 320, 325; attack on 1224, 346–9, 351; at siege of Bedford, 363–4; witnesses 1225 Charter, 388; returns to office with Bp Peter 1232, 393; murderer of Arthur of Brittany?, 138, 138 n.19; close associate of Bp Peter, 139–40, 249, 251, 256, 260–2, 270;

Maulay, Peter de—*contd*
  collects ransoms, 46, 197, 197 n.14,
  275; and Hubert, 338 n.34; oath to keep
  custodies safe until king of age, 123,
  251; as sheriff of Somerset-Dorset, 56
  n.4, 72, 120, 120 n.45, 146, 250, 274–5
  (removal)
Mauléon, family of, 156
Mauléon, Savari de, 14 n.6, 28 n.7, 105,
  139, 151, 229; as seneschal of Poitou,
  267–8, 372–3; offends towns and Hugh
  de Lusignan, 295, 309–10; defence of
  Poitou 1224, 370–2
Mauzé (Deux-Sèvres), castle of, 309–
  310
Mauzé, Porteclie de, 309
McFarlane, K.B., 11
Meath, 345
Meekings, C.A.F., 79 n.5
Melbourne (Derbs), 26, 119, 269, 282,
  284
Melksham (Wilts), forest of, 121
Melle (Deux-Sèvres), castle of, 358
Melrose abbey, chronicle of, 69
Melun, viscount of, 42
Mere (Wilts), 88, 121, 147, 162, 176, 274
  n.17
Merpins (Charente), castle of, 267, 279,
  291, 310 n.5
Merton (Surrey), 187
Middlesex, deforestation of after 1227,
  392
Milborne Port (Som), 346, 349
Military household, king's, *see* John, Henry III
Minority of Henry III, significance of,
  1–4, 396; threats to royal power in,
  1–2, 51–2, 109, 118–27, 329–33, 397;
  problems of government after war, 50–
  6; date of king's majority, fourteen as
  against twenty-one, 123–4, 240–3, 245;
  concessions until completion of king's
  fourteenth year, 19, 123, 123 n.62,
  125–6, 269–70; disputes over sheriffdoms 1217–18, 66, 70–1; pressures for
  patronage, 26, 51, 55–6, 68, 78–9,
  92–3, 95–6, 117–19; inauguration of
  king's seal, 94–5; king's second coronation, a turning point, 187–91, 236–7;
  significance of age fourteen as term of
  king's pupilage, 240–1, 257–8, 268–9;
  development of faction in 1221, 260–2,
  399; resumption of demesne 1222, 279–
  89; prospect of king assuming power,

268, 280, 289; king's confirmation of
  Charters 1223, 295–7; papal letters of
  April 1223, 301–6, 310, 315–17, 321;
  king takes control of his seal, resumes
  his castles and sheriffdoms, 321–9;
  situation of new government Jan. 1224,
  343–4; significance of siege of Bedford,
  343–4, 369–70; situation of kingship
  1225, 376, 385–8; king begins to grant
  charters Jan 1227, 389; minority never
  formally ended, 389; influence of
  minority on later programmes of reform, 407–11; *see* Finance, Forest, Justice, Henry III, Magna Carta, Oaths,
  Rebels, Resumption
Mitchell, S.K., 93
Mitford (Northumb), castle of, 57–8,
  83–6, 109, 130, 145, 147, 162, 168,
  174–6, 187, 189, 194, 197–8, 201, 203–
  5, 207–8, 211, 214, 220, 227, 234–5,
  239, 255, 289, 333, 338, 397–401; *see
  also* Bertram, Roger, and Oldcoates,
  Philip of
Monk, Eustace the, 43–4
Monmouth, John of, 14 n.6, 78, 78 n.3, 85
  n.6, 109; witnesses 1225 Charter, 388
Montbegon, Roger de, 191, 234; struggle
  to recover lands after war, 58–9, 170,
  179, 182, 191, 216, 234, 269, 338, 401
Montfort, Amaury de, 344
Montfort, Simon de (d.1265), 409
Montgomery, 69, 76, 311–17, 320, 322
  n.6, 326, 344, 365, 389, 395; new castle
  of 1223, its strategic importance,
  311–13
Montreuil-Bellay (Maine-et-Loire), 370
Moresk (Cornwall), 349, 352, 356
Mortimer, Hugh de, 255, 255 n.3; and
  Maelienydd, 77 n.7, 192, 194 n.4;
  witnesses 1225 Charter, 388
Mortimer, William de, 56, 102
Moulton, Thomas of, 78; justice in eyre
  1218, 101 n.44; justice of bench, 336; at
  siege of Bedford, 365
Mountsorrel (Leics), 34–5, 45, 60; siege
  of, 35–6, 357; destruction of castle, 40
Mowbray, William de, 6, 33–4, 40, 46,
  234; and Hubert, 141, 338–9; treat-
  ment of his debts, 339; boycotts York-
  shire forest eyre, 277
Mucegros, Richard, senior or junior, 249,
  250; senior, 251 n.9
Mucegros, Robert, 250
Munster, 140

Muntfichet, Richard de, 6; at siege of Bedford 1224, 365; one of twenty-five of 1215 attesting 1225 Charter, 388

Munchensy, Warin de, 287

Musard, Ralph, familiar of earls of Pembroke, 17, 19, 68, 230, 332, 332 n.11; urges Marshal to accept regency, 16; as sheriff of Gloucestershire (and Hubert), 194, 213, 220; 'dismissal' 1223, 316–18, 327–8

Nafferton [in Ovingham] (Northumb), castle of, 88, 202

Narberth (Pembroke), 218

Nassington (Northants), 72, 148–9, 158, 199, 228 n.3

Navarre, Queen Berengar of, Richard I's widow, 200–1, 212, 215, 217, 223–4

Nether Went, lordship of, 49, 307 n.5, 319

Nevers, Hervé de Donz, count of, 29

Neville, Geoffrey de, 171, 197, 205, 228–30, 281–2, 283 n.18, 284; as sheriff of Yorkshire, 80–1, 115, 115 n.27, 116, 146, 163, 185, 195 n.6, 210–11 (and 1220 carucage), 225, 328 n.12; as seneschal of Poitou, 80, 82, 154–6, 167–8 (resignation), 177, 179, 202, 214, 377; missions to Poitou, 178, 295, 310, 345, 345 n.6, 348; commands 1224 expedition, 355–6, 370–1; witnesses 1225 Charter, 388

Neville, Hugh de, 6, 12, 90 n.1, 99; and struggle to recover Northamptonshire forest, 72, 73 n.12, 85, 147, 199, 199 n.5, 234–5, 401; attack on Falkes 1224, 353–4, 367; as forest chief justice 1224–5, 354, 384; protest over Dorset perambulation 1225, 385, 392

Neville, John de, 171

Neville, Ralph de, bishop of Chichester (1224–44), keeper of the seal, 143, 146, 170, 351, 354; entrusted with seal 1218, 94–5; Pandulf's orders about its keeping, 130–1, 131 n.13, 132; place in triumvirate, 133–4; and papal letters of April 1223, 301–2, 306, 321; significance of his career, 407–11; views about great councils, 94–5, 410

Newark (Notts), 36, 89; castle of, 12, 20, 43 n.36, 56, 86, 109, 229, 232; siege of, 84–5, 88, 108–9, 198, 227, 229, 232, 262, 289, 333, 366–7, 397, 400, 408

Newburn (Northumb), 225

Newbury (Berks), 92, 92 n.9

Newcastle-under-Lyme (Staffs), 119; castle of, 125

Newcastle upon Tyne, 57, 68, 72, 119, 283 n.20; castle of, 20, 86, 221, 226

Newnham (Gloucs), 89, 119, 281, 283 n.18

Newport (Shrops), 364 n.14

Newport Pagnell (Bucks), 283 n.18, 284

Newton (Norfolk), 140 n.28

Nicholas, Ralph fitz, steward of e. of Derby, 52; sheriff of Hereford, 318, 327

Hay, Nicola de, 20, 36, 66–7, 159, 175

Niort (Deux-Sèvres), 154, 156

Norfolk, 33, 59 n.16; sheriff to uphold rights of crown, 116; see also Norfolk-Suffolk

Norfolk, Hugh Bigod, earl of 1221–5, 48; supports government 1223–4, 326, 333, 349; at siege of Bedford, 365; one of twenty-five of 1215 (when Hugh Bigod) attesting 1225 Charter, 388; wardship of his lands, 376

Norfolk, Roger Bigod, earl of (1189–1221), 6, 46

Norfolk-Suffolk, sheriffdom of, 53, 116, 122, 265, 327, 332 n.11; Hubert accounts for profits from, 329–30; carucage in 1220, 224; fifteenth of 1225, 380

Norgate, Kate, 5, 25 n.5, 195 n.6, 266, 297 n.5, 302 n.4, 303 n.6

Norham (Northumb), 152, 196

Normandy, 7, 45, 139, 177, 261–2, 273, 309, 345, 381 n.12; proposed invasion 1223, 310–11

Normans, lands of, 347

Northampton, 13, 29, 36, 67, 69–70, 116, 158–9, 175, 198, 230, 233, 303, 303 n.5, 357; castle of, 12, 20, 32, 116, 199, 250, 332 n.10; Christmas court at 1223, 324–6, 331, 333, 353 n.8, 397, 400; great council at June 1224, 361–2; its purpose, 358–60

Northamptonshire, 51, 198–9, 222, 273, 357; carucage of 1220, 224; fifteenth of 1225, 224; forest of, 73 n.12, 147, 199; forest eyres in: 1212, 277; postponed 1221, 236, 252, 276; takes place 1222, 277, 337 n.33; deforestation after 1227, 393; sheriffdom of, 117, 332 n.10

Northern rebels, political rehabilitation of, 196–8, 234, 336, 365

Northumberland, 51, 71, 197; carucage of 1220, 224; amercements of eyre in, 146; sheriffdom of, 197, 216, 220, 235, 328 n.12, 329; exaction of revenue above county farm, 226–7, 235; proclamation of Magna Carta in 1225, 383 n.6; forest in, 392 n.12

Northumbria, 196

North Wheatley (Notts), 58, 170

Norton, Greens Norton (Northants), 272–3; hundred of, 273, 273 n.15

Norwich, 160; bishopric of, 133; castle of, 25, 327, 332 n.11

Nottingham, 26, 40, 130, 198, 233, 298; castle of, 20, 199, 250, 324

Nottinghamshire, 59, 59 n.20, 181, 216, 401; events in county court, 59, 179; demands for deforestation, 89–90, 91 n.5, 151, 403; protest to Pandulf over assarts, 151, 159; deforestation in 1225, 385, 385 n.16; modified in 1227, 392; forest eyre postponed 1221, 236, 252, 276; and 1222, 277 n.6; takes place 1223, 337; see also Sherwood forest, and The Clay

Nottinghamshire-Derbyshire, sheriffdom of, 51, 117, 324, 328 n.12; protests over number of shrieval officials, 115, 181

Oaths: to king and Charters (1218), 73–4; banning permanent alienations (1218), 95, 142, 190, 215; to protect king's rights (1218), 98, 108, 190; oath at 1220 coronation to surrender custodies, 189–90, 196, 198

Odiham (Hants), 119, 281, 293, 305, 329–30; castle of, 317, 326–8, 328 n.15, 332 n.10, 346

Oilly, Henry de, 11

Oldcoates, Philip of, references to in sequence: 20, 51, 57–8, 68, 72, 83–8, 96, 104, 109, 128–30, 145, 147–8, 162, 168, 174–6, 182, 184, 187, 189, 194, 197–8, 201–5, 208–9, 211, 214–17, 221, 226–7, 230, 235, 237, 255, 287, 289, 397–8, 408; early career, 57, and bishop of Durham, 145, 148, 148 n.11; ideas about great councils, 130, 408; and Hubert de Burgh, 174–5, 182, 201, 204, 214, 216–17; grants to, 68, 72, 96, 162, 168; and Harbottle castle, 202, 208–9, 214; letters of conduct for, 104–5, 128–30; and Mitford, 57–8,

83–6, 130, 145, 147, 162, 168, 174–5, 184, 187, 189, 194, 197–8 (surrender of), 211, 214, 227, 255, 289, 397–8, 400; and Mere, 88, 147, 162, 176; his castle at Nafferton, 88; northern enemies of, 88, 197, 201–2, 214, 216; and Pandulf, 168, 174–6, 214; promises to, 72, 87–8, 216; as seneschal of Poitou, 168, 201–3, 211, 214, 216–17; and Richard de Umfraville, 88, 202; and Vesci custody, 71, 84–7, 130, 147, 168, 186, 205; death, 221, 226–7

Oléron, isle of, 178, 178 n.8, 179, 193, 217, 221, 345, 345 n.7, 349, 358

Ombersley and Horwell (Worcs), forest of, 96, 115

Orby, Philip of, 152, 152 n.5

Ordinances of 1311, 412

Orford (Suffolk), castle of, 25, 327, 332 n.11

Osmotherley (Yorks), 102, 129 n.6

Osney abbey (in Oxford), chronicle of, 395

Oswaldbeck (Notts), 58, 269

Oswestry (Shrops), 313

Otto, Master, papal envoy, 386

Ouse and Derwent, forest between (Yorks), 181, 278; deforestation 1225, 385; reversed after 1227, 393; deforested again 1234, 393 n.13

Owain ap Gruffud, 77 n.7

Oxford, 25, 46, 67, 128–30, 135, 148, 249, 290–1, 295, 297 n.5, 355; castle of, 20, 250, 317, 326, 332 n.10; great councils at: in 1217, 43; August 1220, 192, 202–8, 210–13, 219, 222, 225, 230, 236, 238, 241; Christmas court of 1220, 227–8, 231–2

Oxford, countess of, 274

Oxford, Robert de Vere, e. of (1214–21), 191, 198, 200, 205; elevation to the bench, 180, 182, 191, 335–6; judgement founded on Magna Carta on praecipe, 335; wardship of his lands, 274

Oxfordshire, 51, 368 n.47; demands for deforestation in, 180–1; general eyre of 1218–19 in, 101; sheriffdom of, 51, 117, 122, 326, 332 n.10; deforestation after 1227, 392

d'Oyry, Fulk, 99, 102

Painter, Sidney, 19

Pandulf, papal legate 1218–21, bp elect of Norwich, 53, 107–8, 129, 158, 167, 177,

Pandulf—*contd*
200, 206, 219, 291, 319 n.5; early career, 133; appointment, powers and position, 93, 103, 106–7, 128, 132–3; regent entrusts king to, 106–7; initial dispute with Hubert and Bp Peter, 130–1; his letter about the keeping of the seal, 131, 131 n.13; men of Nottinghamshire-Derbyshire protest to over forest assarts, 151, 159; and disorders at Tickhill, 160–1; and king's second coronation, 187, 189; and settlement with king of Scotland, 152–3, 165, 196; and Harbottle castle, 202, 208–9; and resumption of Bristol castle, 229; and e. of Pembroke's marriage and the resumption of Marlborough, 244–8, 398; resignation and achievements, 254–6; mission to Poitou, 266–8, 279, 295; last advice to Hubert, 398; aims and outlook, 142, 146, 153, 397–8; and taking of counsel, 171, 175; and rights of crown and programme of resumption, 118, 142–3, 185, 189–90, 229, 239, 247–8, 253–6, 263, 397–8; and papal letters calling for act of resumption: in 1219, 142, 146, 398; in 1220, 142, 189–90, 398; in 1221, 142, 248, 398; vital role in sponsoring programme of resumption, 397–8; and ecclesiastical vacancies, 143; loans to government, 133, 178, 200, 215–17, 224, 233, 248; on sheriffs, 118, 146; taxation imposed by, 223; and cooperation with Hubert and Bp Peter, 128, 145–6, 151–3, 155, 160–1, 167; and Hubert, especially 134, 152, 170–1, 173–4, 185, 187, 213–14, 229; criticism of Hubert, 214, 217, 266, 338; cooperation with Hubert 1221, 243–4; and Bp Peter, 107, 213–14, 229, 243 (suspicions of as king's tutor), 258; and c. of Aumale, 166–7, 229, 233; and Roger Bertram, 205; and Henry fitz Count, 161–2, 213–15, 398; and Abp Langton, 133, 254, 263; and Llywelyn, 142, 151–2, 171, 174; and Philip of Oldcoates, 168, 174–6, 398; *see also* Triumvirate
Paper Constitution of 1244, 4, 83, 95; influence of Hubert's career on, 395; influence of minority on, 410–11
Paris, 264, 323, 374
Paris Temple, 350
Paris, Matthew, 32–3, 47; and Hubert, 43

n.37, 138, 141, 245 n.11, 290–1, 394; and Falkes, 357 n.11, 367–8
Parthenay, William l'Archevêque, lord of, 279
Passelewe, Robert, in service of Falkes, 117; procures papal letters of April 1223, 304, 304 n.11; envoy to pope, 1223–4, 325, 331, 347, 350–1, 350 n.5, 363; probable author of Falkes' *querimonia*, 305, 368; returns to office with Bp Peter, 1232, 393
Pattishall, Martin of, 64, 183 ns, 3–4, 213 n.6; and triumvirate, 133–4, 134 n.22; and siege of Bedford, 365
Pattishall, Simon of, 64
Pattishall, Walter of, 353
The Peak, honour, castle of (Peverel castle, Castleton, Derbs), 17–19, 41, 114, 119, 119 n.40, 269, 283 n.18, 284–5, 326; forest of, 124
Pembroke, 14; lordship of, 43, 77, 218–20, 307–8, 313
Pembroke, Richard Marshal, e. of 1231–4, 196 n.12; rebels against Bp Peter's regime, 394; rescues Hubert from Devizes, 394
Pembroke, William Marshal, e. of (1199–1219) the regent (1216–19), 9, 14 n.6, 59, 60 n.2, 68, 95, 103, 135, 319 n.15; early career and outlook, 14–16, 31–2, 55, 126; and John, 14–15, 23, 77, 106, 405; becomes regent, 14, 16–17, 21–2; as regent, 17–127 *passim*; and battle of Lincoln, 36–40, 396–7; and peace of Kingston/Lambeth, 44–9; structure and problems of his peacetime government, 50–6, 84, 88–9, 94, 103–4 (increasing role of Bp Peter), 106, 118, 397; and act of resumption, 67–8; and treaty of Worcester, 74, 77; and southwest Wales, 76–7; and Bytham, 57, 85–7; and Mitford, 57, 83, 85, 109; and Newark, 43 n.36, 58, 85–6, 108–9; and Rockingham, 72, 109; inauguration of king's seal/general eyre, 94–103; last illness and death, 104–8; resignation and decision about his successor, 106–7, 106 n.13; achievements, 108–9, 396–8; legacy, 85–6, 109–27; and bench, 64–5, 70; and exchequer, 65, 65 n.9, 70; and great councils, 54–5; government based on consent, need for support, 14, 17, 86, 106–7, 128, 183; as sheriff of Essex-Herts, 115–16, 116

Pembroke, William—*contd*
n.28; and process of settlement, 49, 55, 58, 81–4, 86, 91, 101–3; and demands for deforestation, 89–91, 108; defence of rights of crown, 18–19, 55, 67–8, 91, 94–5, 108, 398; and finance, 26, 51–2, 70, 73, 88–9, 93–4, 113 n.17, 118; and patronage, 18, 43 n.36, 51, 55–6, 68, 73, 78–9, 81, 88–9, 96, 117, 285; desire for rewards himself, 91–2; and lands of c. of Perche, 92; marriages of his daughters, 48–9, 63, 91; Matilda, wife of Hugh Bigod, 48; Isabella, wife of Gilbert de Clare, 49, 63, 91; Eva, wife of William de Braose, 91; and Caerleon, 70, 77; and Marlborough, 29–30, 30 n.15, 55 n.23, 91, 104, 124; and Falkes, 78–9, 117; difficulties with e. of Chester, 26–7, 77; and Guala, 52–3; and difficulties with Hubert, 21–2, 27, 53, 59, 65–6, 77–8, 103–4; and Llywelyn, 43, 76–7, 91, 109; and e. of Salisbury, 92, 92 n.12; and Nicholas de Stuteville, 41, 46, 55 n.23; and Bp Peter, 53, 59, 65, 67, 77, 94, 103–4, 106–7

Pembroke, William Marshal, e. of (1219–31), William Marshal junior, 47, 54, 107, 177, 196 n.12, 200, 205, 233, 241, 255, 266, 275, 281, 290; his desertion of Louis, 27, 29–30, 32; at battle of Lincoln, 39; and Thomas of Berkeley 1220, 203–4; and 1220 carucage, 225; and Llywelyn's invasion of South Wales, 217–20; surrenders Fotheringhay, 220; proposed marriage to king's sister, 244–9; surrenders Marlborough, 247–249; and Christmas crisis of 1221, 271–274; and act of resumption 1221, 270; and resumption of demesne 1222, 282, 282 n.17, 287; conquest of south Wales 1223, 301, 307–9, 314–15; supported by Hubert 1223, 308–9, 315; and attack on Falkes 1224, 347, 354–6, 358, 367; becomes justiciar of Ireland, May 1224, 354–6; defeats Hugh de Lacy, 370; break-up of alliance with Hubert, 390; but accepts him becoming justiciar for life, 407; conflicts with Falkes, 148–9, 164–5, 165 n.16, 175–6, 203, 243–4, 247, 249, 272–3, 281, 293–4, 314, 334, 338; his familiar, Fulk fitz Warin, 294, 294 n.11; dispute with e. of Gloucester, 290, 320; and Hubert, 149, 157–8, 165, 182, 185, 204, 212, 219–20,
243–9 (formation of alliance 1221), 250, 271–3, 287, 290, 294, 308–9; the alliance in 1223–4, 315–17, 319, 325, 333, 345–9, 377; its importance, 399–400; conflicts with Llywelyn, 192, 217–20, 253, 253 n.9, 279, 307–9, 314–15, 399; and Pandulf, 244; and Reginald de Braose, 218, 260 n.26, 314, 320 n.7; alliance with e. of Salisbury, 27, 303–4 (quarrel with), 287, 308–9; born in Normandy, 36, 261–2, 273; and Caerleon, 192, 299, 308, and Cemais, 293–4, 314; and exchange, 73, 77, 200–1; and Fotheringhay, 145, 148–9, 158, 165, 184, 187, 189, 196, 199–200, 211, 219–20, 230; and Marlborough, 29–30, 30 n.15, 165, 185, 239, 244, 247–9 (surrender of 1221), 397–8; and marriage to king's sister, 244–9, 255, 271–2, 341, 346, 354, 408); his relief, 191; and lands of c. of Perche, 244, 287, 400; and support for resumption, 249, 315, 333

Perche, Geoffrey, c. of (d.1202), 92

Perche, Thomas, c. of (d.1217), 33, 36, 48, 92; death at Lincoln, 39

Perche, lands of c. of, 92, 195, 287, 400

Percy, Richard de, 234, 277; one of twenty-five of 1215, 277; at siege of Bedford, 365

Percy, Robert de, 100, 129 n.6; and acceptance of king's justice, 102

Percy, William de, 102

Perigueux (Dordogne), 154, 377

Perigueux, count of, 377

Peterborough abbey, chronicle of, 13

Peverel, William II, 17, 26 n.14, 124

Philip Augustus, king of France (1180–1223), 1, 7, 9, 15, 45, 161, 201, 221, 245; and renewal of truce, 104, 153, 155–6, 172–3, 177; death, 301, 309; on the children of John, 109; and Poitou and Gascony, 153, 167; revenues of compared to king of England's, 186

Philip, clerk of William Marshal, 107

Pickering (Yorks), castle of, 116, 385

Piis, family of (of La Réole), 295, 377

Pitney and Wearne, manors with joint farm in Somerton (Som), 119, 283 n.19, 284, 286 n.35

Plympton (Devon), castle of, 78–9, 184, 347–8, 352, 356, 367, 369

Poitevin scutage, 136, 339, 339 n.45

Poitiers, 153

Poitou, 1–2, 4, 7, 28 n.7, 45, 135, 139, 145, 262; affairs of, 109, 153–6, 167–8, 177–9, 188, 191–4, 196, 201–3, 206, 211, 214–17, 221, 223–4, 229–30, 266–8, 279–80, 291–2, 294–5, 297–9, 303–4, 309–10, 328 n.12, 343–5, 348–9, 355, 358–62, 364, 368–79 (loss of), 389, 393; revenues, 168; seneschalship of, 80, 82, 167, 173, 177–8, 193, 201–3, 214, 221, 229; situation of king of England within, 156; truce in 1222 arranged by Pandulf, 279, 291; truce 1223, 298; warnings of Geoffrey de Neville 1219, 154–5; see Lusignan, Hugh de

Pons, Reginald de, 267, 279

Pons, Reginald de, junior, 201 n.11

de Pont de l'Arche, William de, 32

Portchester (Hants), castle of, 27, 317, 327, 333 n.12

Portsmouth (Hants), 283 n.20, 310, 311, 315, 359

Possonière, Guy de La, 173, 177

Powicke, Sir Maurice, 5, 118 n.36, 143, 265, 267, 307, 326, 360; and papal letters of April 1223, 302

Powys, southern, 69, 76, 309, 313–14

Preston, Walter of, 72, 117, 199, 235, 401

Private wars and truces, 66, 71, 184

Provisions of Oxford, 411–12

Prudhoe (Northumb), castle of, 58, 88, 202

Puy, Bartholomew de, 167, 291, 373

Quincy, Margaret de, marriage to John de Lacy, 103

Quincy, Roger de, 266

Ragnall (Notts), 282

Ramsay, Sir James, 112

Ramsey (Hunts), abbey of, and Falkes as sheriff, 334

Ransoms, see Rebels, former

Rayleigh (Essex), honour of, 141, 291, 389, 395

Reading (Berks), 130–1, 347; great council at, 1219, 106, 259

Reading, abbot of, 107, 333

Rebels, former, ransoms of, 46–7, 101–2, 129, 197, 197 n.14, 339 n.40; and process of settlement after war, 45–9, 56–60, 81–4, 101–3, 108, 179–182, 190–1, 196–9, 205, 216, 227, 234–235, 255, 333–41, 365, 388; as judges,

101–2, 101 n.44, 180, 336; support for government: at Newark, 86, 333, 400; over Mitford, 196–7, 333, 400; over Bytham and the c. of Aumale, 234, 333, 400; over resumption of demesne, 288–9, 333, 400; in Dec. 1223, 325–6, 333; at seige of Bedford, 365, 400; see also Magna Carta under 'clauses obeyed', and 'takes root in minority'; and see individual rebels, notably Albini, William de; Beauchamp, William de; Bertram, Roger; Braose, Reginald de; Braybrooke, Henry of; Cauz, Matilda de; Coleville, Wiliam de; Essex, William de Mandeville, e. of; Moulton, Thomas of; Gant, Gilbert de; Lacy, John de; Lancaster, William of; Marsh, William de; Montbegon, Roger de; Mowbray, William de; Neville, Hugh de; Oxford, Robert de Vere, e. of; Ros, Robert de; Preston, Walter of; Walter, Robert fitz; Winchester, Saer de Quincy, e. of; see also Kingston/Lambeth, peace of

Redvers, Baldwin de, and siege of Exeter castle 1136, 366

Redvers, Margaret de, wife of Falkes, 78, 353–4, 366, 368–9

Regis, Richard fitz, 185, 226–7

Reinfrey, Gilbert fitz, 197, 340 n.46

Resumption, programme of, related ideas: ban on permanent alienations while king under age, 18–19, 95–6, 108, 142–3, 215, 227, 322, 322 n.6, 389, 401; coronation oath to protect rights of crown, 143, 189; resumption of alienations since start of war, 95–7, 206, 215; oath to surrender custodies 1220, 189; papal letters calling for act of resumption: in 1219, 118, 142, 146, 185, 206, 398; in 1220, 118, 123, 142, 189–90, 199, 206, 286, 398; in 1221, 142, 248, 398; papal letter of April 1223 commands resumption and overcomes problem of king's minority, 301–2; sheriffdoms and county farms outside exchequer control, 72, 78, 80–1, 89, 116, 118–22, 185, 188–9, 215, 253, 263, 274–6; county farms, increasing revenue from, 276, 292–3, 415–16; revenues above the county farm, exaction of, 114–15, 226–7, 235, 328–9; royal demesne, revenue from, 114, 185, 283; granting away of demesne manors,

Resumption Programme—*contd*
68, 88–9, 96, 118–19; demesne, in-alienability of, 285–6; resumption of individual manors, 163, 199, 222, 226, 235, 239, 253, 263; attempted resumptions: in 1217, 67–8, 91, 279; in 1220, 187, 203, 206–7, 222, 230, 235, 269, 279, 287; in 1221, 269–70, 279, 287; resumption achieved 1222, 266, 279–89, 292–3, 296, 298; proceeds of, 283; castellans irremovable until king of age, 71, 79, 81, 123–4, 185, 251, 289, 302, 332–3; hereditary claims to castles and sheriffdoms, 124–5; resumption of individual castles, 185, 198, 221, 229, 235, 251, 253, 281, 285–5; resumption of castles and sheriffdoms achieved 1223, 325–9; *see also* Minority, Oaths

Rheims, archbishop of, 200, 309

Rhys Gryg, 43, 77 n.7, 217–19, 218 n.2, 307, 313–14

Rhys Ieuanc, 77 n.7, 219, 219 n.6, 253, 253 n.9, 307

Richard, king of England, 14, 62, 90, 124, 136, 156, 200

Richard (of Cornwall), brother of Henry III, 241, 386; recovery of Gascony 1225, 375–7

Richard, John fitz, 386

Richmond (Yorks), castle of, 33, 33 n.12; honour of, 33, 82

Richmondshire, 33, 102, 197, 279 n.13; revenues outside exchequer control, 122

Ridel, Elyas of Bergerac, 154; submits 1225, 377–8

Rivaux, Peter des, 139, 139 n.23, 242 n.14, 259, 259 n.16; dismissal from king's household 1223–4, 322

Robert, John fitz, at siege of Bedford, 365

Rochefort-sur-Loire (Maine-et-Loire), 173

Rochester, Benedict de Sausetun, bishop of (1215–26), baron of exchequer, 53, 345, 349

Rochester, castle of, 25 n.3, 26–7, 264, 264 n.3, 327–8, 332 n.11; great council at 1219, 104; siege of 1215, 46, 48

Rockingham (Northants), 148; castle of, 34–5, 46, 72, 84, 145, 166–7, 187, 189, 193, 211, 221, 231, 235, 239, 251, 256, 262; siege of, 198–200, 233, 366–7; forest of, 72, 199, 401

Rome, 187, 228, 302–4, 310, 325, 329, 331, 347, 350–1, 355, 368, 373

Rome, Giles of, 258

Ros, Robert de, 60, 60 n.23, 80, 160, 196, 234, 278; supports government 1223–4, 326, 333; at siege of Bedford, 365; one of twenty-five of 1215 attesting 1225 Charter, 388; his debts, 340; favours to, 340; disseisins and resistance to judgments, 99, 102, 195–6, 340; and king's justice, 102, 195

Ros, William de, son of Robert, 40; at siege of Bedford, 365

Ros, William de, of Tydd, 100, 165, 175

Roumare, William de (d.1161), 34, 40

Roumare, William de (d.1198), 40

Rowde (Wilts), 119

Rughedon, William de, 275–6, 246

Runnymede (Berks), 12, 324

Rusceus, Peter de, 56 n.4

Russell, Hugh, 282

Russell, John, retains custodies 1223, 327–8

Rutland, 357; deforestation 1225, 385; reversal of 1225 deforestation, 1227, 392; sheriffdom of, 117 n.33

Rye (Sussex), 27

Sacy, Emery de, 267

St Albans, 19; abbey, abbot of, 19, 26, 357, 357 n.11, 368–9

St Briavels (Gloucs), 290

St Clears, lordship of, 77, 77 n.7, 219, 307, 314

St David's, 307, 307 n.5

St Émilion (Gironde), 374

St Frideswide's, Oxford, prior and canons of, 256

St Germain, Robert de, 19

St Jean d'Angély (Charente-Maritime), 156, 193, 295, 370

St Macaire (Gironde), 291, 374

St Martin, Adam de, 283 n.18, 284, 284 n.24

St Martin of Tours, chronicle of, 370 n.3, 371

St Paul's cathedral, 229; canons of and Falkes as sheriff, 334

Saintes (Charente-Maritime), 178–9, 193, 217, 221, 310, 345, 349, 358

Saintonge, the, 178–9, 193, 221, 349

Salaries for judges, *see* Judges

Salisbury, 170, 323, 379; castle of, 31, 125, 317, 327–8, 330, 333 n.13

Salisbury, Ela, countess of, daughter of William fitz Patrick, wife of William Longespee, 30, 30 n.17, 92 n.12

Salisbury, Richard le Poore, bishop of 1217–28, bishop of Chichester 1215–17, bishop of Durham 1228–37; 121, 171, 240 n.3, 290, 309, 327, 333; executor of John, 14 n.6, 323 n.9; early career, 323; at centre of government from Dec. 1223, 343, 345–7, 349, 355–6, 400; collection of 1225 tax, 379–80, 411; and Magna Carta, 387; withdraws from court, 390

Salisbury, William fitz Patrick, e. of, 30

Salisbury, William Longespee, e. of (1196–1226), 34, 47, 51, 66, 68, 83, 93, 122, 163 n.10, 171, 205–6, 222, 229, 267, 303, 333 n.13; rebellion against John, 6, 12, 30; demands that Hubert surrenders Dover, 12, 21; desertion of Louis, 27, 30–1; at battle of Lincoln, 39; and Devon, Somerset and Peter de Maulay, 31, 35, 66, 71, 121–2, 121 n.48, 250, 275; claim to Lincoln castle, 66–7, 125, 159, 175, 184, 186, 271, 377; struggle to secure Vesci custody, 71–2, 84–5, 130, 147, 205, 274; and Mere, 88, 121, 147, 176, 274 n.17; and Berkeley castle, 194–5, 203–4; and Harbottle castle, 208–9; and 1220 carucage, 225; and Christmas crisis of 1221, 270–4, 399; and act of resumption 1221, 270; and resumption of 1222, 281, 282 n.17, 283, 283 n.18, 285, 287, 399; retains custodies/gains more 1223, 327–9; attack on Falkes 1224, 347, 356; leads Gascon expedition 1225, 376–8; death 1226, 390; grievances and ambitions, 30–1, 119–21, 125; ideas about great councils, 4, 54, 127, 209, 209 n.8, 409; native-born, 273; grants of royal manors to, 68, 88–9, 92, 163, 270 (see also 1222 resumption); and sheriffdom of Lincoln, 40, 55, 66–7, 119–21, 125, 125 n.72, 146, 159–60, 163, 271, 274–5 (vacates), 376–7; as sheriff of Wiltshire, 31, 120–1, 125, 125 n.72, 328; independence as sheriff, 121, 330; and c. of Aumale, 178, 229, 233; and Roger Bertram, 88, 205; and Falkes's accusations, 272–3; and Hubert, 163, 194–5 (their alliance 1220), 204, 244, 250, 271–4 (during Christmas crisis of 1221), 287, 299, 308–9; the alliance in 1223–4, 317, 319, 325, 332–3, 345, 349, 365, 377, 399; importance of, 399–400; and Marshal family, 92, 92 n.12; alliance with e. of Pembroke, 27, 203–4 (quarrel with), 244, 271–3, 287, 308–9; and lands of c. of Perche, 92, 244, 287; and Trowbridge castle, 30, 35, 59, 195, 326

Sancto Albino, William de, 280, 355; and papal letters of April 1223, 303–4, 310; congratulates king on delivery of his patrimony, 329

Sandwich, battle off, 43–4, 136, 138, 394

Santiago (Spain), Bp Peter's pilgrimage to, 239, 243, 245, 245 n.9, 251

Santo Ciriaco, Rome, 368

Saumur (Maine-et-Loire), 358

Sauvey (Leic), 72, 166–7, 198–9

Scarborough (Yorks), castle of, 115 n.27, 116, 328 n.12

Scaccario, Henry de, 226

Scotale, abolition of, 191, 340

Scotland, 179, 188, 246; Anglo-Scottish treaties of 1209 and 1212, 152, 152 n.2, 196; see Alexander II, king of

Seagrave, Stephen of, as justice of bench, 64, 336 n.26; sheriff of Lincoln, 275; as custodian of Tower, 319 n.15

Secular, Nicholas, 283 n.15

Selborne (Hants.), 283 n.19

Senlis, bishop of, 350

Sens, bishop of, 350

Shaftesbury (Dorset), 219

Shakespeare, William, his play King John, 139

Sherborne (Dorset), 71, 214; castle of, 31, 35, 250, 274–5, 327

Sherwood forest (Notts), 90, 392

Shoreham-by-Sea (Sussex), 27

Shrewsbury, 152–3, 191–2, 218, 253–4, 298, 313, 355, 358; castle of, 326, 328, 332 n.10, 346

Shrivenham (Berks), 92, 92 n.10, 119, 244, 244 n.5, 282 n.17, 287, 287 n.46

Shropshire, 51; sheriffdom of, 326, 328, 332 n.10, 346; revenues outside exchequer control, 80–1, 119–22, 185, 189, 239, 253, 255, 274, 276; 1220 carucage in, 225; men of try to reduce number of shrieval officials, 115, 235 n.1; eyre in 1221, 255; reversal of 1225 deforestation 1227, 392

Sicily, kingdom of, 123, 409

Skenfrith (Monmouth), 138, 212, 276, 290; *see* Three Castles

Skipsea (Yorks), 230, 233

Skipton in Craven (Yorks), 57, 233

Slaughter (Gloucs), 271, 283 n.18, 284

Sleaford (Lincs), castle of, 25 n.3, 229, 232

Sneinton (Notts), 119

Somerset, 27, 31, 35, 66, 71, 121–2, 250; demands for deforestation within, 129, 403; forest eyre 1223, 337; private wars in, 66, 71; sheriffdom of, 327

Somerset-Dorset, sheriffdom of, 296; revenues outside exchequer control, 72, 120, 146, 186, 189, 263, 274–6; offer for removal of Peter de Maulay, 274

Somerton (Som), 283 n.19

Sotherton (Suffolk), 140 n.28

Southampton, 68, 163, 186, 222, 283 n.20; castle of, 27, 317, 327

Southern, Sir Richard, 302

South Petherton (Som), 214

Spain, 257, 259

Sowerby, Walter of, leads boycott of Yorkshire forest eyre, 277–8, 277 n.7, 403

Speen (Berks), 30 n.15

Stacey, R. C., 119 n.40, 231, 381, 381 n.12

Stafford, castle of, 125

Staffordshire, 51, 125; sheriffdom of, 326, 328, 332 n.10, 346; revenues outside exchequer control, 80–1, 119–21, 185, 189, 239, 253, 274, 276; and 1220 carucage, 225; forest eyre in 1223, 337; reversal of 1225 deforestation 1227, 392

Staines (Surrey) tournament at, 157–8

Stainton (Yorks), 233

Stamford (Lincs), 57, 85–6

Stanley (Wilts), 171; abbot of, 290

Stenton, Lady, 129 n.5, 255

Stephen, king of England, 34, 40, 366; his reign, 9, 90, 180; parallels with minority, 33, 50, 67, 109, 125–6, 396

Stevenson, W. B., 261

Stogursey (Som), castle, honour of, 348, 354, 356, 364, 367–9

Stowell, Adam of, 290

Stratford Langthorne (Essex), Richard abbot of, 257

Sturminster, (Dorset), 73

Stuteville, Nicholas I de, 6, 40, 46 n.12, 59 n.19, 63; and Knaresborough, 33–5, 59 n.19; his ransom, 41, 46, 55 n.23

Stuteville, Nicholas II de, 234, 277 n.7, 306, 337; boycotts Yorkshire forest eyre 1222, 277–8, 403; faithful service 1224, 365

Suffolk, 33, 59 n.16; sheriffdom of, *see* Norfolk-Suffolk

Surrey, reversal of 1225 deforestation in 1227, 392; sheriffdom of, 66, 122, 328, 333 n.13

Surrey, Hamelin de Warenne, e. of (1164–1202), 261

Surrey, William de Warenne, e. of (1202–40), 6, 12, 31, 80, 83, 108, 141 n.31, 155, 160, 185, 187–8, 233, 333 n.13; deserts Louis 1217, 32, 42; and peace negotiations, 47; and 1220 carucage, 225; his knights in army of Montgomery, 318, 326; supports government 1223–4, 325, 333, 345, 349, 365; retains custodies, 329, 332; exploitation of 1225 Charter, 387; not an alien, 261; and Hubert, 140, 161, 161 n.17, 164, 246, 407; private forests of, 388; as sheriff of Surrey, 66, 71, 96, 328

Sussex, deforestation 1227, 392; sheriffdom of, 66, 328 n.12, 332 n.9

Sutton (Kent), 165, 203, 282 n.15, 354, 367

Sutton, King's Sutton (Northants), hundred of, 273, 273 n.15

Swansea, castle of, 43, 217

Talbot, William, familiar of e. of Salisbury, 220 n.17, 274 n.17, 288 n.48

Talmont (La Vendée), 267

Taunton (Som), 140, 260

Taxation, carucages 1198 and 1200, 207; thirteenth of 1207, 207, 223, 379; scutage of 1217, 54, 67, 67 n.16, 70, 73, 93–4; tallage 1217, 67; carucage 1220, 110, 203, 206–7, 215, 220, 223–5, 248, 379; resistance to it in Yorkshire, 210–11, 211 n.13; clerical aid 1220, 223–4, 223 n.6, 224 n.9; taxation for crusade 1220, 223; scutage of Bytham, 234 n.33; tallage 1223, 296, 299 n.15; scutage of Montgomery 1223, 313; clerical carucage 1224, 364–5; scutage of Bedford, 365 n.26; fifteenth on movables 1225, 110, 376, 379; rules governing its expenditure, 379, 408; its assessment and collection, 380–1; proceeds, 380–1; distinction between scutages and aids, 61 n.4

Teifi, river, 308

Templars, master of, 14 n.6

Tendring (Essex), hundred of, 393

Tewkesbury abbey, annals of, on Falkes, 100, 122, 369

Theobald, Nicholas, fitz, 60 n.23

Thomas, Master, surgeon, 365

Thorney, abbey of (Cambs), oppressed by Falkes as sheriff, 334

Thorney, Robert, *quondam* abbot of, 162, 186 n.11, 187

Thouars, Aimeri VII, vicomte of, 139, 200–1, 224, 295, 344, 350; agreement with Louis, 370, 373

Thouars, family of, 156

Thouars, Hugh de, 372

Three Castles [Grosmont, Skenfrith, Whitecastle] (Monmouth), 138–9, 149 n.19, 246, 247 n.16, 263, 324, 338, 389, 395, 405 n.11

Titchfield (Hants), 346, 349

Tickhill, castle/honour of (Yorks), 89, 160, 187, 261, 275, 320, 397; constable of, 80, 145, 157; derides king as a boy, 160, 162

Tirel, Ralph, 66

Toddington (Bucks), 92, 92 n.9

Toeny, Ralph de, 283 n.18, 284

Torksey (Lincs), 253, 283 n.21

Totnes (Devon), castle of, 85, 141, 179, 216, 235, 246, 401

Toulouse, 153, 344, 378; c. of, 355

Touraine, The, 136, 139, 179, 251, 260, 324

Tournaments, forbidden, 50, 93, 149 n.15, 157–8, 166, 215, 238 n.9

Tours (Indre-et-Loire), 370

Tours, St Martin of, 139

Towy, valley of river, 76

Tracy, Henry de, 35, 66, 85, 87, 87 n.12, 179

Trim (Meath), 370

Triumvirate, The, creation, 128–34; initial crisis within, 128, 130–1; problems facing, 126–7, 134, 145, 153–5; aims, approach, programme of resumption, 142–5, 186, 189–90, 235–7, 398–9; process of its decision making, 128, 134, 146, 152–3, 169–73; changing balance of power within, 170, 172 n.14, 182–4, 237–43; position after first year, 184–6; situation Aug. 1220, 211; achievements, 234–7; beginnings of break-up, 238–43; and Bytham, 166–7, 184, 187,
211, 227–34; and 1220 carucage, 206–7; and Cornwall, 161, 184–5, 187, 211–14; decision to seek king's second coronation, 162; disorder around Tickhill, 160; initiative over eyre amercements, 146; policy on deforestation, 150–1, 168–9, 236; initiative over forest assarts, 150–1, 159, 163–4; and forest eyres, 236; and Fotheringhay, 165, 184, 187, 196, 211, 219–20; and great councils/need for support, 128, 134, 190–1, 196–8, 211, 234, 236; renews truce with king of France, 155, 172–3, 176–7; and Ireland, 205–6, 211; and Llywelyn 168, 171, 174, 191–2; and local society, 235–6; and Mitford/Philip of Oldcoates, 147, 162, 174–6, 184, 187, 197, 204–5, 208, 211; and Poitou, 167–8, 173–4, 177–9, 192–4, 200–3, 216–17, 221, 229; and process of settlement after war, 179–82, 190–1, 196–8, 205, 234–5 (*see also* Bytham, Mitford, Rockingham); and resumption of demesne, 163, 185–7, 203, 206, 211, 226, 135; and Rockingham, 166–7, 198–9, 211; and Vesci wardship, 147

Trowbridge (Wilts), castle of, 30, 46, 59, 195, 317, 326

Trubleville, Henry de, 377

Trubleville, Ralph de, 172, 282 n.15

Trumpington, William of, 101 n.44

Turri, Gregory de, 220, 232 n.22

Turri, William de, 71

Twenty-five barons of Magna Carta 1215's security clause: individual members, 58, 180, 277; those attesting Magna Carta 1225, 388; for the clause itself, *see* Magna Carta

Tyburn (London), 291

Tyerman, C. J., 28 n.7

Tynedale, 152 n.2; mines of, 157

Ulster, 306, 345–6, 370

Ulster, e. of, *see* Lacy, Hugh de

Umfraville, Richard de, 58, 197, 234, 310, 315; ally of Roger Bertram, 58, 58 n.13, 88, 88 n.18, 202; 'faithful service' in 1224, 365; and Harbottle castle, 202, 207–10; and Magna Carta, 137, 209, 403; and Philip of Oldcoates, 88, 202, 208–9; and Robert de Vieuxpont, 88, 88 n.18, 208–9

Upavon (Wilts), 346–9, 393

Usk (Monmouth), castle of, 70; river, 77

Vaux, Robert de, of Gilsland (Cumb), 6, 60, 68, 196–7, 234, 308
Vercelli (Italy), Guala's house of canons at, 68, 95
Verdun, Nicholas de, 60
Verdun, Walter de, 115–16, 270, 282, 283 n.18, 284, 319 n.15
Vernay, Henry de, 356
Vesci, Eustace de, 6, 63, 71; wardship of his lands, 63, 71, 79, 84–6, 109, 130, 147, 168, 186, 274
Vieuxpont, Robert de, 36, 69, 80, 100–2, 230; dissident in 1223, 320, 324; attack on 1224, 346, 349, 351; witnesses 1225 Charter, 388; ally of Roger Bertram, 88, 88 n.18; and of Richard de Umfraville, 88, 88 n.18, 208–9; and Harbottle castle, 208–10; and Hubert, 157–8, 160, 169, 182, 187–8, 275; ideas about great councils, 4, 54, 127, 209, 209 n.7, 236, 409; and Philip of Oldcoates, 88; private forest of, 388; and sheriffdom of Cumberland, 88–9, 119–20, 150, 160, 188, 274–6; his claim to Tickhill, 89, 187–8, 191, 275, 338, 397; and lordship of Westmorland, 35, 124 n.67
Vilers, Roger de, 56 n.4
Vincent, Nicholas, 68 n.23, 71 n.5, 135, 139, 139 ns.21, 23, 25, 303 n.8
Vivonne, Hugh de, 51, 171, 228, 235; as castellan of Bristol/ refusal to surrender Barton, 83–4, 105, 109, 118, 122, 147, 151, 229, 255; as seneschal of Poitou, 123, 229, 266–7; supports government in 1223, 324; assessment of situation in Gascony 1224, 374; a Poitevin in England, 171, 262, 262 n.36; letter proclaiming his fidelity, 105

Wales, 1, 4, 20, 42–3, 69, 74–7, 109, 145, 152, 188, 191–2, 212, 217, 243, 290, 299, 305, 307, 311, 313–14, 316, 330, 340 n.51
Wales, south, 42–3, 187, 211–13, 215, 218, 294, 301, 307–9, 311, 313–14, 316
Wales, Gerald of, 29
Wallingford (Oxon), 85, 94, 170, 172; castle of, 185
Walker, R. F., 308
Walter, Robert fitz, 6, 31, 45, 47, 48 n.27, 56, 83, 87, 94, 233, 339 n.45; loyalty to Louis, 33–5; at battle of Lincoln, 37, 37

n.9, 40; on crusade, 103; exempted from 1217 scutage, 94; and from 1220 carucage, 225; his knights in army of Montgomery, 326; supports government 1223–4, 325, 333, 399; one of twenty-five of 1215 attesting 1225 Charter, 388; political rehabilitation, 101
Waltham (Lincs), 282 n.17
Waltham Abbey (Essex), 319, 324
Wanborough (Wilts), 92, 92 n.12
Wantage (Berks), 294, n.11
Wardon (Beds), abbey of, and Falkes, 368
Wareham (Dorset), 250
Warin, Eudo fitz, 287
Warin, Fulk fitz, 294, 294 n.11, 298
Warin, William fitz, 119
Warren, W. L., 85, 126
Warwick, Henry e. of (1213–29), supports government 1223, 326
Warwickshire, petty assizes in, 195
Warwickshire-Leicestershire, sheriffdom of, 163, 320, 327, 332 n.10
Wash, The, 188
Waterford, 370
Waverley abbey (Surrey), chronicle of, 5–6, 29, 235; on the eyre of 1218–19 and Magna Carta, 100, 103, 335, 402; on Hubert becoming justiciar, 135; on Bp Peter as justiciar, 137
Weald of Kent, the, 27, 29
Weald, Willikin of the, see Kensham, William of
Wearne, see Pitney
Welland, river, 72
Wells (Som), 170
Welshpool (Powys), 313
Wendover, Roger of, monk of St Albans, chronicler, 21, 33 n.14, 37 n.9, 39, 48, 84, 198, 227, 232, 296, 302 n.4, 311, 313, 320, 326, 333, 359, 366, 369, 380, 384–5; and date of confirmation of Magna Carta 1223, 297 n.5; on Henry III, 404–5
West Derby (Lancs), forest of, 392 n.12
West Dereham (Norfolk), priory of, and Falkes as sheriff, 334
Westall, in Cheltenham (Gloucs), 119, 283 n.18
Westminster, 56, 70, 81, 94, 129, 131, 164, 169, 177, 203, 213, 220, 225 n.21, 226, 238, 244, 248–9, 254, 256, 268–9, 276, 281, 284, 290, 296, 298, 301, 306, 311, 314, 321, 323, 335, 348, 355; for councils at see Councils

Westminster abbey, and king's first coronation, 20, 20 n.6; and second coronation, 182, 187–8; abbot of, 290

Westmorland, 35; knights and men of, complaints about private forests 1225, 388

Wexcombe (Wilts), 30 n.15

Whitecastle (Monmouth), 138, 212, 213 n.6; see Three Castles

Whittington (Shrops), castle of, 294, 298, 307, 313

Whitwell, a member of Fordington (Dorset) in Stockland (Devon), 282 n.15

Widigada, commote of, 77 n.7

William, William fitz, 282 n.15

William the Lion, king of Scotland, 60 n.23, 152

Wiltshire, 27, 29, 51, 121; knights of deposit 1225 Charter in Lacock abbey, 384; deforestation after 1227, 393; sheriffdom of 31, 31 n.20, 125, 328, 330, 333 n.13; its revenue outside exchequer control, 120–1

Wimborne Minister (Dorset), 290

Winchelsea (Sussex), 27

Winchester, 29, 31, 36, 169, 171, 174; castle of, 28

Winchester, Peter des Roches, bp of (1205–38), (Bp Peter), 14 n.6, 20 n.6, 31, 59, 71, 96, 98, 103–6, 106 n.13, 108, 171, 191, 206, 248, 285, 319 n.15, 333 n.12, 337, 360; appointed king's tutor, 17, 106; at battle of Lincoln, 37, 39–40, 136, 397; relations with regent/place in his government, 53, 65, 65 n.9, 77, 94, 103–4, 106; refusal to pay 1217 scutage, 48, 67, 94; early career, outlook, 135–40; role under John, 136–7, 140, 243; claims custody of king, seizes him by head 1219, 106–7, 135, 259; controls government after regent's resignation, 128–9, 135; rejected as regent's successor, 129–40; initial place in triumvirate, 129–32; later eclipse, 170, 182–4, 213, 238–43; pilgrimage 1221, 239, 243, 245, 245 n.9; accused of treason, 249–52; return to England, 256; threats to his tutorship of king, 240–3; distrusted as such by Pandulf, 243; loses tutorship, 239, 241–3, 257–60, 399; failure to influence king, 259; and development of faction, 260–2; his projected crusade, 258, 270; working relationship with Hubert 1222, 280–1, 291; continuing influence 293–4, 299; plans to dislodge Hubert, 280, 300; secures papal letters of April 1223 to do so, 301–6; and their withdrawal, 310–11; dissident in 1223, 316–20; accuses Hubert, 321; surrenders custodies, 327–8; disappears from central government 322, 343, 345–6; munitions Farnham, 348; and siege of Bedford, 361, 363–4; helps with that of Stogursey, 364; loan for 1225 Gascon expedition, 380; witnesses 1225 Charter, 388; secures Hubert's dismissal 1232, 393; his own regime 1232–4, its absolutist tendencies, 137, 393–4, 405; dismissal, death, 394–5; political approach, behaviour, 135–40, 225, 239–40, 243, 398–9; an alien in England, 135–6, 139, 262; and attestation of royal letters, 53, 103–4, 128–9, 132, 135, 182–3, 259; and the bench, 164, 164 n.14, 166; and exchequer, 53, 65, 65 n.9, 132, 135–6, 162, 166, 225, 259, 265, 298, 304; left in charge at Westminster, 166 (breaches custom of kingdom), 168, 220, 225–6 (autocratic use of his independence), 238 n.9, 298; as sheriff of Hampshire, 116, 144, 256, 327 (surrenders), 330; imposes harsh terms for repayment of *debita Judeorum*, 137; tries to put out king of France 1220, 177; and royal forest, Charter of the Forest, 129, 137, 144, 150, 159, 170, 330; and Magna Carta, 137–9, 166, 334, 388, 393–4; and process of settlement after war, 179–80; and affairs of Poitou, 291–2, 295, 310; and rights of crown, 143–4; support for great local governorships, 332, 333 n.14; and c. of Aumale, 140, 158–9, 166, 198–9, 232, 239, 262, 325; and Falkes, 140, 260–2, 270, 325, 361, 363–4; and e. of Chester, 260–1, 271, 321, 325, 361; close links with Engelard, 139, 249–51, 260–2, 325, 393; supports his evasion of resumption of demesne 1222, 293; and Hubert: in 1219, 104, 129, 129–32, 132, 138–9; early co-operation, 1219–20, 143–72, 176, 179; May 1220 into 1221, 198–9, 213–14, 217, 220, 229; increasing tensions with 1220–21, 170, 172, 182–3, 225–6, 238–43; position, co-operation, friction with Hubert

Winchester, Peter—*contd*
1221–3, 259–60, 263, 267, 275, 280–1, 293, 295, 298–300, 304–6; as king's tutor, 17, 17 n.20, 53, 78 n.1, 106, 132, 160, 169–70, 172, 238, 238 n.10, 240–3; and Abp Langton, 136, 138–9, 258; and Henry fitz Count, 161–2, 213–15; and Pandulf, 107, 130–1, 134, 143, 146, 149–53, 161, 167–72, 213–14, 229, 243 (distrusted by as king's tutor); close associate of Peter de Maulay, 139, 249–51, 256, 260–2, 270, 325, 393; and Philip of Oldcoates, 104–5, 128–30, 162, 176; and Peter des Rivaux, 139, 259, 259 n.16; see also Triumvirate, Dissidents of 1223–4

Winchester, Saer de Quincy, e. of (1207–19), 6, 30–1, 36, 45, 48, 48 n.27, 56, 83, 93; loyalty to Louis, 33–5; at battle of Lincoln, 37, 37 n.9, 40; rehabilitation after war, 48, 60, 68, 74, 103; on crusade, 103; and Chesterton, 60, 68, 124, 222; and Mountsorrel, 34, 34 n.19, 103

Windsor (Berks), 119, 131, 281, 293, 333, 348; castle of, 7, 20, 249–50, 317, 326–30, 332 n.10, 346; forest of, 308

Wiston (Pembroke), 218

Witham, river, 36

Woodstock (Oxon), 78, 243, 331 n.5

Worcester, 26, 67, 74, 76–8, 168, 170–1, 174–5, 308; castle of, 55; cathedral, monks of, 55; treaty of 1218, 74, 76–8, 217–19, 293, 308–9, 313–14

Worcester, Sylvester bishop of (1216–18), 14 n.6, 115

Worcester, William de Blois, bishop of (1218–36), 96, 285

Worcestershire, Magna Carta proclaimed in, 1217, 42; deforestation after 1227, 392; sheriffdom of, 125, 328 n.12, 332 n.9

Wormegay (Norfolk), castle/honour of, 141, 160

Writ of common seisin, 56, 58, 101

Writtle (Essex), 68, 88, 119, 281, 283 n.18

Wrockwardine (Shrops), 286 n.35

Wulfstan, St, translation of, 78 n.1

Wye, river, 77; valley of, 212

Yardley Hastings (Northants), 149

Yarmouth, Great (Norfolk), 160

Yarwell (Northants), 72, 148–9, 158, 199, 228 n.3

York, 194–9, 210–11, 219–20, 225, 238, 245, 245 n.11, 250, 253, 277, 277 n.7; castle of, 33–4, 46; and Christmas crisis 1221, 268, 268 n.1, 270–1; hospital of St Leonard at, 280

York, Walter de Grey, abp of (1215–55), 95, 129, 130, 130 n.7, 158, 205, 208, 233, 240 n.3, 310, 327

Yorkshire, *debita Judeorum* in, 341; difficulties of justices in eyre in 1218–19, 99, 129, 129 n.6, 195, 255; difficulties of sheriff in, 80, 84, 115, 146, 151, 195; disorder in, 195; sheriffdom of, 292, 328 n.12, 329 n.18; proclamation of 1225 Charter in, 383 n.6; its exploitation, 384, 387, 404; forest in, 151; demands for deforestation, 181, 277–8, 391; deforestation 1225, 385; reversal after 1227, 392; deforestation 1234, 393 n.13 (*see also* Galtres, and Ouse and Derwent, forest between); forest eyres: in 1212, 279; in 1221, 236; postponed, 252, 276; protest over eyre of 1222 (as breach of Forest Charter), 277–9, 288; financial issues of, 337; collection postponed, 337, 340 n.51; resistance to 1220 carucage as breach of Magna Carta, 210–11, 211 n.13, 220, 224, 278, 403; fifteenth of 1225, 224, 380

DATE DUE
